FOLD ALONG DOTTED LINE.

A surprise for the Japanese.

The German art of folding.

To the delight of Audi owners and the surpri[se] of the motor industry, Audi has folded.

The boot of the new Audi 80 now has a capaci[ty] of 430 litres (four suitcases to you and me).

This can be extended to 712 litres by foldin[g] down the rear seats. But the Audi engineer[s'] ingenuity has left room for even more spac[e.]

The seats can also be folded in 60/4[0] proportions, allowing you to carry long item[s] (like skis, for example) and still comfortab[ly] use one or two rear seats.

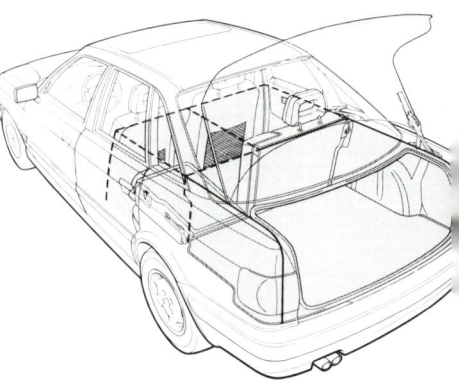

Access to this bumper boot is also easier a[s] the boot opening now extends down to bumpe[r] level. The lid is also wider.

There is, however, no keeping the lid o[n] the fact that as well as being a practical car, th[e] new Audi 80 is an exciting one.

There are five engines to choose from, th[e] top of the range being the 2.8 litre V6 whic[h] accelerates from 0-62 in 8 seconds and has [a] top speed of 137mph.

And talk about torque. The new Audi 80 ha[s] incredible pulling power in low gears.

But power (unless handled carefully) c[an] be a dangerous thing.

The new Audi 80 has electronic ABS brakes as standard on every car in the range.

New torsion beam rear suspension means that handling often suspends belief.

And the option of quattro four-wheel drive allows you to get even more of a grip.

Of course, accidents will and do happen.

So the new Audi 80 has an exceptionally rigid body structure.

And, in order to tackle side-on collisions head-on, it has side-protection bars.

The Procon-Ten safety system will also, of course, protect your head in a frontal collision by pulling you away from the steering wheel and pulling the steering wheel into the dashboard.

So although the engineers at Audi have increased the load-carrying capacity of the new Audi 80, they've also made sure it protects its most valuable cargo.

You.

THE NEW AUDI 80 FROM £13,855*.

For an information pack on the new Audi 80 and to arrange a test drive, please complete the coupon and send to: Audi Information Department, FREEPOST, Yeomans Drive, Blakelands, Milton Keynes MK14 5EY. Or call free on 0800 585685.

Mr/Mrs/Miss/Ms   Initials   Surname

Address

                                          Postcode
Phone   Phone
Home   Business

VORSPRUNG DURCH TECHNIK.

*PRICE CORRECT AT TIME OF GOING TO PRESS AND INCLUDES NUMBER PLATES AND DELIVERY

GCG/F/92

PRICE CORRECT AT TIME OF GOING TO PRESS. (INCLUDES NUMBER PLATES AND DELIVERY

First we protect the car from the environment.

100% zinc galvanised steel. 10 year anti-corrosion warranty. Lead and cadmium-free paintwork. Asbestos-free clutch

AUDI INFORMATION DEPT., FREEPOST, YEOMANS DRIVE, BLAKELANDS, MILTON KEYNES MK14 5EY.

Audi

VORSPRUNG DURCH TECHNIK.

Then we protect the environment from the car.

linings and brake pads. 3-way catalytic converter. 75% recyclable. The new Audi 80. From £13,855. Phone 0800 585 685.

SWING INTO STYLE WITH THE AUDI DRIVING RANGE

ALL NEW FOR '92
In a rapidly changing world keeping pace is no longer sufficient. Fortunately Audi continue to design for the future. With lifestyles, safety and environmental considerations very much in mind they have changed or substantially improved every model in their extensive range during the last twelve months. Audi's philosophy of 'progress through technology' (Vorsprung durch Technik) brings us a sophisticated range of safety enhanced, environmentally conscious, luxury cars in a marriage of elegance and efficiency.

RANGE PAR EXCELLENCE
The new Audi 100 is available in over 20 versions including the spacious estate; the radically updated Audi 80 offers engines from 90 bhp to 174 bhp and includes the exciting 16 valve; the Audi coupe has been updated and will include Audi's new 2.8 V6 engine as an option for the first time; the Audi V8 has a new 280 bhp engine and the chic new Cabriolet makes it's right hand drive debut in the UK this summer. Apart from the Cabriolet, you will find any model you choose, available in a four wheel drive version whilst the galvanised bodies allow Audi to give all cars a 10 year anti - rust warranty.

Audi Coupe S2

ARRIVING SAFELY
Features standard across the range include ABS anti-lock brakes and Audi's revolutionary Procon-Ten safety system. The ABS brakes reduce the odds of an impact but should the worst occur the Procon-Ten system comes into play. Audi's unique system pulls the steering wheel out of the way whilst gently increasing the tension on seat-belts to prevent front seat passengers from being thrown foward. Apart from diesel versions the entire catalyst equipped range runs exclusively on unleaded fuel.

NEW AUDI 80: VERSATILE LOAD SPACE
With the new Audi 80 you don't have to sacrifice style for practicality. Its through load facility provided by the 40/60 split-folding rear seat increases the 15.2 cu. ft boot capacity to over 25 cu. ft. New suspension and a more rigid bodyshell provide a quieter, smoother ride. Pulling power has also been improved and there is a detachable towbar option. Available in versions ranging from the *remarkably fuel efficient direct injection 1.9 litre 90 bhp turbo diesel to the 2.8 V6 with its top speed of 137 mph (where legally permitted).

Audi 80

* Government fuel consumption figures: urban cycle - 41.5 mpg; 56mph - 67.3mpg; 75mph - 51.4mpg

NEW AUDI 100: POWER, COMFORT, LUXURY, AND THE GREEN LINK
The Audi 100 engines range from a 2 litre 115 bhp to a stunning 230 bhp turbo intercooled 2.2 litre 20 valve. Each saloon is matched by an equally prestigious estate version. The aerodynamic estate offers a potential 50.7 cu. ft of space and a rear door that opens down to bumper level.

The Audi 100 clearly demonstrates Audi's green philosophy. Production processes have been refined with all scrap metal plastic and paper being recycled, and the plastic batteries are 100% recyclable. Amazingly, over 80% of the car can be recycled.

Audi 100    *Audi 100 Estate*

AUDI COUPE: THE PRACTICAL SPORTS CAR
This sleek coupe offers unusual versatility with its variable loading facility and spacious luxury for five. The updated coupe has new interior trim and equipment. Choice of 4, 5 or 6 cylinders with a 20 valve, 5 cylinder giving 0 to 60 in under 6 seconds at the top of the range (S2).

AUDI V8: HIGH PERFORMANCE PERMANENT FOUR WHEEL DRIVE

With an all new 4.2 litre 280 bhp V8 engine the 1992 Audi V8 is more responsive under all conditions and has superb traction . The driver chooses sport, economy or manual driving modes and the impressive equipment includes leather upholstery, full climate control and through load facility from the boot. Top speed is 155 mph, (where legally permitted).

AUDI CABRIOLET

This model will be available initially with a 2.3 litre 5 cylinder engine, producing 133 bhp. Enjoy all the Audi quality, reliability and technology with the added sporting cachet of a Cabriolet to be launched in the summer of '92.

Audi V8 *Audi Cabriolet*

For further information contact your nearest Audi dealer or write to:
Audi Information Service,
FREEPOST,
Yeomans Drive,
Milton Keynes,
MK14 5EY
or call FREE on 0800 585685

Audi Coupe

CADE'S
AUDI GOLF COURSE GUIDE
1 9 9 2

The visiting golfers guide to courses and accommodation throughout Britain and Ireland

Compiled and Edited by - Reg Cade and Barry Gallafent

Advertising Sales Manager - Andrew Wiltshire Tel: (0908) 643022

Published by
Marwain Publishing Limited, Marwain House, Clarke Road, Mount Farm, Milton Keynes, MK1 1LG.

Designed and Computer Typset by
Marwain Print Services Limited, Marwain House, Clarke Road, Mount Farm, Milton Keynes, MK1 1LG.

Printed by
Grillford Limited, Granby, Milton Keynes, MK1 1QZ.

Distributed by
(Newsagents and Bookshops)
Springfield Books Limited, Springfield House, Norman Road, Denby Dale, Huddersfield, HD8 8TH.

(Golf Trade, Clubs and Shops)
Marwain Publishing Limited.

ISBN 0 - 905377 - 55 - 9

Acknowledgements

Marwain Publishing Limited would like to thank the following people without whose help and encouragement this guide would not have been possible:-

Northern Ireland Tourist Board, St Anne's Court, 59 North Street, Belfast, BT1 1NB.

Irish Tourist Tourist Board (London), 150 New Bond Street, London, W1Y 0AQ.

Mark Webber PGA

Robin W Mann PGA

Steve Hill

Rod Parker

Dave Goodson

Peter Hewitson

Norman Stevenson

Special thanks to Mark Chamberlain - the resident professional and officials at The Northampton Golf Club. (Front cover photograph)

Club Secretaries and Professionals throughout Britain and Ireland - too numerous to mention individually but equally as important.

Text Copyright ©1992 Marwain Publishing Limited
Marwain House
Clarke Road
Mount Farm
Milton Keynes
MK1 1LG

All rights reserved. No part of this publication may be reproduced, stored in a retrieval system, or transmitted in any form or by any means, electronic, mechanical, photocopying, recording or otherwise, without the prior written permission of the copyright owners.

CONTENTS

Foreword	13
Iron Byron	14
Introduction	15
How to use this guide	17
Taking up the game of golf	18
Golf tips for the beginner	20
1992 European Fixture List including WPG Tour	22

ENGLAND

Avon	27
Bedfordshire	28
Berkshire	29
Buckinghamshire	31
Cambridgeshire	33
Channel Islands	35
Cheshire	35
Cleveland	38
Cornwall	39
Cumbria	41
Derbyshire	44
Devon	45
Dorset	49
Durham	51
Essex	54
Gloucestershire	57
Greater London	58
Greater Manchester	66
Hampshire	72
Hereford and Worcestershire	77
Hertfordshire	80
Humberside	84
Isle Of Man	87
Isle Of Wight	87
Kent	88
Lancashire	92
Leicestershire	96
Lincolnshire	97
Merseyside	99
Norfolfk	101
Northamptonshire	103
Northumberland	104
Nottinghamshire	106
Oxon	108
Salop	110
Somerset	112
Staffordshire	113
Suffolk	116
Surrey	120
Sussex (East)	124
Sussex (West)	128
Tyne and Wear	129
Warwickshire	132
West Midlands	133
Wiltshire	138
North Yorkshire	139
South Yorkshire	141
West Yorkshire	145

WALES

Clwyd	151
Dyfed	152
Mid Glamorgan	154
South Glamorgan	156
West Glamorgan	157
Gwent	158
Gwynedd	159
Powys	162

SCOTLAND

Borders	165
Central	166
Dumfries and Galloway	168
Fife	170
Grampian	174
Highland	178
Lothian	181
Orkneys	187
Strathclyde	187
Tayside	198

NORTHERN IRELAND

County Antrim	203
County Armagh	205
Belfast	206
County Down	208
County Fermanagh	210
County Londonderry	211
County Tyrone	212

REPUBLIC OF IRELAND

County Carlow	215
County Cavan	215
County Clare	215
County Cork	216
County Donegal	217
County Dublin	218
County Galway	221
County Kerry	222
County Kildare	223
County Kilkenny	223
County Laois	224
County Limerick	224
County Longford	224
County Louth	224
County Mayo	225
County Meath	225
County Monaghan	225
County Offaly	226
County Sligo	226
County Tipperary	226
County Waterford	227
County Westmeath	227
County Wexford	227
County Wicklow	228

A Complete Directory of AUDI Dealerships Throughout Britain and Ireland.	229
INDEX	235
MAP SECTION	248

FOREWORD

I take great pleasure in writing this foreword since most of my working life I have been involved with clubs and courses.

The Audi Golf Course Guide is a tribute to Golf Courses in Britain and Ireland, so many are mentioned and such details provided for the golfer advising him or her where they can play, how much it will cost and of the facilities available to them.

Golf courses in Britain and Ireland provide such an enormous array of hills, trees, sand and water that knowing the various types, the length and degree of difficulty that each course provides is important to every golfer. This book is just the sort of reading that every conscientious golfer should have at their fingertips, preferably kept in the glovebox of their car.

Not only does this guide cover the Major Championship courses, it also provides details on some lesser known nine hole courses and so - a course for everyone!

Through the game of golf many friends have been made, with the help of this book I hope that you will make many more. The information contained within these pages will help and enrich golfers from all over including visitors from overseas enabling them to play on courses that they may never previously have heard of.

Enjoy your game.

MARK WEBBER P.G.A.
Golf Professional

Iron Byron by Steve Hill

If we were all an Iron Byron
    a mechanical swinging arm,
we wouldn't suffer the disaster hole
    and the subsequent golfing yarn.

We wouldn't vary from par to bogey
    and double bogey too,
You would play just like me
    and I'd play just like you.

There'd be no competition
    there'd be no winning putt,
They'd all get through La Manga
    and always make the cut.

The Masters would be average
    the open would never end,
And everyone would drive so straight
    it would drive us round the bend.

So if you've ever hankered
    to play like a machine,
Just thank the lord that your'e so bad
    but still so very keen!

              13th December 1988.

INTRODUCTION

Welcome to The Cade's - Audi Golf Course Guide 1992 - The visiting golfers guide to courses and accommodation in the United Kingdom. This guide is intended to be an invaluable source of reference to any golfer travelling the country either on business or for pleasure alone, with family or with friends.

All the courses in this guide welcome visitors. Some may have restrictions at certain times but these are noted within the listing. Where restrictions have not been made clear to the publishers, the guide always errs on the side of the golfer so that you do not embark upon any wasted journeys. You are of course always advised to check by telephone prior to your visit, to ensure that the facilities you particularly require will be available during your visit.

Only golf courses that have responded to our intensive questionnaire or have been interviewed on the telephone by our trained staff, have been included in our guide. It has long since been a policy of the publisher only to include such information that it knows or believes to be accurate and that information is maintained and updated annually.

You may notice if you are looking for a particular club that it is not listed. It may be that it has declined an entry because either it does not accept visitors, or it already has a steady compliment of visitors and that to encourage more might offend its valued members.

Where an entry includes accommodation details, such information has been provided by the club and you are advised to confirm beforehand that it is suitable for you personally.

We hope that you find this guide a valuable addition to your golf equipment and that you will choose it again annually to find out what new courses have opened since we went to press this year. Your comments and criticisms are always welcome, should you feel that we can improve this publication in any way or would like to see anything else included please write to the editor at the publishers address.

Barry M Gallafent
Director
Marwain Publishing Limited
For Cade's - Audi Golf Course Guide.

ATTENTION AUDI OWNERS!

The Audi Quattro Cup

An Annual Golf Tournament
Exclusive to Audi Owners.

Anybody wishing to take part should contact:

Mike Brosnan at the Tournament Office
on 071 - 537 - 2051

Audi

Vorsprung durch technik

HOW TO USE THIS GUIDE

Golf Courses are listed throughout this publication in the following order; County, Town, Golfcourse Name, (alphabetically in ascending order where applicable).

The re-drawing of County Boundaries some years ago caused much confusion over the actual whereabouts of many towns, for example CHISLEHURST, formerly in KENT - is now in THE LONDON BOROUGH OF BROMLEY. There are many examples around Greater London, Greater Manchester and Merseyside. We have endeavoured to include each town in the county appropriate to its current Geographical Gazetteer listing as it should now be shown. The same principal has been applied to Scotland resulting in the demise of many shires in favour of far less grand Regional names.

At the back of the guide you will find a list of club names in alphabetical order. This may help you locate some clubs that do not appear to be in the expected county.

Class One Hotel: Accommodation rated at three stars or above.

Class two Hotel: Accommodation which may be small Family-run Hotels, Guest Houses, Inns, Farmhouses etc..

(Hotel information has been provided by clubs for the assistance of visiting golfers and the publishers recommend that you verify the Hotel suitability and star rating personally before travelling).

Caddies: Where an entry specifies caddies available, this is mostly during school holidays. Should you have a specific requirement, you should check with the club in advance.

Telephone Numbers: All telephone numbers show the STD code in brackets. Republic of Ireland telephone numbers show their regional STD code, to telephone from the United Kingdom you should refer to the telephone book or B.T. operator for specific international dialling information.

All distances (travel) are approximate. All times and Green Fees are correct as we go to press. Any variable should always be confirmed before travelling.

Golf Course information for both Nortern Ireland and The Republic of Ireland has been compiled with assistance of the respective Tourist Boards and you should refer to the notes at the head of each section which explain the difference in presentation of information.

The information in this guide has been supplied by an official at each establishment and is reproduced by the publishers in good faith. No responsibility can be accepted by the publishers (Marwain Publishing Ltd.) or V.A.G.(United Kingdom) Ltd. (for Audi), for any loss or inconvenience arising from its use, whatsoever.

TAKING UP THE GAME OF GOLF

When taking up golf there are definitely some important Do's and Don'ts that can save you time, money and lots of mental frustration. At Fynn Valley Golf Centre we see thousands of people start the game, the large percentage of people visit the golf centre many times and just hit balls and get frustrated because they don't improve when practising, (also practising lots of faults) so:-

DO have one or two half hour golf lessons from a qualified P.G.A. Professional in the first month (you wouldn't dream of taking a car on the road for the first time without an instructor, golf's the same).

DO stay on the Driving Range at first before going onto the golf course. Playing the course before you are ready can cost a fortune in golf balls, let alone destroying your confidence.

DO if possible take the game up with a friend, if having golf lessons try to watch the tips each of you receive when being taught, so that when your coach is not there you can remind each other of recurring faults. Plus it adds a competitive element in the learning cycle.

DON'T read too much literature on the game of golf, it is very easy to think over the top of your head so early in your golf development.

DON'T go to an assortment of different golf coaches, pick one and stick with them, you will develop a good understanding. Your coach will learn to understand you and the way you tick and be able to give you the right instruction and "Thought Patterns" for your golf. Most good coaches have either been good players and now teach after retiring or are current top regional players who also have the ability to control the ball and make good golf scores.

DON'T buy an expensive set of golf clubs when starting, just buy a fairly inexpensive half or full set of clubs that have a good trade-in value. When starting it is easy to take large divots from the ground hitting stones and taking chunks out of the clubs causing large devaluation.

SOME USEFUL GOLF TIPS TO HELP CLEAR YOUR MIND

To play the game of golf very well, to a standard you can enjoy and be proud of, is a lot easier if you can do as the top Professionals do when they practise. The reasons the top Professionals are consistently playing well is because they have very sound basic fundamentals in both their set-up and their golf swings. Here are a few points that they all work on.

1. Take your time checking the set-up routine **A** Club-face, **B** Grip, **C** Stance and Ball Position and **D** Posture (balance). When the ball is there it is easy to rush and just keep hitting balls, "Quality NOT Quantity". Think of the set-up as your course work and the swing as the exam, it will help you to develop a good shot routine.

2. As I have just stated, it is easy to rush when the ball is there. Therefore use the slow

motion swing as an exercise, take ten seconds to make a practise swing, it is a great way of developing good "Tempo" and feeling the muscular movements of a golf swing.

3. In 80 percent of golfers there is too much lower body movement (waist down) these are **A** Moving the body laterally or, **B** Spinning the lower body. Both are in the backswing and downswing. The main use of your lower body is as an anchor or platform on which you build a wind and unwind of the shoulders. A great exercise to help you keep both the lower body still and develop your shoulder turn is the exercise of keeping heels, toes and knees together. When swinging try to retain the knees together, firstly with just one swing, and as you develop it with two or three continuous swings.

4. Another main difference between an average club golfer and a top class Professional is the way a club golfer will hit "at the ball" and the top Professional will hit "through the ball". Always make sure that you don't stop the follow through at waist or chest height, try to always reach a full follow through. Because the flight of the ball is effected by the club-head from impact to waist high in the follow through, plus the club-head must always be accelerating through impact. Train yourself with your practise swing and then do the same when hitting the ball.

Just remember, good basic fundamentals make your golf swing repeat more frequently, it is so easy to think of too complicated thoughts which cannot be implemented in a golf swing.

ROBIN W MANN
DIRECTOR OF GOLF - FYNN VALLEY GOLF CENTRE

Robin Mann turned professional in 1972. Seven times Suffolk Professional Champion, twice East Anglian Open Champion, United Kingdom Club Professional Champion European Tour player since 1975, currently playing the 1992 European Tour, having just led the Firenze Open - Italy in March 1992.

Qualified member of the Professional Golfers Association since 1975, with credits in teaching, to being heavily involved in teaching and the development of golf at Fynn Valley and with Suffolk Youngsters.

Robin W Mann - Director Of Golf

GOLF TIPS FOR THE BEGINNER
BY STEVE HILL

Clubs
Replace worn grips regularly. Clean grips with a rag soaked in petrol. (Don't forget the putter). Occasionally wipe steel shafts with WD40 or similar

Mark the sweetspot on your putter for more accuracy. Do this by grasping the putter grip between finger and thumb and holding the putter aloft in front of you. With one finger of the other hand tap the face of the putter on the toe, hard enough to make it twist. Keep tapping whilst working your finger towards the center of the face. When you reach the sweetspot the club will move squarely, like a pendulum, with no twisting. Check several times then mark this exact spot with a fine hacksaw cut across the top of the putter head. Always line this mark behind thecentre of the ball when putting.

If you use a trolley but find it tends to drag behind you try improving the balance so that all the weight is on the wheels rather than pulling against you. To do this slide the bag up the trolley cradle until the trolley balances with the handle at just the right height for you. Now you will need to bend the bottom support up to meet the bag or find some other method of securing the bag in this position.

The Grip
Your grip should be firm but not tense. Apply the left hand tothe club first. The grip should lie across the base of the fingers. Position the left thumb on top of the grip and pointing directly down the shaft slightly to the righthand side.

A good test is to ask someone to stand in front of you and try to pull the club out of your hand. Your grip should be firm enough to resist this.

Now apply the right hand using your favoured method (interlock,overlap, or baseball). The right thumb must be on the grip slightly to the left side so as to form two 'V's from the thumbs and forefingers.

The Stance
Feet should be approximately shoulder width apart, wider perhaps for a wood off the tee, and feet and shoulders should be square to the ball.

Posture
With the clubhead behind the ball and legs straight, let your weight transfer slightly back onto your heels until the clubhead starts to lift clear of the ground. Now bend slightly at the knees to restore balance and return the clubhead to the ground.

Pre-Shot Routine

You should adopt the same pre-shot routine before every shot. One that many professionals teach is known as GRASP.

GRip Aim Stance Posture

So first grip the club correctly, then aim (to aim always stand behind the ball and look at the target, then stand to the ball and place the clubhead squarely behind it). Now take your stance and lastly adopt the correct posture.

Off The Tee

Always approach the tee from the rear. As you walk forward keep your eyes on the target. Place the ball on a tee peg with just the thickness of your fingers between the ball and the ground, (a bit more for a driver, a bit less for a shorter iron). Align the name on the ball along the target line. Now stand square to the name and position the clubhead behind the ball. You should now be on target.

Don't rest the clubhead on the tee. Remember you are intending to hit the ball not the tee peg, it is best to let the clubhead hover just behind the ball before commencing the backswing.

Learning to use a Wood

If you are just learning to use a wood off the tee remember to swing slow and don't try to hit the ball too hard. Also remember to position the ball more to the left of centre than you would for an iron. This is so the clubhead contacts the ball on the upswing after passing the bottom of the swing arc.

Ball Position

As a general rule if you shift your hips to the left through the swing (like a Pro) the ball will need to be positioned to the left of centre so that the clubhead is behind the ball at the bottom of your swing arc. If you have a more wooden swing with little or no side shift then try positioning the ball more to the centre of your stance.

When pitching or chipping on to the green from close range remember to always take as much care as you would for a putt. Take lots of practise swings to get the feel for the distance then carefully aim the clubhead at the pin (allowing for any borrow on the green). Take your swing and finish the follow through with the clubhead pointing at the target.

You might achieve more consistency by always using the same clubs for close range pitching and chipping. For example, always using the pitching wedge for chipping when you want the ball to roll to the pin and always using the sand wedge when you want the ball to stop quickly.

Never be afraid to use the putter when you are just off the green. Your worst putt is often better than your best chip when it comes to getting close to the pin.

If you find difficulty in judging the distance when putting from the fringe and always leave the putts short, then try putting past the pin by the amount that you are off the green. In other words if you are three feet off the green try to putt three feet past the pin, six feet off, six feet past etc. You may need to vary this to suit your own putting strength.

1992 EUROPEAN FIXTURE LIST INCLUDINGWPG TOUR

May
- 7-10 Benson and Hedges International Open, St Mellion.
- 7-10 (WPG) AGF Ladies Open de Paris, La Boulie.
- 14-17 Peugeot Spanish Open, Club de Campo, Madrid.
- 14-17 (WPG) Italian Classic (Venue to be arranged).
- 21-24 (WPG) BMW European Masters, Bercuit, Brussels
- 22-25 Volvo PGA Championship, Wentworth.
- 28-31 Dunhill Masters, Woburn.
- 28-31 (WPG) Spanish Classic, La Manga.

June
- 4-7 Carrolls Irish Open, Killarney.
- 11-14 Mitsubishi Austrian Open, Gut Altentann, Salzburg.
- 18-21 Lyon Open, Lyon.
- 25-28 Peugeot French Open, National Club Paris.
- 25-28 (WPG) Lufthansa European Open, Beuerberg, Munich.

July
- 1-4 Monte Carlo, Mont Agel.
- 8-11 Bell's Scottish Open, Gleneagles.
- 9-12 (WPG) Hennessy Ladies Cup, Refrath, Cologne.
- 16-19 Open Championship, Muirfield.
- 23-26 Heineken Dutch Open, Noordwijk.
- 30-2 Aug Scandanivian Masters, Barseback, Malmo.
- 30-2 Aug (WPG) English Open, Tytherington.

August
- 6-9 BMW International Open, Golfplatz, Munich.
- 13-16 European Pro-Celebrity (Venue to be arranged).
- 20-23 Volvo German Open, Hubbelrath, Dusseldorf.
- 20-23 (WPG) Netherlands Ladies Open, Rijswijk, The Hague.
- 27-30 (WPG) IBM Ladies Open, Haninge, Stockholm.
- 28-31 Murphy's English Open, The Belfry.

September
- 3-6 Canon European Masters / Swiss Open, Crans-sur-Sierre.
- 10-13 GA European Open Sunningdale.
- 17-20 Equity and Law Challenge, Royal Mid-Surrey.
- 17-20 Lancome Trophy, St Nom-la-Breteche, France.
- 17-20 (WPG) Italian Open, (Venue to be arranged).
- 24-27 Belgian European Open (Venue to be arranged).
- 27-30 (WPG) Weetabix British Open, Woburn.

October
- 1-4 Mercedes German Masters, Stuttgart.
- 1-4 (WPG) Solheim Cup, Dalmahoy.

Cade's - Audi Golf Course Guide

8-11	Toshiba PC Open, Gut Kaden, Hamburg.
8-11	Toyota World Matchplay Championship, Wentworth.
15-18	Dunhill Cup, St Andrews.
22-25	Iberia Madrid Open, Puerta de Hierro.
22-25	(WPG) Longines Classic, Barcelona.
29-1 Nov	Volvo Masters, Valderrama.

November
5-8	World Cup of Golf by Philip Morris (Venue to be arranged).
5-8	Four Tours Championship (Venue to be arranged).

MEN'S AMATEUR

May
2-3	Berkshire Trophy, Berkshire.
2-3	Lytham Trophy, Royal Lytham and St Annes.
9-10	West of Scotland Open, Cardross.
15-17	Brabazon Trophy, Nottingham.
22-24	Welsh Open Strokeplay Championship, Royal St Davids.
27-28	Lagonda Trophy, Gog Magog, Cambridge.
27-29	English Open Seniors Championship, Fulford & York.
28-30	International European Mid-Amateur Championship, Venice.
30-31	St Andrews Links Trophy, St Andrews.

June
1	East of Ireland Amateur Open Championship, County Louth.
2-6	Irish Youths Internationals and Youths Championships, Northumberland.
13-14	Scottish Open Strokeplay, Mortonhall & Bruntsfield Links.
19	Scotland versus Ireland Youths Match, Carnoustie.
20-21	Scottish Youths Amateur Open Championship, Carnoustie.
26-27	St Andrews Trophy, Royal Cinque Ports.
26-27	Midland Amateur Open Championship, Little Aston & 666Sutton Coldfield.
27-28	East of Scotland Open, Lundin Links.
27-28	Irish Youths Amateur Open Championship, Clandeboye, County Down.

July
1-3	Scottish Boys Open Amateur Strokeplay Championship, Royal Burgess Golfing Society.
7	Scottish Boys Under-16 Open Strokeplay Championship, King James VI Golf Club.
8-12	European Boys' Team Championship, Conwy, Gwynedd.
13-17	North of Ireland Amateur Open Championship, Royal Portrush, Co Antrim.

WOMEN'S AMATEUR

May
1	West of Scotland Championship, Haggs Castle.
10-12	Welsh Ladies Amateur Open Championship, Newport, Gwent.
19-20	English Seniors Spring Tournament, Enville.
19-23	English Ladies Close Amateur Championship, St Annes Old Links, Lancs.
19-23	Irish Ladies Close Amateur Championship, County Louth.
19-23	Scottish Ladies Close Amateur Championship, Royal Aberdeen.
30	South of scotland Championship, Portpatrick, Dunskey.
30-31	St Rule Trophy, St Andrews.

June
1	Critchley Salver, Sunningdale.
3	Astor Salver, Berkshire.
4	Guinness Trophy, Burhill.
5	Wentworth Scratch Trophy, Wentworth.
5-6	Curtis Cup, Royal Liverpool.
10-14	British Open Amateur Championship, Saunton, Devon.
27-28	Irish Ladies' Senior Cup, Athlone, Co Roscommon.
27-28	Welsh Open Amateur, 54 - hole Strokeplay Championship, Royal Porthcawl.

July
2	Stoke Poges Scratch, Stoke Poges.
6	Pleasington Putter, Pleasington.
6-8	North Of Scotland Championship, Murrayshall.
8-12	European Ladies' Amateur Team Championship, Golf National, Versailles, France.

Cade's - Audi Golf Course Guide

The new Audi 100 S4 estate

WHAT'S HAPPENING IN THE WORLD OF GOLF?

Find out from your local newsagent every week

Golf Weekly's got all the answers
- The game's liveliest and most extensive coverage from the European tour.
- All the news from home and abroad, brought to you with expert analysis and opinion.
- Results and statistics, gossip, instruction, puzzles and plenty more besides...

ENGLAND

AVON

BATH
Fosseway Golf Club, Charlton Lane, Midsomer Norton, Bath, Avon. BA3 4BD. Tel: 412214 (0761)
Secretary: R F Jones　　　　　　Tel: 412214 (0761)
Location: Off A367 midway between Bath and Wells.
Description: Parkland.
9 holes, 2,139 yards, Par 66, S.S.S. 65, Course record 54.
Membership: 450
Visitors: Welcome. Not Saturdays a.m., not Sundays a.m.. Not wednesdays after 5p.m..
Green Fees: £10, Saturdays and Bank Holidays £15.
Facilities: Lunch. Dinner. Bar Snacks. Full Catering. Changing Room. Golf Shop.
Class One Hotel: Centurion, Midsomer Norton. Tel: 417711 (0761)

BATH
Lansdown Golf Club, Lansdown, Bath, Avon. BA1 9BT. Tel: 425007 (0225)
Secretary: Ron Smith　　　　　　Tel: 422138 (0225)
Professional: Terry Mercer　　　　Tel: 420242 (0225)
Description: Flat parkland course.
18 holes, 6,299 yards, Par 70, S.S.S. 70, Course record 64.
Membership: 780
Visitors: Welcome. Handicap certificate required.
Green Fees: Mon-Fri £24, Weekends £30, Bank Holidays £24.
Facilities: Lunch. Dinner. Bar Snacks. Full Catering. Changing Room. Golf Shop. Club Hire. Trolley Hire. Caddies available.
Class One Hotel: Queen Anne House, Bath, 4 mile(s). Tel: 337992 (0225)
Class Two Hotel: The Huntsman, Bath, 3 mile(s). Tel: 428812 (0225)

BRISTOL
Bristol and Clifton Golf Club, Beggar Bush Lane, Failand, Bristol, Avon. BS8 3TH. Tel: 393474 (0275)
Secretary: Cdr P A Woolings　　　Tel: 393474 (0275)
Professional: Peter Mawson　　　 Tel: 393031 (0275)
Location: Exit 19 off M5, 2 miles west across Clifton Suspension Bridge.
Description: Dry parkland course.
18 holes, 6,294 yards, Par 70, S.S.S. 70.
Membership: 800
Visitors: Welcome. Handicap certificate required. Letter of Introduction required. Some tee time restrictions apply, please telephone in advance.
Green Fees: Weekdays £25, weekends and Bank Holidays £30.
Facilities: Lunch. Dinner. Bar Snacks. Full Catering. Changing Room. Golf Shop. Club Hire. Driving Range. Trolley Hire.
Class One Hotel: Redwood Lodge, Failand. Tel: 393501 (0275)

Cade's - Audi Golf Course Guide

BRISTOL
Filton Golf Club, Golf Course Lane, Filton, Bristol, Avon. BS12 1UL. Tel: 694169 (0272)
Professional: J C N Lumb　　　　Tel: 694158 (0272)
Location: 5 Miles north of Bristol.
Description: Open parkland.
18 holes, 6,020 yards, Par 69, S.S.S. 69, Course record 65.
Membership: 800
Visitors: Welcome. Handicap certificate required. Casual Visitors Monday to Friday, with a member at weekends.
Green Fees: £20 per round, £25 at weekends.
Facilities: Lunch. Dinner. Bar Snacks. Changing Room. Golf Shop. Trolley Hire.
Class One Hotel: Stakis Leisure Lodge, Almondsbury, 5 mile(s). Tel: 201144 (0272)
Class Two Hotel: Strathcona Hotel, Patchway, 4 mile(s). Tel: 612271 (0454)

BRISTOL
Henbury Golf Club, Henbury Hill, Westbury-On-Trym Bristol, Avon. BS10 7QB. Tel: 500660 (0272)
Secretary: J R Leeming　　　　　Tel: 500044 (0272)
Professional: Nick Riley　　　　　Tel: 502121 (0272)
Location: M5 junc 17, A4018 to Westbury-On-Trym 3 miles. Next to Blaise castle.
Description: Wooded parkland.
White course 18 holes, 6,039 yards, Par 70, S.S.S. 70, Course record 62.
Ladies 18 holes, 5,469 yards, Par 72, S.S.S. 72, Course record 66.
Membership: 650
Visitors: Welcome. Handicap certificate required. With a member at weekends and Bank Holidays. Advisable to telephone.
Green Fees: £20 (with a member £9).
Facilities: Lunch. Dinner. Bar Snacks. Full Catering. Changing Room. Golf Shop. Club Hire. Trolley Hire.
Class One Hotel: Henbury Lodge, Henbury, 1 mile(s). Tel: 502615 (0272)
Class Two Hotel: White Swan, Almondsbury, 4 1/2 mile(s). Tel: 612332 (0454)

BRISTOL
Knowle Golf Club, Fairway, Brislington, Bristol, Avon. BS4 5DF. Tel: 776341 (0272)
Secretary: Mrs J D King　　　　　Tel: 770660 (0272)
Professional: G M Brand　　　　　Tel: 779193 (0272)
Description: Parkland.
18 holes, 6,104 yards, Par 69, S.S.S. 69.
Membership: 800
Visitors: Welcome. Handicap certificate required. Dinner by arrangement.
Green Fees: Weekdays £21 per round, £26 per day. Weekends £26 per round, £31 per day.
Facilities: Lunch. Dinner. Bar Snacks. Full Catering. Changing Room. Golf Shop. Club Hire. Trolley Hire. Buggy Hire.
Class One Hotel: Grange, Keynsham, 3 mile(s). Tel: 869181 (0272)
Class Two Hotel: Imperial Guest House, Knowle, 2 mile(s). Tel: 779186 (0272)

BRISTOL

Mangotsfield Golf Club, Carsons Road, Mangotsfield, Bristol, Avon. BS12 3LW. Tel: 565501 (0272)
Secretary: Terry Bindon Tel: 697032 (0272)
Professional: Craig Trewin Tel: 565501 (0272)
Location: 3 miles from M32.
Description: Undulating parkland.
18 holes, 5,337 yards, Par 68, S.S.S. 66, Course record 63.
Membership: 700
Visitors: Welcome. No restrictions.
Green Fees: £8 weekdays, £10 weekends.
Facilities: Lunch. Bar Snacks. Full Catering. Changing Room. Golf Shop. Club Hire. Trolley Hire. Buggy Hire.
Class One Hotel: Forte Crest, Bristol, 3 mile(s). Tel: 564242 (0272)
Class Two Hotel: Grange, Bristol, 3 mile(s). Tel: 869181 (0272)

CHIPPING SODBURY

Chipping Sodbury Golf Club, Chipping Sodbury, Avon. BS17 6PU. Tel: 319042 (0454)
Secretary: K G Starr Tel: 319042 (0454)
Professional: Mike Watts Tel: 314087 (0454)
Description: Parkland.
New Course 18 holes, 6,912 yards, Par 73, S.S.S. 73, Course record 64.
Old Course 9 holes, 3,076 yards, Par 73, S.S.S. 73.
Membership: 700
Visitors: Welcome. Handicap certificate required. Afternoons only at weekends on New Course.
Green Fees: Weekdays £20, weekends £25 (New Course). Old Course £5.
Facilities: Lunch. Dinner. Bar Snacks. Full Catering. Changing Room. Golf Shop. Club Hire. Trolley Hire.
Class One Hotel: Crosshands, Old Sodbury, 2 mile(s). Tel: 313000 (0454)
Class Two Hotel: Moda, Chip. Sodbury, 1/2 mile(s). Tel: 312135 (0454)

CLEVEDON

Clevedon Golf Club, Castle Road, Clevedon, Avon. BS21 7AA. Tel: 874057 (0275)
Secretary: M Sullivan Tel: 874057 (0275)
Location: 2 miles from junc 20 M5.
Description: Spectacularly beautiful hilly parkland.
18 holes, 5,887 yards, Par 69, S.S.S. 69, Course record 66.
Membership: 700
Visitors: Welcome. Handicap certificate required. Not wednesday a.m.. Always telephone beforehand.
Green Fees: Weekdays £20, weekends and Bank Holidays £30.
Facilities: Lunch. Dinner. Bar Snacks. Full Catering. Changing Room. Golf Shop. Club Hire. Trolley Hire.
Class One Hotel: Walton Park, Clevedon, 1 mile(s). Tel: 874253 (0272)

BEDFORDSHIRE

AMPTHILL

Millbrook Golf Course, Millbrook, Ampthill, Beds. MK45 2JB. Tel: 840252 (0525)
Secretary: Mrs M Brackley Tel: 840252 (0525)
Professional: Mr T K Devine Tel: 402269 (0525)
Location: 1 mile from Ampthill town centre. M1 junc 12 from south, junc 13 from the north. On A418 off A507.
Description: Hilly tree-lined parkland, one of the longest courses in Britain.
18 holes, 6,779 yards, Par 74, S.S.S. 73.
Membership: 550
Visitors: Welcome. Weekdays only. Closed Thursdays.
Green Fees: Before 10 a.m. £15, after 10 a.m. £20, day ticket £25.
Facilities: Lunch. Dinner. Bar Snacks. Changing Room. Golf Shop. Trolley Hire.
Class One Hotel: Flitwick Manor, Flitwick, 2 1/2 mile(s). Tel: 712242 (0525)

ASPLEY GUISE

Aspley Guise & Woburn Sands Golf Club, West Hill, Aspley Guise, Milton Keynes, Beds. MK17 8DX. Tel: 583596 (0908)
Secretary: M A Beadle Tel: 583596 (0908)
Professional: T Hill Tel: 582974 (0908)
Location: 2 miles west of junc 13 M1, between Aspley Guise and Woburn sands.
Description: Parkland.
18 holes, 6,248 yards, Par 71, S.S.S. 70, Course record 67.
Membership: 660
Visitors: Welcome. Handicap certificate required. Weekdays, with member at weekends.
Green Fees: £23.50 per day, £18 per round.
Facilities: Lunch. Dinner. Bar Snacks. Full Catering. Changing Room. Golf Shop. Trolley Hire.
Class One Hotel: Moore Place Hotel, Aspley Guise, 1/4 mile(s). Tel: 281888 (0908)
Class Two Hotel: Sands Lodge, Woburn Sands, 1 mile(s). Tel: 584183 (0908)

BEDFORD

Mowsbury Golf Club, Cleaton Hill, Kimbolton Road, Bedford. MK41 8DQ. Tel: 771493 (0234)
Secretary: L W Allan Tel: 771041 (0234)
Professional: Paul Ashwell Tel: 216374 (0234)
Location: On B660 at northern limit of town boundary.
Description: Municipal parkland course with ponds.
18 holes, 6,510 yards, Par 72, S.S.S. 71.
Membership: 900
Visitors: Welcome. No societies Fridays or weekends.
Green Fees: On application from pro-shop.
Facilities: Lunch. Dinner. Bar Snacks. Full Catering. Changing Room. Golf Shop. Club Hire. Driving Range. Trolley Hire.

DUNSTABLE

Dunstable Downs Golf Club, Whipsnade Road, Dunstable, Beds. LU6 2NB. Tel: 604472 (0582)
Secretary: P J Nightingale Tel: 604472 (0582)
Professional: Mike Weldon Tel: 662806 (0582)
Location: South Dunstable.
Description: Downland.
18 holes, 6,184 yards, Par 70, S.S.S. 70, Course record 65.
Membership: 669

Visitors: Welcome. Handicap certificate required.
Green Fees: £25 per day or round.
Facilities: Lunch. Dinner. Bar Snacks. Full Catering. Changing Room. Golf Shop. Trolley Hire.
Class One Hotel: Old Palace Lodge, Dunstable, 2 mile(s). Tel: 662201 (0582)

LEIGHTON BUZZARD

Ivinghoe Golf Club, Ivinghoe, Near Leighton Buzzard, Beds. LU7 9EF. Tel: 668696 (0296)
Secretary: S E Garrad   Tel: 668696 (0296)
Professional: P W Garrad   Tel: 668696 (0296)
Location: Just off main road through village. Tring 5 miles. Dunstable 7 miles.
Description: Tight testing nine hole course with water hazards.
9 holes, 4,508 yards, Par 62, S.S.S. 62, Course record 61.
Membership: 250
Visitors: Welcome. Members only before 8 am. Tee time bookings required for weekends.
Green Fees: £6 weekdays, £8 weekends.
Facilities: Lunch. Bar Snacks. Full Catering. Changing Room. Golf Shop. Club Hire. Trolley Hire.
Class One Hotel: Stocks, Aldbury, 3 mile(s). Tel: 341 (044285)

LEIGHTON BUZZARD

Leighton Buzzard Golf Club, Plantation Road, Leighton Buzzard, Beds. LU7 7JF. Tel: 373811 (0525)
Secretary: J Burchell   Tel: 373811 (0525)
Professional: Lee Muncey   Tel: 372143 (0525)
Description: Part woodland, part parkland.
18 holes, 6,101 yards, Par 71, S.S.S. 70, Course record 71.
Membership: 700
Visitors: Welcome. Handicap certificate required. With member only at weekends and Bank Holidays. Tuesday's Ladies day.
Green Fees: Weekdays £25 per day, £18 per round. With member £10 per round or day. Weekends with member only, £14 per round or day.
Facilities: Lunch. Dinner. Bar Snacks. Full Catering. Changing Room. Golf Shop. Club Hire. Trolley Hire.
Class Two Hotel: Swan Hotel, L/Buzzard, 1 mile(s). Tel: 372148 (0525)

SANDY

John O'Gaunt Golf Club, Sutton Park, Sandy, Beds. SG19 2LY. Tel: 260360 (0767)
Secretary: I M Simpson   Tel: 260360 (0767)
Professional: P Round   Tel: 260094 (0767)
Location: B1040 between Potton and Biggleswade.
Description: 2 courses, one parkland and one heathland.
John O'Gaunt 18 holes, 6,214 yards, Par 71, S.S.S. 70, Course record 64.
Carthagena 18 holes, 5,590 yards, Par 69, S.S.S. 67.
Membership: 1400
Visitors: Welcome. Handicap certificate required at weekends.
Green Fees: Weekdays £35, weekends and Bank Holidays £50.

Facilities: Lunch. Dinner. Bar Snacks. Full Catering. Changing Room. Golf Shop. Trolley Hire. Buggy Hire.
Class One Hotel: Stratton House, Biggleswade, 3 mile(s). Tel: 312442 (0767)
Class Two Hotel: Rose and Crown, Potton, 3 mile(s). Tel: 260221 (0767)

WYBOSTON

Wyboston Lakes Golf Club, Wyboston Lakes, Wyboston, Beds. MK44 3AL. Tel: 219200 (0480)
Secretary: B Chinn   Tel: 219200 (0480)
Professional: P Ashwell   Tel: 212501 (0480)
Location: Off A1 and A45, south of St Neots.
Description: Parkland around 5 lakes.
18 holes, 5,803 yards, Par 69, S.S.S. 69.
Membership: 300
Visitors: Welcome. Pay and Play, book starting times at weekends 1 week in advance.
Green Fees: On application.
Facilities: Lunch. Bar Snacks. Changing Room. Golf Shop. Club Hire. Driving Range. Trolley Hire.
Class One Hotel: Wyboston Motel, On Course. Tel: 219200 (0480)

BERKSHIRE

ASCOT

Berkshire Golf Club, Swinley Road, Ascot, Berks. SL5 8AY. Tel: 21495 (0344)
Secretary: Major P D Clarke   Tel: 21496 (0344)
Professional: K A MacDonald   Tel: 22351 (0344)
Location: Between Ascot and Bagshot on A332.
Description: Undulating heathland championship course, host of The Berkshire Trophy and the Astor Salver. Established in 1928.
Red 18 holes, 6,369 yards, Par 72, S.S.S. 70.
Blue 18 holes, 6,260 yards, Par 71, S.S.S. 70.
Membership: 980
Visitors: Welcome. Handicap certificate required. With members only at weekends. Caddies available with notice.
Green Fees: On application.
Facilities: Lunch. Dinner. Bar Snacks. Full Catering. Changing Room. Golf Shop. Club Hire. Trolley Hire. Buggy Hire.
Class One Hotel: Berystede, Ascot, 3 mile(s). Tel: 23311 (0344)

ASCOT

Lavender Park, Swinley Road, Ascot, Berks. SL5 8BD. Tel: 884074 (0344)
Professional: Tony Bowers   Tel: 886096 (0344)
Description: Small nine hole par 3.
9 holes, 1,104 yards, Par 28, S.S.S. 28.
Visitors: Welcome. No restrictions.
Green Fees: Weekdays £2.95, Weekends £3.95.
Facilities: Lunch. Bar Snacks. Golf Shop. Club Hire. Driving Range.
Class One Hotel: Royal Berkshire, Ascot, 2 mile(s). Tel: 23322 (0344)
Class Two Hotel: Royal Foresters, Ascot, 2 mile(s). Tel: 884747 (0344)

ASCOT

Swinley Forest Golf Club, Coronation Road, Ascot, Berks. SL5 9LE. Tel: 20197 (0344)
Secretary: I L Pearce   Tel: 20197 (0344)
Professional: R C Parker   Tel: 874811 (0344)
Location:
Description: Heathland and pine.
18 holes, 5,952 yards, Par 68, S.S.S. 69, Course record 64.
Membership: 240
Visitors: Letter of Introduction required. Only on introduction of a member.
Green Fees: £65.
Facilities: Lunch. Bar Snacks. Full Catering. Changing Room. Golf Shop. Club Hire. Trolley Hire. Caddies available.
Class One Hotel: Berystede, Ascot, 2 mile(s). Tel: 23311 (0344)
Class Two Hotel: Brockenhurst, Ascot, 1 mile(s). Tel: 21912 (0344)

CROWTHORNE

East Berkshire Golf Club, Ravenswood Avenue, Crowthorne, Berks. RG11 6BD. Tel: 772041 (0344)
Secretary: W H Short   Tel: 772041 (0344)
Professional: Arthur Roe   Tel: 774112 (0344)
Location: Near Crowthorne station.
Description: Heathland.
18 holes, 6,345 yards, Par 69, S.S.S. 70, Course record 65.
Membership: 700
Visitors: Welcome. Handicap certificate required. No visitors at weekends.
Green Fees: £33 per round or day.
Facilities: Lunch. Bar Snacks. Changing Room. Golf Shop. Trolley Hire.
Class One Hotel: Waterloo, Crowthorne, 1/2 mile(s). Tel: 777711 (0344)
Class Two Hotel: Dial House, Crowthorne, 1/2 mile(s). Tel: 776941 (0344)

MAIDENHEAD

Maidenhead Golf Club, Shoppenhangers Road, Maidenhead, Berks. SL6 2PZ. Tel: 20545 (0344)
Secretary: Iain Lindsay   Tel: 24693 (0628)
Professional: Clive Dell   Tel: 24067 (0628)
Location: Adjacent to Maidenhead Station (south side), 1 mile from M4.
Description: Flat.
18 holes, 6,344 yards, Par 70, S.S.S. 70, Course record 66.
Visitors: Welcome. Handicap certificate required. Not after 12p.m. Fridays. Societies Wednesdays and Thursdays.
Green Fees: £27 per round/day.
Facilities: Lunch. Dinner. Bar Snacks. Changing Room. Golf Shop. Trolley Hire. Buggy Hire.
Class One Hotel: Fredericks, Maidenhead. Tel: 35934 (0628)
Class Two Hotel: Kingswood, Maidenhead, 2 mile(s). Tel: 33598 (0628)

NEWBURY

Newbury and Crookham Golf Club, Bury's Bank Road, Newbury, Berks. RG15 8BZ. Tel: 40035 (0635)
Secretary: Mrs J R Hearsey   Tel: 40035 (0635)
Professional: Mr D Harris   Tel: 31201 (0635)
Location: 3 miles west of Newbury off A34.
Description: A short course with varied challenging interest.
18 holes, 5,880 yards, Par 68, S.S.S. 68.
Membership: 500
Visitors: Welcome. Handicap certificate required. With members at weekends and Bank Holidays.
Green Fees: £27.50.
Facilities: Lunch. Dinner. Bar Snacks. Full Catering. Changing Room. Golf Shop. Trolley Hire.
Class One Hotel: Hilton, Newbury, 1 mile(s). Tel: 529000 (0635)

NEWBURY

West Berkshire Golf Club, Chaddleworth, Newbury, Berks. RG16 0HS. Tel: 574 (04882)
Secretary: W Richardson   Tel: 574 (04882)
Professional: David Shepard   Tel: 8851 (04882)
Location: Close to junc's 13 and 14 M4.
Description: Downland.
18 holes, 7,069 yards, Par 73, S.S.S. 74.
Membership: 800
Visitors: Welcome. Not weekends.
Green Fees: £22 per day
Facilities: Dinner. Bar Snacks. Full Catering. Changing Room. Golf Shop. Club Hire. Trolley Hire. Buggy Hire.
Class One Hotel: The Bear, Hungerford, 10 mile(s). Tel: 682512 (0488)
Class Two Hotel: Queen's Arms, Newbury, 4 mile(s). Tel: 47547 (0635)

NORTH ASCOT

Mill Ride Golf Club, Mill Ride Estate, North Ascot, Berks. SL5 8LT. Tel: 886777 (0344)
Secretary: J K Deeming   Tel: 8867777 (0344)
Professional: Bob Newman   Tel: 886777 (0344)
Location: 1 mile from Ascot Racecourse.
Description: Parkland with lakes.
18 holes, 6,689 yards, Par 72, S.S.S. 72, Course record 68.
Membership: 250
Visitors: Welcome. Handicap certificate required. Visitor times available.
Green Fees: £40 Monday to Friday.
Facilities: Lunch. Dinner. Bar Snacks. Full Catering. Changing Room. Golf Shop. Club Hire. Driving Range. Trolley Hire. Caddies available
Class One Hotel: Mill Ride (On Course), Ascot. Tel: 886777 (0344)

READING

Reading Golf Club, 17 Kidmore End Road, Emmer Green, Reading, Berks. RG4 8SG. Tel: 472169 (0734)
Secretary: John Weekes   Tel: 472909 (0734)
Professional: Tim Morrison   Tel: 476115 (0734)
Location: 2 miles north of Reading, 1 mile north of Caversham, off B481 Peppard road.

Description: Parkland.
18 holes, 6,212 yards, Par 70, S.S.S. 70, Course record 67.
Membership: 700
Visitors: Welcome. Handicap certificate required. With member Friday, Saturday and Sunday.
Green Fees: £12 with member, £26 without.
Facilities: Lunch. Dinner. Bar Snacks. Full Catering. Changing Room. Golf Shop. Club Hire. Trolley Hire.
Class One Hotel: Caversham Hotel, Caversham, 1 mile(s). Tel: 391818 (0734)
Class Two Hotel: Rainbow Corner Hotel, Caversham, 1 mile(s). Tel: 588140 (0734)

STREATLEY ON THAMES
Goring and Streatley Golf Club, Streatley On Thames, Berks.   . Tel: 872688 (0491)
Secretary: J Menzies   Tel: 873229 (0491)
Professional: Roy Mason   Tel: 873715 (0491)
Location: 10 miles north-west of Reading, on Reading-Wantage road A417.
Description: Overlooking Berkshire Downland (National Trust) course of scenic beauty.
18 holes, 6,286 yards, Par 71, S.S.S. 70, Course record 65.
Membership: 750
Visitors: Welcome. Not weekends.
Green Fees: £27 per day.
Facilities: Lunch. Dinner. Bar Snacks. Full Catering. Changing Room. Golf Shop. Club Hire. Trolley Hire.
Class One Hotel: The Swann Diplomat, Streatley, 3/4 mile(s). Tel: 873737 (0491)
Class Two Hotel: Beetle and Wedge, Moulsford, 4 mile(s). Tel: 651381 (0491)

SUNNINGDALE
Sunningdale Golf Club, Ridgemont Road, Sunningdale, Berks.   SL5 9RR. Tel: 21681 (0344)
Secretary: Mr Stuart Zuill   Tel: 21681 (0344)
Professional: Mr K Maxwell   Tel: 20128 (0344)
Location: Situated close to the centre of Sunningdale.
Description: Both Old and New courses feature flat and undulating heathland. Old Course (championship) established in 1902. New Course established in 1904.
Old 18 holes, 6,586 yards, Par 71, S.S.S. 71, Course record 66.
New 18 holes, 6,676 yards, Par , S.S.S. 71, Course record 65.
Membership: 800
Visitors: Welcome. Handicap certificate required. Letter of Introduction required. With members only at weekends and Bank Holidays. Always book in advance.
Green Fees: £80 per day.
Facilities: Lunch. Bar Snacks. Full Catering. Changing Room. Golf Shop. Club Hire. Trolley Hire. Caddies available.
Class One Hotel: Berystede, Ascot, 2 mile(s). Tel: 23311 (0344)

WOKINGHAM
Downshire Golf Course, Easthampstead Park, Wokingham, Berks.   RG11 3DH. Tel: 422708 (0344)
Professional: Paul Watson   Tel: 302030 (0344)

Location: 2 miles from Wokingham, 2 miles from Bracknell.
Description: Natural parkland municipal course.
18 holes, 6,395 yards, Par , S.S.S. .
Membership: 600
Visitors: Welcome.
Green Fees: Weekdays £7.70, weekends £8.70 (winter rates).
Facilities: Lunch. Dinner. Bar Snacks. Full Catering. Changing Room. Golf Shop. Club Hire. Driving Range. Trolley Hire. Buggy Hire.
Class One Hotel: St Annes Manor, Wokingham, 2 mile(s). Tel: 772550 (0734)

BUCKINGHAMSHIRE

AYLESBURY
Chiltern Forest Golf Club, Aston Hill, Halton, Aylesbury, Bucks.   HP22 5HQ. Tel: 630899 (0296)
Secretary: L E A Clark   Tel: 631267 (0296)
Professional: Christopher Skeet   Tel: 631817 (0296)
Description: 14 lake layout until July 1992, then 18 lakes. Hilly and wooded.
14 Lake layout 18 holes, 5,942 yards, Par 72, S.S.S. 70, Course record 68.
18 Lake layout 18 holes, 5.755 yards, Par 70, S.S.S. 69.
Membership: 600
Visitors: Welcome. With members at weekends, when handicap certificate is required. Certain catering restrictions apply, please confirm beforehand.
Green Fees: April 92 £21, from August 92 £24.
Facilities: Lunch. Dinner. Bar Snacks. Full Catering. Changing Room. Golf Shop.
Class One Hotel: The Bell Inn, Aston Clinton, 1 mile(s). Tel: 630252 (0296)
Class Two Hotel: West Lodge Hotel, Aston Clinton, 1 mile(s). Tel: 630331 (0296)

AYLESBURY
Weston Turville Golf and Squash Club, New Road, Weston Turville, Near Aylesbury, Bucks. HP22 5QT. Tel: 25949 (0296)
Secretary: Mr Barry Hill   Tel: 24084 (0296)
Professional: Tom Jones   Tel: 24084 (0296)
Location: 1 1/2 miles south of Aylesbury, just off A41.
Description: Parkland with views of the Chiltern Hills.
18 holes, 6,002 yards, Par 69, S.S.S. 69, Course record 73.
Membership: 600
Visitors: Welcome.
Green Fees: Weekdays £15, weekends £20.
Facilities: Lunch. Dinner. Bar Snacks. Full Catering. Changing Room. Golf Shop. Club Hire. Trolley Hire.
Class One Hotel: Forte Crest, Aston Clinton, 3 mile(s). Tel: 393388 (0296)

BEACONSFIELD
Beaconsfield Golf Club Ltd., Seer Green, Near Beaconsfield, Bucks.   HP9 2UR. Tel: 676545 (0494)

Secretary: P I Anderson Tel: 676545 (0494)
Professional: Mike Brothers Tel: 676616 (0494)
Description: A well bunkered, tree lined parkland golf course which plays longer than the card, easy walking.
18 holes, 6,487 yards, Par 72, S.S.S. 71.
Membership: 850
Visitors: Welcome. Handicap certificate required. Not weekends or Thursdays a.m..
Green Fees: £33 per round, £40 per day.
Facilities: Lunch. Dinner. Bar Snacks. Full Catering. Changing Room. Golf Shop. Trolley Hire.
Class One Hotel: Bellhouse Hotel, Beaconsfield, 3 mile(s). Tel: 887211 (0753).
Class Two Hotel: Old Jordans Quaker Guest House, Jordans, 1 mile(s). Tel: 74586 (0240)

CHALFONT ST GILES
Harewood Downs Golf Club, Cokes Lane, Chalfont St Giles, Bucks. HP8 4TA. Tel: 762184 (0494)
Secretary: M R Cannon Tel: 762184 (0494)
Professional: G C Morris Tel: 764102 (0494)
Location: A413 2miles east of Amersham.
Description: Natural tree lined course, sloping greens, lovely views.
18 holes, 5,958 yards, Par 69, S.S.S. 69, Course record 64.
Membership: 700
Visitors: Welcome. Handicap certificate required. Ladies day Tuesday. Some catering restrictions apply, please confirm in advance.
Green Fees: £20 per round, £27 per day.
Facilities: Lunch. Dinner. Bar Snacks. Full Catering. Changing Room. Golf Shop. Trolley Hire.
Class One Hotel: The Crown, Old Amersham, 2 mile(s). Tel: 721541 (0494)

GERRARDS CROSS
Gerrards Cross Golf Club, Chalfont Park, Gerrards Cross, Bucks. SL9 0QA. Tel: 883263 (0753)
Secretary: P H Fisher Tel: 883263 (0753)
Professional: A P Barr Tel: 885300 (0753)
Location: Adjacent to A413.
Description: Parkland.
18 holes, 6,295 yards, Par 69, S.S.S. 70, Course record 65.
Visitors: Welcome. Handicap certificate required. Letter of Introduction required. No visitors at weekends.
Green Fees: £26 per round, £33 per day.
Facilities: Lunch. Bar Snacks. Changing Room. Golf Shop. Trolley Hire.
Class One Hotel: Bull Hotel, Gerrards Cross, 3 mile(s). Tel: 885995 (0753)

HIGH WYCOMBE
Flackwell Heath Golf Club Ltd., Treadaway Road, Flackwell Heath, High Wycombe, Bucks. HP10 9PE. Tel: 520027 (0628)
Secretary: Peter Jeans Tel: 520927 (0628)
Professional: Steven Bryan Tel: 523017 (0628)
Location: Junc 3 M40. Towards Oxford, 3 miles from High Wycombe.
Description: Hilly parkland/heathland.
18 holes, 6,207 yards, Par 71, S.S.S. 70, Course record 65.

Membership: 800
Visitors: Welcome. Handicap certificate required. With members only at weekends. Tuesday is ladies day.
Green Fees: £27, £10 with member.
Facilities: Lunch. Dinner. Bar Snacks. Full Catering. Changing Room. Golf Shop. Trolley Hire.
Class One Hotel: Bellhouse, Beaconsfield, 2 mile(s). Tel: 887211 (0753)

HIGH WYCOMBE
Hazlemere Golf and Country Club Ltd., Penn Road, Hazlemere, Near High Wycombe, Bucks. HP15 7LR. Tel: 714722 (0494)
Secretary: Mrs D Hudson Tel: 714722 (0494)
Professional: Mr S Morvell Tel: 718298 (0494)
Location: 3 miles on A404 from High Wycombe (junc 4 on M40) entrance on B474 approx 400 yards from Hazlemere Crossroads.
Description: Undulating parkland.
18 holes, 5,652 yards, Par 70, S.S.S. 68, Course record 64.
Membership: 800
Visitors: Welcome. With members only at weekends.
Green Fees: Weekdays £22 per round.
Facilities: Lunch. Dinner. Bar Snacks. Full Catering. Changing Room. Golf Shop. Club Hire. Trolley Hire. Buggy Hire.
Class One Hotel: The Bellhouse, Beaconsfield, 4 1/2 mile(s). Tel: 887211 (0753)
Class Two Hotel: The Chiltern, High Wycombe, 4 mile(s). Tel: 452597 (0494)

LITTLE CHALFONT
Little Chalfont Golf Club, Lodge Lane, Little Chalfont, Bucks. HP8 4AJ. Tel: 764877 (0494)
Secretary: J M Dunne Tel: 764877 (0494)
Professional: J M Dunne Tel: 762942 (0494)
Location: 2 miles from M25 junc 18, off A404 between Chorleywood and Little Chalfont.
Description: Gently undulating nine hole parkland.
9 holes, 5,532 yards, Par 68, S.S.S. 68, Course record 66.
Visitors: Welcome.
Green Fees: £9 for 18 holes weekdays, £11 for 18 holes weekends and Bank Holidays.
Facilities: Lunch. Dinner. Bar Snacks. Full Catering. Changing Room. Golf Shop. Club Hire. Trolley Hire. Buggy Hire.
Class One Hotel: Bedford Arms, Chenies, 2 mile(s). Tel: 283601 (0923)
Class Two Hotel: Two Brewers, Chipperfield, 3 mile(s). Tel: 265266 (0923)

MILTON KEYNES
Abbey Hill Golf Club, Abbey Hill, Monks Way, Two Mile Ash, Milton Keynes. MK8 8AA. Tel: 562408 (0908)
Secretary: Mr I D Grieve Tel: 562408 (0908)
Professional: S Harlock Tel: 563845 (0908)
Location: Junction of A422 and A5.
Description: Undulating parkland. Public course with private club.
18 holes, 6,177 yards, Par 68, S.S.S. 69, Course record 67.
Membership: 500
Visitors: Welcome.
Green Fees: Weekdays £6, weekends £8.50.

Facilities: Lunch. Dinner. Bar Snacks. Full Catering. Changing Room. Golf Shop. Club Hire. Trolley Hire.
Class One Hotel: Friendly Lodge, Milton Keynes, 1/8th mile(s). Tel: 561666 (0908)
Class Two Hotel: Bull Hotel, Stony Stratford, 3 mile(s). Tel: 567104 (0908)

MILTON KEYNES
Three Locks Golf Club, Partridge House, Great Brickhill, Milton Keynes, Bucks. MK17 9BH. Tel: 270050 (0525)
Secretary: Bill Stevenson Tel: 270470 (0525)
Professional: Colin Anssell Tel: 270050 (0525)
Description: Flat parkland course, with wide fairways with river running through the course and several lakes.
9 holes, 3,327 yards, Par 70, S.S.S. 72.
Membership: 450
Visitors: Welcome. Members have priority bookings at weekends.
Green Fees: Weekdays £5 for 9 holes, £8 for 18 holes. Weekends £7 for 9 holes, £9.50 for 18 holes.
Facilities: Bar Snacks. Changing Room. Golf Shop. Club Hire. Trolley Hire.
Class Two Hotel: Partridge House, On Course. Tel: 270470 (0525)

MILTON KEYNES
Wavendon Golf Centre, Lower End Road, Wavendon, Milton Keynes, Bucks. MK17 8DA. Tel: 281811 (0908)
Secretary: Cynthia Cheney Tel: 281811 (0908)
Professional: Nick Elmer Tel: 281811 (0908)
Location: Alongside A421 link road connecting M1 junc 13 to Milton Keynes.
Description: Parkland course set in mature trees, six water hazards.
18 holes, 5,479 yards, Par 67, S.S.S. 67, Course record 73.
9 holes, 2,848 yards, Par 27, S.S.S. 27.
Membership: 450
Visitors: Welcome.
Green Fees: 18 holes weekdays £9, weekends £12.
Facilities: Lunch. Dinner. Bar Snacks. Full Catering. Changing Room. Golf Shop. Club Hire. Driving Range. Trolley Hire.
Class One Hotel: Coach House, Newport Pagnell, 5 mile(s). Tel: 613688 (0908)
Class Two Hotel: Bell Hotel, Woburn, 5 mile(s). Tel: 290280 (0525)

MILTON KEYNES
Woburn Golf and Country Club, Bow Brickhill, Milton Keynes, Bucks. MK17 9LJ. Tel: 370756 (0908)
Secretary: Mrs G Beasley Tel: 370756 (0908)
Managing Director and Professional: Alex Hay Tel: 647987 (0908)
Location: Approx 4 miles west of junc 13 M1, 1 mile east of A5 at Little Brickhill.
Description: Both championship courses were carved from a large pine forest and the holes are played through avenues of trees and are bordered by heather, gorse and rhododendrons.
Duke's 18 holes, 6,940 yards, Par 72, S.S.S. 74, Course record 64.
Duchess 18 holes, 6.641 yards, Par 72, S.S.S. 72.
Visitors: Welcome. Handicap certificate required. Monday to Friday only by prior arrangement.
Green Fees: On application.
Facilities: Lunch. Dinner. Changing Room. Golf Shop. Trolley Hire. Buggy Hire. Caddies available.
Class One Hotel: Bedford Arms, Woburn, 3 mile(s). Tel: 290441 (0525)
Class Two Hotel: The Bell Inn, Woburn, 3 mile(s). Tel: 290280 (0525)

PRINCES RISBOROUGH
Whiteleaf Golf Club Ltd., Whiteleaf, Princes Risborough, Aylesbury, Bucks. HP17 0LY. Tel: 3097 (08444)
Secretary: D G Bullard Tel: 274058 (0844)
Professional: K S Ward Tel: 5472 (08444)
Location: On main Aylesbury road, 1 mile from Princes Risborough.
Description: 9 holes played off 18 tees, set in the Chiltern Hills.
9 holes, 5,391 yards, Par 66, S.S.S. 66, Course record 63.
Membership: 350
Visitors: Welcome. Handicap certificate required. Letter of Introduction required. Prior arrangement with secretary only. Not weekends.
Green Fees: £18 per round, £25 per day.
Facilities: Lunch. Dinner. Bar Snacks. Full Catering. Changing Room. Golf Shop. Trolley Hire.
Class Two Hotel: George and Dragon, P. Risborough, 1 1/2 mile(s). Tel: 3808 (08444)

CAMBRIDGESHIRE

CAMBRIDGE
Cambridge Moat House Hotel Golf Club, Bar Hill, Cambs. CB3 8EU. Tel: 780555 (0954)
Secretary: G Huggett Tel: 780555 (0954)
Professional: G Huggett Tel: 780098 (0954)
Description: Undulating parkland with lake and ditches.
18 holes, 6,734 yards, Par 72, S.S.S. 72, Course record 68.
Membership: 500
Visitors: Welcome. Handicap certificate preferred.
Green Fees: W/days £19, w/ends and Bank Holidays £25.
Facilities: Lunch. Dinner. Bar Snacks. Full Catering. Changing Room. Golf Shop. Club Hire. Trolley Hire. Buggy Hire.
Class One Hotel: Cambridgeshire Moat House, On Course. Tel: 780555 (0954)

CAMBRIDGE
Girton Golf Club, Dodford Lane, Girton, Cambs. CB3 0QE. Tel: 276169 (0223)
Secretary: Mrs M A Cornwal Tel: 276169 (0223)
Professional: S Thompson Tel: 276991 (0223)
Location: 2 miles north of Cambridge.
Description: Parkland.
18 holes, 6,085 yards, Par 69, S.S.S. 69.
Membership: 700
Visitors: Welcome. Weekdays only.
Green Fees: £18 per day with handicap certificate, £23 without.

Facilities: Lunch. Dinner. Bar Snacks. Full Catering. Changing Room. Golf Shop. Club Hire. Trolley Hire.
Class One Hotel: Post House, Impington, 3 mile(s). Tel: 237000 (0223)

CAMBRIDGE

Gog Magog Golf Club, Shelford Bottom, Cambs. CB2 4AB. Tel: 247626 (0223)
Secretary: John E Riches   Tel: 247626 (0223)
Professional: Ian Bamborough   Tel: 246058 (0223)
Description: Open and undulating.
Old 18 holes, 6,386 yards, Par 70, S.S.S. 70, Course record 64.
New 18 holes, 5,805 yards, Par 68, S.S.S. 68.
Membership: 1050
Visitors: Welcome. Handicap certificate required. With members at weekends, Handicap 22 or better.
Green Fees: £27.50 per round, £33 per day. New Course £18.
Facilities: Lunch. Dinner. Bar Snacks. Full Catering. Changing Room. Golf Shop. Trolley Hire.
Class One Hotel: Garden House, Cambridge, 3 mile(s). Tel: 63421 (0223)
Class Two Hotel: Centennial, Cambridge, 2 mile(s). Tel: 314652 (0223)

ELY

Ely City Golf Course, Cambridge Road, Ely, Cambs. CB7 4HX. Tel: 662751 (0353)
Secretary: Mr G A Briggs   Tel: 662751 (0353)
Professional: Fred Rowden   Tel: 663317 (0353)
Description: Slightly undulating parkland.
18 holes, 6,602 yards, Par 72, S.S.S. 72, Course record 66.
Visitors: Welcome. Handicap certificate required. Dress rule - no jeans, tee shirts or trainer shoes.
Green Fees: £22 per day weekdays, £30 per day at weekends.
Facilities: Lunch. Dinner. Bar Snacks. Full Catering. Changing Room. Golf Shop. Club Hire. Trolley Hire.
Class One Hotel: Lamb Hotel, Ely, 1 mile(s). Tel: 663000 (0353)
Class Two Hotel: Nyton House, Ely, 1/4 mile(s). Tel: 662459 (0353)

MARCH

March Golf Club, Frogs Abbey, Grange Road, March, Cambs. PE15 0YH. Tel: 52364 (0354)
Secretary: W D Evans   Tel: 57804 (0354)
Professional: Richard Keys   Tel: 52364 (0354)
Location: Adjacent to A141 March by-pass. 1 mile south of town centre.
Description: Parkland.
9 holes, 6,210 yards, Par 70, S.S.S. 70, Course record 67.
Membership: 350
Visitors: Welcome. Handicap certificate required. Some catering restrictions apply, please telephone in advance.
Green Fees: £15 Monday to Friday only.
Facilities: Lunch. Dinner. Bar Snacks. Full Catering. Changing Room. Golf Shop. Club Hire. Trolley Hire.
Class Two Hotel: Griffin Hotel, March, 1 mile(s). Tel: 52517 (0354)

PETERBOROUGH

Orton Meadows Golf Course, Ham Lane, Oundle Road, Peterborough, Cambs. PE2 0UU. Tel: 237478 (0733)
Secretary: K Boyer
Professional: N Grant and M D Booker   Tel: 237478 (0733)
Location: 2 miles south west of Peterborough on the old A605.
Description: Partly in Ferry Meadows Country Park and on reclaimed flood plain, lakes and water fowl. Also 12 hole pitch and putt.
18 holes, 5,800 yards, Par 68, S.S.S. 66, Course record 71.
Membership: 850
Visitors: Welcome. No restrictions, but please book weekends and Bank Holidays. Some catering restrictions apply, please telephone in advance.
Facilities: Lunch. Dinner. Bar Snacks. Full Catering. Changing Room. Golf Shop. Club Hire. Trolley Hire.
Class One Hotel: Swallow Hotel, Peterborough, 1/2 mile(s). Tel: 371111 (0733)

PETERBOROUGH

Thorpe Wood Golf Course, Thorpe Wood, Peterborough, Cambs. PE3 6SE. Tel: 267701 (0733)
Secretary: R Palmer
Professional: Dennis and Roger Fitton   Tel: 267701 (0733)
Location: 3 miles west of town on A47.
Description: Parkland.
18 holes, 7,086 yards, Par 73, S.S.S. 74, Course record 73.
Membership: 800
Visitors: Welcome. No restrictions, but please book. Some catering restrictions apply, please telephone in advance.
Green Fees: £6.70 weekdays, £9.40 weekends and Bank Holidays.
Facilities: Lunch. Dinner. Bar Snacks. Full Catering. Changing Room. Golf Shop. Club Hire. Trolley Hire.
Class One Hotel: Peterborough Moat House, Peterborough, 1/8th mile(s). Tel: 260000 (0733)
Class Two Hotel: Hollies Farm, Castor, 2 mile(s). Tel: 380273 (0733)

ST NEOTS

Abbotsley Golf Club, St Neots, Cambs. PE19 4XN. Tel: 215153 (0480)
Secretary: Miss Jenny Wisson   Tel: 215153 (0480)
Professional: Vivien Saunders & Allen Robertson Tel: 406463 (0480)
Location: Signposted from Abbotsley Village, 2 miles south east of St Neots.
Description: Two courses pleasantly undulating and tree lined with plenty of water hazards. Regular for local championships.
Eynesbury Hardwicke 18 holes, 5,829 yards, Par 73, S.S.S. 71.
Cromwell 18 holes, 6,087 yards, Par 70, S.S.S. 69.
Membership: 700
Visitors: Welcome. Limited on Eynesbury Hardwicke course at weekends, booking essential.
Green Fees: Eynesbury Hardwicke - weekdays £16,

weekends £18. Cromwell - £8 weekdays, £10 weekends.
Facilities: Lunch. Dinner. Bar Snacks. Full Catering. Changing Room. Golf Shop. Club Hire. Driving Range. Trolley Hire. Buggy Hire.
Class One Hotel: Abbotsley Golf Hotel, On complex. Tel: 747000 (0480)
Class Two Hotel: Nags Head, Eynesbury, 3 mile(s). Tel: 74038 (0480)

CHANNEL ISLANDS

ALDERNEY
Alderney Golf Club, Longis Road, Alderney, Channel Islands. . Tel: 822835 (0481)
Secretary: N Soane-Sands   Tel: 823448 (0481)
Location: 1/2 mile east of St Anne.
Description: Challenging 9 hole course with beautiful views of the English Channel and the French Coast.
9 holes, 2,528 yards, Par 32, S.S.S. 65.
Membership: 400
Visitors: Welcome. Not before 10.30a.m. weekends. Parties of 4 or more must telephone to confirm in advance.
Green Fees: Weekdays £12, weekends £18.
Facilities: Lunch. Bar Snacks. Changing Room. Golf Shop. Club Hire. Trolley Hire.
Class One Hotel: Belle Vue, St Anne, 3/4 mile(s). Tel: 822844 (0481)
Class Two Hotel: The Town House, St Anne, 1/2 mile(s). Tel: 822330 (0481)

GUERNSEY
Royal Guernsey Golf Club, L'Ancresse, Vale, Guernsey, Channel Islands. . Tel: 47022 (0481)
Secretary: Mr De Laune   Tel: 46523 (0481)
Professional: Mr N Wood   Tel: 45070 (0481)
Location: 3 miles north of St Peter Port on main north road.
Description: Links course with 2 ponds and several ditches.
18 holes, 6,200 yards, Par 70, S.S.S. 70, Course record 64.
Membership: 750
Visitors: Welcome. Handicap certificate required. Sunject to availability. Members and guests only until 12p.m. on Saturdays. Not before 5p.m. on Sundays.
Green Fees: Weekdays £23 per day, weekends £23 per round. £75 per week.
Facilities: Lunch. Dinner. Bar Snacks. Full Catering. Changing Room. Golf Shop. Club Hire. Driving Range. Trolley Hire.
Class One Hotel: Pembroke Hotel, Adjacent, 0 mile(s). Tel: 47573 (0481)

JERSEY
La Moye Golf Club, St Brelade, Jersey, Channel Islands. JE3 8GQ. Tel: 47166 (0534)
Secretary: Mr P Clash   Tel: 43401 (0534)
Professional: Mr D Melville   Tel: 43130 (0534)
Location: 5 miles west of St Helier on the coast road A2.
Description: Championship links course, extremely difficult and subject to prevailing winds. Overlooking St Ouens Bay.
18 holes, 6,698 yards, Par 72, S.S.S. 72, Course record 69.
Membership: 1348
Visitors: Welcome. Handicap certificate required. Letter of Introduction required. Wednesdays Ladies Day. Only between 9.30a.m. and 11a.m. and 2.30p.m. to 4p.m. weekdays. Not before 2.30p.
Green Fees: Weekdays £30 per round, weekends £35 per round.
Facilities: Lunch. Dinner. Bar Snacks. Full Catering. Changing Room. Golf Shop. Club Hire. Driving Range. Trolley Hire.
Class One Hotel: L'Horizon, St Brelades Bay, 2 mile(s). Tel: 43101 (0534)
Class Two Hotel: Chateau Valeuse, St Brelades Bay, 2 mile(s). Tel: 46281 (0534)

JERSEY
Royal Jersey Golf Club, Grouville, Jersey, Channel Islands. . Tel: 52234 (0534)
Secretary: Mr R C Leader   Tel: 54416 (0534)
Professional: Mr T Horton   Tel: 52234 (0534)
Location: 1 mile west of Gorey along the coast road.
Description: Links course with coastal views. 120 years old.
18 holes, 6,059 yards, Par 70, S.S.S. 70, Course record 64.
Membership: 1242
Visitors: Welcome. Handicap certificate required. Only between 10a.m. and 12p.m. and 2p.m. to 4p.m. weekdays and not before 2.30p.m. weekends.
Green Fees: Weekdays £30 per round, weekends £35 per round.
Facilities: Lunch. Dinner. Bar Snacks. Full Catering. Changing Room. Golf Shop. Club Hire. Trolley Hire.
Class One Hotel: Les Arches, Gorey, 3 mile(s). Tel: 53839 (0534)
Class Two Hotel: Mondesir Guest House, Grouville, 1/4 mile(s). Tel: 54809 (0534)

CHESHIRE

CHESTER
Upton-By-Chester Golf Club, Upton Lane, Chester, Cheshire. CH2 1EE. Tel: 381183 (0244)
Secretary: J B Durban   Tel: 381183 (0244)
Professional: P A Gardner   Tel: 381333 (0244)
Location: A41 near Zoo traffic lights.
Description: Flat parkland.
18 holes, 5,808 yards, Par 69, S.S.S. 68, Course record 62.
Membership: 800
Visitors: Welcome. Handicap certificate required.
Green Fees: £16 weekdays per round, £21 per day or one round weekends.
Facilities: Lunch. Dinner. Bar Snacks. Full Catering. Changing Room. Golf Shop. Trolley Hire. Buggy Hire.

Class One Hotel: Dene, Chester, 1 1/2 mile(s). Tel: 321165 (0244)
Class Two Hotel: Glann, Chester, 1 1/2 mile(s). Tel: 344800 (0244)

CREWE

Crewe Golf Club, Fields Road, Haslington, Crewe, Cheshire. CW1 1TB. Tel: 584227 (0270)
Secretary: David G Elias   Tel: 584099 (0270)
Location: Off A534, between Crewe and Sandbach.
Description: Parkland.
18 holes, 6,201 yards, Par 70, S.S.S. 70.
Membership: 600
Visitors: Welcome. Handicap certificate required. With members only at weekends.
Green Fees: On application.
Facilities: Lunch. Dinner. Bar Snacks. Full Catering. Changing Room. Golf Shop. Club Hire. Trolley Hire.
Class One Hotel: Alvaston Hall, Nantwich, 6 mile(s). Tel: 624341 (0270)
Class Two Hotel: Saxon Cross Motel, Sandbach, 4 mile(s). Tel: 763281 (0270)

CREWE

Onneley Golf Club, Barrhill Road, Onneley, Near Crewe, Cheshire. CW3 5QF. Tel: 750577 (0782)
Secretary: L Kennedy   Tel: 661842 (0270)
Location:
Description: Open parkland on gentle slope.
9 holes, 5,584 yards, Par 70, S.S.S. 67, Course record 67.
Membership: 400
Visitors: Welcome.
Green Fees: £12.50, with member £6.
Facilities: Bar Snacks. Changing Room.
Class One Hotel: Clayton Lodge, N/castle U Lyme, 6 mile(s). Tel: 613093 (0782)
Class Two Hotel: Wheatsheaf Inn, Adjacent. Tel: 751582 (0782)

CREWE

Queens Park Golf Course, Queens Park Drive, Crewe, Cheshire. CW2 7SB. Tel: 666724 (0270)
Secretary: K F Lear   Tel: 628352 (0270)
Professional: H Bilton   Tel: 666724 (0270)
Location: Adjacent to Queens Park Gardens, approx 1 mile from town centre.
Description: Parkland.
Nine holes twice 9 holes, 4,920 yards, Par 64. Course record 69.
Membership: 180
Visitors: Welcome. Some catering restrictions apply, telephone in advance. Tee reserve Sunday mornings.
Green Fees: 18 Holes £3.30 weekdays, £4.20 weekends and Bank Holidays.
Facilities: Lunch. Dinner. Bar Snacks. Full Catering. Changing Room. Golf Shop. Club Hire. Trolley Hire.

HELSBY

Helsby Golf Club, Towers Lane, Helsby, Warrington, Cheshire. WA6 0JB. Tel: 723407 (0928)
Secretary: G A Johnson   Tel: 722021 (0928)

Have you played probably the best municipal golf course in the North of England?

WALTON HALL GOLF COURSE
WARRINGTON
managed by
GOLDEN GATES LEISURE

== WARRINGTON ==
will challenge the best!
Green Fees from £4.10
Tel : 0925 263061
WORKING TOGETHER
IN THE COMMUNITY

Bramallford
WINWICK ROAD WARRINGTON TEL 51111

Professional: Ian Wright   Tel: 725457 (0928)
Location: Junc 14 M56. A5117 to Helsby, through traffic lights, 1 mile 1st right into Primrose Lane, then 1st right into Towers Lane.
Description: Flat parkland.
18 holes, 6,204 yards, Par 70, S.S.S. 70, Course record 67.
Membership: 600
Visitors: Welcome. Handicap certificate required. Societies Tuesdays and Thursdays only. No visitors at weekends unless with a member. No catering on Monday.
Green Fees: £18 per round.
Facilities: Lunch. Dinner. Bar Snacks. Full Catering. Changing Room. Golf Shop. Club Hire. Trolley Hire. Buggy Hire. Caddies available.
Class One Hotel: Runcorn Crest, Runcorn, 3 mile(s). Tel: 714000 (0928)

HIGHER WALTON

Walton Hall Municipal Golf Club, Warrington Road, Higher Walton, Warrington, Cheshire. . Tel: 263061 (0925)
Secretary: M Youd   Tel: 266775 (0925)
Location: Just off A56 Warrington to Chester road, 3 miles from Warrington.
Description: Probably the best municipal golf course in the region. Home The Warrington Classic. Magnificent parkland course on the old Walton Hall Estate. Walton Hall Golf Club also based at the course.
18 holes, 6,849 yards, Par 72, S.S.S. 73, Course record 70.
Visitors: Welcome. Not Sundays before 10 a.m., most other times available. Booking six days in advance available by credit card. Very busy, especially weekends.
Green Fees: Weekdays £5.40, weekends £6.80. Reduc-

tions for juniors and senior citizens.
Facilities: Dinner. Full Catering. Driving Range. Buggy Hire. Caddies available.
Class One Hotel: Lord Daresbury, Daresbury, 1 mile(s). Tel: 265050 (0925)
Class Two Hotel: Walton Arms, Walton. Tel: 262659 (0925)

KNUTSFORD

Mere Golf and Country Club, Chester Road, Knutsford, Cheshire. WA16 6LJ. Tel: 830155 (0565)
Location: 2 miles east of junc 19 M6, 3 miles west of junc 7 M56.
Description: One of the finest parkland championship courses in the country.
18 holes, 6,817 yards, Par 71, S.S.S. 73, Course record 69.
Visitors: Welcome. Handicap certificate required. Groups and societies Mondays, Tuesdays and Thursdays only. All bookings by prior arrangement.
Green Fees: £45 weekdays, £55 weekends.
Facilities: Lunch. Dinner. Bar Snacks. Full Catering. Changing Room. Golf Shop. Driving Range. Trolley Hire. Buggy Hire. Caddies available.
Class One Hotel: The Swan Hotel, Mere, 1/2 mile(s). Tel: 830295 (0565)
Class Two Hotel: The Vicarage, Knutsford, 1 mile(s). Tel: 652221 (0565)

MACCLESFIELD

Macclesfield Golf Club, Hollins Road, Macclesfield, Cheshire. SK11 7AE. Tel: 423227 (0625)
Secretary: N H Edwards   Tel: 615845 (0625)
Professional: A Taylor   Tel: 616952 (0625)
Location: From town left off Neap Road into Windmill Street, right fork after 1/3 mile.
Description: Parkland. New extension to open 1993.
9 holes, 5,974 yards, Par 69, S.S.S. 69, Course record 63.
Membership: 450
Visitors: Welcome. Handicap certificate required. Telephone in advance either professional or secretary.
Green Fees: Weekdays £15, weekends £17.
Facilities: Lunch. Dinner. Full Catering. Changing Room. Golf Shop.
Class One Hotel: Sutton Hall, Sutton, 1 1/2 mile(s). Tel: 3211 (02605)

MACCLESFIELD

Prestbury Golf Club, Macclesfield Road, Prestbury, Near Macclesfield, Cheshire. SK10 4BJ. Tel: 828241 (0625)
Secretary: A W J Wilkinson   Tel: 828241 (0625)
Professional: Nick Summerfield   Tel: 828242 (0625)
Description: Parkland.
18 holes, 6,359 yards, Par 71, S.S.S. 71, Course record 66.
Membership: 747
Visitors: Welcome. Handicap certificate required. Not weekends. Societies Thursdays. Tuesdays Ladies Day.
Green Fees: £25.
Facilities: Lunch. Dinner. Bar Snacks. Full Catering. Changing Room. Golf Shop. Trolley Hire.
Class One Hotel: Bridge, Prestbury, 1 mile(s). Tel: 829326 (0625)

Class Two Hotel: Park Vale Guest House, Macclesfield, 2 mile(s). Tel: 500025 (0625)

MACCLESFIELD

The Tytherington Club, Manchester Road, Macclesfield, Cheshire. SK10 2JP. Tel: 434562 (0625)
Secretary: R Dawson   Tel: 434562 (0625)
Professional: Sandy Wilson   Tel: 434562 (0625)
Location: 1 mile North of Macclesfield on A523 .
Description: Championship course. Home of The Women Professional Golfers European Tour. Mature parkland with lakes and streams, beautifully manicured.
Mens 18 holes, 6,756 yards, Par 72, S.S.S. 72, Course record 68.
Womens 18 holes, 5,645 yards, Par 73, S.S.S. 74, Course record 66.
Membership: 600
Visitors: Welcome. Handicap certificate required. Any weekday, weekends with a member.
Green Fees: Individuals weekdays (18 holes) £22, (36 holes) £32, Socities (18 holes) £20, (36 holes) £30.
Facilities: Lunch. Dinner. Bar Snacks. Full Catering. Changing Room. Golf Shop. Club Hire. Driving Range. Trolley Hire. Buggy Hire. Caddies availabl
Class One Hotel: Chadwick House, Macclesfield, mile(s). Tel: 615558 (0625)

POYNTON

Davenport Golf Club, Middlewood Road, Poynton, Stockport, Cheshire. SK 12 1TS. Tel: 877321 (0625)
Secretary: Brian Commins   Tel: 876951 (0625)
Professional: Wyn Harris   Tel: 877319 (0625)
Location: A6 from Stockport, Macclesfield road from Hazel Grove left at Poynton church.
Description: Undulating parkland.
18 holes, 6,065 yards, Par 68, S.S.S. 69.
Membership: 740
Visitors: Welcome. Tee booking in operation, arranged through club professional.
Green Fees: £24 weekdays, £30 weekends.
Facilities: Lunch. Dinner. Bar Snacks. Full Catering. Changing Room. Golf Shop. Trolley Hire.

RUNCORN

Runcorn Golf Club, Clifton Road, Runcorn, Cheshire. WA7 4SU. Tel: 572093 (0928)
Secretary: W B Reading   Tel: 574214 (0928)
Professional: I Sephton   Tel: 564791 (0928)
Location: Signposted The Heath from A557.
Description: High parkland course.
18 holes, 6,035 yards, Par 69, S.S.S. 69, Course record 66.
Membership: 550
Visitors: Welcome. Handicap certificate required. Not on Tuesday mornings. No visitors weekends or Bank Holidays except with a member. Societies by arrangement Mondays.
Green Fees: £16 weekdays.
Facilities: Lunch. Dinner. Bar Snacks. Full Catering. Changing Room. Golf Shop. Trolley Hire.

Class One Hotel: Forte Crest, Runcorn, 3 mile(s). Tel: 714000 (0928)

SANDBACH

Malkins Bank Golf Club, Betchton Road, Sanbach, Cheshire. CW11 0XN.
Secretary: Ken Lea
Professional: David Wheeler   Tel: 765931 (0270)
Location: Junc 17 M6, south-east of town off A533.
Description: Fairly flat parkland, municipal course.
18 holes, 6,071 yards, Par 70, S.S.S. 69.
Membership: 500
Visitors: Welcome.
Green Fees: Weekdays £5, weekends £6.
Facilities: Bar Snacks. Changing Room. Golf Shop. Club Hire. Trolley Hire.
Class Two Hotel: Old Hall, Sandbach, 1 1/2 mile(s). Tel: 761221 (0270)

WARRINGTON

Birchwood Golf Club, Kelvin Close, Birchwood, Warrington, Cheshire. WA3 7PB. Tel: 818819 (0925)
Secretary: R G Jones   Tel: 818819 (0925)
Professional: D Cooper   Tel: 818819 (0925)
Location: Junc 11 M62 2 miles Leigh-Warrington.
Description: Testing parkland course with water.
Pilgrims 18 holes, 6,808 yards, Par 71, S.S.S. 73, Course record 68.
Progress 18 holes, 6,440 yards, Par 71, S.S.S. 72.
Membership: 680
Visitors: Welcome. Handicap certificate required. Not Sundays. Society meetings Monday, Wednesday and Thursday only.
Green Fees: Weekdays £22, weekends and Bank Holidays £30.
Facilities: Lunch. Dinner. Bar Snacks. Full Catering. Changing Room. Golf Shop. Trolley Hire.
Class One Hotel: Holiday Inn, Warrington, 2 mile(s). Tel: 831158 (0925)

WARRINGTON

Leigh Golf Club, Kenyon Hall, Broseley Lane, Culcheth, Warrington, Cheshire. WA3 4BG. Tel: 762943 (0925)
Secretary: G D Riley   Tel: 762943 (0925)
Professional: A Baguley   Tel: 762013 (0925)
Location: Off East Lancs road (A580) 5 miles from Leigh, 7 miles from Warrington.
Description: Parkland.
18 holes, 5,863 yards, Par 69, S.S.S. 68.
Membership: 520
Visitors: Welcome. Handicap certificate required.
Green Fees: Weekdays £20, weekends and Bank Holidays £25. £7 with member.
Facilities: Lunch. Dinner. Bar Snacks. Full Catering. Changing Room. Golf Shop. Trolley Hire.
Class One Hotel: Thistle Hotel, Haydock, 4 mile(s). Tel: 272000 (0942)

WARRINGTON

Poulton Park Golf Club, Dig Lane, Cinnamon Brow, Warrington, Cheshire. WA2 0SH. Tel: 812034 (0925)
Secretary: J Reekie   Tel: 812034 (0925)
Professional: A Cuppello   Tel: 825220 (0925)
Location: From A574 take Crab Lane for 300 yards.
Description: Wooded parkland. Nine holes, eighteen tees.
9 holes, 5,400 yards, Par 68, S.S.S. 66, Course record 66.
Membership: 400
Visitors: Welcome. At peak times telephone professional.
Green Fees: £16 weekdays, £18 weekends.
Facilities: Lunch. Dinner. Bar Snacks. Full Catering. Changing Room. Golf Shop. Club Hire.
Class One Hotel: Holiday Inn, Warrington, 1/2 mile(s). Tel: 831158 (0925)

WINSFORD

Knights Grange Sports Complex, Grange Lane, Winsford, Cheshire. CW7 2PT. Tel: 552780 (0606)
Secretary: R Wright   Tel: 552780 (0606)
Location: 1 mile north of A54, signposted fron Winsford town centre.
Description: Municipal pay and play.
9 holes, 2,860 yards, Par 68, S.S.S. 72.
Visitors: Welcome.
Green Fees: Weekdays 9 holes £2.40, 18 holes £3.20. Weekends 18 holes £4.80.
Facilities: Changing Room. Golf Shop. Club Hire. Driving Range. Trolley Hire.

CLEVELAND

HARTLEPOOL

Castle Eden and Peterlee Golf Club, Castle Eden, Hartlepool, Cleveland. TS27 4SS. Tel: 836220 (0429)
Secretary: Peter Robinson   Tel: 836510 (0429)
Professional: Graham J Laidlaw   Tel: 836689 (0429)
Location: 2 miles south of Peterlee, use exits from A19.
Description: Picturesque parkland course.
18 holes, 6,262 yards, Par 70, S.S.S. 70, Course record 66.
Membership: 700
Visitors: Welcome. 9.30 - 11.30a.m., 1.45 - 3.30p.m. Not Tuesdays p.m.
Green Fees: £18, weekends and Bank Holidays £25.
Facilities: Lunch. Dinner. Bar Snacks. Full Catering. Changing Room. Golf Shop. Club Hire. Driving Range. Trolley Hire. Buggy Hire.
Class One Hotel: Three Tuns, Durham, 8 mile(s). Tel: 486 4326 (091)

HARTLEPOOL

Seaton Carew Golf Club, Tees Road, Seaton Carew, Hartlepool, Cleveland. TS25 1DE. Tel: 266249 (0429)
Secretary: T Waite   Tel: 266249 (0429)
Professional: W Hector   Tel: 266249 (0429)
Description: Links championship course, over 118 years old. Venue for R & A England Golf Union and Ladies Golf Union events.

Old 18 holes, 6,630 yards, Par 72, S.S.S. 72.
Brabazon 18 holes, 6,800 yards, Par 72, S.S.S. 73, Course record 66.
Membership: 450
Visitors: Welcome. Handicap certificate required.
Green Fees: Weekdays £20 per day, weekends and Bank Holidays £28.
Facilities: Lunch. Dinner. Bar Snacks. Full Catering. Changing Room. Golf Shop. Club Hire. Trolley Hire. Buggy Hire.
Class One Hotel: Grand, Hartlepool, 1 mile(s). Tel: 266345 (0429)
Class Two Hotel: Staincliffe, Hartlepool, 1/2 mile(s). Tel: 264301 (0429)

REDCAR
Cleveland Golf Club, Queen Street, Redcar, Cleveland. TS10 1BT. Tel: 471798 (0642)
Secretary: L R Manley   Tel: 471798 (0642)
Professional: D J Masey   Tel: 483462 (0642)
Location: 1/2 mile west of Redcar town centre.
Description: Links.
White 18 holes, 6,707 yards, Par 72, S.S.S. 72, Course record 70.
Yellow 18 holes, 6,233 yards, Par 71, S.S.S. 70, Course record 65.
Membership: 799
Visitors: Welcome. Handicap certificate required. No parties at weekends or Bank Holidays.
Green Fees: Weekdays £14.50, weekends £25.
Facilities: Lunch. Dinner. Bar Snacks. Full Catering. Changing Room. Golf Shop.
Class One Hotel: Park, Redcar, 1 mile(s). Tel: 490888 (0642)

CORNWALL
CAMBORNE
Tehidy Park Golf Club, Camborne, Cornwall. TR14 0HH. Tel: 842208 (0209)
Secretary: John Prosser   Tel: 842208 (0209)
Professional: James Dumbreck   Tel: 842914 (0209)
Description: Parkland.
18 holes, 6,241 yards, Par 72, S.S.S. 70, Course record 64.
Membership: 950
Visitors: Welcome. Handicap certificate required.
Green Fees: Weekdays £20/£25, weekends £25/£30.

Facilities: Lunch. Dinner. Bar Snacks. Full Catering. Changing Room. Golf Shop. Club Hire. Trolley Hire.
Class One Hotel: Penventon, Redruth, 3 mile(s). Tel: 214141 (0209)
Class Two Hotel: Basset Arms, Portreath, 1 mile(s). Tel: 842077 (0209)

FALMOUTH
Falmouth Golf Club, Swanpool Road, Falmouth, Cornwall. TR11 5BQ. Tel: 311262 (0326)
Secretary: D Sizer   Tel: 40525 (0326)
Professional: D T Short   Tel: 316229 (0326)
Location: 1/4 mile west of Swanpool beach, Falmouth. On the road to Maenporth beach.
Description: Parkland on coast and inland position.
18 holes, 5,680 yards, Par 70, S.S.S. 67.
Membership: 600
Visitors: Welcome. Handicap certificate required. Tuesday is Ladies day. 10a.m. - 2p.m. Advisable to telephone any day. Some catering restrictions apply, please telephone in advance.
Green Fees: £15 per round, £20 per day.
Facilities: Lunch. Dinner. Bar Snacks. Full Catering. Changing Room. Golf Shop. Club Hire. Trolley Hire.
Class One Hotel: Royal Duchy, Falmouth, 3/4 mile(s). Tel: 313042 (0326)
Class Two Hotel: Parkgrove, Falmouth, 1 mile(s). Tel: 311020 (0326)

NEWQUAY
Newquay Golf Club, Tower Road, Newquay, Cornwall. TR7 1LT. Tel: 874354 (0637)
Secretary: G Binney   Tel: 874354 (0637)
Professional: P Muscroft   Tel: 874830 (0637)
Location: Adjacent to Fistral beach.
Description: Seaside course.
18 holes, 6,140 yards, Par 69, S.S.S. 69, Course record 63.
Membership: 600
Visitors: Welcome. Handicap certificate required. Always telephone in advance.
Green Fees: Weekdays £18, weekends £25.
Facilities: Lunch. Dinner. Bar Snacks. Full Catering. Changing Room. Golf Shop. Club Hire. Trolley Hire.
Class One Hotel: Hotel Bristol, Newquay, 1/2 mile(s). Tel: 875181 (0637)
Class Two Hotel: Tregarn, Newquay. Tel: 874483 (0637)

TRELOY TOURIST PARK

400 yards from Treloy Golf Club.
A Friendly Family site for touring vans, tents and dormobiles.
* Heated Swimming Pool * Modern Facilities
* Licenced Club/Family Room * Free Entertainment
* Electric Hook Ups * Coarse Fishing nearby
Golfing packages available April, May and September.
CONCESSIONS FOR GOLFERS STAYING ON SITE.
For **FREE** Colour Brochure, Please Ring: **0637 872063.**

NEWQUAY
Treloy Golf Club, Newquay, Cornwall. TR7 4JN. Tel: 878554 (0637)
Secretary: Jim Reid　　　　　　Tel: 878554 (0637)
Location: 2 miles from Newquay, on A3059 St Columb Major to Newquay Road.
Description: A delightful, well maintained parkland course with American style sculptured greens.
9 holes, 2,143 yards, Par 32, S.S.S. 31.
Visitors: Welcome.
Green Fees: £7.50 for 9 holes, £11.50 for 18 holes.
Facilities: Changing Room. Golf Shop. Trolley Hire.
Class One Hotel: Barrowfield, Newquay, 2 mile(s). Tel: 879490 (0637)
Class Two Hotel: White Lodge, Mawgan Porth, 4 mile(s). Tel: 860512 (0637)

PADSTOW
Trevose Golf and Country Club, Constantine Bay, Padstow, Cornwall. PL28 8JB. Tel: 520208 (0841)
Secretary: L Grindley　　　　　Tel: 520208 (0841)
Location: Off B3276 4 miles west of Padstow at Constantine Bay.
Description: Seaside championship links course.
18 holes, 6,461 yards, Par , S.S.S. 71.
Membership: 800
Visitors: Welcome. Handicap certificate required. Please check by telephone beforehand in case course is closed or has restrictions. Four balls very restricted in summer months.
Green Fees: £20 - £30, depending upon season.
Facilities: Lunch. Dinner. Bar Snacks. Full Catering. Changing Room. Golf Shop. Club Hire. Driving Range. Trolley Hire. Buggy Hire.
Class One Hotel: Treglos, Constantine Bay, 1/4 mile(s). Tel: 520727 (0841)
Class Two Hotel: Trevose Golf & Country Club, On course. Tel: 520208 (0841)

PENZANCE
Cape Cornwall Golf and Country Club, St Just, Penzance, Cornwall. TR19 7NL. Tel: 788611 (0736)
Secretary: Mr J Osborne　　　Tel: 788611 (0736)
Professional: Mr B Hamilton　Tel: 786611 (0736)
Description: Coastal parkland course.
18 holes, 5,665 yards, Par , S.S.S. 68.
Membership: 800
Visitors: Welcome.
Green Fees: £14 weekdays.
Facilities: Lunch. Dinner. Bar Snacks. Changing Room. Golf Shop. Club Hire. Trolley Hire.
Class One Hotel: Boswedden House, St Just. Tel: 788733 (0736)
Class Two Hotel: Commercial, St Just, 1 mile(s). Tel: 788455 (0736)

PERRANPORTH
Perranporth Golf Club, Budnick Hill, Perranporth, Cornwall. TR6 0AB. Tel: 572454 (0872)
Secretary: P D R Barnes　　　Tel: 573701 (0872)
Professional: D Michell　　　　Tel: 572317 (0872)
Description: Links type, designed by James Braid, with breathtaking sea views.
18 holes, 6,286 yards, Par 72, S.S.S. 70. Course record 65.
Membership: 650
Visitors: Welcome. Handicap certificate required. Handicap certificate required weekends only.
Green Fees: Weekdays £19 per day, weekends and Bank Holidays £24 per day.
Facilities: Lunch. Dinner. Bar Snacks. Full Catering. Changing Room. Golf Shop. Club Hire. Trolley Hire.
Class One Hotel: Ponsmere, Perranporth, 1/2 mile(s). Tel: 572225 (0872)

SALTASH
St Mellion Golf and Country Club, St Mellion, Saltash, Cornwall. PL12 6SD. Tel: 50101 (0579)
Secretary: David Webb　　　　Tel: 50101 (0579)
Professional: Tony Moore　　Tel: 50724 (0579)
Location: A388 Saltash to Callington road.
Nicklaus 18 holes, 6,626 yards, Par 72, S.S.S. 72.
Old 18 holes, 5,927 yards, Par 70, S.S.S. 68.
Membership: 750
Visitors: Welcome. Handicap certificate required.
Green Fees: Nicklaus £42, Old £22.
Facilities: Lunch. Dinner. Bar Snacks. Full Catering. Changing Room. Golf Shop. Club Hire. Driving Range. Trolley Hire. Buggy Hire.
Class One Hotel: St Mellion, On complex. Tel: 50101 (0579)
Class Two Hotel: The Weary Friar, Pillaton, 3 mile(s). Tel: 50238 (0579)

ST AUSTELL
St Austell Golf Club, Tregongeeves, St Austell, Cornwall. PL26 7DS. Tel: 74756 (0726)
Secretary: S H Davey　　　　Tel: 74756 (0726)
Professional: Mark Rowe　　Tel: 68621 (0726)
Location: On Truro Road.
Description: Parkland.
18 holes, 6,089 yards, Par 69, S.S.S. 69.
Membership: 700
Visitors: Welcome. Handicap certificate required. Letter of Introduction required. Always telephone in advance.
Green Fees: £15.
Facilities: Lunch. Dinner. Bar Snacks. Full Catering. Changing Room. Golf Shop. Trolley Hire. Buggy Hire.
Class One Hotel: Carlyon Bay Hotel, St Austell, 5 mile(s). Tel: 2304 (072681)

ST IVES
West Cornwall Golf Club, Church Lane, Lelant, Lelant, St Ives, Cornwall. TR26 3DZ. Tel: 753319 (0736)
Secretary: W S Richards　　Tel: 753401 (0736)
Professional: P Atherton　　Tel: 753177 (0736)
Description: Traditional links with spectacular coastal views.
18 holes, 5,879 yards, Par 69, S.S.S. 68. Course record 65.
Membership: 450
Visitors: Welcome. Handicap certificate required. Letter of Introduction required. Not Tuesday or Wednesday afternoons.

Cade's - Audi Golf Course Guide

Green Fees: Weekdays £20 flat rate, weekends £25 flat rate.
Facilities: Lunch. Dinner. Bar Snacks. Changing Room. Golf Shop. Trolley Hire.

TRURO
Killiow Park Golf Club, Killiow, Kea, Truro, Cornwall. TR3 6AS. Tel: 70246 (0872)
Secretary: John Crowson   Tel: 72768 (0872)
Location: 3 miles from Truro adjacent to A39 Truro/Falmouth Road.
Description: Picturesque rolling parkland.
18 holes, 3,448 yards, Par 60, S.S.S. 57.
Membership: 400
Visitors: Welcome. Handicap certificate required. With members only at weekends and Bank Holidays until 10.30a.m.. Telephone for bookings.
Green Fees: Weekdays £8.50, weekends £10.50.
Facilities: Changing Room. Golf Shop. Club Hire. Driving Range. Trolley Hire.

TRURO
Truro Golf Club, Treliske, Truro, Cornwall. TR1 3LG. Tel: 78684 (0872)
Secretary: B E Heggie   Tel: 78684 (0872)
Professional: N K Bicknell   Tel: 76595 (0872)
Description: Undulating parkland.
18 holes, 5,357 yards, Par 66, S.S.S. 66, Course record 61.
Visitors: Welcome. Handicap certificate required. Competition days, Tuesdays and weekends, tees restricted between certain times, telephone for availability.
Green Fees: £17 weekdays, £22 weekends and Bank Holidays.
Facilities: Lunch. Dinner. Bar Snacks. Full Catering. Changing Room. Golf Shop. Club Hire. Trolley Hire. Buggy Hire.
Class One Hotel: Alverton Manor, Truro, 3 mile(s). Tel: 76633 (0872)
Class Two Hotel: Carlton, Truro, 1 1/2 mile(s). Tel: 72450 (0872)

WADEBRIDGE
St Enodoc Golf Club, Rock, Wadebridge, Cornwall. PL27 6LB. Tel: 863216 (0208)
Secretary: Mr L Guy   Tel: 863216 (0208)
Professional: Mr N Williams   Tel: 862402 (0208)
Location: 6 miles north west of Wadebridge, signposted Rock.
Description: Championship links type course designed by James Braid. Established in 1891. Host of English Mens County Championships. Well known for large bunkers.
Church 18 holes, 6,207 yards, Par 69, S.S.S. 70, Course record 65.
Holywell 18 holes, 4,142 yards, Par 63, S.S.S. 61.
Membership: 1400
Visitors: Welcome. Handicap certificate required. Letter of Introduction required.
Green Fees: Church - £22 per round, £35 per day. Holywell - £12 per round, £18 per day. Both courses £28.

Facilities: Lunch. Dinner. Bar Snacks. Full Catering. Changing Room. Golf Shop. Club Hire. Driving Range. Trolley Hire. Buggy Hire.
Class One Hotel: St Moritz, Trebetherick, 3 mile(s). Tel:862242 (0208)

CUMBRIA

ALSTON
Alston Moor Golf Club, The Hermitage, Alston, Cumbria. CA9 3DB. Tel: 381675 (0434)
Secretary: A Dodd   Tel: 381242 (0434)
Location: Two miles outside Alston on Middleton Teesdale (Scotch Corner) Road.
Description: Meadowland Course with panoramic views of the South Tyne Valley.
9 holes, 5,386 yards, Par 66, S.S.S. 66, Course record 67.
Membership: 200
Visitors: Welcome. Handicap certificate required.
Green Fees: Weekdays £5, weekends and Bank Holidays £8.
Facilities: Lunch. Dinner. Bar Snacks. Full Catering. Changing Room.
Class One Hotel: Lovelady Shield, Nenthead, 2 mile(s). Tel: 381203 (0434)
Class Two Hotel: George and Dragon, Alston, 2 mile(s). Tel: 381293 (0434)

CARLISLE
Dalston Hall Golf Club, Dalston, Carlisle, Cumbria. CA5 7JX. Tel: 710165 (0228)
Secretary: Jane Simpson   Tel: 710165 (0228)
Location: Off junc 42 M6, take Dalston sign, through village for 1 mile, golf club on right hand side.
Description: Parkland.
9 holes, 5,294 yards, Par , S.S.S. 67.
Visitors: Welcome. Ladies Day Tuesdays. Booking is essential weekends and during the Summer. Some catering restrictions apply, please telephone in advance.
Green Fees: £4 per 9 holes, £7 per 18 holes.
Facilities: Lunch. Dinner. Bar Snacks. Full Catering. Changing Room. Golf Shop. Club Hire. Caddies available.
Class One Hotel: Dalston Hall, Carlisle. Tel: 710271 (0228)

EMBLETON
Cockermouth Golf Club, The Clubhouse, Embleton, Cockermouth, Cumbria. CA13 9SG. Tel: 76223 (07687)
Secretary: R D Pollard   Tel: 822650 (0900)
Location: Second exit on A66 to Embleton across Old Road and up 1 in 5 hill.
Description: Scenic fell land.
18 holes, 5,457 yards, Par 69, S.S.S. 67, Course record 64.
Membership: 532
Visitors: Welcome. With members at weekends.
Green Fees: £10 weekdays, £15 weekends and Bank Holidays.
Facilities: Bar Snacks. Changing Room.

41

GRANGE-OVER-SANDS

Grange-Over-Sands Golf Club, Meathop Road, Grange-Over-Sands, Cumbria. LA11 6QX. Tel: 33180 (05395)
Secretary: J R Green　　　　　Tel: 33754 (05395)
Location: Leave A590 at roundabout signposted Grange. Take the B5277 for 3 miles. Course on outskirts of Grange-Over-Sands.
Description: Flat parkland with tree plantations and water courses.
18 holes, 5,670 yards, Par 69, S.S.S. 68.
Membership: 575
Visitors: Welcome. Handicap certificate required. Some catering restrictions apply, please telephone in advance.
Green Fees: Weekdays £15 per round, £20 per day. Weekends and Bank Holidays £20 per round, £25 per day.
Facilities: Lunch. Dinner. Bar Snacks. Full Catering. Changing Room. Trolley Hire.
Class One Hotel: Grange, Grange-O-Sands, 1/2 mile(s). Tel: 33666 (05395)
Class Two Hotel: Clare House, Grange-O-Sands, 2 mile(s). Tel: 33026 (05395)

KENDAL

Kendal Golf Club, The Heights, Kendal, Cumbria. LA9 4PQ. Tel: 733708 (0539)
Secretary: R E Maunder　　　　Tel: 733708 (0539)
Professional: D Turner　　　　　Tel: 723499 (0539)
Location: A6 and A591 close to town centre (signposted).
Description: Elevated.
18 holes, 5,534 yards, Par 66, S.S.S. 67, Course record 57.
Membership: 730
Visitors: Welcome. Handicap certificate required. Ladies Day Tuesdays. Tee reserved 1p.m. to 2.30p.m. and 4.30p.m. to 6.30p.m.. Members reservation 1p.m. to 2p.m. weekdays.
Green Fees: Weekdays £16, weekends £20.
Facilities: Lunch. Dinner. Bar Snacks. Full Catering. Changing Room. Golf Shop. Club Hire. Trolley Hire.
Class One Hotel: Woolpack, Kendal, 1/4 mile(s). Tel: 723852 (0529)
Class Two Hotel: Rainbow, Kendal, 1/4 mile(s). Tel: 724178 (0539)

KESWICK

Keswick Golf Club Ltd., Threlkeld Hall, Keswick, Cumbria. LA11 8PZ. Tel: 79324 (07687)
Secretary: Richard Bell　　　　Tel: 79324 (07687)
Location: A66 4 miles east of Keswick.
Description: Woodland and parkland.
18 holes, 6,175 yards, Par 71, S.S.S. 72, Course record 71.
Membership: 840
Visitors: Welcome. Thursday is Ladies day. Please telephone in advance.
Green Fees: Weekdays £12, weekends and Bank Holidays £15 (temporary membership).
Facilities: Lunch. Dinner. Bar Snacks. Full Catering. Changing Room. Golf Shop. Trolley Hire.
Class One Hotel: Keswick, Keswick, 4 mile(s). Tel: 72020 (07687)
Class Two Hotel: Linnett Hill, Keswick, 4 mile(s). Tel: 73109 (07687)

Class One Hotel: Armathwaite Hall, Cockermouth, 3 mile(s). Tel: 76551 (07687)

KIRKBY LONSDALE

Kirkby Lonsdale Golf Club, Scaleber Lane, Barbon, Kirkby Lonsdale, Cumbria. LA6 2LE. Tel: 36365 (0468)
Secretary: P Jackson　　　　　Tel: 36365 (0468)
Description: Parkland.
18 holes, 6,285 yards, Par 70, S.S.S. 70.
Membership: 600
Visitors: Welcome. Handicap certificate required. Letter of Introduction required.
Green Fees: £14 weekdays, £18 weekends.
Facilities: Lunch. Dinner. Bar Snacks. Full Catering. Changing Room. Golf Shop. Trolley Hire.

MARYPORT

Maryport Golf Club, Bankend, Maryport, Cumbria. CA15 6PA. Tel: 812605 (0900)
Secretary: N H Cook　　　　　Tel: 815652 (0900)
Location: 1 mile north of Maryport on B5300 to Silloth.
Description: Links with 6 holes adjoining the beach.
18 holes, 6,272 yards, Par 71, S.S.S. 71, Course record 70.
Membership: 418
Visitors: Welcome. No restrictions.
Green Fees: £10 weekdays, £15 weekends and Bank Holidays.
Facilities: Lunch. Dinner. Bar Snacks. Changing Room.
Class Two Hotel: Ellenbank, Maryport, 1 mile(s). Tel: 815233 (0900)

MILLOM

Silecroft Golf Club, Silecroft, Millom, Cumbria. LA18 4NX. Tel: 774250 (0229)
Secretary: M Wilson　　　　　Tel: 774160 (0229)
Description: Seaside course, mostly flat.
9 holes, 5,712 yards, Par 68, S.S.S. 68, Course record 68.
Membership: 370
Visitors: Welcome. Not Bank Holidays or Saturdays and Sundays p.m. April to August inclusive.
Green Fees: £10 per day.
Facilities: Changing Room.
Class Two Hotel: Bankfield House, Kirksanton, 1 mile(s). Tel: 772276 (0229)

PENRITH

Penrith Golf Club, Salkeld Road, Penrith, Cumbria. CA11 8SG. Tel: 62217 (0768)
Secretary: J Carruthers　　　　Tel: 62217 (0768)
Professional: Bryan Thomson　Tel: 62217 (0768)
Description: Parkland.
18 holes, 6,026 yards, Par 69, S.S.S. 69, Course record 64.
Membership: 800
Visitors: Welcome. Handicap certificate required. Letter of Introduction required. Telephone in advance for booking.
Green Fees: Weekdays £15, weekends and Bank Holidays £22.
Facilities: Lunch. Dinner. Bar Snacks. Full Catering. Changing Room. Golf Shop. Club Hire. Driving Range.
Class Two Hotel: Norcroft Guest House, Penrith, 1 mile(s). Tel: 62365 (0768)

SEASCALE

Seascale Golf Club, The Banks, Seascale, Cumbria. CA20 1QL. Tel: 28202 (09467)
Secretary: Colin Taylor　　　　　　Tel: 28202 (09467)
Location: Off A595, on the coast to the north of Seascale.
Description: Undulating links course, generally considered a difficult, but fair, test for golfers of all standards.
White 18 holes, 6,419 yards, Par 71, S.S.S. 71, Course record 67.
Yellow 18 holes, 6,173 yards, Par 71, S.S.S. 69, Course record 67.
Membership: 780
Visitors: Welcome. Some catering restrictions apply on Mondays and Tuesdays, please telephone in advance.
Green Fees: Weekdays £18 per day, weekends £22 per day.
Facilities: Lunch. Dinner. Bar Snacks. Full Catering. Changing Room. Golf Shop. Club Hire. Trolley Hire.
Class Two Hotel: Scawfell, Seascale, 1/4 mile(s). Tel: 28400 (09467)

SEDBERGH

Sedbergh Golf Club, Catholes-Abbot Howie, Sedbergh, Cumbria. LA10 5SS. Tel: 20993 (05396)
Secretary: David Lord　　　　　　Tel: 20993 (05396)
Location: 1 mile out of Sedbergh on road to Dent. Well signposted.
Description: Superbly scenic 9 hole course in the Yorkshire Dales National Park. New course opening in 1993. Temporary course open now.
Main 9 holes, 5,800 yards, Par 70, S.S.S. 69.
Temporary 9 holes, 4,178 yards, Par 64, S.S.S. 62, Course record 71.
Membership: 150
Visitors: Welcome. Prior booking essential at weekends.
Green Fees: £8 weekdays, £10 weekends.
Facilities: Lunch. Changing Room. Club Hire. Trolley Hire.
Class Two Hotel: The Dalesman, Sedbergh, 1 mile(s). Tel: 21183 (05396)

SILLOTH

Silloth on Solway Golf Club, The Clubhouse, Silloth, Cumbria. CA5 4BL. Tel: 31304 (06973)
Secretary: J G Proudlock　　　　　Tel: 31304 (06973)
Professional: J Burns　　　　　　Tel: 31304 (06973)
Location: Junc 43 M6, take A595 to Thursby, then A596 to Wigton, then B5302 to Silloth.
Description: Seaside links.
18 holes, 6,026 yards, Par 72, S.S.S. 71, Course record 68.
Membership: 1000
Visitors: Welcome. Handicap certificate required. Restricted to 40 visitors on Saturdays and Sundays.
Green Fees: Weekdays £18 per day, Sundays £23 per round.
Facilities: Lunch. Dinner. Bar Snacks. Full Catering. Changing Room. Golf Shop. Trolley Hire.
Class One Hotel: Golf Hotel, Silloth, 1/10 mile(s). Tel: 31438 (06973)
Class Two Hotel: Skinburness, Silloth, 2 mile(s). Tel: 32332 (06973)

ULVERSTON

Ulverston Golf Club Ltd., Bardsea Park, Ulverston, Cumbria. LA12 9QJ. Tel: 52824 (0229)
Secretary: I D Procter
Professional: M R Smith　　　　　Tel: 52806 (0229)
Location: M6 junc 36 onto A590 to Barrow, in Ulverston turn left onto A5087 to Bardsea.
Description: Wooded undulating parkland.
18 holes, 6,148 yards, Par 71, S.S.S. 69, Course record 66.
Membership: 700
Visitors: Welcome. Handicap certificate required. Accredited golf club members only. Not Saturdays in summer. Not Tuesdays. Some catering restrictions apply, please telephone in advance.
Green Fees: March to October weekdays £20, weekends £25. November to February weekdays £14, Weekends £18. Juniors half price.
Facilities: Lunch. Dinner. Bar Snacks. Changing Room. Golf Shop. Trolley Hire.
Class One Hotel: Abbey House, Barrow, 8 mile(s). Tel: 838282 (0229)
Class Two Hotel: Lonsdale House, Ulverston, 2 mile(s). Tel: 52598 (0229)

WINDERMERE

Windermere Golf Club, Cleabarrow, Windermere, Cumbria. LA23 3NB. Tel: 43123 (05394)
Secretary: K R Moffat　　　　　　Tel: 43123 (05394)
Professional: W S M Rooke　　　　Tel: 43550 (05394)
Location: 1 1/4 miles from Bowness-On-Winderemere.
Description: Idyllic National Park setting.
18 holes, 5,006 yards, Par 67, S.S.S. 65, Course record 58.
Visitors: Welcome. Handicap certificate required. 9 a.m. to 12 noon, 2 to 4.30 p.m. or before 9 a.m. by arrangement.
Green Fees: Weekdays £18, £25 weekends and Bank Holidays.
Facilities: Lunch. Dinner. Bar Snacks. Full Catering. Changing Room. Golf Shop. Club Hire. Trolley Hire.
Class One Hotel: Wild Boar, Crook, 1 1/2 mile(s). Tel: 45225 (05394)
Class Two Hotel: Fayrer Holme, Bowness-On-W, 1 mile(s). Tel: 88195 (05394)

WORKINGTON

Workington Golf Club, Branthwaite Road, Workington, Cumbria. CA14 4SS. Tel: 603460 (0900)
Secretary: J K Walker　　　　　　Tel: 605420 (0900)
Professional: A Drabble　　　　　Tel: 67828 (0900)
Location: 2 miles south-east of town on A596.
Description: Undulating meadowland.
18 holes, 6,202 yards, Par 72, S.S.S. 70, Course record 65.
Membership: 700
Visitors: Welcome. Handicap certificate required. Restricted to members 12 to 1.30 each day.
Green Fees: On application.
Facilities: Lunch. Dinner. Bar Snacks. Full Catering. Changing Room. Golf Shop. Club Hire. Trolley Hire.
Class One Hotel: Westland, Workington. Tel: 604544 (0900)
Class Two Hotel: Hunday Manor, Workington, 1 mile(s). Tel: 61798 (0900)

Cade's - Audi Golf Course Guide

DERBYSHIRE

BUXTON
Cavendish Golf Club Ltd., Gadley Lane, Buxton, Derbys. SK17 6XD.
Secretary: S Doyle-Davidson   Tel: 23494 (0298)
Professional: John Nolan   Tel: 25052 (0298)
Description: Downland.
18 holes, 6,026 yards, Par 68, S.S.S. 68, Course record 63.
Membership: 530
Visitors: Welcome. Handicap certificate required. Not at weekends.
Green Fees: Weekdays £22, weekends £33.
Facilities: Lunch. Bar Snacks. Changing Room. Golf Shop. Club Hire. Driving Range. Trolley Hire.
Class One Hotel: Lee Wood, Buxton, 1 mile(s). Tel: 23002 (0298)

CHAPEL-EN-LE-FRITH
Chapel-En-Le-Frith Golf Club, The Cockyard, Manchester Road, Chapel-En-Le-Frith, Derbys. SK12 6UH. Tel: 812118 (0298)
Secretary: Mr W Dranfield   Tel: 813943 (0298)
Professional: Mr D J Cullen   Tel: 812118 (0298)
Location: 11 miles south of Stockport on B5470.
Description: Scenic parkland.
18 holes, 6,089 yards, Par 70, S.S.S. 69.
Membership: 675
Visitors: Welcome. Advisable to telephone professional for convenient tee time at weekends. Some catering restrictions apply, please telephone stewardess.
Green Fees: £15 weekdays, £20 weekends and Bank Holidays.
Facilities: Lunch. Dinner. Bar Snacks. Changing Room. Golf Shop. Club Hire. Trolley Hire.

CHESTERFIELD
Stanedge Golf Club, Walton Hay Farm, Walton, Chesterfield, Derbys. S45 0LW. Tel: 566156 (0246)
Secretary: W C Tyzack   Tel: 276568 (0246)
Location: Off B5057 near Red Lion public house 5 miles west of Chesterfield town centre.
Description: Moorland. Tight nine holes with excellent views.
9 holes, 4,867 yards, Par 64, S.S.S. 64, Course record 64.
Membership: 300
Visitors: Welcome. Handicap certificate required. Without member before 2 p.m. Monday to Friday. With member only at weekends.
Green Fees: £10 per round (18 holes), £5 with member.
Facilities: Bar Snacks. Changing Room. Trolley Hire.
Class One Hotel: Chesterfield, Chesterfield, 5 mile(s). Tel: 271141 (0246)
Class Two Hotel: Glen Stuart, Chesterfield, 5 mile(s). Tel: 276052 (0246)

CODNOR
Ormonde Fields Golf Club, Nottingham Road, Codnor, Derbys. DE5 9RG. Tel: 742987 (0773)

Secretary: R N Walters   Tel: 742987 (0773)
Professional: D Bird   Tel: 742987 (0773)
Location: Off M1 junc 26 take A610 Ripley Road.
Description: Undulating.
18 holes, 6,020 yards, Par 69, S.S.S. 69, Course record 63.
Visitors: Welcome. Not weekends.
Green Fees: Weekdays £12, £8 with member.
Facilities: Lunch. Dinner. Bar Snacks. Full Catering. Changing Room. Golf Shop. Trolley Hire.
Class One Hotel: Swallow, Alfreton, 4 mile(s). Tel: 812000 (0773)

DERBY
Breadsall Priory Hotel Golf & Country Club, Moor Road, Morley, Derbys. DE7 6DL. Tel: 832235 (0332)
Secretary: Pat Wolf   Tel: 832534 (0332)
Professional: Andrew Smith   Tel: 834425 (0332)
Location: A61 from Derby 4 miles north, through Breadsall Village.
Description: Parkland course where full use has been made of natural features and fine old trees.
Priory 18 holes, 6,202 yards, Par 72, S.S.S. 70, Course record 66.
Moorland 18 holes, 6,037 yards, Par 71, S.S.S. 69.
Membership: 750
Visitors: Welcome. Handicap certificate required. Caddies available with seven days notice.
Green Fees: 18 holes £22.50 Monday to Friday, day card £31 Monday to Friday, £26 Weekends and Bank Holidays.
Facilities: Lunch. Dinner. Bar Snacks. Full Catering. Changing Room. Golf Shop. Club Hire. Trolley Hire. Buggy Hire. Caddies available.
Class One Hotel: Breadsall Priory, On complex. Tel: 832235 (0332)

HATHERSAGE
Sickleholme Golf Club, Bamford, Near Hathersage, Derbys. S30 2BH.
Secretary: P H Taylor   Tel: 51306 (0433)
Professional: P H Taylor   Tel: 51252 (0433)
Location: A625 from Sheffield.
Description: Picturesque Peak District golf club.
18 holes, 6,064 yards, Par 69, S.S.S. 69, Course record 62.
Membership: 600
Visitors: Welcome. Handicap certificate required. Letter of Introduction required. Wednesdays a.m. Ladies. Not weekends on competition days.
Green Fees: Weekdays £20 per day, weekends £27 per day.
Facilities: Lunch. Dinner. Bar Snacks. Full Catering. Changing Room. Golf Shop. Trolley Hire.

ILKESTON
Erewash Valley Golf Club, Stanton-by-Dale, Near Ilkeston, Derbys. DE7 4QR. Tel: 322984 (0602)
Secretary: J A Beckett   Tel: 322984 (0602)
Professional: M Ronan   Tel: 324667 (0602)
Description: 2 holes in an old quarry.
18 holes, 6,487 yards, Par 72, S.S.S. 72, Course record 68.
Visitors: Welcome.
Green Fees: £25 per day, £20 per round.

Cade's - Audi Golf Course Guide

Facilities: Lunch. Dinner. Bar Snacks. Full Catering. Changing Room. Golf Shop. Trolley Hire.
Class One Hotel: Hilton International, Kegworth, 8 mile(s). Tel: 674000 (0509)

ILKESTON

Ilkeston Borough Golf Club, Peewit Municipal Golf Course, West End Drive, Ilkeston, Derbys. . Tel: 307704 (0602)
Secretary: S J Rossington   Tel: 320304 (0602)
Professional: P Law   Tel: 307704 (0602)
Location: From Ilkeston market place take Wharncliff Road, then West End Drive. Approx 1/2 mile from market place.
Description: Slightly undulating.
9 holes, 4,100 yards, Par 60, S.S.S. 60.
Membership: 115
Visitors: Welcome.
Green Fees: £5.25.
Facilities: Changing Room. Golf Shop. Club Hire.

MICKLEOVER

Mickleover Golf Club, Uttoxeter Road, Mickleover, Derbys. DE3 5AD. Tel: 513339 (0332)
Secretary: D Rodgers   Tel: 516011 (0332)
Professional: Paul Wilson   Tel: 518662 (0332)
Location: 3 miles west of Derby on A516/B5020.
18 holes, 5,708 yards, Par 68, S.S.S. 68.
18 holes, 5,631 yards, Par 69, S.S.S. 67.
Membership: 650
Visitors: Welcome. Handicap certificate required. Handicap certificate required only at weekends.
Green Fees: Weekdays £17 per day, Weekends and Bank Holidays £24.
Facilities: Lunch. Dinner. Bar Snacks. Full Catering. Changing Room. Golf Shop. Club Hire. Trolley Hire.
Class One Hotel: Forte Crest, Derby, 1 1/2 mile(s). Tel: 514933 (0332)

MICKLEOVER

Pastures Golf Club, Pastures Hospital, Mickleover, Derbys. DE3 5DQ. Tel: 513921 (0332)
Secretary: Mr S McWilliams   Tel: 513921 (0332)
Location: 4 miles west of Derby in the village of Mickleover.
Description: Undulating meadowland.
9 holes, 5,005 yards, Par 64, S.S.S. 64, Course record 62.
Membership: 320
Visitors: Welcome. Letter of Introduction required. All visitors must be introduced by a member.
Green Fees: £8 per day.
Facilities: Bar Snacks. Changing Room.
Class One Hotel: Forte Crest, Derby, 2 mile(s). Tel: 514933 (0332)
Class Two Hotel: Plews Guest House, Derby 3, 3 mile(s). Tel: 44325 (0332)

QUARNDON

Kedleston Park Golf Club, Kedleston, Quarndon, Derbys. DE6 4JD. Tel: 840035 (0332)
Secretary: K Wilson   Tel: 840035 (0332)
Professional: J Hetherington   Tel: 841685 (0332)
Location: 4 miles north of Derby, situated on Kedleston Hall Estate.
Description: Parkland.
18 holes, 6,585 yards, Par 72, S.S.S. 71, Course record 65.
Membership: 968
Visitors: Welcome. Handicap certificate required. Letter of Introduction required. Weekdays only, must be reserved prior to visit.
Green Fees: £25 per round, £30 per day.
Facilities: Lunch. Dinner. Bar Snacks. Full Catering. Changing Room. Golf Shop. Club Hire. Trolley Hire.
Class One Hotel: Kedleston Country Hotel, Quarndon, 1/2 mile(s). Tel: 559202 (0332)
Class Two Hotel: Mundy Arms, Mackworth, 2 mile(s). Tel: 824254 (0332)

RENISHAW

Renishaw Park Golf Club, Golf House, Station Road, Renishaw, Derbys. S3 9YZ. Tel: 432044 (0246)
Secretary: G B Denison   Tel: 432044 (0246)
Professional: Simon Elliott   Tel: 435484 (0246)
Description: Parkland.
18 holes, 6,253 yards, Par 71, S.S.S. 70, Course record 64.
Membership: 400
Visitors: Welcome. Handicap certificate required. Letter of Introduction required. Not weekends. Weekdays after 9.30, tee reserved for members 12 to 1.30 p.m.
Green Fees: £18 per round, £25 per day.
Facilities: Lunch. Dinner. Bar Snacks. Full Catering. Changing Room. Golf Shop. Trolley Hire.
Class One Hotel: Sitwell Arms, Renishaw, 1/4 mile(s). Tel: 435226 (0246)
Class Two Hotel: Mosborough Hall, Mosborough, 2 mile(s). Tel: 484353 (0742)

SHIRLAND

Shirland Golf Club, Lower Delves, Shirland, Derbys. DE5 6AU. Tel: 834935 (0773)
Secretary: Mrs C S Fincham   Tel: 832515 (0773)
Professional: Neville Hallam   Tel: 834935 (0773)
Description: Tree lined rolling parkland.
Mens 18 holes, 5,802 yards, Par 70, S.S.S. 68, Course record 71.
Ladies 18 holes, 5,291 yards, Par 73, S.S.S. 71.
Visitors: Welcome. Book through professional.
Green Fees: On application
Facilities: Lunch. Dinner. Bar Snacks. Full Catering. Changing Room. Golf Shop. Club Hire. Trolley Hire.
Class One Hotel: Swallow, South Normanton, 4 mile(s). Tel: 812000 (0773)
Class Two Hotel: Higham Farm, Alfreton, 2 mile(s). Tel: 833812 (0773)

DEVON

AXMOUTH

Axe Cliff Golf Club, Squires Lane, Axmouth, Seaton, Devon. EX12 4AB. Tel: 20499 (0297)
Secretary: Mrs D Rogers   Tel: 24371 (0297)

Location: Through village of Axmouth along riverside until you reach bridge, turn left.
Description: 18 holes part countryside, part cliff.
18 holes, 4,867 yards, Par 67, S.S.S. 64, Course record 64.
Membership: 400
Visitors: Welcome. Handicap certificate required. Not before 11 a.m. anyday.
Green Fees: Weekdays £12, weekends £16.
Facilities: Lunch. Dinner. Bar Snacks. Full Catering. Changing Room. Trolley Hire.
Class Two Hotel: Anchor Inn, Beer, 2 mile(s). Tel: 20386 (0297)

BRAUNTON

Saunton Golf Club, Saunton, Nr Braunton, Devon. EX33 1LG. Tel: 812436 (0271)
Secretary: Bill Geddes   Tel: 812436 (0271)
Professional: Jimmy McGhee   Tel: 812013 (0271)
Location: 8 miles from Barnstaple, on th Braunton/Croyde road.
Description: Links course.
East 18 holes, 6,703 yards, Par 71, S.S.S. 73, Course record 66.
West 18 holes, 6,356 yards, Par 71, S.S.S. 71, Course record 68.
Membership: 1100
Visitors: Welcome. Handicap certificate required. Not before 9.30 a.m. daily.
Green Fees: Weekdays £25, weekends and Bank Holidays £30 (per day).
Facilities: Lunch. Dinner. Bar Snacks. Full Catering. Changing Room. Golf Shop. Club Hire. Trolley Hire.
Class One Hotel: Saunton Sands, Saunton, 1/2 mile(s). Tel: 890212 (0271)
Class Two Hotel: Kittiwell House, Croyde, 1 1/2 mile(s). Tel: 890247 (0271)

BRIXHAM

Churston Golf Club, Churston, Brixham, Devon. . Tel: 842751 (0803)
Secretary: A M Chaundy   Tel: 842751 (0803)
Professional: R Penfold   Tel: 842894 (0803)
Description: Seaside course.
18 holes, 6,219 yards, Par 70, S.S.S. 70, Course record 64.
Membership: 700
Visitors: Welcome. Handicap certificate required. Ladies Day Tuesdays, With members only at weekends.
Green Fees: Weekdays £20, weekends and Bank Holidays £25.
Facilities: Lunch. Dinner. Bar Snacks. Full Catering. Changing Room. Golf Shop. Trolley Hire.

CHULMLEIGH

Chulmleigh Golf Course, Leigh Road, Chulmleigh, Devon. EX18 7BL. Tel: 80519 (0769)
Secretary: P N Callow   Tel: 80519 (0769)
Professional: Michael Blackwell   Tel: 81069 (0769)
Location: Midway between Barnstaple and Crediton. Just off A377.
Description: Undulating meadowland. Unique par 3 course used for the first junior/celebrity golf on BBC television.

18 holes, 1,450 yards, Par 54, S.S.S. 54, Course record 52.
Membership: 150
Visitors: Welcome.
Green Fees: £4.50 one round, £6.50 two rounds, £9 all day. Reductions for juniors under 17.
Facilities: Bar Snacks. Changing Room. Golf Shop. Club Hire. Trolley Hire.
Class One Hotel: Thelbridge Cross Inn, Thelbridge, 8 mile(s). Tel: 860316 (0884)
Class Two Hotel: Sampson Barton (Farm), Kings Nympton, 5 mile(s). Tel: 52466 (0769)

CREDITON

Downes Crediton Golf Club, Hookway, Crediton, Devon. EX17 3PT. Tel: 773025 (0363)
Secretary: W J Brooks   Tel: 773025 (0363)
Professional: H Finch   Tel: 774464 (0363)
Location: Off A377 Exeter to Barnstaple road, on Exeter side of Crediton.
Description: Parkland with water features. Flat front nine, hilly back nine.
Mens 18 holes, 5,917 yards, Par 69, S.S.S. 68.
Ladies 18 holes, 5,408 yards, Par 72, S.S.S. 72.
Membership: 720
Visitors: Welcome. Handicap certificate required. Telephone first to avoid disappointment. Some catering restrictions apply, please telephone in advance.
Green Fees: Weekdays £16, weekends £22.
Facilities: Lunch. Dinner. Full Catering. Changing Room. Golf Shop. Club Hire. Trolley Hire.
Class Two Hotel: Fairpark, Crediton, 1/4 mile(s). Tel: 772686 (0363)

DAWLISH

Warren Golf Club, Dawlish, Devon.   EX7 0NF. Tel: 862255 (0626)
Secretary: D M Beesley   Tel: 862255 (0626)
Professional: G Wicks   Tel: 864002 (0626)
Location: 12 miles south-west of Exeter, off A379.
Description: Links course lying on spit of land at the mouth of the River Exe.
18 holes, 5,968 yards, Par 69, S.S.S. 69.
Membership: 700
Visitors: Welcome. Handicap certificate required. Thursdays limited number only.
Green Fees: Weekdays £19, weekends £21.
Facilities: Lunch. Dinner. Bar Snacks. Full Catering. Changing Room. Golf Shop. Trolley Hire.
Class One Hotel: Langstone Cliff, Dawlish Warren, 1/2 mile(s). Tel: 865155 (0626)
Class Two Hotel: Barton Hey, Dawlish, 3 mile(s). Tel: 862728 (0626)

EXETER

Exeter Golf and Country Club, Countess Weare, Exeter, Devon. EX2 7AE. Tel: 874139 (0392)
Secretary: Chris Greetham   Tel: 874139 (0392)
Professional: Mike Rowett   Tel: 875028 (0392)
Description: Parkland.
18 holes, 6,000 yards, Par 69, S.S.S. 69.
Membership: 850

Visitors: Welcome. Handicap certificate required. With member only at weekends. Thursday is society day.
Green Fees: £23.
Facilities: Lunch. Dinner. Bar Snacks. Full Catering. Changing Room. Golf Shop. Driving Range. Trolley Hire.
Class One Hotel: Countess Wear Lodge, Exeter, 1/2 mile(s). Tel: 875441 (0392)

HOLSWORTHY

Holsworthy Golf Club, Holsworthy, Devon. EX22 6XU. Tel: 253177 (0409)
Secretary: Barry Megson   Tel: 253177 (0409)
Professional: Tim McSherry   Tel: 254771 (0409)
Location: 1 1/2 miles west of Holsworthy on Bude road.
Description: Parkland.
18 holes, 6,025 yards, Par 70, S.S.S. 69, Course record 66.
Membership: 700
Visitors: Welcome. Not Sunday mornings.
Green Fees: Weekdays £13, weekends and Bank Holidays £16.
Facilities: Lunch. Dinner. Bar Snacks. Full Catering. Changing Room. Golf Shop. Club Hire. Trolley Hire.

HONITON

Honiton Golf Club, Middlehills, Honiton, Devon. EX14 8TR. Tel: 47167 (0404)
Secretary: J L Carter   Tel: 44422 (0404)
Professional: A Cave   Tel: 42943 (0404)
Location:
Description: Flat parkland.
18 holes, 5,940 yards, Par 69, S.S.S. 68.
Membership: 750
Visitors: Welcome. Handicap certificate required. Not wednesdays or weekend competition days.
Green Fees: Weekdays £18, weekends and Bank Holidays £23.
Facilities: Lunch. Dinner. Bar Snacks. Full Catering. Changing Room. Golf Shop. Club Hire. Trolley Hire.
Class Two Hotel: Heathfield, Honiton, 1 mile(s). Tel: 45321 (0404)

ILFRACOMBE

Ilfracombe Golf Club, Hele Bay, Ilfracombe, Devon. EX34 9RT. Tel: 862176 (0271)
Secretary: Rodney C Beer   Tel: 862176 (0271)
Professional: David Hoare   Tel: 863328 (0271)
Location: On coast road from Ilfracombe to Combe Martin.
Description: Cliff top parkland type course, providing a good test of golf and offering spectacular views of sea and moorland.
18 holes, 5,893 yards, Par 70, S.S.S. 68, Course record 66.
Membership: 664
Visitors: Welcome. Handicap certificate required. Members only 12 to 2 p.m. daily and until 10 a.m. weekends and Bank Holidays.
Green Fees: £16 daily, £18 weekends and Bank Holidays, £70 five day ticket.
Facilities: Lunch. Dinner. Bar Snacks. Full Catering. Changing Room. Golf Shop. Club Hire. Trolley Hire.

Class One Hotel: Woolacombe Bay, Woolacombe, 6 mile(s). Tel: 870388 (0271)
Class Two Hotel: Colindale, Ilfracombe, 1 mile(s). Tel: 863770 (0271)

NEWTON ABBOT

Newton Abbot (Stover) Golf Club, Bovey Road, Newton Abbot, Devon. TQ12 6QQ. Tel: 52460 (0626)
Secretary: R Smith   Tel: 52460 (0626)
Professional: M Craig   Tel: 62078 (0626)
Location: 3 miles of Newton Abbot on A382.
Description: Parkland, wooded with stream running through course.
18 holes, 5,886 yards, Par 69, S.S.S. 68, Course record 63.
Membership: 800
Visitors: Welcome. Handicap certificate required. Telephone prior to visit.
Green Fees: £21 daily.
Facilities: Lunch. Dinner. Bar Snacks. Full Catering. Changing Room. Golf Shop. Trolley Hire.
Class One Hotel: Edgemoor, Bovey Tracey, 3 mile(s). Tel: 832466 (0626)
Class Two Hotel: Dolphin, Bovey Tracey, 2 mile(s). Tel: 832413 (0626)

OKEHAMPTON

Okehampton Golf Club, Off Tors Road, Okehampton, Devon. EX20 1EF. Tel: 52113 (0837)
Secretary: Spencer Chave   Tel: 52113 (0837)
Professional: Philip J Blundell   Tel: 53541 (0837)
Location: A30 from Exeter 25 miles.
Description: Picturesque moorland course.
18 holes, 5,200 yards, Par 68, S.S.S. 67, Course record 62.
Membership: 550
Visitors: Welcome. Handicap certificate required. Handicap limits of 24 mens and 30 ladies on saturdays.
Green Fees: Weekdays £13, Saturdays £20, Sundays £17.
Facilities: Lunch. Dinner. Bar Snacks. Full Catering. Changing Room. Golf Shop. Club Hire. Trolley Hire.
Class One Hotel: Rougemont, Exeter, 25 mile(s). Tel: 54982 (0392)
Class Two Hotel: Oxenham Arms, South Zeal, 7 mile(s). Tel: 840244 (0837)

PLYMOUTH

Staddon Heights Golf Club, Staddon Heights, Plymstock, Plymouth, Devon. PL9 9SP. Tel: 402475 (0752)
Secretary: Mike Holliday   Tel: 402475 (0752)
Professional: John Cox   Tel: 492630 (0752)
Location: From Plymstock follow signs to Hoe. Follow signs to Staddon Heights.
Description: Parkland with sea views.
18 holes, 5,945 yards, Par 68, S.S.S. 68, Course record 67.
Membership: 750
Visitors: Welcome. Handicap certificate required.
Green Fees: Weekdays £15 per day, weekends and Bank Holidays £20.
Facilities: Lunch. Dinner. Bar Snacks. Full Catering. Changing Room. Golf Shop. Club Hire. Trolley Hire.

SIDMOUTH

Sidmouth Golf Club, Cotmaton Road, Sidmouth, Devon. EX10 8SX. Tel: 513451 (0395)
Secretary: Mr I M Smith Tel: 513451 (0395)
Professional: Mervyn Kemp Tel: 516407 (0395)
Description: Parkland with beautiful coastal views. Seven par 3 holes reduce overall par.
18 holes, 5,100 yards, Par 66, S.S.S. 65.
Membership: 600
Visitors: Welcome. Handicap certificate required. Please telephone for tee reservation.
Green Fees: £18 per day.
Facilities: Lunch. Dinner. Bar Snacks. Full Catering. Changing Room. Golf Shop. Club Hire. Trolley Hire.
Class One Hotel: Riviera, Sidmouth, 1 mile(s). Tel: 515201 (0395)
Class Two Hotel: Mount Pleasant, Sidmouth, 1 1/2 mile(s). Tel: 514694 (0395)

SOUTH BRENT

Wrangaton (South Devon) Golf Club, Golf Links Road, Wrangaton, South Brent, Devon. TQ10 9HJ. Tel: 73229 (0364)
Secretary: Mr R R Hine Tel: 73229 (0364)
Professional: Alistair Cardwell Tel: 72161 (0364)
Location: Modbury and Yealmpton exit from A38 28 miles south of Exeter, 17 miles north of Plymouth.
Description: Nine moorland holes (Dartmoor), nine parkland holes, panoramic views (850 feet above sea level) at South Hams.
18 holes, 6,041 yards, Par 69, S.S.S. 69, Course record 68.
Membership: 700
Visitors: Welcome. Handicap certificate required. Regular municipal course golfers etc. will be allowed to play at pros discretion. Weds. p.m. Ladies competitions. Telephone for weekends.
Green Fees: £16 weekdays, £20 Weekends and Bank Holidays.
Facilities: Lunch. Bar Snacks. Full Catering. Changing Room. Golf Shop. Trolley Hire.
Class One Hotel: Glazebrook, South Brent, 1 mile(s). Tel: 73322 (0364)
Class Two Hotel: Packhorse, South Brent, 2 mile(s). Tel: 72283 (0364)

TAVISTOCK

Tavistock Golf Club, Down Road, Tavistock, Devon. PL19 9AQ. Tel: 612344 (0822)
Secretary: B G Steer Tel: 612344 (0822)
Professional: R Cade Tel: 612316 (0822)
Description: Moorland.
18 holes, 6,250 yards, Par 70, S.S.S. 70.
Membership: 750
Visitors: Welcome. Handicap certificate required. Letter of Introduction required. Visitors must book in advance.
Green Fees: Weekdays £18, weekends and Bank Holidays £22.
Facilities: Lunch. Dinner. Bar Snacks. Full Catering. Changing Room. Golf Shop. Club Hire. Trolley Hire.
Class One Hotel: Bedford Hotel, Tavistock, 2 mile(s). Tel: 613221 (0822)

THURLESTONE

Thurlestone Golf Club, Thurlestone, Kingsbridge, Devon. TQ7 3NZ. Tel: 560405 (0548)
Secretary: R Marston Tel: 560405 (0548)
Professional: N Whitley Tel: 560715 (0548)
Location: Off A379 Plymouth to Salcombe road near Kingsbridge.
Description: Downland with magnificent sea and coastal views. An enjoyable course.
18 holes, 6,300 yards, Par 70, S.S.S. 70, Course record 67.
Membership: 700
Visitors: Welcome. Handicap certificate required.
Green Fees: £24 per day.
Facilities: Lunch. Bar Snacks. Full Catering. Changing Room. Golf Shop. Club Hire. Trolley Hire.
Class One Hotel: Thurlestone Hotel, Thurlstone, 1/2 mile(s). Tel: 560382 (0548)
Class Two Hotel: Cottage Hotel, Hope Cove, 3 mile(s). Tel: 561555 (0548)

TIVERTON

Tiverton Golf Club, Post Hill, Tiverton, Devon. EX16 4NE.
Secretary: M Crouch Tel: 252187 (0884)
Professional: R E Freeman Tel: 254836 (0884)
Description: Parkland with tree lined fairways.
18 holes, 6,263 yards, Par 71, S.S.S. 71, Course record 65.
Membership: 900
Visitors: Welcome. Handicap certificate required.
Green Fees: On application.
Facilities: Lunch. Dinner. Bar Snacks. Full Catering. Changing Room. Golf Shop. Trolley Hire.
Class One Hotel: Tiverton Hotel, Tiverton, 2 mile(s). Tel: 256120 (0884)
Class Two Hotel: Bridge Guest House, Tiverton, 3 mile(s). Tel: 252804 (0884)

TORQUAY

Torquay Golf Club, Petitor Road, St Marychurch, Torquay, Devon. TQ1 4QF. Tel: 314591 (0803)
Secretary: B G Long Tel: 314591 (0803)
Professional: M Ruth Tel: 329113 (0803)
Location: From Torquay, take road to St Marychurch, from there well signposted.
Description: Parkland with sea views.
18 holes, 6,198 yards, Par 69, S.S.S. 69.
Membership: 700
Visitors: Welcome. Handicap certificate required. Letter of Introduction required. Please telephone for bookings.
Green Fees: Weekdays £20, weekends £25.
Facilities: Lunch. Dinner. Bar Snacks. Full Catering. Changing Room. Golf Shop. Club Hire. Trolley Hire. Buggy Hire.
Class One Hotel: Imperial, Torquay, 2 mile(s). Tel: 294301 (0803)

WESTWARD HO!

Royal North Devon Golf Club, Golf Links Road, Westward Ho! Bideford, Devon. EX39 1HD. Tel: 473817 (0237)
Professional: Mr G Johnston Tel: 477598 (0237)
Location: Between Westward Ho and Northam.
Description: Links.

Cade's - Audi Golf Course Guide

18 holes, 6,662 yards, Par 71, S.S.S. 72, Course record 65.
Membership: 600
Visitors: Welcome. Handicap certificate required. Thursday mornings Ladies. Weekdays no play before 9.30a.m.. Telephone in advance.
Green Fees: Weekdays £19 per round, £23 per day. Weekends £23 per round.
Facilities: Lunch. Dinner. Bar Snacks. Full Catering. Changing Room. Golf Shop. Driving Range. Trolley Hire.
Class One Hotel: Royal, Bideford, 2 1/2 mile(s). Tel: 472005 (0237)

YELVERTON

Yelverton Golf Club, Golf Links Road, Yelverton, Devon. PL20 6BN. Tel: 852824 (0822)
Secretary: Major D R Bettany   Tel: 852824 (0822)
Professional: I Parker   Tel: 853593 (0822)
Location: A386 Plymouth to Tavistock (signposted).
Description: Moorland.
18 holes, 6,293 yards, Par 70, S.S.S. 73.
Membership: 600
Visitors: Welcome. Handicap certificate required. Telephone in advance.
Green Fees: £20 per day.
Facilities: Lunch. Bar Snacks. Full Catering. Changing Room. Golf Shop. Driving Range. Trolley Hire.
Class One Hotel: Moorland Links Hotel, Yelverton, 1/2 mile(s). Tel: 852245 (0822)

DORSET

BLANDFORD

Ashley Wood Golf Club, Wimbourne Road, Blandford, Dorset. DT11 9HN. Tel: 452253 (0258)
Secretary: P Lillford   Tel: 452253 (0258)
Professional: S Taylor   Tel: 480379 (0258)
Description: Downland with magnificent views over the Dorset countryside.
9 holes, 6,274 yards, Par 70, S.S.S. 70, Course record 67.
Membership: 500
Visitors: Welcome. Handicap certificate required. Ladies only, Tuesday a.m.
Green Fees: Weekdays £17, weekends £24.
Facilities: Lunch. Dinner. Bar Snacks. Full Catering. Changing Room. Golf Shop. Trolley Hire. Buggy Hire.
Class One Hotel: The Crown, Blandford, 1 mile(s). Tel: 456626 (0258)
Class Two Hotel: Damory Arms, Blandford, 1 mile(s). Tel: 452741 (0258)

BOURNEMOUTH

Bournemouth & Meyrick Park Golf Club, Meyrick Park, Bournemouth, Dorset. BH2 6LI I. Tel: 290307 (0202)
Secretary: Ms J Bennett   Tel: 290307 (0202)
Professional: J Waring   Tel: 290862 (0202)
Location: One mile from town centre.
Description: Playing over municipal course (Meyrick Park), beautiful woodland.
18 holes, 5,663 yards, Par 68, S.S.S. 68.
Membership: 500
Visitors: Welcome. Pay as you play, no restrictions. Tees bookable on (0202) 290871. Some catering restrictions apply unless booked in by member.
Green Fees: £10.40 in summer, £8.90 in winter. (Subject to increase in April.)
Facilities: Lunch. Dinner. Bar Snacks. Full Catering. Changing Room. Golf Shop. Club Hire. Trolley Hire.
Class One Hotel: Collingwood, Bournemouth, 1 mile(s). Tel: 557575 (0202)
Class Two Hotel: The Manchester, Bournemouth, 2 mile(s). Tel: 553333 (0202)

BOURNEMOUTH

Knighton Heath Golf Club, Francis Avenue, Bournemouth, Dorset. BH11 8NX. Tel: 572633 (0202)
Secretary: R C Bestwick   Tel: 572633 (0202)
Professional: Jane Miles   Tel: 578275 (0202)
Location: At junc of A348 and A3049.
Description: Undulating heathland.
18 holes, 6,120 yards, Par 69, S.S.S. 69.
Membership: 700
Visitors: Welcome. Handicap certificate required. With members only at weekends.
Green Fees: On application.
Facilities: Lunch. Bar Snacks. Full Catering. Changing Room. Golf Shop. Trolley Hire. Buggy Hire.

BRIDPORT

Bridport and West Dorset Golf Club, East Cliff, West Bay, Bridport, Dorset. DT6 4EP. Tel: 421095 (0308)
Secretary: P J Ridler   Tel: 421095 (0308)
Professional: J Parish   Tel: 421491 (0308)
Location: South of Bridport at West Bay.
Description: Cliff top course.
18 holes, 5,246 yards, Par 67, S.S.S. 66, Course record 61.
Membership: 696
Visitors: Welcome. Handicap certificate required. Letter of Introduction required. Ladies Tuesday a.m., Veterans Thursday a.m. and competitions Sundays a.m.. No play before 9.30a.m.. Betwe
Green Fees: Weekdays £18, weekends £25.
Facilities: Lunch. Dinner. Bar Snacks. Full Catering. Changing Room. Golf Shop. Trolley Hire.

BROADSTONE

Broadstone (Dorset) Golf Club, Wentworth Drive, Broadstone, Dorset. BH18 8DQ. Tel: 692595 (0202)
Secretary: J M Cowan   Tel: 692595 (0202)
Professional: Nigel Tokely   Tel: 692835 (0202)
Location: 4 miles from Poole.
Description: Parkland.
18 holes, 6,183 yards, Par 69, S.S.S. 70, Course record 66.
Visitors: Welcome. Handicap certificate required. Not weekends. Thursday Ladies Day.
Green Fees: Weekdays £30 per day, weekends £40.
Facilities: Lunch. Dinner. Bar Snacks. Full Catering. Changing Room. Golf Shop. Club Hire. Trolley Hire. Caddies available.
Class One Hotel: Fairlight, Broadstone, 1/4 mile(s). Tel: 694316 (0202)
Class Two Hotel: Broadstone Hotel, Broadstone, 1/4 mile(s). Tel: 694220 (0202)

49

CHRISTCHURCH

Christchurch Golf Club, Iford Bridge, Christchurch, Dorset. . Tel: 473817 (0202)
Secretary: J Lucas   Tel: 303958 (0202)
Professional: P Troth   Tel: 473817 (0202)
Location: Signposted from the Iford Bridge roundabout.
Description: Flat public course.
9 holes, 4,754 yards, Par 68, S.S.S. 63, Course record 63.
Membership: 400
Visitors: Welcome.
Green Fees: Weekdays £4, weekends £5.35.
Facilities: Bar Snacks. Golf Shop. Driving Range. Trolley Hire.

DORCHESTER

Came Down Golf Club, Came Downs, Dorchester, Dorset. DT2 8NR. Tel: 813494 (0305)
Secretary: D Matthews   Tel: 813494 (0305)
Professional: R Preston   Tel: 812670 (0305)
Location: Off Dorchester to Weymouth Road.
Description: Downland.
18 holes, 6,224 yards, Par 70, S.S.S. 71, Course record 67.
Membership: 700
Visitors: Welcome. Handicap certificate required. Not before 11a.m. Sundays.
Green Fees: Weekdays £20 per day, weekends £25 per day.
Facilities: Lunch. Dinner. Bar Snacks. Full Catering. Changing Room. Golf Shop. Club Hire. Trolley Hire.

FERNDOWN

Ferndown Golf Club, 119 Golf Links Road, Ferndown, Dorset. BH22 8BU. Tel: 874602 (0202)
Secretary: E Robertson   Tel: 874602 (0202)
Professional: D Sewell   Tel: 873825 (0202)
Location: Travel along A31, then take A348, take second turning on right into Golf Links Road, it is about 1 1/2 miles along this road.
Description: Wooded heathland.
18 holes, 6,210 yards, Par 71, S.S.S. 71.
9 holes, 2,797 yards, Par 35, S.S.S. .
Membership: 700
Visitors: Welcome. Handicap certificate required. Thursday Ladies Day. Restricted at weekends. Societies allowed on Tuesdays and Fridays.
Green Fees: Weekdays £35, weekends £40.
Facilities: Lunch. Dinner. Bar Snacks. Full Catering. Changing Room. Golf Shop. Club Hire. Driving Range. Trolley Hire. Buggy Hire.
Class One Hotel: Dormy, Ferndown, 1/3 mile(s). Tel: 872121 (0202)
Class Two Hotel: Bridge Inn, Longham, 3 mile(s). Tel: 578828 (0202)

HIGHCLIFFE

Highcliffe Castle Golf Club, 107 Lymington Road, Highcliffe-on-Sea, Dorset. BH23 4LA. Tel: 272953 (0425)
Secretary: Mrs E Thompson   Tel: 272210 (0425)
Professional: R Crockford   Tel: 276640 (0425)
Description: Flat, narrow fairways, well wooded with excellent greens.
18 holes, 4,686 yards, Par 64, S.S.S. 63, Course record 58.
Membership: 450
Visitors: Welcome. Handicap certificate required. Not on competition days. Please enquire at pro-shop.
Green Fees: Weekdays £18, weekends £27.
Facilities: Lunch. Dinner. Bar Snacks. Full Catering. Changing Room. Golf Shop. Trolley Hire.
Class One Hotel: Avonmouth, Christchurch, 1 1/2 mile(s). Tel: 483434 (0425)

LYME REGIS

Lyme Regis Golf Club, Timber Hill, Lyme Regis, Dorset. DT7 3HQ. Tel: 442043 (0297)
Secretary: R G Fry   Tel: 442693 (0297)
Professional: A Black   Tel: 443822 (0297)
Location: Just off A35 turn for Lyme Regis, 1 mile north of Lyme Regis.
Description: Cliff top undulating meadowland course with fine views of Lyme Bay and Golden Cap.
18 holes, 6,220 yards, Par 71, S.S.S. 70, Course record 68.
Membership: 570
Visitors: Welcome. Handicap certificate required. Not before 9.30 a.m. Not before 1.30 p.m. Thursdays, Not before 12.30 p.m. Sundays.
Green Fees: £24 per day, £20 after 2.00 p.m.
Facilities: Lunch. Dinner. Bar Snacks. Full Catering. Changing Room. Golf Shop. Trolley Hire.
Class One Hotel: Fairwater Head, Hawkchurch, 6 mile(s). Tel: 349 (02977)
Class Two Hotel: Springfield Guest House, Lyme Regis, 1 mile(s). Tel: 443409 (0297)

POOLE

Parkstone Golf Club, Links Road, Poole, Dorset. BH14 9JU. Tel: 707138 (0202)
Secretary: A S Kinnear
Professional: M Thomas
Description: Parkstone offers a challenging test for all golfers, in an area of outstanding natural beauty with pine-fringed fairways.
18 holes, 6,250 yards, Par 72, S.S.S. 70, Course record 65.
Membership: 700
Visitors: Welcome. Handicap certificate required. Letter of Introduction required. Must book in writing.
Green Fees: £24 per round, £32 per day.
Facilities: Lunch. Dinner. Bar Snacks. Full Catering. Changing Room. Golf Shop. Club Hire. Trolley Hire. Caddies available.
Class One Hotel: Haven, Poole, 3 mile(s). Tel: 707333 (0202)

STUDLAND

Isle of Purbeck Golf Club, Studland, Swanage, Dorset. BH19 3AB. Tel: 210 (092944)
Location: 2 miles from Swanage on B3351 Corfe Castle to Studland Road.
Description: Undulating heathland.
Purbeck 18 holes, 6,295 yards, Par 70, S.S.S. 71.
Dene 9 holes, 2,007 yards, Par 60, S.S.S. 60.
Membership: 600
Visitors: Welcome. Handicap certificate required for

Purbeck course.
Green Fees: Purbeck - weekdays £22.50 per round, £30 per day. Weekends £27.50 per round, £35 per day. Dene - weekdays £10 per day, weekends £12 per
Facilities: Lunch. Bar Snacks. Full Catering. Changing Room. Golf Shop. Club Hire. Trolley Hire. Buggy Hire.

WAREHAM
East Dorset Golf Club, Hyde, Wareham, Dorset. BH20 7NT. Tel: 472244 (0929)
Secretary: D F C Thomas   Tel: 472244 (0929)
Professional: G Packer   Tel: 472272 (0929)
Description: Lakeland difficult course with water hazards. Woodland course through trees and rhododendrons.
Lakeland 18 holes, 6,556 yards, Par 71, S.S.S. 71.
Woodland 18 holes, 4,853 yards, Par 66, S.S.S. 64.
Membership: 600
Visitors: Welcome. Handicap certificate required. Telephone for tee reservations.
Green Fees: Lakeland £22 weekdays £30 weekends. Woodland £20 weekdays, £26 weekends.
Facilities: Lunch. Dinner. Bar Snacks. Full Catering. Changing Room. Golf Shop. Club Hire. Driving Range. Trolley Hire. Buggy Hire.
Class One Hotel: Kemps, Wareham, 3 mile(s). Tel: 462563 (0929)
Class Two Hotel: Hyde Woods, Wareham, 1 mile(s). Tel: 471087 (0929)

WAREHAM
Wareham Golf Club, Sandford Road, Wareham, Dorset. BH20 4DH. Tel: 554156 (0929)
Secretary: J L Holloway   Tel: 554147 (0929)
Location: Adjoining A351 near Wareham railway station.
Description: Partly wooded and undulating.
18 holes, 5,603 yards, Par 69, S.S.S. 67.
Membership: 550
Visitors: Welcome. Handicap certificate required. After 9.30 a.m. With members only at weekends.
Green Fees: £15 per round, £20 per day.
Facilities: Lunch. Dinner. Bar Snacks. Full Catering. Changing Room. Trolley Hire.
Class One Hotel: Springfield, Wareham, 2 mile(s). Tel: 552177 (0929)
Class Two Hotel: Worgret Manor, Wareham, 1 mile(s). Tel: 552957 (0929)

WEYMOUTH
Wessex Golf Centre, Radipole Lane, Weymouth, Dorset. Tel: 784737 (0352)
Professional: H Stathor   Tel: 784737 (0352)
Location: Off Weymouth by-pass behind football stadium.
9 holes, 1,385 yards, Par 27, S.S.S. .
Visitors: Welcome.
Green Fees: £2.90 per round, £4.50 with club hire.
Facilities: Golf Shop. Club Hire. Driving Range.

WEYMOUTH
Weymouth Golf Club, Links Road, Weymouth, Dorset. DT4 0PF. Tel: 773981 (0305)
Secretary: Colin Robinson   Tel: 773981 (0305)
Professional: Des Lochrie   Tel: 773997 (0305)
Description: Undulating parkland.
18 holes, 6,009 yards, Par 70, S.S.S. 69, Course record 63.
Membership: 750
Visitors: Welcome. Handicap certificate required.
Green Fees: Weekdays £16, weekends and Bank Holidays £22.
Facilities: Lunch. Dinner. Bar Snacks. Full Catering. Changing Room. Golf Shop. Club Hire. Driving Range. Trolley Hire.
Class One Hotel: Moonfleet Manor, Weymouth, 4 mile(s). Tel: 786948 (0305)
Class Two Hotel: Ponderosa, Weymouth, 2 mile(s). Tel: 812501 (0305)

DURHAM

BARNARD CASTLE
Barnard Castle Golf Club, Harmire Road, Barnard Castle, County Durham. DL12 8QN. Tel: 37237 (0833)
Secretary: A W Lavender   Tel: 38355 (0833)
Professional: J Harrison   Tel: 31980 (0833)
Location: North of town on Middleton-in-Teesdale road.
Description: Heathland.
18 holes, 5,838 yards, Par 71, S.S.S. 68.
Membership: 600
Visitors: Welcome. Booking system for weekends. Limited catering on Mondays.
Green Fees: Weekdays £13.50, weekends £20.
Facilities: Lunch. Dinner. Bar Snacks. Full Catering. Changing Room. Golf Shop. Club Hire. Trolley Hire.
Class Two Hotel: Marwood View, Barnard Castle, 1/2 mile(s). Tel: 37493 (0833)

BISHOP AUCKLAND
Bishop Auckland Golf Club, High Plains, Durham Road, Bishop Auckland, County Durham. DL14 8DL. Tel: 602198 (0388)
Secretary: Mr G Thatcher   Tel: 663648 (0388)
Professional: Mr D Skiffington Tel: 661618 (0388)
Location: Leave the Market Place on the main road to Spennymoor and Durham, entrance 1/2 mile on the left.
Description: Parkland course, excellent views up Wear valley and over Bishops Palace.
18 holes, 6,420 yards, Par 72, S.S.S. 71, Course record 65.
Membership: 900
Visitors: Welcome. No catering Mondays. Ladies day Tuesdays. No Visiting parties weekends.
Green Fees: Weekdays £16 per round, £20 per day, (parties over 20 reduced to £16). Weekends £22 per round.
Facilities: Lunch. Dinner. Bar Snacks. Full Catering. Changing Room. Golf Shop. Driving Range. Trolley Hire.
Class One Hotel: Parkhead Hotel, Bishop Auckland, 1 mile(s). Tel: 661727 (0388)
Class Two Hotel: Queens, Bishop Auckland, 1/2 mile(s). Tel: 603477 (0388)

BRANCEPETH

Brancepeth Castle Golf Club, Brancepeth, County Durham. DH7 8EA.
Secretary: J T Ross　　　　　Tel: 378 0075 (091)
Professional: D C Howdon　　Tel: 378 0183 (091)
Location: 4 miles west of Durham City on A690 Durham to Crook road.
18 holes, 6,415 yards, Par 70, S.S.S. 71, Course record 65.
Membership: 650
Visitors: Welcome. No parties at weekends. Indviduals by prior arrangement.
Green Fees: £23 weekdays, £30 weekends.
Facilities: Lunch. Dinner. Bar Snacks. Full Catering. Changing Room. Golf Shop. Trolley Hire.
Class One Hotel: Royal County, Durham, 4 mile(s). Tel: 386 6821 (091)
Class Two Hotel: Duke Of Wellington, Durham, 3 mile(s). Tel: 384 2735 (091)

CHESTER-LE-STREET

Chester-le-Street Golf Club, Lumley Park, Chester-le-Street, County Durham. DH3 4NS. Tel: 388 3218 (091)
Secretary: W B Dodds　　　Tel: 388 3218 (091)
Professional: A Hartley　　　Tel: 389 0157 (091)
Location: 1/2 mile east of Chester-le-street.
Description: Parkland.
White 18 holes, 6,054 yards, Par 70, S.S.S. 69, Course record 67.
Yellow 18 holes, 5,767 yards, Par 70, S.S.S. 68.
Membership: 650
Visitors: Welcome. Handicap certificate required. Letter of Introduction required. Weekdays not before 9.30 a.m. or between 12 and 1.30 p.m. Weekends and Bank Holidays, not before 10.30 a
Green Fees: £18 weekdays, £25 weekends and Bank Holidays.
Facilities: Lunch. Dinner. Bar Snacks. Full Catering. Changing Room. Golf Shop. Club Hire. Trolley Hire.
Class One Hotel: Lumley Castle, Chester-le-St.. Tel: 389 1111 (091)
Class Two Hotel: Manse Guest House, Birtley, 4 mile(s). Tel: 410 2486 (091)

CONSETT

Consett and District Golf Club, Elmfield Road, Consett, County Durham. DH8 5NN. Tel: 502186 (0207)
Secretary: Mr J Horrill　　　　Tel: 562261 (0207)
Professional: S Corbally
Description: Parkland.
18 holes, 6,013 yards, Par 71, S.S.S. 69, Course record 64.
Membership: 650
Visitors: Welcome. Competition day Wednesday. Telephone for weekends.
Green Fees: Weekdays £15, weekends and Bank Holidays £20.
Facilities: Lunch. Dinner. Bar Snacks. Full Catering. Changing Room. Golf Shop.
Class One Hotel: Raven, Broomhill, 2 mile(s). Tel: 560367 (0207)

CROOK

Crook Golf Club, Low Jobs Hill, Crook, County Durham. DL15 9AA. Tel: 762429 (0388)
Secretary: R King　　　　　Tel: 746400 (0388)
18 holes, 6,075 yards, Par 68, S.S.S. 69, Course record 64.
Membership: 600
Visitors: Welcome. No catering Mondays. Restrictions at weekends and competition days.
Green Fees: £10 weekdays, £15 per day weekends and Bank Holidays.
Facilities: Lunch. Dinner. Bar Snacks. Full Catering. Changing Room. Driving Range.
Class One Hotel: Three Tuns, Durham, 6 mile(s). Tel: 386 4326 (091)

DARLINGTON

Blackwell Grange Golf Club, Briar Close, Blackwell, Darlington, County Durham. DL3 8QX. Tel: 464464 (0325)
Secretary: F Hewitson　　　Tel: 464458 (0325)
Professional: R Given　　　Tel: 462088 (0325)
Location: 1 mile south of Darlington on A66, turn into Blackwell.
Description: Parkland course.
18 holes, 5,621 yards, Par 68, S.S.S. 67, Course record 63.
Membership: 650
Visitors: Welcome. Handicap certificate required. Ladies Wednesdays. Mens competition Sundays. Visiting parties weekdays only.
Green Fees: On application.
Facilities: Lunch. Dinner. Bar Snacks. Full Catering. Changing Room. Golf Shop. Club Hire. Trolley Hire.
Class One Hotel: Moat House, Darlington, 1/2 mile(s). Tel: 380888 (0325)
Class Two Hotel: Grange, Darlington, 1 mile(s). Tel: 464555 (0325)

DARLINGTON

Darlington Golf Club, Haughton Grange, Darlington, County Durham. DL1 3JD. Tel: 463936 (0325)
Secretary: G E Callender　　Tel: 355324 (0325)
Professional: Ian Todd　　　Tel: 462955 (0325)
Location: Northern outskirts of town A1150 off A167.
Description: Parkland.
18 holes, 6,271 yards, Par 71, S.S.S. 70.
Visitors: Welcome. Handicap certificate required. With members only at weekends. Groups maximum 40.
Green Fees: £20 per day.
Facilities: Lunch. Dinner. Bar Snacks. Full Catering. Changing Room. Golf Shop. Club Hire. Trolley Hire.
Class One Hotel: White Horse, Darlington, 1 1/2 mile(s). Tel: 382121 (0325)
Class Two Hotel: Aberlady Guest House, Darlington, 3 mile(s). Tel: 461449 (0325)

DARLINGTON

Dinsdale Spa Golf Club, Neasham Road, Middleton-St-George, Darlington, Co. Durham. DL2 1DW. Tel: 332297 (0325)
Secretary: P J Wright　　　Tel: 332297 (0325)
Professional: David Dodds　Tel: 332515 (0325)
Location: Near Teeside Airport.

Cade's - Audi Golf Course Guide

Description: Parkland.
18 holes, 5,667 yards, Par 69, S.S.S. 71, Course record 64.
Membership: 800
Visitors: Welcome. Handicap certificate required. Ladies Day Tuesday. With member only on Sundays.
Green Fees: £15 per round, £18 per day.
Facilities: Lunch. Dinner. Bar Snacks. Full Catering. Changing Room. Golf Shop. Club Hire. Trolley Hire.
Class One Hotel: Devonport, Middleton Row, 2 mile(s). Tel: 332255 (0325)

DARLINGTON

Stressholme Golf Club, Snipe Lane, Darlington, County Durham. . Tel: 353073 (0325)
Secretary: Graham Patrick   Tel: 353073 (0325)
Professional: Tim Jenkins   Tel: 461002 (0325)
Location: 1 mile south-west of Darlington town centre on A66.
Description: Greenland course.
18 holes, 6,511 yards, Par 71, S.S.S. 71, Course record 63.
Membership: 600
Visitors: Welcome. Handicap certificate required. Dinner by arrangement.
Green Fees: On application.
Facilities: Lunch. Dinner. Bar Snacks. Full Catering. Changing Room. Golf Shop. Club Hire. Trolley Hire.
Class One Hotel: Blackwell Grange Moat House, Darlington, 1/4 mile(s). Tel: 380888 (0325)
Class Two Hotel: Croft Spar, Darlington, 1 1/2 mile(s). Tel: 720319 (0325)

DURHAM

Mount Oswald Golf Club, South Road, Durham. DH1 3TQ. Tel: 386 7527 (091)
Location: West of the City of Durham on the A1050 approx 2 miles from city centre.
Description: Parkland.
18 holes, 6,101 yards, Par 71, S.S.S. 69, Course record 64.
Membership: 120
Visitors: Welcome.
Green Fees: £10 per round weekdays, £12 per round weekends.
Facilities: Lunch. Dinner. Bar Snacks. Full Catering. Changing Room. Club Hire. Trolley Hire.
Class One Hotel: Royal County, Durham, 2 mile(s). Tel: 386 6821 (091)

NEWTON AYCLIFFE

Aycliffe Golf Course & Driving Range, Oakley Sports Complex, School Aycliffe Lane, Newton Aycliffe, County Durham. DL5 6QZ. Tel: 310820 (0325)
Professional: Robert Lister   Tel: 310820 (0325)
Location: From Darlington A68 turn off Heighington By-Pass towards Newton Aycliffe.
Description: Parkland.
9 holes, 2,981 yards, Par , S.S.S. 69.
Membership: 250
Visitors: Welcome. Not before 8a.m. Saturdays and not before 9a.m. on Sundays.

Green Fees: Weekdays £3.60, weekends £4.60.
Facilities: Lunch. Dinner. Bar Snacks. Full Catering. Golf Shop. Club Hire. Driving Range. Trolley Hire.

NEWTON AYCLIFFE

Woodham Golf and Country Club, Burnhill Way, Newton Aycliffe, County Durham. DL5 4PN. Tel: 320574 (0325)
Description: Parkland course with streams and lakes.
18 holes, 6,727 yards, Par 73, S.S.S. 73.
Membership: 650
Visitors: Welcome. Handicap certificate required. After 10.30 a.m. at weekends.
Green Fees: £15 per round, £20 per day weekdays. £20 per round, £25 per day weekends and Bank Holidays.
Facilities: Lunch. Dinner. Bar Snacks. Full Catering. Changing Room. Golf Shop. Club Hire. Trolley Hire. Buggy Hire.
Class One Hotel: Redworth Hall, Redworth, 6 mile(s). Tel: 772442 (0388)
Class Two Hotel: Old Manor House, West Auckland, 6 mile(s). Tel: 834834 (0388)

STANLEY

Beamish Park Golf Club, Stanley, County Durham. DH9 0RH. Tel: 370 1382 (091)
Secretary: L Gilbert   Tel: 370 1382 (091)
Professional: C Cole   Tel: 370 1984 (091)
Location: Follow signs to Beamish Museum.
Description: Parkland.
18 holes, 6,205 yards, Par 71, S.S.S. 70, Course record 67.
Membership: 520
Visitors: Welcome. Not weekends.
Green Fees: £16 per round, £20 per day.
Facilities: Lunch. Dinner. Bar Snacks. Full Catering. Changing Room. Golf Shop. Club Hire. Driving Range. Trolley Hire.

STANLEY

South Moor Golf Club, The Middles, Craghead, Stanley, County Durham. DH9 6AG. Tel: 232848 (0207)
Secretary: B Davison   Tel: 239719 (0207)
Professional: S Cowell   Tel: 283525 (0207)
Location: 8 miles north of Durham City, 2 miles south of Beamish museum, 1 mile south of Stanley at Craghead.
Description: Parkland/moorland.
18 holes, 6,445 yards, Par 72, S.S.S. 71, Course record 66.
Membership: 600
Visitors: Welcome. Handicap certificate required. Members only before 9.30 a.m. and 12.00 to 2.00 p.m. weekdays. No casual visitors weekends or Bank Holidays unless with a member.
Green Fees: Weekdays £14 per round, £21 per day. Weekends and Bank Holidays £25.
Facilities: Lunch. Dinner. Bar Snacks. Full Catering. Changing Room. Golf Shop. Club Hire. Trolley Hire.
Class One Hotel: Swallow, Gateshead, 10 mile(s). Tel: 477 1105 (091)
Class Two Hotel: Lambton Arms, Chester-le-St., 6 mile(s). Tel: 387 1302 (091)

ESSEX

BASILDON

Basildon Golf Club, Clay Hill Lane, Basildon, Essex. .
Secretary: A M Burch   Tel: 533849 (0268)
Professional: G Hill   Tel: 533532 (0268)
Location: Off A13, take A176 to Basildon off at Kingswood roundabout.
Description: Undulating wooded grassland.
18 holes, 6,122 yards, Par 70, S.S.S. 69, Course record 67.
Membership: 150
Visitors: Welcome. Letter of Introduction required. Tee reservations at weekends, please telephone in advance.
Green Fees: Weekdays £7 per round, weekends £13 per round.
Facilities: Lunch. Dinner. Bar Snacks. Full Catering. Changing Room. Golf Shop. Club Hire. Trolley Hire.

BRAINTREE

Braintree Golf Club, Kings Lane, Stisted, Braintree, Essex. CM7 8DA. Tel: 46079 (0376)
Secretary: H W Hardy   Tel: 46079 (0376)
Professional: A K Parcell   Tel: 43465 (0376)
Location: 1 mile east of Braintree By-Pass off A120.
Description: Parkland.
18 holes, 6,161 yards, Par 70, S.S.S. 69, Course record 65.
Membership: 750
Visitors: Welcome. No handicap certificate required Monday to Thursday. Visitors not encouraged Friday to Sunday.
Green Fees: Monday to Thursday £24 per day. Friday to Sunday £40 per day.
Facilities: Lunch. Dinner. Bar Snacks. Full Catering. Changing Room. Golf Shop. Trolley Hire.

BRAINTREE

Towerlands Golf Club, Panfiedd Road, Braintree, Essex. CM7 5BJ. Tel: 326802 (0376)
Secretary: Mr K Cooper   Tel: 326802 (0376)
Professional: Mr A Boulter   Tel: 347951 (0376)
Location: On B1053 north of Braintree.
Description: Undulating course.
9 holes, yards, Par , S.S.S. 66.
Membership: 350
Visitors: Welcome. No green fees before 12.30 p.m. Saturdays and Sundays.
Green Fees: 9 Hholes £8.50, 18 holes £10.50, 18 holes weekends and Bank Holidays £12.50.
Facilities: Lunch. Dinner. Bar Snacks. Full Catering. Changing Room. Golf Shop. Club Hire. Driving Range. Trolley Hire. Buggy Hire. Caddies available.

BRENTWOOD

Bentley Golf Club, Ongar Road, Brentwood, Essex. CM15 9SS. Tel: 373179 (0277)
Professional: Keith Bridges   Tel: 372933 (0277)
Location: On A128 mid-way between Brentwood and Ongar.
Description: Parkland.

18 holes, 6,709 yards, Par 72, S.S.S. 72.
Membership: 550
Visitors: Welcome. Handicap certificate required. Not wednesdays. With members at weekends. After 11.00 a.m. on Bank Holidays. Some catering restrictions apply, please telephone in advan
Green Fees: £18.50 per round, £24 per day.
Facilities: Lunch. Dinner. Bar Snacks. Full Catering. Changing Room. Golf Shop. Trolley Hire.
Class One Hotel: Moat House, Brentwood, 5 mile(s). Tel: 225252 (0277)
Class Two Hotel: Furlongs Bed & Breakfast, Brentwood, 5 mile(s). Tel: 213758 (0277)

BRENTWOOD

Warley Park Golf Club, Magpie Lane, Little Warley, Brentwood, Essex. CM13 3DX. Tel: 224891 (0277)
Secretary: K Reagan   Tel: 224891 (0277)
Professional: P O'Connor   Tel: 212552 (0277)
Location: Leave M25 at junc 29, A127 towards Southend, turn left 3/4 mile in to Little Warley Hall Lane and left in to Magpie Lane.
Description: 27 hole parkland course with several water hazards.
1 and 2 18 holes, 5,932 yards, Par 70, S.S.S. 69.
1 and 3 18 holes, 6,124 yards, Par 71, S.S.S. 69.
2 and 3 18 holes, 6,376 yards, Par 71, S.S.S. 70.
Membership: 980
Visitors: Welcome. Handicap certificate required. With members at weekends after 12.00 p.m. only.
Green Fees: £20 per round, £30 per day.
Facilities: Lunch. Bar Snacks. Changing Room. Golf Shop. Club Hire. Trolley Hire. Buggy Hire.
Class One Hotel: Moat House, Brentwood, 1 1/2 mile(s). Tel: 225252 (0277)

BURNHAM-ON-CROUCH

Burnham-on-Crouch Golf Club Ltd., Ferry Road, Creaksea, Burnham-on-Crouch, Essex. CM0 8PQ. Tel: 782282 (0621)
Secretary: A S Hill   Tel: 782282 (0621)
Location: Turn right off B1010 1 mile short of Burnham-on Crouch.
Description: Undulating meadowland.
9 holes, 5,918 yards, Par 68, S.S.S. 68, Course record 66.
Membership: 500
Visitors: Welcome. Handicap certificate required. Not weekends or Bank Holidays and not before 12 noon on Thursdays. Advance order for lunch and dinner.
Green Fees: £20 per round or day.
Facilities: Lunch. Dinner. Bar Snacks. Changing Room. Buggy Hire.

CANVEY ISLAND

Castle Point Golf Club, Somnes Avenue, Canvey Island, Essex. SS8 9FG. Tel: 510830 (0268)
Secretary: Vic Russell   Tel: 698909 (0268)
Professional: John Hudson   Tel: 510830 (0268)
Location: Off A13, A130 to Canvey Island.
Description: Seaside links course.

Cade's - Audi Golf Course Guide

18 holes, 5,627 yards, Par 71, S.S.S. 69, Course record 68.
Membership: 300
Visitors: Welcome. Booking weekends a.m.
Green Fees: Weekdays £8.40, juniors and O.A.P.'s £4.20. Weekends all classes £12.50.
Facilities: Lunch. Dinner. Bar Snacks. Full Catering. Changing Room. Golf Shop. Club Hire. Driving Range. Trolley Hire.
Class One Hotel: Forte Crest, Basildon, 8 mile(s). Tel: 533955 (0268)

CHELMSFORD
Channels Golf Club, Belsteads Farm Lane, Little Waltham, Chelmsford, Essex. CM3 3PT.
Secretary: R J Stubbings   Tel: 440005 (0245)
Professional: I B Sinclair   Tel: 441056 (0245)
Location: On A130 signposted to Little Waltham.
Description: Flat with undulation on back 9 holes.
18 holes, 5,726 yards, Par 70, S.S.S. 69, Course record 67.
Membership: 600
Visitors: Welcome.
Green Fees: £25 per day.
Facilities: Full Catering. Changing Room. Golf Shop. Trolley Hire. Buggy Hire. Caddies available.
Class One Hotel: Swan, Felstead, 5 mile(s). Tel: 820245 (0371)
Class Two Hotel: White Hart, Little Waltham, 1 1/2 mile(s). Tel: 360487 (0245)

CHIGWELL
Chigwell Golf Club, The Clubhouse, High Road, Chigwell, Essex. IG7 5BH. Tel: 500 2059 (081)
Secretary: Mr M McL Farnsworth   Tel: 500 2059 (081)
Professional: R Beard   Tel: 500 2384 (081)
Description: Undulating parkland course.
18 holes, 6,279 yards, Par 71, S.S.S. 70, Course record 66.
Membership: 615
Visitors: Welcome. Handicap certificate required. With members only at weekends. Caddies by arrangement.
Green Fees: £28 per round, £35 per day.
Facilities: Lunch. Bar Snacks. Full Catering. Changing Room. Golf Shop. Club Hire. Trolley Hire. Caddies available.

CHIGWELL
Hainault Forest Golf Club, Chigwell Row, Chigwell, Essex. IG7 4QW. Tel: 500 0385 (081)
Secretary: H G Richards   Tel: 500 0385 (081)
Professional: A E Frost   Tel: 500 2131 (081)
Location: Travel along A12, turn off at Chigwell, signposted to Municipal golf course.
Description: Undulating parkland.
One 18 holes, 5,900 yards, Par 71, S.S.S. 71, Course record 65.
Two 18 holes, 6,600 yards, Par 71, S.S.S. 71, Course record 68.
Membership: 780
Visitors: Welcome. Bookings for weekends, 10 days in advance.

Green Fees: Weekdays £7.80, weekends £10.
Facilities: Lunch. Dinner. Bar Snacks. Full Catering. Changing Room. Golf Shop. Club Hire. Trolley Hire.

COLCHESTER
Birch Grove Golf Club, Layer Road, Colchester, Essex. CO2 0HS. Tel: 734276 (0206)
Secretary: Mrs M Marston   Tel: 734276 (0206)
Location: On B1026, 2 miles south of Colchester town centre.
Description: Undulating parkland, very challenging.
9 holes, 4,038 yards, Par 62, S.S.S. 60, Course record 61.
Membership: 250
Visitors: Welcome. After 1.00 p.m. Sundays. Ladies after 1.00 p.m. Saturdays and Sundays. Dinner by arrangement.
Green Fees: On application.
Facilities: Lunch. Dinner. Bar Snacks. Full Catering. Changing Room. Golf Shop. Trolley Hire.
Class One Hotel: Marks Tey Hotel, Colchester, 2 mile(s). Tel: 210001 (0206)
Class Two Hotel: Kingsford Park, Colchester, 1/3 mile(s) Tel: 734301 (0206)

COLCHESTER
Colchester Golf Club, Braiswick, Colchester, Essex. CO4 5AU. Tel: 852946 (0206)
Secretary: Mrs J Boorman   Tel: 853396 (0206)
Professional: Mark Angel   Tel: 853920 (0206)
Location: B1508 3/4 mile north-west of Colchester North station towards West Bergholt.
Description: Parkland.
18 holes, 6,319 yards, Par 70, S.S.S. 70, Course record 63.
Membership: 750
Visitors: Welcome. Handicap certificate required. Weekends only wih member before 2.00 p.m.
Green Fees: £22 per day.
Facilities: Lunch. Bar Snacks. Full Catering. Changing Room. Golf Shop. Club Hire. Trolley Hire.
Class One Hotel: Marks Tey Hotel, Colchester, 6 mile(s). Tel: 210001 (0206)
Class Two Hotel: Kingsford Park, Colchester, 6 mile(s). Tel: 34301 (0206)

COLCHESTER
Stoke by Nayland Golf Club, Keepers Lane, Leavenheath, Colchester, Essex. CO6 4PZ. Tel: 262836 (0206)
Secretary: J Loshak   Tel: 262836 (0206)
Professional: K Lovelock   Tel: 262769 (0206)
Location: On B1068 off A134 between Colchester and Sudbury.
Description: Undulating parkland, with water hazards.
Gainsborough 18 holes, 6,516 yards, Par 72, S.S.S. 71, Course record 66.
Constable 18 holes, 6,544 yards, Par 72, S.S.S. 71, Course record 67.
Membership: 1450
Visitors: Welcome. Handicap certificate required at weekends. Telephone call advised.
Green Fees: £25 per day.
Facilities: Lunch. Dinner. Bar Snacks. Full Catering. Chang-

55

ing Room. Golf Shop. Club Hire. Trolley Hire. Buggy Hire.
Class One Hotel: Maison Talbooth, Dedham, 8 mile(s). Tel: 322367 (0206)
Class Two Hotel: Angel Inn, Stoke b Nayland, 2 mile(s). Tel: 263245 (0206)

EPPING

Theydon Bois Golf Club, Theydon Road, Epping, Essex. CM16 4EH. Tel: 831054 (0992)
Secretary: Ian McDonald	Tel: 813054 (0992)
Professional: Robert Joyce	Tel: 812460 (0992)
Location: M25 junc 26, A121 to Epping turn right at Bell Hotel 1 mile on left.
Description: Wooded parkland.
18 holes, 5,472 yards, Par 68, S.S.S. 68, Course record 66.
Membership: 630
Visitors: Welcome. Handicap certificate required. Not wednesdays or Thursdays a.m., not November to March.
Green Fees: Weekdays £23, weekends and Bank Holidays £34.
Facilities: Lunch. Bar Snacks. Full Catering. Changing Room. Golf Shop. Driving Range. Trolley Hire.
Class One Hotel: The Bell, Epping, 1 mile(s). Tel: 73137 (0992)
Class Two Hotel: Parsonage Farm Guest House, Theydon Bois, 2 mile(s). Tel: 814242 (0378)

HARLOW

Canons Brook Golf Club, Elizabeth Way, Harlow, Essex. CM19 5BE.
Secretary: G E Chambers	Tel: 421482 (0279)
Professional: R Yates	Tel: 418357 (0279)
Description: Parkland.
18 holes, 6,728 yards, Par 73, S.S.S. 73.
Membership: 700
Visitors: Welcome. Not weekends. Must telephone in advance for weekdays.
Green Fees: £25 per day.
Facilities: Lunch. Dinner. Bar Snacks. Full Catering. Changing Room. Golf Shop. Trolley Hire.

LOUGHTON

Loughton Golf Club, Clay's Lane, Loughton, Essex. IG10 2RZ. Tel: 502 2923 (081)
Professional: B Davies	Tel: 502 2923 (081)
Location: Just north of Loughton on edge Epping Forest.
Description: Parkland.
9 holes, 4,700 yards, Par 64, S.S.S. 63, Course record 65.
Membership: 350
Visitors: Welcome. Telephone to book.
Green Fees: Weekdays 9 holes £4, 18 holes £6. Weekends 9 holes £5.30, 18 holes £9.50.
Facilities: Bar Snacks. Changing Room. Golf Shop. Club Hire. Trolley Hire.
Class One Hotel: St Olaves, Loughton, 2 mile(s). Tel: 508 1699 (081)

MALDON

Forrester Park Golf Club, Forrester Park, Beckingham Road, Great Totham, Near Maldon, Essex. CM9 8EA. Tel: 891406 (0621)

Secretary: D Everett	Tel: 891406 (0621)
Location: 3 1/2 miles north of Maldon on B1022.
Description: Rural Essex countryside parkland.
18 holes, 6,073 yards, Par 71, S.S.S. 69.
Membership: 850
Visitors: Welcome. Members only before 12.30 p.m. Saturdays and Sundays. Full catering for societies only.
Green Fees: Weekdays £13, weekends £18.
Facilities: Lunch. Bar Snacks. Full Catering. Changing Room. Golf Shop.
Class One Hotel: Rivenhall Motor Inn, Rivenhall, 2 mile(s). Tel: 516969 (0376)
Class Two Hotel: The Star Guest House, Maldon, 3 1/2 mile(s). Tel: 853527 (0621)

MALDON

Maldon Golf Club, Beeleigh, Langford, Maldon, Essex. CM9 6LL. Tel: 853212 (0621)
Secretary: G R Bezant	Tel: 853212 (0621)
Location: B1019 2 miles north-west of Maldon, turn off at the Essex water works.
Description: Parkland bounded by the River Chelmer and the Blackwater Canal.
9 holes, 6,197 yards, Par 71, S.S.S. 69.
Membership: 480
Visitors: Welcome. Handicap certificate required. With members only at weekends (no Sunday mornings). Priorities: Ladies Tuesdays a.m., Veterans Wednesdays a.m. Catering for groups only.
Green Fees: £15 per round, £20 per day.
Facilities: Changing Room. Golf Shop.
Class One Hotel: Blue Boar, Maldon, 2 mile(s). Tel: 852681 (0621)
Class Two Hotel: The Benbridge, Heybridge, 1/2 mile(s). Tel: 857666 (0621)

MALDON

Quiet Waters Golf and Country Club, Colchester Road, Tolleshunt Knights, Maldon, Essex. CM9 8HX. Tel: 860410 (0621)
Secretary: P D Keeble	Tel: 860410 (0621)
Professional: Gary Pike and Clive Tucker	Tel: 860576 (0621)
Location: Approx 8 miles south of Colchester.
Links 18 holes, 6,222 yards, Par 71, S.S.S. 70.
Lakes 18 holes, 6,767 yards, Par 72, S.S.S. 72.
Membership: 600
Visitors: Welcome. Please telephone in advance for bookings.
Green Fees: Links - Weekdays £18 round, £25 day. Weekends £22.50 round, £30 day. Lakes - Weekdays £40 round, £50 day. Weekends £60 round, £80 day.
Facilities: Lunch. Dinner. Bar Snacks. Full Catering. Changing Room. Golf Shop. Trolley Hire. Buggy Hire.
Class One Hotel: Quiet Waters Country Club, Tolleshunt. Tel: 860410 (0621)

OCKENDON

Belhus Park Golf Club, Belhus Park, South Ockendon, Essex. RM15 4QR. Tel: 852248 (0708)
Secretary: D A Faust	Tel: 46224 (04024)

Cade's - Audi Golf Course Guide

Professional: Gary Lunn　　　Tel: 854260 (0708)
Location: Near A13/M25 junc 26.
Description: Parkland.
18 holes, 4,900 yards, Par 68, S.S.S. 68.
Membership: 300
Visitors: Welcome.
Green Fees: Weekdays £10.25.
Facilities: Lunch. Dinner. Bar Snacks. Full Catering. Changing Room. Golf Shop. Club Hire. Driving Range. Trolley Hire.

ORSETT

Orsett Golf Club, Brentwood Road, Orsett, Essex. RM16 3DS. Tel: 891352 (0375)
Secretary: P M Pritchard　　　Tel: 891226 (0375)
Professional: R Newberry　　　Tel: 891797 (0375)
Location: 4 miles north-east of Grays at junction of A13 and A128.
18 holes, 6,614 yards, Par 72, S.S.S., Course record 68.
Membership: 900
Visitors: Welcome. Handicap certificate required. Weekdays only and when course restrictions allow.
Green Fees: On application.
Facilities: Lunch. Dinner. Bar Snacks. Full Catering. Changing Room. Golf Shop. Trolley Hire. Buggy Hire.
Class One Hotel: Plough Motel, Bulphan, 4 mile(s). Tel: 891592 (0375)

ROCHFORD

Ballards Gore Golf Club, Gore Road, Canewdon, Near Rochford, Essex. SS4 2DA. Tel: 258917 (0702)
Secretary: N G Patient　　　Tel: 258917 (0702)
Professional: Ian Marshall　　　Tel: 258924 (0702)
Location: From London via A127 to Southend Airport (3 miles away) through Rochford to club 2 miles on.
Description: Parkland with lakes.
18 holes, 7,062 yards, Par 73, S.S.S. 74.
Membership: 750
Visitors: Welcome. Weekdays only. With members at weekends.
Green Fees: £20.
Facilities: Lunch. Bar Snacks. Changing Room. Golf Shop. Trolley Hire.
Class One Hotel: The Renouf, Rochford, 1 1/2 mile(s). Tel: 541334 (0702)

SOUTHEND-ON-SEA

Thorpe Hall Golf Club, Thorpe Hall Avenue, Thorpe Bay, Southend-on-Sea, Essex. SS1 3AT. Tel: 582205 (0702)
Secretary: G Winkless　　　Tel: 582205 (0702)
Professional: G Harvey　　　Tel: 588195 (0702)
Location: 1 mile from Southend-on-Sea east along coast road.
Description: Parkland course.
18 holes, 6,286 yards, Par 71, S.S.S. 71, Course record 68.
Membership: 1100
Visitors: Welcome. Handicap certificate required. With members only at weekends. Some catering restrictions apply, please telephone in advance.
Green Fees: £27.
Facilities: Lunch. Bar Snacks. Full Catering. Changing Room. Golf Shop, Club Hire. Trolley Hire.
Class One Hotel: Roslin, Southend, 1/2 mile(s). Tel: 586375 (0702)
Class Two Hotel: West Park, Southend, 3 mile(s). Tel: 334252 (0702)

STAPLEFORD ABBOTTS

Stapleford Abbotts Golf Club, Horsemans Side, Tysea Hill, Stapleford Abbotts, Essex. RM4 1JU. Tel: 81108 (04023)
Secretary: Keith Fletcher　　　Tel: 81108 (04023)
Professional: Scott Cranfield　　　Tel: 81278 (04023)
Location: 3 miles from junc 28 M25 off main Romford to Ongar road B175 at Stapleford Abbotts.
Description: Flat parkland with numerous lakes.
Abbotts 18 holes, 6,432 yards, Par 72, S.S.S. 71.
Priors 18 holes, 5,711 yards, Par 69, S.S.S. 67.
Friars 9 holes, 1,140 yards, Par 27.
Membership: 1000
Visitors: Welcome. Weekdays only. Tee reservations, Abbotts: 70040 (04023), Priors: 373344 (0277).
Green Fees: Abbotts £20, Priors £15, Friars £5.
Facilities: Lunch. Dinner. Bar Snacks. Full Catering. Changing Room. Golf Shop. Club Hire. Trolley Hire. Buggy Hire.
Class One Hotel: Post House, Brentwood, 3 mile(s). Tel: 260260 (0277)

GLOUCESTERSHIRE

COLEFORD

Royal Forest of Dean Golf Club, Lords Hill, Coleford, Gloucs. GL16 8BD. Tel: 832583 (0594)
Secretary: Mrs K Cave　　　Tel: 832583 (0594)
Professional: Mr J Nicol　　　Tel: 833689 (0594)
Description: Parkland course with own hotel adjacent to the first tee, in the beautiful Forest of Dean.
Competition 18 holes, 5,535 yards, Par 69, S.S.S. 67.
Yellow 18 holes, 5,188 yards, Par 67, S.S.S. 65.
Membership: 500
Visitors: Welcome. Society days Mondays to Thursdays. Visitors welcome at all times. Tee times required.
Green Fees: £14 weekdays, £16 weekends. £23 society day including lunch and three course dinner.
Facilities: Lunch. Dinner. Bar Snacks. Full Catering. Changing Room. Golf Shop. Club Hire. Trolley Hire. Buggy Hire.
Class Two Hotel: Bell Hotel, On course. Tel: 832583 (0594)

MINCHINHAMPTON

Minchinhampton Golf Club, New Course, Minchinhampton, Stroud, Gloucs. GL6 9BE. Tel: 833866 (0453)
Secretary: D R Vickers　　　Tel: 833866 (0453)
Professional: C Steele　　　Tel: 833860 (0453)
Location: (New course) - 2 miles east of Minchinhampton on Avening Road. (Old course) - 2 miles west of Minchinhampton, on Minchinhampton Common.
Description: New Course - Parkland. Old Course - Cotswold grassland.
New 18 holes, 6,675 yards, Par 72, S.S.S. 72, Course record 66.

Old 18 holes, 6,295 yards, Par 72, S.S.S. 70, Course record 65.
Visitors: Welcome. Handicap certificate required. Not Monday or Tuesday mornings on New Course.
Green Fees: New Course - Weekdays £22.50, weekends £28. Old Course - £10.
Facilities: Lunch. Dinner. Bar Snacks. Full Catering. Changing Room. Golf Shop. Club Hire. Trolley Hire.
Class One Hotel: Hare and Hounds, Westonbirt, 5 mile(s). Tel: 233 (066688)
Class Two Hotel: Amberley Inn, Amberley, 4 mile(s). Tel: 872565 (0453)

PAINSWICK

Painswick Golf Club, Painswick, Near Stroud, Gloucs. GL6 6TL. Tel: 812180 (0452)
Secretary: R J May   Tel: 812180 (0452)
Location: Off A46 i mile north of Painswick Village, between Stroud and Cheltenham.
Description: Common land hilly course.
18 holes, 4,895 yards, Par 67, S.S.S. 64, Course record 62.
Membership: 420
Visitors: Welcome. Only with member Saturday p.m. or Sundays a.m. No play on Sundays p.m. Some catering restrictions apply, please telephone in advance.
Green Fees: £8 per round weekdays, £12 weekends and Bank Holidays.
Facilities: Lunch. Dinner. Bar Snacks. Changing Room.
Class One Hotel: Painswick, Painswick, 1 mile(s). Tel: 812160 (0452)
Class Two Hotel: Beechmount Guest House, Birdlip, 2 mile(s). Tel: 862162 (0452)

TETBURY

Westonbirt Golf Course, c/o Bursar, Westonbirt School Ltd, Westonbirt, Near Tetbury, Gloucs. GL8 8QG. Tel: 880242 (0666)
Secretary: Mr J R Watts   Tel: 880242 (0666)
Professional: C Steele   Tel: 880242 (0666)
Location: 3 1/2 miles from Tetbury towards Bath on A433, as you come through Westonbirt the Arbotetum is on your right, take the next turning on rig
Description: Parkland.
9 holes, 5,404 yards, Par , S.S.S. 61.
Membership: 157
Visitors: Welcome.
Green Fees: £6 per day weekdays, £6 per round (18 holes) weekends and Bank Holidays.
Facilities: Changing Room.
Class One Hotel: Hare and Hounds, Westonbirt, 1 mile(s). Tel: 880233 (0666)
Class Two Hotel: Tavern House, Willesley, 1 1/2 mile(s). Tel: 880254 (0666)

WOTTON-UNDER-EDGE

Cotswold Edge Golf Club, Upper Rushmire, Wotton-under-Edge, Gloucs. GL12 7PT. Tel: 844167 (0453);
Secretary: N J Newman   Tel: 844167 (0453)
Professional: D Gosling   Tel: 844398 (0453)
Location: 8 miles from junc 14 M5 on B4058 Tetbury road.
Description: Fairly flat, set in magnificient countryside

offering unrivalled views.
18 holes, 5,816 yards, Par 71, S.S.S. 68.
Visitors: Welcome. Handicap certificate required. Letter of Introduction required. With member only at weekends.
Green Fees: £15.
Facilities: Lunch. Bar Snacks. Changing Room. Golf Shop. Club Hire. Trolley Hire. Buggy Hire.
Class One Hotel: Hare and Hounds, Westonbirt, 7 mile(s). Tel: 880233 (0666)

GREATER LONDON

BARKINGSIDE

Fairlop Waters Golf Club, Forest Road, Barkingside, Ilford, Essex. IG6 3JA. Tel: 500 9911 (081)
Secretary: Keith Robson   Tel: 500 9911 (081)
Professional: Tony Bowers   Tel: 501 1881 (081)
Location: A12 from London (Eastern Avenue) signposted from Gantshill roundabout. A12 south (signposted from Moby Dick Public House).
Description: Open country parkland. Municipal course.
18 holes, 6,281 yards, Par 72, S.S.S. 70.
Visitors: Welcome.
Green Fees: Weekdays £7 for 18 holes, £4.25 for 9 holes. Weekends £10 for 18 holes, £6 for 9 holes. Concessions mid-week for Senior Citizens and Jun
Facilities: Lunch. Dinner. Bar Snacks. Full Catering. Changing Room. Golf Shop. Club Hire. Driving Range. Trolley Hire.

BECKENHAM

Braeside Golf Club, Beckenham Place Park, Beckenham Hill, Beckenham, BR3 2BH. Tel: 650 2292 (081)
Secretary: Mr R Oliver   Tel: 304 3818 (081)
Professional: Mr Woodman   Tel: 658 5374 (081)
Location: From Bromley, take Bromley Road towards Catford, 3 to 4 miles on left hand side.
Description: Undulating parkland.
18 holes, 5,722 yards, Par 68, S.S.S. 68, Course record 62.
Membership: 150
Visitors: Welcome.
Green Fees: On application.
Facilities: Lunch. Bar Snacks. Golf Shop. Club Hire. Trolley Hire.
Class One Hotel: Bromley Court, Bromley, 3 mile(s). Tel: 464 5011 (081)
Class Two Hotel: Stowcroft Guest House, Chislehurst, 3 mile(s). Tel: 467 7406 (081)

BECKENHAM

Langley Park Golf Club, Barnfield Wood Road, Beckenham, Kent. BR3 2SZ. Tel: 658 6849 (081)
Secretary: John L Smart   Tel: 658 6849 (081)
Professional: George Ritchie Tel: 650 1663 (081)
Location: 1 mile from South Bromley Station.
Description: Flat parkland.
18 holes, 6,488 yards, Par 69, S.S.S. 71, Course record 65.
Membership: 650
Visitors: Welcome. Handicap certificate required. Monday to Friday only, by arrangement with professionals.

Cade's - Audi Golf Course Guide

Green Fees: £30 per round or day.
Facilities: Lunch. Bar Snacks. Changing Room. Golf Shop. Club Hire. Trolley Hire.
Class One Hotel: Bromley Court, Bromley, 2 mile(s). Tel: 464 5011 (081)
Class Two Hotel: Bickley Manor, Bickley, 4 mile(s). Tel: 467 3851 (081)

BEXLEY HEATH
Bexley Heath Golf Club, Mount Row, Mount Road, Bexley Heath, Kent. DA6 8JS. Tel: 303 6951 (081)
Secretary: Mr Squires   Tel: 303 6951 (081)
Location: Adjacent to A2 in Bexley Heath.
Description: Open parkland.
9 holes, 5,239 yards, Par 66, S.S.S. 66, Course record 60.
Membership: 400
Visitors: Welcome. With members only at weekends.
Green Fees: £15 per day.
Facilities: Lunch. Dinner. Bar Snacks. Full Catering. Changing Room.
Class One Hotel: The Crest, Bexley Heath, 1 1/2 mile(s). Tel: 526900 (0322)

BROMLEY
Bromley Golf Club, Magpie Hall Lane, Bromley, London. BR2 14AF. Tel: 462 7014 (081)
Professional: Alan Hodgson   Tel: 462 7014 (081)
Location:
Description: 9 hole public course.
9 holes, 2,745 yards, Par 35.
Visitors: Welcome.
Green Fees: Weekdays £3.50 adults, juniors and O.A.P.'s £2.00. Weekends £4.25 all classes.
Facilities: Bar Snacks. Golf Shop. Club Hire. Trolley Hire.
Class One Hotel: Bromley Court, Bromley, 2 mile(s). Tel: 464 5011 (081)

CHESSINGTON
Chessington Golf Club, Garrison Lane, Chessington, Surrey. KT9 2LW. Tel: 974 1705 (081)
Secretary: Mr T Maxted   Tel: 974 1705 (081)
Professional: Mr R Cornwall   Tel: 391 0948 (081)
Location: 1 mile south of Chessington on Garrison Lane.
Description: Open, tree lined parkland, gently undulating.
9 holes, 1,400 yards, Par 54, S.S.S. 50, Course record 54.
Membership: 250
Visitors: Welcome. With members only Saturday and Sunday mornings.
Green Fees: Weekdays £3.10, weekends £3.75.
Facilities: Lunch. Dinner. Bar Snacks. Full Catering. Changing Room. Golf Shop. Club Hire. Driving Range. Trolley Hire.

CHESSINGTON
Surbiton Golf Club, Woodstock Lane, Chessington, Surrey. KT9 1UG. Tel: 398 2056 (081)
Secretary: Mr G A Keith MBE   Tel: 398 3101 (081)
Professional: Mr P Milton   Tel: 398 6619 (081)
Location: 1 1/2 miles south east of Esher off A3 westbound from London, turn off for Esher and Claygate.
Description: Undulating, tree lined, open parkland.

18 holes, 6,211 yards, Par 70, S.S.S. 70, Course record 64.
Membership: 750
Visitors: Welcome. Handicap certificate required. With members only at weekends. Tuesdays Ladies Day.
Green Fees: £27 per round, £40.50 per day.
Facilities: Lunch. Dinner. Bar Snacks. Full Catering. Changing Room. Golf Shop. Club Hire. Trolley Hire.
Class Two Hotel: The Haven, Esher, 1 1/2 mile(s). Tel: 398 0023 (081)

CHINGFORD
West Essex Golf Club, Bury Road, Sewardstonebury, Chingford, London. E4 7QL. Tel: 529 7558 (081)
Secretary: P H Galley MBE   Tel: 529 7558 (081)
Professional: C Cox   Tel: 529 6347 (081)
Location: 2 miles north of Chingford station. Junc 26 (M25) Waltham Abbey.
Description: Parkland in Epping forest.
18 holes, 6,289 yards, Par 71, S.S.S. 70, Course record 65.
Membership: 652
Visitors: Welcome. Handicap certificate required. Not before 11 a.m. Tuesdays. Not after 12 noon Thursdays. With member at weekends.
Green Fees: £28 per round, £35 per day. With member £14.
Facilities: Lunch. Dinner. Bar Snacks. Full Catering. Changing Room. Golf Shop. Trolley Hire. Buggy Hire.
Class One Hotel: Swallow, Waltham Abbey, 3 mile(s). Tel: 717170 (0992)
Class Two Hotel: Forest View, Chingford, 2 mile(s). Tel: 529 1387 (081)

CHISLEHURST
Chislehurst Golf Club, Camden Park Road, Chislehurst, Kent. BR7 5HJ. Tel: 467 2782 (081)
Secretary: N Pearson   Tel: 467 2782 (081)
Professional: S Corstorphine   Tel: 467 6798 (081)
Location: A20-A222 2 1/2 miles from Bromley.
Description: Parkland.
18 holes, 5,128 yards, Par 66, S.S.S. 65, Course record 62.
Membership: 750
Visitors: Welcome. Handicap certificate required. With members at weekends. 36 hole societies Thursdays only. Some catering restrictions apply, please telephone in advance.
Green Fees: £25 per day.
Facilities: Lunch. Dinner. Bar Snacks. Changing Room. Golf Shop. Club Hire. Trolley Hire.
Class One Hotel: Bromley Court, Bromley, 2 mile(s). Tel: 464 5011 (081)
Class Two Hotel: Meadowcroft Lodge, Eltham, 1 1/2 mile(s). Tel: 859 1488 (081)

COULSDON
Coulsdon Court, Coulsdon Road, Coulsdon, Surrey. CR5 2LL. Tel: 660 0468 (081)
Professional: Colin Staff   Tel: 660 6083 (081)
Location: On B2030 near South Croydon. Minutes from main road and rail links in to London.
Description: Rolling parkland.
18 holes, 6,037 yards, Par 70, S.S.S. 69, Course record 66.

Visitors: Welcome.
Green Fees: Weekdays £10.25, weekends £12.80.
Facilities: Lunch. Dinner. Bar Snacks. Full Catering. Golf Shop. Club Hire. Trolley Hire.
Class One Hotel: Coulsdon Court, On course, 0 mile(s). Tel: 668 0414 (081)

COULSDON
Woodcote Park Golf Club, Meadow Hill, Bridle Way, Coulsdon, Surrey. CR5 2QQ. Tel: 668 2788 (081)
Description: Meadowland.
18 holes, 6,624 yards, Par 71, S.S.S. 71.
Membership: 600
Visitors: Welcome. Handicap certificate required. With members only at weekends. Not Tuesday a.m.
Green Fees: £25.
Facilities: Lunch. Dinner. Bar Snacks. Full Catering. Changing Room. Golf Shop. Club Hire. Trolley Hire.

CROYDON
Croham Hurst Golf Club, Croham Road, South Croydon, Surrey. CR2 7HJ. Tel: 657 5581 (081)
Secretary: R Passingham   Tel: 657 5581 (081)
Professional: E Stillwell   Tel: 657 7705 (081)
Location: 1 1/2 miles from Croydon on Selsdon Road.
18 holes, 6,286 yards, Par 70, S.S.S. 70, Course record 64.
Membership: 900
Visitors: Welcome. Handicap certificate required. Members only at weekends.
Green Fees: Weekdays £32.
Facilities: Lunch. Bar Snacks. Full Catering. Changing Room. Golf Shop. Club Hire. Trolley Hire.

CROYDON
Selsdon Park Hotel Golf Course, Sanderstead, South Croydon, Surrey. CR2 8YA. Tel: 657 8811 (081)
Professional: Mr O'Keefe   Tel: 657 4129 (081)
Location: 3 miles south east of Croydon on A2022.
Description: Steeply undulating tree lined open parkland. A championship course.
18 holes, 6,402 yards, Par 73, S.S.S. 71, Course record 68.
Visitors: Welcome. Caddies available with 24 hrs notice.
Green Fees: Weekdays £20 per round, Saturdays £25 per round, Sundays and Bank Holidays £30 per round.
Facilities: Lunch. Dinner. Bar Snacks. Full Catering. Changing Room. Golf Shop. Club Hire. Driving Range. Trolley Hire.
Class One Hotel: Selsdon Park Hotel, On Course, 0 mile(s). Tel: 657 8811 (081)

CROYDON
Shirley Park Golf Club, 194 Addiscombe Road, Croydon, Surrey. CR0 7LB. Tel: 654 1143 (081)
Secretary: Mr A Baird   Tel: 654 1143 (081)
Professional: Mr H Stott   Tel: 654 8767 (081)
Location: On A232 from Croydon towards West Wickham and Orpington. 1 1/2 miles from Croydon.
Description: Open gently undulating parkland, wooded in places with several ponds and ditches. Championship course.
18 holes, 6,210 yards, Par 71, S.S.S. 70, Course record 66.

Membership: 1000
Visitors: Welcome. With members only at weekends. Ladies Thursday mornings. Caddies available with 7 days notice.
Green Fees: £26 per day or round.
Facilities: Lunch. Dinner. Bar Snacks. Full Catering. Changing Room. Golf Shop. Trolley Hire.

DULWICH
Dulwich and Sydenham Golf Club, Grange Lane, College Road, Dulwich, London. SE21 7LH. Tel: 693 1221 (081)
Secretary: Mrs S Alexander   Tel: 693 3961 (081)
Professional: David Baillie   Tel: 693 8491 (081)
Location: 6 miles south of central London, follow signs to Camberwell and Dulwich.
Description: Hilly open parkland, 2 small ponds, overlooks the City of London.
18 holes, 6,051 yards, Par 69, S.S.S. 69.
Membership: 800
Visitors: Welcome. Handicap certificate required. Tuesdays Ladies Day. With members only at weekends.
Green Fees: £25 per round, £30 per day.
Facilities: Lunch. Dinner. Bar Snacks. Full Catering. Changing Room. Golf Shop. Club Hire. Trolley Hire. Buggy Hire.
Class One Hotel: The Queens Hotel, Crystal Palace, 3 mile(s). Tel: 653 6622 (081)

ELTHAM
Eltham Warren Golf Club, Bexley Road, Eltham, London. SE9 2PE. Tel: 850 1166 (081)
Secretary: D J Clare   Tel: 850 4477 (081)
Professional: R V Taylor   Tel: 859 7909 (081)
Location: A210 1/2 mile north of Eltham.
Description: Parkland.
9 holes, 5,840 yards, Par 69, S.S.S. 68, Course record 66.
Membership: 450
Visitors: Welcome. Handicap certificate required. Weekdays only.
Green Fees: £25 per day.
Facilities: Lunch. Dinner. Bar Snacks. Full Catering. Changing Room. Golf Shop. Club Hire. Trolley Hire.
Class One Hotel: Crest, Bexley, 3 mile(s). Tel: 526900 (0322)
Class Two Hotel: Elthham Hotel, Eltham, 1/4 mile(s). Tel: 850 8222 (081)

ENFIELD
Enfield Golf Club, Old Park Road South, Enfield, London. EN2 7DA.
Secretary: Mr N Challis   Tel: 363 3970 (081)
Professional: Mr Fickling   Tel: 366 4492 (081)
Location: 2 miles north of Enfield on the Windmill Hill Road.
Description: Wooded undulating parkland with a brook running through the course, an ancient Anglo Saxon moat forms part of the course.
18 holes, 6,200 yards, Par 72, S.S.S. 70, Course record 65.
Membership: 650
Visitors: Welcome. Handicap certificate required. Tuesdays Ladies Day. With members only at weekends.

Cade's - Audi Golf Course Guide

Green Fees: £20 per round, £30 per day.
Facilities: Lunch. Dinner. Full Catering. Changing Room. Golf Shop. Club Hire. Trolley Hire.
Class One Hotel: The West Lodge Park, Enfield, 3 mile(s). Tel: 440 8311 (081)

ENFIELD

Whitewebbs Golf Club, Clay Hill, Beggars Hollow, Enfield, London. EN2 9JN. Tel: 363 2951 (081)
Secretary: Mr I V Graan   Tel: 363 4454 (081)
Professional: Mr D Lewis   Tel: 363 4454 (081)
Location: A10 junc with M25 2 miles north of Enfield.
Description: Undulating wooded parkland with streams.
18 holes, 5,863 yards, Par 68, S.S.S. 68, Course record 62. Membership: 300
Visitors: Welcome. Pay as you play course.
Green Fees: Weekdays £7.60 per round, weekends £9.40.
Facilities: Bar Snacks. Changing Room. Golf Shop. Club Hire. Trolley Hire.
Class One Hotel: The Royal Chace, Enfield, 2 mile(s). Tel: 366 6500 (081)

FINCHLEY

Finchley Golf Club, Nether Court, Frith Lane, Mill Hill, London. NW7 1PU. Tel: 346 2436 (081)
Secretary: J R Pearce   Tel: 346 2436 (081)
Professional: D Brown   Tel: 346 5086 (081)
Location: Close to Mill Hill East tube station and M1.
Description: Wooded course.
18 holes, 6,411 yards, Par 72, S.S.S. 71, Course record 65. Membership: 530
Visitors: Welcome. Not Thursdays.
Green Fees: Weekdays £28 per round, £33 per day. Weekends £37.
Facilities: Lunch. Dinner. Bar Snacks. Full Catering. Changing Room. Golf Shop. Club Hire. Trolley Hire. Buggy Hire.
Class One Hotel: Hendon Hall, Hendon, 1 mile(s). Tel: 203 3341 (081)

GREENFORD

Ealing Golf Club, Perivale Lane, Greenford, London. UB6 8SS. Tel: 997 0937 (081)
Secretary: M Scargill   Tel: 997 0937 (081)
Professional: A Stickley   Tel: 997 3959 (081)
Location: Off A40 westbound opposite Hoover building.
Description: Parkland.
18 holes, 6,216 yards, Par 70, S.S.S. 70, Course record 65. Membership: 700
Visitors: Welcome. Handicap certificate required. With a member weekends and Bank Holidays.
Green Fees: £30 per day or round.
Facilities: Lunch. Dinner. Bar Snacks. Full Catering. Changing Room. Golf Shop. Club Hire. Trolley Hire. Buggy Hire.
Class One Hotel: The Bridge, Greenford, 1 mile(s). Tel: 566 6246 (081)
Class Two Hotel: Grange Lodge, Ealing, 2 mile(s). Tel: 567 1049 (081)

GREENFORD

Horsenden Hill Golf Club, Woodland Rise, Greenford, London. UB6 0RD. Tel: 902 4555 (081)
Secretary: Mr Pyemont   Tel: 902 4555 (081)
Professional: Mr T Martin   Tel: 902 4555 (081)
Location: 2 miles north of Greenford along the Greenford to Sudbury Hill road.
Description: Hilly, difficult course on wooded parkland.
9 holes, 1,632 yards, Par 28, S.S.S. 28, Course record 25. Membership: 160
Visitors: Welcome.
Green Fees: Weekdays £3.75 per round, weekends £5.60 per round.
Facilities: Lunch. Dinner. Bar Snacks. Full Catering. Changing Room. Golf Shop. Club Hire. Trolley Hire.
Class One Hotel: The Bridge, Greenford, 2 mile(s). Tel: 566 6246 (081)

HAMPSTEAD

Hampstead Golf Club, Winnington Road, Hampstead, London. N2 0TU. Tel: 455 0203 (081)
Secretary: K F Young   Tel: 455 0203 (081)
Professional: P J Brown   Tel: 455 7089 (081)
Location:
Description: Undulating parkland with trees.
9 holes, 5,812 yards, Par 68, S.S.S. 68, Course record 65. Membership: 500
Visitors: Welcome. Handicap certificate required. Limited at weekends and on Tuesdays. Always telephone professional first for availability.
Green Fees: Weekdays £23 per round, £28 per day. Weekends £30 per round.
Facilities: Bar Snacks. Changing Room. Golf Shop. Trolley Hire.

HAMPTON HILL

Fulwell Golf Club, Wellington Road, Hampton Hill, London. TW2 5PE. Tel: 977 2733 (081)
Secretary: Mr C Brown   Tel: 977 2733 (081)
Professional: Mr D Haslum   Tel: 977 3844 (081)
Location: Off A3136 1/2 mile west of Twickenham.
Description: Flat and wooded championship course with streams, brooks and ponds.
18 holes, 6,490 yards, Par 71, S.S.S. 71, Course record 68. Membership: 700
Visitors Welcome. Letter of Introduction required. Thursdays Ladies Day. With members only at weekends.
Green Fees: £25 per day.
Facilities: Lunch. Dinner. Bar Snacks. Full Catering. Changing Room. Golf Shop. Club Hire. Trolley Hire. Buggy Hire.

HAMPTON WICK

Home Park Golf Club, Hampton Wick, Kingston-upon-Thames, London. KT1 4AD. Tel: 977 2423 (081)
Secretary: Mr O'Farrell   Tel: 977 2423 (081)
Professional: Mr L Roberts   Tel: 977 2658 (081)
Location: 1 1/2 miles south of Kingston across the Kingston Bridge.
Description: Wooded parkland in the grounds of Hampton Court Palace.
18 holes, 6,616 yards, Par 72, S.S.S. , Course record 65. Membership: 600
Visitors: Welcome. Handicap certificate required. Tuesdays Ladies Day.

61

Cade's - Audi Golf Course Guide

Green Fees: W/days £15 per day, w/ends £20 per round.
Facilities: Lunch. Dinner. Bar Snacks. Full Catering. Changing Room. Golf Shop. Club Hire. Trolley Hire. Buggy Hire.
Class One Hotel: Kingston Lodge, Kingston, 1 mile(s). Tel: 541 4481 (081)

HENDON

Hendon Golf Club, Off Sanders Lane, Mill Hill, Hendon, London. NW7 1DG. Tel: 346 6023 (081)
Secretary: Mr D Cooper   Tel: 346 6023 (081)
Professional: Mr S Murray   Tel: 346 8990 (081)
Location: 8 miles north of central London, follow signs to Hendon.
Description: Wooded parkland.
18 holes, 6,266 yards, Par 70, S.S.S. 70, Course record 66.
Membership: 500
Visitors: Welcome. With members only at weekends and Bank Holidays.
Green Fees: Weekdays £23 per day, weekends £35 per day.
Facilities: Lunch. Dinner. Bar Snacks. Full Catering. Changing Room. Golf Shop. Club Hire. Trolley Hire.
Class One Hotel: Hendon Hall, Hendon, 3 mile(s). Tel: 203 3341 (081)

HIGHGATE

Highgate Golf Club, Denewood Road, Highgate, London. N6 4AH. Tel: 340 1906 (081)
Secretary: Mr Monktelow   Tel: 340 3745 (081)
Professional: Mr R Turner   Tel: 340 5467 (081)
Location: 5 miles north of central London on A1.
Description: Gently undulating tree lined parkland.
18 holes, 5,985 yards, Par 69, S.S.S. 69, Course record 66.
Membership: 700
Visitors: Welcome. Handicap certificate required. Wednesdays Ladies Day. With members only at weekends.
Green Fees: £27 per round, £36 per day.
Facilities: Lunch. Dinner. Bar Snacks. Full Catering. Changing Room. Golf Shop. Club Hire. Trolley Hire.

HILLINGDON

Hillingdon Golf Club, 18 Dorset Way, Hillingdon, Uxbridge, London. UB10 0JR. Tel: 239810 (0895)
Secretary: Mr R J Goodfellow   Tel: 233956 (0895)
Professional: Mr Holmes   Tel: 251980 (0895)
Location: 1/2 mile east of Uxbridge on the Uxbridge to Ealing road.
Description: Undulating tree lined parkland course.
9 holes, 5,490 yards, Par 68, S.S.S. 67, Course record 66.
Membership: 500
Visitors: Welcome. Handicap certificate required. Thursdays Ladies Day. With members only at weekends and Bank Holidays.
Green Fees: £17.50 per round, £25 per day.
Facilities: Lunch. Dinner. Bar Snacks. Full Catering. Changing Room. Golf Shop. Trolley Hire.
Class One Hotel: The Master Brewer, Uxbridge, 2 mile(s). Tel: 51199 (0895)

HOUNSLOW

Airlinks Golf Club, Southall Lane, Hounslow, London. TW5 9PE. Tel: 561 1418 (081)
Secretary: Mr N Hutchins   Tel: 561 1418 (081)
Professional: Mr K Wickham   Tel: 561 1418 (081)
Location: 12 miles west of London along M4 junc 3.
Description: Open, flat, parkland course, with 2 lakes and streams.
18 holes, 5,885 yards, Par 71, S.S.S. 68, Course record 65.
Membership: 600
Visitors: Welcome. Pay as you play course. Book 7 days in advance.
Green Fees: Weekdays £9.50 per round, weekends £12.50 per round.
Facilities: Lunch. Dinner. Bar Snacks. Full Catering. Changing Room. Golf Shop. Club Hire. Driving Range. Trolley Hire. Buggy Hire. Caddies available.

ILFORD

Ilford Golf Club, 291 Wanstead Road, Ilford, Essex. .
Secretary: P H Newson   Tel: 554 2930 (081)
Professional: S Dowsett   Tel: 554 0094 (081)
Description: Parkland. Play 1st and 3rd to make 18 holes.
16 holes, 5,787 yards, Par 68, S.S.S. 69, Course record 62.
Membership: 600
Visitors: Welcome. By appointment weekdays, restricted at weekends.
Green Fees: Weekdays £13.50 per round, £20 per day. Weekends £16 per round.
Facilities: Lunch. Dinner. Bar Snacks. Full Catering. Changing Room. Golf Shop. Trolley Hire.

MILL HILL

Mill Hill Golf Club, 100 Barnet Way, Mill Hill, London. NW7 3AL. Tel: 959 2282 (081)
Secretary: Mr Scott   Tel: 959 2339 (081)
Professional: Mr Daniel   Tel: 959 7261 (081)
Location: 1/2 mile from Mill Hill centre on A1 Barnet Way.
Description: Open wooded parkland with lake.
18 holes, 6,247 yards, Par 69, S.S.S. 70, Course record 65.
Membership: 500
Visitors: Welcome. Handicap certificate required. Letter of Introduction required. Must book in advance for weekends.
Green Fees: Weekdays £22 per round, £28 per day. Weekends £36.
Facilities: Lunch. Dinner. Bar Snacks. Full Catering. Changing Room. Golf Shop. Club Hire. Driving Range. Trolley Hire.

MITCHAM

Mitcham Golf Club, Carshalton Road, Mitcham Junction, Mitcham, Surrey. CR4 4HN. Tel: 648 1508 (081)
Secretary: Mr C A McGahan   Tel: 648 4197 (081)
Professional: Mr J A Godfrey   Tel: 640 4280 (081)
Location: 2 miles south of Mitcham on the Carshalton Road.
Description: Wooded common land surrounded by scenic countryside.
18 holes, 5,935 yards, Par 69, S.S.S. 68, Course record 66.
Membership: 500.

Cade's - Audi Golf Course Guide

Visitors: Welcome. Advisable to book 2 days in advance.
Green Fees: £9 per round.
Facilities: Lunch. Bar Snacks. Full Catering. Changing Room. Golf Shop. Trolley Hire.
Class One Hotel: Forte, Croydon, 5 mile(s). Tel: 688 5185 (081)

NORTHWOOD

Sandy Lodge Golf Club, Sandy Lodge Lane, Northwood, London. HA6 2JD. Tel: 825429 (0923)
Secretary: Mr Blair   Tel: 825429 (0923)
Professional: Mr A M Fox   Tel: 825321 (0923)
Location: 4 miles south of Watford on the Northwood Road.
Description: Links type course, no water, huge sand bunkers 100ft across surrounded by scenic countryside.
18 holes, 6,342 yards, Par 70, S.S.S. 70, Course record 64.
Membership: 700
Visitors: Welcome. Handicap certificate required. Letter of Introduction required. Tuesdays Ladies Day. With members only at weekends.
Green Fees: On application.
Facilities: Lunch. Bar Snacks. Full Catering. Changing Room. Golf Shop. Trolley Hire.
Class One Hotel: The Dean Park, Watford, 5 mile(s). Tel: 229212 (0923)

ORPINGTON

Cray Valley Golf Club, Sandy Lane, St Pauls Cray, Orpington, Kent. BR5 3HY.
Secretary: Ron Hill   Tel: 839677 (0689)
Professional: John Gregory   Tel: 837909 (0689)
Description: Open parkland.
18 holes, 5,600 yards, Par 70, S.S.S. 67, Course record 67.
9 holes, 2,300 yards, Par 32, S.S.S. 64.
Membership: 850
Visitors: Welcome. Bookings required at weekends.
Green Fees: On application
Facilities: Bar Snacks. Changing Room. Golf Shop. Club Hire. Driving Range. Trolley Hire.

ORPINGTON

Lullingstone Park Golf Club, Park Gate, Chelsfield, Nr Orpington, London. BR6 7PX. Tel: 32928 (0959)
Secretary: Mr G S Childs   Tel: 34297 (0959)
Professional: Mr D Cornford   Tel: 34542 (0959)
Location: 3 miles south east of Orpington on A224 (Orpington By-Pass). Signposted from M25 junc 4.
Description: Undulating, tree lined parkland. Championship course.
18 holes, 6,779 yards, Par 72, S.S.S. 72, Course record 71.
9 holes, 2,432 yards, Par 33.
Visitors: Welcome. Booking card required, for weekend telephone reservations.
Green Fees: Weekdays 18 holes £8.50, 9 holes £5.50. Weekends 18 holes £13.50, 9 holes £7.
Facilities: Lunch. Dinner. Bar Snacks. Full Catering. Changing Room. Golf Shop. Club Hire. Driving Range. Trolley Hire. Buggy Hire.
Class Two Hotel: The Mary Rose, St Marys Cray, 5 mile(s). Tel: 871917 (0689)

ORPINGTON

Ruxley Park Golf Centre Ltd., Sandy Lane, St Pauls Cray, Orpington, Kent. BR5 3HY. Tel: 871490 (0689)
Secretary: Les Dyke   Tel: 871490 (0689)
Professional: John Gregory   Tel: 871490 (0689)
Description: Undulating parkland.
18 holes, 4,466 yards, Par 65, S.S.S. 65.
Membership: 300
Visitors: Welcome. Not before 1p.m. weekends.
Green Fees: Weekdays £10, weekends £14.50.
Facilities: Lunch. Bar Snacks. Changing Room. Golf Shop. Club Hire. Driving Range. Trolley Hire.
Class One Hotel: The Eltham Hotel, Eltham, 3 mile(s). Tel: 850 8222 (081)
Class Two Hotel: Toronto, Sidcup, 2 mile(s). Tel: 300 4674 (081)

PINNER

Grims Dyke Golf Club, Oxhey Lane, Hatch End, Pinner, London. HA5 4AL. Tel: 428 4539 (081)
Secretary: Mr P Payne   Tel: 428 4539 (081)
Professional: Mr C Williams   Tel: 428 7484 (081)
Description: Gently undulating tree lined parkland.
18 holes, 5,600 yards, Par 69, S.S.S. 67, Course record 65.
Membership: 580
Visitors: Welcome. Handicap certificate required. Thursdays Ladies Day. With members only at weekends.
Green Fees: £25 per day.
Facilities: Lunch. Dinner. Bar Snacks. Full Catering. Changing Room. Golf Shop. Trolley Hire.
Class One Hotel: The Grims Dyke Manor House, Harrow, 1/2 mile(s). Tel: 954 4227 (081)

PINNER

Pinner Hill Golf Club, Southview Road, Pinner Hill, London. HA5 3YA. Tel: 866 0963 (081)
Secretary: J P Devitt   Tel: 868 4817 (081)
Professional: Mr M Grieve   Tel: 866 2109 (081)
Location: 1 mile west of Pinner Green.
Description: A hilly parkland course designed by J H Taylor, with magnificent views.
18 holes, 6,280 yards, Par 72, S.S.S. 70, Course record 63.
Visitors: Welcome. Handicap certificate required. Letter of Introduction required. Wednesdays and Thursdays (no access to Clubhouse). Society meetings, Mondays, Tuesdays and Fridays. Telep
Green Fees: £25 weekdays, £32 Saturdays by prior arrangement only. Public days (Wednesdays and Thursdays) £7.80 per round, £10.70 per day.
Facilities: Golf Shop.

ROMFORD

Maylands Golf Club, Colchester Road, Harold Park, Romford, Essex. RM3 0AZ. Tel: 42055 (04023)
Secretary: P S Taylor
Professional: John Hopkin   Tel: 46466 (04023)
Description: Parkland.
18 holes, 6,351 yards, Par 71, S.S.S. 70, Course record 67.

63

Membership: 600
Visitors: Welcome. Handicap certificate required. Letter of Introduction required.Weekdays only. With members at weekends and Bank Holidays.
Green Fees: £20 per round, £30 per day.
Facilities: Lunch. Dinner. Bar Snacks. Full Catering. Changing Room. Golf Shop. Trolley Hire. Buggy Hire.
Class One Hotel: Post House, Brentwood, 1 1/2 mile(s). Tel: 260260 (0277)
Class Two Hotel: Gidea Park, Romford, 3 mile(s). Tel: 746676 (0708)

RUISLIP

Ruislip Golf Club, Ickenham Road, Ruislip, London. HA4 7DQ. Tel: 638081 (0895)
Secretary: Mr Channing   Tel: 638835 (0895)
Professional: Mr D Nash   Tel: 632004 (0895)
Location: On Ickenham Road between Uxbridge and Ruislip.
Description: Short, flat course tree lined, with 2 lakes.
18 holes, 5,213 yards, Par 67, S.S.S. 68, Course record 63.
Membership: 600
Visitors: Welcome. Tuesdays and Thursdays Ladies Day. Societies Wednesdays. Book 7 days in advance.
Green Fees: Weekdays £7 per round, weekends £10 per round.
Facilities: Lunch. Dinner. Bar Snacks. Full Catering. Changing Room. Golf Shop. Club Hire. Driving Range. Trolley Hire. Buggy Hire.
Class One Hotel: The Master Brewer, Uxbridge, 2 mile(s). Tel: 51199 (0895)

SHOOTERS HILL

Shooters Hill Golf Club, Eaglesfield Road, Shooters Hill, London. SE18 3DA. Tel: 854 1216 (081)
Secretary: B R Adams   Tel: 854 6368 (081)
Professional: Michael Ridge   Tel: 854 0073 (081)
Location: On A207 2 miles east of Blackheath.
Description: Hilly.
18 holes, 5,736 yards, Par 69, S.S.S. 68, Course record 62.
Membership: 965
Visitors: Welcome. Handicap certificate required. Letter of Introduction required.Not at weekends.
Green Fees: £27.
Facilities: Lunch. Dinner. Bar Snacks. Full Catering. Changing Room. Golf Shop. Club Hire. Driving Range. Caddies available.

SOUTHGATE

Trent Park Golf Club, Bramley Road, Southgate, London. N14. Tel: 366 7432 (081)
Secretary: T Sadler
Professional: Craig Easton   Tel: 366 7432 (081)
Location: Opposite Oakwood Underground Station.
Description: Undulating parkland with many water hazards.
18 holes, 6,008 yards, Par 69, S.S.S. 68, Course record 64.
Membership: 800
Visitors: Welcome.
Green Fees: Weekdays £7.50, weekends £9.50.

Facilities: Lunch. Dinner. Bar Snacks. Full Catering. Changing Room. Golf Shop. Trolley Hire.
Class One Hotel: West Lodge Park, Cockfosters, 3 mile(s). Tel: 440 8311 (081)
Class Two Hotel: Royal Chase, Enfield, 4 mile(s). Tel: 366 6500 (081)

STANMORE

Stanmore Golf Club, 29 Gordon Avenue, Stanmore, London. HA7 2RL. Tel: 954 4661 (081)
Secretary: Mr J Pertwee   Tel: 954 2599 (081)
Professional: Mr V Law   Tel: 954 2646 (081)
Location: 10 miles north of London on A41 turn into Stanmore the golf club is signposted.
Description: Undulating wooded parkland.
18 holes, 5,884 yards, Par 68, S.S.S. 68, Course record 67.
Membership: 350
Visitors: Welcome. Handicap certificate required. Mondays and Fridays open to public. Tuesdays, Wednesdays and Thursdays only with a letter of Introduction.
Green Fees: Mondays and Fridays £7.80 per round, Tuesdays, Wednesdays and Thursdays £22.50 per round.
Facilities: Lunch. Dinner. Bar Snacks. Full Catering. Changing Room. Golf Shop. Club Hire. Trolley Hire.
Class One Hotel: The Madonna Halley, Edgeware, 3 mile(s). Tel: 951 5959 (081)

TWICKENHAM

Strawberry Hill Golf Club, Wellesley Road, Twickenham, London. TW2 5SD. Tel: 894 0165 (081)
Secretary: Mr F E Ingoldby   Tel: 894 1246 (081)
Professional: Mr P Buchan   Tel: 898 2802 (081)
Location: 2 miles south east of Twickenham along Heath Road.
Description: Long Par 3, brook running through every hole with one exception, tree lined.
9 holes, 4,762 yards, Par 64, S.S.S. 62, Course record 61.
Membership: 400
Visitors: Welcome. Thursdays Ladies Day. With members only at weekends.
Green Fees: £18 per round, £25 per day, £9 with member.
Facilities: Lunch. Dinner. Bar Snacks. Full Catering. Changing Room. Golf Shop. Trolley Hire.

WANSTEAD

Wanstead Golf Club, Overton Drive, Wanstead, London. E11 2LW. Tel: 989 0604 (081)
Secretary: Mr K Jones   Tel: 989 3938 (081)
Professional: Mr G Jacom   Tel: 989 9876 (081)
Location: Off Eastern Avenue at the Redbridge roundabout in Wanstead.
Description: Open parkland with a lake. Borders on the Epping Forest.
18 holes, 6,282 yards, Par 69, S.S.S. 69, Course record 62.
Membership: 750
Visitors: Welcome. Handicap certificate required.
Green Fees: On application.
Facilities: Lunch. Dinner. Bar Snacks. Full Catering. Changing Room. Golf Shop. Trolley Hire.

Cade's - Audi Golf Course Guide

WEMBLEY
Sudbury Golf Club, Bridgewater Road, Wembley, London. HA0 1AL. Tel: 902 3713 (081)
Secretary: Mr A Poole   Tel: 902 3713 (081)
Professional: Mr N Jordan   Tel: 902 7910 (081)
Location: 2 miles west of Wembley on the Ealing Road.
Description: Flat parkland, tree lined, adjacent to a canal.
18 holes, 6,282 yards, Par 69, S.S.S. 70, Course record 63.
Membership: 530
Visitors: Welcome. Handicap certificate required. Letter of Introduction required. Tuesdays Ladies Day. With members only at weekends.
Green Fees: Weekdays £26 per round, £40 per day.
Facilities: Lunch. Dinner. Bar Snacks. Full Catering. Changing Room. Golf Shop. Trolley Hire.

WEST DRAYTON
Holiday Inn Golf Club, Stockley Road, West Drayton, London. . Tel: 444232 (0895)
Secretary: P A Davies   Tel: 561 3471 (081)
Professional: P Coles   Tel: 444232 (0895)
Description: Wide open course with trees. Hard to par.
18 holes, 4,222 yards, Par 60, S.S.S. 62, Course record 61.
Membership: 198
Visitors: Welcome.
Green Fees: Weekdays £5, weekends £6.50.
Facilities: Lunch. Dinner. Bar Snacks. Full Catering. Changing Room. Golf Shop. Club Hire.
Class One Hotel: Holiday Inn, West Drayton, 0 mile(s). Tel: 445555 (0895)

WHETSTONE
North Middlesex Golf Club, Friern Barnet Lane, Whetstone, London. N20 0NL. Tel: 445 1732 (081)
Secretary: Mr Reding   Tel: 445 1604 (081)
Professional: Mr Roberts   Tel: 445 3060 (081)
Location: 2 miles north of Finchley along the A1000 Great North Road.
Description: Gently undulating parkland with 2 lakes and copses. Attractive Manor House setting.
18 holes, 5,625 yards, Par 69, S.S.S. 67, Course record 65.
Membership: 600
Visitors: Welcome. Wednesdays Ladies Day. Must book in advance for play at weekends.
Green Fees: Weekdays £22 per round, £27.50 per day. Weekends and Bank Holidays £30 per round.
Facilities: Lunch. Dinner. Bar Snacks. Full Catering. Changing Room. Golf Shop. Trolley Hire.

WIMBLEDON
London Scottish Golf Club, Windmill Road, Wimbledon, London. SW19 5NQ. Tel: 788 0135 (081)
Secretary: J Johnson   Tel: 789 7517 (081)
Professional: M Barr   Tel: 789 1207 (081)
Description: Heathland.
Yellow 18 holes, 5,247 yards, Par 66, S.S.S. 66, Course record 63.
White 18 holes, 5,438 yards, Par 68, S.S.S. 66, Course record 64.
Membership: 250
Visitors: Welcome. Handicap certificate required. Not at weekends. Must wear red top garment.
Green Fees: £13.50 per round, £20 per day.
Facilities: Lunch. Dinner. Bar Snacks. Full Catering. Changing Room. Golf Shop. Trolley Hire.
Class One Hotel: Richmond Gate, Richmond, 3/4 mile(s). Tel: 940 0061 (081)
Class Two Hotel: The Wimbledon, Wimbledon, 1 mile(s). Tel: 946 9265 (081)

WIMBLEDON
Wimbledon Common Golf Club, 19 Camp Road, Wimbledon, London. SW19 4UW. Tel: 946 0294 (081)
Secretary: B K Cox   Tel: 946 7571 (081)
Professional: J S Jukes   Tel: 946 0294 (081)
Location:
Description: Wooded heathland.
18 holes, 5,438 yards, Par 68, S.S.S. 66, Course record 63.
Membership: 250
Visitors: Welcome. With a member at weekends.
Green Fees: £13.50 per round, £20 per day.
Facilities: Lunch. Bar Snacks. Changing Room. Golf Shop. Trolley Hire.
Class One Hotel: Cannizaro House, Wimbledon, 1/2 mile(s). Tel: 879 1464 (081)

WIMBLEDON
Wimbledon Park Golf Club, Home Park Road, Wimbledon, London. SW19 7HR. Tel: 946 1002 (081)
Secretary: M K Hale   Tel: 946 1250 (081)
Professional: D Wingrove   Tel: 946 4053 (081)
Description: Parkland.
18 holes, 5,417 yards, Par 66, S.S.S. 66, Course record 63.
Membership: 710
Visitors: Welcome. Handicap certificate required. Most weekends after 3.30p.m.. Some catering restrictions apply, please telephone in advance.
Green Fees: On application.
Facilities: Lunch. Dinner. Bar Snacks. Full Catering. Changing Room. Golf Shop. Trolley Hire.
Class One Hotel: Cannizaro House, Wimbledon, 1 mile(s). Tel: 879 1464 (081)
Class Two Hotel: Trochee, Wimbledon, 2 mile(s). Tel: 946 1579 (081)

WINCHMORE HILL
Bush Hill Park Golf Club, Bush Hill, Winchmore Hill, London. N21 2BU.
Secretary: Mr K Maplesden   Tel: 360 5738 (081)
Professional: Mr G Low   Tel: 360 4103 (081)
Location: 1 mile west of Enfield along the London Road.
Description: Parkland, tree lined with 1 lake. The Clubhouse is an old Hunting Lodge.
18 holes, 5,809 yards, Par 70, S.S.S. 68, Course record 65.
Membership: 700
Visitors: Welcome. Handicap certificate required. Wednesdays Ladies Day. With members only at weekends.
Green Fees: £20 per round, £25 per day.
Facilities: Lunch. Dinner. Bar Snacks. Full Catering. Changing Room. Golf Shop. Trolley Hire. Caddies available.
Class One Hotel: The Royal Chace, Enfield, 2 mile(s). Tel: 366 6500 (081)

WOOD GREEN
Muswell Hill Golf Club, Rhodes Avenue, Wood Green, London. N22 4UT. Tel: 888 2044 (081)
Secretary: J A B Connors　　　Tel: 888 1764 (081)
Professional: I B Roberts　　　Tel: 888 8046 (081)
Location: 1 mile from Bounds Green Underground Station.
Description: Parkland.
18 holes, 6,491 yards, Par 71, S.S.S. 71, Course record 67.
Membership: 550
Visitors: Welcome. Pre-book with professional for Saturdays and Sundays.
Green Fees: Weekdays £23 per round, £33 per day. Weekends £35 per round.
Facilities: Lunch. Dinner. Bar Snacks. Changing Room. Golf Shop. Trolley Hire. Buggy Hire.

GREATER MANCHESTER

ALTRINCHAM
Dunham Forest Golf and Country Club, Oldfield Lane, Altrincham, Manchester. WA14 4TY. Tel: 928 2605 (061)
Secretary: Mrs S Klaus　　　Tel: 928 2605 (061)
Professional: Mr I Wrigley　　　Tel: 928 2727 (061)
Location: 9 miles south of Manchester off A56.
Description: Wooded parkland.
18 holes, 6,636 yards, Par 72, S.S.S. 72.
Visitors: Welcome. Handicap certificate required. Details on application.
Green Fees: On application.
Facilities: Lunch. Dinner. Bar Snacks. Full Catering. Changing Room. Golf Shop. Trolley Hire.
Class One Hotel: Cresta Court, Altrincham, 1 mile(s). Tel: 927 7272 (061)
Class Two Hotel: George & Dragon, Altrincham, 3/4 mile(s). Tel: 928 9933 (061)

ALTRINCHAM
The Ringway Golf Club, Hale Road, Halebarns, Altrincham, Manchester. WA15 8SW. Tel: 980 2630 (061)
Secretary: Mr D Wright　　　Tel: 980 2630 (061)
Professional: Mr N Ryan　　　Tel: 980 8432 (061)
Location: Off M56 junc 6, take A538 to Altrincham.
Description: Gently undulating, tree lined parkland.
18 holes, 6,474 yards, Par 71, S.S.S. 71, Course record 67.
Membership: 700
Visitors: Welcome. Handicap certificate required. Tuesdays Ladies Day. Not on Fridays. Saturdays is competition day.
Green Fees: Weekdays £24 per round/day. Weekends and Bank Holidays £30.
Facilities: Lunch. Dinner. Bar Snacks. Full Catering. Changing Room. Golf Shop. Club Hire. Trolley Hire.
Class One Hotel: The Cresta Court, Altrincham, 2 mile(s). Tel: 927 7272 (061)
Class Two Hotel: Unicorn, Halebarns, 1/2 mile(s). Tel: 980 4347 (061)

ASHTON-IN-MAKERFIELD
Ashton-in-Makerfield Golf Club, Garswood Park, Ashton-in-Makerfield, Manchester. WN4 0YT. Tel: 727267 (0942)
Secretary: J R Hay　　　Tel: 719330 (0942)
Professional: P S Allan　　　Tel: 724229 (0942)
Location: Close to junc 24 M6.
Description: Parkland.
18 holes, 6,169 yards, Par 70, S.S.S. 69, Course record 66.
Membership: 800
Visitors: Welcome. Handicap certificate required. Not Wednesdays. With members only at weekends.
Green Fees: £20.
Facilities: Lunch. Dinner. Bar Snacks. Full Catering. Changing Room. Golf Shop. Trolley Hire.
Class One Hotel: Thistle, Haydock, 4 mile(s). Tel: 272000 (0942)

ASHTON-UNDER-LYNE
Ashton-under-Lyne Golf Club, Gorsey Way, Ashton-under-Lyne, Manchester. OL6 9HT. Tel: 330 1537 (061)
Secretary: Mr G Musgrave　　　Tel: 339 8655 (061)
Professional: Mr C Boyle　　　Tel: 308 2095 (061)
Location: 1 mile east from Ashton-under-Lyne along the Queens Road.
Description: Flat parkland with streams surrounded by scenic countryside.
18 holes, 6,209 yards, Par 70, S.S.S. 70, Course record 658668.
Membership: 500
Visitors: Welcome. Handicap certificate required. Wednesdays Ladies Day. With members only at weekends.
Green Fees: £20 per round, £8 with a member.
Facilities: Lunch. Dinner. Bar Snacks. Full Catering. Changing Room. Golf Shop. Club Hire. Trolley Hire.
Class One Hotel: York House, Ashton-u-Lyne, 2 mile(s). Tel: 330 5899 (061)

AUDENSHAW
Fairfield Golf and Sailing Club, Booth Road, Audenshaw, Manchester. M34 5GA. Tel: 370 1641 (061)
Secretary: Mr J Humphries　　　Tel: 336 3950 (061)
Professional: Mr D Butler　　　Tel: 370 2292 (061)
Location: 3 miles east of Manchester centre on Ashton Old Road.
Description: Undulating, open parkland.
18 holes, 4,956 yards, Par 70, S.S.S. 68, Course record 65.
Membership: 300
Visitors: Welcome. Not before 4.30p.m. Saturdays or 2.30p.m. Sundays. Thursdays Ladies Day.
Green Fees: Weekdays £16 per round, weekends £18 per round.
Facilities: Lunch. Dinner. Bar Snacks. Full Catering. Changing Room. Golf Shop. Club Hire. Trolley Hire.

BOLTON
Deane Golf Club, Broadford Road, Deane, Bolton, Manchester. BL3 4NB. Tel: 61944 (0204)
Secretary: P Flaxman　　　Tel: 651808 (0204)
Professional: D Martindale　　　Tel: 61944 (0204)
Location: 2 miles from Bolton town centre on Wigan Road.

1 mile east of junc 5 M61.
Description: Parkland with a few hills. Course has a number of small ravines giving interesting shots to the green.
18 holes, 5,583 yards, Par 68, S.S.S. 67, Course record 62.
Membership: 400
Visitors: Welcome. Handicap certificate required. No catering on Mondays.
Green Fees: Weekdays £16.50, weekends and Bank Holidays £22.50.
Facilities: Lunch. Dinner. Bar Snacks. Full Catering. Changing Room. Golf Shop. Trolley Hire.
Class One Hotel: Crest, Bolton, 1/2 mile(s). Tel: 651511 (0204)

BOLTON
Dunscar Golf Club, Longworth Lane, Bromley Cross, Bolton, Manchester. BL7 9QY. Tel: 53321 (0204)
Secretary: T M Yates Tel: 51090 (0204)
Professional: G Treadgold Tel: 592992 (0204)
Location: 1/2 mile off A666 approx 1 3/4 miles from Bolton.
Description: Moorland course with uninterrupted views.
18 holes, 6,050 yards, Par 71, S.S.S. 69, Course record 66.
Membership: 400
Visitors: Welcome. Handicap certificate required. Not Mondays or weekends.
Green Fees: On application.
Facilities: Lunch. Dinner. Bar Snacks. Full Catering. Changing Room. Golf Shop. Club Hire. Driving Range. Trolley Hire.
Class One Hotel: Last Drop, Bolton, 1 mile(s). Tel: 591131 (0204)
Class Two Hotel: Egerton House, Bolton, 1 mile(s). Tel: 57171 (0204)

BRAMHALL
Bramhall Golf Club Ltd., The Clubhouse, Ladythorn Road, Bramhall, Stockport, Manchester. SK7 2EY. Tel: 439 4057 (061)
Secretary: J G Lee Tel: 439 6092 (061)
Professional: B Nield Tel: 439 1171 (061)
Description: Parkland course with good views.
18 holes, 6,361 yards, Par 71, S.S.S. 70.
Visitors: Welcome. Handicap certificate required. Letter of Introduction required. Not Thursdays or Competition Saturdays (i.e. most Saturdays).
Green Fees: On application.
Facilities: Lunch. Dinner. Bar Snacks. Full Catering. Changing Room. Golf Shop. Trolley Hire.
Class One Hotel: Bramhall Moat House, Bramhall, 1 mile(s). Tel: 439 8116 (061)

BURY
Bury Golf Club, Unsworth Hall, Blackford Bridge, Bury, Manchester. BL9 8TJ. Tel: 766 2213 (061)
Secretary: Mr J Meikle Tel: 766 4897 (061)
Professional: Mr Peel Tel: 766 2213 (061)
Location: 5 miles north west of Manchester centre on A56.
Description: Moorland course part of which is adjacent to a stream.
18 holes, 5,961 yards, Par 69, S.S.S. 69, Course record 66.

Membership: 625
Visitors: Welcome. Handicap certificate required. Not before 9.30a.m. and not between 12p.m. and 2p.m. every day.
Green Fees: Weekdays £17.50 per day, weekends and Bank Holidays £25.
Facilities: Lunch. Dinner. Bar Snacks. Full Catering. Changing Room. Golf Shop. Club Hire. Trolley Hire.
Class One Hotel: Red Hall, Ramsbottom, 3 mile(s). Tel: 822476 (0706)

BURY
Greenmount Golf Club, Greenhaigh Fold Farm, Greenmount, Bury, Manchester. BL8. Tel: 883712 (0204)
Secretary: G J Lowe Tel: 883712 (0204)
Location: 3 miles north of Bury town centre.
Description: Undulating parkland.
9 holes, 4,980 yards, Par 66, S.S.S. 64, Course record 62.
Membership: 280
Visitors: Welcome. Handicap certificate required. Weekends with member only. Ladies Day Tuesday, also Monday and Thursday evenings. No catering for visitors.
Green Fees: £10 per day, £5 per day with member.
Facilities: Changing Room.
Class One Hotel: Red Hall, Walmersley, 5 mile(s). Tel: 822476 (0706)
Class Two Hotel: The Old Mill, Ramsbottom, 4 mile(s). Tel: 822991 (0706)

BURY
Lowes Park Golf Club Ltd., Hill Top, Bury, Manchester. Tel: 764 1231 (061)
Secretary: E Brierley Tel: 367331 (0706)
Description: Hilly. Usually windy.
9 holes, 6,009 yards, Par 70, S.S.S. 69.
Membership: 300
Visitors: Welcome. Handicap certificate required.
Green Fees: Weekdays £10, weekends and Bank Holidays £15.
Facilities: Lunch. Dinner. Bar Snacks. Full Catering. Changing Room.
Class Two Hotel: Woolfield House, Bury, 1 mile(s). Tel: 797 9775 (061)

BURY
Walmersley Golf Club, Garretts Close, Whitecar Lane, Walmersley, Bury, Manchester. BL9 6TE. Tel: 764 1429 (061)
Secretary: Mr C Stock Tel: 764 5057 (061)
Location: Off M66 junc 1 take A56 to Bury (south).
Description: Moorland, tree lined course with 2 ponds.
9 holes, 6,200 yards, Par 72, S.S.S. 70, Course record 65.
Membership: 320
Visitors: Welcome. Not on Saturdays. With members only on Sundays.
Green Fees: £12 per day, £6 per day with a member.
Facilities: Lunch. Dinner. Bar Snacks. Full Catering. Changing Room. Golf Shop. Caddies available.
Class One Hotel: Red Hall, Walmersley, 1 mile(s). Tel: 822476 (0706)

Cade's - Audi Golf Course Guide

CHEADLE
Cheadle Golf Club, Cheadle, Manchester. SK8 1HW.
Tel: 428 2160 (061)
Secretary: Mr P P Webster   Tel: 491 4452 (061)
Professional: Mr Redrup   Tel: 428 9878 (061)
Location: From M63 junc 11, follow signs for Cheadle for 2 1/2 miles.
Description: Gently undulating parkland with a stream.
9 holes, 5,006 yards, Par 64, S.S.S. 65.
Membership: 325
Visitors: Welcome. Handicap certificate required. Letter of Introduction required. Not on Saturdays. Tuesdays Ladies Day.
Green Fees: Weekdays £12 per round, Sundays and Bank Holidays £23.
Facilities: Lunch. Dinner. Bar Snacks. Full Catering. Changing Room. Golf Shop.
Class One Hotel: Village Leisure Hotels, Cheadle, 1/8 mile(s). Tel: 428 0404 (061)

CHORLTON-CUM-HARDY
Chorlton-cum-Hardy Golf Club, Barlow Hall Road, Chorlton-cum-Hardy, Manchester. M21 2JJ. Tel: 881 3139 (061)
Secretary: Mr Stuart   Tel: 881 5830 (061)
Professional: Mr Screeton   Tel: 881 9911 (061)
Location: 4 miles south of Manchester on A5103 or A5145.
Description: Undulating, tree lined meadowland. Club founded in 1903, clubhouse dates back to 1547.
18 holes, 6,003 yards, Par 69, S.S.S. 69, Course record 65.
Membership: 780
Visitors: Welcome. Handicap certificate required. Society meetings Thursdays. Not before 9.30a.m. or between 12.30p.m. and 1.30p.m.. Tuesdays Ladies Day.
Green Fees: Weekdays £20 per day, weekends £25 per day.
Facilities: Lunch. Dinner. Bar Snacks. Full Catering. Changing Room. Golf Shop. Club Hire. Trolley Hire.

DUKINFIELD
Dukinfield Golf Club, Yew Tree Lane, Dukinfield, Manchester. SK16 5DB. Tel: 338 2340 (061)
Secretary: Mr Holmes   Tel: 406 6939 (061)
Professional: Mr A Boyle   Tel: 335 0376 (061)
Location: 2 miles west of Ashton-under-Lyne. Well signposted.
Description: Hillside course, copses, scenic with Tight greens.
18 holes, 5,586 yards, Par 68, S.S.S. 67, Course record 62.
Membership: 450
Visitors: Welcome. Wednesdays Ladies Day. With members only at weekends.
Green Fees: Weekdays £14.50 per round.
Facilities: Lunch. Dinner. Bar Snacks. Full Catering. Changing Room. Golf Shop. Trolley Hire.

ECCLES
Worsley Golf Club, Stableford Avenue, Monton, Eccles, Manchester. M30 8AP. Tel: 789 4202 (061)
Secretary: B Dean   Tel: 789 4202 (061)
Professional: Ceri Cousins   Tel: 789 4202 (061)
Description: Parkland.
18 holes, 6,252 yards, Par 72, S.S.S. 70, Course record 66.
Membership: 700
Visitors: Welcome. Handicap certificate required. Letter of Introduction required.
Green Fees: Weekdays £18 per round, £22 per day. Weekends £25.
Facilities: Lunch. Dinner. Bar Snacks. Full Catering. Changing Room. Golf Shop. Club Hire. Trolley Hire.
Class One Hotel: Wendover Hotel, Eccles, 1 mile(s). Tel: 789 7811 (061)

HYDE
Werneth Low Golf Club, Werneth Low, Hyde, Manchester. SK14 3AF. Tel: 368 2503 (061)
Secretary: R Watson   Tel: 368 7388 (061)
Professional: T Bacchus   Tel: 336 6908 (061)
Description: Hilly moorland course with excellent greens.
9 holes, 6,114 yards, Par , S.S.S. 66.
Membership: 400
Visitors: Welcome. No catering Wednesdays.
Green Fees: Weekdays £15 per day.
Facilities: Lunch. Dinner. Bar Snacks. Full Catering. Changing Room. Golf Shop.
Class One Hotel: The Village, Hyde, 2 mile(s). Tel: 368 1456 (061)
Class Two Hotel: Needhams Farm, Hyde. Tel: 368 4610 (061)

LEIGH
Pennington Golf Club, St Helens Road, Leigh, Manchester. WN7 3PA.
Secretary: Mr P Cartwright   Tel: 794 5316 (061)
Professional: Mr T Kershaw   Tel: 607278 (0942)
Location: 1 mile south of Leigh on St Helens Road.
Description: Flat parkland with brooks, streams and ponds.
9 holes, 2,895 yards, Par 35, S.S.S. 68, Course record 68.
Membership: 150
Visitors: Welcome. Pay as you play.
Green Fees: Weekdays £2.40 per round, weekends £3.50 per round.
Facilities: Golf Shop. Club Hire. Trolley Hire.
Class One Hotel: The Thistle, Haydock, 2 1/2 mile(s). Tel: 272000 (0942)

LEVENSHULME
Houldsworth Golf Club, Wingate House, Longford Road West, Higher Levenhulme, Manchester M19 3JW. Tel: 224 5055 (061)
Secretary: Mr S Zielinski   Tel: 224 5055 (061)
Professional: Mr D Naylor   Tel: 224 4571 (061)
Location: On the A6, 4 miles south of Manchester.
Description: Open parkland with streams and large ponds.
18 holes, 6,083 yards, Par 70, S.S.S. 69, Course record 62.
Membership: 550
Visitors: Welcome. Not on Wednesdays or competition days. Tuesday is Ladies day. With members only at weekends.
Green Fees: £13 per round weekdays.
Facilities: Lunch. Dinner. Bar Snacks. Full Catering. Chang-

68

Cade's - Audi Golf Course Guide

ing Room. Golf Shop. Club Hire. Trolley Hire.
Class One Hotel: The Rudyard Toby Hotel, Stockport, 3 mile(s). Tel: 432 2753 (061)

LITTLEBOROUGH

Whittaker Golf Club, Whittaker Lane, Littleborough, Manchester. OL15 0LH. Tel: 378310 (0706)
Secretary: Mr G A Smith   Tel: 428546 (0484)
Location: 1 mile from Littleborough centre, off Blackstone Edge Old Road.
Description: Moorland.
9 holes, 5,632 yards, Par 68, S.S.S. 67, Course record 61.
Membership: 150
Visitors: Welcome. Not Tuesday p.m. or Sundays.
Green Fees: £8 - £10.
Facilities: Changing Room.

MANCHESTER

Blackley Golf Club, Victoria Avenue East, Blackley, Manchester. M9 2HW. Tel: 643 2980 (061)
Secretary: C B Leggott   Tel: 654 7770 (061)
Professional: M Barton   Tel: 643 3912 (061)
Location: 5 miles north of city centre.
Description: Parkland.
18 holes, 6,237 yards, Par , S.S.S. 70, Course record 65.
Membership: 600
Visitors: Welcome. Thursdays and weekends with member only.
Green Fees: £15.
Facilities: Lunch. Dinner. Bar Snacks. Full Catering. Changing Room. Golf Shop. Trolley Hire.
Class One Hotel: Bower, Hollinwood, 2 mile(s). Tel: 682 7254 (061)

MIDDLETON

Manchester Golf Club, Hopwood Cottage, Rochdale Road, Middleton, Manchester. M24 2QP. Tel: 643 2718 (061)
Secretary: K G Flett   Tel: 643 3202 (061)
Professional: B Connor   Tel: 643 2638 (061)
Location: From M62 junc 20 take A627(M) signposted Oldham/Manchester. Leave at first exit A664 to Middleton. Follow A664 signs, club on right over b
Description: Moorland/parkland championship course.
18 holes, 6,454 yards, Par 72, S.S.S. 72, Course record 67.
Membership: 700
Visitors: Welcome. Handicap certificate required. Monday to Friday subject to availability. Weekends very restricted. Some catering restrictions apply please telephone in advance.
Green Fees: Weekdays £25, weekends and Bank Holidays £30.
Facilities: Lunch. Dinner. Bar Snacks. Full Catering. Changing Room. Golf Shop. Driving Range. Trolley Hire. Buggy Hire.
Class One Hotel: Norton Grange, Castleton, 1 mile(s). Tel: 30788 (0706)

NORTHENDEN

Northenden Golf Club, Palatine Road, Northenden, Manchester. M22 4FR. Tel: 998 4738 (061)
Secretary: Mr T Holcroft   Tel: 998 4738 (061)
Professional: Mr W McColl   Tel: 945 3386 (061)
Location: 3 miles south of Manchester on the Wilmslow to Barlow Moor Road.
Description: Tree lined open parkland. First six holes adjacent to the River Mersey.
18 holes, 6,469 yards, Par 72, S.S.S. 71, Course record 64.
Membership: 800
Visitors: Welcome. Handicap certificate required. Saturday is competition day. Not before 10.30a.m. Sundays.
Green Fees: Weekdays £20 per round, weekends £25 per round.
Facilities: Lunch. Dinner. Bar Snacks. Full Catering. Changing Room. Golf Shop. Trolley Hire.
Class One Hotel: Post House, Northenden, 2 mile(s). Tel: 998 7090 (061)
Class Two Hotel: The Dane Lodge, Sale, 3 mile(s). Tel: 973 6666 (061)

ROCHDALE

Lobden Golf Club, Whitworth, Near Rochdale, Manchester. OL12 8XJ. Tel: 343228 (0706)
Secretary: C Buchanan   Tel: 343197 (0706)
Location: 3 1/2 miles north of Rochdale on A681.
Description: Moorland.
9 holes, 5,780 yards, Par 70, S.S.S. 68, Course record 64.
Membership: 230
Visitors: Welcome. Handicap certificate required. Not Saturdays or other competition days.
Green Fees: Weekdays £7, weekends and Bank Holidays £10 without member.

ROCHDALE

Rochdale Golf Club, The Clubhouse, Bagslate, Rochdale, Manchester. OL11 5YR. Tel: 46024 (0706)
Secretary: Mr S Cockroft   Tel: 43818 (0706)
Professional: Mr A Laverty   Tel: 522104 (0706)
Location: 2 miles north-west of Rochdale on A680.
Description: Open, flat tree lined parkland with open ditches and scenic countryside.
White 18 holes, 6,002 yards, Par 71, S.S.S. 69, Course record 65.
Yellow 18 holes, 5,780 yards, Par 71, S.S.S. 68.
Membership: 750
Visitors: Welcome. Handicap certificate required. Not before 4p.m. Saturdays.
Green Fees: £18 per day, Sundays £22.
Facilities: Lunch. Bar Snacks. Full Catering. Changing Room. Golf Shop. Club Hire. Trolley Hire.
Class Two Hotel: The Midway, Castleton, 2 1/2 mile(s). Tel: 32881 (0706)

SADDLEWORTH

Saddleworth Golf Club, Mountain Ash, Ladcastle Road, Uppermill, Near Oldham, Manchester. OL3 6LT. Tel: 873653 (0457)
Secretary: Mr H Morgan   Tel: 873653 (0457)
Professional: Mr T Shard   Tel: 873653 (0457)
Location: 4 miles east of Oldham on the Oldham Road.
Description: Tree lined moorland course with scenic views and small ponds.

18 holes, 5,976 yards, Par 71, S.S.S. 69, Course record 61.
Membership: 720
Visitors: Welcome. Handicap certificate required. No parties at weekends.
Green Fees: Weekdays £22 per day, with member £7. Weekends and Bank Holidays £25, with member £10.
Facilities: Lunch. Dinner. Bar Snacks. Full Catering. Changing Room. Golf Shop. Club Hire. Trolley Hire. Buggy Hire.
Class One Hotel: The Green Ash, Saddleworth, 2 1/2 mile(s). Tel: 871035 (0457)
Class Two Hotel: The Farrars, Saddleworth, 1 mile(s). Tel: 872124 (0457)

SALE

Ashton on Mersey Golf Club, Church Lane, Ashton on Mersey, Sale, Manchester. M33 5QQ. Tel: 973 3220 (061)
Secretary: Mr Edwards   Tel: 973 3220 (061)
Professional: Mr Preston   Tel: 962 3727 (061)
Description: Open tree lined undulating parkland, with streams ponds and lakes, overlooking the River Mersey.
9 holes, 6,146 yards, Par 72, S.S.S. 69, Course record 67.
Membership: 350
Visitors: Welcome. Handicap certificate required. Ladies day is Tuesday. With members only at weekends.
Green Fees: £16 per day, £8 with member.
Facilities: Lunch. Dinner. Bar Snacks. Full Catering. Changing Room. Golf Shop. Club Hire. Trolley Hire.
Class One Hotel: The Cresta Court, Altrincham, 3 mile(s). Tel: 927 7272 (061)
Class Two Hotel: Amblehurst, Sale, 1/2 mile(s). Tel: 973 8800 (061)

SALE

Sale Golf Club, Sale Lodge, Golf Road, Sale, Manchester. M33 2LU. Tel: 973 3404 (061)
Secretary: Mr J Blair   Tel: 973 1638 (061)
Professional: Mr M Stewart   Tel: 973 1730 (061)
Location: 2 miles south of Sale on the Northenden Road.
Description: Flat open parkland, tree lined with streams.
White 18 holes, 6,346 yards, Par 71, S.S.S. 70, Course record 67.
Yellow 18 holes, 6,093 yards, Par 71, S.S.S. 69.
Membership: 1000
Visitors: Welcome. Saturday is competition day. Tuesday is Ladies day until 1p.m..
Green Fees: Weekdays £20 per day, £7 with a member, weekends £30 per day £10 with a member.
Facilities: Lunch. Dinner. Bar Snacks. Full Catering. Changing Room. Golf Shop. Trolley Hire.
Class One Hotel: Post House, Northenden, 2 mile(s). Tel: 998 7090 (061)

STOCKPORT

Hazel Grove Golf Club, Buxton Road, Hazel Grove, Stockport, Manchester. SK7 6LU. Tel: 483 3978 (061)
Secretary: H A G Carlisle   Tel: 483 3978 (061)
Professional: M E Hill   Tel: 483 7272 (061)
Location: On A6 Stockport to Buxton Road.
Description: Parkland.
18 holes, 6,380 yards, Par 71, S.S.S. 70, Course record 65.
Membership: 550

Visitors: Welcome. Handicap certificate required.
Green Fees: Weekdays £22.50, weekends £27.50
Facilities: Lunch. Dinner. Bar Snacks. Full Catering. Changing Room. Golf Shop. Club Hire. Trolley Hire.
Class One Hotel: Alma Lodge, Stockport, 2 mile(s). Tel: 483 4431 (061)

STOCKPORT

Heaton Moor Golf Club, Mauldeth Road, Heaton Mersey, Stockport, Manchester. SK4 3NX. Tel: 432 2134 (061)
Secretary: A D Townsend   Tel: 432 2134 (061)
Professional: C R Loydall   Tel: 432 0846 (061)
Description: Flat parkland.
18 holes, 5,909 yards, Par 70, S.S.S. 68, Course record 66.
Membership: 700
Visitors: Welcome. By arrangement.
Green Fees: Weekdays £18, weekends and Bank Holidays £30.
Facilities: Lunch. Dinner. Bar Snacks. Full Catering. Changing Room. Golf Shop. Club Hire. Trolley Hire.

STOCKPORT

Mellor and Townscliffe Golf Club, Gibb Lane, Mellor, Stockport, Manchester. SK6 5NA.
Secretary: D A Ogden   Tel: 427 2208 (061)
Professional: Michael J Williams   Tel: 427 5759 (061)
Location: 7 miles south east of Stockport off A626.
Description: Wooded parkland.
White 18 holes, 5,925 yards, Par 70, S.S.S. 69.
Yellow 18 holes, 5,721 yards, Par 70, S.S.S. 68.
Membership: 650
Visitors: Welcome. Handicap certificate required. No casual visitors weekends. No parties weekends. No catering Tuesdays.
Green Fees: Weekdays £16.
Facilities: Lunch. Dinner. Bar Snacks. Full Catering. Changing Room. Golf Shop. Trolley Hire.
Class One Hotel: Alma Lodge, Stockport, 7 mile(s). Tel: 483 4431 (061)
Class Two Hotel: West Towers, Marple, 4 mile(s). Tel: 426 0086 (061)

STOCKPORT

Romiley Golf Club, Goosehouse Green, Romiley, Stockport, Manchester. SK6 4LJ. Tel: 430 2392 (061)
Secretary: Mr F Beard   Tel: 430 7257 (061)
Professional: Mr Butler   Tel: 430 7122 (061)
Location: 4 miles east of Stockport, follow signs to Romiley Village, turn in to Carlton Avenue.
Description: Part open, part wooded parkland with scenic countryside.
White 18 holes, 6,421 yards, Par 70, S.S.S. 70, Course record 64.
Yellow 18 holes, 6,142 yards, Par 69, S.S.S. 69.
Membership: 750
Visitors: Welcome. Handicap certificate required. With members only at weekends. Two days notice required for caddies.
Green Fees: Weekdays £20 per round, £25 per day. Weekends and Bank Holidays £30 per round, £40 per day.

Facilities: Lunch. Bar Snacks. Full Catering. Changing Room. Golf Shop. Club Hire. Trolley Hire.
Class One Hotel: The Alma Lodge, Stockport, 4 mile(s). Tel: 483 4431 (061)

STOCKPORT

Stockport Golf Club, Offerton Road, Offerton, Stockport, Manchester. SK2 5HL. Tel: 427 2001 (061)
Secretary: Mr Moorhead   Tel: 427 8369 (061)
Professional: Mr Tattersall   Tel: 427 2421 (061)
Location: 4 miles south of Stockport on A6.
Description: Open parkland, wooded scenic countryside.
18 holes, 6,390 yards, Par 71, S.S.S. 71, Course record 67.
Membership: 500
Visitors: Welcome. Tuesday is Ladies day. Not before 12.30p.m. weekends unless guest of a member. Caddies available summer months only.
Green Fees: Weekdays £25 per round, £35 per day. Weekends £35 per round, £45 per day.
Facilities: Lunch. Dinner. Bar Snacks. Full Catering. Changing Room. Golf Shop. Club Hire. Trolley Hire.
Class One Hotel: The Alma Lodge, Stockport, 3 mile(s). Tel: 483 4431 (061)

SWINTON

Swinton Park Golf Club, East Lancashire Road, Swinton, Manchester. M27 1LX. Tel: 794 1785 (061)
Secretary: F Slater   Tel: 794 0861 (061)
Professional: J Wilson   Tel: 793 8077 (061)
Location: On A580 Manchester to Liverpool Road, 5 miles from central Manchester.
Description: Parkland.
18 holes, 6,712 yards, Par 73, S.S.S. 72, Course record 66.
Membership: 600
Visitors: Welcome. Handicap certificate required. With members at weekends and Bank Holidays. Ladies Day Thursdays.
Green Fees: On application.
Facilities: Lunch. Dinner. Bar Snacks. Full Catering. Changing Room. Golf Shop. Trolley Hire.
Class Two Hotel: The Gay Willows, Clifton, 2 mile(s). Tel: 794 3761 (061)

URMSTON

Davyhulme Park Golf Club, Gleneagles Road, Urmston, Manchester. . Tel: 748 2260 (061)
Secretary: Mr Langworthy   Tel: 748 2260 (061)
Professional: Mr Lewis   Tel: 748 3931 (061)
Description: Flat open parkland surrounded by scenic countryside.
18 holes, 6,237 yards, Par 72, S.S.S. 70.
Visitors: Welcome. Handicap certificate required. Ladies day is Wednesday. With members only at weekends.
Green Fees: £19, or £9 with a member.
Facilities: Lunch. Dinner. Bar Snacks. Full Catering. Changing Room. Golf Shop. Trolley Hire.

WHITEFIELD

Stand Golf Club, The Dales, Ashbourne Grove, Whitefield, Manchester. M25 7NL. Tel: 766 2388 (061)
Secretary: Mr E B Taylor   Tel: 766 3197 (061)

Professional: Mr M Dance   Tel: 766 2214 (061)
Location: 5 miles north of Manchester. M62 junc 17.
Description: Parkland/moorland.
18 holes, 6,411 yards, Par 72, S.S.S. 71, Course record 67.
Membership: 700
Visitors: Welcome. Visiting societies Wednesday and Fridays. Ladies Day Tuesdays.
Green Fees: Weekdays £18, weekends £20.
Facilities: Lunch. Dinner. Bar Snacks. Full Catering. Changing Room. Golf Shop.

WHITEFIELD

Whitefield Golf Club, Higher Lane, Whitefield, Manchester. M25 7EZ. Tel: 766 2904 (061)
Secretary: Mrs R L Vidler   Tel: 766 2904 (061)
Professional: Mr Paul Reeves   Tel: 766 3096 (061)
Location: 5 miles north of Manchester from junc 17 M62.
Description: Parkland.
18 holes, 6,041 yards, Par 69.
Membership: 500
Visitors: Welcome. Handicap certificate required. Not Sunday mornings or Monday mornings. Socities Tuesday to Friday. Prior booking essential.
Green Fees: £21 package deal £28.
Facilities: Lunch. Dinner. Full Catering. Changing Room. Golf Shop. Trolley Hire.

WIGAN

Gathurst Golf Club, Miles Lane, Shevington, Wigan, Manchester. WN6 8EW. Tel: 2861 (02575)
Secretary: H Marrow   Tel: 5234 (02575)
Professional: D Clarke   Tel: 4909 (02575)
Location: 5 miles from Wigan, 1 mile south of M6 junc 27.
Description: Parkland.
9 holes, 6,308 yards, Par 72, S.S.S. 70, Course record 68.
Visitors: Welcome. Handicap certificate required. Wednesdays, weekends and Bank Holidays with a member. Catering only during licensing hours or by arrangement.
Green Fees: £17.
Facilities: Lunch. Dinner. Bar Snacks. Full Catering. Changing Room. Golf Shop.

WIGAN

Haigh Hall Golf Club, Haigh Country Park, Aspull, Near Wigan, Manchester. WN2 1PE. Tel: 831107 (0942)
Secretary: Jim Parker   Tel: 833337 (0942)
Professional: Ian Lee   Tel: 831107 (0942)
18 holes, 6,423 yards, Par 70, S.S.S. 71, Course record 66.
Visitors: Welcome.
Green Fees: Weekdays £5.50, weekends £8.
Facilities: Lunch. Dinner. Bar Snacks. Full Catering. Golf Shop. Club Hire. Driving Range. Trolley Hire.
Class One Hotel: Kilhey Court, Standish, 2 mile(s). Tel: 472100 (0257)
Class Two Hotel: Red Rock Country Guest House, Syandish, 1/2 mile(s). Tel: 832330 (0942)

WIGAN

Hindley Hall Golf Club, Hall Lane, Hindley, Wigan, Manchester. WN2 2SQ. Tel: 55131 (0942)
Secretary: R Bell   Tel: 55131 (0942)

Professional: N Brazell   Tel: 55991 (0942)
Location: Off exit 6 M61, follow signds to Wigan Pier and Haigh Hall.
Description: Undulating parkland.
18 holes, 5,875 yards, Par 69, S.S.S. 68, Course record 63.
Membership: 450
Visitors: Welcome. Handicap certificate required. Not before 9.45a.m. or between 11.45a.m. and 1.45p.m..
Green Fees: Weekdays £18, weekends £25.
Facilities: Lunch. Dinner. Bar Snacks. Full Catering. Changing Room. Golf Shop. Trolley Hire.
Class One Hotel: Georgian House, Westhaughton, 3 mile(s). Tel: 814958 (0942)

WIGAN

Wigan Golf Club, Arley Hall, Haigh, Wigan, Manchester. WN1 2UH. Tel: 421360 (0257)
Secretary: E Walmsley   Tel: 44429 (0942)
Location: 3 miles north of Wigan near Standish.
Description: Parkland.
9 holes, 6,058 yards, Par 70, S.S.S. 68, Course record 64.
Membership: 255
Visitors: Welcome. Handicap certificate required. Ladies Day Tuesdays. Not Saturdays. Some catering restrictions apply, please telephone in advance.
Green Fees: On application.
Facilities: Lunch. Dinner. Bar Snacks. Full Catering. Changing Room.
Class One Hotel: Kilhey Court, Standish, 1 mile(s). Tel: 472100 (0257)
Class Two Hotel: The Beeches, Standish, 1 1/2 mile(s). Tel: 426432 (0257)

WORSLEY

Ellesmere Golf Club, Old Clough Lane, Worsley, Manchester. M28 4AZ. Tel: 790 2122 (061)
Secretary: A C Kay   Tel: 799 0554 (061)
Professional: T Morley   Tel: 790 8591 (061)
Location: Off A580 East Lancs Road, adjacent to M62 northbound (eastbound) access.
Description: Wooded parkland.
18 holes, 5,954 yards, Par 69, S.S.S. 69.
Membership: 500
Visitors: Welcome. Handicap certificate required. Not Bank Holidays or during club competitions (Wednesday afternoons, Thursday afternoons, Saturday and Sunday mornings).
Green Fees: Weekdays £16 per round, £20 per day. Weekends £20 per round, £25 per day.
Facilities: Lunch. Dinner. Bar Snacks. Full Catering. Changing Room. Golf Shop. Club Hire. Trolley Hire.

HAMPSHIRE

ALTON

Alton Golf Club, Old Odiham Road, Alton, Hants. GU34 4BU.
Location: Turn off Alton High Street at Crown Hotel, follow Old Odiham Road for 1 1/2 miles club is on the left.
Description: Undulating.

9 holes, 5,744 yards, Par 68, S.S.S. 68, Course record 65.
Membership: 342
Visitors: Welcome. Weekends and Bank Holidays with member or maximum handicap of 18.
Green Fees: £12 per round, £16 per day weekdays. £20 per round, £30 per day weekends and Bank Holidays.
Facilities: Changing Room. Golf Shop. Trolley Hire.
Class One Hotel: Alton House, Alton, 2 mile(s). Tel: 80033 (0420)
Class Two Hotel: Wheatsheaf, Alton, 2 mile(s). Tel: 83316 (0420)

AMPFIELD

Ampfield Par Three Golf Club, Ampfield, Near Romsey, Hants. SO51 9BQ. Tel: 68480 (0794)
Secretary: Mrs Stella Baker   Tel: 68480 (0794)
Professional: Richard Benfield   Tel: 68750 (0794)
Location: A31 Winchester to Romsey. Approx 4 miles east of Romsey.
Description: 18 par three holes set in parkland. Designed by Henry Cotton.
18 holes, 2,478 yards, Par 54, S.S.S. 53, Course record 49.
Membership: 500
Visitors: Welcome. Handicap certificate required weekends and Bank Holidays. Telephone for availability. Recognised golf shoes must be worn. Dinner, societies only.
Green Fees: On application.
Facilities: Lunch. Bar Snacks. Changing Room. Golf Shop. Club Hire. Trolley Hire.
Class One Hotel: Potters Heron, Ampfield, 1 1/2 mile(s). Tel: 266611 (0703)

ANDOVER

Andover Golf Club, 51 Winchester Road, Andover, Hants. SP10 2EF. Tel: 323980 (0264)
Secretary: D A Fairweather   Tel: 358040 (0264)
Professional: A Timms   Tel: 324151 (0264)
Location: 1/2 mile south of town centre on A3057.
Description: Sloping downland. Second nine played from different tees.
9 holes, 5,933 yards, Par 69, S.S.S. 68, Course record 67.
Visitors: Welcome. Not before noon weekends and Bank Holidays.
Green Fees: Weekdays £12, weekends and Bank Holidays £22.
Facilities: Lunch. Dinner. Bar Snacks. Full Catering. Changing Room. Golf Shop. Club Hire. Trolley Hire.
Class One Hotel: Danebury, Andover, 1/2 mile(s). Tel: 323332 (0264)
Class Two Hotel: Amberley, Andover, 1 mile(s). Tel: 352224 (0264)

BASINGSTOKE

Bishopswood Golf Club, Bishopswood Lane, Tadley, Basingstoke, Hants. RG26 6AT. Tel: 815213 (0734)
Secretary: M W Phillips   Tel: 812200 (0734)
Professional: Steve Ward   Tel: 815213 (0734)
Location: 6 miles north of Basingstoke off A340.
Description: Wooded parkland with water hazards.
9 holes, 6,474 yards, Par 72, S.S.S. 71, Course record 68.
Membership: 500

Cade's - Audi Golf Course Guide

Visitors: Welcome. Members only at weekends. Societies welcome by prior arrangement.
Green Fees: £7.15 9 holes, £12.25 18 holes.
Facilities: Lunch. Dinner. Bar Snacks. Full Catering. Changing Room. Golf Shop. Driving Range. Trolley Hire.

BROCKENHURST

Brockenhurst Manor Golf Club, Sway Road, Brockenhurst, Hants. SO42 7SG. Tel: 22383 (0590)
Secretary: R E Stallard   Tel: 23332 (0590)
Professional: Brian Plucknett   Tel: 23092 (0590)
Description: Beautiful forest course, designed by Colt with some very interesting holes, particularly the 4 par 3's and the 17th.
18 holes, 6,222 yards, Par 70, S.S.S. 70, Course record 64.
Membership: 650
Visitors: Welcome. Handicap certificate required. Please telephone in advance. Not Tuesdays. Society day is Thursday, small parties welcome on other days. Closures & restrictions on certain days.
Green Fees: Weekdays £25 per round, £30 per day. Weekends and Bank Holidays £35 per day/round.
Facilities: Lunch. Dinner. Bar Snacks. Full Catering. Changing Room. Golf Shop. Trolley Hire.
Class One Hotel: Balmer Lawn, Brockenhurst, 2 mile(s). Tel: 23116 (0590)
Class Two Hotel: Whitly Ridge, Brockenhurst, 2 1/4 mile(s). Tel: 22354 (0590)

CRONDALL

Oak Park Golf Complex, Heath lane, Crondall, Odiham, GU10 5PB. Tel: 850880 (0252)
Secretary: Mrs R Smythe   Tel: 850880 (0252)
Professional: S Coaker   Tel: 850066 (0252)
Location: Off A287 Farnham-Odiham Road, M3 junc 5, 4 miles distant.
Description: Gently undulating parkland.
18 holes, 6,437 yards, Par 72, S.S.S. 71.
Membership: 400
Visitors: Welcome. Tee reservations at weekends and Bank Holidays, telephone pro shop also telephone for caddies.
Green Fees: Weekdays £15, weekends and Bank Holidays £22.
Facilities: Lunch. Dinner. Bar Snacks. Full Catering. Changing Room. Golf Shop. Club Hire. Driving Range. Trolley Hire. Caddies available.
Class One Hotel: Bishops Table, Farnham, 3 mile(s). Tel: 710222 (0252)

FLEET

North Hants Golf Club, Minley Road, Fleet, Hants. GU13 8RE. Tel: 616443 (0252)
Secretary: Mr Goodliffe   Tel: 616443 (0252)
Professional: Mr S Porter   Tel: 616655 (0252)
Description: Heathland.
18 holes, 6,257 yards, Par 69, S.S.S. 70, Course record 67.
Membership: 650
Visitors: Welcome. Handicap certificate required. Not at weekends. Thursdays Ladies Day. Societies Tuesdays and Wednesdays.

Green Fees: £21 per round, £25 per two rounds.
Facilities: Lunch. Dinner. Bar Snacks. Full Catering. Changing Room. Golf Shop. Trolley Hire.
Class One Hotel: Lismoyne, Fleet, 1/8 mile(s). Tel: 628555 (0252)

GOSPORT

Fleetland Golf Club, Fareham Road, Gosport, Hants. PO13 0AW. Tel: 822351 (0705)
Secretary: Mr A Eade   Tel: 822351 (0705)
Location: From Fareham take Gosport Road for 2 miles, club on left hand side.
Description: Flat and wooded.
9 holes, 4,777 yards, Par 65, S.S.S. 63, Course record 63.
Membership: 150
Visitors: Welcome. Not Saturdays p.m. (Ladies Day). All visitors must play with a member at all times.
Green Fees: Weekday £3, weekends £5.
Facilities: Bar Snacks. Full Catering. Changing Room. Club Hire.
Class One Hotel: The Bridgemary Manor, Gosport, 3/4 mile(s). Tel: 232946 (0329)

GOSPORT

Gosport and Stokes Bay Golf Club, Haslar, Gosport, Hants. .
Secretary: A P Chubb   Tel: 527941 (0705)
Location: South coast of Gosport, along Fort Road to Haslar.
Description: 9 hole links, plenty of gorse, water and natural hazards using ten greens with different tees on the back nine.
9 holes, 5,800 yards, Par 71, S.S.S. 68, Course record 69.
Membership: 500
Visitors: Welcome. Handicap certificate preffered. Restricted on Sundays and Thursdays (Ladies day).
Green Fees: £10 weekday, £16 weekend.
Facilities: Lunch. Dinner. Bar Snacks. Full Catering. Changing Room. Golf Shop. Club Hire. Trolley Hire.
Class Two Hotel: Anglesey Hotel, Gosport, 1 1/2 mile(s). Tel: 527712 (0705)

HARTLEY WINTNEY

Hartley Wintney Golf Club, London Road, Hartley Wintney, Hants. RG27 8PT. Tel: 842214 (0252)
Secretary: B Powell   Tel: 844211 (0252)
Professional: Martin Smith   Tel: 843779 (0252)
Location: A30 between Camberley and Basingstoke, 7 miles south of Camberley.
Description: Parkland.
9 holes, 6,096 yards, Par 70, S.S.S. 69, Course record 63.
Membership: 380
Visitors: Welcome. With members only at weekends. Not Wednesday mornings.
Green Fees: £17 per round, £25 per day.
Facilities: Lunch. Dinner. Bar Snacks. Full Catering. Changing Room. Golf Shop. Trolley Hire.
Class One Hotel: Basingstoke Country Hotel, Hook, 5 mile(s). Tel: 764161 (0256)
Class Two Hotel: Lismoyne Hotel, Fleet, 4 mile(s). Tel: 628555 (0252)

HAVANT

Rowlands Castle Golf Club, 31 Links Lane, Rowlands Castle, Havant, Hants. PO9 6AE. Tel: 412784 (0705)
Secretary: A W Aird   Tel: 412784 (0705)
Professional: P Klepacz   Tel: 412785 (0705)
Location: Nine miles south of Petersfield. 1st exit off A3(M) towards Havant. 4 miles north of Havant.
Description: Mostly flat parkland.
White 18 holes, 6,627 yards, Par 72, S.S.S. 72, Course record 70.
Yellow 18 holes, 6,381 yards, Par 72, S.S.S. 70, Course record 70.
Membership: 800
Visitors: Welcome. Handicap certificate preferred. Weekends with members only. Maximum 12 (green fees).
Green Fees: £22 per round or day weekdays, £28 Sundays and Bank Holidays.
Facilities: Lunch. Bar Snacks. Full Catering. Changing Room. Golf Shop. Trolley Hire. Buggy Hire.
Class One Hotel: Brookfield, Havant, 4 mile(s). Tel: 373363 (0243)
Class Two Hotel: Fountain Inn, Rowlands castle, 1/2 mile(s). Tel: 412291 (0705)

HAYLING ISLAND

Hayling Golf Club, Ferry Road, Hayling Island, Hants. PO11 0BX. Tel: 463777 (0705)
Secretary: Mr Stokes   Tel: 464446 (0705)
Professional: Mr Gadd   Tel: 464491 (0705)
Location: 5 miles south of Havant on A3023.
Description: Links.
18 holes, 6,489 yards, Par 71, S.S.S. 71, Course record 66.
Membership: 850
Visitors: Welcome. Handicap certificate required. Letter of Introduction required. Ladies Day Thursday. Societies Tuesdays and Wednesdays. Weekends restricted.
Green Fees: Weekdays £24, weekends £30.
Facilities: Lunch. Bar Snacks. Full Catering. Changing Room. Golf Shop. Club Hire. Trolley Hire.
Class One Hotel: Post House, Hayling Island, 4 1/2 mile(s). Tel: 465011 (0705)
Class Two Hotel: Rook Hollow, Hayling Island, 2 mile(s). Tel: 467080 (0705)

LEE-ON-THE-SOLENT

Lee-on-the-Solent Golf Club, Brune Lane, Lee-on-the-Solent, Hants. PO13 6PB. Tel: 551170 (0705)
Secretary: P A Challis   Tel: 551170 (0705)
Professional: J Richardson   Tel: 551181 (0705)
Description: Parkland.
18 holes, 5,959 yards, Par 69, S.S.S. 69, Course record 65.
Visitors: Welcome. Handicap certificate required. Usually with members at weekends.
Green Fees: £20 per day weekdays, £24 weekends.
Facilities: Lunch. Dinner. Bar Snacks. Full Catering. Changing Room. Golf Shop. Trolley Hire.
Class One Hotel: Bellvue, Leigh-on-Solent, 2 mile(s). Tel: 550258 (0705)

LIPHOOK

Liphook Golf Club, Wheatsheaf Enclosure, Liphook, Hants. GU30 7EH. Tel: 723271 (0428)
Secretary: Major Morgan M.B.E.   Tel: 723785 (0428)
Professional: Mr Large   Tel: 723271 (0428)
Location: Liphook A3 to Petersfield, 1/2 mile on left.
Description: Championship golf course with heather, silver birch and pines.
18 holes, 6,247 yards, Par 70, S.S.S. 70.
Membership: 800
Visitors: Welcome. Handicap certificate required. Restricted at weekends. Ladies Day Tuesdays. Please telephone in advance.
Green Fees: Weekdays £24 per round, £33 per day. Weekends £35 per round, £45 per day.
Facilities: Lunch. Bar Snacks. Full Catering. Changing Room. Golf Shop. Club Hire. Driving Range. Trolley Hire. Caddies available.
Class One Hotel: The Georgian, Hazelmere, 6 mile(s). Tel: 651555 (0428)

LIPHOOK

Old Thorns Golf Course & Hotel, Longmoor Road, Liphook, Hants. GU30 7PE. Tel: 724555 (0428)
Secretary: Mr G M Jones   Tel: 724555 (0428)
Professional: Mr P Loxley   Tel: 724555 (0428)
Location: 2 miles south west of Liphook on B2131 Longmoor Road.
Description: Wooded parkland with 8 lakes.
18 holes, 6,500 yards, Par 72, S.S.S. 71, Course record 66.
Visitors: Welcome. Pay as you play.
Green Fees: Weekdays £24 per round, £42 per day. Weekends £35 per round.
Facilities: Lunch. Dinner. Bar Snacks. Full Catering. Changing Room. Golf Shop. Club Hire. Driving Range. Trolley Hire. Buggy Hire.
Class One Hotel: Old Thorns Golf Hotel, Liphook. Tel: 724555 (0428)

LYNDHURST

Bramshaw Golf Club, Brook, Lyndhurst, Hants. SO4 7HE. Tel: 813433 (0703)
Secretary: R D Tingey   Tel: 813433 (0703)
Professional: Clive Bonner   Tel: 813434 (0703)
Location: 1 mile from M27 junc 1 on to B3078 towards Fordingbridge on righthand side.
Description: The oldest golf club in Hampshire with two different courses. The Forest course runs through the New Forest and The Manor course is in a well maintained park/woodland setting.
Manor 18 holes, 6,233 yards, Par 71, S.S.S. 70, Course record 69.
Forest 18 holes, 5,774 yards, Par 69, S.S.S. 68, Course record 67.
Membership: 1400
Visitors: Welcome. Handicap certificate required. No visitors at weekends unless resident in club's hotel (The Bell Inn), when reserved tee times are given.
Green Fees: £26 per day.
Facilities: Lunch. Dinner. Bar Snacks. Full Catering. Changing Room. Golf Shop. Trolley Hire. Buggy Hire.

Cade's - Audi Golf Course Guide

Class One Hotel: The Bell Inn, On course. Tel: 812214 (0703)

LYNDHURST

New Forest Golf Club, Southampton Road, Lyndhurst, Hants. SO43 7BU. Tel: 282450 (0703)
Secretary: Mr W Swann   Tel: 282752 (0703)
Professional: Mr K Gilhespy   Tel: 282450 (0703)
Location: On A35 towards Southampton from Lyndhurst, 1/2 mile on left.
Description: Open forest course, natural surroundings including wild New Forest ponies wandering around the course.
18 holes, 5,742 yards, Par 69, S.S.S. 68, Course record 64.
Membership: 900
Visitors: Welcome. Pay and play system. Bookings and reservations excepted 1 week in advance. No jeans or trainers.
Green Fees: Weekdays £10 per round/day, weekends £12 per round/day.
Facilities: Lunch. Dinner. Bar Snacks. Full Catering. Changing Room. Golf Shop. Trolley Hire. Caddies available.
Class One Hotel: Knightwood Lodge, Lyndhurst, 1/4 mile(s). Tel: 282502 (0703)

PETERSFIELD

Petersfield Golf Club, The Heath, Petersfield, Hants. GU31 4EJ. Tel: 63725 (0730)
Secretary: Mr P Heraud   Tel: 62386 (0730)
Professional: Mr S Clay   Tel: 67732 (0730)
Location: 1 mile ast of Petersfield on A3, turn into Heath Road.
Description: Combined heath and parkland.
18 holes, 5,649 yards, Par 69, S.S.S. 67.
Membership: 800
Visitors: Welcome. Not before mid-day weekends and Bank Holidays. Tuesdays Ladies Day.
Green Fees: Weekdays £15 per round, £21 per day. Weekends £21 per round.
Facilities: Lunch. Bar Snacks. Full Catering. Changing Room. Golf Shop. Trolley Hire.

PORTSMOUTH

Great Salterns Municipal Golf Course, Eastern Road, Portsmouth, Hants. PO3 6QB. Tel: 664549 (0705)
Professional: Mr T Healy   Tel: 664549 (0705)
Description: Parkland course. Magnificent lake through centre of course adjoining Langstone Harbour.
18 holes, 5,894 yards, Par 71, S.S.S. 68, Course record 64.
Visitors: Welcome. Previous day bookings. Municipal course.
Green Fees: £8.90 per round, £13.30 per day April to September. £6.60 per round October to March.
Facilities: Lunch. Dinner. Bar Snacks. Full Catering. Golf Shop. Club Hire. Driving Range. Trolley Hire.
Class One Hotel: Inn Lodge, Portsmouth, 1/4 mile(s). Tel: 650510 (0705)

PORTSMOUTH

Waterlooville Golf Club, Cherry Tree Avenue, Cowplain, Portsmouth, Hants. PO8 8AP. Tel: 263388 (0705)

Secretary: Mr C Chamberlain   Tel: 263388 (0705)
Professional: Mr J Hay   Tel: 256911 (0705)
Location: From Portsmouth to Waterlooville A3, signposted in 2 miles.
Description: Parkland tree lined course.
18 holes, 6,647 yards, Par 72, S.S.S. 72, Course record 67.
Membership: 750
Visitors: Welcome. Handicap certificate required. Not weekends. Tuesdays Ladies Day.
Green Fees: Weekdays £20 per round, £30 per day.
Facilities: Lunch. Dinner. Bar Snacks. Full Catering. Changing Room. Golf Shop. Trolley Hire. Buggy Hire.
Class One Hotel: Langstone Hotel, Havant, 8 mile(s). Tel: 452349 (0705)

RINGWOOD

Burley Golf Club, Cott Lane, Burley, Ringwood, Hants. BH24 4BB. Tel: 2431 (04253)
Secretary: Major G R Kendall   Tel: 2431 (04253)
Professional: Bill Brampton   Tel: 477880 (0425)
Location: Four miles south east of Ringwood. Leave A31 at Picket Post. Drive through Burley Village, Clubhouse on left as you leave Burley on Lymingington Road.
Description: Undulating heathland.
9 holes, 6,149 yards, Par 71, S.S.S. 69, Course record 68.
Membership: 520
Visitors: Welcome. Handicap certificate required. No visitors on Saturdays, Ladies Day Wednesday until 1.45p.m. Telephone club prior to visit.
Green Fees: Weekdays £13, weekends £15.
Facilities: Lunch. Bar Snacks. Full Catering. Changing Room.
Class One Hotel: Moorhill House, Burley, 1/4 mile(s). Tel: 3285 (04253)
Class Two Hotel: The White Buck Inn, Burley, 1/2 mile(s). Tel: 2264 (04253)

ROMSEY

Dunwood Manor Golf Club, Shootash Hill, Near Romsey, Hants. SO51 0GF. Tel: 40549 (0794)
Secretary: Mr P Dawson   Tel: 40549 (0794)
Professional: Mr T Pearce   Tel: 40663 (0794)
Location: On A27 3 miles from Romsey.
Description: Undulating parkland.
18 holes, 5,885 yards, Par 69, S.S.S. 68, Course record 61.
Membership: 700
Visitors: Welcome. With members only at weekends.
Green Fees: Weekdays £20 per round, £30 per day. Weekends £30 per round.
Facilities: Lunch. Dinner. Bar Snacks. Full Catering. Changing Room. Golf Shop. Club Hire. Trolley Hire.
Class One Hotel: White Horse, Romsey, 3 mile(s). Tel: 512431 (0794)

SOUTHAMPTON

Corhampton Golf Club, Sheeps Pond Lane, Droxford, Southampton, Hants. SO3 1QZ. Tel: 877279 (0489)
Secretary: Mr P Taylor   Tel: 877279 (0489)
Professional: Mr G Stubbington   Tel: 877638 (0489)
Location: From Bishops Waltham take Corhampton Road for 5 miles, course is on right hand side.

75

Description: Flat downland course.
18 holes, 6,088 yards, Par 69, S.S.S. 69, Course record 64.
Membership: 700
Visitors: Welcome. Handicap certificate required. Not weekends. Ladies Day Tuesdays. Mondays and Fridays are Society days.
Green Fees: £20 per round, £32 per day.
Facilities: Lunch. Dinner. Bar Snacks. Full Catering. Changing Room. Golf Shop. Driving Range. Trolley Hire. Buggy Hire.

SOUTHAMPTON
Meon Valley Golf and Country Club, Sandy Lane, Shedfield, Southampton, Hants. SO3 2HQ. Tel: 833455 (0329)
Secretary: Mr McMenemy   Tel: 833455 (0329)
Professional: Mr J Stirling   Tel: 833850 (0329)
Location: Junc 7 on M27 onto A334 through Botley Village to Wickham for 2 miles.
Description: Gently undulating parkland, good test from the back tees championship course.
Meon 18 holes, 6,519 yards, Par 71, S.S.S. 71, Course record 69.
Valley 9 holes, 2,714 yards, Par 35.
Membership: 500
Visitors: Welcome. Handicap certificate required. Booking is essential upto 8 days in advance.
Green Fees: Weekdays £22 per round, £36 per day. Weekends £30 per round. For 9 holes £10 per round weekdays, £15 weekends.
Facilities: Lunch. Dinner. Bar Snacks. Full Catering. Changing Room. Golf Shop. Club Hire. Trolley Hire. Buggy Hire.
Class One Hotel: Meon Valley, Shedfield. Tel: 833455 (0339)

SOUTHAMPTON
Southampton Golf Club, Municipal Golf Course, Golf Course Road, Southampton, Hants. SO1 7LE. Tel: 767996 (0703)
Secretary: Mr. Kennard   Tel: 767996 (0703)
Professional: Mr J Cave   Tel: 768407 (0703)
Location: 5 miles north of Southampton on the Avenue left hand side.
Description: Tree lined open park land.
18 holes, 6,123 yards, Par 69, S.S.S. 70.
9 holes, 2,385 yards, Par 33, S.S.S. 33.
Membership: 800
Visitors: Welcome. Booking advised 7 days in advance.
Green Fees: Weekdays £7.60 per round (18 holes), £3.40 per round (9 holes). Weekends and Bank Holidays £10.80 per round (18 holes), £5.60 per round
Facilities: Lunch. Bar Snacks. Full Catering. Changing Room. Golf Shop. Club Hire. Trolley Hire.
Class One Hotel: Hilton National, Southampton, 1/2 mile(s). Tel: 702700 (0703)

SOUTHAMPTON
Stoneham Golf Club, Bassett Green Road, Bassett, Southampton, Hants. SO2 3NE. Tel: 768151 (0703)
Secretary: Mrs A M Wilkinson   Tel: 769272 (0703)
Professional: Ian Young   Tel: 768349 (0703)
Location: 2 miles north of Southampton on A27.

Description: Heather and gorse, subsoil-sand or peat, undulating.
18 holes, 6,310 yards, Par 72, S.S.S. 70, Course record 65.
Membership: 780
Visitors: Welcome. Handicap certificate required. Letter of Introduction required. Weekends by arrangement. Some catering restrictions apply, please telephone in advance.
Green Fees: Weekdays £25 per round or day, weekends £27.50 per round or day.
Facilities: Lunch. Dinner. Bar Snacks. Full Catering. Changing Room. Golf Shop. Club Hire. Trolley Hire. Caddies available.
Class One Hotel: Hilton National, Southampton, 1/2 mile(s). Tel: 702700 (0703)
Class Two Hotel: Wessex Hotel, Southampton, 2 mile(s). Tel: 631744 (0703)

TIDWORTH
Tidworth Garrison Golf Club, Bulford Road, Tidworth, Hants. SP9 7AF. Tel: 42301 (0980)
Secretary: Lt Col D F T Tucker   Tel: 42301 (0980)
Professional: Terry Gosden   Tel: 42393 (0980)
Description: Downland course set in wooded area with superb views of the Salisbury Plain.
18 holes, 6,075 yards, Par 69, S.S.S. 69, Course record 65.
Membership: 800
Visitors: Welcome. With members at weekends, unless after 2.00p.m. Sandwiches only on Mondays.
Green Fees: £18 per day, £25 weekends, £15 after 2p.m. weekends.
Facilities: Lunch. Dinner. Bar Snacks. Full Catering. Changing Room. Golf Shop. Club Hire. Trolley Hire.

WATERLOOVILLE
Portsmouth Golf Club, Crookhorn Lane, Widley, Waterlooville, Hants. PO7 5QL.
Secretary: D Houlihan   Tel: 201827 (0705)
Professional: R Brown   Tel: 372210 (0705)
Location: 2 miles from A3(M) on B2150.
Description: Parkland on hills overlooking Portsmouth Harbour.
18 holes, 6,139 yards, Par 69, S.S.S. 70, Course record 66.
Membership: 800
Visitors: Welcome. Handicap certificate required.
Green Fees: £9.20.
Facilities: Lunch. Dinner. Bar Snacks. Full Catering. Changing Room. Golf Shop. Club Hire. Trolley Hire. Buggy Hire.
Class One Hotel: The Bear, Havant, 3 mile(s). Tel: 486501 (0705)
Class Two Hotel: Corner House, Waterlooville, 2 mile(s). Tel: 374079 (0705)

WINCHESTER
Royal Winchester Golf Club, Sarum Road, Winchester, Hants. SO22 5QE. Tel: 852462 (0962)
Secretary: David Williams   Tel: 852462 (0962)
Professional: David Williams   Tel: 852462 (0962)
Location: 1 mile west of Winchester, left of A272, right at A31.
Description: Downland.

18 holes, 6,780 yards, Par , S.S.S. 70.
Membership: 750
Visitors: Welcome. Handicap certificate required. With members only at weekends.
Green Fees: Weekdays £25.
Facilities: Lunch. Dinner. Bar Snacks. Full Catering. Changing Room. Golf Shop. Club Hire. Trolley Hire.

HEREFORDSHIRE & WORCESTERSHIRE

ALVECHURCH
Kings Norton Golf Club Ltd., Brockhill Lane, Weatheroak, Alvechurch, Here/Worcs. B48 7ED. Tel: 826789 (0564)
Secretary: L N W Prince   Tel: 826789 (0564)
Professional: C Haycock   Tel: 822822 (0564)
Description: Parkland, on a number of holes, three courses.
Blue/Red 18 holes, 7,046 yards, Par 72, S.S.S. 74, Course record 65.
Red/Yellow 18 holes, 6,791 yards, Par 72, S.S.S. 73.
Membership: 980
Visitors: Welcome. Handicap certificate required. Not weekends, Bank Holidays, Easter Tuesday or between Christmas Day and New Years Day.
Green Fees: £27 per round, £29.50 per day.
Facilities: Lunch. Dinner. Bar Snacks. Full Catering. Changing Room. Golf Shop. Club Hire. Trolley Hire. Buggy Hire.
Class One Hotel: Country Court, Bromsgrove, 6 mile(s). Tel: 447 7888 (021)
Class Two Hotel: The Old rectory, Alvechurch, 4 mile(s). Tel: 445 6136 (021)

BEWDLEY
Little Lakes Golf Club, Lye Head, Bewdley, Worcs. DY12 2UX. Tel: 266385 (0299)
Secretary: R A Norris   Tel: 67495 (0562)
Professional: M Laing   Tel: 266385 (0299)
Location: Two miles west of Bewdley off A456, turn left opposire Alton Glasshouses.
Description: Parkland.
9 holes, 6,247 yards, Par 73, S.S.S. 72.
Membership: 420
Visitors: Welcome. Handicap certificate required. Weekends only by invitation of a member.
Green Fees: £15 per round, £18 per day.
Facilities: Lunch. Dinner. Bar Snacks. Changing Room. Golf Shop. Club Hire. Trolley Hire.
Class One Hotel: Heath, Bewdley, 5 mile(s). Tel: 400900 (0299)
Class Two Hotel: Black Boy, Bewdley, 5 mile(s) Tel: 402199 (0299)

BROMYARD
Sapey Golf Club, Upper Sapey, Near Bromyard, Here/Worcs. WR6 6XT. Tel: 288 (08867)
Secretary: Mrs Shirley Dykes   Tel: 288 (08867)
Professional: Chris Knowles   Tel: 288 (08867)
Location: Twenty minutes from M5 Droitwich on B4203 Bromyard to Great Witley Road.
Description: Undulating parkland with water hazards (lakes and streams). Seven of the holes set in an area of outstanding natural beauty, looking towards the Malvern Hills.
18 holes, 5,900 yards, Par 69, S.S.S. 68, Course record 65.
Membership: 400
Visitors: Welcome. Handicap certificate required.
Green Fees: Weekdays £12 per round, weekends £19 per round.
Facilities: Lunch. Dinner. Bar Snacks. Full Catering. Changing Room. Golf Shop. Club Hire. Driving Range. Trolley Hire. Buggy Hire.
Class One Hotel: The Hundred House, Great Witley, 6 mile(s). Tel: 896888 (0299)
Class Two Hotel: The Granary, Bromyard, 2 mile(s). Tel: 410345 (0885)

DROITWICH
Droitwich Golf and Country Club, Westford House, Ford Lane, Droitwich, Here/Worcs. WR9 0BQ. Tel: 774344 (0905)
Secretary: M J Taylor   Tel: 774344 (0905)
Professional: C Thompson   Tel: 770207 (0905)
Location: Junction 5 on M5 off A38 one mile north of town.
Description: Undulating parkland.
18 holes, 6,040 yards, Par 70, S.S.S. 69, Course record 63.
Membership: 870
Visitors: Welcome. Handicap certificate required. Letter of Introduction required. With member only at weekends.
Green Fees: £22 per day.
Facilities: Lunch. Dinner. Bar Snacks. Full Catering. Changing Room. Golf Shop. Trolley Hire.
Class One Hotel: Raven, Droitwich, 3 mile(s). Tel: 772224 (0905)
Class Two Hotel: St Andrews, Droitwich, 4 mile(s). Tel: 779677 (0905)

DROITWICH
Ombersley Golf Club, Bishops Wood Road, Lineholt, Ombersley, Droitwich, Here/Worcs. WR9 0LE. Tel: 620747 (0905)
Secretary: Mr Robert Dowty   Tel: 620747 (0905)
Professional: Mr Graham Glenister   Tel: 620747 (0905)
Location: one and a half miles north of Ombersley off A449.
Description: High undulating course above the Severn Valley.
18 holes, 6,289 yards, Par 72, S.S.S. 68.
Visitors: Welcome.
Green Fees: Weekdays £9, weekends £12, reductions for veterans and juniors.
Facilities: Lunch. Dinner. Bar Snacks. Full Catering. Changing Room. Golf Shop. Club Hire. Driving Range. Trolley Hire. Buggy Hire.
Class One Hotel: Stourport Moat House, Stourport, 3 mile(s). Tel: 827733 (0299)
Class Two Hotel: Crown and Sandys Arms, Ombersley, 1 1/2 mile(s). Tel: 620252 (0905)

77

HAGLEY

Hagley Country Club Golf Club, Wassell Grove, Hagley, Here/Worcs. DY9 9JW. Tel: 883701 (0562)
Secretary: Mr G F Yardley   Tel: 883701 (0562)
Professional: Mr I Clark   Tel: 883852 (0562)
Location: On A456, 6 miles south of Birmingham, signposted into Wassell Grove.
Description: Tree lined open parkland.
18 holes, 6,353 yards, Par 72, S.S.S. 72, Course record 71.
Membership: 650
Visitors: Welcome. Not weekends. Wednesdays Ladies Day.
Green Fees: Weekdays £20 per round, £25 per day.
Facilities: Lunch. Dinner. Bar Snacks. Full Catering. Changing Room. Golf Shop. Driving Range. Trolley Hire. Buggy Hire.
Class One Hotel: The Stone Manor, Kidderminster, 3 mile(s). Tel: 777555 (0562)

HEREFORD

Belmont House Golf Club, Belmont House, Belmont, Hereford, Here/Worcs. HR2 9SA. Tel: 352666 (0432)
Secretary: Mrs Caulsley   Tel: 352666 (0432)
Professional: Mr M Welch   Tel: 352717 (0432)
Description: Alongside River Wye, gently undulating parkland. Surrounded by scenic Herefordshire countryside.
18 holes, 6,480 yards, Par 71, S.S.S. 71, Course record 71.
Membership: 350
Visitors: Welcome.
Green Fees: Weekdays £14 per round, £24 per day. Weekends £18 per round, £28 per day.
Facilities: Dinner. Bar Snacks. Full Catering. Changing Room. Golf Shop. Trolley Hire. Caddies available.
Class One Hotel: Belmont Golf Hotel, On Course. Tel: 352666 (0432)
Class Two Hotel: The Ancient Camp Public House, Ruckhall, 6 mile(s). Tel: 250449 (0981)

HEREFORD

Burghill Valley Golf Club, Tillington Road, Burghill, Hereford. HR4 7RW. Tel: 760456 (0432)
Professional: Mr T Morgan   Tel: 760456 (0432)
Location: 3 miles south of Hereford on Tillington Road to Burghill.
Description: Open parkland with a lake, adjacent to a cider orchard.
White 9 holes, 3,073 yards, Par 36, S.S.S. 70.
Red 9 holes, 2,728 yards, Par 36, S.S.S. 70.
Membership: 250
Visitors: Welcome. Must book 5 days in advance. No jeans, trainers or shorts.
Green Fees: £6 for 9 holes, £10 for 18 holes.
Facilities: Lunch. Dinner. Bar Snacks. Full Catering. Changing Room. Golf Shop. Club Hire. Trolley Hire.

HEREFORD

Herefordshire Golf Club, Ravens Causeway, Wormsley, Hereford. HR4 8LY. Tel: 71219 (0432)
Secretary: Mr B Bullock   Tel: 71219 (0432)
Professional: Mr D Hemming   Tel: 71465 (0432)
Location: 6 miles from Hereford on the Hereford to Weobley Road B493.
Description: Hilly woodland course with lakes.
18 holes, 6,036 yards, Par 70, S.S.S. 69, Course record 65.
Membership: 800
Visitors: Welcome. Handicap certificate required.
Green Fees: Weekdays £14 per round, £20 per day. Weekends £18 per round, £26 per day.
Facilities: Lunch. Dinner. Bar Snacks. Full Catering. Changing Room. Golf Shop. Club Hire. Trolley Hire. Buggy Hire.

HOLLYWOOD

Gay Hill Golf Club, Hollywood Lane, Hollywood, Here/Worcs. B47 5PP. Tel: 430 7077 (021)
Secretary: Mrs E K Devitt   Tel: 430 8544 (021)
Professional: Andrew Hill   Tel: 474 6001 (021)
Location: On A435 Birmingham to Evesham Road.
Description: Parkland.
18 holes, 6,500 yards, Par 72, S.S.S. 71, Course record 67.
Membership: 660
Visitors: Welcome. Handicap certificate required. Not weekends and Bank Holidays. Tuesdays Ladies Day. Societies Thursdays. Caddies by prior arrangement.
Green Fees: £28.50 per day.
Facilities: Lunch. Dinner. Bar Snacks. Full Catering. Changing Room. Golf Shop. Club Hire. Trolley Hire.
Class One Hotel: The George, Solihull, 5 mile(s). Tel: 711 2121 (021)
Class Two Hotel: Inkford Cottage, Wythall, 1 mile(s). Tel: 824330 (0564)

KIDDERMINSTER

Habberley Golf Club, Trimpley Road, Habberley, Kidderminster, Here/Worcs. . Tel: 745756 (0562)
Secretary: Mr D Lloyd   Tel: 745756 (0562)
Location: 2 miles west of Kidderminster on the Bridgnorth Road.
Description: Open parkland, hilly and a tight course.
9 holes, 5,481 yards, Par 69, S.S.S. 68, Course record 55.
Membership: 300
Visitors: Welcome. Letter of Introduction required. With members only at weekends and Bank Holidays.
Green Fees: £12 per day, £5 with a member.
Facilities: Lunch. Dinner. Bar Snacks. Full Catering. Changing Room.
Class One Hotel: The Gainsborough House, Kidderminster, 2 mile(s). Tel: 820041 (0562)

KIDDERMINSTER

Kidderminster Golf Club, Russell Road, Kidderminster, Here/Worcs. DY10 3HT. Tel: 822303 (0562)
Secretary: Alan Biggs   Tel: 822303 (0562)
Professional: Nick Underwood   Tel: 740090 (0562)
Location: Signposted off A449 Worcester-Wolverhampton Road.
Description: Mainly flat parkland course.
18 holes, 6,405 yards, Par 72, S.S.S. 71.
Visitors: Welcome. Handicap certificate required. With members only at weekends.
Green Fees: £22.
Facilities: Lunch. Dinner. Bar Snacks. Full Catering. Changing Room. Golf Shop. Club Hire. Trolley Hire.

Cade's - Audi Golf Course Guide

Class One Hotel: Stone Manor, Kidderminster, 2 mile(s). Tel: 83555 (0562)
Class Two Hotel: Gordon House, Kidderminster, 1/2 mile(s). Tel: 822900 (0562)

KINGTON

Kington Golf Club, Bradnor Hill, Kington, Here/Worcs. HR5 3RE. Tel: 230340 (0544)
Secretary: G E Long   Tel: 820542 (0497)
Professional: D Oliver   Tel: 231320 (0544)
Location: Take B4355 Presteigne Road off A44 at Kington, left turn 200 yards.
Description: Natural mountain course, highest 18 holes in England.
18 holes, 5,840 yards, Par 70, S.S.S. 68, Course record 65.
Membership: 530
Visitors: Welcome. Handicap certificate required. Telephone club first.
Green Fees: Weekdays £16 per day, £13 per round. Weekends and Bank Holidays £22 per day, £18 per round.
Facilities: Lunch. Dinner. Bar Snacks. Full Catering. Changing Room. Golf Shop. Trolley Hire.
Class Two Hotel: The Burton, Kington, 1 1/2 mile(s). Tel: 230323 (0544)

LEOMINSTER

Leominster Golf Club, Ford Bridge, Leominster, Here/Worcs. HR6 0LE. Tel: 612863 (0568)
Secretary: John A Ashcroft   Tel: 880493 (0432)
Professional: Russell Price   Tel: 611402 (0568)
Location: Three miles south of Leominster on A49 Leominster By-pass. Clearly signed.
Description: Meadowland by River Lugg and some undulating higher ground.
18 holes, 6,045 yards, Par 69, S.S.S. 69.
Membership: 650
Visitors: Welcome. Weekends by prior booking. Tuesday Ladies Day. No catering Mondays.
Green Fees: £17 weekdays. £21 weekends and Bank Holidays.
Facilities: Lunch. Dinner. Bar Snacks. Full Catering. Changing Room. Golf Shop. Club Hire. Trolley Hire.
Class One Hotel: Talbot, Leominster, 3 mile(s). Tel: 616347 (0568)

MALVERN WELLS

The Worcestershire Golf Club Ltd., Wood Farm, Malvern Wells, Worcs. WR14 4PP. Tel: 575992 (0684)
Secretary: G R Scott   Tel: 575992 (0684)
Professional: G M Harris   Tel: 564428 (0684)
Location: 2 miles south of Great Malvern, near junc of A449 and B4209.
Description: Attractively situated with the Malvern Hills on the east side and good views over the Vale of Evesham and Cotswolds to the west. The course gently undulates among streams and wooded areas.
White 18 holes, 6,449 yards, Par 71, S.S.S. 71.
Yellow 18 holes, 5,970 yards, Par 69, S.S.S. 69.
Membership: 780
Visitors: Welcome. Handicap certificate required. Not before 10a.m. at weekends.

Green Fees: Weekdays £22 per day, weekends £25 per day.
Facilities: Lunch. Dinner. Bar Snacks. Full Catering. Changing Room. Golf Shop. Club Hire. Trolley Hire.
Class One Hotel: Abbey, Malvern, 2 mile(s). Tel: 892332 (0684)
Class Two Hotel: Essington, Malvern Wells, 1/2 mile(s). Tel: 561177 (0684)

REDDITCH

Abbey Park Golf and Country Club, Abbey Park, Dagnell End Road, Redditch, Here/Worcs. B98 7BD. Tel: 63918 (0527)
Secretary: Mr Bradley   Tel: 63918 (0527)
Professional: Mr R Morrell   Tel: 68006 (0527)
Location: From Redditch take A441, 1 mile turn into Dagnell End Road, 1 mile on the right.
Description: Undulating parkland with a number of large lakes.
18 holes, 6,500 yards, Par 71, S.S.S. 71, Course record 69.
Membership: 1000
Visitors: Welcome. Pay as you play. Booking 6 days in advance. Limited games weekends. 1 weeks notice required for Caddies.
Green Fees: Weekdays £10 per round, weekends £12.50 per round.
Facilities: Lunch. Dinner. Bar Snacks. Full Catering. Changing Room. Golf Shop. Club Hire. Driving Range. Trolley Hire.
Class One Hotel: Abbey Park Golf & Country Club, On Course. Tel: 63918 (0527)

REDDITCH

Redditch Golf Club, Green Lane, Lower Grinsty, Callow Hill, Redditch, Here/Worcs. B97 5PJ. Tel: 543309 (0527)
Secretary: C Holman   Tel: 543309 (0527)
Professional: F Powell   Tel: 546372 (0527)
Location: Three miles west of town centre, off Redditch/Bromsgrove A448.
Description: First nine parkland, second nine wooded.
White 18 holes, 6,671 yards, Par 72, S.S.S. 72, Course record 68.
Yellow 18 holes, 6,285 yards, Par 70, S.S.S. 70.
Visitors: Welcome. Weekends with members only. Some catering restrictions apply. Please telephone in advance.
Green Fees: £25. £7.50 with member.
Facilities: Lunch. Dinner. Bar Snacks. Full Catering. Changing Room. Golf Shop.
Class One Hotel: Southcrest, Redditch, 2 mile(s). Tel: 541511 (0527)
Class Two Hotel: Montville, Redditch, 2 1/2 mile(s). Tel: 544411 (0527)

ROSS-ON-WYE

Ross-on-Wye Golf Club, Two Park, Gorsley, Ross-on-Wye, Here/Worcs. HR9 7UT. Tel: 82660 (0989)
Secretary: Mr G H Cason   Tel: 82267 (0989)
Professional: Mr A M Catchpole   Tel: 82439 (0989)
Location: Adjacent to junc 3 M50.
Description: Open parkland.
18 holes, 6,500 yards, Par 72, S.S.S. 73, Course record 69.

79

Membership: 750
Visitors: Welcome. Society days Wednesdays, Thursdays and Fridays. Ladies Day Tuesdays. Visitors play after 9.30a.m.. Bookings 24 hours in advance.
Green Fees: Weekdays £25, weekends £30 all day.
Facilities: Lunch. Dinner. Bar Snacks. Full Catering. Changing Room. Golf Shop. Club Hire. Driving Range. Trolley Hire.
Class One Hotel: The Chase, Ross-on-Wye, 4 mile(s). Tel: 763161 (0989)

WORCESTER
Tolladine Golf Club, The Fairway, Tolladine Road, Worcester, Here/Worcs. WR4 9BA. Tel: 21074 (0905)
Secretary: A J Wardle   Tel: 21074 (0905)
Location: North east of Worcester City Centre/south west junction 6 M5 Warndon.
Description: Nine hole hilly open parkland.
9 holes, 5,440 yards, Par 68, S.S.S. 67, Course record 65.
Membership: 360
Visitors: Welcome. With members at weekends. Ladies Day Tuesday, not after 2p.m. Wednesdays.
Green Fees: £12, with member £5, with member weekends £6.
Facilities: Changing Room. Golf Shop.
Class One Hotel: The Giffard, Worcester, 3 mile(s). Tel: 726262 (0905)
Class Two Hotel: Dilmore House, Worcester, 3 mile(s). Tel: 51543 (0905)

HERTFORDSHIRE

BARNET
Arkley Golf Club, Rowley Green Road, Barnet, Herts. EN5 3HL.
Secretary: Mr G Taylor   Tel: 499 0394 (081)
Professional: Mr Squire   Tel: 440 8473 (081)
Location: 2 miles from Barnet, towards A1 for 1 1/2 miles turn right into Rowley Lane.
Description: Open parkland, 9 holes played off 18 tees.
9 holes, 6,045 yards, Par 69, S.S.S. 69.
Visitors: Welcome. Handicap certificate required. With members only at weekends.
Green Fees: £20 per round, £25 per day.
Facilities: Lunch. Dinner. Bar Snacks. Full Catering. Changing Room. Golf Shop. Trolley Hire.

BARNET
Hadley Wood Golf Club, Beech Hill, Near Barnet, Herts. EN4 0JJ. Tel: 449 4486 (081)
Secretary: Mr P Bryan   Tel: 449 4328 (081)
Professional: Mr A McGinn   Tel: 449 3285 (081)
Location: On A111, 1 mile south of Potters Bar on right hand side.
Description: Wooded and undulating.
18 holes, 6,473 yards, Par 72, S.S.S. 71, Course record 67.
Membership: 550
Visitors: Welcome. Handicap certificate required. With members only at weekends. Tuesday morning is Ladies day.

Green Fees: £30 per round, £37.50 per day.
Facilities: Lunch. Dinner. Bar Snacks. Full Catering. Changing Room. Golf Shop. Club Hire. Trolley Hire.
Class One Hotel: West Lodge Park, Cockfosters, 1/2 mile(s). Tel: 440 8311 (081)

BARNET
Old Fold Manor Golf Club, Hadley Green, Barnet, Herts. EN5 4QN. Tel: 440 9185 (081)
Secretary: D V Dalingwater   Tel: 440 9185 (081)
Professional: P Jones   Tel: 440 7488 (081)
Location: Junc 23 M25, A1000 1 mile north of Barnet.
Description: Scenic heathland.
18 holes, 6,449 yards, Par 71, S.S.S. 71, Course record 66.
Membership: 520
Visitors: Welcome. Handicap certificate required. Mondays and Wednesdays. With a member only at weekends on non-competition days. Some catering restrictions apply, please telephone in ad
Green Fees: £27 per round, £30 per day.
Facilities: Lunch. Dinner. Bar Snacks. Full Catering. Changing Room. Golf Shop. Club Hire. Trolley Hire. Buggy Hire.
Class One Hotel: West Lodge Park, Cockfosters, 2 mile(s). Tel: 440 8311 (081)
Class Two Hotel: Hadley Hotel, Barnet, 1 1/2 mile(s). Tel: 449 0161 (081)

BERKHAMSTED
Ashridge Golf Club, Little Gaddesden, Berkhamsted, Herts. HP4 1LY. Tel: 842244 (0442)
Secretary: Mrs M West   Tel: 842244 (0442)
Professional: Mr G Pook   Tel: 842307 (0442)
Location: A41 from London through Berkhamsted onto the B4056.
Description: Open parkland set on National Trust land.
18 holes, 6,547 yards, Par 72, S.S.S. 71, Course record 64.
Membership: 700
Visitors: Welcome. Handicap certificate required. Ladies Day Thursdays. Not at weekends or Summer months.
Green Fees: On application.
Facilities: Lunch. Dinner. Full Catering. Changing Room. Golf Shop. Club Hire. Trolley Hire.

BERKHAMSTED
Berkhamsted Golf Club, The Common, Berkhamsted, Herts. HP4 2QB. Tel: 863730 (0442)
Secretary: Mr I Wheater   Tel: 865832 (0442)
Professional: Mr Proudfoot   Tel: 865851 (0442)
Location: Off A41 Berkhamsted.
Description: Heathland, gorse, wooded, every hole is different. No bunkers.
White 18 holes, 6,605 yards, Par 71, S.S.S. 72, Course record 69.
Yellow 18 holes, 6,212 yards, Par 70, S.S.S. 70.
Membership: 760
Visitors: Welcome. Handicap certificate required. Book 2 days in advance.
Green Fees: Weekdays £24 per round, £36 per day. Weekends £30.50 per round, £41 per day.
Facilities: Lunch. Dinner. Bar Snacks. Full Catering. Changing Room. Golf Shop. Club Hire. Trolley Hire.

Class One Hotel: The Penny Farthing, Berkhamsted, 1 mile(s). Tel: 872828 (0442)

BUSHEY

Bushey Hall Golf Club, Bushey Hall Drive, Bushey, Herts. . Tel: 229759 (0923)
Secretary: Mr C A Brown　　　　　　Tel: 225802 (0923)
Professional: Mr D Fitzsimmons　　　Tel: 222253 (0923)
Location: 6 miles south of Watford on the Aldenham Road.
Description: Open parkland, water running through course, undulating and tree lined.
Yellow 18 holes, 6,003 yards, Par 68, S.S.S. 68.
White 18 holes, 6,099 yards, Par 70, S.S.S. 69, Course record 66.
Membership: 600
Visitors: Welcome. Handicap certificate required. With members only at weekends.
Green Fees: £21 per round, £29.50 per day.
Facilities: Lunch. Dinner. Bar Snacks. Full Catering. Changing Room. Golf Shop. Club Hire. Trolley Hire.
Class One Hotel: Hilton International, Watford, 2 mile(s). Tel: 31333 (0923)
Class Two Hotel: Lindal Guest House, Harrow, 8 mile(s). Tel: 863 3164 (081)

BUSHEY HEATH

Hartsbourne Golf and Country Club, Hartsbourne Avenue, Bushey Heath, Herts. WD2 1JW. Tel: 950 1133 (081)
Secretary: David J Woodman　　　　Tel: 950 1133 (081)
Professional: Geoff Hunt　　　　　　Tel: 950 2836 (081)
Location: Between Stanmore and Watford off A414.
Description: Undulating parkland.
White 18 holes, 6,333 yards, Par 72, S.S.S. 70, Course record 62.
Blue 9 holes, 2,716 yards, Par 34, S.S.S. 33.
Membership: 950
Visitors: Welcome. Handicap certificate required. Only with members.
Green Fees: On application.
Facilities: Lunch. Dinner. Bar Snacks. Full Catering. Changing Room. Golf Shop. Club Hire. Trolley Hire. Buggy Hire. Caddies available.
Class One Hotel: Hilton National, Watford, 2 mile(s). Tel: 35881 (0923)

CHESHUNT

Cheshunt Golf Club, The Clubhouse, Park Lane, Cheshunt, Herts. EN7 6QD. Tel: 29777 (0992)
Secretary: Mr J G Duncan　　　　　Tel: 29777 (0992)
Professional: Chris Newton　　　　　Tel: 24009 (0992)
Location: M25 junc 25 take A10 towards Hertford, at second traffic lights turn left, at mini roundabout turn right.
Description: Parkland.
18 holes, 6,604 yards, Par 71, S.S.S. 69, Course record 65.
Membership: 550
Visitors: Welcome. Societies by arrangement with professional. Catering facilities are in public cafeteria.
Green Fees: W/days £7, w/ends and B/Holidays £9. Senior Citizens and Juniors w/days £3.50, w/ends full fee.
Facilities: Golf Shop. Club Hire. Trolley Hire. Buggy Hire.
Class One Hotel: Marriot, Cheshunt, 1 mile(s). Tel: 451245 (0992)

DAGNALL

Whipsnade Golf Club, Studham Lane, Dagnall, Herts. HP4 1RH. Tel: 842330 (0442)
Secretary: Mr Whalley　　　　　　Tel: 842330 (0442)
Professional: Mr M Lewendon　　　Tel: 842310 (0442)
Location: A4146 from Hemel Hempstead towards Leighton Buzzard, turn in to Dagnall Village 1/4 mile up the hill.
Description: Scenic, flat, open part of the course runs alongside Whipsnade Zoo.
18 holes, 6,735 yards, Par 72, S.S.S. 72, Course record 66.
Membership: 550
Visitors: Welcome. Not weekends.
Green Fees: £20 per round, £30 per day.
Facilities: Lunch. Bar Snacks. Full Catering. Changing Room. Golf Shop. Club Hire. Trolley Hire. Buggy Hire.
Class One Hotel: Crows Nest Travel Inn, Tring, 2 mile(s). Tel: 4819 (044282)

GRAVELEY

Chesfield Downs Family Golf Centre, Graveley, Herts. SG4 7EQ. Tel: 482929 (0462)
Secretary: Marion Holmes　　　　　Tel: 482929 (0462)
Professional: Dale Brightman　　　　Tel: 482929 (0462)
Location: Just off A1(M) approx 1 1/2 miles B197, north of the Village of Graveley.
Description: Inland links/downland.
Chesfield Downs 18 holes, 6,630 yards, Par 70, S.S.S. 72, Course record 69
Lannock Links 9 holes, 975 yards, Par 27, S.S.S. 27.
Membership: 700
Visitors: Welcome. Advance bookings are available to reserve tee times. One weeks notice preferred.
Green Fees: Chesfield - Weekdays £11, with member £10. Weekends £20, with member £15. Lannock - Weekdays £3, weekends £4.
Facilities: Lunch. Dinner. Bar Snacks. Full Catering. Changing Room. Golf Shop. Club Hire. Driving Range. Trolley Hire. Buggy Hire.
Class One Hotel: Novotel, Knebworth Park, 3 mile(s). Tel: 742299 (0438)

HATFIELD

Brookmans Park Golf Club, Golf Club Road, Brookmans Park, Hatfield, Herts. AL9 7AT. Tel: 52487 (0707)
Secretary: P A Gill　　　　　　　　Tel: 52487 (0707)
Professional: I Jelley　　　　　　　Tel: 52468 (0707)
Location: Exit 24 on M25 off A1000.
Description: Parkland.
18 holes, 6,454 yards, Par 71, S.S.S. 71, Course record 66.
Membership: 764
Visitors: Welcome. Handicap certificate required. With members at weekends. Not Tuesdays. Dinner for socities.
Green Fees: £25 per round, £30 per day.
Facilities: Lunch. Bar Snacks. Full Catering. Changing Room. Golf Shop. Trolley Hire.
Class One Hotel: Crest Hotel, South Mimms, 4 mile(s). Tel: 43311 (0707)
Class Two Hotel: Brookmans Park Hotel, Brookmans Park, 1 mile(s). Tel: 53577 (0707)

HEMEL HEMPSTEAD
Little Hay Golf Complex, Box Lane, Bovingdon, Hemel Hempstead, Herts. HP3 0DQ. Tel: 833798 (0442)
Secretary: Mr D Johnson   Tel: 833798 (0442)
Professional: Mr S Proudfoot   Tel: 833798 (0442)
Location: Take A41 from Hemel Hempstead centre.
Description: Wooded parkland.
White 18 holes, 6,678 yards, Par 72, S.S.S. 72.
Yellow 18 holes, 6,311 yards, Par 70, S.S.S. 70.
Visitors: Welcome. Public course, booking advised 7 days in advance.
Green Fees: Weekdays £6.25 per round, weekends £9.25 per round.
Facilities: Lunch. Dinner. Bar Snacks. Full Catering. Changing Room. Golf Shop. Club Hire. Driving Range. Trolley Hire. Buggy Hire.
Class One Hotel: The Bobsleigh, Boxmoor, 1/4 mile(s). Tel: 833276 (0442)

HERTFORD
Brickendon Grange Golf & Country Club, Brickendon, Near Hertford, Herts. SG13 8PD. Tel: 494 (099286)
Secretary: Mr N Martin   Tel: 258 (099286)
Professional: Mr J Hamilton   Tel: 218 (099286)
Location: 3 miles from Hertford on Brickendon Lane.
Description: Open parkland.
18 holes, 6,349 yards, Par 71, S.S.S. 71, Course record 66.
Membership: 600
Visitors: Welcome. Handicap certificate required. Wednesday is Ladies day. With members only at weekends.
Green Fees: Weekdays £24 per round, £30 per day.
Facilities: Lunch. Dinner. Bar Snacks. Full Catering. Changing Room. Golf Shop. Club Hire. Driving Range. Trolley Hire. Buggy Hire.

KNEBWORTH
Knebworth Golf Club, Deards End Lane, Knebworth, Herts. SG3 6NL. Tel: 812752 (0438)
Secretary: Mr J Wright   Tel: 812752 (0438)
Professional: Mr Mitchell   Tel: 812757 (0438)
Location: 1 mile from Stevenage south, junc 7 A1, then follow signs to Knebworth.
Description: Championship course, open parkland.
18 holes, 6,492 yards, Par 71, S.S.S. 71, Course record 64.
Membership: 600
Visitors: Welcome. Handicap certificate required. Letter of Introduction required. With members only at weekends.
Green Fees: £27 per round/day, £13 with member.
Facilities: Lunch. Dinner. Bar Snacks. Full Catering. Changing Room. Golf Shop. Club Hire. Trolley Hire. Buggy Hire.
Class One Hotel: The Roebuck, Stevenage, 3 mile(s). Tel: 365444 (0438)

LETCHWORTH
Letchworth Golf Club, Letchworth Lane, Letchworth, Herts. LU6 3AN. Tel: 683203 (0462)
Secretary: A R Bailey   Tel: 683203 (0462)
Professional: J Mutimer   Tel: 682713 (0462)
Location: 1/2 mile of A505 south at Letchworth.
Description: Parkland.
18 holes, 6,181 yards, Par 70, S.S.S. 69.
Membership: 500
Visitors: Welcome. Handicap certificate required. Not Tuesdays. No catering Mondays.
Green Fees: Weekdays £23.50 per round, £32.50 per day. Weekends £30 per round, £37 per day.
Facilities: Lunch. Dinner. Bar Snacks. Full Catering. Changing Room. Golf Shop.
Class One Hotel: Letchworth Hall, Letchworth, 1/8 mile(s). Tel: 683747 (0462)
Class Two Hotel: Greenlawns, Letchworth, 1 mile(s). Tel: 683143 (0462)

POTTERS BAR
Potters Bar Golf Club, Darkes Lane, Potters Bar, Herts. EN6 1DF. Tel: 52020 (0707)
Secretary: A St J Williams   Tel: 52020 (0707)
Professional: K Hughes   Tel: 52986 (0707)
Description: Wooded parkland with water.
18 holes, 6,273 yards, Par 71, S.S.S. 70, Course record 65.
Membership: 520
Visitors: Welcome. Handicap certificate required. Only with members at weekends.
Green Fees: £29.40 per round.
Facilities: Lunch. Bar Snacks. Full Catering. Changing Room. Golf Shop. Trolley Hire. Buggy Hire. Caddies available.
Class One Hotel: South Mimms Crest, South Mimms, 1 mile(s). Tel: 43311 (0707)

RADLETT
Porters Park Golf Club, Shenley Hill, Radlett, Herts. WD7 7AZ. Tel: 854127 (0923)
Secretary: J H Roberts   Tel: 854127 (0923)
Professional: D Gleeson   Tel: 854366 (0923)
Location: 1/2 mile north of Radlett Station.
Description: Parkland with pine trees and a stream.
18 holes, 6,313 yards, Par 70, S.S.S. 70, Course record 65.
Membership: 650
Visitors: Welcome. Handicap certificate required. Letter of Introduction required. Telephone to book. Reserved for Ladies on Tuesdays, socieites Wednesdays and Thursdays. Weekends with mem
Green Fees: £28 per round.
Facilities: Lunch. Bar Snacks. Full Catering. Changing Room. Golf Shop. Club Hire. Trolley Hire.
Class Two Hotel: Pinks, Shenley, 1 mile(s). Tel: 43106 (0707)

RICKMANSWORTH
Moor Park Golf Club, Moor Park, Rickmansworth, Herts. WD3 1QN. Tel: 773146 (0923)
Secretary: Mr J A Davies   Tel: 773146 (0923)
Professional: Mr R Whitehead   Tel: 773146 (0923)
Location: 1 mile south east of Rickmansworth off A404.
Description: Championship course, open parkland.
West 18 holes, 5,815 yards, Par 69, S.S.S. 68, Course record 63.
High 18 holes, 6,713 yards, Par 72, S.S.S. 72, Course record 67.
Membership: 1800
Visitors: Welcome. Handicap certificate required. Thurs-

days Ladies Day. Not at weekends.
Green Fees: West - £25 per round. High - £30 per round, £50 per day.
Facilities: Lunch. Bar Snacks. Full Catering. Changing Room. Golf Shop. Club Hire. Trolley Hire. Buggy Hire. Caddies available.
Class One Hotel: Bedford Arms, Chorleywood, 3 mile(s). Tel: 284335 (0923)

RICKMANSWORTH

Rickmansworth Public Golf Course, Moor Lane, Rickmansworth, Herts. WD3 1QL. Tel: 775278 (0923)
Secretary: W F Stokes   Tel: 772948 (0923)
Professional: Iain Duncan   Tel: 775278 (0923)
Location: From town centre along A404 to waterworks, left on B4504 then first right signposted Moor Park Mansion.
Description: Testing undulating parkland.
18 holes, 4,493 yards, Par 63, S.S.S. 62, Course record 63. Pitch & Putt 9 holes, yards, Par .
Membership: 300
Visitors: Welcome. Book 7 days in advance for weekends.
Green Fees: Estimated from April 1992 weekdays £8, weekends £15. Telephone pro for confirmation.
Facilities: Lunch. Dinner. Bar Snacks. Full Catering. Changing Room. Golf Shop. Club Hire. Trolley Hire.

ST ALBANS

Batchwood Golf Club, Batchwood Hall, Batchwood Drive, St Albans, Herts. AL3 5XA. Tel: 44250 (0727)
Professional: J Thomson   Tel: 52101 (0727)
Location: Off M25 junc 21A, junc 6 M1, follow signs for St Albans.
Description: Undulating parkland.
18 holes, 6,141 yards, Par 69, S.S.S. 69, Course record 67.
Visitors: Welcome. Not before 10a.m. weekends and not before 10a.m. Tuesdays.
Green Fees: Weekdays £7, weekends £9.
Facilities: Bar Snacks. Changing Room. Golf Shop. Club Hire. Trolley Hire.
Class One Hotel: St Michaels Manor, St Albans, 2 mile(s). Tel: 864444 (0727)

ST ALBANS

Redbourn Golf Club, Kinsbourne Green Lane, Redbourn, Near St Albans, Herts. AL3 7QA. Tel: 793363(0582)
Secretary: W M Dunn   Tel: 792150 (0582)
Professional: Steve Baldwin   Tel: 793493 (0582)
Location: 1 mile south of M1 from junc 9.
Description: Parkland.
18 holes, 6,407 yards, Par 70, S.S.S. 71, Course record 67
9 holes, 1,361 yards, Par 27.
Visitors: Welcome. No visitors weekdays between 4.15 - 6p.m., or weekends before 3p.m.
Green Fees: Weekdays £14 per round, weekends and Bank Holidays £17 per round.
Facilities: Lunch. Dinner. Bar Snacks. Full Catering. Changing Room. Golf Shop. Club Hire. Driving Range. Trolley Hire. Buggy Hire.
Class One Hotel: Aubrey Park, Redbourn, 3 mile(s). Tel: 792105 (0582)

ST ALBANS

Verulam Golf Club, 226 London Road, St Albans, Herts. AL1 1JG. Tel: 53327 (0727)
Secretary: G D Eastwood   Tel: 53327 (0727)
Professional: P Anderson   Tel: 861401 (0727)
Location: A1085 south west of St Albans City Centre.
Description: Parkland.
18 holes, 6,452 yards, Par 72, S.S.S. 71, Course record 65.
Membership: 650
Visitors: Welcome. Monday to Friday, with members at weekends. Full catering for societies only.
Green Fees: Monday £11 per round, £18 per day. Tuesday to Friday £20 per round, £25 per day.
Facilities: Lunch. Bar Snacks. Changing Room. Golf Shop. Club Hire. Trolley Hire.
Class One Hotel: Lake Holiday Hotel, St Albans, 1/4 mile(s). Tel: 40904 (0727)
Class Two Hotel: Apples, St Albans, 1/2 mile(s). Tel: 44111 (0727)

WARE

Chadwell Springs Golf Club, Hertford Road, Ware, Herts. SG12 9LE. Tel: 461447 (0920)
Secretary: Mr Evans   Tel: 461447 (0920)
Professional: Mr A Shearn   Tel: 461447 (0920)
Location: 5 miles south of Hertford off A10 towards Ware.
Description: Open parkland.
18 holes, 6,024 yards, Par 72, S.S.S. 68, Course record 64.
Membership: 600
Visitors: Welcome. Thursdays Ladies Day. Not at weekends.
Green Fees: £14 per round/day.
Facilities: Lunch. Dinner. Bar Snacks. Full Catering. Changing Room. Golf Shop. Trolley Hire.
Class One Hotel: Ware Moat House, Ware, 5 mile(s). Tel: 465011 (0920)

WATFORD

Aldenham Golf Club, Church Lane, Aldenham, Near Watford, Herts. WD2 8AL. Tel: 853929 (0923)
Secretary: D W Phillips   Tel: 853929 (0923)
Professional: A McKay   Tel: 857889 (0923)
Description: Parkland, 3 x 9 hole courses.
Red/Yellow 18 holes, 6,455 yards, Par 70, S.S.S. 71.
White/Yellow 18 holes, 5,780 yards, Par 70, S.S.S. 70.
Visitors: Welcome. Handicap certificate required. Not before 1p.m. on main course.
Green Fees: £18 weekdays, £26 weekends.
Facilities: Lunch. Dinner. Bar Snacks. Full Catering. Changing Room. Golf Shop. Club Hire. Driving Range. Trolley Hire. Buggy Hire.
Class One Hotel: Hilton National, Watford, 1/2 mile(s). Tel: 235881 (0923)
Class Two Hotel: The Willow, Radlett, 2 mile(s). Tel: 857543 (0923)

WATFORD

West Herts Golf Club Ltd., Cassiobury Park, Watford, Herts. WD1 7SL. Tel: 236484 (0923)
Secretary: A D Bluck			Tel: 236484 (0923)
Professional: C Gough			Tel: 220352 (0923)
Location: Off A412 between Watford and Rickmansworth.
Description: Parkland.
18 holes, 6,488 yards, Par , S.S.S. 71, Course record 68.
Membership: 694
Visitors: Welcome. Handicap certificate required. Not weekends or Bank Holidays. Some catering restrictions apply, please telephone in advance.
Green Fees: £20 per round, £30 per day.
Facilities: Lunch. Dinner. Bar Snacks. Full Catering. Changing Room. Golf Shop. Trolley Hire.
Class One Hotel: The Two Brewers, Chipperfield, 5 mile(s). Tel: 265266 (0923)
Class Two Hotel: Grove End, Watford, 9 mile(s). Tel: 226798 (0923)

WELWYN GARDEN CITY

Panshanger Municipal Golf Club, Herns Lane, Welwyn Garden City, Herts. AL7 2ED. Tel: 333350 (0707)
Secretary: Mr Travers			Tel: 332837 (0707)
Professional: Mr M Corlass		Tel: 333350 (0707)
Location: 1 mile north of Welwyn Garden City on Herns Lane.
Description: Open parkland with scenic views overlooking the Mimram Valley.
18 holes, 6,700 yards, Par 72, S.S.S. 72.
Visitors: Welcome. Bookings 7 days in advance.
Green Fees: Weekdays £9.80 per round, weekends £10.80 per round.
Facilities: Lunch. Dinner. Bar Snacks. Full Catering. Changing Room. Golf Shop. Club Hire. Trolley Hire.
Class One Hotel: The Clock, Welwyn Gdn City, 3 mile(s). Tel: 6911 (0707)
Class Two Hotel: Tewin Bury Farm House, Welwyn Gdn City, 1/3 mile(s). Tel: 7793 (0707)

WELWYN GARDEN CITY

Welwyn Garden City Golf Club, Mannicotts, High Oaks Road, Welwyn Garden City, Herts. AL8 7RP.
Secretary: Mr J L Carragher		Tel: 325243 (0707)
Professional: Mr Bishop			Tel: 325525 (0707)
Location: From Welwyn Garden City take A1 north for 1 1/2 miles.
Description: Wooded parkland with lots of ponds, ditches and dells.
18 holes, 6,074 yards, Par 70, S.S.S. 69, Course record 64.
Membership: 600
Visitors: Welcome. Handicap certificate required. Not on Sundays.
Green Fees: Weekdays £25 per round/day, weekends £33 per round.
Facilities: Lunch. Dinner. Bar Snacks. Full Catering. Changing Room. Golf Shop. Trolley Hire. Buggy Hire.
Class One Hotel: The Crest, Welwyn Gdn City, 1 1/2 mile(s). Tel: 324336 (0707)

WHEATHAMPSTEAD

Mid-Herts Golf Club, Gustard Wood, Wheathampstead, St Albans, Herts. AL4 8RS. Tel: 2242 (058283)
Secretary: Mr R Jordan			Tel: 2242 (058283)
Professional: Mr N Brown		Tel: 2788 (058283)
Location: 8 miles north of St Albans on the St Albans to Wheathampstead Road.
Description: Parkland, heathland, well wooded, small greens.
18 holes, 6,094 yards, Par 69, S.S.S. 69, Course record 66.
Membership: 650
Visitors: Welcome. Tuesdays Ladies Day. Wednesday afternoons competitions.
Green Fees: £21 per round, £31 per day.
Facilities: Lunch. Bar Snacks. Full Catering. Changing Room. Golf Shop. Trolley Hire.
Class One Hotel: Glen Eagle, Harpenden, 4 1/2 mile(s). Tel: 760271 (0582)

HUMBERSIDE

BRIDLINGTON

Bridlington Golf Club, Belvedere Road, Bridlington, Humberside. YO15 3NA. Tel: 672092 (0262)
Secretary: Mr C Wilson			Tel: 674679 (0262)
Professional: Mr D Rands		Tel: 674721 (0262)
Location: 2 miles from Bridlington on A165 Hull Road.
Description: Parkland with coastal views.
18 holes, 6,491 yards, Par 71, S.S.S. 71, Course record 65.
Membership: 500
Visitors: Welcome. Wednesday is Ladies day. With members only on Sunday mornings. No jeans on course.
Green Fees: Weekdays £14 per day, weekends £20 per day.
Facilities: Lunch. Bar Snacks. Full Catering. Changing Room. Golf Shop. Trolley Hire.
Class One Hotel: The Expanse, Bridlington, 2 mile(s). Tel: 675347 (0262)
Class Two Hotel: The Harmony Guest House, Bridlington, 2 mile(s). Tel: 671607 (0262)

BRIDLINGTON

Flamborough Head Golf Club, Flamborough, Bridlington, Humberside. YO15 1AR. Tel: 850333 (0262)
Secretary: Mr W R Scarle		Tel: 676494 (0262)
Professional: Mr England
Location: 1 mile from Flamborough church, signposted from Flamborough.
Description: Clifftop links.
18 holes, 5,438 yards, Par 66, S.S.S. 66, Course record 63.
Membership: 600
Visitors: Welcome. Members only Sunday mornings.
Green Fees: Weekdays £12, weekends £16.
Facilities: Lunch. Dinner. Bar Snacks. Full Catering. Changing Room. Golf Shop.
Class One Hotel: Flamborough Hotel, Flamborough, 5 mile(s). Tel: 850284 (0262)

Cade's - Audi Golf Course Guide

Elsham Golf Club, Barton Road, Elsham, Near Brigg, Humberside. DN20 0LS. Tel: 680291 (0652)
Secretary: B P Nazer　　　　　　Tel: 680291 (0652)
Professional: S Brewer　　　　　Tel: 680291 (0652)
Location: Off M180 junc 5, 3 miles from Brigg on Barton Road.
Description: Parkland.
18 holes, 6,411 yards, Par 71, S.S.S. 71, Course record 68.
Membership: 650
Visitors: Welcome. Handicap certificate required. Not Thursdays. With members at weekends.
Green Fees: £20 per round or day.
Facilities: Lunch. Dinner. Bar Snacks. Full Catering. Changing Room. Golf Shop. Club Hire. Trolley Hire.
Class One Hotel: Briggate Lodge, Brigg, 4 mile(s). Tel: 650770 (0652)
Class Two Hotel: Queens' Arms, Brigg, 3 mile(s). Tel: 653174 (0652)

BROUGH

Brough Golf Club, Cave Road, Brough, Humberside. HU15 1HB. Tel: 667374 (0482)
Secretary: Mr W G Burley　　　　Tel: 667291 (0482)
Professional: Mr G Townshill　　Tel: 667483 (0482)
Location: Follow M62 onto A63, turn off at South Cave junc and follow signs.
Description: Parkland.
18 holes, 6,153 yards, Par 68, S.S.S. 69, Course record 66.
Membership: 650
Visitors: Welcome. Handicap certificate required. Letter of Introduction required. With members only at weekends. Ladies day Wednesday. Caddies by arrangement.
Green Fees: Weekdays £22.50 per round, weekends £30.
Facilities: Lunch. Dinner. Bar Snacks. Full Catering. Changing Room. Golf Shop. Club Hire. Trolley Hire.
Class One Hotel: The Crest, Ferriby, 5 mile(s). Tel: 645212 (0482)
Class Two Hotel: Green Dragon, Welton, 2 1/2 mile(s). Tel: 666700 (0482)

CLEETHORPES

Cleethorpes Golf Club, Golf House, Kings Road, Cleethorpes, Humberside. DN35 0PN. Tel: 812059 (0472)
Secretary: Mr G B Standaloft　　Tel: 814060 (0472)
Professional: Mr P Davies　　　Tel: 814060 (0472)
Location: 1 mile south of Cleethorpes on the coast road.
Description: Flat meadowland, intersected by wide dykes.
18 holes, 6,018 yards, Par 70, S.S.S. 69, Course record 64.
Membership: 760
Visitors: Welcome. Ladies day Wednesday afternoon. Men only Saturday afternoons and Sunday mornings.
Green Fees: Weekdays £17, weekends £22, reductions when playing with a member.
Facilities: Lunch. Dinner. Bar Snacks. Full Catering. Changing Room. Golf Shop. Trolley Hire.
Class One Hotel: Kingsway, Cleethorpes, 1 mile(s). Tel: 601122 (0472)
Class Two Hotel: Blundell Park, Cleethorpes, 2 mile(s). Tel: 691970 (0472)

CONISTON

Ganstead Park Golf Club, Longdales Lane, Coniston, Hull, Humberside. HU11 4LB. Tel: 811121 (0482)
Secretary: Mrs J Kirby　　　　　Tel: 874754 (0482)
Professional: Mike Smee　　　　Tel: 811121 (0482)
Description: Flat parkland.
18 holes, 6,495 yards, Par 73, S.S.S. 71.
Visitors: Welcome. Handicap certificate required. Not Sunday a.m.. Not Wednesday 9.30a.m. to 12p.m..
Green Fees: £14 per round.
Facilities: Lunch. Dinner. Bar Snacks. Full Catering. Changing Room. Golf Shop. Club Hire. Trolley Hire.

COTTINGHAM

Hessle Golf Club, Westfield Road, Raywell, Cottingham, Humberside. HU16 5YL. Tel: 650171 (0482)
Secretary: Mr R I Dorsey　　　　Tel: 650171 (0482)
Professional: Mr G Fieldsend　　Tel: 650190 (0482)
Location: 3 miles south-west of Cottingham, follow golf club signs.
Description: Parkland.
Yellow 18 holes, 6,290 yards, Par 72, S.S.S. 70.
White 18 holes, 6,638 yards, Par 72, S.S.S. 72, Course record 67.
Membership: 700
Visitors: Welcome. Tuesday is Ladies day. Not before 11a.m weekends and Bank Holidays.
Green Fees: Weekdays £15 per round, £20 per day. Weekends and Bank Holidays £20 per round.
Facilities: Lunch. Dinner. Bar Snacks. Full Catering. Changing Room. Golf Shop. Trolley Hire.
Class One Hotel: Willowby Manor, Willowby, 5 mile(s). Tel: 652616 (0482)

GRIMSBY

Grimsby Golf Club, Littlecoats Road, Grimsby, Humberside. DN34 4LU. Tel: 342823 (0472)
Secretary: Mr A D Houlihan　　　Tel: 342630 (0472)
Professional: Mr S Houltby　　　Tel: 356981 (0472)
Location: 3 miles south west of Grimsby on the Immingham Road.
Description: Open parkland.
18 holes, 6,058 yards, Par 70, S.S.S. 69, Course record 66.
Membership: 725
Visitors: Welcome. Handicap certificate required. Tuesday afternoons Ladies Day, competitions permitting play all week.
Green Fees: Weekdays £17 per day, weekends £22 per day.
Facilities: Lunch. Dinner. Bar Snacks. Changing Room. Golf Shop. Club Hire. Driving Range. Trolley Hire. Caddies available.
Class One Hotel: Forte Crest, Grimsby. Tel: 350295 (0472)

HORNSEA

Hornsea Golf Club, Rolston Road, Hornsea, Humberside. HU18 1XG. Tel: 535488 (0964)
Secretary: Mr Kirton　　　　　　Tel: 532020 (0964)
Professional: Mr Thompson　　　Tel: 534989 (0964)

Location: From M62 follow signs to Beverley, then to Hornsea Pottery. Golf club is 200 yards past Hornsea Pottery.
Description: Parkland.
18 holes, 6,475 yards, Par 71, S.S.S. 71.
Membership: 600
Visitors: Welcome. With member on Tuesdays and weekends.
Green Fees: £16.50 per round, £23 per day.
Facilities: Lunch. Dinner. Bar Snacks. Full Catering. Changing Room. Golf Shop. Club Hire. Trolley Hire.
Class One Hotel: Tickton Grange, Tickton, 7 mile(s). Tel: 54366 (04012)
Class Two Hotel: Burton Lodge, Brandesburton, 6 mile(s). Tel: 542847 (0964)

HULL
Hull Golf Club, The Hall, 27 Packman Lane, Kirk Ella, Hull, Humberside. HU10 7TJ. Tel: 658919 (0482)
Secretary: Mr Toothill   Tel: 658919 (0482)
Professional: Mr D Jagger   Tel: 653074 (0482)
Location: M62 to A63 turn off at Humber Bridge, northern approach road to Beverley, 4 miles to club, signposted.
Description: Parkland.
18 holes, 6,250 yards, Par 70, S.S.S. 70, Course record 64.
Membership: 780
Visitors: Welcome. Handicap certificate required. With members at weekends. Visitors are advised to telephone Professional in advance.
Green Fees: £23 per round/day.
Facilities: Lunch. Dinner. Bar Snacks. Full Catering. Changing Room. Golf Shop. Club Hire. Trolley Hire.
Class One Hotel: Willowby Manor, Willowby, 1 mile(s). Tel: 652616 (0482)

HULL
Sutton Park Municipal Golf Club, Salthouse Road, Hull, Humberside. HU8 9HF. Tel: 74242 (0482)
Secretary: Mr Platten   Tel: 74242 (0482)
Professional: Mr Rushworth   Tel: 711450 (0482)
Location: 3 miles from Hull city centre on Holdenness Road, turn left to Sutton on Salthouse Road, club on left hand side.
Description: Parkland with small narrow greens.
18 holes, 6,251 yards, Par 70, S.S.S. 70, Course record 63.
Membership: 430
Visitors: Welcome. Bookings only on Sundays.
Green Fees: Weekdays £3.65, weekends £5.10 per round.
Facilities: Lunch. Dinner. Bar Snacks. Full Catering. Changing Room. Golf Shop. Club Hire. Driving Range. Trolley Hire.

IMMINGHAM
Immingham Golf Club, Church Lane, Immingham, Humberside. DN40 2EU. Tel: 575298 (0469)
Professional: N Harding   Tel: 575493 (0469)
Location: Behind St Andrews Church, Immingham.
Description: Parkland.
18 holes, 6,100 yards, Par 71, S.S.S. 69.
Membership: 650
Visitors: Welcome.

Green Fees: £11 per round weekdays, £18 per round weekends and Bank Holidays.
Facilities: Lunch. Dinner. Bar Snacks. Full Catering. Changing Room. Golf Shop. Buggy Hire.

SCUNTHORPE
Grange Park Golf Club, Butterwick Road, Messingham, Scunthorpe, Humberside. DN17 3PP. Tel: 762945 (0724)
Secretary: Ian Cannon   Tel: 762945 (0724)
Location: 5 miles south of Scunthorpe, between Messingham and East Butterwick.
Description: New parkland course offering wide fairways, ideal for the mid to high handicap golfer, whilst providing a challenging game.
9 holes, 2,970 yards, Par 35, S.S.S. 69, Course record 34.
Visitors: Welcome. 8a.m. to dusk.
Green Fees: £4 weekdays, £6 weekends, Juniors (under 16) half price.
Facilities: Changing Room. Golf Shop. Club Hire. Driving Range. Trolley Hire.
Class One Hotel: Wortley House, Scunthorpe, 5 mile(s). Tel: 853344 (0724)
Class Two Hotel: Ivy Lodge Guest House, Scotter, 2 mile(s). Tel: 763723 (0724)

SCUNTHORPE
Holme Hall Golf Club, Holme Lane, Bottesford, Scunthorpe, Humberside. DN16 3RF. Tel: 849185 (0724)
Secretary: G D Smith   Tel: 862078 (0724)
Professional: R McKeirnan   Tel: 851816 (0724)
Location: Approx 3 miles south of Scunthorpe just off M180.
Description: Attractive heathland course. Regular venue of County Championships.
18 holes, 6,475 yards, Par 71, S.S.S. 71, Course record 66.
Membership: 700
Visitors: Welcome. Handicap certificate required. With a member at weekends. No catering Mondays.
Green Fees: £15 per round or day weekdays.
Facilities: Lunch. Dinner. Bar Snacks. Full Catering. Changing Room. Golf Shop. Trolley Hire.
Class One Hotel: Wortley, Scunthorpe, 3 mile(s). Tel: 842223 (0724)
Class Two Hotel: Briggate Lodge Inn, Broughton, 2 mile(s). Tel: 650770 (0652)

SCUNTHORPE
Normanby Golf Club, Normanby Park, Near Scunthorpe, Humberside. DN16 9HU. Tel: 720252 (0724)
Secretary: Mr G Kirk   Tel: 844303 (0724)
Professional: C Mann   Tel: 720226 (0724)
Location: 3 miles north of Scunthorpe on Normanby Road.
Description: Wooded parkland.
White 18 holes, 6,548 yards, Par 72, S.S.S. 71, Course record 68.
Yellow 18 holes, 6,398 yards, Par 72, S.S.S. 70.
Membership: 700
Visitors: Welcome.
Green Fees: Weekdays £9.50 per round, £15 per day. Weekends £15 per round.

Facilities: Lunch. Dinner. Bar Snacks. Full Catering. Changing Room. Golf Shop. Club Hire. Trolley Hire.
Class One Hotel: The Royal, Scunthorpe, 5 mile(s). Tel: 282233 (0724)

SCUNTHORPE

Scunthorpe Golf Club, Burringham Road, Scunthorpe, Humberside. DN17 2AB. Tel: 842913 (0724)
Secretary: Mr E Willsmore   Tel: 866561 (0724)
Professional: Mr A Lawson   Tel: 868972 (0724)
Location: From Scunthorpe towards Barclays Circle on to Scotterbottom Road for 1 1/2 miles, at roundabout turn right, club is 500 yards on left.
Description: Parkland.
18 holes, 6,900 yards, Par 71, S.S.S. 72, Course record 67.
Membership: 900
Visitors: Welcome. Not Sundays. Saturdays with member only. Ladies Tuesday.
Green Fees: Weekdays £16 per round or day, weekends £20 per round or day.
Facilities: Lunch. Dinner. Bar Snacks. Full Catering. Changing Room. Golf Shop. Club Hire. Trolley Hire.
Class One Hotel: Royal, Scunthorpe, 1 mile(s). Tel: 282233 (0724)

ISLE OF MAN

ONCHAN

King Edward Bay Golf Club, Howstrake, Groudle Road, Onchan, Isle of Man. . Tel: 620430 (0624)
Secretary: Miss K Nightingale   Tel: 676794 (0624)
Description: Headland links overlooking Douglas Bay.
18 holes, 5,457 yards, Par 67, S.S.S. 66.
Membership: 360
Visitors: Welcome. Handicap certificate required. Not Sundays before 10a.m..
Green Fees: Weekdays £6 per round, weekends and Bank Holidays £8.
Facilities: Lunch. Dinner. Bar Snacks. Full Catering. Changing Room. Club Hire. Trolley Hire.
Class One Hotel: Empress, Douglas, 2 mile(s). Tel: 661155 (0624)

PEEL

Peel Golf Club, Rheast Lane, Peel, Isle of Man.Tel: 842227 (0624)
Secretary: T P Kissack   Tel: 843456 (0624)
Description: Heathland designed by James Braid.
18 holes, 5,914 yards, Par 69, S.S.S. 68, Course record 62.
Membership: 890
Visitors: Welcome. Handicap certificate required. Advance notice required for parties at weekends.
Green Fees: Weekdays £12 per day, weekends and Bank Holidays £16 per day.
Facilities: Lunch. Dinner. Bar Snacks. Full Catering. Changing Room. Golf Shop. Trolley Hire.
Class One Hotel: Empress, Douglas, 10 mile(s). Tel: 661155 (0624)
Class Two Hotel: Ascot, Douglas, 10 mile(s). Tel: 675081 (0624)

RAMSEY

Ramsey Golf Course, Ramsey, Isle of Man. Tel: 812244 (0624)
Secretary: Mrs S Birchall   Tel: 812244 (0624)
Professional: Mr P Lowry   Tel: 814736 (0624)
Description: Parkland.
18 holes, 6,019 yards, Par 70, S.S.S. 69, Course record 64.
Membership: 1000
Visitors: Welcome. Handicap certificate required. Ladies only Tuesdays a.m.. Not between 10a.m. and 12p.m. or between 2p.m. and 4p.m.. No parties at weekends.
Green Fees: Winter - weekdays £10, weekends £12. Summer - weekdays £15, weekends £18.
Facilities: Lunch. Dinner. Bar Snacks. Full Catering. Changing Room. Golf Shop. Club Hire. Driving Range. Trolley Hire.
Class One Hotel: Grand Island, Ramsey, 2 mile(s). Tel: 812455 (0624)
Class Two Hotel: Eskdale Private Hotel, Ramsey, 2 mile(s). Tel: 813283 (0624)

ISLE OF WIGHT

COWES

Cowes Golf Club, Crossfield Avenue, Cowes, IOW. PO31 8HN. Tel: 292303 (0983)
Secretary: D C Weaver   Tel: 292303 (0983)
Description: Parkland.
9 holes, 5,934 yards, Par 70, S.S.S. 68, Course record 65.
Membership: 300
Visitors: Welcome. Not Sunday mornings or Thursdays between 11a.m. and 3.30p.m..
Green Fees: Weekdays £15, weekends £18.
Facilities: Lunch. Bar Snacks. Changing Room. Club Hire.
Class One Hotel: New Holmwood, Cowes, 2 mile(s). Tel: 292508 (0983)
Class Two Hotel: Cowes Hotel, Cowes, 2 mile(s). Tel: 291541 (0983)

EAST COWES

Osborne Golf Club, Osborne House, East Cowes, IOW. PO32 6JX. Tel: 295421 (0983)
Secretary: Mr Jones   Tel: 295421 (0983)
Professional: Mr A Scullion
Location: Southampton to East Cowes on Red Funnel Ferry, follow road to Osborne House. Golf club is in the grounds of Osborne House.
Description: Flat wooded parkland with some coastal views.
9 holes, 5,934 yards, Par 70, S.S.S. 70, Course record 58.
Membership: 375
Visitors: Welcome. Ladies day Tuesday mornings. Not before noon weekends.
Green Fees: W/days £15 per day, w/ends £18 per day.
Facilities: Lunch. Dinner. Bar Snacks. Full Catering. Changing Room. Golf Shop. Trolley Hire.
Class One Hotel: The Calvert, Newport, 5 mile(s). Tel: 528372 (0983)
Class Two Hotel: The Wheatsheaf, Newport, 5 mile(s). Tel: 523865 (0983)

FRESHWATER

Freshwater Bay Golf Club, Afton Down, Freshwater, IOW. . Tel: 752955 (0983)
Secretary: Mr Smith   Tel: 752955 (0983)
Location: Off Military Road in Freshwater Bay.
Description: Links course overlooking Freshwater Bay, Solent and the Channel.
18 holes, 5,662 yards, Par 68, S.S.S. 68, Course record 64.
Membership: 600
Visitors: Welcome. Handicap certificate required.
Green Fees: Weekdays £16, weekends and Bank Holidays £20.
Facilities: Lunch. Dinner. Bar Snacks. Full Catering. Changing Room. Club Hire. Driving Range. Trolley Hire.
Class One Hotel: Farringford, Freshwater Bay, 1 mile(s). Tel: 752500 (0983)

RYDE

Ryde Golf Club, Binstead Road, Ryde, IOW. PO33 3NF. Tel: 614809 (0983)
Secretary: A Clark   Tel: 614809 (0983)
Description: Parkland.
9 holes, 5,287 yards, Par 66, S.S.S. 66, Course record 67.
Membership: 418
Visitors: Welcome. Handicap certificate required. Not Sunday mornings.
Green Fees: £15 w/days, £20 w/ends and Bank Holidays.
Facilities: Lunch. Dinner. Bar Snacks. Full Catering. Changing Room. Golf Shop.
Class One Hotel: Yelfs, Ryde, 2 mile(s). Tel: 64062 (0983)
Class Two Hotel: Newlands, Ryde, 2 mile(s). Tel: 62719 (0983)

SANDOWN

Shanklin and Sandown Golf Club, The Fairway, Lake, Sandown, IOW. PO36 9PR. Tel: 403170 (0983)
Secretary: Mr Wormald   Tel: 403217 (0983)
Professional: Mr Hammond   Tel: 404424 (0983)
Location: 1/2 mile west of Sandown on A3035.
Description: Heathland and links type course.
18 holes, 6,068 yards, Par 70, S.S.S. 69, Course record 65.
Membership: 700
Visitors: Welcome. Handicap certificate required. Tuesdays Ladies Day. Not before 1p.m. weekends.
Green Fees: Weekdays £19 per round, £23 per day. Weekends £23 per round.
Facilities: Lunch. Dinner. Bar Snacks. Full Catering. Changing Room. Golf Shop. Club Hire. Trolley Hire. Caddies available.

VENTNOR

Ventnor Golf Club, Steephill Down Road, Ventnor, IOW. Tel: 853326 (0983)
Secretary: R Hose   Tel: 853198 (0983)
Description: Undulating downland with sidehill lies. 600 to 700 feet above sea level, good views but windy.
9 holes, 5,752 yards, Par 68, S.S.S. 70, Course record 73.
Membership: 230
Visitors: Welcome.
Green Fees: £12 weekdays, Ladies £10. Sundays £14, Ladies £12.
Facilities: Bar Snacks. Changing Room. Club Hire. Trolley Hire.
Class One Hotel: Royal, Ventnor, 1 mile(s). Tel: 852186 (0983)
Class Two Hotel: Central, Ventnor, 2 mile(s). Tel: 852473 (0983)

KENT

ASHFORD

Ashford (Kent) Golf Club, Sandyhurst Lane, Ashford, Kent. TN25 4NT. Tel: 620180 (0233)
Secretary: A H Story   Tel: 622655 (0233)
Professional: H Sherman   Tel: 629644 (0233)
Location: 1 1/2 miles west of town centre just off A20.
Description: Parkland with streams, good test of golf.
18 holes, 6,246 yards, Par 71, S.S.S. 70, Course record 67.
Membership: 650
Visitors: Welcome. Handicap certificate required Please telephone in advance.
Green Fees: Weekdays £24, weekends £40.
Facilities: Lunch. Dinner. Bar Snacks. Full Catering. Changing Room. Golf Shop. Trolley Hire.
Class One Hotel: International, Ashford, 1 mile(s). Tel: 611444 (0233)
Class Two Hotel: Croft, Ashford, 1 1/2 mile(s). Tel: 622140 (0233)

BIGGIN HILL

Cherry Lodge Golf Club, Jail Lane, Biggin Hill, Kent. TN16 3AX. Tel: 572250 (0959)
Secretary: Mr J R MacArthur   Tel: 576712 (0959)
Professional: N Child   Tel: 572989 (0959)
Description: Undulating parkland.
18 holes, 6,522 yards, Par 72, S.S.S. 72.
Membership: 750
Visitors: Welcome. With a member at weekends.
Green Fees: £29 per round, £36 per day.
Facilities: Lunch. Dinner. Bar Snacks. Full Catering. Changing Room. Golf Shop. Trolley Hire. Buggy Hire.
Class One Hotel: Bromley Court, Bromley, 10 mile(s). Tel: 464 5011 (081)
Class Two Hotel: Kings Arms, Westerham, 5 mile(s). Tel: 62990 (0959)

BROADSTAIRS

North Foreland Golf Club, The Clubhouse, Convent Road, Broadstairs, Kent. CT10 3PU. Tel: 62140 (0843)
Secretary: Mr B J Preston   Tel: 62140 (0843)
Professional: Mr M Lee   Tel: 69628 (0843)
Location: 1 1/2 miles from Broadstairs station, take the coast road.
Description: Chalk base clifftop course with coastal views from every hole.
Long 18 holes, 6,382 yards, Par 71, S.S.S. 71, Course record 65.
Short 18 holes, 1,720 yards, Par 54, Course record 49.
Membership: 1150

Visitors: Welcome. Handicap certificate required. Societies Wednesdays and Fridays.
Green Fees: Weekdays £20 per round, £30 per day. Weekends £30.
Facilities: Lunch. Dinner. Bar Snacks. Full Catering. Changing Room. Golf Shop. Club Hire. Trolley Hire. Buggy Hire.
Class One Hotel: The Fayrness, Kingsgate, 1/2 mile(s). Tel: 61103 (0843)
Class Two Hotel: The Rothsay, Broadstairs, 1 1/2 mile(s). Tel: 62646 (0843)

CRANBROOK

Cranbrook Golf Club, Benenden Road, Cranbrook, Kent. TN17 4AL. Tel: 712833 (0580)
Location: M25 junc 5. A21 towards Hastings, turn left onto A62 towards Cranbrook, then Sissinghurst, turn right at Bull Public House, 2 1/2 miles on
Description: Wooded parkland.
18 holes, 6,351 yards, Par 70, S.S.S. 70, Course record 65.
Membership: 450
Visitors: Welcome. Not Tuesday or Thursday. Not before 10.30 a.m. weekdays or before 11.30 a.m. weekends.
Green Fees: Weekdays £19, weekends £27.50.
Facilities: Lunch. Dinner. Bar Snacks. Full Catering. Changing Room. Driving Range. Trolley Hire.
Class One Hotel: Kennel Holt Country House, Cranbrook, 1 1/2 mile(s). Tel: 712032 (0580)
Class Two Hotel: Willersley, Cranbrook, 1 mile(s). Tel: 713555 (0580)

DARTFORD

Dartford Golf Club Ltd., The Clubhouse, Dartford Heath, Dartford, Kent. DA1 2TN. Tel: 223616 (0322)
Secretary: Margaret Gronow   Tel: 226455 (0322)
Professional: A Blackburn   Tel: 226409 (0322)
Location: Backing onto A2, 1 mile from Dartford Tunnel and M25.
Description: Flat Parkland.
18 holes, 5,914 yards, Par 69, S.S.S. 68.
Visitors: Welcome. Handicap certificate required. With member at weekends. Please telephone to reserve weekdays. Catering only if booked in advance.
Green Fees: On application.
Facilities: Changing Room. Golf Shop.
Class One Hotel: Royal Victoria, Dartford, 1 mile(s). Tel: 223104 (0322)

DEAL

Royal Cinque Ports Golf Club, Golf Road, Deal, Kent. CT14 6RF. Tel: 374007 (0304)
Secretary: C W Greaves   Tel: 374007 (0304)
Professional: A Reynolds   Tel: 374170 (0304)
Location: A258 from Dover, north end of Deal.
Description: Traditional links, site of many national championships.
18 holes, 6,407 yards, Par 70, S.S.S. 71, Course record 65.
Membership: 700
Visitors: Welcome. Handicap certificate required. Letter of Introduction required. Not weekends or Wednesdays a.m., some catering restrictions apply, please telephone in advance.

Cade's - Audi Golf Course Guide

Green Fees: Summer £50 per day, £40 after 1 p.m.
Facilities: Lunch. Bar Snacks. Changing Room. Golf Shop. Club Hire. Driving Range. Trolley Hire. Buggy Hire. Caddies available.
Class One Hotel: Royal, Deal, 1 mile(s). Tel: 375555 (0304)
Class Two Hotel: Chequers, On course, 1/2 mile(s). Tel: 374289 (0304)

DEAL

Walmer and Kingsdown Golf Club, The Leas, Kingsdown, Deal, Kent. CT14 8ET. Tel: 373256 (0304)
Secretary: B W Cockerill   Tel: 373256 (0304)
Professional: I A Coleman   Tel: 363017 (0304)
Location: Signposted on Dover-Deal road A258 at Ringwould, 5 miles from Dover.
Description: Seaside links on White Cliffs.
18 holes, 6,451 yards, Par 72, S.S.S. 71.
Membership: 650
Visitors: Welcome. Handicap certificate required. Not before 12 noon weekends and Bank Holidays.
Green Fees: Weekdays £20, Weekends £22.
Facilities: Lunch. Dinner. Bar Snacks. Full Catering. Changing Room. Golf Shop. Club Hire. Trolley Hire.
Class One Hotel: Royal, Deal, 4 mile(s). Tel: 375555 (0304)
Class Two Hotel: Blencathra, Kingsdown, 1/2 mile(s). Tel: 373725 (0304)

FAVERSHAM

Faversham Golf Club Ltd., Belmont Park, Faversham, Kent. ME13 0PJ. Tel: 890561 (0795)
Secretary: David Christie   Tel: 890561 (0795)
Professional: Gordon Nixon   Tel: 890275 (0795)
Location: M2 junc 6 Faversham-Ashford. Turn towards Faversham then Sittingbourne, first left turn Brogdale Road. Follow golf club signs.
Description: Parkland.
18 holes, 6,030 yards, Par 70, S.S.S. 69, Course record 65.
Membership: 700
Visitors: Welcome. Handicap certificate required. With members at weekends.
Green Fees: £21 per round, £28 per day.
Facilities: Lunch. Dinner. Bar Snacks. Full Catering. Changing Room. Golf Shop. Club Hire. Trolley Hire. Buggy Hire.

HAWKHURST

Hawkhurst Golf Club, High Street, Hawkhurst, Kent. TN18 4JS. Tel: 752396 (0580)
Secretary: Richard C Fowles   Tel: 752396 (0580)
Professional: Tony Collins   Tel: 753600 (0580)
Location: On A268 from Hawkhurst to Flimwell.
Description: Parkland. 9 hole course with eighteen different tee positions.
9 holes, 5,769 yards, Par 72, S.S.S. 68, Course record 70.
Membership: 480
Visitors: Welcome. Handicap certificate required. Some catering restrictions apply, please telephone in advance.
Green Fees: 9 holes £9, 18 holes £18. With member £10. Day ticket £25.

89

Facilities: Lunch. Dinner. Bar Snacks. Full Catering. Changing Room. Golf Shop. Trolley Hire. Buggy Hire.
Class One Hotel: Tudor Court, Cranbrook, 6 mile(s). Tel: 752312 (0580)
Class Two Hotel: Queens Head, Hawkhurst, 1 mile(s). Tel: 753577 (0580)

LONGFIELD

Corinthian Golf Club, Fawkham Road, Fawkham, Longfield, Kent. DA3 8LZ. Tel: 707559 (0474)
Secretary: John Wood   Tel: 707559 (0474)
Location: South-east of Dartford.
Description: Nine holes with astro-turf greens and tees.
9 holes, 6,045 yards, Par 72, S.S.S. 70, Course record 79.
Membership: 400
Visitors: Welcome. Not weekends before noon. Some catering restrictions apply, please telephone in advance.
Green Fees: £10, £6 with member.
Facilities: Bar Snacks. Full Catering. Changing Room.
Class One Hotel: Brands Hatch Thistle, West Kingsdown, 2 1/2 mile(s). Tel: 854900 (0474)

MAIDSTONE

Bearsted Golf Club, Ware Street, Bearsted, Maidstone, Kent. ME14 4PQ. Tel: 38198 (0622)
Secretary: Mrs L M Siems   Tel: 38198 (0622)
Professional: Tim Simpson   Tel: 38024 (0622)
Location: Junc 7 off M20.
Description: Parkland with North Down views.
18 holes, 6,253 yards, Par , S.S.S. 70.
Membership: 700
Visitors: Welcome. Handicap certificate required. Letter of Introduction required.Not Tuesday mornings. With members at weekends. Please telephone in advance.
Green Fees: £22 per round, £30 per day.
Facilities: Lunch. Dinner. Bar Snacks. Full Catering. Changing Room. Golf Shop. Trolley Hire.
Class One Hotel: Stakis Country Court, Maidstone, 1 1/2 mile(s). Tel: 34322 (0622)

MAIDSTONE

Leeds Castle Golf Course, Leeds Castle, Leeds, Maidstone, Kent. ME17 1PL. Tel: 880467 (0622)
Secretary: Jill Skinner   Tel: 880467 (0622)
Professional: Chris Miller PGA   Tel: 880467 (0622)
Location: M20, A20 near Maidstone.
Description: Nine hole course in the grounds of Leeds Castle.
9 holes, 2,880 yards, Par 34, Course record 32.
Visitors: Welcome. Bookings taken 6 days in advance. Catering is provided in The Parkgate Inn situated in the Golf car park.
Green Fees: £8.50 for 9 holes.
Facilities: Lunch. Dinner. Bar Snacks. Full Catering. Changing Room. Golf Shop. Club Hire. Trolley Hire.
Class One Hotel: Great Danes, Hollingbourne, 1 mile(s). Tel: 30022 (0622)
Class Two Hotel: Sonnenhof Bed and Breakfast, Maidstone, 4 mile(s). Tel: 670537 (0622)

MAIDSTONE

West Malling Golf Club, London Road, Addington, Maidstone, Kent. ME19 5AR. Tel: 844795 (0732)
Secretary: M R Ellis   Tel: 844795 (0732)
Professional: P Foston   Tel: 844022 (0732)
Description: Parkland.
Spitfire 18 holes, 6,142 yards, Par 70, S.S.S. 70, Course record 68.
Hurricane 18 holes, 6,011 yards, Par 70, S.S.S. 69, Course record 71.
Visitors: Welcome. Handicap certificate required. With members at weekends, not before noon.
Green Fees: £18 per round, £25 per day.
Facilities: Lunch. Dinner. Bar Snacks. Full Catering. Changing Room. Golf Shop. Trolley Hire. Buggy Hire.
Class One Hotel: Larkfield Priory, Maidstone, 3 mile(s). Tel: 846858 (0732)

RAMSGATE

St Augustines Golf Club, Cottington Road, Cliffsend, Ramsgate, Kent. CT12 5JN. Tel: 590333 (0843)
Secretary: R James   Tel: 590333 (0843)
Professional: D B Scott   Tel: 590222 (0843)
Description: Attractive parkland course, not long but tight and challenging for the club golfer.
White 18 holes, 5,197 yards, Par 69, S.S.S. 65, Course record 59.
Yellow 18 holes, 4,999 yards, Par 69, S.S.S. 64.
Membership: 550
Visitors: Welcome. Handicap certificate required.
Green Fees: Weekdays £20, weekends and Bank Holidays £22.
Facilities: Lunch. Dinner. Bar Snacks. Full Catering. Changing Room. Golf Shop. Trolley Hire. Buggy Hire.
Class One Hotel: The Bell, Sandwich, 4 mile(s). Tel: 613388 (0304)
Class Two Hotel: St Hilary, Ramsgate, 3 mile(s). Tel: 591427 (0843)

ROCHESTER

Rochester and Cobham Park Golf Club, Park Pale, By Rochester, Kent. ME2 3UL. Tel: 3411 (047482)
Secretary: J W Irvine   Tel: 3411 (047482)
Professional: M Henderson   Tel: 3658 (047482)
Location: On A2, 2 miles east of Gravesend.
Description: Undulating parkland.
18 holes, 6,450 yards, Par 72, S.S.S. 71, Course record 66.
Membership: 650
Visitors: Welcome. Handicap certificate required. Societies Tuesdays and Thursdays. Not weekends.
Green Fees: £25.
Facilities: Lunch. Dinner. Bar Snacks. Full Catering. Changing Room. Golf Shop. Club Hire. Trolley Hire.
Class One Hotel: Inn On The Lake, Shorne, 2 mile(s). Tel: 3333 (047482)
Class Two Hotel: The Cedars, Rochester, 2 mile(s). Tel: 290277 (0634)

SANDWICH

Prince's Golf Club, Princes Drive, Sandwich Bay, Sandwich, Kent. CT13 9QB. Tel: 611118 (0304)

Secretary: Geoff Ramm Tel: 611118 (0304)
Professional: Phil Sparks Tel: 613797 (0304)
Location: Sandwich Bay 4 1/4 miles from Sandwich railway station.
Description: On traditional links terrain. One of the Great British tests of golf in 3 loops, each of 9 holes which can be amalgamated to make three seperate championship courses, all used for pro. golf.
Himalayas/Shore 18 holes, 6,500 yards, Par 71, S.S.S. 71.
Shore/Dunes 18 holes, 6,690 yards, Par 72, S.S.S. 72.
Membership: 450
Visitors: Welcome. Handicap certificate required.
Green Fees: Weekdays £26.50 per round, £29 per day. Saturdays £31 per round, £34 per day. Sundays £31 per round, £39 per day.
Facilities: Lunch. Dinner. Bar Snacks. Full Catering. Changing Room. Golf Shop. Club Hire. Driving Range. Trolley Hire. Buggy Hire.
Class One Hotel: The Bell, Sandwich, 4 1/2 mile(s). Tel: 613388 (0304)
Class Two Hotel: Fleur de Lys, Sandwich, 4 1/2 mile(s). Tel: 611131 (0304)

SANDWICH

Royal St Georges Golf Club, Sandwich, Kent. CT13 9PB. Tel: 613090 (0304)
Secretary: Mr G E Watts Tel: 613090 (0304)
Professional: Niall Cameron Tel: 615236 (0304)
Location: 1 1/2 miles from Sandwich.
Description: Links.
18 holes, 6,534 yards, Par .
Membership: 675
Visitors: Welcome. Handicap certificate required. Letter of Introduction required.Not at weekends. Caddies must be booked in advance.
Green Fees: £45 per round, £65 per day.
Facilities: Lunch. Dinner. Bar Snacks. Full Catering. Changing Room. Golf Shop. Club Hire. Trolley Hire. Caddies available.
Class One Hotel: The Bell, Sandwich, 1 1/2 mile(s). Tel: 613380 (0304)
Class Two Hotel: St Crispin Inn, Worth, 2 1/2 mile(s). Tel: 612081 (0304)

SEVENOAKS

Darenth Valley Golf Club Ltd., Station Road, Shoreham, Near Sevenoaks, Kent. TN14 7SA. Tel: 2944 (09592)
Secretary: R N Morgan Tel: 2944 (09592)
Professional: Scott Fotheringham Tel: 2922 (09592)
Description: Parkland.
18 holes, 6,356 yards, Par 71, S.S.S. 71, Course record 68.
Visitors: Welcome. Functions and societies catered for by arrangement with clubhouse manager.
Green Fees: £10 weekdays, £13 weekends and Bank Holidays.
Facilities: Lunch. Dinner. Bar Snacks. Full Catering. Changing Room. Golf Shop. Club Hire. Trolley Hire.

SEVENOAKS

Knole Park Golf Club, Seal Hollow Road, Sevenoaks, Kent. TN15 0HJ. Tel: 452709 (0732)

Secretary: D J L Hoppe Tel: 452150 (0732)
Professional: P E Gill Tel: 451740 (0732)
Location: 1 mile south-east of Sevenoaks.
Description: Parkland.
18 holes, 6,249 yards, Par 70, S.S.S. 70.
Membership: 550
Visitors: Welcome. Handicap certificate required. Not weekends or Bank Holidays. Always by appointment only.
Green Fees: 18 holes £25.50, 36 holes £36.
Facilities: Lunch. Full Catering. Changing Room. Golf Shop. Trolley Hire.
Class One Hotel: Sevenoaks Park, Sevenoaks, 1/4 mile(s). Tel: 454245 (0732)

SEVENOAKS

Wrotham Heath Golf Club, Seven Mile Lane, Comp, Sevenoaks, Kent. TN15 8QZ. Tel: 884800 (0732)
Secretary: Mr T J Fensom Tel: 884800 (0732)
Professional: Mr H Dearden Tel: 883854 (0732)
9 holes, 5,918 yards, Par 69, S.S.S. 68, Course record 66.
Membership: 376
Visitors: Welcome. Handicap certificate required. Letter of Introduction required.With member at weekends. Not Bank Holidays.
Green Fees: £20 per round, £30 per day.
Facilities: Lunch. Dinner. Bar Snacks. Full Catering. Changing Room. Golf Shop. Trolley Hire.
Class One Hotel: Post House, Wrotham Heath, 1 mile(s). Tel: 883311 (0732)

SHEERNESS

Sheerness Golf Club, Power Station Road, Sheerness, Kent. ME12 3AE. Tel: 662585 (0795)
Secretary: J W Gavins Tel: 662585 (0795)
Professional: A Gillard Tel: 666840 (0795)
Location: M20 or M2 to A249 then A250, 1/2 mile east of Sheerness.
Description: Marsh/meadowland course with many water hazards.
18 holes, 6,460 yards, Par 72, S.S.S. 71, Course record 68.
Membership: 650
Visitors: Welcome. With members only at weekends.
Green Fees: £15, weekends £12.
Facilities: Lunch. Dinner. Bar Snacks. Full Catering. Changing Room. Golf Shop. Trolley Hire.
Class One Hotel: Coniston, Sittingbourne, 10 mile(s). Tel: 472131 (0795)
Class Two Hotel: Abbey Motel, Minster, 2 1/2 mile(s). Tel: 872873 (0795)

SITTINGBOURNE

Sittingbourne & Milton Regis G C, Wormdale, Newington, Sittingbourne, Kent. ME9 7PX. Tel: 842261 (0795)
Secretary: H D G Wylie Tel: 842261 (0795)
Professional: J Hearn Tel: 842775 (0795)
Location: 1 mile north of M2 junc 5 (A249).
Description: Undulating wooded parkland.
18 holes, 6,121 yards, Par 70, S.S.S. 69.
Membership: 624
Visitors: Welcome. Handicap certificate required. Letter of Introduction required.Not weekends.

Green Fees: 18 holes £20, 36 holes £32.
Facilities: Lunch. Dinner. Bar Snacks. Full Catering. Changing Room. Golf Shop. Trolley Hire.
Class One Hotel: Newington Manor, Newington, 1 mile(s). Tel: 842053 (0795)

TENTERDEN

Tenterden Golf Club, Woodchurch Road, Tenterden, Kent. TN30 7DR. Tel: 3987 (05806)
Secretary: D F Hunt   Tel: 3987 (05806)
Professional: G Potter   Tel: 2409 (05806)
Location: On B2067, 1 mile east of town.
Description: Parkland.
18 holes, 6,030 yards, Par 70, S.S.S. 69, Course record 64.
Membership: 650
Visitors: Welcome. With members at weekends. Ladies Tuesday. Busy Wednesdays.
Green Fees: £18 per day.
Facilities: Lunch. Dinner. Bar Snacks. Full Catering. Changing Room. Golf Shop. Trolley Hire. Buggy Hire.
Class One Hotel: White Lion, Tenterden, 1 mile(s). Tel: 5077 (05806)
Class Two Hotel: Little Silver Country Hotel, Tenterden, 1 1/2 mile(s). Tel: 850321 (0233)

TUNBRIDGE WELLS

Tunbridge Wells Golf Club, Langton Road, Tunbridge Wells, Kent. TN4 8XH. Tel: 523034 (0892)
Secretary: E M Goulden   Tel: 536918 (0892)
Professional: K Smithson   Tel: 541386 (0892)
Location: Behind Spa Hotel, access to rear of Marchants Garage.
Description: Undulating parkland course, surrounded by trees, with lake and water hazards.
9 holes, 4,560 yards, Par 65, S.S.S. 62, Course record 59.
Visitors: Welcome. Handicap certificate required. With members at weekends. Some catering restrictions apply, please telephone in advance.
Green Fees: £21 per round, £28 per day.
Facilities: Lunch. Dinner. Bar Snacks. Full Catering. Changing Room. Golf Shop. Trolley Hire.
Class One Hotel: Royal Wells, Tunbridge Wells, 1/2 mile(s). Tel: 511188 (0892)
Class Two Hotel: The Swan, Tunbridge Wells, 1 mile(s). Tel: 541450 (0892)

LANCASHIRE

ACCRINGTON

Accrington Golf Club, Devon Avenue, Oswaldtwistle, Accrington, Lancs. BB5 4LS. Tel: 232734 (0254)
Secretary: J Pilkington   Tel: 235070 (0254)
Professional: W Harling   Tel: 231091 (0254)
Location: On A679 2mls from Blackburn.
Description: Pleasant moorland.
18 holes, 5,954 yards, Par 70, S.S.S. 69, Course record 64.
Membership: 600
Visitors: Welcome.
Green Fees: Weekdays £13, weekends £18.
Facilities: Lunch. Dinner. Bar Snacks. Full Catering. Changing Room. Golf Shop. Club Hire. Trolley Hire.
Class One Hotel: Dunqenhalgh, Accrington, 2 mile(s). Tel: 398021 (0254)

BARNOLDSWICK

Ghyll Golf Club, Ghyll Brow, Barnoldswick, Lancs. BB8 6JQ. Tel: 842764 (0282)
Secretary: Mr Gill   Tel: 813205 (0282)
Location: 4 miles from Colne, between Colne and Skipton.
Description: Open undulating parkland, with panoramic views of the Lake District and Pennines. 9 holes played twice.
9 holes, 5,900 yards, Par 68, S.S.S. 68, Course record 64.
Membership: 350
Visitors: Welcome. Tuesdays Ladies Day. With members only Friday evenings and Sundays.
Green Fees: Weekdays £12, weekends £16.
Facilities: Changing Room.

BLACKBURN

Blackburn Golf Club, Beardwood Brow, Blackburn, Lancs. BB2 7AX. Tel: 51122 (0254)
Secretary: P D Haydock   Tel: 51122 (0254)
Professional: A Rodwell   Tel: 55942 (0254)
Description: Challenging 18 hole course with superb views of Lancashire coast and Pennine hills.
18 holes, 6,147 yards, Par 71, S.S.S. 70, Course record 63.
Membership: 800
Visitors: Welcome. Not competition days or Tuesdays.
Green Fees: £16 weekdays, £19 weekends. (Reductions for parties of 12 or more).
Facilities: Lunch. Dinner. Bar Snacks. Full Catering. Changing Room. Golf Shop. Trolley Hire.
Class One Hotel: Moat House, Blackburn, 1/2 mile(s). Tel: 264441 (0254)

BLACKBURN

Whalley Golf Club, Portfield Lane, Whalley, Blackburn, Lancs. BB6 9DR. Tel: 822236 (0254)
Secretary: R Bolsover   Tel: 824259 (0254)
Professional: H Smith   Tel: 824766 (0254)
Description: Parkland course with splendid views of Ribble Valley.
9 holes, 5,912 yards, Par , S.S.S. 69.
Membership: 320
Visitors: Welcome. Not Thursdays p.m. or weekends.
Green Fees: £12.
Facilities: Lunch. Dinner. Bar Snacks. Full Catering. Changing Room. Golf Shop. Club Hire. Trolley Hire.

BLACKPOOL

Blackpool North Shore Golf Club, Devonshire Road, Blackpool, Lancs. FY2 0RD. Tel: 51017 (0253)
Secretary: D S Walker   Tel: 52054 (0253)
Professional: Brendan Ward   Tel: 54640 (0253)
Location: 1 mile north of town centre.
Description: Undulating parkland.
18 holes, 6,400 yards, Par 71, S.S.S. 71, Course record 67.
Membership: 550
Visitors: Welcome. Not Thursdays. Spare tee times rarely available at weekends.

Cade's - Audi Golf Course Guide

Green Fees: Weekdays £21 per round, weekends £30.
Facilities: Lunch. Dinner. Bar Snacks. Full Catering. Changing Room. Golf Shop. Club Hire. Trolley Hire.

BLACKPOOL

Blackpool Park Golf Club, North Park Drive, Blackpool, Lancs. FY3 8LS. Tel: 393960 (0253)
Secretary: Terence Lee   Tel: 397916 (0253)
Professional: Brian Purdie   Tel: 396001 (0253)
Location: Within the boundary of Stanley Park.
Description: Parkland.
18 holes, 6,061 yards, Par 69, S.S.S. 69, Course record 64.
Membership: 700
Visitors: Welcome.
Green Fees: £7.50 weekdays, £8.50 weekends and Bank Holidays.
Facilities: Lunch. Dinner. Bar Snacks. Full Catering. Changing Room. Golf Shop. Club Hire. Trolley Hire.
Class Two Hotel: Sheraton, Blackpool, 3 mile(s). Tel: 52723 (0253)

BURNLEY

Burnley Golf Club, Glen View, Burnley, Lancs. BB11 3RW. Tel: 21045 (0282)
Secretary: G J Butterfield   Tel: 54434 (0282)
Professional: W Tighe   Tel: 55266 (0282)
Location: 300 yards from junc of A56 and A646 on Glen View Road.
Description: Moorland, superb views.
18 holes, 5,899 yards, Par 69, S.S.S. 69, Course record 65.
Membership: 350
Visitors: Welcome. Handicap certificate required. Not Saturdays. Thursday is Ladies day. Some catering restrictions apply, please telephone in advance.
Green Fees: Weekdays £14, weekends and Bank Holidays £23.
Facilities: Lunch. Dinner. Bar Snacks. Full Catering. Changing Room. Golf Shop. Trolley Hire.
Class One Hotel: Keirby, Burnley, 2 mile(s). Tel: 27611 (0282)
Class Two Hotel: Rosehill House, Burnley, 1 mile(s). Tel: 53931 (0282)

CHORLEY

Chorley Golf Club, Hall O'the Hill, Heath Charnock, Chorley, Lancs. PR6 9HX. Tel: 480263 (0257)
Secretary: A K Tyrer   Tel: 480263 (0257)
Professional: Paul Wesselingh Tel: 481245 (0257)
Location: Just off A673 at junc with A6 south of Chorley.
Description: Challenging scenic course.
18 holes, 6,317 yards, Par 71, S.S.S. 70, Course record 65.
Membership: 500
Visitors: Welcome. Handicap certificate required. Not Mondays, weekends or Bank Holidays
Green Fees: £20 per round, £22.50 per day.
Facilities: Lunch. Dinner. Bar Snacks. Full Catering. Changing Room. Golf Shop. Trolley Hire.
Class One Hotel: Park Hall, Charnock Rich., 6 mile(s). Tel: 452090 (0257)
Class Two Hotel: Gladmar, Adlington, 2 mile(s). Tel: 480398 (0257)

CHORLEY

Shaw Hill Hotel Golf & Country Club, Preston Road, Whittle-le-Woods, Chorley, Lancs. PR6 7PP. Tel: 269221 (0257)
Secretary: Bernard Brodrick   Tel: 269221 (0257)
Professional: David Clark   Tel: 279222 (0257)
Location: 1 mile north of junc 8 M61, 2 miles from junc 28 M6.
Description: Mature rolling parkland with lakes.
18 holes, 6,405 yards, Par 72, S.S.S. 71, Course record 67.
Membership: 500
Visitors: Welcome. Handicap certificate required. Buggy hire summer only.
Green Fees: Weekdays £30 per round, weekends £40 per round.
Facilities: Lunch. Dinner. Bar Snacks. Full Catering. Changing Room. Golf Shop. Club Hire. Driving Range. Trolley Hire. Caddies available.
Class One Hotel: Shawhill, On course.. Tel: 269221 (0257)

COLNE

Colne Golf Club, Law Farm, Old Skipton Road, Colne, Lancs. BB8 7EB. Tel: 863391 (0282)
Secretary: K Hargreaves   Tel: 864907 (0282)
Location: Leave Colne End off M65 carry on to next roundabout, take extreme left exit up hill for 3/4 mile.
Description: Flat moorland course with many trees in play.
9 holes, 5,961 yards, Par 70, S.S.S. 69, Course record 63.
Membership: 300
Visitors: Welcome. Not on competition days. Two balls only on Thursdays. Not on Bank Holidays.
Green Fees: £10 weekdays, £12 weekends.
Facilities: Lunch. Dinner. Bar Snacks. Full Catering. Changing Room.
Class One Hotel: Keirby, Burnley, 6 mile(s). Tel: 27611 (0282)
Class Two Hotel: Stirk House, Gisburn, 6 mile(s). Tel: 445581 (0200)

DARWEN

Darwen Golf Club, Winter Hill, Darwen, Lancs. BB3 0LB. Tel: 701287 (0254)
Secretary: J Kenyon   Tel: 704367 (0254)
Professional: Wayne Lennon   Tel: 776370 (0254)
Location: On A666 approx 1 1/2 miles from town centre.
Description: Moorland.
18 holes, 5,752 yards, Par 68, S.S.S. 68, Course record 66.
Membership: 600
Visitors: Welcome. Handicap certificate required. Letter of Introduction required. Not Tuesdays and Saturdays. Sundays by prior arrangement. Some catering restrictions apply, please teleph
Green Fees: Weekdays £15, weekends £20.
Facilities: Lunch. Dinner. Bar Snacks. Full Catering. Changing Room. Golf Shop.

FLEETWOOD

Fleetwood Golf Club, Golf House, Princes Way, Fleetwood, Lancs. FY7 8AF. Tel: 873661 (0253)

Secretary: H Fielding Msc Bsc Tel: 873661 (0253)
Professional: C Burgess Tel: 873661 (0253)
Location: 1 mile west of Fleetwood.
Description: Links course adjacent to beach and sea. White 18 holes, 6,723 yards, Par 72, S.S.S. 72. Yellow 18 holes, 6,433 yards, Par 72, S.S.S. 71, Course record 64.
Visitors: Welcome. Handicap certificate required.
Green Fees: £20 weekdays, £25 weekends.
Facilities: Lunch. Dinner. Bar Snacks. Full Catering. Changing Room. Golf Shop. Trolley Hire.
Class One Hotel: North Euston, Fleetwood, 1 1/2 mile(s). Tel: 876525 (0253)
Class Two Hotel: Boston, Fleetwood, 1 1/4 mile(s). Tel: 874644 (0253)

HASLINGDEN
Rossendale Golf Club, Ewood Lane Head, Haslingden, Lancs. BB4 6LH. Tel: 831339 (0706)
Secretary: Mr J R Swain Tel: 831339 (0706)
Professional: S Nicholls Tel: 213616 (0706)
Description: Parkland with superb views. Interesting short holes nos. 1 and 13.
18 holes, 6,293 yards, Par 72, S.S.S. 70, Course record 68.
Membership: 700
Visitors: Welcome. Not Saturdays during the season.
Green Fees: Weekdays £20, weekends and Bank Holidays £25.
Facilities: Lunch. Dinner. Bar Snacks. Full Catering. Changing Room. Golf Shop. Trolley Hire.
Class One Hotel: Red Hall, Bury, 5 mile(s). Tel: 82247 (0706)
Class Two Hotel: Sykeside, Haslingden, 1 mile(s). Tel: 831163 (0706)

HEYSHAM
Heysham Golf Club, Trumacar Park, Middleton Road, Heysham, Lancs. LA3 3TH. Tel: 851240 (0524)
Secretary: Mr F A Blond Tel: 851011 (0524)
Professional: S Fletcher Tel: 852000 (0524)
Location: 5 miles from M6 via Lancaster and Morecambe.
Description: Wooded parkland.
18 holes, 6,338 yards, Par 69, S.S.S. 70, Course record 65.
Membership: 1000
Visitors: Welcome. Handicap certificate required. Not weekends.
Green Fees: £20.
Facilities: Lunch. Dinner. Bar Snacks. Full Catering. Changing Room. Golf Shop. Trolley Hire.

LANCASTER
Lancaster Golf and Country Club, Ashton Hall, Ashton-with-Stodday, Lancaster, Lancs. LA2 0AJ. Tel: 751247 (0524)
Secretary: Mrs J Hayhurst Tel: 751247 (0524)
Professional: Mr David Sutcliffe Tel: 751802 (0524)
Location: South of Lancaster, Glasson Dock Road.
Description: Parkland.
18 holes, 6,465 yards, Par 71, S.S.S. 71.
Membership: 950

Visitors: Welcome. Handicap certificate required. Not at weekends.
Green Fees: £25.
Facilities: Lunch. Dinner. Bar Snacks. Full Catering. Golf Shop.

LANCASTER
Lansil Golf Club, Caton Road, Lancaster, Lancs. LA1 3PE. Tel: 39269 (0524)
Secretary: Derrick Crutchley Tel: 418007 (0524)
Location: M6 junc 34. A683 towards Lancaster, 3/4 from motorway.
Description: Parkland. Quite hilly.
9 holes, 5,608 yards, Par , S.S.S. 67.
Membership: 450
Visitors: Welcome. Handicap certificate required. Not competition days or Sundays
Green Fees: £6 with a member, £12 without.
Facilities: Lunch. Bar Snacks. Changing Room.
Class One Hotel: Forte Post House, Lancaster, 1/8 mile(s). Tel: 65999 (0524)

LYTHAM ST ANNES
Royal Lytham and St Annes Golf Club, Links Gate, Lytham St Annes, Lancs. FY8 3LQ. Tel: 724206 (0253)
Secretary: Major A S Craven Tel: 724206 (0253)
Professional: E Birchenough Tel: 720094 (0253)
Location: 1 mile from centre of St Annes.
Description: Championship links course.
18 holes, 6,673 yards, Par 71, S.S.S. 73, Course record 65.
Visitors: Welcome. Handicap certificate required. Letter of Introduction required. Between 9.30 a.m. and 12 noon and 2.30 and 4.00 p.m. Not weekends or Tuesdays a.m. Caddies by arrangeme
Green Fees: On application.
Facilities: Lunch. Dinner. Bar Snacks. Full Catering. Changing Room. Golf Shop. Driving Range. Trolley Hire.

MORECAMBE
Morecambe Golf Club, Bare, Morecambe, Lancs. Morecambe, LA4 6AJ. Tel: 418050 (0524)
Secretary: T H Glover Tel: 412841 (0524)
Professional: P De Valle Tel: 415596 (0524)
Location: On A589 coastal road, leaving Morecambe towards Carnforth.
Description: Parkland course offering superb views affected by sea breezes.
18 holes, 5,766 yards, Par 67, S.S.S. 68.
Membership: 800
Visitors: Welcome. Handicap certificate required. Tees are reserved Monday to Saturday 8.00-9.30 a.m. and Sundays until 11.30 and again 12.00-1.30 p.m.
Green Fees: Weekdays £19, weekends and Bank Holidays £24.
Facilities: Lunch. Dinner. Bar Snacks. Full Catering. Changing Room. Golf Shop. Trolley Hire.
Class One Hotel: The Elms, Morecambe, 1/4 mile(s). Tel: 411501 (0524)

Cade's - Audi Golf Course Guide

NELSON

Nelson Golf Club, King's Causeway, Brierfield, Nelson, Lancs. BB9 0EU. Tel: 614583 (0282)
Secretary: R W Baldwin   Tel: 611834 (0282)
Professional: M J Herbert   Tel: 617000 (0282)
Location: 2 miles from junc 12 M65.
Description: Moorland with trees.
18 holes, 5,967 yards, Par 70, S.S.S. 69, Course record 65.
Membership: 500
Visitors: Welcome. Handicap certificate required. Not Thursdays or Saturdays. Some catering restrictions apply, please telephone in advance.
Green Fees: Weekdays £16, weekends £18.
Facilities: Lunch. Dinner. Bar Snacks. Full Catering. Changing Room. Golf Shop. Trolley Hire.
Class One Hotel: Oaks, Burnley, 1 1/2 mile(s). Tel: 414141 (0282)
Class Two Hotel: Higher Trap, Simonstone, 3 mile(s). Tel: 72781 (0282)

PRESTON

Ashton and Lea Golf Club, Tudor Avenue, Lea, Preston, Lea, Lancs. PR4 0XA. Tel: 726480 (0772)
Secretary: Mr M G Gibbs   Tel: 735282 (0772)
Professional: Mr P G Laugher   Tel: 720374 (0772)
Description: Parkland with water hazards.
18 holes, 6,289 yards, Par 71, S.S.S. 70.
Membership: 850
Visitors: Welcome. To reserve tee times - telephone professional, especially weekends.
Green Fees: Monday to Thursday £18, Friday £20, weekends and Bank Holidays £24.
Facilities: Lunch. Dinner. Bar Snacks. Full Catering. Changing Room. Golf Shop. Club Hire. Trolley Hire.
Class One Hotel: Broughton Park, Preston, 4 mile(s). Tel: 864087 (0772)
Class Two Hotel: Whitburn House, Preston, 2 mile(s). Tel: 717973 (0772)

PRESTON

Fishwick Hall Golf Club, Glenluce Drive, Farringdon Park, Preston, Lancs. PR1 5TD. Tel: 798300 (0772)
Secretary: R R Gearing   Tel: 708300 (0772)
Professional: S Bence   Tel: 795870 (0772)
Location: Off M6 junc 31.
Description: Parkland. Part wooded bounded by River Ribble.
White 18 holes, 6,092 yards, Par 70, S.S.S. 69.
Yellow 18 holes, 5,753 yards, Par 69, S.S.S. 68.
Membership: 650
Visitors: Welcome.
Green Fees: £20 weekdays, £25 weekends and Bank Holidays.
Facilities: Lunch. Dinner. Bar Snacks. Full Catering. Changing Room. Golf Shop. Club Hire. Trolley Hire.
Class One Hotel: Tickled Trout, Preston, 1 mile(s). Tel: 877671 (0772)
Class Two Hotel: Carrside, Preston, 3 mile(s). Tel: 700612 (0772)

PRESTON

Longridge Golf Club, Fell Barn, Jeffrey Hill, Longridge, Preston, Lancs. PR3 2TU. Tel: 783291 (0772)
Secretary: J Greenwood   Tel: 782765 (0772)
Professional: N James   Tel: 783291 (0772)
Location: 8 miles north-east of Preston off B6243 on Fell Road.
Description: Moorland with extensive spectacular views.
18 holes, 5,726 yards, Par 70, S.S.S. 68, Course record 66.
Membership: 600
Visitors: Welcome. Handicap certificate required. Weekends restricted to accomodate club competitions.
Green Fees: Monday to Thursday £15 per day. Friday, Saturday and Sunday £18 per day.
Facilities: Lunch. Dinner. Bar Snacks. Full Catering. Changing Room. Golf Shop. Trolley Hire.

PRESTON

Penwortham Golf Club Ltd., Blundell Lane, Penwortham, Preston, Lancs. PR1 0AX. Tel: 743207 (0772)
Secretary: Mr J Parkinson   Tel: 744630 (0772)
Professional: Mr J Wright   Tel: 742345 (0772)
Location: 1 mile west of Preston off A59.
Description: Parkland.
18 holes, 5,667 yards, Par 69, S.S.S. 68.
Membership: 975
Visitors: Welcome. Handicap certificate required. Not Tuesdays.
Green Fees: £22 per round, £25 per day.
Facilities: Lunch. Dinner. Bar Snacks. Full Catering. Changing Room. Golf Shop. Trolley Hire.
Class One Hotel: Crest, Preston, 3 mile(s). Tel: 59411 (0772)
Class Two Hotel: Claremont, Preston, 3 mile(s). Tel: 700917 (0772)

PRESTON

Preston Golf Club, Fulwood Hall Lane, Fulwood, Preston, Lancs. PR2 4DD. Tel: 700011 (0772)
Secretary: J B Dickinson   Tel: 700011 (0772)
Professional: P A Wells   Tel: 700022 (0772)
Description: Rolling parkland.
18 holes, 6,233 yards, Par 71, S.S.S. 70, Course record 65.
Membership: 800
Visitors: Welcome. Handicap certificate required. Not at weekends. Limited number weekdays, please telephone in advance.
Green Fees: £20 per round, £25 per day.
Facilities: Lunch. Dinner. Bar Snacks. Full Catering. Changing Room. Golf Shop. Trolley Hire.
Class One Hotel: Broughton Park, Preston, 3 mile(s). Tel: 864087 (0772)
Class Two Hotel: Briarfield, Preston, 1/2 mile(s). Tel: 700917 (0772)

SILVERDALE

Silverdale Golf Club, Redbridge Lane, Silverdale, Carnforth, Lancs. LA5 0SP. Tel: 701300 (0524)
Secretary: P J Watts   Tel: 701307 (0524)
Location: M6 to carnforth, 2 miles west adjacent to railway station.

95

Description: Heathland course with rock outcrops.
9 holes, 5,256 yards, Par 70, S.S.S. 67, Course record 66.
Membership: 500
Visitors: Welcome. Ladies day Wednesday. No visitors on Sundays unless with a member.
Green Fees: £12 per day weekdays, £17 weekends and Bank Holidays.
Facilities: Changing Room. Golf Shop. Trolley Hire.
Class Two Hotel: Wheatsheaf, Beetham, 4 mile(s). Tel: 2123 (04482)

SKELMERSDALE

Beacon Park Golf Club, Beacon Lane, Dalton, Up Holland, Skelmersdale, Lancs. . Tel: 622700 (0695)
Secretary: J C McIlroy   Tel: 892930 (0704)
Professional: R Peters   Tel: 622700 (0695)
Location: 5 miles from Ormskirk.
Description: Woodland.
18 holes, 5,995 yards, Par 72, S.S.S. 69, Course record 68.
Membership: 370
Visitors: Welcome.
Green Fees: £5.50 weekends, £3.9 weekdays.
Facilities: Trolley Hire. Buggy Hire. Caddies available.
Class One Hotel: Martin Inn, Burscough, 6 mile(s). Tel: 892309 (0704)

LEICESTERSHIRE

ASHBY DE LA ZOUCH

Willesley Park Golf Club Ltd., Measham Road, Ashby de la Zouch, Leics. LE6 5PF. Tel: 414596 (0530)
Secretary: N H Jones   Tel: 414596 (0530)
Professional: C Hancock   Tel: 414820 (0530)
Location: 2 miles south of Ashby on B5006.
Description: Parkland.
18 holes, 6,304 yards, Par 70, S.S.S. 70, Course record 65.
Membership: 600
Visitors: Welcome. Handicap certificate required. Tuesdays Ladies Day.
Green Fees: Weekdays £25, weekends and Bank Holidays £30.
Facilities: Lunch. Dinner. Bar Snacks. Full Catering. Changing Room. Golf Shop. Trolley Hire.
Class One Hotel: Fallen Knight, Ashby-D-L-Zouch, 1 mile(s). Tel: 412230 (0530)

COSBY

Cosby Golf Club, Chapel Lane, off Broughton Road, Cosby, Leics. LE9 5RG. Tel: 864759 (0533)
Secretary: M D Riddle   Tel: 864759 (0533)
Professional: D Bowring   Tel: 848275 (0533)
Location: 8 miles south of Leicester, 4 miles from junc 21 of M1.
Description: Undulating parkland course.
18 holes, 6,277 yards, Par 71, S.S.S. 70, Course record 65.
Membership: 680
Visitors: Welcome. Handicap certificate required. Weekdays before 4 p.m. Weekends and Bank Holidays with members only.
Green Fees: £18 per round, £20 per day.
Facilities: Lunch. Dinner. Bar Snacks. Full Catering. Changing Room. Golf Shop. Club Hire. Trolley Hire.
Class One Hotel: Time Out Hotel and Leisure, Blaby, 4 mile(s). Tel: 787898 (0533)
Class Two Hotel: Charnwood, Narborough, 2 mile(s). Tel: 862218 (0533)

HINCKLEY

Hinckley Golf Club, Leicester Road, Hinckley, Leics. LE10 3DR. Tel: 615124 (0455)
Secretary: J Toon   Tel: 615124 (0455)
Professional: R Jones   Tel: 615014 (0455)
Location: 1 miles north east of Hinckley on A47.
Description: Parkland with lakeside features.
18 holes, 6,592 yards, Par 71, S.S.S. 71, Course record 64.
Membership: 680
Visitors: Welcome. Handicap certificate required. Visitors by appointment only.
Green Fees: £20 per 18 holes, £25 per 27 to 36 holes. £10 with member.
Facilities: Lunch. Dinner. Bar Snacks. Full Catering. Changing Room. Golf Shop. Trolley Hire. Buggy Hire.

KIRBY MUXLOE

Kirby Muxloe Golf Club, Station Road, Kirby Muxloe, Leics. LE9 9EP. Tel: 393107 (0533)
Secretary: S F Aldwinckle   Tel: 393457 (0533)
Professional: R T Stephenson   Tel: 392813 (0533)
Location: 5 miles west of Leicester off A47.
Description: Parkland with lake.
Medal 18 holes, 6,303 yards, Par 71, S.S.S. 70, Course record 65.
Standard 18 holes, 5,956 yards, Par 70, S.S.S. 69.
Membership: 745
Visitors: Welcome. Handicap certificate required. With members at weekends. Advisable to telephone in advance.
Green Fees: £20 per round, £25 per day. With member £5 per round, £7.50 per day.
Facilities: Lunch. Dinner. Bar Snacks. Full Catering. Changing Room. Golf Shop. Driving Range. Trolley Hire.
Class One Hotel: Leicester Forest Moat House, L/Forest East, 1 1/2 mile(s). Tel: 394661 (0533)
Class Two Hotel: Forest Lodge, Kirby Muxloe, 1/2 mile(s). Tel: 393125 (0533)

LOUGHBOROUGH

Longcliffe Golf Club, Snell's Nook Lane, Nanpantan, Loughborough, Leics. LE11 3YA. Tel: 216321 (0509)
Secretary: G Harle   Tel: 239129 (0509)
Professional: Ian Bailey   Tel: 231450 (0509)
Location: Junc 23 M1, take A512 to Loughborough.
Description: Heathland.
18 holes, 6,551 yards, Par 72, S.S.S. 71.
Membership: 625
Visitors: Welcome. Handicap certificate required. Wednesdays, Thursdays and Fridays. With members only at weekends.
Green Fees: £22 per round, £9 with member. £27 per day.
Facilities: Lunch. Dinner. Bar Snacks. Full Catering. Changing Room. Golf Shop. Trolley Hire.
Class One Hotel: Kings Head, Loughborough, 2 mile(s). Tel: 233222 (0509)

WOODHOUSE EAVES
Lingdale Golf Club, Joe Moore's Lane, Woodhouse Eaves, Near Loughborough, Leics. LE12 8TF. Tel: 890703 (0509)
Secretary: M Green Tel: 890703 (0509)
Professional: P Sellears Tel: 890684 (0509)
Location: On B5330 Anstey to Shepshed Road, 3 miles from M1 junc 23.
Description: Parkland and woodland.
18 holes, 6,545 yards, Par 71, S.S.S. 71.
Membership: 580
Visitors: Welcome.
Green Fees: Weekdays £16, weekends £20.
Facilities: Lunch. Dinner. Bar Snacks. Full Catering. Changing Room. Golf Shop. Driving Range. Trolley Hire.
Class Two Hotel: The Brant Inn, Groby, 2 mile(s). Tel: 872703 (0533)

LINCOLNSHIRE

BOSTON
Boston Golf Club, Cowbridge, Horncastle Road, Boston, Lincs. PE22 7EL. Tel: 362306 (0205)
Secretary: D E Smith Tel: 350589 (0205)
Professional: T R Squires Tel: 362306 (0205)
Location: 2 miles north of Boston on B1183 main Boston to Horncastle Road.
Description: Parkland with water featuring on 10 holes and "true fast" greens.
18 holes, 5,825 yards, Par 69, S.S.S. 68, Course record 66.
Membership: 650
Visitors: Welcome. Handicap certificate required. No societies at weekends or Bank Holidays.
Green Fees: Weekdays £14 per round, £20 per day. Weekends and Bank Holidays £20 per round, £30 per day.
Facilities: Lunch. Dinner. Bar Snacks. Full Catering. Changing Room. Golf Shop. Club Hire. Trolley Hire.
Class One Hotel: White Hart, Boston, 2 1/2 mile(s). Tel: 364877 (0205)
Class Two Hotel: Burton House, Boston, 2 mile(s). Tel: 362307 (0205)

GRANTHAM
Belton Park Golf Club, Londonthorpe Lane, Grantham, Lincs. NG3 9SH. Tel: 67399 (0476)
Secretary: T Measures Tel: 67399 (0476)
Professional: B McKee Tel: 63911 (0476)
Location: 2 miles of Grantham off A1.
Description: Parkland.
Brownlow 18 holes, 6,420 yards, Par 71, S.S.S. 71, Course record 65.
Ancaster 18 holes, 6,252 yards, Par 70, S.S.S. 70.
Membership: 950
Visitors: Welcome. Handicap certificate required. No societies or weekends.
Green Fees: Weekdays £16 for 18 holes, £21 for 27 holes. Weekends £26 for 18 holes, £31 for 27 holes.
Facilities: Lunch. Dinner. Bar Snacks. Full Catering. Changing Room. Shop. Club Hire. Driving Range. Trolley Hire.
Class One Hotel: Angel and Royal, Grantham, 2 mile(s). Tel: 65816 (0476)

GRANTHAM
Stoke Rochford Golf Club, Stoke Rochford, Near Grantham, Lincs. NG33 5EW. Tel: 83275 (0476)
Secretary: J Butler Tel: 67030 (0476)
Professional: A Dow Tel: 83218 (0476)
Location: 5 miles south of Grantham.
Description: Parkland.
18 holes, 6,251 yards, Par 70, S.S.S. 70, Course record 65.
Membership: 550
Visitors: Welcome. Handicap certificate required. Essential to check with professional before visit.
Green Fees: Weekdays £17 per round, £24 per day. Weekends £26 per round, £35 per day.
Facilities: Lunch. Dinner. Bar Snacks. Full Catering. Changing Room. Golf Shop. Club Hire. Trolley Hire.
Class One Hotel: Angel and Royal, Grantham, 6 mile(s). Tel: 65816 (0476)

LINCOLN
Blankney Golf Club, Blankney, Metheringham, Lincoln, Lincs. LN4 3AZ. Tel: 20263 (0526)
Secretary: D A Priest Tel: 20263 (0526)
Professional: G Bradley Tel: 20202 (0526)
Location: On B118 8 miles south of Lincoln.
Description: Parkland.
18 holes, 6,378 yards, Par 71, S.S.S. 71, Course record 64.
Membership: 675
Visitors: Welcome. With a member at weekends.
Green Fees: On application.
Facilities: Lunch. Dinner. Bar Snacks. Full Catering. Changing Room. Golf Shop. Club Hire. Trolley Hire.
Class One Hotel: Golf Hotel, Woodhall Spa, 9 mile(s). Tel: 53555 (0526)
Class Two Hotel: Dower House, Woodhall Spa, 9 mile(s). Tel: 52588 (0526)

LINCOLN
Canwick Park Golf Club, Canwick Park, Washingborough Road, Lincoln, Lincs. LN4 1EF. Tel: 522166 (0522)
Secretary: A C Hodgkinson Tel: 791757 (0522)
Professional: S Williamson Tel: 536870 (0522)
Location: 1 1/2 miles east of Lincoln.
Description: Wooded parkland.
18 holes, 6,257 yards, Par 70, S.S.S. 70.
Membership: 650
Visitors: Welcome. Not before 3p.m. at weekends.
Green Fees: Mondays £10 per round, £17 per day. Tuesdays to Fridays £12 per round, £18 per day. Weekends £13 per round, £20 per day.
Facilities: Lunch. Dinner. Bar Snacks. Full Catering. Changing Room. Golf Shop. Club Hire. Trolley Hire. Buggy Hire.
Class One Hotel: Forte Crest, Lincoln, 2 mile(s). Tel: 520341 (0522)
Class Two Hotel: Washingborough Hall, Washingborough, 2 mile(s). Tel: 790340 (0522)

MARKET RASEN
Market Rasen and District Golf Club, Legsby Road, Market Rasen, Lincs. LN8 3DZ. Tel: 842319 (0673)
Secretary: E Hill Tel: 842319 (0673)
Professional: Tony Chester Tel: 842416 (0673)

Description: Heathland wooded course.
18 holes, 6,043 yards, Par 70, S.S.S. 69, Course record 65.
Membership: 550
Visitors: Welcome. Handicap certificate required. Not after 10.30 a.m. Ladies day Wednesday. Weekends with members only.
Green Fees: On application.
Facilities: Lunch. Dinner. Bar Snacks. Full Catering. Changing Room. Golf Shop. Club Hire. Trolley Hire.
Class Two Hotel: Gordon Arms, Market Rasen, 1 mile(s). Tel: 842364 (0673)

SKEGNESS

North Shore Hotel and Golf Club, North Shore Road, Skegness, Lincs. PE25 1DN. Tel: 763398 (0754)
Secretary: Chris Thompson   Tel: 763298 (0754)
Professional: John Cornelius   Tel: 763298 (0754)
Location: North of Skegness town centre on A52. Right on the coast.
Description: 18 hole twin looped, designed in 1910 by James Braid. Half parkland, half links.
18 holes, 6,134 yards, Par 71, S.S.S. 69, Course record 69.
Membership: 590
Visitors: Welcome. Handicap certificate required. Letter of Introduction required.
Green Fees: £14 weekdays, £20 weekends. Special rates for societies.
Facilities: Lunch. Dinner. Bar Snacks. Full Catering. Changing Room. Golf Shop. Club Hire. Trolley Hire.

SKEGNESS

Seacroft Golf Club, Drummond Road, Skegness, Lincs. PE25 3AU. Tel: 763020 (0754)
Secretary: H K Brader   Tel: 763020 (0754)
Professional: R Lawie   Tel: 763020 (0754)
Location: Southern boundary of Skegness.
Description: Links.
18 holes, 6,501 yards, Par 71, S.S.S. 71, Course record 68.
Membership: 600
Visitors: Welcome. Handicap certificate required. Not before 9.30 a.m.
Green Fees: Weekdays £20 per round, £25 per day. Weekends and Bank Holidays £25 per round, £35 per day.
Facilities: Lunch. Dinner. Bar Snacks. Full Catering. Changing Room. Golf Shop. Trolley Hire.
Class One Hotel: Vine, Skegness, 1 mile(s). Tel: 72228 (0754)

SLEAFORD

Sleaford Golf Club, Willoughby Road, South Rauceby, Sleaford, Lincs. NG34 8PL. Tel: 273 (05298)
Secretary: D B R Harris   Tel: 326 (05298)
Professional: Steve Harrison   Tel: 644 (05298)
Location: 1 mile west of Sleaford on A153.
Description: Inland links type course, lightly wooded and fairly flat.
18 holes, 6,443 yards, Par 72, S.S.S. 71, Course record 65.
Membership: 650
Visitors: Welcome. Handicap certificate required. Parties of 9 or more by prior arrangement only. No visitors winter Sundays. No 4 balls before noon on Tuesdays.

Green Fees: Weekdays £17 per day or round. Weekends and Bank Holidays £25 per day or round.
Facilities: Lunch. Dinner. Bar Snacks. Changing Room. Golf Shop. Trolley Hire.
Class One Hotel: Lincolnshire Oak, Sleaford, 3 mile(s). Tel: 413807 (0529)
Class Two Hotel: Nags Head Inn, Heckington, 6 mile(s). Tel: 60218 (0529)

STAMFORD

Luffenham Heath Golf Club, Ketton, Stamford, Lincs. PE9 3UU. Tel: 720205 (0780)
Secretary: I F Davenport   Tel: 720205 (0780)
Professional: J A Lawrence   Tel: 720298 (0780)
Description: Heathland. Established in 1911, designed by James Braid. Limestone grassland, butterflies etc..
18 holes, 6,250 yards, Par 70, S.S.S. 70, Course record 64.
Membership: 520
Visitors: Welcome. Handicap certificate required. No societies weekends. Weekdays and Bank Holidays by prior arrangement.
Green Fees: £30 weekdays, £35 weekends and Bank Holidays.
Facilities: Lunch. Bar Snacks. Changing Room. Golf Shop. Club Hire. Trolley Hire.
Class One Hotel: George, Stamford, 6 mile(s). Tel: 55171 (0780)
Class Two Hotel: Kings Arms, Wing, 6 mile(s). Tel: 85315 (0572)

SUTTON-ON-SEA

Sandilands Golf Club, Sea Lane, Sandilands, Sutton-on-Sea, Mablethorpe, Lincs. LN12 2RJ. Tel: 441432 (0507)
Secretary: D Mumby   Tel: 441617 (0507)
Professional: D Vernon   Tel: 441600 (0507)
Location: A52, 2 miles south of Sutton-on-Sea.
Description: Flat links, adjacent to sea.
18 holes, 5,995 yards, Par 70, S.S.S. 69, Course record 66.
Membership: 300
Visitors: Welcome.
Green Fees: Weekdays £18 per day, £12 per round. Weekends and Bank Holidays £18 per round.
Facilities: Lunch. Dinner. Bar Snacks. Full Catering. Changing Room. Golf Shop. Club Hire. Trolley Hire.
Class One Hotel: Grange and Links, Sutton-on-Sea, 1/4 mile(s). Tel: 441334 (0507)

WOODHALL SPA

Woodhall Spa Golf Club, Woodhall Spa, Lincs. LN10 6PU. Tel: 52511 (0526)
Secretary: B H Fawcett   Tel: 52511 (0526)
Professional: P Fixter   Tel: 53229 (0526)
Description: Flat wooded heathland.
18 holes, 6,907 yards, Par 73, S.S.S. 73, Course record 68.
Membership: 450
Visitors: Welcome. Caddies available during school holidays.
Green Fees: Weekdays £22 per round, £32 per day. Weekends £25 per round, £35 per day.
Facilities: Lunch. Dinner. Bar Snacks. Full Catering. Changing Room. Golf Shop. Club Hire. Trolley Hire.
Class One Hotel: Golf Hotel, Woodhall Spa, 1/4 mile(s).

MERSEYSIDE

BEBINGTON
Brackenwood Golf Club, Bracken Lane, Bebington, Merseyside. L63 2LY. Tel: 608 5394 (051)
Secretary: N D Taylor　　　　　Tel: 327 2387 (051)
Professional: Colin Disbury　　　Tel: 608 3093 (051)
Location: M53 junc 7 Clatterbridge roundabout.
Description: Parkland.
18 holes, 6,200 yards, Par 70, S.S.S. 70, Course record 67.
Membership: 250
Visitors: Welcome. Ladies Day up to 10a.m. Wednesdays. Not before 10.30a.m. Sundays.
Green Fees: £5.
Facilities: Golf Shop. Club Hire. Trolley Hire.
Class Two Hotel: Thornton Hall, Thornton Hough, 2 mile(s). Tel: 336 3938 (051)

BIRKENHEAD
Prenton Golf Club, Golf Links Road, Prenton, Birkenhead, Merseyside. L42 8LW. Tel: 608 1053 (051)
Secretary: W F W Disley　　　　Tel: 608 1053 (051)
Professional: R Thompson　　　Tel: 608 1636 (051)
Location: Junc 3 off M53 on A552 towards Birkenhead.
Description: Parkland.
18 holes, 6,411 yards, Par 71, S.S.S. 71, Course record 67.
Membership: 650
Visitors: Welcome. Handicap certificate required.
Green Fees: W/days £23, w/ends and Bank Holidays £25.
Facilities: Lunch. Dinner. Bar Snacks. Full Catering. Changing Room. Golf Shop. Club Hire. Trolley Hire.
Class One Hotel: Leasowe Castle, Wallasey, 4 mile(s). Tel: 606 9191 (051)
Class Two Hotel: Bowler Hat, Birkenhead, 1 mile(s). Tel: 652 4931 (051)

FORMBY
Formby Golf Club, Golf Road, Formby, Liverpool, Merseyside. L37 1LQ. Tel: 73090 (07048)
Secretary: A Thirlwell　　　　　Tel: 72164 (07048)
Professional: C F Harrison　　　Tel: 73090 (07048)
Location: 5 miles south of Southport on A565.
Description: Links with trees.
18 holes, 6,790 yards, Par 72, S.S.S. 73.
Membership: 600
Visitors: Welcome. Handicap certificate required. Not Wednesdays, weekends or Bank Holidays.
Green Fees: £40.
Facilities: Lunch. Dinner. Bar Snacks. Full Catering. Changing Room. Golf Shop. Trolley Hire. Caddies available.
Class One Hotel: Scarisbrick, Southport, 4 mile(s). Tel: 543000 (0704)

FORMBY
Formby Ladies' Golf Club, Golf Road, Formby, Liverpool, Merseyside. L37 1LQ.
Secretary: Mrs Bailey　　　　　Tel: 73493 (07048)
Professional: C F Harrison　　　Tel: 73090 (07048)
Location: 5 miles south of Southport on A565.
Description: Links with trees.
18 holes, 4,900 yards, Par 71, S.S.S. 71, Course record 63.
Membership: 500
Visitors: Welcome. Handicap certificate required. Not Thursdays or before 11.30a.m. weekends and Bank Holidays.
Green Fees: Weekdays £25, weekends £31.
Facilities: Lunch. Dinner. Bar Snacks. Full Catering. Changing Room. Golf Shop. Trolley Hire. Caddies available.
Class One Hotel: Scarisbrick, Southport, 4 mile(s). Tel: 543000 (0704)

HESWALL
Heswall Golf Club, Cottage Lane, Gayton, Wirral, Merseyside. L60 8PB. Tel: 342 2193 (051)
Secretary: R Calvert　　　　　Tel: 342 1237 (051)
Professional: Alan E Thompson　Tel: 342 7431 (051)
Location: On A540 8 miles north west of Chester.
Description: Parkland alongside River Dee.
18 holes, 6,472 yards, Par 72, S.S.S. 72, Course record 63.
Membership: 900
Visitors: Welcome. Handicap certificate required.
Green Fees: Weekdays £25 per round, £30 per day. Weekends £30 per round, £35 per day.
Facilities: Lunch. Bar Snacks. Full Catering. Changing Room. Golf Shop. Club Hire. Trolley Hire.

HOYLAKE
Royal Liverpool Golf Club, Meols Drive, Hoylake, Wirral, Merseyside. L47 4AL. Tel: 632 3101 (051)
Secretary: R H White　　　　　Tel: 632 3101 (051)
Professional: J Heggarty　　　　Tel: 632 5868 (051)
Location: 10 miles west of Liverpool.
Description: Links course with superb greens and challenging bunkers.
Green 18 holes, 6,821 yards, Par 72, S.S.S. 74.
Yellow 18 holes, 6,128 yards, Par 71, S.S.S. 71.
Membership: 400
Visitors: Welcome. Handicap certificate required. Ladies Day Thursday (a.m. only). Letter of introduction preferred.
Green Fees: Weekdays £35 per round, £50 per day. Weekends £50 per round, £75 per day.
Facilities: Lunch. Dinner. Bar Snacks. Full Catering. Changing Room. Golf Shop. Club Hire. Driving Range. Trolley Hire. Caddies available.
Class One Hotel: Thornton Hall, Thornton Hough, 10 mile(s). Tel: 336 3938 (051)
Class Two Hotel: Kings Gap Court, Hoylake, 1/2 mile(s). Tel: 632 2073 (051)

HUYTON
Huyton and Prescot Golf Club, Hurst Park, Huyton Lane, Huyton, Merseyside. L36 1UA. Tel: 489 1138 (051)
Secretary: Mrs E Holmes　　　Tel: 489 3948 (051)
Professional: R Pottage　　　　Tel: 489 2022 (051)
Location: Alongside junc 2 M57.
Description: Undulating parkland.
18 holes, 5,779 yards, Par 68, S.S.S. 68, Course record 67.
Membership: 750
Visitors: Welcome. Handicap certificate required. Not

weekends. Weekdays not before 9.30a.m. or between 12p.m. and 2p.m. and not after 4p.m..
Green Fees: £18.
Facilities: Lunch. Dinner. Bar Snacks. Full Catering. Changing Room. Golf Shop. Trolley Hire.
Class One Hotel: The Derby Lodge, Huyton, 1 1/2 mile(s). Tel: 480 4440 (051)

LIVERPOOL
Dudley Golf Club, Allerton Municipal Golf Course, Allerton, Liverpool, Merseyside. L18. Tel: 428 8510 (051)
Secretary: Dave Howard   Tel: 428 8510 (051)
Professional: Barry Large   Tel: 428 1046 (051)
Location: End of M62 about 2 miles towards Airport.
Description: Woodland.
18 holes, 5,494 yards, Par 67, S.S.S. 67, Course record 62.
9 holes, 2,790 yards, Par 29, S.S.S. 29.
Membership: 700
Visitors: Welcome.
Green Fees: £4.50, reduced rate for OAP's and children.
Facilities: Lunch. Dinner. Bar Snacks. Full Catering. Golf Shop. Club Hire. Trolley Hire.

LIVERPOOL
The Childwall Golf Club Ltd., Naylors Road, Liverpool, Merseyside. L27 2YB. Tel: 487 9982 (051)
Secretary: Mr L Upton   Tel: 487 0654 (051)
Professional: N M Parr   Tel: 487 9871 (051)
Location: 2 miles from exit 6 M62 towards Huyton.
Description: Parkland.
18 holes, 6,025 yards, Par 69, S.S.S. 65, Course record 65.
Membership: 636
Visitors: Welcome. Handicap certificate required. Tuesdays Ladies Day. Not weekends.
Green Fees: £19.50.
Facilities: Lunch. Dinner. Bar Snacks. Full Catering. Changing Room. Golf Shop. Club Hire. Trolley Hire.
Class One Hotel: Logwood Mill, Liverpool, 2 mile(s). Tel: 449 2341 (051)

LIVERPOOL
West Derby Golf Club, Yew Tree Lane, West Derby, Liverpool, Merseyside. L12 9HQ. Tel: 254 1034 (051)
Secretary: S Young   Tel: 254 1034 (051)
Professional: N Brace   Tel: 220 5478 (051)
Description: Flat wooded parkland.
18 holes, 6,346 yards, Par 72, S.S.S. 70.
Membership: 450
Visitors: Welcome.
Green Fees: Weekdays £20, weekends £28.
Facilities: Lunch. Dinner. Bar Snacks. Full Catering. Changing Room. Golf Shop. Trolley Hire.

LIVERPOOL
Woolton Golf Club, Doe Park, Speke Road, Woolton, Liverpool, Merseyside. L25 7TZ. Tel: 486 1601 (051)
Secretary: K G Jennions   Tel: 486 2298 (051)
Professional: M Edwards   Tel: 486 1298 (051)
Location: South of Liverpool, 1 mile from Woolton Village.
Description: Parkland.
18 holes, 5,706 yards, Par 67, S.S.S. 68, Course record 63.

Membership: 600
Visitors: Welcome. Handicap certificate required. Ladies day is Tuesday. Not before 9.30a.m., or between 12 and 1p.m. in winter.
Green Fees: Weekdays £18, weekends £25.
Facilities: Lunch. Dinner. Bar Snacks. Full Catering. Changing Room. Golf Shop. Trolley Hire. Buggy Hire.

NEWTON-LE-WILLOWS
Haydock Park Golf Club, Golborne Park, Newton-le-Willows, Merseyside. WA12 0HX. Tel: 224389 (0925)
Secretary: G Tait   Tel: 228525 (0925)
Professional: P Kenwright   Tel: 226944 (0925)
Location: Off at junc 28 M6 towards Manchester.
Description: Flat parkland.
18 holes, 6,043 yards, Par 70, S.S.S. 69.
Membership: 500
Visitors: Welcome. Visitors must have membership card from home golf club. Tuesdays Ladies Day. With members only at weekends.
Green Fees: Weekdays £22, £6 with members.
Facilities: Lunch. Dinner. Bar Snacks. Full Catering. Changing Room. Golf Shop. Trolley Hire.
Class Two Hotel: Kirkfield, Newton-l-Willow, 1 mile(s). Tel: 228196 (0925)

SOUTHPORT
Hillside Golf Club, Hastings Road, Hillside, Southport, Merseyside. PR8 2LU. Tel: 66902 (0704)
Secretary: Mr P Ray   Tel: 67169 (0704)
Professional: Mr B Seddon   Tel: 68360 (0704)
Location: 25 miles north west of Liverpool on A565 to Southport.
Description: Undulating links, well bunkered, with 2 lakes. Rated number 19 in the top 50 by Golf World in 1990.
18 holes, 6,850 yards, Par 72, S.S.S. 74, Course record 67.
Visitors: Welcome. Handicap certificate required. With members only at weekends. Tuesday mornings Ladies only. Caddies available with 7 days notice.
Green Fees: £35 per round, £45 per day.
Facilities: Lunch. Dinner. Bar Snacks. Full Catering. Changing Room. Golf Shop. Club Hire. Trolley Hire. Buggy Hire.
Class One Hotel: Shelbourne, Southport, 2 mile(s). Tel: 541252 (0704)
Class Two Hotel: Lockerbie House, Southport, 1 mile(s). Tel: 65298 (0704)

SOUTHPORT
Southport Municipal Golf Club, Park Road West, Southport, Merseyside. PR9 0JS. Tel: 535286 (0704)
Secretary: J Turner   Tel: 530133 (0704)
Professional: William Fletcher Tel: 535286 (0704)
Description: Flat seaside links.
18 holes, 6,139 yards, Par 70, S.S.S. 69, Course record 67.
Membership: 605
Visitors: Welcome. Societies welcome weekdays only. Booking system operates up to six days in advance.
Green Fees: Weekdays £4.40 adult, £2.20 junior. Weekends and Bank Holidays £6.05.
Facilities: Lunch. Dinner. Bar Snacks. Full Catering. Changing Room. Golf Shop. Club Hire. Trolley Hire.

Class One Hotel: Prince of Wales, Southport, 1/2 mile(s). Tel: 536688 (0704)
Class Two Hotel: Victorian Licensed Hotel, Southport, 1/4 mile(s). Tel: 530755 (0704)

SOUTHPORT

Southport Old Links Golf Club, Moss Lane, Churchtown, Southport, Merseyside. PR9 7QS. Tel: 28207 (0704)
Secretary: Mr G Rimington   Tel: 28207 (0704)
Description: Tree lined links course.
9 holes, 6,378 yards, Par 72, S.S.S. 71.
Membership: 350
Visitors: Welcome. Handicap certificate required. No visitors Sundays or Wednesdays.
Green Fees: Weekdays £15, weekends £20.
Facilities: Lunch. Dinner. Bar Snacks. Full Catering. Changing Room.
Class One Hotel: Royal Clifton, Southport, 2 mile(s). Tel: 533771 (0704)
Class Two Hotel: The Gilton, Southport, 2 mile(s). Tel: 530646 (0704)

ST HELENS

Grange Park Golf Club, Prescot Road, St Helens, Merseyside. WA10 3AD. Tel: 26318 (0744)
Secretary: David A Wood   Tel: 26318 (0744)
Professional: Paul G Evans   Tel: 28785 (0744)
Location: 1 1/2 miles south west of St Helens on A58.
Description: Parkland.
White 18 holes, 6,429 yards, Par 72, S.S.S. 71, Course record 65.
Yellow 18 holes, 6,209 yards, Par 70, S.S.S. 70.
Membership: 700
Visitors: Welcome. Handicap certificate required. Mondays, Wednesdays and Thursdays.
Green Fees: £21.
Facilities: Lunch. Dinner. Bar Snacks. Full Catering. Changing Room. Golf Shop. Club Hire. Trolley Hire. Buggy Hire.
Class One Hotel: Haydock Thistle, St Helens, 5 mile(s). Tel: 272000 (0942)
Class Two Hotel: Griffin, St Helens, 1 mile(s). Tel: 27907 (0744)

NORFOLK

BAWBURGH

Bawburgh Golf Club, Long Lane, Bawburgh, Norwich, Norfolk. NR9 3LX. Tel: 746390 (0603)
Secretary: R J Mapes   Tel: 606776 (0953)
Professional: Chris Potter   Tel: 742323 (0603)
Location: West of Norwich at intersection of A47 and Norwich southern by-pass. Adjacent to Showground.
Description: Existing 9 hole course-parkland being expanded to 18 holes for July 1992.
18 holes, 6,066 yards, Par 70.
Membership: 500
Visitors: Welcome. Handicap certificate required. Dress restrictions. Telephone for availability.
Green Fees: On application.
Facilities: Bar Snacks. Changing Room. Golf Shop. Driving Range. Trolley Hire.
Class One Hotel: Friendly Lodge, Norwich, 1 mile(s). Tel: 741161 (0603)

CAISTER-ON-SEA

Great Yarmouth and Caister Golf Club, Beach House, Caister-on-Sea, Near Great Yarmouth, Norfolk. NR30 5TD. Tel: 728699 (0493)
Secretary: Mrs H M Marsh   Tel: 728699 (0493)
Professional: Robert Foster   Tel: 720421 (0493)
Location: Adjoining Yarmouth racecourse between Great Yarmouth and Caister.
Description: Links.
18 holes, 6,330 yards, Par 70, S.S.S. 70, Course record 65
Membership: 760
Visitors: Welcome. Ladies day Tuesday. Restrictions weekends, Bank Holidays and race days. Always telephone in advance.
Green Fees: Weekdays £20, weekends £24.
Facilities: Lunch. Dinner. Bar Snacks. Full Catering. Changing Room. Golf Shop. Club Hire. Trolley Hire.
Class One Hotel: Imperial, Great Yarmouth, 2 mile(s). Tel: 851113 (0493)
Class Two Hotel: Windy Shore, Great Yarmouth, 2 mile(s). Tel: 844145 (0493)

CROMER

Links Country Park Hotel & Golf Club, West Runton, Cromer, Norfolk. NR27 9QH. Tel: 691 (026375)
Professional: Mr Mike Jubb   Tel: 838215 (0263)
Location: On north Norfolk Coast Road A140 from Norwich (Cromer 2 miles).
Description: Rolling parkland with well guarded greens.
9 holes, 4,814 yards, Par 66, S.S.S. 64, Course record 64.
Membership: 300
Visitors: Welcome.
Green Fees: Weekdays £19, weekends £23.
Facilities: Lunch. Dinner. Bar Snacks. Full Catering. Changing Room. Golf Shop. Club Hire. Trolley Hire. Caddies available.
Class One Hotel: Links Country Park, On course. Tel: 838383 (0263)

CROMER

Royal Cromer Golf Club, 145 Overstrand Road, Cromer, Norfolk. NR27 0JH. Tel: 512884 (0263)
Secretary: B A Howson   Tel: 512884 (0263)
Professional: R J Page   Tel: 512267 (0263)
Location: 1 mile east of town centre on Coast Road.
Description: Undulating seaside course.
18 holes, 6,508 yards, Par 72, S.S.S. 71, Course record 68.
Membership: 670
Visitors: Welcome. Handicap certificate required. Booking essential 1st April to 31st October.
Green Fees: Weekdays £25, weekends £30.
Facilities: Lunch. Dinner. Bar Snacks. Full Catering. Changing Room. Golf Shop. Trolley Hire.
Class One Hotel: Dormy House, West Runton, 6 mile(s). Tel: 75537 (0263)
Class Two Hotel: Anglia Court, Cromer, 2 mile(s). Tel: 512443 (0263)

DEREHAM

Dereham Golf Club, Quebec Road, Dereham, Norfolk. NR19 2DS. Tel: 695900 (0362)
Secretary: George Dalrymple   Tel: 695900 (0362)
Professional: Steven Fox   Tel: 695631 (0362)
Location: 1/4 mile from town centre on Fakenham Road.
Description: Undulating parkland.
9 holes, 6,225 yards, Par 71, S.S.S. 70, Course record 68.
Membership: 447
Visitors: Welcome. Handicap certificate required. Not weekends. Prior notification required.
Green Fees: £16.
Facilities: Lunch. Dinner. Bar Snacks. Full Catering. Changing Room. Golf Shop. Club Hire. Trolley Hire.
Class One Hotel: Phoenix, Dereham, 1 mile(s). Tel: 692276 (0362)
Class Two Hotel: Croft Guest House, Dereham, 1/4 mile(s). Tel: 693417 (0362)

FAKENHAM

Fakenham Golf Club, Gallow Sports Centre, Hempton Road, Fakenham, Norfolk. . Tel: 862867 (0328)
Secretary: Mr G G Cocker   Tel: 855665 (0328)
Professional: J Westwood   Tel: 863534 (0328)
Location: Approx 1/2 mile from town on Swaffham Road.
Description: Parkland.
9 holes, 6,000 yards, Par 71, S.S.S. 69, Course record 67.
Membership: 540
Visitors: Welcome. Handicap certificate required. Ladies day Monday. Not before 3p.m. weekends and B/ Holidays.
Green Fees: Weekdays £14, w/ends and B/ Holidays £18.
Facilities: Lunch. Bar Snacks. Changing Room. Trolley Hire.
Class One Hotel: The Crown, Fakenham, 3/4 mile(s). Tel: 851418 (0328)
Class Two Hotel: The Mill House, Fakenham, 1/2 mile(s). Tel: 710739 (0328)

GORLESTON

Gorleston Golf Club, Warren Road, Gorleston, Near Great Yarmouth, Norfolk. NR31 6JT. Tel: 661911 (0493)
Secretary: C B Court   Tel: 661911 (0493)
Professional: R L Moffitt   Tel: 662103 (0493)
Location: Off A12 on the coast halfway between Lowestoft and Great Yarmouth.
Description: Seaside course.
18 holes, 6,400 yards, Par 71, S.S.S. 71, Course record 68.
Membership: 900
Visitors: Welcome. Handicap certificate required. Always telephone in advance.
Green Fees: Weekdays £18, weekends £25.
Facilities: Lunch. Dinner. Bar Snacks. Full Catering. Changing Room. Golf Shop. Club Hire.
Class One Hotel: Imperial, Great Yarmouth, 4 mile(s). Tel: 851113 (0493)

HUNSTANTON

Hunstanton Golf Club, Golf Course Road, Old Hunstanton, Norfolk. PE36 6JQ. Tel: 532811 (0485)
Secretary: R H Cotton   Tel: 532811 (0485)
Professional: J Carter   Tel: 532751 (0485)

Location: Through Hunstanton off coast road, follow signs.
Description: Seaside links.
18 holes, 72 yards, Par 72, S.S.S. 65.
Membership: 650
Visitors: Welcome. Handicap certificate required. Letter of Introduction required. Not Bank Holidays. Restrictions every weekend. Advance booking advisable.
Green Fees: Weekdays £28, weekends £34. Special rates available after 4p.m..
Facilities: Lunch. Dinner. Bar Snacks. Full Catering. Changing Room. Golf Shop. Club Hire. Trolley Hire. Buggy Hire. Caddies available.
Class One Hotel: Le Strange Arms, Old Hunstanton, 1/2 mile(s). Tel: 534411 (0485)
Class Two Hotel: Links Way, Old Hunstanton, 1/8 mile(s). Tel: 532209 (0485)

NORWICH

Barnham Broom Hotel, Golf & Country Club, Honingham Road, Norwich, Norfolk. NR9 4DD. Tel: 393 (060545)
Secretary: Peter Ballingall   Tel: 393 Ex 138 (060545)
Professional: Steve Beckham   Tel: 393 Ex 132 (060545)
Location: 8 miles S.W. of Norwich, between A11 and A47.
Description: Valley Course; River valley, wooded parkland. Hill Course; Undulating parkland.
Valley 18 holes, 6,470 yards, Par 71, S.S.S. 71, Course record 69.
Hill 18 holes, 6,628 yards, Par 72, S.S.S. 72.
Membership: 600
Visitors: Welcome. Always telephone in advance.
Green Fees: £25 per round, £35 per day.
Facilities: Lunch. Dinner. Bar Snacks. Full Catering. Changing Room. Golf Shop. Trolley Hire. Buggy Hire.
Class One Hotel: Barnham Broom, On course. Tel: 393 (060545)
Class Two Hotel: Abbey, Wymondham, 4 mile(s). Tel: 602148 (0953)

NORWICH

Costessey Park Golf Club, Old Costessey, Norwich, Norfolk. NR8 5AL. Tel: 746333 (0603)
Secretary: Mr C L House   Tel: 746333 (0603)
Professional: Simon Cook   Tel: 747085 (0603)
Location: Off A47 past Norfolk showground follow signs for Old Costessey.
Description: Part wooded, part parkland.
18 holes, 5,650 yards, Par 71, S.S.S. 67.
Membership: 550
Visitors: Welcome. Must book weekends and Bank Holidays. Caddies by prior arrangement.
Green Fees: Weekdays £14, £8 with a member. £17 weekends and Bank Holidays, £10 with a member.
Facilities: Lunch. Bar Snacks. Changing Room. Golf Shop. Club Hire. Trolley Hire.
Class One Hotel: Lenwade House, Norwich, 3 mile(s). Tel: 872288 (0603)

NORWICH

Eaton Golf Club, Newmarket Road, Norwich, Norfolk. NR4 6SF. Tel: 51686 (0603)
Secretary: D L P Sochon   Tel: 51686 (0603)

Professional: Frank Hill　　　　　Tel: 52478 (0603)
Location: Off A11 1 1/2 miles south west of Norwich.
Description: Parkland.
18 holes, 6,135 yards, Par 70, S.S.S. 69, Course record 64.
Membership: 850
Visitors: Welcome. Handicap certificate required. Not before 11.30a.m. at weekends.
Green Fees: Weekdays £25, weekends £30.
Facilities: Lunch. Dinner. Bar Snacks. Full Catering. Changing Room. Golf Shop. Club Hire. Trolley Hire.
Class One Hotel: Forte Post House, Norwich, 1 mile(s). Tel: 56431 (0603)

SWAFFHAM
Swaffham Golf Club, Cley Road, Swaffham, Norfolk. PE37 8AE. Tel: 721611 (0760)
Secretary: R Joslin　　　　　Tel: 721611 (0760)
Professional: P Field　　　　　Tel: 721611 (0760)
Location: 1 1/2 miles from centre of Swaffham on Cockley Cley Road.
Description: Heathland.
9 holes, 6,252 yards, Par 72, S.S.S. 70, Course record 64.
Membership: 500
Visitors: Welcome. Handicap certificate required. With members only at w/ends. No catering Monday or Tuesday.
Green Fees: £18 per day or round.
Facilities: Lunch. Dinner. Bar Snacks. Full Catering. Changing Room. Golf Shop. Club Hire. Trolley Hire.
Class One Hotel: George, Swaffham, 1 1/2 mile(s). Tel: 721238 (0760)

THETFORD
Thetford Golf Club, Brandon Road, Thetford, Norfolk. IP24 3NE. Tel: 752169 (0842)
Secretary: R J Ferguson　　　Tel: 752169 (0842)
Professional: N Arthur　　　　Tel: 752662 (0842)
Location: On B1107 1/2 mile off A11 at Thetford.
Description: Wooded heathland. A course of Character.
18 holes, 6,879 yards, Par 72, S.S.S. 73, Course record 68.
Membership: 700
Visitors: Welcome. Handicap certificate required. With members at weekends and Bank Holidays.
Green Fees: £26.
Facilities: Lunch. Dinner. Bar Snacks. Full Catering. Changing Room. Golf Shop. Club Hire. Trolley Hire.
Class One Hotel: The Bell, Thetford, 1 mile(s). Tel: 754455 (0842)
Class Two Hotel: Wereham House, Thetford, 1 mile(s). Tel: 761956 (0842)

NORTHAMPTONSHIRE

CHURCH BRAMPTON
Northamptonshire County Golf Club, Church Brampton, Northants.　NN6 8AZ. Tel: 842170 (0604)
Secretary: Mr Wadley　　　　Tel: 843025 (0604)
Professional: M T Rouse　　　Tel: 842226 (0604)
Location: 6 miles north west of Northampton between M1 and town centre.
Description: Tree lined heathland with ditches and a brook running through the course.
18 holes, 6,503 yards, Par 70, S.S.S. 71, Course record 63.
Membership: 750
Visitors: Welcome. Handicap certificate required. Society meetings Wednesdays. Tuesdays Ladies Day.
Green Fees: £30 per round or day.
Facilities: Lunch. Dinner. Bar Snacks. Full Catering. Changing Room. Golf Shop. Club Hire. Driving Range. Trolley Hire.

COLD ASHBY
Cold Ashby Golf Club, Cold Ashby, Northants.　NN6 7EP. Tel: 740548 (0604)
Secretary: David Croxton　　　Tel: 740548 (0604)
Professional: Tony Skingle　　Tel: 740099 (0604)
Location: 12 miles north of Northampton. 5 miles east of junc 18 (M1).
Description: Undulating parkland with natural streams and super views.
18 holes, 6,010 yards, Par 70, S.S.S. 69, Course record 64.
Membership: 700
Visitors: Welcome. With members at weekends.
Green Fees: £13.50 per round, £19 per day.
Facilities: Lunch. Dinner. Bar Snacks. Full Catering. Changing Room. Golf Shop. Club Hire. Trolley Hire.
Class One Hotel: Post House, Crick, 5 mile(s). Tel: 822101 (0788)
Class Two Hotel: Broom Hill Hotel, Spratton, 5 mile(s). Tel: 845959 (0604)

HARLESTONE
Northampton Golf Club, Harlestone, Northants.　NN7 4EF. Tel: 845102 (0604)
Secretary: I M Kirkwood　　　Tel: 845155 (0604)
Professional: M Chamberlain　Tel: 845167 (0604)
Location: On A428 4 miles north-west of Northampton towards Rugby, pass through the Village of Harlestone.
Description: Parkland.
18 holes, 6,534 yards, Par 72, S.S.S. 71.
Membership: 889
Visitors: Welcome. Handicap certificate required. Letter of Introduction required. Not Wednesdays. With members only at weekends.
Green Fees: £25 per day.
Facilities: Lunch. Dinner. Bar Snacks. Full Catering. Changing Room. Golf Shop. Club Hire. Trolley Hire.
Class One Hotel: Broomhill, Spratton, 4 mile(s). Tel: 845959 (0604)

KETTERING
Kettering Golf Club, Headlands, Kettering, Northants. NN15 6XA. Tel: 512074 (0536)
Secretary: B C L Rumary　　　Tel: 511104 (0536)
Professional: K Theobald　　　Tel: 81014 (0536)
Description: Meadowland.
18 holes, 6,035 yards, Par 69, S.S.S. 69, Course record 65.
Membership: 680
Visitors: Welcome. Handicap certificate required. With members at weekends. Some catering restrictions apply, please telephone in advance.

Green Fees: £20.
Facilities: Lunch. Dinner. Bar Snacks. Full Catering. Changing Room. Golf Shop. Trolley Hire.
Class One Hotel: George, Kettering, 1 mile(s). Tel: 518500 (0536)
Class Two Hotel: Headlands, Kettering, 1 mile(s). Tel: 524624 (0536)

NORTHAMPTON
Collingtree Park Golf Club, Windingbrook Lane, Northampton, Northants. NN4 0XN. Tel: 700000 (0604)
Secretary: Mrs G Peters   Tel: 700000 (0604)
Professional: Mr John Cook   Tel: 700000 (0604)
Location: On A508 1 1/2 miles from junc 15 M1.
Description: Parkland 18th hole is an island green.
18 holes, 6,692 yards, Par , S.S.S. 72.
Membership: 600
Visitors: Welcome. Handicap certificate required. Anytime, weekends after 1 p.m. Telephone in advance.
Green Fees: Summer weekdays £35, winter weekday £25, weekends £50. (18 hole rates).
Facilities: Lunch. Dinner. Bar Snacks. Full Catering. Changing Room. Golf Shop. Club Hire. Driving Range. Buggy Hire.
Class One Hotel: Stakis Country Court, Northampton, 2 mile(s). Tel: 700666 (0604)

WELLINGBOROUGH
Rushden Golf Club, Kimbolton Road, Chelveston, Wellingborough, Northants. NN9 6AN. Tel: 312581 (0933)
Secretary: E W Richardson   Tel: 314910 (0933)
Location: On A45 2 miles east of Higham Ferrers.
Description: Undulating parkland.
9 holes, 6,335 yards, Par 71, S.S.S. 70.
Membership: 360
Visitors: Welcome. Not Wednesday afternoons. With members at weekends. Some catering restrictions apply, please telephone in advance.
Green Fees: £12 per round, £8 with member.
Facilities: Lunch. Dinner. Bar Snacks. Changing Room.

WELLINGBOROUGH
Wellingborough Golf Club, Harrowden Hall, Great Harrowden, Wellingborough, Northants. NN9 5AD. Tel: 673022 (0933)
Secretary: Roy Tomlin   Tel: 677234 (0933)
Professional: David Clifford   Tel: 678752 (0933)
Location: 1 mile north of Wellingborough at Great Harrowden crossroads on A509.
Description: Undulating parkland, with trees and lakes.
18 holes, 6,620 yards, Par 72, S.S.S. 72, Course record 69.
Membership: 850
Visitors: Welcome. Handicap certificate required. With members at weekends.
Green Fees: £22 per round, £27 per day.
Facilities: Lunch. Dinner. Bar Snacks. Full Catering. Changing Room. Golf Shop. Trolley Hire. Buggy Hire.
Class One Hotel: Tudor Gate, Finedon, 2 mile(s). Tel: 680408 (0933)
Class Two Hotel: Oak House, Wellingborough, 2 mile(s). Tel: 271133 (0933)

NORTHUMBERLAND

ALNWICK
Alnwick Golf Club, Swansfield Park, Alnwick, Northumberland.
Secretary: L E Stewart   Tel: 602499 (0665)
Location: At Alnwick turn left off A1 in to Willowburn Ave, over roundabout 2nd left in to Swansfield Park Road, left at park gates and then first right.
Description: Mature parkland.
9 holes, 5,387 yards, Par 66, S.S.S. 66.
Membership: 420
Visitors: Welcome. Handicap certificate required.
Green Fees: Weekdays £10 per round, £15 per day. Weekends and Bank Holidays £15 per round, £20 per day.
Facilities: Lunch. Bar Snacks. Full Catering. Changing Room. Trolley Hire.
Class One Hotel: White Swan, Alnwick, 1 mile(s). Tel: 602109 (0665)
Class Two Hotel: The Oaks, Alnwick, 1 mile(s). Tel: 510014 (0665)

ALNWICK
Dunstanburgh Castle Golf Club, Embleton, Alnwick, Northumberland. NE66 3XQ. Tel: 576562 (0665)
Secretary: Dr P F C Gilbert   Tel: 576562 (0665)
Location: 7 miles north-east of Alnwick off A1.
Description: Links course in area of outstanding natural beauty, founded in 1905 - remodelled by James Braid in 1922.
18 holes, 6,039 yards, Par 70, S.S.S. 69.
Membership: 370
Visitors: Welcome.
Green Fees: Weekdays £10.50, weekends and Bank Holidays £12.75 per round, £16.50 per day.
Facilities: Lunch. Dinner. Bar Snacks. Full Catering. Changing Room. Golf Shop. Trolley Hire.
Class Two Hotel: Dunstanburgh Castle, Embleton, 1/2 mile(s). Tel: 203 (066576)

BAMBURGH
Bamburgh Castle Golf Club, Bamburgh, Northumberland. NE69 7DE. Tel: 378 (06684)
Secretary: T C Osborne   Tel: 321 (06684)
Location: Between Alnwick and Berwick-Upon-Tweed east of A1 take B1341 or B1342 to Bamburgh Village.
Description: Links course with outstanding views of Holy Island and Farne Islands.
18 holes, 5,465 yards, Par 68, S.S.S. 67.
Membership: 650
Visitors: Welcome. Handicap certificate required. Not Bank Holidays or competition weekends. No catering Tuesdays.
Green Fees: Weekdays £20 per day or round, weekends £25 per round, £30 per day.
Facilities: Lunch. Dinner. Bar Snacks. Full Catering. Changing Room. Trolley Hire. Buggy Hire.
Class Two Hotel: Sunningdale, Bamburgh, 1 mile(s). Tel: 324 (06684)

BEDLINGTON

Bedlingtonshire Golf Club, Acorn Bank, Bedlington, Northumberland. NE22 6AA. Tel: 822457 (0670)
Secretary: B W Munro   Tel: 822457 (0670)
Professional: Marcus Webb   Tel: 822087 (0670)
Location: 1 mile south-west of Bedlington on A1086.
Description: Parkland.
18 holes, 6,813 yards, Par 73, S.S.S. 73.
Membership: 830
Visitors: Welcome. Handicap certificate required. Letter of Introduction required. Society meetings catered for. Applications to Chief Leisure Officer, Town Hall, Ashington.
Green Fees: Weekdays £12 per round, £15 per day. Weekends £14.50 per round, £19 per day.
Facilities: Lunch. Dinner. Bar Snacks. Full Catering. Changing Room. Golf Shop. Club Hire. Trolley Hire.

BERWICK-UPON-TWEED

Berwick-upon-Tweed (Goswick) Golf Club, Beal, Berwick-upon-Tweed, Northumberland. TD15 2RW. Tel: 87256 (0289)
Secretary: R C Oliver   Tel: 87256 (0289)
Professional: P Terras   Tel: 87380 (0289)
Location: Off A1 3 miles south of Berwick-Upon-Tweed.
Description: Links.
18 holes, 6,400 yards, Par 72, S.S.S. 71, Course record 63.
Membership: 450
Visitors: Welcome. Times restricted, please telephone in advance.
Green Fees: Weekdays £14 per round £18 per day. Weekends £18 per round £24 per day.
Facilities: Lunch. Bar Snacks. Changing Room. Golf Shop. Trolley Hire.
Class One Hotel: Kings Arms, Berwick, 5 mile(s). Tel: 307454 (0289)

BLYTH

Blyth Golf Club, New Delaval, Blyth, Northumberland. NE24. Tel: 367728 (0670)
Secretary: Miss J Tate   Tel: 540110 (0670)
Professional: Mr B Rumney
Location: 2 miles from town centre.
Description: Parkland.
18 holes, 6,300 yards, Par 72, S.S.S. 70, Course record 64.
Membership: 800
Visitors: Welcome. Not after 3 p.m. weekdays. With a member at weekends.
Green Fees: £12 per round £14 per day.
Facilities: Lunch. Bar Snacks. Changing Room. Golf Shop.

HALTWHISTLE

Haltwhistle Golf Course, Banktop, Greenhead, Near Haltwhistle, Northumberland. CA6 7HN. Tel: 47367 (06977)
Secretary: Bill Barnes   Tel: 320337 (0434)
Professional: Joe Metcalfe   Tel: 47367 (06977)
Location: Off A69, 2 miles west of Haltwhistle on Gilsland Road.
Description: Hillside country course, with magnificent views.
12 holes, 5,973 yards, Par 72, S.S.S. 69, Course record 74.
Membership: 300
Visitors: Welcome. Ladies day is Monday. Not before 4 p.m. Sundays. Some catering restrictions apply, please telephone in advance.
Green Fees: £10 per day.
Facilities: Bar Snacks. Changing Room. Golf Shop. Club Hire.
Class One Hotel: Gilsland Spa, Gilsland, 2 mile(s). Tel: 47203 (06977)
Class Two Hotel: Greenhead, Gilsland, 1/4 mile(s). Tel: 47411 (06977)

HEXHAM

Allendale Golf Club, Thornley Gate, Allendale, Hexham, Northumberland. NE47 9LG.
Secretary: Jim Hall   Tel: 267 5875 (091)
Location: 10 miles south of Hexham on B6295.
Description: Hilly parkland.
9 holes, 4,488 yards, Par 66, S.S.S. 63, Course record 63.
Membership: 130
Visitors: Welcome. Handicap certificate required. Not Sundays a.m. from May to September. Not August Bank Holiday Monday.
Green Fees: Weekdays £4, weekends and Bank Holidays £5.
Facilities: Changing Room. Golf Shop.
Class One Hotel: Bishopfields, Allendale, 1 mile(s). Tel: 683248 (0434)
Class Two Hotel: Heatherlea, Allendale, 1 mile(s). Tel: 233706 (0434)

HEXHAM

Bellingham Golf Club, Bogglehole, Bellingham, Northumberland. NE48 2JU. Tel: 220530 (0434)
Secretary: T H Thompson   Tel: 220281 (0434)
Location: 4 miles west of A38.
Description: Upland.
9 holes, 5,245 yards, Par 67, S.S.S. 66, Course record 63.
Membership: 250
Visitors: Welcome. Not during club competitions.
Green Fees: Weekdays £7, weekends and Bank Holidays £10.
Facilities: Lunch. Dinner. Full Catering. Changing Room.
Class One Hotel: Riverdale Hall, Bellingham, 1/2 mile(s). Tel: 220254 (0434)
Class Two Hotel: Cheviot, Bellingham, 1/2 mile(s). Tel: 220216 (0434)

HEXHAM

Hexham Golf Club, Spital Park, Hexham, Northumberland. NE46 3RZ. Tel: 602057 (0434)
Secretary: J C Oates   Tel: 603072 (0434)
Professional: Ian Waugh   Tel: 604904 (0434)
Location: 1 mile west of town centre.
Description: Undulating parkland.
18 holes, 6,000 yards, Par 70, S.S.S. 68, Course record 65.
Membership: 700
Visitors: Welcome. Handicap certificate required. No society bookings at weekends. Always telephone in advance. Caddies by prior arrangement.

Green Fees: Weekdays £18 per round, £24 per day. Weekends £24 per round, £30 per day.
Facilities: Lunch. Dinner. Bar Snacks. Full Catering. Changing Room. Golf Shop. Club Hire. Trolley Hire.
Class One Hotel: Beaumont, Hexham, 1 mile(s). Tel: 602331 (0434)

PONTELAND

Ponteland Golf Club, 57, Bell Villas, Ponteland, Northumberland. NE20 9BD. Tel: 22689 (0661)
Secretary: Mr Hillyer   Tel: 22689 (0661)
Professional: Alan Crosby   Tel: 22689 (0661)
Location: On the southern perimeter of Ponteland Village, 2 miles from Newcastle airport on A696.
Description: Partly wooded.
18 holes, 6,524 yards, Par 72, S.S.S. 71, Course record 67.
Membership: 766
Visitors: Welcome. Handicap certificate required. Parties and societies on Tuesdays and Thursdays only. With member only Fridays, Saturdays, Sundays and Bank Holidays.
Green Fees: £21 per day.
Facilities: Lunch. Dinner. Bar Snacks. Full Catering. Changing Room. Golf Shop. Trolley Hire.
Class One Hotel: The Airport Moat House, Ponteland, 1 1/2 mile(s). Tel: 24911 (0661)

ROTHBURY

Rothbury Golf Club, Old Race Course, Thropton Road, Rothbury, Northumberland. NE65 7TL. Tel: 21271 (0669)
Secretary: W T Bathgate   Tel: 20718 (0669)
Location: Leave A1 at Morpeth on to A987, turn off to Rothbury at Weldon Bridge. Follow signs to Rothbury.
Description: Parkland.
9 holes, 5,560 yards, Par 68, S.S.S. 67.
Membership: 400
Visitors: Welcome. Ladies day Tuesday. Weekends mostly competitions and members only, occasional visitors by prior arrangement.
Green Fees: Weekdays £9, weekends £14.
Class One Hotel: Coquet Vale, Rothbury, 1/2 mile(s). Tel: 20305 (0669)

SEAHOUSES

Seahouses Golf Club, Beadnell Road, Seahouses, Northumberland. NE68 7XT. Tel: 720794 (0665)
Secretary: J A Stevens   Tel: 720794 (0665)
Description: Links type course with water hazards.
18 holes, 5,457 yards, Par 67, S.S.S. 67, Course record 65.
Membership: 490
Visitors: Welcome.
Green Fees: Weekdays £13 per day, weekends £16.50 per day.
Facilities: Lunch. Dinner. Bar Snacks. Full Catering. Changing Room.
Class One Hotel: Marine House, Alnmouth, 7 mile(s). Tel: 830349 (0665)
Class Two Hotel: Links, Seahouses, 1 mile(s). Tel: 720062 (0665)

STOCKSFIELD

Stocksfield Golf Club, New Ridley, Stocksfield, Northumberland. NE43 7RE. Tel: 843041 (0661)
Secretary: D B Moon   Tel: 843041 (0661)
Professional: K Driver   Tel: 843041 (0661)
Location: 15 miles west of Newcastle-On-Tyne on A69. 3 miles east of A68.
Description: Part woodland and part open countryside.
18 holes, 5,594 yards, Par 68, S.S.S. 68, Course record 64.
Membership: 760
Visitors: Welcome. Handicap certificate required. Weekdays. Weekends after 4 p.m. Telephone for reservations.
Green Fees: Weekdays £15 per round, £20 per day. Weekends £20 per round.
Facilities: Bar Snacks. Changing Room. Golf Shop. Club Hire. Trolley Hire.
Class One Hotel: Royal Derwent, Allensford, 6 mile(s). Tel: 592000 (0207)
Class Two Hotel: Broomhaugh, Riding Mill, 6 mile(s). Tel: 682256 (0434)

NOTTINGHAMSHIRE

BULWELL

Bulwell Forest Golf Club, Hucknall Road, Bulwell, Notts. NG5 9LQ. Tel: 770576 (0602)
Secretary: D Stubbs   Tel: 770576 (0602)
Professional: C D Hall   Tel: 763172 (0602)
Location: 3 miles from junc 26 M1, follow signs to Nottingham then Bulwell.
Description: Moorland municipal course.
18 holes, 5,893 yards, Par 68, S.S.S. 67, Course record 65.
Membership: 420
Visitors: Welcome. Always telephone for booking in advance.
Green Fees: Weekdays £6.80, weekends £8.50.
Facilities: Lunch. Bar Snacks. Changing Room. Golf Shop. Club Hire. Trolley Hire.
Class One Hotel: The Moat House, Nottingham, 1 1/2 mile(s). Tel: 602621 (0602)

BULWELL

Nottingham City Golf Club, Lawton Drive, Bulwell, Notts. NG6 8BL. Tel: 278021 (0602)
Secretary: D A Griffiths   Tel: 278021 (0602)
Professional: Cyril Jepson   Tel: 272767 (0602)
Location: 3 miles north of Nottingham junc 26 M1.
Description: Parkland.
18 holes, 6,218 yards, Par 69, S.S.S. 70, Course record 65.
Membership: 400
Visitors: Welcome. Not at weekends.
Green Fees: Weekdays £7, weekends £8.50.
Facilities: Lunch. Dinner. Bar Snacks. Full Catering. Changing Room. Golf Shop. Club Hire. Trolley Hire.

EAST LEAKE

Rushcliffe Golf Club, Stocking Lane, East Leake, Near Loughborough. LE12 5RL. Tel: 852959 (0509)
Secretary: D J Barnes   Tel: 852959 (0509)

Location: 4 miles north of Loughborough off junc 24 M1 on A453 signposted Gotham.
Description: Rural well wooded and hilly.
18 holes, 6,058 yards, Par 70, S.S.S. 69, Course record 62.
Membership: 700
Visitors: Welcome. Handicap certificate required. Weekends between 9.30 - 11.00 a.m. and 3.00 - 4.30 p.m.
Green Fees: Weekdays £22, weekends £25.
Facilities: Lunch. Dinner. Bar Snacks. Full Catering. Changing Room. Golf Shop. Trolley Hire.

KIRKBY-IN-ASHFIELD

Notts. (Hollinwell) Golf Club Ltd., Derby Road, Kirkby-in-Ashfield, Notts. NG17 7QR. Tel: 753225 (0623)
Secretary: J R Walker   Tel: 753225 (0623)
Professional: Brian Waites   Tel: 753087 (0623)
Location: On A611 3 miles from junc 27 M1.
Description: Championship heathland.
Long 18 holes, 7,020 yards, Par 72, S.S.S. 74, Course record 67.
Membership: 500
Visitors: Welcome. Handicap certificate required. Letter of Introduction required. Not between 12.00-1.00 p.m. Mons & Tues, or 12.00-2.00 p.m. Weds & Thurs. Fri Ladies only until 12.30 p.m.
Green Fees: £30 per round, £38 per day.
Facilities: Lunch. Dinner. Bar Snacks. Full Catering. Changing Room. Golf Shop. Club Hire. Driving Range. Trolley Hire. Caddies available.
Class One Hotel: Swallow, South Normanton, 5 mile(s). Tel: 812000 (0773)
Class Two Hotel: Pine Lodge, Mansfield, 3 mile(s). Tel: 22308 (0623)

MANSFIELD

Mansfield Woodhouse Golf Club, Leeming Lane North, Mansfield, Notts. NG19 9EU. Tel: 23521 (0623)
Secretary: T Mason   Tel: 33769 (0623)
Professional: L Highfield Jnr. Tel: 23521 (0623)
Location: On main A60 Mansfield to Worksop road.
Description: Flat parkland.
9 holes, 4,892 yards, Par 68, S.S.S. 64, Course record 68.
Membership: 130
Visitors: Welcome. Not before 11a.m. Saturdays. Caddies at weekends only.
Green Fees: £2.60 for 9 holes, £3.75 for 18 holes.
Facilities: Lunch. Dinner. Bar Snacks. Full Catering. Golf Shop. Club Hire.
Class One Hotel: Pine Lodge, Mansfield, 7 mile(s). Tel: 22308 (0623)

MANSFIELD

Sherwood Forest Golf Club, Eakring Road, Mansfield, Notts. NG18 3EW. Tel: 26689 (0623)
Description: Traditional heathland course designed at the turn of the century by H S Colt, subsequently re-designed by James Braid.
18 holes, 6,710 yards, Par 71, S.S.S. 73, Course record 68.
Membership: 749
Visitors: Welcome. Handicap certificate required. Letter of Introduction required. Not Saturday, Sunday, Tuesday or Wednesday.
Green Fees: £28 per round, £33 per day.
Facilities: Lunch. Dinner. Bar Snacks. Full Catering. Changing Room. Golf Shop. Club Hire. Trolley Hire.

NEWARK

Newark Golf Club, Coddington, Newark, Notts. NG24 2QX. Tel: 626241 (0636)
Secretary: A W Morgans   Tel: 626282 (0636)
Professional: H A Bennett   Tel: 626492 (0636)
Location: On A17 from Newark.
Description: Flat parkland.
18 holes, 6,421 yards, Par 71, S.S.S. 71, Course record 71.
Membership: 600
Visitors: Welcome. Handicap certificate required. Weekdays. Always telephone in advance.
Green Fees: Weekdays £16.50 per round, £20.50 per day. Weekends £20.50 per round or day.
Facilities: Lunch. Dinner. Bar Snacks. Full Catering. Changing Room. Golf Shop. Trolley Hire.

NOTTINGHAM

Beeston Fields Golf Club, Old Drive, Woollaton Road, Beeston, Notts. NG9 3DD. Tel: 257062 (0602)
Secretary: J E L Grove   Tel: 257062 (0602)
Professional: A Wardle   Tel: 220872 (0602)
Location: Off A52 1 mile from Beeston.
White 18 holes, 6,414 yards, Par 71, S.S.S. 71, Course record 67.
Yellow 18 holes, 6,166 yards, Par 71, S.S.S. 69, Course record 67.
Visitors: Welcome. Handicap certificate required. Not Tuesdays.
Green Fees: Weekdays £25, Weekends £30.
Facilities: Lunch. Dinner. Bar Snacks. Full Catering. Changing Room. Golf Shop. Trolley Hire.
Class One Hotel: Royal Moat House, Nottingham, 3 mile(s). Tel: 414444 (0602)
Class Two Hotel: The Hylands, Beeston, 2 mile(s). Tel: 257456 (0602)

NOTTINGHAM

Mapperley Golf Club, Plains Road, Mapperley, Nottingham, Notts. NG3 5RH. Tel: 265611 (0602)
Secretary: A Newton   Tel: 265611 (0602)
Professional: R Daibell   Tel: 202227 (0602)
Location: 3 miles north-east of City Centre on Woodborough road.
Description: Hilly parkland.
18 holes, 6,300 yards, Par 71, S.S.S. 70.
Membership: 600
Visitors: Welcome. Not Saturdays in summer. Some catering restrictions apply, please telephone in advance.
Green Fees: Weekdays £14 per round, £9 with member. Weekends £16 per round, £11 with member.
Facilities: Lunch. Dinner. Bar Snacks. Full Catering. Changing Room. Golf Shop. Trolley Hire.
Class One Hotel: Woodville Hotel, Carrington, 1 mile(s). Tel: 606436 (0602)

RADCLIFFE-ON-TRENT

Radcliffe-on-Trent Golf Club, Dewberry Lane, Cropwell Road, Radcliffe-On-Trent, Notts. NG12 2JH. Tel: 333000 (0602)
Secretary: Major B C Hodgson   Tel: 333000 (0602)
Professional: N Burkitt   Tel: 333000 (0602)
Description: Parkland.
18 holes, 6,423 yards, Par 71, S.S.S. 70, Course record 71.
Visitors: Welcome. Handicap certificate required. Letter of Introduction required. Must be members of another club. Ladies day Tuesday. Visiting parties Wednesdays.
Green Fees: Weekdays £21, weekends £26.
Facilities: Lunch. Dinner. Bar Snacks. Full Catering. Changing Room. Golf Shop.

RETFORD

Retford Golf Club Ltd., Brecks Road, Ordsall, Retford, Notts. DN22 7UA. Tel: 703733 (0777)
Secretary: A Harrison   Tel: 860682 (0777)
Professional: S Betteridge   Tel: 703733 (0777)
Location: 1 1/2 miles south of A620, between Worksop and Retford.
Description: Parkland and woodland.
18 holes, 6,301 yards, Par 71, S.S.S. 70, Course record 71.
Membership: 700
Visitors: Welcome. With members only at weekends.
Green Fees: Weekdays £15 per round, £20 per day. Weekends £20.
Facilities: Lunch. Dinner. Bar Snacks. Full Catering. Changing Room. Golf Shop. Trolley Hire.
Class One Hotel: Ye Olde Bell, Barnby Moor, 4 mile(s). Tel: 705121 (0777)

WEST BRIDGFORD

Edwalton Municipal Golf & Social Club, Wellin Lane, Edwalton, West Bridgford, Notts. NG12 4AS. Tel: 234775 (0602)
Secretary: E Watts   Tel: 231576 (0602)
Professional: J A Staples   Tel: 234775 (0602)
Location: 1 1/2 south of Trentbridge off A606 Melton Mowbray Road.
Description: Undulating Parkland.
One 9 holes, 3,336 yards, Par 36, S.S.S. 72.
Two 9 holes, 1,563 yards, Par 27.
Membership: 800
Visitors: Welcome. Bookings required for same day. Six days in advance for weekends.
Green Fees: One: £4 nine holes. Two: £2.20 nine holes.
Facilities: Lunch. Dinner. Bar Snacks. Full Catering. Changing Room. Golf Shop. Club Hire. Trolley Hire.
Class One Hotel: The Beeches, West Bridgford, 1 1/2 mile(s). Tel: 818753 (0602)
Class Two Hotel: Edwalton Hall, Edwalton, 1/2 mile(s). Tel: 452323 (0602)

WORKSOP

Kilton Forest Golf Club, Blyth Road, Worksop, Notts. S81 0TL. Tel: 472488 (0909)
Secretary: P W Foster   Tel: 486563 (0909)
Professional: E L James   Tel: 477427 (0909)
Location: B6045 1 mile north of Worksop.
Description: Undulating, no steep hills.
18 holes, 6,450 yards, Par 72, S.S.S. 72, Course record 69.
Membership: 450
Visitors: Welcome. Not during club competitions (most Sundays through spring and summer).
Green Fees: On application.
Facilities: Bar Snacks. Changing Room. Golf Shop. Club Hire. Trolley Hire.
Class Two Hotel: Regancy, Worksop, 1 mile(s). Tel: 474108 (0909)

WORKSOP

Lindrick Golf Club, Lindrick Common, Worksop, Notts. S81 8BH. Tel: 485802 (0909)
Secretary: G Bywater   Tel: 475282 (0909)
Professional: P Cowen   Tel: 475820 (0909)
Location: On A57 4 miles west of Worksop.
Description: Heathland.
18 holes, 6,615 yards, Par 71, S.S.S. 72.
Membership: 500
Visitors: Welcome. Handicap certificate required. By arrangement with the Secretary's office. Not Tuesdays. Not weekends in winter.
Green Fees: Weekdays £35 per day, weekends £45 per round.
Facilities: Lunch. Dinner. Bar Snacks. Full Catering. Changing Room. Golf Shop. Trolley Hire. Caddies available.

WORKSOP

Worksop Golf Club, Windmill Lane, Worksop, Notts. S80 2SQ. Tel: 472696 (0909)
Secretary: P G Jordan   Tel: 477731 (0909)
Location: Between junc 31 M1 and A1 on A57.
Description: Heathland.
18 holes, 6,651 yards, Par 72, S.S.S. 73, Course record 67.
Membership: 600
Visitors: Welcome. Handicap certificate required. Ladies day Tuesday. No catering on Mondays. Always telephone in advance.
Green Fees: Weekdays £18 per round, £25 per day. Weekends £25.
Facilities: Lunch. Dinner. Bar Snacks. Full Catering. Changing Room. Golf Shop. Trolley Hire.
Class One Hotel: Travelodge, Worksop, 2 mile(s). Tel: 850950 (0800)

OXON

ABINGDON

Frilford Heath Golf Club, Abingdon, Oxon. OX13 5NW. Tel: 390864 (0865)
Secretary: J W Kleynhans   Tel: 390864 (0865)
Professional: Derek Craik   Tel: 390887 (0865)
Location: On A338, 8 miles west of Oxford, 6 miles west of Abingdon.
Description: Heathland.
Red 18 holes, 6,768 yards, Par 73, S.S.S. 73, Course record 68.
Green 18 holes, 6,006 yards, Par 69, S.S.S. 69, Course record 65.

Membership: 1000
Visitors: Welcome. Handicap certificate required. Letter of Introduction required.Only by prior arrangement. Societies Mondays, Wednesdays and Fridays. With members only at weekends.
Green Fees: Weekdays £37, weekends and Bank Holidays £47.
Facilities: Lunch. Dinner. Bar Snacks. Full Catering. Changing Room. Golf Shop. Club Hire. Trolley Hire. Buggy Hire.
Class One Hotel: Upper Reaches, Abingdon, 6 mile(s). Tel: 522311 (0235)
Class Two Hotel: The Doghouse, Frilford Heath, 1/2 mile(s). Tel: 390830 (0865)

BANBURY

Cherwell Edge Course, Chacombe, Banbury, Oxon. OX17 2EN. Tel: 711591 (0295)
Professional: Richard Davies   Tel: 711591 (0295)
Location: 3 miles east of Banbury. M40 junc 11.
Description: Parkland.
18 holes, 5,802 yards, Par 70, S.S.S. 68.
Visitors: Welcome.
Green Fees: Weekdays £5.20, weekends £6.80.
Facilities: Lunch. Dinner. Bar Snacks. Full Catering. Changing Room. Golf Shop. Club Hire. Trolley Hire.
Class One Hotel: Whatley Hall, Banbury, 4 mile(s). Tel: 263451 (0925)

BANBURY

Tadmarton Heath Golf Club, Wigginton, Banbury, Oxon. OX15 5HL.
Secretary: R E Wackrill   Tel: 737278 (0608)
Professional: L Bond   Tel: 730047 (0608)
Location: 4 miles west of Banbury on B4035, turn left before Tadmarton Village, then 1 mile on left.
Description: Heathland.
18 holes, 5,917 yards, Par 69, S.S.S. 69.
Membership: 600
Visitors: Welcome. Handicap certificate required. Ladies day Thursday. With members only at weekends. Visitors by arrangement.
Green Fees: £26.
Facilities: Lunch. Dinner. Bar Snacks. Full Catering. Changing Room. Golf Shop. Club Hire. Trolley Hire.
Class One Hotel: Banbury Moat House, Banbury, 4 mile(s). Tel: 259361 (0295)
Class Two Hotel: Lissmore, Banbury, 4 mile(s). Tel: 267661 (0295)

BURFORD

Burford Golf Club, Burford, Oxon.   OX18 4JG. Tel: 822583 (0993)
Secretary: Richard Cane   Tel: 822583 (0993)
Professional: Norman Allen   Tel: 822344 (0993)
Location: Off A40 at Burford roundabout.
Description: Flat parkland.
18 holes, 6,405 yards, Par 71, S.S.S. 71, Course record 68.
Membership: 800
Visitors: Welcome. Handicap certificate required. Ladies day Tuesday. Members only Tuesdays, weekends and Bank Holidays. Visitors only by prior arrangement.

Green Fees: £25.
Facilities: Lunch. Dinner. Bar Snacks. Full Catering. Changing Room. Golf Shop. Club Hire. Trolley Hire.
Class Two Hotel: Cotswold Gateway, Burford, 1/8 mile(s). Tel: 822695 (0993)

CHIPPING NORTON

Chipping Norton Golf Club, Southcombe, Chipping Norton, Oxon. OX7 5QH. Tel: 642383 (0608)
Secretary: John Norman   Tel: 642383 (0608)
Professional: Robert Gould   Tel: 643356 (0608)
Location: Off main A3400, halfway between Stratford and Oxford. Take A44 Evesham road, Take Chipping Norton turn, golf course on corner.
Description: Hilly.
18 holes, 6,280 yards, Par 70, S.S.S. 70.
Membership: 889
Visitors: Welcome. Not weekends or Bank Holidays.
Green Fees: £22 per day.
Facilities: Lunch. Dinner. Bar Snacks. Full Catering. Changing Room. Golf Shop. Club Hire. Trolley Hire.
Class One Hotel: Crown and Cushion, Chipping Norton, 1 mile(s). Tel: 642533 (0608)
Class Two Hotel: Southcombe Guest House, Southcombe. Tel: 643068 (0608)

HENLEY-ON-THAMES

Badgemore Park Golf Club, Badgemore, Henley-On-Thames, Oxon. RG9 4NR. Tel: 572206 (0491)
Secretary: R Park   Tel: 572206 (0491)
Professional: Mark Wright   Tel: 574175 (0491)
Location: 1 mile from town centre of Henley on the Peppard road.
Description: Easy walking parkland.
18 holes, 6,112 yards, Par 69, S.S.S. 69.
Membership: 912
Visitors: Welcome. Handicap certificate required. By prior arrangement. Weekends and Bank Holidays a.m., with members only.
Green Fees: Weekdays £26, weekends and Bank Holidays £29.
Facilities: Lunch. Dinner. Bar Snacks. Full Catering. Changing Room. Golf Shop. Trolley Hire. Buggy Hire.
Class One Hotel: Red Lion, Henley, 1 mile(s). Tel: 572161 (0491)
Class Two Hotel: The Royal, Henley, 1 mile(s). Tel: 577526 (0491)

HENLEY-ON-THAMES

Henley Golf Club, Harpsden, Henley-on-Thames, Oxon. RG9 4HG. Tel: 575742 (0491)
Secretary: John Hex   Tel: 575742 (0491)
Professional: M Howell   Tel: 575710 (0491)
Description: Parkland with many interesting holes.
18 holes, 6,130 yards, Par 70, S.S.S. 70.
Membership: 820
Visitors: Welcome. Handicap certificate required. With members only at weekends and Bank Holidays.
Green Fees: £30 per round/day, November to March £20 per round/day.
Facilities: Lunch. Dinner. Bar Snacks. Full Catering. Chang-

ing Room. Golf Shop. Club Hire. Trolley Hire.
Class One Hotel: Red Lion, Henley, 2 mile(s). Tel: 572161 (0491)
Class Two Hotel: Little White Hart, Henley, 2 mile(s). Tel: 574145 (0491)

OXFORD

North Oxford Golf Club, Banbury Road, Oxford, Oxon. OX2 8EZ. Tel: 54924 (0865)
Secretary: W Forster　　　　　　Tel: 54924 (0865)
Professional: Bob Harris　　　　　Tel: 53977 (0865)
Location: Off A40, follow signs to Kidlington then Oxford. Follow road to golf club, which is Banbury Road.
Description: Parkland.
18 holes, 5,736 yards, Par 67, S.S.S. 67, Course record 64.
Membership: 750
Visitors: Welcome. With members only at weekends and bank Holidays.
Green Fees: £25 per day.
Facilities: Lunch. Dinner. Bar Snacks. Full Catering. Changing Room. Golf Shop. Club Hire. Trolley Hire.
Class One Hotel: Moat House, Oxford, 1/2 mile(s). Tel: 59933 (0865)

OXFORD

Southfield Golf Club, Hill Top Road, Oxford, Oxon. OX4 1PF. Tel: 242158 (0865)
Secretary: A Hopcraft　　　　　Tel: 242158 (0865)
Professional: Tony Rees　　　　Tel: 244258 (0865)
Location: Near Oxford Poly.
Description: Undulating parkland. Southfields hosts Oxford University Golf Club, Oxford City and Oxford Ladies.
18 holes, 6,300 yards, Par 69, S.S.S. 70, Course record 66.
Membership: 600
Visitors: Welcome. With members only at weekends.
Green Fees: Weekdays £24, £15 with member.
Facilities: Lunch. Dinner. Bar Snacks. Full Catering. Changing Room. Golf Shop. Club Hire. Trolley Hire. Buggy Hire.

SALOP

CHURCH STRETTON

Church Stretton Golf Club, Trevor Hill, Church Stretton, Salop. SY6 6JH. Tel: 722281 (0694)
Secretary: R Broughton　　　　Tel: 722633 (0694)
Location: 1 mile west of A49 through town adjoining Cardingmill Valley.
Description: Hillside with spectacular views.
18 holes, 5,008 yards, Par 66, S.S.S. 65, Course record 64.
Membership: 460
Visitors: Welcome. Handicap certificate required. Not between 9.00-10.30 a.m. and 1.00-2.30 p.m. Saturdays. Not before 10.30 a.m. and not between 12.30-3.00 p.m. on Sundays.
Green Fees: Weekdays £12, weekends and Bank Holidays £18.
Facilities: Lunch. Dinner. Bar Snacks. Full Catering. Changing Room. Golf Shop.
Class One Hotel: Longmynd, Church Stretton, 1 1/2 mile(s). Tel: 722244 (0694)

Class Two Hotel: Denehurst, Church Stretton, 1/2 mile(s). Tel: 722699 (0694)

LUDLOW

Ludlow Golf Club, Bromfield, Ludlow, Salop. SY8 2HL. Tel: 77285 (0584)
Secretary: M Cropper　　　　　Tel: 77285 (0584)
Professional: G J Farr　　　　　Tel: 77366 (0584)
Location: Off A49 2 miles north of Ludlow.
Description: Well drained parkland.
18 holes, 6,239 yards, Par 70, S.S.S. 70.
Membership: 550
Visitors: Welcome. Handicap certificate required. Societies by arrangement. Casual visitors should telephone professional in advance.
Green Fees: Weekdays £18, weekends £24.
Facilities: Lunch. Dinner. Bar Snacks. Full Catering. Changing Room. Golf Shop. Trolley Hire.

MARKET DRAYTON

Market Drayton Golf Club, Sutton, Market Drayton, Salop. TF9 2HX. Tel: 652266 (0630)
Secretary: J J Moseley　　　　　Tel: 653661 (0630)
Professional: R Clewes　　　　　Tel: 652266 (0630)
Location: 1 1/4 miles south-west of Market Drayton town centre.
Description: Undulating parkland.
18 holes, 6,214 yards, Par 71, S.S.S. 70.
Membership: 500
Visitors: Welcome. Not weekends or Bank Holidays.
Green Fees: £20 per day in summer, £20 per round in winter.
Facilities: Lunch. Dinner. Bar Snacks. Full Catering. Changing Room. Golf Shop. Trolley Hire.
Class One Hotel: Four Alls Motel, Market Drayton, 1 mile(s). Tel: 652995 (0630)
Class Two Hotel: Tern Hill Hall, Tern Hill, 2 mile(s). Tel: 638310 (0630)

OSWESTRY

Llanymynech Golf Club, Pant, Near Oswestry, Salop. SY10 8LB. Tel: 830542 (0691)
Secretary: N Clews　　　　　　Tel: 830983 (0691)
Professional: A Griffiths　　　　Tel: 830879 (0691)
Location: 1 mile west of A483 Oswestry to Welshpool Road. Turn by Cross Guns Inn, Pant.
Description: Upland course with extensive views.
18 holes, 6,114 yards, Par 70, S.S.S. 69, Course record 64.
Membership: 786
Visitors: Welcome. Handicap certificate required. Ladies Day Thursday. Telephone in advance.
Green Fees: Weekdays £13 per round, £18 per day. Weekends £19 per round, £23 per day.
Facilities: Lunch. Dinner. Bar Snacks. Full Catering. Changing Room. Golf Shop. Club Hire. Trolley Hire.
Class One Hotel: Wynnstay, Oswestry, 5 mile(s). Tel: 655261 (0691)
Class Two Hotel: Lion, Llanymynech, 1 mile(s). Tel: 830234 (0691)

OSWESTRY

Oswestry Golf Club, Aston Park, Oswestry, Salop. SY11 4JJ. Tel: 221 (069188)
Secretary: Mrs P M Lindner   Tel: 535 (069188)
Professional: D Skelton   Tel: 448 (069188)
Location: Off A5, 2 miles east from Mile End roundabout.
Description: Undulating parkland.
18 holes, 6,038 yards, Par 70, S.S.S. 69.
Membership: 740
Visitors: Welcome. Handicap certificate required. Ladies day Tuesday. Restricted at weekends and Bank Holidays - by prior arrangement only.
Green Fees: Weekdays £17, weekends and Bank Holidays £25.
Facilities: Lunch. Dinner. Bar Snacks. Full Catering. Changing Room. Golf Shop. Trolley Hire.
Class One Hotel: Wynnstay Hotel, Oswestry, 2 mile(s). Tel: 655261 (0691)

SHIFNAL

Shifnal Golf Club, Decker Hill, Shifnal, Salop. TF11 8QL. Tel: 460330 (0952)
Secretary: P W Holden   Tel: 460330 (0952)
Professional: J Flanagan   Tel: 460457 (0952)
Location: 1 mile north of Shifnal.
Description: Parkland.
18 holes, 6,260 yards, Par 71, S.S.S. 71, Course record 67.
Membership: 550
Visitors: Welcome. Handicap certificate required. Members only at weekends and Bank Holidays.
Green Fees: £25 per day.
Facilities: Lunch. Dinner. Bar Snacks. Full Catering. Changing Room. Golf Shop. Trolley Hire.
Class One Hotel: Park House, Shifnal, 2 mile(s). Tel: 460128 (0952)
Class Two Hotel: Jerningham Arms, Telford, 2 mile(s). Tel: 460411 (0952)

SHREWSBURY

Shrewsbury Golf Club, Condover, Shrewsbury, Salop. SY5 7BL. Tel: 722976 (0743)
Secretary: Mrs S Kenny   Tel: 722977 (0743)
Professional: P Seal   Tel: 723751 (0743)
Location: Off A49 south of Shrewsbury 3 miles.
Description: First 9 holes flat parkland, second 9 holes undulating with good views of Stretton Hills.
18 holes, 6,205 yards, Par 70, S.S.S. 70, Course record 60.
Membership: 700
Visitors: Welcome. Handicap certificate required. Weekends only between 10a.m. and 12p.m. or after 2.15p.m.. Not on Wednesdays. Advisable to telephone and check availability.
Green Fees: Weekdays £15 per round, £20 per day. Weekends and Bank Holidays £25 per round/day.
Facilities: Lunch. Dinner. Bar Snacks. Full Catering. Changing Room. Golf Shop. Club Hire. Trolley Hire.
Class One Hotel: Prince Rupert, Shrewsbury, 5 mile(s). Tel: 236000 (0743)
Class Two Hotel: The Pengwern, Shrewsbury, 4 mile(s). Tel: 343871 (0743)

Cade's - Audi Golf Course Guide

TELFORD

Telford Hotel, Golf and Country Club, Great Hay, Sutton Hill, Telford, Salop. TF7 4DT. Tel: 585642 (0952)
Secretary: John Brigham   Tel: 585642 (0952)
Professional: Graham Farr   Tel: 586052 (0952)
Location: A442 south of Telford to Brockton Roundabout, then follow brown signs to Telford golf club.
Description: Parkland.
The Great Hay 18 holes, 6,766 yards, Par 72.
Membership: 5000
Visitors: Welcome. Handicap certificate required. Societies only Mondays to Fridays unless resident. No dogs. Dress rules apply. Caddies by prior arrangement weekends and holidays.
Green Fees: Weekdays £25 per round, weekends and Bank Holidays £35.
Facilities: Lunch. Dinner. Bar Snacks. Full Catering. Changing Room. Golf Shop. Club Hire. Driving Range. Trolley Hire. Buggy Hire.
Class One Hotel: Telford hotel, On course, Tel: 585642 (0952)
Class Two Hotel: Hundred House, Norton, 5 mile(s). Tel: 353 (095271)

TELFORD

Wrekin Golf Club, Ercall Lane, Wellington, Telford, Salop. TF1 2DF. Tel: 244032 (0952)
Secretary: S Leys   Tel: 255586 (0952)
Professional: K Housden   Tel: 223101 (0952)
Location: M54 junc 6, take A5 towards Wellington, turn right at Wickets Public House.
Description: Undulating parkland.
18 holes, 5,699 yards, Par 66, S.S.S. 67, Course record 64.
Membership: 500
Visitors: Welcome. Dress rules apply.
Green Fees: W/days £18, w/ends and Bank Holidays £25.
Facilities: Lunch. Dinner. Bar Snacks. Full Catering. Changing Room. Golf Shop. Club Hire. Trolley Hire. Buggy Hire.
Class One Hotel: Buckatree Hall, Wellington, 2 mile(s). Tel: 641821 (0952)

WEM

Hawkstone Park Leisure Ltd., Hawkstone, Wem, Salop. SY4 5UY. Tel: 200611 (0939)
Professional: Keith Williams   Tel: 200209 (0939)
Location: Off A49 12 miles north of Shrewsbury.
Description: Undulating parkland.
Hawkstone 18 holes, 6,450 yards, Par 72, S.S.S. 71, Course record 66.
Weston 18 holes, 5,100 yards, Par 65, S.S.S. 65, Course record 65.
Membership: 650
Visitors: Welcome. Handicap certificate required. Reserved times for Hotel residents and members. Telephone in advance for booking.
Green Fees: Hawkstone; weekdays £25 per round, weekends £28. Weston; weekdays £12, £15 weekends
Facilities: Lunch. Dinner. Bar Snacks. Full Catering. Changing Room. Golf Shop. Club Hire. Trolley Hire. Buggy Hire.
Class One Hotel: Hawkstone Park Hotel, On course, Tel: 200611 (0939)

Class Two Hotel: The Bear, Hodnet, 3 mile(s). Tel: 214 (063084)

WHITCHURCH

Hill Valley Golf and Country Club, Kerrich Road, Whitchurch, Salop. SY13 4JZ. Tel: 3584 (0948)
Secretary: R B Walker   Tel: 3584 (0948)
Professional: Tony Minshall   Tel: 3032 (0948)
Location: 1 mile north of Whitchurch off A41 at junc of A49.
Description: Young woodland.
Hill Valley 18 holes, 6,517 yards, Par 72, S.S.S. 71, Course record 68.
Hill Valley II 18 holes, 4,406 yards, Par 63, S.S.S. 62.
Membership: 650
Visitors: Welcome. Handicap certificate required. Special visitor times, prior arrangement must be made.
Green Fees: Hill Valley - Weekdays £18 per round, weekends and Bank Holidays £24 per round. Hill Valley II - Weekdays £9, weekends and Bank Holidays
Facilities: Lunch. Dinner. Bar Snacks. Full Catering. Changing Room. Golf Shop. Club Hire. Trolley Hire. Buggy Hire.
Class One Hotel: Hill Valley Golf & C Club, On Course, Tel: 3584 (0948)

WORFIELD

Worfield Golf Club, Roughton, Worfield, Near Bridgenorth, Salop. . Tel: 372 (07464)
Secretary: W Weaver   Tel: 546 (07464)
Professional: D Thorp   Tel: 372 (07464)
Location: On A454 Bridgenorth to Wolverhampton Road 3 miles from Bridgenorth.
Description: Undulating course with feature lakes.
18 holes, 6,798 yards, Par 73, S.S.S. 72, Course record 73.
Visitors: Welcome. Handicap certificate required. Members have priority until 10a.m. and between 12.30p.m. and 2p.m..
Green Fees: Weekdays £15, weekends £20.
Facilities: Lunch. Bar Snacks. Full Catering. Changing Room. Golf Shop. Club Hire. Driving Range. Trolley Hire.
Class One Hotel: Old Vicarage, Worfield, 1 mile(s). Tel: 497 (07464)

SOMERSET

BRIDGWATER

Enmore Park Golf Club, Enmore, Bridgwater, Somerset. TA5 2AN. Tel: 671244 (0278)
Secretary: Mr D Weston   Tel: 671481 (0278)
Professional: Mr N Wixon   Tel: 671519 (0278)
Location: M5 exit 23 left at lights in town, 1 mile, course signposted 2 miles after left turn. Entry on the right.
Description: Undulating wooded parkland.
Gents 18 holes, 6,406 yards, Par 71, S.S.S. 71, Course record 66.
Ladies 18 holes, 5,714 yards, Par 74, S.S.S. 74, Course record 70.
Membership: 750
Visitors: Welcome. Handicap certificate required at weekends. No visitors on competition days.
Green Fees: Weekdays £18 per round, £25 per day.

Weekends £25 per round, £30 per day.
Facilities: Lunch. Dinner. Bar Snacks. Full Catering. Changing Room. Golf Shop. Club Hire. Buggy Hire.
Class Two Hotel: York House Inn, Minehead, 15 mile(s). Tel: 705151 (0643)

BURNHAM-ON-SEA

Brean Golf Club, Coast Road, Brean, Burnham-on-Sea, Somerset. TA8 2RF. Tel: 751570 (0278)
Secretary: W S Martin   Tel: 751570 (0278)
Professional: G Coombe   Tel: 751570 (0278)
Description: Meadowland.
18 holes, 5,630 yards, Par 69, S.S.S. 67, Course record 63.
Membership: 700
Visitors: Welcome. Handicap certificate required. Weekends and Bank Holidays after 1.30p.m..
Green Fees: Weekdays £12 per round, £20 per day. Weekends £15 per round.
Facilities: Lunch. Dinner. Bar Snacks. Full Catering. Changing Room. Golf Shop. Club Hire. Trolley Hire.

BURNHAM-ON-SEA

Burnham and Berrow Golf Club, St Christopher's Way, Burnham-on-Sea, Somerset.   TA8 2PE. Tel: 783137 (0278)
Secretary: Mrs E L Sloman   Tel: 785760 (0278)
Professional: M Crowther-Smith   Tel: 784545 (0278)
Location: M5 junc 22 1 mile north of Burnham.
Description: Seaside links championship course.
Championship 18 holes, 6,327 yards, Par 71, S.S.S. 72, Course record 66.
9 holes, 6,332 yards, Par 72, S.S.S. 70.
Membership: 940
Visitors: Welcome. Handicap certificate required. Handicap of 22 and under on championship course. Not before 2.30p.m. on Saturdays and only a few times available on Sundays.
Green Fees: 18 hole £28, £40 at weekends. 9 hole £8.
Facilities: Lunch. Dinner. Bar Snacks. Full Catering. Changing Room. Golf Shop. Club Hire. Trolley Hire. Caddies available.
Class One Hotel: Royal Pier, Weston-S-Mare, 12 mile(s). Tel: 626644 (0934)
Class Two Hotel: Batch Farm County Hotel, Lympshaw, 5 mile(s). Tel: 750371 (0934)

CHARD

Windwhistle Golf, Squash & Country Club Ltd, Cricket St Thomas, Chard, Somerset. TA20 4DG. Tel: 30231 (0460)
Secretary: Ian N Dodd   Tel: 30055 (0460)
Professional: Ivor Yard   Tel: 30055 (0460)
Location: On A30 between Chard and Crewkerne, 12 miles from junc 25 on M5 and 12 miles from Lyme Bay.
Description:
18 holes, 6,443 yards, Par 73, S.S.S. 71.
9 holes, 3,094 yards, Par 72, S.S.S. 70.
Membership: 600
Visitors: Welcome. Handicap certificate required. Letter of Introduction required. Please telephone for starting times and booking.

Cade's - Audi Golf Course Guide

Green Fees: On request.
Facilities: Lunch. Dinner. Bar Snacks. Full Catering. Changing Room. Golf Shop. Club Hire. Driving Range. Trolley Hire. Buggy Hire. Caddies availabl

MINEHEAD
Minehead and West Somerset Golf Club, The Warren, Minehead, Somerset. TA24 5SJ. Tel: 702057 (0643)
Secretary: L S Harper   Tel: 702057 (0643)
Professional: I M Read   Tel: 704378 (0643)
Location: 1 mile east of town at end of sea front past Butlins Camp.
Description: Links Course.
18 holes, 6,228 yards, Par 71, S.S.S. 71, Course record 68.
Visitors: Welcome. Not before 9.30a.m..
Green Fees: Weekdays £19.50, weekends £23.
Facilities: Lunch. Dinner. Bar Snacks. Full Catering. Changing Room. Golf Shop. Club Hire. Trolley Hire.
Class Two Hotel: York Hotel Inn, Minehead, 1 mile(s). Tel: 705151 (0643)

SHEPTON MALLET
Mendip Golf Club Ltd., Gurney Slade, Shepton Mallet, Near Bath, Somerset. BA3 4UT. Tel: 840570 (0749)
Secretary: Mrs J P Howe   Tel: 840570 (0749)
Professional: Mr R F Lee   Tel: 840793 (0749)
Location: 3 miles north of Shepton Mallet on A37.
Description: Undulating hilltop.
18 holes, 6,330 yards, Par 71, S.S.S. 70, Course record 65.
Membership: 780
Visitors: Welcome.
Green Fees: On application.
Facilities: Lunch. Dinner. Bar Snacks. Full Catering. Changing Room. Golf Shop. Club Hire. Trolley Hire.
Class One Hotel: Charlton House, Shepton Mallet, 3 mile(s). Tel: 342008 (0749)
Class Two Hotel: Star, Wells, 5 mile(s). Tel: 673055 (0749)

TAUNTON
Vivary Park Golf Course, Vivary Park, Taunton, Somerset. TA1 3JW. Tel: 333875 (0823)
Secretary: Keith Hunt
Professional: Jeremy Wright   Tel: 333875 (0823)
Location: Close to Taunton town centre.
Description: Overlooked by the Quantock and Blackdown Hills. Ideal for all standards of player. Public parkland course.
18 holes, 4,620 yards, Par 63, S.S.S. 63, Course record 63.
Membership: 500
Visitors: Welcome.
Green Fees: £6.80 per round.
Facilities: Lunch. Dinner. Bar Snacks. Full Catering. Changing Room. Golf Shop. Club Hire. Trolley Hire.
Class One Hotel: Runwell Manor, Taunton, 3 mile(s). Tel: 461902 (0823)
Class Two Hotel: Heatherton Grange, Taunton, 4 mile(s).

Tel: 461777 (0823)

WELLS
Wells (Somerset) Golf Club, East Horrington Road, Wells, Somerset. BA5 3DS. Tel: 675005 (0749)
Secretary: G E Ellis   Tel: 675005 (0749)
Professional: A England   Tel: 679059 (0749)
Description: Rolling wooded parkland.
18 holes, 5,354 yards, Par 67, S.S.S. 66, Course record 64.
Membership: 800
Visitors: Welcome. Not before 9.30a.m. weekends. Handicap certificates required at weekends and Bank Holidays.
Green Fees: Weekdays £16 per round, £19 per day. Weekends £20 per round, £22 per day.
Facilities: Lunch. Dinner. Bar Snacks. Full Catering. Changing Room. Golf Shop. Club Hire. Trolley Hire.
Class One Hotel: Swan, Wells, 1 1/2 mile(s). Tel: 678877 (0749)
Class Two Hotel: Bekynton Guest House, Wells, 1 mile(s). Tel: 672222 (0749)

YEOVIL
Yeovil Golf Club, Sherborne Road, Yeovil, Somerset. BA21 5BW. Tel: 75949 (0935)
Secretary: J Riley   Tel: 22965 (0935)
Professional: Geoff Kite   Tel: 73763 (0935)
Location: 1 mile from town centre on A30 to Sherborne/Salisbury Road on right hand side.
Description: Parkland.
Old course 18 holes, 6,144 yards, Par 72, S.S.S. 70, Course record 64.
Newton 9 holes, 2,508 yards, Par 34, S.S.S. 66.
Membership: 800
Visitors: Welcome. Handicap certificate required. Letter of Introduction required. Some catering restrictions apply, please telephone in advance.
Green Fees: Weekdays £20 per day, weekends £25 per day. 9 hole course on application.
Facilities: Lunch. Dinner. Bar Snacks. Full Catering. Changing Room. Golf Shop. Club Hire. Trolley Hire.
Class One Hotel: Manor Crest, Yeovil, 2 mile(s). Tel: 23116 (0935)
Class Two Hotel: Seeburgh Guest House, Yeovil, 1 mile(s). Tel: 72159 (0935)

STAFFORDSHIRE

BARLASTON
Barlaston Golf Club, Meaford Road, Barlaston, Stone, Staffs. ST15 5UX. Tel: 392795 (0781)
Secretary: M J Degg   Tel: 392867 (0781)
Professional: I Rogers   Tel: 392795 (0781)
18 holes, 5,800 yards, Par 69, S.S.S. 68, Course record 68.
Membership: 600
Visitors: Welcome. Not before 10a.m. weekends.
Green Fees: Weekdays £18, weekends £22.50.
Facilities: Lunch. Dinner. Bar Snacks. Full Catering. Changing Room. Golf Shop. Trolley Hire.
Class One Hotel: Crown, Stone, 3 mile(s). Tel: 813535 (0785)

BURTON-ON-TRENT

Branston Golf Club, Burton Road, Branston, Burton-on-Trent, Staffs. DE14 3DP. Tel: 43207 (0283)
Secretary: K L George   Tel: 66984 (0283)
Professional: S D Warner   Tel: 43207 (0283)
Description: Parkland alongside River Trent.
18 holes, 6,541 yards, Par 72, S.S.S. 71, Course record 67.
Membership: 600
Visitors: Welcome.
Green Fees: Weekdays £18, weekends £22.
Facilities: Lunch. Dinner. Bar Snacks. Full Catering. Changing Room. Golf Shop. Club Hire. Driving Range. Trolley Hire.
Class One Hotel: Riverside, Branston, 1/2 mile(s). Tel: 511234 (0283)
Class Two Hotel: Dog & Partridge, Tutbury, 4 mile(s). Tel: 813030 (0283)

BURTON-ON-TRENT

Burton-on-Trent Golf Club, 43 Ashby Road East, Burton-on-Trent, Staffs. DE15 0TZ. Tel: 68708 (0283)
Secretary: D Hartley   Tel: 44551 (0283)
Professional: Gary Stafford   Tel: 62240 (0283)
Description: A mature undulating parkland course with many testing holes especially the par 3's
18 holes, 6,555 yards, Par 71, S.S.S. 71.
Membership: 700
Visitors: Welcome. Handicap certificate required. Letter of Introduction required. Some catering restrictions apply, please telephone in advance. Ladies Day Tuesday. With members at weeken
Green Fees: Weekdays £20 per round, £25 per day. Weekends and Bank Holidays £25 per round, £30 per day.
Facilities: Lunch. Dinner. Bar Snacks. Full Catering. Changing Room. Golf Shop. Club Hire. Trolley Hire.
Class One Hotel: Stanhope Arms, Burton-on-Trent, 1/2 mile(s). Tel: 217954 (0283)
Class Two Hotel: Edgecote, Burton-on-Trent, 2 mile(s). Tel: 68966 (0283)

BURTON-ON-TRENT

Craythorne Golf Centre, Craythorne Road, Stretton, Burton-on-Trent, Staffs. DE13 0AZ. Tel: 64329 (0283)
Secretary: J Bissell   Tel: 64329 (0283)
Professional: Steve Hadfield   Tel: 33745 (0283)
Description: Parkland.
18 holes, 5,243 yards, Par 68, S.S.S. 66.
Membership: 500
Visitors: Welcome. Booking necessary at weekends.
Green Fees: Weekdays £12, Saturdays £14 and Sundays £16.
Facilities: Lunch. Dinner. Bar Snacks. Full Catering. Changing Room. Golf Shop. Club Hire. Driving Range. Trolley Hire.
Class One Hotel: Brookhouse Inn, Rolleston, 1 mile(s). Tel: 814188 (0283)
Class Two Hotel: Craythorne Farm Hotel, Stretton, Tel: 31648 (0283)

CANNOCK

Beau Desert Golf Club Ltd., Hazel Slade, Cannock, Staffs. WS12 5PJ. Tel: 422626 (0543)
Secretary: Mr A J R Fairfield   Tel: 422626 (0543)
Professional: Mr B Stevens   Tel: 422492 (0543)
Location: 4 miles north east of Cannock.
Description: Woodland and heather.
18 holes, 6,285 yards, Par 70, S.S.S. 71, Course record 64.
Membership: 500
Visitors: Welcome. Handicap certificate required. Letter of Introduction required.
Green Fees: £30 Monday to Thursday.
Facilities: Lunch. Dinner. Bar Snacks. Full Catering. Changing Room. Golf Shop. Trolley Hire.
Class One Hotel: The Cedar Tree, Rugeley, 3 mile(s). Tel: 584241 (0889)
Class Two Hotel: Longdon Old Hall, Rugeley, 5 mile(s). Tel: 682267 (0543)

CANNOCK

Cannock Park Golf Club, Stafford Road, Cannock, Staffs. WS11 2AL. Tel: 578850 (0543)
Professional: David Dunk   Tel: 578850 (0543)
Location: On A34 Stafford Road 1/2 mile out of Cannock centre.
Description: Parkland course on Cannock Chase.
18 holes, 5,300 yards, Par 66, S.S.S. 65.
Visitors: Welcome.
Green Fees: Weekdays £4.10, weekends £6.15, half price for juniors.
Facilities: Lunch. Dinner. Bar Snacks. Full Catering. Changing Room. Golf Shop. Club Hire. Trolley Hire.
Class One Hotel: Roman Way, Cannock, 2 mile(s). Tel: 502749 (0543)

LEEK

Leek Golf Club, Birchall, Cheddleton Road, Leek, Staffs. ST13 5RE. Tel: 384779 (0538)
Secretary: Frank Cutts   Tel: 384779 (0538)
Professional: P A Stubbs   Tel: 384767 (0538)
Description: Undulating semi moorland.
18 holes, 6,240 yards, Par 70, S.S.S. 70.
Membership: 750
Visitors: Welcome. Handicap certificate required.
Green Fees: Weekdays £22.50, weekends £30.
Facilities: Lunch. Dinner. Bar Snacks. Full Catering. Changing Room. Golf Shop. Club Hire. Trolley Hire.
Class One Hotel: Three Horse Shoes, Leek, 4 mile(s). Tel: 300296 (0538)
Class Two Hotel: Bank End Farm, Leek, 2 mile(s). Tel: 383638 (0538)

LEEK

Westwood Golf Club, Wallbridge, Newcastle Road, Leek, Staffs. ST13 7AA. Tel: 383060 (0538)
Secretary: Colin Plant   Tel: 399119 (0538)
Description: Parkland.
18 holes, 6,156 yards, Par 69, S.S.S. 69, Course record 71.
Membership: 550
Visitors: Welcome. No visitors Saturdays p.m. or Sundays.

Green Fees: £15.
Facilities: Lunch. Dinner. Bar Snacks. Full Catering. Changing Room.
Class One Hotel: The Jester, Leek, 2 mile(s). Tel: 383997 (0538)
Class Two Hotel: Peakweavers, Leek, 1 1/2 mile(s). Tel: 383729 (0538)

LICHFIELD

Whittington Barracks Golf Club, Tamworth Road, Lichfield, Staffs. WS14 9PW. Tel: 432317 (0543)
Secretary: D W J Macalester   Tel: 432317 (0543)
Professional: Adrian Sadler   Tel: 432261 (0543)
Location: Between Lichfield and Tamworth on A51.
Description: Heathland.
18 holes, 6,457 yards, Par 69, S.S.S. 71, Course record 65.
Membership: 600
Visitors: Welcome. Handicap certificate required. With members only at weekends and Bank Holidays. Tuesdays Ladies Day.
Green Fees: £28 per day.
Facilities: Lunch. Dinner. Bar Snacks. Full Catering. Changing Room. Golf Shop. Club Hire. Trolley Hire.
Class One Hotel: The George, Lichfield, 3 1/2 mile(s). Tel: 414822 (0543)
Class Two Hotel: Oakleigh House, Lichfield, 3 1/2 mile(s). Tel: 262688 (0543)

RUGELEY

Lakeside Golf Club, Rugeley Power Station, Armitage Road, Rugeley, Staffs. WS15 1PR. Tel: 583181 (0889)
Secretary: Mr E G Jones   Tel: 584472 (0889)
Location: 2 miles from Rugeley town centre.
Description: Parkland with holes adjacent to River Trent and to the Power Station.
18 holes, 5,508 yards, Par 68, S.S.S. 67.
Membership: 450
Visitors: Welcome. Must be with a member.
Green Fees: £6.
Facilities: Bar Snacks. Changing Room. Trolley Hire.
Class One Hotel: Cedar Tree, Rugeley, 2 mile(s). Tel: 584241 (0889)

STAFFORD

Ingestre Park Golf Club, Ingestre, Near Stafford, Staffs. ST18 0RE. Tel: 270061 (0889)
Secretary: D Humphries   Tel: 270845 (0889)
Professional: Danny Scullion   Tel: 270304 (0889)
Location: 6 miles east of Stafford off Tixall Road or A51.
Description: Undulating parkland.
18 holes, 6,334 yards, Par 70, S.S.S. 70, Course record 65.
Membership: 690
Visitors: Welcome. Handicap certificate required. Only with member at weekends.
Green Fees: £20 per day, £8 with member.
Facilities: Lunch. Dinner. Bar Snacks. Full Catering. Changing Room. Golf Shop. Trolley Hire.
Class One Hotel: Tillington Hall, Stafford, 6 mile(s). Tel: 53531 (0889)
Class Two Hotel: Forte Travel Lodge, Rugeley, 5 mile(s). Tel: 570096 (0889)

Cade's - Audi Golf Course Guide

STAFFORD

Stafford Castle Golf Club, Newport Road, Stafford, Staffs. ST16 1BP. Tel: 223821 (0785)
Secretary: M H Fisher   Tel: 223821 (0785)
Location: M6 junc 13 or 14, 2 miles from club.
Description: Parkland.
9 holes, 6,073 yards, Par 71, S.S.S. 69.
Membership: 400
Visitors: Welcome. Handicap certificate required. No visitors Sunday mornings.
Green Fees: Weekdays £14, weekends £18.
Facilities: Lunch. Dinner. Bar Snacks. Full Catering. Changing Room. Golf Shop. Trolley Hire.
Class One Hotel: Tillington Hall, Stafford, 6 mile(s). Tel: 5351 (0785)

STOKE-ON-TRENT

Alsager Golf and Country Club, Audley Road, Alsager, Stoke-on-Trent, Staffs. ST7 2UR. Tel: 875700 (0270)
Secretary: Mr Moffit   Tel: 875700 (0270)
Professional: N Routhe   Tel: 877432 (0270)
Location: Junc 16 M6 take A500 towards Stoke-on-Trent for 1 1/2 miles, take first exit turn left towards Alsager.
Description: Undulating parkland.
18 holes, 6,400 yards, Par 71, S.S.S. 71, Course record 67.
Membership: 454
Visitors: Welcome. Handicap certificate required. Not weekends and Bank Holidays. Societies Mondays, Wednesdays and Thursdays.
Green Fees: £18 per day, £7.50 with a member. 36 hole package for societies, £28 for morning coffee and biscuits, soup and sandwich lunch, 3 course
Facilities: Lunch. Dinner. Bar Snacks. Full Catering. Changing Room. Golf Shop. Trolley Hire. Buggy Hire. Caddies available.
Class One Hotel: The Manor House, Alsager, 0 mile(s). Tel: 884000 (0270)

STOKE-ON-TRENT

Trentham Golf Club, 14 Barlaston Road, Stoke-on-Trent, Staffs. ST4 8HB. Tel: 659827 (0782)
Secretary: Mr R B Irving   Tel: 658109 (0782)
Professional: Mr M Budz   Tel: 657309 (0782)
Location: 5 miles south of Newcastle-under-Lyme off A34.
Description: Open, wooded parkland with 3 lakes.
18 holes, 6,644 yards, Par 72, S.S.S. 72, Course record 64.
Membership: 500
Visitors: Welcome. Handicap certificate required. Letter of Introduction required. With members only at weekends. Tuesdays Ladies Day.
Green Fees: £25 per round, £30 per day.
Facilities: Lunch. Dinner. Bar Snacks. Full Catering. Changing Room. Golf Shop. Club Hire. Trolley Hire. Buggy Hire. Caddies available.
Class Two Hotel: The White House Private Hotel, Stoke-on-Trent, 3 mile(s). Tel: 642460 (0782)

STOKE-ON-TRENT

Trentham Park Golf Club, Trentham Park, Stoke-on-Trent, Staffs. ST4 8AE. Tel: 644130 (0782)
Secretary: Mr Lindop　　　　　Tel: 658800 (0782)
Professional: Mr R Clarke　　　Tel: 642125 (0782)
Location: 3 1/2 miles south of Stoke-on-Trent on A34.
Description: Woodland course with lake, over 100 years old.
18 holes, 6,403 yards, Par 70, S.S.S. 69, Course record 67.
Membership: 640
Visitors: Welcome. Handicap certificate required. Tuesdays Ladies Day. Members and their guests have priority at weekends.
Green Fees: Weekdays £20 per day, weekends £25 per day.
Facilities: Lunch. Dinner. Bar Snacks. Full Catering. Changing Room. Golf Shop. Club Hire. Trolley Hire.
Class One Hotel: Clayton Lodge, N/castle-u-Lyme, 2 mile(s). Tel: 613093 (0782)

STONE

Stone Golf Club, Filleybrooks, Stone, Staffs. ST15 0NB. Tel: 813103 (0785)
Secretary: M G Pharaoh　　　　Tel: 224 (08897)
Location: 3/4 mile north of Stone on A34.
Description: Parkland
9 holes, 6,299 yards, Par 71, S.S.S. 70, Course record 65.
Membership: 401
Visitors: Welcome. Not weekends or Bank Holidays.
Green Fees: £15 per round, £20 per day.
Facilities: Lunch. Dinner. Bar Snacks. Full Catering. Changing Room.
Class One Hotel: Stone House, Stone, 1/2 mile(s). Tel: 815531 (0785)

TAMWORTH

Drayton Park Golf Club, Drayton Manor Drive, Fazeley, Tamworth, Staffs. B78 3TN. Tel: 251139 (0827)
Secretary: Mr A O Rammell　　　Tel: 251139 (0827)
Professional: Mr M W Passmore　Tel: 251478 (0827)
Location: 4 miles off M42, 2 miles south of Tamworth on A456.
Description: Open parkland, tree lined, surrounded by scenic countryside. Adjacent to Drayton Manor Park and Zoo.
18 holes, 6,414 yards, Par 71, S.S.S. 71.
Membership: 600
Visitors: Welcome. Handicap certificate required. Letter of Introduction required. With members only at weekends. Wednesdays Ladies Day.
Green Fees: £25 per day.
Facilities: Lunch. Dinner. Bar Snacks. Full Catering. Changing Room. Golf Shop. Trolley Hire. Buggy Hire.
Class One Hotel: The Gungate, Tamworth, 3 mile(s). Tel: 63120 (0827)
Class Two Hotel: The Buxton, Fazeley, 1 mile(s). Tel: 284842 (0827)

UTTOXETER

Uttoxeter Golf Club, Wood Lane, Uttoxeter, Staffs. ST14 8JR. Tel: 565108 (0889)
Secretary: Mrs G Davies　　　Tel: 566552 (0889)
Professional: Mr J Pearsall　　Tel: 564884 (0889)
Description: Picturesque, undulating.
18 holes, 5,456 yards, Par 69, S.S.S. 67, Course record 68.
Visitors: Welcome. Handicap certificate required. Restrictions on "Major" days, please telephone in advance.
Green Fees: Weekdays £13 per day, weekends and Bank Holidays £17 per day.
Facilities: Lunch. Dinner. Bar Snacks. Full Catering. Changing Room. Golf Shop. Club Hire. Trolley Hire. Buggy Hire.
Class Two Hotel: Bank House, Uttoxeter, 1/2 mile(s). Tel: 566922 (0889)

SUFFOLK

BECCLES

Wood Valley Golf Club, The Common, Beccles, Suffolk. NR34 9BX. Tel: 712244 (0502)
Secretary: Mrs L Allen　　　　Tel: 712479 (0502)
Location: On A146 between Norwich and Lowestoft.
Description: Heathland.
9 holes, 5,562 yards, Par 68, S.S.S. 67, Course record 54.
Membership: 150
Visitors: Welcome. With a member on Sunday. Lunch only to order. Closed 1.30p.m. to 5.30p.m. Sunday afternoons April 1 to September 30.
Green Fees: Weekdays £9, weekends and Bank Holidays £10.
Facilities: Bar Snacks. Changing Room. Golf Shop. Trolley Hire.
Class One Hotel: The Kings Head, Beccles, 1/2 mile(s). Tel: 712147 (0502)
Class Two Hotel: Waveney House, Beccles, 1/2 mile(s). Tel: 712270 (0502)

BUNGAY

Bungay and Waveney Valley Golf Club, Outney Common, Bungay, Suffolk. NR35 1DS. Tel: 892337 (0986)
Secretary: W J Stevens　　　Tel: 892337 (0986)
Professional: N Whyte　　　　Tel: 892337 (0986)
Location: 1/2 mile from Bungay alongside A143.
Description: Heath/Glen.
18 holes, 5,950 yards, Par 69, S.S.S. 68.
Membership: 724
Visitors: Welcome. With members only at weekends. Some catering restrictions apply, please telephone in advance.
Green Fees: £18 per day or round.
Facilities: Lunch. Dinner. Bar Snacks. Full Catering. Changing Room. Golf Shop. Club Hire. Trolley Hire.

BURY ST EDMUNDS

Fornham Park Golf and Country Club, St Johns Hill Plantation, The Street, Fornham All saints, Bury St Edmunds, Suffolk. IP28 6JQ. Tel: 706777 (0284)
Secretary: Sean Clark　　　　Tel: 706777 (0284)

Professional: Sean Clark   Tel: 706777 (0284)
Description: Flat parkland with interesting water features. 18 holes, 6,229 yards, Par 71, S.S.S. 70, Course record 67.
Membership: 525
Visitors: Welcome. Not Tuesdays p.m. After 1 p.m. at weekends.
Green Fees: Weekdays £15 per round, £20 per day. Weekends £25 per round.
Facilities: Lunch. Dinner. Bar Snacks. Full Catering. Changing Room. Golf Shop. Club Hire. Trolley Hire.
Class One Hotel: Angel, Bury St Edmunds, 3 mile(s). Tel: 753926 (0284)

BURY ST EDMUNDS
Royal Worlington & Newmarket Golf Club, Worlington, Bury St Edmunds, Suffolk. IP28 8SD. Tel: 712216 (0638)
Secretary: C P Simpson   Tel: 712216 (0638)
Professional: M Hawkins   Tel: 715224 (0638)
Location: 6 miles north-east of Newmarket just off A11.
Description: Inland links type course. Reputed to be the best nine hole course in the country.
9 holes, 3,105 yards, Par 35, Course record 28.
Membership: 310
Visitors: Welcome. Handicap certificate required. Weekdays only. Always telephone in advance. Some catering restrictions apply, please telephone in advance.
Green Fees: £24 per day.
Facilities: Lunch. Bar Snacks. Changing Room. Golf Shop. Club Hire. Trolley Hire.

FELIXSTOWE
Felixstowe Ferry Golf Club, Ferry Road, Felixstowe, Suffolk. IP11 9RY. Tel: 286834 (0394)
Secretary: I H Kimber   Tel: 286834 (0394)
Professional: Ian McPherson   Tel: 283975 (0394)
Description: Links.
18 holes, 6,324 yards, Par 72, S.S.S. 70, Course record 66.
Membership: 850
Visitors: Welcome. Handicap certificate required.
Green Fees: Weekdays £21, weekends £24.
Facilities: Lunch. Dinner. Bar Snacks. Full Catering. Changing Room. Golf Shop. Trolley Hire.
Class One Hotel: Orwell Moat House, Felixstowe, 1 mile(s). Tel: 5511 (0394)
Class Two Hotel: Flyover Arms, Felixstowe, 1 mile(s). Tel: 282879 (0392)

HAVERHILL
Haverhill Golf Club, Coupals Road, Haverhill, Suffolk. CB9 7UW. Tel: 61951 (0440)
Secretary: Mrs J Webster   Tel: 61951 (0440)
Professional: Mr S P Mayfield   Tel: 712628 (0440)
Location: Haverhill 1 mile off A604 signs to Calford Green.
Description: 9 hole parkland course with water hazards on 4 fairways.
9 holes, 5,707 yards, Par 68, S.S.S. 68, Course record 66.
Membership: 445
Visitors: Welcome. With members on Bank Holidays.
Green Fees: Weekdays £15, weekends and Bank Holidays £21.
Facilities: Bar Snacks. Changing Room. Golf Shop. Club Hire. Trolley Hire.
Class Two Hotel: Rose and Crown, Haverhill, 1 mile(s). Tel: 708446 (0440)

IPSWICH
Alnesbourne Priory Golf Club, Priory Park, Nacton Road, Ipswich, Suffolk. IP10 0JT. Tel: 727393 (0473)
Secretary: Fergus Little   Tel: 726373 (0473)
Location: Off A45 Ipswich By-Pass take Europark/Airport exit. 300 yards from A45 small entrance on right hand side, follow signs to Caravan park.
Description: A very attractive 9 hole course enjoying a superb setting on the banks of the River Orwell. Non competetive course with a relaxed and friendly ambiance.
9 holes, 1,700 yards, Par 29.
Membership: 200
Visitors: Welcome. Closed Tuesdays.
Green Fees: From £8.
Facilities: Lunch. Bar Snacks. Full Catering. Changing Room.
Class One Hotel: Suffolk Grange, Ipswich, 1 1/2 mile(s). Tel: 272244 (0473)

IPSWICH
Fynn Valley Golf Club, Witnesham, Ipswich, Suffolk. IP6 9JA. Tel: 785465 (0473)
Secretary: Tony Tyrrell   Tel: 785267 (0473)
Professional: Robin Mann   Tel: 785463 (0473)
Location: 3 miles north of Ipswich on B1077.
Description: Undulating course set along the edge of the Fynn Valley preservation area.
9 holes, 2,750 yards, Par 34, S.S.S. 66, Course record 64.
18 holes, 5,680 yards, Par 69, S.S.S. 68.
Membership: 500
Visitors: Welcome. 18 hole course opens July 1992. Not Sunday mornings. Thursday mornings Ladies only.
Green Fees: 9 holes - £7.50. 18 holes - £12, £15 per day.
Facilities: Lunch. Bar Snacks. Golf Shop. Club Hire. Driving Range. Trolley Hire.
Class One Hotel: Marlborough, Ipswich, 3 mile(s). Tel: 257677 (0473)
Class Two Hotel: Whitton Lodge, Ipswich, 3 mile(s). Tel: 240909 (0473)

IPSWICH
Ipswich Golf Club, Purdis Heath, Bucklesham Road, Ipswich, Suffolk. IP3 8UQ.
Secretary: A P Wright MBE   Tel: 728941 (0473)
Professional: S Whymark   Tel: 724017 (0473)
Location: 2 1/2 miles east of Ipswich off A45.
Description: Tree lined heathland with 3 lakes.
18 holes, 6,415 yards, Par 71, S.S.S. 71, Course record 64.
9 holes, 1,930 yards, Par 31.
Visitors: Welcome. Handicap certificate required. Tuesdays Ladies Day. Always telephone in advance.
Green Fees: Weekdays 18 hole course £28 per day. Weekdays 9 hole course £7.50 per day.
Facilities: Lunch. Dinner. Bar Snacks. Full Catering. Changing Room. Golf Shop. Club Hire. Trolley Hire.

Alnesbourne Priory Golf Club

SUPERB SOUTH FACING PARKLAND SETTING OF FORMER 12th CENTURY MONASTERY
Panoramic Views over Orwell estuary with River Frontage

TESTING 9 HOLE COURSE
7 PAR 3; 2 PAR 4
LARGE CLUBHOUSE, TENNIS COURTS, HEATED POOL IN SUMMER, 5 MINS A45, 10 MINS IPSWICH CENTRE

EXCLUSIVE USE- BOOKINGS TAKEN FOR TUESDAYS, WHEN CLOSED TO MEMBERS & NORMAL GREEN FEES

PRIORY PARK, NACTON ROAD, IPSWICH IP10 OJT

TEL: IPSWICH (0473) 727393

IPSWICH

Rushmere Golf Club, Rushmere Heath, Ipswich, Suffolk. IP4 5QQ. Tel: 727109 (0473)
Secretary: Mr R W Whiting   Tel: 725648 (0473)
Professional: Mr N T J McNeill   Tel: 728076 (0473)
Location: On A12 north of Ipswich.
Description: Gently undulating heathland, mostly gorse and heather with a pond.
18 holes, 6,287 yards, Par 70, S.S.S. 66, Course record 66.
Membership: 800
Visitors: Welcome. Handicap certificate required. Wednesday mornings Ladies. Not before 2.30p.m. weekends.
Green Fees: £18 per day.
Facilities: Lunch. Bar Snacks. Full Catering. Changing Room. Golf Shop. Club Hire. Trolley Hire.

LOWESTOFT

Rookery Park Golf Club, Beccles Road, Carlton Colville, Lowestoft, Suffolk. . Tel: 574009 (0502)
Secretary: Mr Cooper   Tel: 560380 (0502)
Professional: Mr M Elsworthy   Tel: 515103 (0502)
Location: 3 miles west of Lowestoft on Beccles Road.
Description: Open parkland with some lateral water hazards.
18 holes, 6,566 yards, Par 72, S.S.S. 72, Course record 69.
Visitors: Welcome. Handicap certificate required. Letter of Introduction required.Tuesdays Ladies Day.
Green Fees: Weekdays £20, weekends £25.
Facilities: Lunch. Dinner. Bar Snacks. Full Catering. Changing Room. Golf Shop. Club Hire. Trolley Hire.

NEWMARKET

Links Golf Club, Cambridge Road, Newmarket, Suffolk. CB8 0TG. Tel: 663000 (0638)
Secretary: Mrs T N MacGregor   Tel: 663000 (0638)
Professional: Mr J Sharkey   Tel: 662395 (0638)
Location: A1304 12, miles from Cambridge - 1 mile from Newmarket.
Description: Open parkland.
Links 18 holes, 6,424 yards, Par 72, S.S.S. 71, Course record 67.
Membership: 680
Visitors: Welcome. Handicap certificate required. Not Sundays before 11.30 a.m. unless with a member.
Green Fees: Weekdays £22, weekends and Bank Holidays £27.
Facilities: Lunch. Dinner. Full Catering. Changing Room. Golf Shop. Trolley Hire.
Class One Hotel: The Rutland Arms, Newmarket, 1 mile(s). Tel: 662451 (0638)
Class Two Hotel: The Rosery, Exning, 3 mile(s). Tel: 577312 (0638)

SOUTHWOLD

Southwold Golf Club, The Common, Southwold, Suffolk. IP18 6TB. Tel: 723234 (0502)
Secretary: Mr D F Randall   Tel: 723248 (0502)
Professional: Mr B Allen   Tel: 723790 (0502)
Description: Flat common land with sea views.
9 holes, 6,050 yards, Par 70, S.S.S. 69, Course record 65.
Membership: 450
Visitors: Welcome. Ladies day Wednesdays. Restrictions at weekends, please telephone for information.
Green Fees: Weekdays £14 per round, weekends £18 per round.
Facilities: Lunch. Bar Snacks. Full Catering. Changing Room. Golf Shop. Club Hire. Trolley Hire.
Class One Hotel: The Swan, Southwold, 1 mile(s). Tel: 722186 (0502)
Class Two Hotel: Randolph, Reydon, 1 1/2 mile(s). Tel: 723603 (0502)

STOWMARKET

Stowmarket Golf Club, Lower Road, Onehouse, Stowmarket, Suffolk. IP14 3DA.
Secretary: P W Rumball   Tel: 736473 (0449)
Professional: C Aldred   Tel: 736392 (0449)
Location: Off B1115 Stowmarket - Bildeston Road.
Description: Parkland.
18 holes, 6,101 yards, Par 69, S.S.S. 69.
Membership: 635
Visitors: Welcome. Handicap certificate required. Not wednesdays a.m.
Green Fees: Weekdays £18.50, weekends £29.
Facilities: Lunch. Dinner. Bar Snacks. Full Catering. Changing Room. Golf Shop. Driving Range. Trolley Hire.
Class One Hotel: Cedars, Stowmarket, 3 mile(s). Tel: 612668 (0449)
Class Two Hotel: Kiln Farm Guest House, Elmswell, 3 mile(s). Tel: 40442 (0359)

FYNN VALLEY GOLF CENTRE

Fynn Valley is situated on the B1077, 2 miles north of Ipswich in Suffolk. It is set in the Valley of the River Fynn, hence its name, in beautiful Suffolk countryside.

Fynn Valley Golf Centre is one of the new style of golf centre Golf Clubs that are beginning to form in the United Kingdom. It offers the game of golf to all, right from the passing visitors who are wishing to find out if they can use the facility, to the established golfer wishing to play on an 18 hole full length golf course.

The game of golf had been clouded to lots of people because of the "Catch 22" of "No Handicap" - "No Membership" - "No Membership" - "No Handicap". Fynn Valley Golf Centre offers the facilities from day one, your first bucket of golf balls and a hire club at a cost of £2.00 all the way through to being a fully fledged Member of the Golf Club.

The Golf Centre offers you a golf centre open to the general public, its facilities are a 25 bay (10 undercover) floodlit Driving Range open until 9.30p.m. with a three level practice bunker, four Chipping Greens with an 18 hole Putting Green. If you are new to the game, Robin Mann (Director of Golf) and his staff of four golf Professionals offer the facility of first class golf tuition at any time, either individual or group. This is especially good so the new golfer does not start practising a fault.

The next stage can be Fynn Valleys 1,050 yard, 9 hole, Par 3 golf course around the outside of the Golf Centre. A great way to develop the process of learning golf. In 1991-92, Fynn Valley has just completed its latest stage by building a 5,800 yard, 18 hole course with a Membership of 400. Both the 18 hole and the 9 hole golf courses are open to people wishing to pay Green Fees.

For the golfer with no equipment, the Centre has a well stocked Professionals Shop with all equipment for the beginner upwards, famous names stocked like Titleist, Wilson Taylor-made, Lyle & Scott and Relum just to mention a few.

Fynn Valleys motto is "Golf For All" with a friendly welcome.

Robin W Mann (Director of Golf) turned Professional in 1972. Seven times Suffolk Professional Champion, twice East Anglian Open Champion in 1985, United Kingdom Club Professional Champion European Tour player since 1975, currently playing the 1992 European Tour having just led the Firenze Open Italy in March 1992.

Qualified Member of the Professional Golfers Association since 1975, with credits in teaching, to being heavily involved in teaching and the development of golf at Fynn Valley and with Suffolk youngsters.

ASSISTANTS
1. Glenn Crane
2. Paul Wilby
3. Stuart Robertson
All Assistants are in the top 10 of the 1991 Suffolk Professionals Championship.

SUDBURY

Newton Green Golf Club, Newton Green, Sudbury, Suffolk. CO10 0QV. Tel: 77501 (0787)
Secretary: Mr G Bright   Tel: 77217 (0787)
Professional: Mr K Lovelock   Tel: 210910 (0787)
Location: 3 miles east of Sudbury on A134.
Description: Flat heathland, mainly heather and gorse, with ponds and streams situated on a village green.
9 holes, 5,488 yards, Par 68, S.S.S. 65, Course record 59.
Membership: 400
Visitors: Welcome. With members only at weekends. Tuesdays Ladies Day.
Green Fees: £15 per day.
Facilities: Lunch. Dinner. Bar Snacks. Full Catering. Changing Room. Golf Shop. Trolley Hire.
Class One Hotel: The Mill, Sudbury, 3 mile(s). Tel: 75544 (0787)

WOODBRIDGE

Waldringfield Heath Golf Club, Newborne Road, Waldringfield, Woodbridge, Suffolk. IP12 4PT. Tel: 36426 (0473)
Secretary: Mr L J McWade   Tel: 36768 (0473)
Professional: Mr A Dobson   Tel: 36417 (0473)
Location: 3 miles north of Ipswich on Vauxhall Road.
Description: Flat heathland, tree lined with gorse and some ponds. Easy walking.
18 holes, 6,153 yards, Par 71, S.S.S. 69, Course record 69.
Membership: 660
Visitors: Welcome. Not before 12p.m. weekends. Tuesdays Ladies Day.
Green Fees: Weekdays £10 per round, £15 per day.
Facilities: Lunch. Bar Snacks. Full Catering. Changing Room. Golf Shop. Trolley Hire.
Class One Hotel: The Marlborough, Ipswich, 7 mile(s). Tel: 257677 (0473)
Class Two Hotel: The Bull, Woodbridge, Tel: 385688 (0394)

WOODBRIDGE

Woodbridge Golf Club, Bromeswell Heath, Woodbridge, Suffolk. IP12 2PF. Tel: 382038 (0394)
Secretary: Capt L A Harpum   Tel: 382038 (0394)
Professional: L A Jones   Tel: 383213 (0394)
Location: On A1152/B1084 approx 2 miles from Woodbridge.
Description: Undulating Heathland.
18 holes, 6,314 yards, Par 70, S.S.S. 70, Course record 64.
9 holes, 2,243 yards, Par 31, S.S.S. 31.
Membership: 900
Visitors: Welcome. Handicap certificate required. Weekdays only. Not before 9.30 a.m. Advisable to telephone in advance.
Green Fees: £24 (18 holes), £11 (9 holes). Societies £28.
Facilities: Lunch. Dinner. Bar Snacks. Full Catering. Changing Room. Golf Shop.
Class One Hotel: Seckford Hall, Woodbridge, 3 mile(s). Tel: 385678 (0394)
Class Two Hotel: Crown and Castle, Orford, 7 mile(s). Tel: 450205 (0394)

SURREY

BROOKWOOD

West Hill Golf Club, Bagshot Road, Brookwood, Surrey. GU24 0BH. Tel: 474365 (0483)
Secretary: W D Leighton   Tel: 474365 (0483)
Professional: J C Clements   Tel: 473172 (0483)
Location: On A322 between Guildford and Bagshot.
Description: Heathland/woodland.
18 holes, 6,368 yards, Par 69, S.S.S. 70, Course record 65.
Membership: 250
Visitors: Welcome. Handicap certificate required. Not weekends. Only by prior arrangement.
Green Fees: £32 per round, £42 per day.
Facilities: Lunch. Dinner. Bar Snacks. Full Catering. Changing Room. Golf Shop. Club Hire. Driving Range. Trolley Hire. Caddies available.
Class One Hotel: Berystede, Ascot, 7 mile(s). Tel: 23311 (0344)

CAMBERLEY

Camberley Heath Golf Club, Golf Drive, Portsmouth Road, Camberley, Surrey. GU15 1JG. Tel: 23258 (0276)
Secretary: Mr Greenwood   Tel: 23258 (0276)
Professional: Mr G Smith   Tel: 27905 (0276)
Location: 1 mile south east of Camberley.
Description: Gently undulating heathland lined with pine trees with a pond. Course is divided by a road.
18 holes, 6,337 yards, Par 72, S.S.S. 70, Course record 63.
Membership: 600
Visitors: Welcome. Handicap certificate required. Tuesdays Ladies Day. With members only at weekends.
Green Fees: £30 per round.
Facilities: Lunch. Dinner. Bar Snacks. Full Catering. Changing Room. Golf Shop. Club Hire. Trolley Hire. Buggy Hire.
Class One Hotel: Frimley Hall, Camberley, 1/2 mile(s). Tel: 28321 (0276)
Class Two Hotel: Hazel Lodge, Camberley, 1 mile(s). Tel: 64856 (0276)

CHERTSEY

Laleham Golf Course, Laleham Reach, Chertsey, Surrey. KT16 8RP. Tel: 562188 (0932)
Secretary: Miss J Clinton   Tel: 564211 (0932)
Professional: Mr T Witton   Tel: 562877 (0932)
Location: 1 mile north of Chertsey on A320 Chertsey to Staines road.
Description: Flat meadowland.
White 18 holes, 6,210 yards, Par 70, S.S.S. 70, Course record 65.
Yellow 18 holes, 6,041 yards, Par 70, S.S.S. 69.
Membership: 650
Visitors: Welcome. Handicap certificate required. With members only at weekends. Thursdays Ladies Day.
Green Fees: Weekdays £23.50 per round or day.
Facilities: Lunch. Dinner. Bar Snacks. Full Catering. Changing Room. Golf Shop. Trolley Hire.
Class One Hotel: Runnymede Hotel, Egham, 3 1/2 mile(s). Tel: 436171 (0784)

CRANLEIGH
Fernfell Golf and Country Club, Barhatch Lane, Cranleigh, Surrey. GU6 7NG. Tel: 268855 (0483).
Secretary: Miss C Kimberley　　Tel: 268855 (0483)
Professional: Mr T Longmuir　　Tel: 277188 (0483)
Location: 1 mile south of Cranleigh on Ewhurst Road.
Description: Well wooded open parkland with pond, quite tight and challenging.
Medal 18 holes, 5,461 yards, Par 68, S.S.S. 67, Course record 59.
Yellow 18 holes, 5,071 yards, Par 67, S.S.S. 65.
Membership: 1000
Visitors: Welcome. With members only at weekends. Tuesdays Ladies Day.
Green Fees: Weekdays £20 per round, £30 for 36 holes.
Facilities: Lunch. Dinner. Bar Snacks. Full Catering. Changing Room. Golf Shop. Club Hire. Driving Range. Trolley Hire. Buggy Hire.
Class One Hotel: Bramley Grange, Bramley, 3 mile(s). Tel: 893434 (0483)
Class Two Hotel: Cranley Hotel, Cranleigh, 1 mile(s). Tel: 272827 (0483)

DORKING
Dorking Golf Club, Chart Park, Dorking, Surrey. RH5 4BX.
Secretary: R M Payne　　Tel: 886917 (0306)
Professional: P Napier　　Tel: 886917 (0306)
Location: 1 mile south of junc A24/A25.
Description: Parkland. 9 holes, second nine from different tees.
9 holes, 5,163 yards, Par 66, S.S.S. 65, Course record 61.
Membership: 420
Visitors: Welcome. Not wednesdays a.m. With members at weekends.
Green Fees: £16.
Facilities: Lunch. Dinner. Bar Snacks. Full Catering. Changing Room. Golf Shop. Club Hire. Trolley Hire.
Class One Hotel: White Horse, Dorking, 1 mile(s). Tel: 881138 (0306)
Class Two Hotel: Travelodge, Dorking, 1 mile(s). Tel: 740361 (0306)

EFFINGHAM
Effingham Golf Club, Guildford Road, Effingham, Surrey. KT24 5PZ. Tel: 452203 (0372)
Secretary: Lt Col (Rtd) S C Manning OBE　　Tel: 452203 (0372)
Professional: Steve Hoatson　　Tel: 452606 (0372)
Location: Between Guildford and Leatherhead on A246.
Description: Downland course with magnificent views over Surrey towards London.
18 holes, 6,488 yards, Par 71, S.S.S. 71, Course record 63.
Membership: 960
Visitors: Welcome. Handicap certificate required. Letter of Introduction required. With member at weekends and Bank Holidays.
Green Fees: £35 per day, £27.50 after 2 p.m.
Facilities: Lunch. Dinner. Bar Snacks. Full Catering. Changing Room. Golf Shop. Club Hire. Trolley Hire. Buggy Hire.
Class One Hotel: Thatchers Resort, East Horsley, 2 mile(s). Tel: 4291 (04865)
Class Two Hotel: Preston Cross, Effingham, 1 mile(s). Tel: 456642 (0372)

EPSOM
Epsom Golf Club, Longdown Lane South, Epsom, Surrey. KT17 4JR.
Secretary: Mr R R Fry　　Tel: 721666 (0372)
Professional: Bob Wynn　　Tel: 741867 (0372)
Description: Undulating downland. Traditional links type course with very fast greens. Still the original course dating from 1889.
Mens 18 holes, 5,607 yards, Par 69, S.S.S. 67.
Ladies 18 holes, 4,873 yards, Par 72, S.S.S. 68.
Membership: 850
Visitors: Welcome. After mid-day Saturdays and Sundays. Caddies by arrangement, only in school holidays.
Green Fees: Weekdays £14 per round, £22 per day. Weekends £18 after mid-day.
Facilities: Lunch. Dinner. Bar Snacks. Full Catering. Changing Room. Golf Shop. Club Hire. Trolley Hire.
Class One Hotel: Chalk Lane Hotel, Epsom, 1 mile(s). Tel: 721179 (0372)
Class Two Hotel: Drift Bridge Hotel, Burgh Heath, 1 mile(s). Tel: 352163 (0737)

ESHER
Sandown Golf Centre, More Lane, Esher, Surrey. KT10 8AN. Tel: 463340 (0372)
Secretary: P J Barriball　　Tel: 463340 (0372)
Professional: Neal Bedward　　Tel: 463340 (0372)
Location: In centre of Sandown Park racecourse.
Description: Flat parkland.
New Course 9 holes, 2,828 yards, Par 35, S.S.S. 67, Course record 62.
Par 3 9 holes, 1,193 yards, Par 27.
Membership: 550
Visitors: Welcome. Advance booking recommended.
Green Fees: New course £4.80 weekdays, £6 weekends. Par 3 £3.20 weekdays, £3.95 weekends.
Facilities: Lunch. Bar Snacks. Changing Room. Golf Shop. Club Hire. Driving Range. Trolley Hire.
Class One Hotel: Hilton National, Cobham, 5 mile(s). Tel: 864471 (0932)

FARNHAM
Farnham Golf Club Ltd., Sands, Farnham, Surrey. GU10 1PX. Tel: 3163 (02518)
Secretary: Mr J Pevalin　　Tel: 2109 (02518)
Professional: Mr Cowlishaw　　Tel: 2198 (02518)
Location: 2 miles south west of Farnham on A31.
Description: Wooded parkland/heathland.
18 holes, 6,303 yards, Par 72, S.S.S. 70, Course record 67.
Membership: 725
Visitors: Welcome. Handicap certificate required. With members only at weekends. Tuesdays Ladies Day.
Green Fees: £25 per round, £30 per day.
Facilities: Lunch. Dinner. Bar Snacks. Full Catering. Changing Room. Golf Shop. Club Hire. Trolley Hire.
Class One Hotel: The Hogs Back Motel, Seale, 1 mile(s). Tel: 2345 (02518)

GODALMING

Shillinglee Park Golf Club, Chiddingfold, Godalming, Surrey. GU8 4TA. Tel: 653237 (0428) •
Secretary: Roger Mace   Tel: 653237 (0428)
Professional: Roger Mace   Tel: 653237 (0428)
Description: Well maintained undulating parkland.
9 holes, 2,700 yards, Par 32, S.S.S. 65.
Membership: 300
Visitors: Welcome. Always advisable to telephone for starting time. Dinner available for societies.
Green Fees: Weekdays 9 holes £8.50, 18 holes £15, £18 per day. Weekends 9 holes £9, 18 holes £16.50, £19.50 per day.
Facilities: Lunch. Bar Snacks. Full Catering. Changing Room. Golf Shop. Club Hire. Trolley Hire. Buggy Hire.
Class One Hotel: Crown Inn, Chiddingfold, 2 1/2 mile(s). Tel: 682255 (0428)
Class Two Hotel: Old Wharf, Billingshurst, 1 Tel: 784096 (0403)

GUILDFORD

Bramley Golf Club, Bramley, Near Guildford, Surrey. GU5 0AL. Tel: 892696 (0483)
Secretary: Margaret Lambert   Tel: 892696 (0483)
Professional: Gary Peddie   Tel: 893685 (0483)
Location: 3 miles south of Guildford on A281 Horsham Road.
Description: Parkland.
18 holes, 5,990 yards, Par 69, S.S.S. 69.
Membership: 750
Visitors: Welcome. Tuesday mornings reserved for ladies. With members only at weekends. Caddies by arrangement.
Green Fees: £20.50 per round, £25.50 per day.
Facilities: Lunch. Dinner. Bar Snacks. Full Catering. Changing Room. Golf Shop. Club Hire. Driving Range. Trolley Hire. Buggy Hire.
Class One Hotel: Bramley Grange, Bramley, Tel: 893434 (0483)

HINDHEAD

Hindhead Golf Club, Churt Road, Hindhead, Surrey. GU26 6HX. Tel: 604614 (0428)
Secretary: D Browse   Tel: 604614 (0428)
Professional: N Ogilvy   Tel: 604458 (0428)
Location: 1 1/4 miles north of Hinhead crossroads on A287.
Description: Part heathland, part woodland.
18 holes, 6,357 yards, Par 70, S.S.S. 70, Course record 65.
Membership: 900
Visitors: Welcome. Handicap certificate required. Not on competition days.
Green Fees: Weekdays £34 per day, £26 per round (after 2p.m.). Weekends and Bank Holidays £41 per day, £31 per round (after 2p.m.).
Facilities: Lunch. Dinner. Bar Snacks. Full Catering. Changing Room. Golf Shop. Club Hire. Trolley Hire.
Class One Hotel: Frensham Pond Hotel, Frensham, 3 mile(s). Tel: 3175 (025125)
Class Two Hotel: Devils Punch Bowl, Hindhead, 1 1/2 mile(s). Tel: 606565 (0428)

LEATHERHEAD

Leatherhead Golf Club, Kingston Road, Leatherhead, Surrey. KT22 0DP. Tel: 843966 (0372)
Secretary: W G Betts   Tel: 843966 (0372)
Professional: R Hurst   Tel: 843956 (0372)
Location: On A243 Kingston Road, just off junc 9 M25.
Description: 90 year old parkland course.
18 holes, 6,107 yards, S.S.S. 69.
Membership: 610
Visitors: Welcome. Handicap certificate required. Letter of Introduction required. Not a.m. Thursdays, Saturdays or Sundays. Caddies by arrangement
Green Fees: Weekdays £30 (18 holes), £35 (36 holes) Weekends £42.50.
Facilities: Lunch. Dinner. Bar Snacks. Full Catering. Changing Room. Golf Shop. Club Hire. Trolley Hire.
Class One Hotel: Woodlands Park, Cobham, 2 mile(s). Tel: 843933 (0372)
Class Two Hotel: Travel Inn, Chessington, 2 mile(s). Tel: 744060 (0372)

LEATHERHEAD

Tyrrells Wood Golf Club, Leatherhead, Surrey. KT22 8QP. Tel: 372069 (0372)
Secretary: Mrs P Humphries   Tel: 376025 (0372)
Professional: Mr P Taylor   Tel: 375200 (0372)
Location: 1 mile north of Leatherhead on A24.
Description: Open parkland, hilly and wooded.
18 holes, 6,234 yards, Par 71, S.S.S. 70, Course record 68.
Membership: 850
Visitors: Welcome. Handicap certificate required. With members only all day Saturday and Sunday mornings. Tuesdays Ladies Day. Caddies available with 7 days notice.
Green Fees: £30 per round, £45 per day.
Facilities: Lunch. Dinner. Bar Snacks. Full Catering. Changing Room. Golf Shop. Club Hire. Driving Range. Trolley Hire.
Class One Hotel: The Bull, Leatherhead, 1 mile(s). Tel: 372153 (0372)

LINGFIELD

Lingfield Park Golf Club, Racecourse Road, Lingfield Park, Lingfield, Surrey. RH7 6TA. Tel: 834602 (0342)
Secretary: Greer Milne   Tel: 834602 (0342)
Professional: Trevor Collingwood   Tel: 832659 (0342)
Location: Next to Lingfield Park Racecourse. M25 junc 6.
Description: Wooded parkland.
18 holes, 6,473 yards, Par 71, S.S.S. 72, Course record 67.
Membership: 700
Visitors: Welcome. Not before 1 p.m. weekends.
Green Fees: Weekdays £20 per round, £30 per day. £30 per round weekends.
Facilities: Lunch. Dinner. Bar Snacks. Changing Room. Golf Shop. Club Hire. Driving Range. Trolley Hire. Buggy Hire.
Class One Hotel: Copthorne, Copthorne, 1 Tel: 714994 (0342)
Class Two Hotel: Royal Oak, Dormansland, 5 mile(s). Tel: 832383 (0342)

Cade's - Audi Golf Course Guide

OXTED

Limpsfield Chart Golf, Westerham Road, Limpsfield, Oxted, Surrey. RH8 0SL. Tel: 722106 (0883)
Secretary: Mr Bannochier Tel: 723405 (0883)
Location: 2 miles east of Oxted on A25.
Description: 9 hole course played off 18 tees. Tree lined flat heathland over 100 years old.
18 holes, 5,718 yards, Par 70, S.S.S. 68, Course record 62.
Membership: 350
Visitors: Welcome. Handicap certificate required. With members only at weekends. Thursdays Ladies Day.
Green Fees: Weekdays £17 per day.
Facilities: Lunch. Dinner. Bar Snacks. Full Catering. Changing Room.
Class One Hotel: Kings Arms, Westerham, 4 mile(s). Tel: 62990 (0959)

OXTED

Tandridge Golf Club, Godstone Road, Oxted, Surrey. RH8 9NQ. Tel: 712274 (0883)
Secretary: A Survival Tel: 712274 (0883)
Professional: A Farquhar Tel: 713701 (0883)
Location: 5 miles east of Redhill off A25 or M25 junc 6.
Description: Undulating parkland.
18 holes, 6,250 yards, Par 70, S.S.S. 70, Course record 68.
Membership: 750
Visitors: Welcome. Handicap certificate required. Monday, Wednesday and Thursday only. Always telephone in advance.
Green Fees: £40 per day.
Facilities: Lunch. Bar Snacks. Changing Room. Golf Shop. Club Hire. Trolley Hire.
Class One Hotel: Kings Arms, Westerham, 3 mile(s). Tel: 62990 (0959)

PIRBRIGHT

Goal Farm Golf Club, Gole Road, Pirbright, Woking, Surrey. . Tel: 473183 (0483)
Secretary: Mr B Tapsfield Tel: 43868 (09323)
Professional: Mr K Warn Tel: 473183 (0483)
Location: 6 miles north of Guildford off A3222.
Description: Difficult but picturesque. 2 ponds, 15 bunkers, tree lined with ditches.
9 holes, 2,270 yards, Par 54, S.S.S. 48, Course record 51.
Membership: 300
Visitors: Welcome. Not Saturdays before 4p.m.. Thursdays Ladies Day.
Green Fees: £5.75 for 18 holes.
Facilities: Lunch. Bar Snacks. Full Catering. Golf Shop. Club Hire.
Class One Hotel: The Queens, Farnborough, 4 mile(s). Tel: 545051 (0252)

REDHILL

Redhill and Reigate Golf Club, Clarence Lodge, Pendleton Road, Redhill, Surrey. RH1 6LB. Tel: 244626 (0737)
Secretary: Mr F R Cole Tel: 240777 (0737)
Professional: Mr B Davies Tel: 244433 (0737)
Location: 1 1/2 miles south of Redhill on A23 Brighton Road into Pendleton Road.
Description: Wooded common land with ditches situated close to Earlswood Lakes. Scenic countryside.
18 holes, 5,238 yards, Par 67, S.S.S. 66.
Membership: 600
Visitors: Welcome. Members and guests have priority at weekends. Tuesdays Ladies Day.
Green Fees: Weekdays £12 per round, weekends £18 per round.
Facilities: Lunch. Bar Snacks. Full Catering. Changing Room. Golf Shop. Club Hire. Trolley Hire.

REIGATE

Reigate Heath Golf Club, The Clubhouse, Reigate Heath, Reigate, Surrey. RH2 8QR. Tel: 242610 (0737)
Secretary: Mrs D M Howard Tel: 245530 (0737)
Location: Western boundary of Reigate, south of A25.
Description: Heathland.
9 holes, 5,554 yards, Par 67, S.S.S. 67, Course record 65.
Visitors: Welcome. With members at weekends. Some catering restrictions apply, please telephone in advance.
Green Fees: On application.
Facilities: Lunch. Dinner. Bar Snacks. Full Catering. Changing Room.
Class One Hotel: Reigate Manor, Reigate, 2 1/2 mile(s). Tel: 240125 (0737)
Class Two Hotel: Cranleigh, Reigate, 1/2 mile(s). Tel: 240600 (0737)

SUTTON

Banstead Downs Golf Club, Burdon Lane, Belmont, Sutton, Surrey. SM2 7DD. Tel: 642 2284 (081)
Secretary: A W Schooling Tel: 642 2284 (081)
Professional: Ian Marr Tel: 642 6884 (081)
Location: A217 1 mile south of Sutton town centre.
Description: Downland course.
18 holes, 6,169 yards, Par 69, S.S.S. 69, Course record 66.
Visitors: Welcome. Handicap certificate required. Not at weekends.
Green Fees: £30 all day, £20 after noon.
Facilities: Lunch. Dinner. Bar Snacks. Full Catering. Changing Room. Golf Shop. Trolley Hire.
Class One Hotel: Holiday Inn, Sutton, 2 mile(s). Tel: 770 1311 (081)
Class Two Hotel: Dene, Sutton, 2 mile(s). Tel: 642 3170 (081)

TADWORTH

Walton Heath Golf Club, Deans Lane, Tadworth, Surrey. KT20 7TP. Tel: 812060 (0737)
Professional: Ken MacPherson Tel: 812152 (0737)
Location: Junc 8 M25, take A217 towards London, 3rd roundabout take B2032 towards London, turning righthand side Deans Lane.
Description: Two heathland courses laid out over Walton heath. Between 600-700 feet above sea level. Heather, bracken, gorse, pine and birch. Large rolling greens, deep bunkers.
Old 18 holes, 6,883 yards, Par 73, S.S.S. 73.
New 18 holes, 6,659 yards, Par 72, S.S.S. 72.
Membership: 1000
Visitors: Welcome. Handicap certificate required. Not at weekends. Only by prior arrangement weekdays.

Green Fees: £55, £45 after 11.30 a.m.
Facilities: Lunch. Changing Room. Golf Shop. Club Hire. Trolley Hire. Caddies available.
Class One Hotel: Heathside, Burgh Heath, 2 mile(s). Tel: 353355 (0737)
Class Two Hotel: Chalk Lane, Epsom, 4 mile(s). Tel: 721179 (0372)

VIRGINIA WATER
Wentworth Club Ltd., Wentworth Drive, Virginia Water, Surrey. GU25 4LS. Tel: 842201 (0344)
Secretary: G R James   Tel: 842201 (0344)
Professional: B Gallacher   Tel: 843353 (0344)
Description: 3 excellent heathland courses heather lined fairways with birch and pine trees in the main.
West 18 holes, 6,947 yards, Par 73, S.S.S. 73, Course record 63.
East 18 holes, 6,176 yards, Par 68, S.S.S. 69, Course record 62.
Edinburgh 18 holes, 6,979 yards, Par 72, S.S.S. 71, Course record 67.
Membership: 2000
Visitors: Welcome. Handicap certificate required. Letter of Introduction required.With members only at weekends and Bank Holidays. Caddies available 48 hours notice required.
Green Fees: West - £80, East - £55, Edinburgh - £55. (Special rates for parties over 24 persons).
Facilities: Lunch. Dinner. Bar Snacks. Full Catering. Changing Room. Golf Shop. Club Hire. Driving Range. Trolley Hire.
Class One Hotel: Royal Berkshire, Ascot, 2 mile(s). Tel: 23322 (0344)
Class Two Hotel: Milton Park Farm, Egham, 4 mile(s). Tel: 439295 (0784)

WEST BYFLEET
West Byfleet Golf Club, Sheerwater Road, West Byfleet, Surrey. KT14 6AA. Tel: 345230 (0932)
Secretary: Mr D G Smith   Tel: 343433 (0932)
Professional: Mr D Regan   Tel: 346584 (0932)
Location: 2 miles north of Byfleet, 2 miles south of M25.
Description: Flat open parkland, tree lined with a pond. 18 holes, 5,211 yards, Par 70, S.S.S. 70, Course record 65.
Membership: 700
Visitors: Welcome. With members only at weekends. Thursdays Ladies Day. Caddies available, 3 days notice required.
Green Fees: Weekdays £27 per round, £33 per day.
Facilities: Lunch. Dinner. Bar Snacks. Full Catering. Changing Room. Golf Shop. Trolley Hire.
Class One Hotel: The Hilton, Cobham, 5 mile(s). Tel: 864471 (0932)
Class Two Hotel: Claremont, Byfleet, 1/2 mile(s). Tel: 345048 (0932)

WEYBRIDGE
St George's Hill Golf Club, St George's Hill, Weybridge, Surrey. KT13 0NL. Tel: 842406 (0932)
Secretary: M R Tapsell   Tel: 847758 (0932)
Professional: A C Rattue   Tel: 843523 (0932)

Location: 1 mile from junc 10 M25.
Description: Undulating heathland with pine, birch, heather and rhododendrons.
A + B 18 holes, 6,569 yards, Par 70, S.S.S. 71.
B + C 18 holes, 6,210 yards, Par 70, S.S.S. 70.
C + A 18 holes, 6,097 yards, Par 70, S.S.S. 69.
Membership: 650
Visitors: Welcome. Handicap certificate required. Letter of Introduction required.Caddies by prior arrangement with caddy master, telephone 858175 (0932).
Green Fees: On application.
Facilities: Full Catering. Changing Room. Golf Shop. Club Hire. Trolley Hire.
Class One Hotel: Cedar House, Cobham, 2 mile(s). Tel: 863424 (0932)
Class Two Hotel: Warbeck House, Weybridge, 1 mile(s). Tel: 848764 (0932)

WOKING
Windlemere Golf Club, Windlesham Road, West End, Woking, Surrey. GU24 9QL. Tel: 858727 (0276)
Secretary: Mr S Hodsdon   Tel: 857405 (0276)
Professional: A Kelso   Tel: 858727 (0276)
Description: Undulating parkland.
9 holes, 2,673 yards, Par 34, S.S.S. 33.
Visitors: Welcome. Booking 7 days in advance.
Green Fees: On application.
Facilities: Bar Snacks. Changing Room. Golf Shop. Club Hire. Driving Range. Trolley Hire.
Class One Hotel: Pennyhill Park Country Club, Bagshot, 4 mile(s). Tel: 71774 (0276)
Class Two Hotel: Park Gate Hotel, Bagshot, 3 mile(s). Tel: 73667 (0276)

SUSSEX (EAST)

BEXHILL-ON-SEA
Cooden Beach Golf Club, Cooden Sea Road, Bexhill-on-Sea, E Sussex. TN39 4TR. Tel: 2040 (04243)
Secretary: C R Cope   Tel: 2040 (04243)
Professional: Keith Robson   Tel: 3938 (04243)
Location: A259 Eastbourne to Hastings Road.
Description: Seaside course.
18 holes, 6,450 yards, S.S.S. 71, Course record 67.
Membership: 700
Visitors: Welcome. Handicap certificate required. Letter of Introduction required.Prior booking essential.
Green Fees: Weekdays £22.50, weekends and bank Holidays £27.50.
Facilities: Lunch. Dinner. Bar Snacks. Full Catering. Changing Room. Golf Shop. Club Hire. Trolley Hire. Caddies available.
Class One Hotel: Cooden Resort, On Course, Tel: 2281 (04243)

BEXHILL-ON-SEA
Highwoods Golf Club, Ellerslie Lane, Bexhill-on-Sea, E Sussex. TN39 4LJ. Tel: 219600 (0424)
Secretary: Mr P Robins   Tel: 212625 (0424)
Professional: Mr M Andrews   Tel: 212770 (0424)

Cade's - Audi Golf Course Guide

Location: 5 miles north of Bexhill on Turkey Road.
Description: Undulating open parklad, wooded with streams.
18 holes, 6,218 yards, Par 70, S.S.S. 70, Course record 65.
Membership: 850
Visitors: Welcome. Handicap certificate required. Tuesdays Ladies Day.
Green Fees: Weekdays £22 per day, weekends £28 per day.
Facilities: Lunch. Dinner. Bar Snacks. Full Catering. Changing Room. Golf Shop. Trolley Hire.
Class One Hotel: Granville, Bexhill, 5 mile(s) Tel: 215437 (0424)

BRIGHTON

Brighton and Hove Golf Club, Dyke Road, Brighton, E Sussex. BN1 8YJ. Tel: 507861 (0273)
Secretary: Mr Cawkwell   Tel: 556482 (0273)
Professional: Mr C Burgess   Tel: 540560 (0273)
Location: 1 1/2 miles north of Brighton on Dyke Road.
Description: Hilly downland.
18 holes, 5,701 yards, Par 68, S.S.S. 67, Course record 67.
Membership: 360
Visitors: Welcome. Not Sunday mornings. Friday mornings Veterans Day. Wednesdays Ladies day. Telephone booking advisable 24 hours in advance.
Green Fees: Weekdays £12.50, weekends £21.
Facilities: Lunch. Dinner. Bar Snacks. Full Catering. Changing Room. Golf Shop. Trolley Hire.
Class One Hotel: The Old Ship, Brighton, 1 1/2 mile(s). Tel: 29001 (0273)

BRIGHTON

Dyke Golf Club, Dyke Road, Brighton, E Sussex. BN1 8YJ. Tel: 857230 (0273)
Secretary: Mr White   Tel: 857296 (0273)
Professional: Mr Longmore   Tel: 857260 (0273)
Location: 3 miles north of Brighton on Dyke Road.
Description: Downland, blackthorn and gorse lined. Founded in 1906.
18 holes, 6,588 yards, Par 72, S.S.S. 71, Course record 68.
Membership: 750
Visitors: Welcome. With members only at weekends. Tuesdays Ladies Day.
Green Fees: £21 per round, £31 per day.
Facilities: Lunch. Dinner. Bar Snacks. Full Catering. Changing Room. Golf Shop. Club Hire. Trolley Hire. Buggy Hire.
Class One Hotel: The Old Ship, Brighton, 3 mile(s). Tel: 29001 (0273)

BRIGHTON

East Brighton Golf Club, Roedean Road, Brighton, E Sussex. BN2 5RA. Tel: 604838 (0273)
Secrctary: K R Head   Tel: 604838 (0273)
Professional: W Street   Tel: 603989 (0273)
Location: East end of Brighton, just of A259 behind Brighton Marina.
Description: Undulating downland.
White 18 holes, 6,346 yards, Par 72, S.S.S. 70, Course record 68.
Red 18 holes, 6,020 yards, Par 70, S.S.S. 68.

Membership: 650
Visitors: Welcome. Handicap certificate required. No catering Mondays.
Green Fees: Weekdays £21 per day, weekends and bank Holidays £30 per day.
Facilities: Lunch. Dinner. Bar Snacks. Full Catering. Changing Room. Golf Shop. Trolley Hire.
Class One Hotel: Old Ship, Brighton, 3 mile(s). Tel: 29001 (0273)
Class Two Hotel: Dudley, Brighton, 5 mile(s). Tel: 736266 (0273)

BRIGHTON

Hollingbury Park Golf Club, Ditchling Road, Brighton, E Sussex. BN1 7HS. Tel: 552010 (0273)
Secretary: J Walling   Tel: 552010 (0273)
Professional: P Brown   Tel: 500086 (0273)
Location: 2 miles from town centre, between A23 and A27.
Description: Public course, undulating downland.
18 holes, 6,500 yards, Par 72.
Membership: 400
Visitors: Welcome. Not before 10a.m. weekends.
Green Fees: Weekdays £12 per round, £17 per day. Weekends £15 per round.
Facilities: Lunch. Bar Snacks. Changing Room. Golf Shop. Club Hire. Trolley Hire. Buggy Hire.
Class One Hotel: Old Ship, Brighton, 2 mile(s). Tel: 29001 (0273)
Class Two Hotel: The Black Lion, Patcham, 1 1/2 mile(s). Tel: 552886 (0273)

BRIGHTON

Pyecombe Golf Club, Clayton Hill, Pyecombe, Brighton, E Sussex. BN45 7FF. Tel: 845372 (0273)
Secretary: W M Wise   Tel: 845372 (0273)
Professional: C R White   Tel: 845398 (0273)
Location: 4 miles north of Brighton on A273 Burgess Hill Road.
Description: Undulating downland with magnificent views.
18 holes, 6,248 yards, Par 71, S.S.S. 70, Course record 67.
Membership: 624
Visitors: Welcome. Weekdays after 9.15a.m., weekends after 2p.m. otherwise with member.
Green Fees: Weekdays £17, weekends £20.
Facilities: Lunch. Dinner. Bar Snacks. Full Catering. Changing Room. Golf Shop. Club Hire. Trolley Hire.

CROWBOROUGH

Crowborough Beacon Golf Club, Beacon Road, Crowborough, E Sussex. TN6 1UJ. Tel: 661511 (0892)
Secretary: M C Swatton   Tel: 661511 (0892)
Professional: D Newnham   Tel: 653877 (0892)
Location: On A26 9 miles south of Tunbridge Wells.
18 holes, 6,318 yards, Par 71, S.S.S. 70, Course record 67.
Membership: 700
Visitors: Welcome. Handicap certificate required. Not at weekends or Bank Holidays unless with a member.
Green Fees: £22.50 per round, £34 per day.
Facilities: Lunch. Dinner. Bar Snacks. Full Catering. Chang-

ing Room. Golf Shop. Club Hire. Trolley Hire. Caddies available.
Class One Hotel: Winston Manor, Crowborough, 1 1/2 mile(s). Tel: 652772 (0892)
Class Two Hotel: Major & Mrs Graham Allt, Maresfield, 7 mile(s). Tel: 762335 (0825)

EASTBOURNE
Eastbourne Downs Golf Club, East Dean Road, Eastbourne, E Sussex. BN20 8ES. Tel: 20827 (0323)
Secretary: D J Eldrett   Tel: 20827 (0323)
Professional: T Marshall   Tel: 32264 (0323)
Description: Downland.
18 holes, 6,635 yards, Par 72, S.S.S. 72, Course record 69.
Membership: 730
Visitors: Welcome.
Green Fees: Weekdays £20.
Facilities: Lunch. Bar Snacks. Full Catering. Changing Room. Golf Shop. Trolley Hire.
Class One Hotel: Lansdowne, Eastbourne, 1 mile(s). Tel: 25174 (0323)
Class Two Hotel: Princes, Eastbourne, 1 mile(s). Tel: 22056 (0323)

EASTBOURNE
Royal Eastbourne Golf Club, Paradise Drive, Eastbourne, E Sussex. BN20 8PB. Tel: 30412 (0323)
Secretary: Mr P Robins   Tel: 29738 (0323)
Professional: Richard Wooller   Tel: 36986 (0323)
Description: Parkland.
18 holes, 6,109 yards, Par 70, S.S.S. 69, Course record 63.
9 holes, 2,147 yards, Par 32, S.S.S. 61.
Membership: 950
Visitors: Welcome. Handicap certificate required. No 3 or 4 balls before 9.15 a.m. any day or before 2 p.m. Tuesdays. Always telephone starter for availability. Societies contact Secretary.
Green Fees: 18 holes - Weekdays £25, weekends and Bank Holidays £35. 9 holes - Weekdays £14, weekends and Bank Holidays £18. Reductions at certain times.
Facilities: Lunch. Dinner. Bar Snacks. Full Catering. Changing Room. Golf Shop. Club Hire. Trolley Hire. Buggy Hire.
Class One Hotel: Lansdowne, Eastbourne, 1 1/2 mile(s). Tel: 25174 (0323)
Class Two Hotel: Wish Tower, Eastbourne, 1 1/2 mile(s). Tel: 22676 (0323)

EASTBOURNE
Willingdon Golf Club, Southdown Road, Eastbourne, E Sussex. BN20 9AA. Tel: 410983 (0323)
Secretary: B Kirby   Tel: 410981 (0323)
Location: 2 miles north of Eastbourne on A22.
Description: Downland course with superb views.
18 holes, 6,049 yards, Par 69, S.S.S. 69.
Membership: 500
Visitors: Welcome. Handicap certificate required. Not Tuesdays, not Sundays a.m.. Very limited weekends.
Green Fees: On application.

Facilities: Lunch. Dinner. Bar Snacks. Full Catering. Changing Room. Golf Shop. Club Hire. Trolley Hire. Caddies available.
Class One Hotel: Lansdowne, Eastbourne, 2 mile(s). Tel: 39721 (0323)
Class Two Hotel: New Willmington, Eastbourne, 2 mile(s). Tel: 21219 (0323)

FOREST ROW
Royal Ashdown Forest New Course, Chapel Lane, Forest Row, E Sussex. RH18 5BB. Tel: 824866 (0342)
Secretary: Mr R L Pratt   Tel: 824866 (0342)
Professional: Martyn Landsborough   Tel: 822047 (0342)
Description: Forest course, tight, with beautiful scenery suitable for the experienced and the not so experienced.
18 holes, 5,549 yards, Par 68, S.S.S. 67.
Membership: 150
Visitors: Welcome. 4 balls at weekends prior to mid-day.
Green Fees: On application.
Facilities: Lunch. Dinner. Bar Snacks. Full Catering. Changing Room. Golf Shop. Trolley Hire.
Class Two Hotel: Ashdown Forest, On Course, Tel: 824866 (0342)

HASTINGS
Beauport Park Golf Club, Battle Road, St Leonards on Sea, Hastings, E Sussex. TN38 0TA. Tel: 852977 (0424)
Secretary: Mr R Thompson   Tel: 852977 (0424)
Professional: Mr M Barton   Tel: 852981 (0424)
Location: 3 miles north of Hastings on A2100 Hastings to Battle Road.
Description: Undulating, tree lined course with scenic views of open countryside.
White 18 holes, 6,248 yards, Par 71, S.S.S. 70, Course record 69.
Yellow 18 holes, 6,033 yards, Par 70, S.S.S. 70.
Membership: 500
Visitors: Welcome. Must book in advance for play before 10.30 a.m. at weekends.
Green Fees: Weekdays £10 per day, weekends £12 per day.
Facilities: Lunch. Dinner. Bar Snacks. Full Catering. Changing Room. Golf Shop. Club Hire. Driving Range. Trolley Hire.
Class One Hotel: Beauport Park, St Leonards, 1/4 mile(s). Tel: 851222 (0424)

HOVE
West Hove Golf Course, Church Farm, Hangleton, Hove, E Sussex. BN3 8AL. Tel: 419738 (0273)
Secretary: R W Charman   Tel: 419738 (0273)
Professional: David Mills   Tel: 413494 (0273)
Description: Undulating downland.
18 holes, 6,266 yards, Par 72, S.S.S. 70.
Membership: 600
Visitors: Welcome.
Green Fees: On application.
Facilities: Lunch. Dinner. Bar Snacks. Full Catering. Chang-

ing Room. Golf Shop. Club Hire. Trolley Hire. Caddies available.
Class One Hotel: Dudley, Hove, 3 mile(s). Tel: 736266 (0273)
Class Two Hotel: Milton, Hove, 2 mile(s). Tel: 738587 (0273)

LEWES

Lewes Golf Club, Chapel Hill, Lewes, E Sussex. BN7 2BB. Tel: 473245 (0273)
Secretary: Mr R B M Moore   Tel: 483474 (0273)
Professional: Mr P Dobson   Tel: 473245 (0273)
Description: Undulating downland with magnificent views of surrounding countryside.
18 holes, 5,951 yards, Par 71, S.S.S. 69, Course record 67.
Membership: 700
Visitors: Welcome. Handicap certificate required. Not before 2p.m. weekends.
Green Fees: Weekdays £15.50 per round or day, weekends £26.
Facilities: Lunch. Dinner. Bar Snacks. Full Catering. Changing Room. Golf Shop. Trolley Hire. Buggy Hire.
Class One Hotel: The Crown, Lewes, 1 mile(s). Tel: 480670 (0273)

NEWHAVEN

Peacehaven Golf Club, The Clubhouse, Brighton Road, Newhaven, E Sussex. BN9 9UH. Tel: 514049 (0273)
Secretary: D Wright   Tel: 512571 (0273)
Professional: G Williams
Location: On A259 1 mile from Newhaven 9 miles from Brighton.
Description: Links, 9 holes, picturesque, short to medium length.
9 holes, 5,926 yards, Par 70, S.S.S. 66, Course record 65.
Membership: 200
Visitors: Welcome. Not Sundays or Bank Holidays a.m.. Saturdays a.m. only with a member.
Green Fees: £16.
Facilities: Lunch. Dinner. Bar Snacks. Full Catering. Changing Room. Golf Shop. Club Hire. Trolley Hire. Caddies available.

RYE

Rye Golf Course, Camber, Rye, E Sussex. TN31 7QS. Tel: 225241 (0797)
Secretary: J M Bradley   Tel: 225241 (0797)
Professional: P Marsh   Tel: 225218 (0797)
Location: From Rye take A259 towards Folkestone, after 3/4 mile turn right to Camber. Golf course is 3 miles along this road.
Description: Typical links course.
Old Course 18 holes, 6,310 yards, Par 68, S.S.S. 71, Course record 64.
Jubilee 9 holes, 6,141 yards, Par 71, S.S.S. 70.
Membership: 1000
Visitors: Welcome. Handicap certificate required. Letter of Introduction required.Only on introduction of a member, not at weekends.
Green Fees: £30 per round.

Facilities: Lunch. Full Catering. Changing Room. Golf Shop. Trolley Hire.
Class One Hotel: Mermaid, Rye, 4 mile(s). Tel: 223065 (0797)
Class Two Hotel: Hope & Anchor, Rye, 4 mile(s). Tel: 222216 (0797)

SEAFORD

Seaford Golf Club, East Blatchington, Seaford, E Sussex. BN25 2JD. Tel: 892442 (0323)
Secretary: M B Hichisson   Tel: 892442 (0323)
Professional: P Stevens   Tel: 894160 (0323)
Location: Turn inland at War Memorial at Seaford and follow road for 1 mile.
Description: Downland with gentle slopes and fine views.
18 holes, 6,233 yards, Par 69, S.S.S. 70, Course record 67.
Visitors: Welcome. Handicap certificate required. Not Tuesdays or weekends.
Green Fees: £30 all day, £24 after 12p.m., £14 after 3p.m..
Facilities: Lunch. Dinner. Bar Snacks. Full Catering. Changing Room. Golf Shop. Driving Range. Trolley Hire. Buggy Hire.
Class Two Hotel: Course Dormy House, On Course, Tel: 892442 (0323)

UCKFIELD

Piltdown Golf Club, Piltdown, Uckfield, E Sussex. TN22 3XB. Tel: 2033 (082572)
Secretary: J C Duncan   Tel: 2033 (082572)
Professional: J Amos   Tel: 2389 (082572)
Location: 1 mile west of Maresfield off A272 signposted Isfield.
Description: Undulating with gorse and heather.
18 holes, 6,030 yards, Par 69, S.S.S. 69, Course record 67.
Visitors: Welcome. Handicap certificate required. Not before 2.30p.m. Sundays. Restrictions Tuesdays and Thursdays. Always telephone in advance. Caddies by arrangement. Dinner by arrangement.
Green Fees: £27.50 per day.
Facilities: Lunch. Bar Snacks. Full Catering. Changing Room. Golf Shop. Club Hire. Trolley Hire. Buggy Hire.
Class One Hotel: The Halland, East Hoathly, 6 mile(s). Tel: 840456 (0825)

WADHURST

Dale Hill Golf Club, Ticehurst, Wadhurst, E Sussex. TN5 7DQ. Tel: 200112 (0580)
Secretary: Lindsey Irvine   Tel: 200112 (0580)
Professional: Mr Ian Connelly   Tel: 201090 (0580)
Location: Off A21 on B2087 towards Ticehurst.
Description: Undulating parkland.
18 holes, 6,060 yards, Par 69, S.S.S. 69.
Membership: 580
Visitors: Welcome. Not before 12p.m. weekends. Some catering restrictions apply, please telephone in advance.
Green Fees: Weekdays £20, weekends £25.
Facilities: Lunch. Dinner. Bar Snacks. Full Catering. Changing Room. Golf Shop. Club Hire. Trolley Hire. Buggy Hire.
Class One Hotel: Dale Hill Golf Hotel, On Course, Tel: 200112 (0580)

SUSSEX (WEST)

CHICHESTER
Goodwood Golf Club, Goodwood, Chichester, W Sussex. PO18 0PN. Tel: 774968 (0243)
Secretary: Mr C Pickup Tel: 774968 (0243)
Professional: Mr K MacDonald Tel: 774994 (0243)
Location: 3 miles north of Chichester on A285 adjacent to Goodwood racecourse.
Description: Tree lined downland with excellent views of Chichester and the Channel.
18 holes, 6,401 yards, Par 72, S.S.S. 71.
Membership: 950
Visitors: Welcome. Handicap certificate required. With members only at weekends. Tuesdays Ladies Day. Always telephone in advance.
Green Fees: Weekdays £25 per day, weekends £35 per day.
Facilities: Lunch. Dinner. Bar Snacks. Full Catering. Changing Room. Golf Shop. Trolley Hire.
Class One Hotel: Chichester Resort Hotel, Chichester, 1 1/2 mile(s). Tel: 786351 (0243)

CRAWLEY
Copthorne Golf Course, Borers Arms Road, Copthorne, Crawley, W Sussex. RH10 3LL. Tel: 712033 (0342)
Secretary: Mr J Appleton Tel: 712508 (0342)
Professional: Mr J Burrell Tel: 712405 (0342)
Location: Midway between Crawley and East Grinstead. Junc 10 M23 onto A264.
Description: Level common heath and woodland. Streams guarding some greens. 1992 is our centenary year.
18 holes, 6,550 yards, Par 71, S.S.S. 71, Course record 68.
Membership: 535
Visitors: Welcome. Not before 1p.m. weekends. Tuesdays Ladies Day.
Green Fees: Weekdays £25 per round, £33 per day. Weekends £40 per round.
Facilities: Lunch. Dinner. Bar Snacks. Full Catering. Changing Room. Golf Shop. Club Hire. Trolley Hire.
Class One Hotel: The Copthorne Hotel, Copthorne, 1/2 mile(s). Tel: 714971 (0342)

CRAWLEY
Ifield Golf and Country Club, Rusper Road, Ifield, Crawley, W Sussex. RH11 0LN. Tel: 520222 (0293)
Secretary: Mr B Gazzard Tel: 520222 (0293)
Professional: Mr J Earl Tel: 523088 (0293)
Location: 1 1/2 miles south of Crawley on Crawley to Rusper Road.
Description: Flat, open parkland, tree lined with ditches, surrounded by scenic countryside.
18 holes, 5,901 yards, Par 70, S.S.S. 68, Course record 67.
Membership: 900
Visitors: Welcome. Handicap certificate required. Tuesdays 9a.m. to 11a.m. Veterans only. Wednesdays Ladies Day.
Green Fees: £20 per round, £27 per day.
Facilities: Lunch. Dinner. Bar Snacks. Full Catering. Changing Room. Golf Shop. Club Hire. Trolley Hire. Buggy Hire.

Class One Hotel: The Copthorne Hotel, Copthorne, 6 1/2 mile(s). Tel: 714971 (0342)
Class Two Hotel: The Ifield Court, Ifield, 1 1/2 mile(s). Tel: 534807 (0293)

EAST GRINSTEAD
Holtye Golf Club, Cowden, Near Edenbridge, East Grinstead, W Sussex. TN8 7ED. Tel: 850635 (0342)
Secretary: Mr J P Holmes Tel: 850576 (0342)
Professional: Mr K Hinton Tel: 850957 (0342)
Location: 4 miles east of East Grinstead on A264.
Description: Tree lined heathland with heather and gorse.
18 holes, 5,325 yards, Par 66, S.S.S. 66, Course record 65.
Membership: 500
Visitors: Welcome. With members only weekends a.m.. Thursday mornings Ladies only.
Green Fees: Weekdays £17, weekends £20.
Facilities: Lunch. Dinner. Bar Snacks. Full Catering. Changing Room. Golf Shop. Trolley Hire.
Class One Hotel: Felbridge Hotel, East Grinstead, 6 mile(s). Tel: 326992 (0342)
Class Two Hotel: White Horse Inn, East Grinstead, Tel: 850640 (0342)

HAYWARDS HEATH
Haywards Heath Golf Club, High Beech Lane, Haywards Heath, W Sussex. RH16 1SL. Tel: 414457 (0444)
Secretary: Mr John Duncan Tel: 414457 (0444)
Professional: Michael Henning Tel: 414866 (0444)
Location: North of Haywards Heath near Ardingly College.
Description: Parkland.
18 holes, 6,204 yards, S.S.S. 70.
Visitors: Welcome. Handicap certificate required. With members only at weekends. Wednesdays or Thursdays Society days. Some catering restrictions apply, please telephone in advance.
Green Fees: Weekdays £20 per round, £25 per day. Weekends and bank Holidays £25 per round, £30 per day.
Facilities: Lunch. Dinner. Bar Snacks. Full Catering. Changing Room. Golf Shop. Club Hire. Trolley Hire.

HORSHAM
Mannings Heath Golf Club, Goldings Lane, Mannings Heath, Horsham, W Sussex. RH13 6JU. Tel: 210228 (0403)
Secretary: Mr J Owen Tel: 210228 (0403)
Professional: Mr M Denny Tel: 210228 (0403)
Location: 3 miles south of Horsham on A281.
Description: Well established mature course, circa 1919. A thinking golfers course. Tree lined on edge of St Leonards Forest.
18 holes, 6,404 yards, Par 73, S.S.S. 71, Course record 65.
Membership: 650
Visitors: Welcome. Must book 7 days in advance. Thursdays Ladies Day.
Green Fees: Weekdays £25 per round, £40 per day. Weekends £33 per round, £50 per day.
Facilities: Lunch. Dinner. Bar Snacks. Full Catering. Changing Room. Golf Shop. Club Hire. Trolley Hire.
Class One Hotel: South Lodge, Horsham, 2 mile(s). Tel: 891711 (0403)

MIDHURST

Cowdray Park Golf Club, Midhurst, W Sussex. GU29 0BB. Tel: 812088 (0730)
Secretary: Mrs J D Huggett   Tel: 813599 (0730)
Professional: Mr S Hall   Tel: 812091 (0730)
Location: 1 mile north of Midhurst on A272.
Description: Gently undulating parkland with scenic views of the South Downs.
18 holes, 6,212 yards, Par 70, S.S.S. 70, Course record 69.
Membership: 750
Visitors: Welcome. Handicap certificate required. Not before 9a.m. weekdays and not before 11a.m. weekends. Tuesdays Ladies Day. Caddies available with 7 days notice.
Green Fees: Weekdays £20 per day, weekends £25 per day.
Facilities: Lunch. Dinner. Bar Snacks. Full Catering. Changing Room. Golf Shop. Club Hire. Trolley Hire.
Class One Hotel: Spread Eagle, Midhurst, 1 mile(s). Tel: 816911 (0730)

PULBOROUGH

West Sussex Golf Club, Hurston Warren, Pulborough, W Sussex. RH20 2EN. Tel: 872563 (0798)
Secretary: Mr G Martindale   Tel: 872563 (0798)
Professional: T Packham   Tel: 872426 (0798)
Location: 1 mile east of Pulborough on A283.
Description: Flat heathland championship course, host of English Ladies Amateur Open and English Men's Seniors.
18 holes, 6,221 yards, Par 68, S.S.S. 70, Course record 62.
Visitors: Welcome. Handicap certificate required. Letter of Introduction required.By prior arrangement only. Not Tuesdays. Not before 9.30a.m.. With members only at weekends. Caddies a
Green Fees: £28 per round, £38 per 2 rounds.
Facilities: Lunch. Dinner. Bar Snacks. Full Catering. Changing Room. Golf Shop. Trolley Hire. Buggy Hire.
Class One Hotel: The Roundabout, W Chiltington, 2 mile(s). Tel: 813838 (0798)
Class Two Hotel: Arun Cosmopolitan, Pulborough, 1 mile(s). Tel: 872162 (0798)

SELSEY

Selsey Golf Club, Golf Links Lane, Selsey, W Sussex. Tel: 602203 (0243)
Secretary: Mr Rackstraw   Tel: 602029 (0243)
Professional: Mr P Grindley   Tel: 602203 (0243)
Location: 7 miles south of Chichester on Chichester to Selsey Road.
Description: 9 holes played twice. Flat links course with hedges and streams.
18 holes, 5,932 yards, Par 68, S.S.S. 68, Course record 66.
Membership: 400
Visitors: Welcome. With members only at weekends.
Green Fees: Weekdays £10 per round, £15 per day.
Facilities: Lunch. Dinner. Bar Snacks. Full Catering. Changing Room. Golf Shop. Trolley Hire.
Class One Hotel: The Seal, Selsey, 1 mile(s). Tel: 602461 (0243)

WORTHING

Hill Barn Golf Course, Hill Barn Lane, Worthing, W Sussex. BN14 9QE. Tel: 233918 (0903)
Secretary: Mr Pettit   Tel: 207179 (0903)
Professional: Mr Higgins   Tel: 237301 (0903)
Location: 1 mile north of Worthing on A24.
Description: Municipal course, tree lined downland.
18 holes, 6,400 yards, Par 70, S.S.S. 70, Course record 63.
Membership: 200
Visitors: Welcome.
Green Fees: Weekdays £10 per round, weekends £11.70.
Facilities: Lunch. Dinner. Bar Snacks. Full Catering. Changing Room. Golf Shop. Club Hire. Trolley Hire. Buggy Hire.
Class One Hotel: The Chatsworth, Worthing, 1 mile(s). Tel: 236103 (0903)
Class Two Hotel: The Village House, Findon, 1 1/2 mile(s). Tel: 872733 (0903)

WORTHING

Worthing Golf Club, Links Road, Worthing, W Sussex. BN14 9QZ. Tel: 260801 (0903)
Secretary: D J Morgan   Tel: 260801 (0903)
Professional: S Rolley   Tel: 260718 (0903)
Location: Central Station 1 1/2 miles (A27) 1/4 mile from A24 junc.
Description: Attractive 36 hole downland course with sea views.
Lower 18 holes, 6,519 yards, Par 71, S.S.S. 72, Course record 66.
Upper 18 holes, 5,243 yards, Par 66, S.S.S. 66.
Membership: 1150
Visitors: Welcome. Handicap certificate required.
Green Fees: Weekdays £28, weekends and bank Holidays £35.
Facilities: Lunch. Dinner. Bar Snacks. Full Catering. Changing Room. Golf Shop. Trolley Hire.
Class One Hotel: Beach, Worthing, 1 1/2 mile(s). Tel: 234001 (0903)
Class Two Hotel: Windsor House, Worthing, 1 1/2 mile(s). Tel: 820775 (0903)

TYNE & WEAR

CHOPWELL

Garesfield Golf Club, Chopwell, Tyne & Wear. NE17 7AP. Tel: 561278 (0207)
Secretary: Mr Peart   Tel: 561309 (0207)
Location: 9 miles south east of Newcastle on A6135 from Rowlands Gill.
Description: Scenic hilly parkland with pond and small stream. Tree lined and wooded.
18 holes, 6,603 yards, Par 72, S.S.S. 72, Course record 69.
Membership: 715
Visitors: Welcome. Not before 4.30p.m. weekends.
Green Fees: Weekdays £11 per round, £14 per day. Weekends and Bank Holidays £14 per round.
Facilities: Lunch. Dinner. Bar Snacks. Full Catering. Changing Room. Golf Shop.

EAST BOLDON

Boldon Golf Club Ltd., Dipe Lane, East Boldon, Tyne & Wear. NE36 0PQ. Tel: 536 4182 (091)
Secretary: Mr R E Jobes　　　　　Tel: 536 5360 (091)
Professional: Phipps Golf　　　　Tel: 536 5835 (091)
Location: 5 miles west of Sunderland on A184.
Description: Open tree lined parkland with pleasant views from the tees.
18 holes, 6,362 yards, Par 72, S.S.S. 70, Course record 67.
Membership: 734
Visitors: Welcome. Not between 9a.m. and 10a.m. or 12.30p.m. and 1.30p.m. weekdays and not before 3.30p.m. weekends.
Green Fees: Weekdays 316 per day, with a member £9. Weekends and Bank Holidays £20 per day. Summer rates £11 per day with a member.
Facilities: Lunch. Dinner. Bar Snacks. Full Catering. Changing Room. Golf Shop. Club Hire. Trolley Hire.
Class One Hotel: The Friendly, Boldon, 1 mile(s). Tel: 519 1999 (091)

GATESHEAD

Heworth Golf Club, Gingling Gate, Heworth, Gateshead, Tyne & Wear. NE10 8XY. Tel: 469 2137 (091)
Secretary: Mr G Holbrow　　　　Tel: 469 9832 (091)
Location: 3 miles east of Gateshead on Felling By-Pass.
Description: Flat, open parkland with some trees surrounded by the Tyne & Wear Green Belt.
18 holes, 6,432 yards, Par 71, S.S.S. 71, Course record 69.
Membership: 700
Visitors: Welcome. With members only at weekends. Wednesdays Ladies Day.
Green Fees: Weekdays £13 per round, £6.50 with a member, £16 per day, £8 with a member. Weekends £8 per round, £16 per day.
Facilities: Lunch. Dinner. Bar Snacks. Full Catering. Changing Room.
Class One Hotel: The Swallow, Gateshead, 3 mile(s). Tel: 477 1105 (091)

GOSFORTH

City of Newcastle Golf Club, Three Mile Bridge, Gosforth, Newcastle upon Tyne, Tyne & Wear. NE3 2DR. Tel: 285 1775 (091)
Secretary: A J Matthew　　　　　Tel: 285 1775 (091)
Professional: A J Matthew　　　　Tel: 285 5481 (091)
Location: 3 miles north of Newcastle.
Description: Parkland.
18 holes, 6,508 yards, Par 72, S.S.S. 71, Course record 67.
Membership: 570
Visitors: Welcome. Not on competition days. Full catering by arrangement.
Green Fees: Weekdays £18.50 per day, with a member £7.50. Weekends and Bank Holidays £20.50 per day, with a member £8.50.
Facilities: Lunch. Dinner. Bar Snacks. Changing Room. Golf Shop. Trolley Hire.
Class One Hotel: Gosforth Park Hotel, Gosforth, 1 mile(s). Tel: 236 4111 (091)

HEDDON-ON-THE-WALL

Close House Golf Club, Heddon-on-the-Wall, Newcastle-upon-Tyne, Tyne & Wear. NE15 0HT. Tel: 852953 (0661)
Secretary: Mrs L Steel　　　　　Tel: 852303 (0661)
Location: 9 miles west of Newcastle on A69.
Description: Open tree lined parkland.
18 holes, 5,587 yards, Par 68, S.S.S. 67, Course record 66.
Membership: 900
Visitors: Welcome. Handicap certificate required. Only with members. Society bookings by prior arrangement with Secretary.
Green Fees: £15 per day.
Facilities: Bar Snacks. Full Catering. Changing Room.

HOUGHTON-LE-SPRING

Houghton-le-Spring Golf Club, Copt Hill, Houghton-le-Spring, Tyne & Wear. . Tel: 584 1198 (091)
Secretary: N Wales　　　　　Tel: 528 6716 (091)
Professional: S Bradbury　　　Tel: 584 6088 (091)
Description: Hillside course.
18 holes, 6,700 yards, Par 72, S.S.S. 71, Course record 67.
Membership: 600
Visitors: Welcome. Not Sundays until late afternoon.
Green Fees: Weekdays £12, weekends and Bank Holidays £18.
Facilities: Lunch. Dinner. Bar Snacks. Full Catering. Changing Room. Golf Shop. Trolley Hire.
Class One Hotel: Tunstall Lodge, Sunderland, 2 mile(s). Tel: 521 0353 (091)

NEWCASTLE UPON TYNE

Gosforth Golf Club, Broadway East, Gosforth, Newcastle upon Tyne, Tyne & Wear. NE3 5ER. Tel: 285 3495 (091)
Secretary: A Sutherland　　　　Tel: 285 3495 (091)
Professional: G Garland　　　　Tel: 285 0553 (091)
Location: 3 miles north of Newcastle of A6125.
Description: Parkland.
18 holes, 6,024 yards, Par 69, S.S.S. 69.
Membership: 550
Visitors: Welcome. Handicap certificate required. Guests of members only weekends and Bank Holidays before 4p.m..
Green Fees: £18.
Facilities: Lunch. Dinner. Bar Snacks. Full Catering. Changing Room. Golf Shop. Trolley Hire.

NEWCASTLE UPON TYNE

Hobson Municipal Golf Club, Hobson, Burnopfield, Newcastle upon Tyne, Tyne & Wear. NE16 6BZ. Tel: 71605 (0207)
Secretary: R J Handrick　　　　Tel: 570189 (0207)
Professional: J W Ord　　　　　Tel: 71605 (0207)
Location: On main A692 Consett to Gateshead Road, opposite Hobson Industrial Estate.
Description: Easy walking parkland.
18 holes, 6,582 yards, Par 71, S.S.S. 71, Course record 67.
Membership: 600
Visitors: Welcome. Booking system for weekends and Bank Holidays.
Green Fees: Weekdays £8 per round, weekends and

Bank Holidays £10 per round.
Facilities: Lunch. Dinner. Bar Snacks. Full Catering. Changing Room. Golf Shop. Club Hire. Trolley Hire.
Class One Hotel: Beamish Park, Stanley, 2 1/2 mile(s). Tel: 230666 (0207)

NEWCASTLE UPON TYNE

Westerhope Golf Club, Whorton Grange, Westerhope, Newcastle upon Tyne, Tyne & Wear. NE5 1PP. Tel: 286 7636 (091)
Secretary: H Simmons Tel: 286 7636 (091)
Professional: N Brown Tel: 286 0594 (091)
Location: West of A1(M). 1 1/2 miles north west of Tyne Bridge. 5 miles west of Newcastle. 2 miles south of Airport.
Description: Parkland with lots of trees.
18 holes, 6,468 yards, Par 72, S.S.S. 71, Course record 66.
Membership: 700
Visitors: Welcome. With members only at weekends and Bank Holidays. Dress rules apply. Some catering restrictions apply, please telephone in advance.
Green Fees: Weekdays £14 per round, with a member £8, £18 per day, with member £12. Weekends £10. Students and Senior Citizens £8, Juniors £7 before
Facilities: Lunch. Dinner. Bar Snacks. Full Catering. Changing Room. Golf Shop. Trolley Hire. Buggy Hire.

NEWCASTLE UPON TYNE

Whickham Golf Club Ltd., Hollinside Park, Whickham, Newcastle upon Tyne, Tyne & Wear. NE16 5BA. Tel: 488 7309 (091)
Secretary: N Weightman Tel: 488 1576 (091)
Professional: B Ridley Tel: 488 8591 (091)
Location: 5 miles south west of Newcastle.
Description: Parkland.
18 holes, 6,129 yards, Par 68, S.S.S. 69, Course record 61.
Membership: 600
Visitors: Welcome. Handicap certificate required. Not weekends or Bank Holidays. Some catering restrictions apply, please telephone in advance.
Green Fees: £16.
Facilities: Lunch. Dinner. Bar Snacks. Full Catering. Changing Room. Golf Shop. Club Hire. Trolley Hire.
Class One Hotel: Gibside Arms, Whickham, 2 mile(s). Tel: 488 9292 (091)

SHIREMOOR

Backworth Golf Club, The Hall, Backworth, Shiremoor, Tyne & Wear. NE27 0AH.
Secretary: R Forester Tel: 253 1110 (091)
Location: B1322 approx 1 mile from Holystone roundabout on A1.
Description: Parkland.
Medal 18 holes, 5,930 yards, Par 71, S.S.S. 69, Course record 66.
Club 18 holes, 5,606 yards, Par 70, S.S.S. 68.
Membership: 460
Visitors: Welcome. Handicap certificate required. Some catering restrictions apply, please telephone in advance.
Green Fees: Weekdays £10, £6 with member. Weekends and Bank Holidays £12.
Facilities: Lunch. Dinner. Bar Snacks. Full Catering. Changing Room.
Class One Hotel: Moat House, Wallsend, 3 mile(s). Tel: 262 8989 (091)

SOUTH SHIELDS

South Shields Golf Club, Cleadon Hills, South Shields, Tyne & Wear. NE34 8EG. Tel: 456 0475 (091)
Secretary: W H Loades Tel: 456 8942 (091)
Professional: Gary Parsons Tel: 456 0110 (091)
Description: A rare breed, a coastal heathland course well maintained, with copses of gorse, and dry stone walls.
18 holes, 6,264 yards, Par 71, S.S.S. 70.
Membership: 800
Visitors: Welcome. Handicap certificate required. Letter of Introduction required.
Green Fees: W/days £20, w/ends and Bank Holidays £25.
Facilities: Lunch. Dinner. Bar Snacks. Full Catering. Changing Room. Golf Shop. Club Hire. Trolley Hire.
Class One Hotel: Sea Hotel, South Shields, 2 mile(s). Tel: 427 0999 (091)
Class Two Hotel: Marsden Inn, South Shields, 3/4 mile(s). Tel: 456 1812 (091)

SOUTH SHIELDS

Whitburn Golf Club, Lizard Lane, South Shields, Tyne & Wear. Tel: 529 2144 (091)
Secretary: Mrs V Atkinson Tel: 529 2144 (091)
Professional: D Stephenson Tel: 529 4210 (091)
Location: Between Sunderland and South Shields parallel to Coast Road.
Description: Parkland.
18 holes, 6,046 yards, Par 70, S.S.S. 69, Course record 65.
Visitors: Welcome. Not on competition days or before 9.30a.m., restricted on Tuesdays (Ladies Day) please ring professional.
Green Fees: Weekdays £15, with member £8. Weekends and Bank Holidays £20, with member £10.
Facilities: Lunch. Dinner. Bar Snacks. Full Catering. Changing Room. Golf Shop.
Class One Hotel: Swallow, Seaburn, 5 mile(s). Tel: 529 4545 (091)
Class Two Hotel: New Crown, South Shields, 5 mile(s). Tel: 455 3472 (091)

WALLSEND

Wallsend Golf Club, Rheydt Avenue, Wallsend, Tyne & Wear. NE29 8XF. Tel: 262 1973 (091)
Secretary: L Rowe Tel: 262 1973 (091)
Professional: K Phillips Tel: 262 4231 (091)
Location: 1 mile west of Wallsend centre, follow brown signs to sports centre.
Description: Municipal, flat course.
18 holes, 6,324 yards, Par 71, S.S.S. 71.
Membership: 750
Visitors: Welcome. Booking system in operation.
Green Fees: Weekdays £10, weekends £12.
Facilities: Lunch. Dinner. Bar Snacks. Full Catering. Changing Room. Golf Shop. Club Hire. Trolley Hire.
Class One Hotel: Newcastle Moat House, Newcastle, 1 1/2 mile(s). Tel: 262 8989 (091)

WHITLEY BAY

Whitley Bay Golf Club, Claremont Road, Whitley Bay, Tyne & Wear. NE26 3UF. Tel: 252 0180 (091)
Secretary: B Dockar　　　　　　　Tel: 252 0180　(091)
Professional: W J Light　　　　　　Tel: 252 5688　(091)
Location: North end of Whitley Bay.
Description: Simulated links.
18 holes, 6,617 yards, Par 71, S.S.S. 72, Course record 68.
Membership: 750
Visitors: Welcome. With members only at weekends. Tuesdays Ladies Day. No Catering Mondays.
Green Fees: £17 per round, £24 per day.
Facilities: Lunch. Dinner. Bar Snacks. Full Catering. Changing Room. Golf Shop. Trolley Hire.
Class One Hotel: The Windsor, Whitley Bay, 1/2 mile(s). Tel: 252 3317 (091)

WARWICKSHIRE

ATHERSTONE

Atherstone Golf Club, The Outwoods, Coleshill Road, Atherstone, Warwicks. CV9 2RL. Tel: 713110 (0827)
Secretary: V A Walton　　　　　　Tel: 892568　(0827)
Location: Approx 1/4 mile from town centre on Coleshill Road.
Description: Undulating parkland.
18 holes, 6,114 yards, Par 73, S.S.S. 70, Course record 65.
Membership: 250
Visitors: Welcome. Handicap certificate required. Not Sundays. Saturday with member.
Green Fees: £17 per day/round. £23 Bank Holidays, £7 with member.
Facilities: Lunch. Dinner. Bar Snacks. Full Catering. Changing Room. Golf Shop.
Class Two Hotel: The Old Red Lion, Atherstone, 1/4 mile(s). Tel: 713156 (0827)

LEAMINGTON SPA

Newbold Comyn Golf Club, Newbold Terrace East, Leamington Spa, Warwicks. . Tel: 422660 (0926)
Secretary: Alan Pierce　　　　　　Tel: 422660　(0926)
Professional: Dan Knight　　　　　Tel: 421157　(0926)
Location: In Leamington Spa follow signs to Newbold Comyn Park.
Description: Municipal course. Undulating parkland.
18 holes, 6,315 yards, Par 70, S.S.S. 70, Course record 69.
Membership: 350
Visitors: Welcome. Must book 7 days in advance for weekends and Bank Holidays.
Green Fees: Weekdays £6.30 per round, weekends £8 per round.
Facilities: Changing Room. Golf Shop. Club Hire. Trolley Hire.
Class One Hotel: Falstaff, Leamington Spa, 2 1/2 mile(s). Tel: 312044 (0926)
Class Two Hotel: The Angel, Leamington Spa, 1 mile(s). Tel: 881296 (0926)

NUNEATON

Nuneaton Golf Club, Golf Drive, Whitestone, Nuneaton, Warwicks. CV11 6QF. Tel: 347810 (0203)
Secretary: G Pinder　　　　　　　Tel: 347810　(0203)
Professional: G Davison　　　　　Tel: 340201　(0203)
Location: 2 miles south of Nuneaton.
Description: Wooded parkland.
18 holes, 5,431 yards, Par 71, S.S.S. 71.
Membership: 657
Visitors: Welcome. Handicap certificate required. Letter of Introduction required. Not at weekends.
Green Fees: Weekdays £22, with member £6.
Facilities: Lunch. Dinner. Bar Snacks. Full Catering. Changing Room. Golf Shop.

NUNEATON

Purley Chase Golf and Country Club, Ridge Lane, Near Nuneaton, Warwicks. CV10 0RB. Tel: 393118 (0203)
Secretary: David Llewellyn　　　　Tel: 393118　(0203)
Professional: David Llewellyn　　　Tel: 395348　(0203)
Location: 2 miles from Nuneaton, 3 miles from Atherstone.
Description: Championship length over 7,000 yards, slightly undulating terrain. Fourth highest spot in Warwickshire, pleasant surroundings.
18 holes, 6,845 yards, Par 71, S.S.S. 71.
Membership: 650
Visitors: Welcome. Handicap certificate required. Not before 12p.m. weekends.
Green Fees: Weekdays £18 per round, with member £10. Day ticket £30. Weekends £25 per round, with member £15.
Facilities: Lunch. Dinner. Bar Snacks. Full Catering. Changing Room. Golf Shop. Driving Range. Trolley Hire.
Class One Hotel: Hinckley Island, Hinckley, 1 Tel: 631122 (0455)

RUGBY

Rugby Golf Club, Clifton Road, Rugby, Warwicks. CV21 3RD. Tel: 542306 (0788)
Secretary: J B Poxon　　　　　　 Tel: 542306　(0788)
Professional: D Sutherland　　　　Tel: 575134　(0788)
Location: North side of Rugby follow signs to Clifton.
Description: Undulating parkland.
18 holes, 5,500 yards, Par 68, S.S.S. 67, Course record 62.
Membership: 550
Visitors: Welcome. Not after 4p.m.. Not weekends and Bank Holidays.
Green Fees: £18 per round, £25 per day.
Facilities: Lunch. Dinner. Bar Snacks. Full Catering. Changing Room. Golf Shop. Trolley Hire.
Class One Hotel: The Grosvenor, Rugby, 1/4 mile(s). Tel: 535686 (0788)

STRATFORD-UPON-AVON

Welcombe Hotel and Golf Course, Warwick Road, Stratford-upon-Avon, Warwicks. CV37 0NR. Tel: 295252 (0789)
Secretary: P J Day　　　　　　　Tel: 295252　(0789)
Location: 1 1/2 miles from Stratford towards Warwick on A439.

Description: Undulating parkland, lakes and waterfall.
18 holes, 6,202 yards, Par 70, S.S.S. 70, Course record 67.
Membership: 450
Visitors: Welcome. Handicap certificate required. Not before mid-day weekends. Telephone call is advisable.
Green Fees: £30 weekdays, £35 weekends.
Facilities: Lunch. Dinner. Bar Snacks. Full Catering. Changing Room. Golf Shop. Club Hire. Driving Range. Trolley Hire. Buggy Hire. Caddies availabl
Class One Hotel: Welcombe, On Course, Tel: 295252 (0789)

WARWICK

Warwick Golf Club, Warwick Golf Centre, Racecourse, Warwick. CV34 6HW. Tel: 494316 (0926)
Secretary: Mrs Dunkley   Tel: 494316 (0926)
Professional: S Hutchinson   Tel: 491284 (0926)
Location: Follow signs to Racecourse.
Description: Municipal, flat.
9 holes, 2,682 yards, Par 34, S.S.S. 66, Course record 67.
Membership: 200
Visitors: Welcome. Not Sundays before 12.30p.m.. Restrictions on race days.
Green Fees: Weekdays £3.80, weekends £5.50.
Facilities: Changing Room. Golf Shop. Club Hire. Driving Range. Trolley Hire.
Class One Hotel: Hilton National, Warwick, 1 1/2 mile(s). Tel: 499555 (0926)
Class Two Hotel: Warwick Arms, Warwick, 1/2 mile(s). Tel: 492759 (0926)

WEST MIDLANDS

COLESHILL

Maxstoke Park Golf Club, Castle Lane, Coleshill, Birmingham, West Midlands. B46 2RD. Tel: 464915 (0675)
Secretary: J C Evans   Tel: 464915 (0675)
Professional: R A Young   Tel: 464915 (0675)
Location: 2 1/2 miles east of Coleshill off B4114.
Description: Parkland with many mature trees, 2 holes cross lake.
18 holes, 6,478 yards, Par 71, S.S.S. 71, Course record 65.
Membership: 550
Visitors: Welcome. With member at weekends.
Green Fees: £20 per round, £30 per day.
Facilities: Lunch. Dinner. Bar Snacks. Full Catering. Changing Room. Golf Shop. Trolley Hire.

COVENTRY

Coventry Hearsall Golf Club, Beechwood Avenue, Coventry, West Midlands. CV5 6DF. Tel: 675809 (0203)
Secretary: W G Doughty   Tel: 713470 (0203)
Location: Off A45 on A429 Coventry to Kenilworth Road, opposite Memorial Park.
Description: Easy walking parkland.
18 holes, 5,983 yards, Par 70, S.S.S. 70.
Membership: 650
Visitors: Welcome. Handicap certificate required. With members only at weekends. Wednesdays Ladies Day.
Green Fees: £23 per day.

Facilities: Lunch. Dinner. Bar Snacks. Full Catering. Changing Room. Golf Shop. Trolley Hire.
Class One Hotel: Post House, Allesley, 2 mile(s). Tel: 402151 (0203)
Class Two Hotel: Hearsall Lodge, Coventry, 1/2 mile(s). Tel: 674543 (0203)

COVENTRY

Grange Golf Club, Copeswood, Coventry, West Midlands. CV3 1HJ. Tel: 562117 (0203)
Secretary: Mr B Melling   Tel: 562082 (0203)
Location: M6 junc 2 take A46 towards Coventry. At traffic lights by Pippin Restaurant turn left.
Description: Easy walking parkland, lots of trees and plenty of water.
9 holes, 6,006 yards, Par 72, S.S.S. 69.
Membership: 260
Visitors: Welcome. Not Saturdays. Not Sundays before 11.30a.m. and not after 2.30p.m. weekdays.
Green Fees: Weekdays £8, weekends £15.
Facilities: Changing Room.
Class One Hotel: Forte Crest, Coventry, 2 mile(s). Tel: 613261 (0203)

DUDLEY

Swindon Golf Club, Bridgnorth Road, Swindon, Dudley, West Midlands. DY3 4PU. Tel: 897031 (0902)
Secretary: E G Greenway   Tel: 897031 (0902)
Location: B4176 Dudley to Bridgnorth Road 3 miles from A449 at Himley.
Description: Woodland and parkland course with exceptional views.
18 holes, 6,042 yards, Par 71, S.S.S. 69.
9 holes, 1,135 yards, Par.
Visitors: Welcome.
Green Fees: Weekdays £15 per round, weekends and Bank Holidays £25 per round.
Facilities: Lunch. Dinner. Bar Snacks. Full Catering. Changing Room. Golf Shop. Driving Range. Trolley Hire. Buggy Hire.
Class One Hotel: Himley Country Club, Himley, 2 mile(s). Tel: 893755 (0902)
Class Two Hotel: Pencroft Guest House, Wolverhampton, 6 mile(s). Tel: 340906 (0902)

HALESOWEN

Halesowen Golf Club, The Leasowes, Halesowen, West Midlands. B62 8QF. Tel: 550 1041 (021)
Secretary: Mrs M Bateman   Tel: 501 3606 (021)
Professional: Mr D Down   Tel: 503 0593 (021)
Location: 2 miles from junc 3 M5.
Description: Parkland.
18 holes, 5,754 yards, Par 69, S.S.S. 68.
Membership: 600
Visitors: Welcome. Not Wednesdays, weekends with member.
Green Fees: £16 per round, £21 per day.
Facilities: Lunch. Dinner. Bar Snacks. Full Catering. Changing Room. Golf Shop. Trolley Hire.
Class One Hotel: Norfolk Hotel, Birmingham, 5 mile(s). Tel: 454 8071 (021)

Class Two Hotel: Studio Restaurant & Hotel, Coldbury, 3 mile(s). Tel: 422 2926 (021)

HANDSWORTH WOOD
Handsworth Golf Club, 11 Sunningdale Close, Handsworth Wood, Birmingham, West Midlands. B20 1NP. Tel: 554 0599 (021)
Location: 5 minutes from junc 1 off M5. 5 minutes from junc 7 M6. Situated 4 1/2 miles from city centre north west of Birmingham.
Description: Parkland course with slight gradients, exceptionally good test of golf. Excellent greens, large practice area adjacent to Clubhouse.
White 18 holes, 6,272 yards, Par 70, S.S.S. 70, Course record 66.
Yellow 18 holes, 6,059 yards, Par 70, S.S.S. 69.
Membership: 820
Visitors: Welcome. Handicap certificate required. With members at weekends.
Green Fees: Weekdays £25, with member £7. £10 weekends.
Facilities: Lunch. Dinner. Bar Snacks. Full Catering. Changing Room. Golf Shop. Club Hire. Trolley Hire.
Class One Hotel: Post House, Great Barr, 2 mile(s). Tel: 357 7444 (021)
Class Two Hotel: Sheriden House, Handsworth Wood, 1 mile(s). Tel: 554 2185 (021)

HARBORNE
Harborne Golf Club, 40 Tennal Road, Harborne, Birmingham, West Midlands. B32 2JE. Tel: 427 1728 (021)
Secretary: E J Humphreys   Tel: 427 3058 (021)
Professional: A Quarterman   Tel: 427 3512 (021)
Location: A4123-A456 B4124 3 miles west of Birmingham City Centre.
Description: Undulating parkland/moorland.
18 holes, 6,235 yards, Par 70, S.S.S. 70, Course record 65.
Membership: 550
Visitors: Welcome. Handicap certificate required. With members only at weekends. Some catering restrictions apply, please telephone in advance.
Green Fees: £27 per day or round.
Facilities: Lunch. Dinner. Bar Snacks. Full Catering. Changing Room. Golf Shop. Club Hire. Trolley Hire.
Class One Hotel: Strathallan, Birmingham, 2 mile(s). Tel: 455 9777 (021)
Class Two Hotel: Claremont, Birmingham, 2 mile(s). Tel: 429 4070 (021)

KINGS HEATH
Moseley Golf Club, Springfield Road, Kings Heath, Birmingham, West Midlands. B14 7DX. Tel: 444 2115 (021)
Secretary: Mr Richardson   Tel: 444 4957 (021)
Professional: G Edge   Tel: 444 2063 (021)
Location: South of Birmingham between Kings Heath and Moseley.
Description: Undulating parkland.
18 holes, 6,285 yards, S.S.S. 70.
Membership: 600
Visitors: Welcome. Handicap certificate required. Letter of Introduction required. Only by prior arrangement. Tuesdays Ladies Day. Dinner available to order.
Green Fees: £30 per day.
Facilities: Lunch. Bar Snacks. Full Catering. Changing Room. Golf Shop. Club Hire. Trolley Hire.
Class One Hotel: Regency, Solihull, 3 1/2 mile(s). Tel: 745 6119 (021)

MERIDEN
Forest of Arden Hotel, Golf & Country Club, Maxstoke Lane, Meriden, West Midlands. CV7 6HR. Tel: 22335 (0676)
Secretary: Richard Woolston   Tel: 22335 (0676)
Professional: Mike Tarn   Tel: 22335 (0676)
Location: Very close to N.E.C. midway between Coventry and Birmingham, 1 mile off A45.
Description: Parkland.
Arden 18 holes, 6,915 yards, Par 72, S.S.S. 73.
Aylsford 18 holes, 6,525 yards, Par 72, S.S.S. 71.
Visitors: Welcome. Handicap certificate required. No non-residential visitors before 1 p.m. at weekends.
Green Fees: On application.
Facilities: Lunch. Dinner. Bar Snacks. Full Catering. Changing Room. Golf Shop. Club Hire. Trolley Hire. Buggy Hire. Caddies available.
Class One Hotel: Forest Of Arden Hotel, On course, Tel: 22335 (0676)

MERIDEN
North Warwickshire Golf Club Ltd., Hampton Lane, Meriden, West Midlands. . Tel: 22259 (0676)
Secretary: E G Barnes   Tel: 22915 (0676)
Professional: Mr Edwin   Tel: 22259 (0676)
Location: Off A45 Coventry to Birmingham Road.
Description: Parkland with a brook and plenty of trees.
9 holes, 6,390 yards, Par 72, S.S.S. 70, Course record 67.
Membership: 330
Visitors: Welcome. Handicap certificate required. Not weekends. Thursday mornings Ladies only. Dinner by prior arrangement.
Green Fees: Weekdays £20 per round, £6 with a member.
Facilities: Lunch. Bar Snacks. Full Catering. Changing Room. Golf Shop.
Class One Hotel: The Manor, Meriden, 1 mile(s). Tel: 22735 (0676)

NORTHFIELD
North Worcestershire Golf Club, Frankley Beeches Road, Northfield, Birmingham, West Midlands. B31 5LP. Tel: 475 1047 (021)
Secretary: E J Pearce   Tel: 475 1047 (021)
Professional: K E Jones   Tel: 475 5721 (021)
Location: Corner of Frankley Beeches Road and Hanging Lane in Northfield.
Description: Easy walking parkland.
18 holes, 5,959 yards, Par 69, S.S.S. 69.
Membership: 600
Visitors: Welcome. Handicap certificate required. Letter of Introduction required. Only by prior arrangement. With members only at weekends.
Green Fees: Weekdays £20 per round, £35 per day, with a member £8. Weekends £15.

Cade's - Audi Golf Course Guide

Facilities: Lunch. Dinner. Bar Snacks. Full Catering. Changing Room. Golf Shop. Trolley Hire.

OLDBURY
Brandhall Golf Club, Heron Road, Oldbury, Birmingham, West Midlands. B68 8AQ. Tel: 552 2195 (021)
Professional: G Mercer   Tel: 552 2195 (021)
Location: 6 miles north of Birmingham on main Wolverhampton road. Junc 2 M5 (Oldbury turn off) 3/4 of a mile.
Description: Undulating parkland.
18 holes, 5,734 yards, Par 70, S.S.S. 68, Course record 68.
Visitors: Welcome. Always telephone in advance. Not Saturdays before 10a.m.. Some catering restrictions apply, please telephone in advance.
Green Fees: On application.
Facilities: Lunch. Dinner. Bar Snacks. Full Catering. Golf Shop. Trolley Hire.

SOLIHULL
Ladbrook Park Golf Club Ltd., Poolhead Lane, Tanworth-in-Arden, Solihull, West Midlands. B94 5ED. Tel: 2220 (05644)
Secretary: Mrs G P Taylor   Tel: 2264 (05644)
Professional: Graham Taylor   Tel: 2581 (05644)
Location: M42 junc 3 signpost Evesham and Redditch.
Description: Easy walking parkland.
18 holes, 6,191 yards, Par 71, S.S.S. 71, Course record 65.
Membership: 735
Visitors: Welcome. Handicap certificate required. Not weekends. By prior arrangement only weekdays.
Green Fees: £27 per day.
Facilities: Lunch. Dinner. Bar Snacks. Full Catering. Changing Room. Golf Shop. Trolley Hire.

SOLIHULL
Robin Hood Golf Club, St Bernards Road, Solihull, West Midlands. B92 7DJ. Tel: 706 0159 (021)
Secretary: A J Hansom   Tel: 706 0061 (021)
Professional: Ray Thompson   Tel: 706 0806 (021)
Location: Half way between A3400 and A41. Between Solihull and Hall Green.
Description: Tree lined parkland.
18 holes, 6,609 yards, Par 72, S.S.S. 72, Course record 68.
Membership: 600
Visitors: Welcome. Not weekends and bank Holidays. Tuesdays not before 12.30p.m.. Wednesdays not after 12p.m.. Dinner only by prior arrangement.
Green Fees: £26 per round, with a member £9, £31 per day.
Facilities: Lunch. Bar Snacks. Full Catering. Changing Room. Golf Shop. Trolley Hire.
Class One Hotel: St Johns Swallow, Solihull, 1 mile(s). Tel: 711 3000 (021)

SOLIHULL
Shirley Golf Club, Stratford Road, Monkspath, Shirley, Solihull, West Midlands. B90 4EW. Tel: 745 7024 (021)
Secretary: A J Phillips   Tel: 744 6001 (021)
Professional: Chris Wicketts   Tel: 745 4979 (021)
Location: M42 junc 4 on A3400 towards Birmingham.
Description: Easy walking parkland.

18 holes, 6,510 yards, Par 72, S.S.S. 71.
Membership: 350
Visitors: Welcome. Handicap certificate required. Not at weekends. Tuesdays Ladies Day. Not during mid-week competitions (Wednesdays). Dinner only by prior arrangement.
Green Fees: £25 per round, £30 per day.
Facilities: Lunch. Bar Snacks. Full Catering. Changing Room. Golf Shop. Trolley Hire.

STOURBRIDGE
Enville Golf Club, Highgate Common, Enville, Stourbridge, West Midlands. DY7 5BN. Tel: 872074 (0384)
Secretary: R J Bannister   Tel: 872074 (0384)
Professional: S Power   Tel: 872551 (0384)
Location: Leave A449 at Stewpony Hotel on A458 Bridgnorth Road, fork right after Fox Inn, follow signs for Halfpenny Green Airport. 5 miles west of
Description: Both courses have nine holes of woodland and nine holes of heathland.
Highgate 18 holes, 6,556 yards, Par 72, S.S.S. 72, Course record 66.
Lodge 18 holes, 6,217 yards, Par 70, S.S.S. 70, Course record 65.
Membership: 900
Visitors: Welcome. Handicap certificate required. With members only at weekends.
Green Fees: 18 holes £22, 27 holes £26.50, 36 holes £32.
Facilities: Lunch. Dinner. Bar Snacks. Full Catering. Changing Room. Golf Shop. Trolley Hire. Buggy Hire.
Class Two Hotel: Anchor, Kinver, 3 mile(s). Tel: 873291 (0384)

STOURBRIDGE
Stourbridge Golf Club, Worcester Lane, Stourbridge, West Midlands. DY8 2RB. Tel: 395566 (0384)
Secretary: F R McLachlan   Tel: 395566 (0384)
Professional: W H Firkins   Tel: 393125 (0384)
Location:
Description: Parkland.
18 holes, 6,231 yards, Par 70, S.S.S. 70, Course record 63.
Membership: 830
Visitors: Welcome. Handicap certificate required. Not wednesday mornings. With members only at weekends.
Green Fees: £22.
Facilities: Lunch. Dinner. Bar Snacks. Full Catering. Changing Room. Golf Shop. Club Hire. Trolley Hire.
Class One Hotel: Pedmore House, Stourbridge, 1 mile(s). Tel: 393132 (0384)
Class Two Hotel: Talbot, Stourbridge, 1 1/2 mile(s). Tel: 394150 (0384)

STREETLY
Little Aston Golf Club, Streetly, Sutton Coldfield, West Midlands. B74 3AW. Tel: 353 2942 (021)
Secretary: Mr Russell   Tel: 353 2942 (021)
Professional: Mr J Anderson   Tel: 353 2942 (021)
Location: 3 miles from Sutton Coldfield.
Description: Undulating parkland with 2 lakes. Established in 1908.
18 holes, 6,724 yards, Par 72, S.S.S. 72, Course record 66.

135

Visitors: Welcome. Handicap certificate required. With members only at weekends. Only by prior arrangement.
Green Fees: On application.
Facilities: Lunch. Dinner. Full Catering. Changing Room. Golf Shop. Trolley Hire.

SUTTON COLDFIELD
Moor Hall Golf Club, Moor Hall Drive, Sutton Coldfield, West Midlands. B75 6LN. Tel: 308 6130 (021)
Secretary: R V Wood　　　　　　　Tel: 308 6130 (021)
Professional: A Partridge　　　　　Tel: 308 5106 (021)
Location:
Description: Parkland.
18 holes, 6,249 yards, Par 70, S.S.S. 70.
Visitors: Welcome.
Green Fees: £25 per round, £32 per day.
Facilities: Lunch. Dinner. Bar Snacks. Full Catering. Changing Room. Golf Shop. Trolley Hire.
Class One Hotel: Moor Hall Hotel, S Coldfield, 1 mile(s). Tel: 308 0103 (021)

SUTTON COLDFIELD
Pype Hayes Golf Club, Eachelhurst Road, Walmley, Sutton Coldfield, West Midlands. . Tel: 351 1014 (021)
Secretary: Keith Haden　　　　　Tel: 351 1014 (021)
Professional: J Bayliss　　　　　　Tel: 351 1014 (021)
Location: M6 junc 6, Kingsbury Road turn left into Chester Road and right into Eachelhurst Road.
Description: Wooded with 4 testing par 3 holes.
18 holes, 5,743 yards, Par 71, S.S.S. 69, Course record 63.
Membership: 250
Visitors: Welcome. Some catering restrictions apply, please telephone in advance.
Green Fees: On application.
Facilities: Lunch. Dinner. Bar Snacks. Changing Room. Golf Shop. Club Hire. Trolley Hire.
Class One Hotel: The Belfry, Curdworth, 2 mile(s). Tel: 470301 (0675)

SUTTON COLDFIELD
The Belfry, Wishaw, Near Sutton Coldfield, West Midlands. B76 9PR. Tel: 470301 (0675)
Secretary: Robert Maxfield　　　Tel: 470301 (0675)
Location: Junc of A446 Coventry to Lichfield Road and A4091 Tamworth Road.
Description: Brabazon - host of the last two Ryder Cups. Brabazon 18 holes, 6,975 yards, Par 73, S.S.S. 73, Course record 63.
Derby 18 holes, 6,103 yards, Par 70, S.S.S. 70.
Membership: 380
Visitors: Welcome. Handicap certificate required.
Green Fees: Brabazon - weekdays £46, weekends £51. Derby - weekdays £20.50, weekends £26.
Facilities: Lunch. Dinner. Bar Snacks. Full Catering. Changing Room. Golf Shop. Club Hire. Driving Range. Trolley Hire. Buggy Hire. Caddies availabl
Class One Hotel: The Belfry, On course, Tel: 470301 (0675)
Class Two Hotel: Penns Hall, S Coldfield, 8 mile(s). Tel: 351 3111 (021)

WALSALL
Calderfield Golf Club Ltd., Aldridge Road, Walsall, West Midlands. WS4 2JS. Tel: 640540 (0922)
Professional: Roger Griffin　　　　Tel: 32243 (0922)
Location: M6 junc 7, A454 entrance next to Dilke Arms Public House.
Description: Parkland with lake.
18 holes, 6,590 yards, Par 73, S.S.S. 72, Course record 71.
Membership: 600
Visitors: Welcome. Not before 11 a.m. Saturdays, not before 12 noon on Sundays.
Green Fees: Weekdays £12 per round, weekends £16 per round.
Facilities: Lunch. Dinner. Bar Snacks. Full Catering. Changing Room. Golf Shop. Club Hire. Trolley Hire.
Class One Hotel: Barons Court, Walsall, 5 mile(s). Tel: 452020 (0543)

WALSALL
Druids Heath Golf Club Ltd., Stonnall Road, Aldridge, Walsall, West Midlands. WS9 8JZ. Tel: 55595 (0922)
Secretary: Mr Smith　　　　　　　Tel: 55595 (0922)
Professional: M P Daubney　　　Tel: 59523 (0922)
Location: North east side of Aldridge off A454.
Description: Testing, undulating, heathland course.
18 holes, 6,914 yards, Par 72, S.S.S. 73, Course record 68.
Membership: 500
Visitors: Welcome. Must be members of another Club or Society. Thursdays Ladies Day. Not before 12p.m. Saturdays and not before 2p.m. Sundays.
Green Fees: Weekdays £22 per day, weekends £29 per day.
Facilities: Lunch. Dinner. Bar Snacks. Full Catering. Changing Room. Golf Shop. Trolley Hire.
Class One Hotel: Fairlawns, Aldridge, 1/2 mile(s). Tel: 55122 (0922)

WALSALL
Walsall Golf Club, Broadway, Walsall, West Midlands. WS1 3EY. Tel: 613512 (0922)
Secretary: E Murray　　　　　　　Tel: 613512 (0922)
Professional: Richard Lambert　　Tel: 26766 (0922)
Location: 1 mile south of Walsall town centre, close to M6 interchange.
Description: Undulating and well wooded.
18 holes, 6,300 yards, Par 70, S.S.S. 70, Course record 65.
Membership: 550
Visitors: Welcome. Handicap certificate required. Weekdays only by prior arrangement.
Green Fees: £30 per round, £40 per day.
Facilities: Lunch. Dinner. Bar Snacks. Full Catering. Changing Room. Golf Shop. Club Hire. Trolley Hire.
Class One Hotel: Forte Crest, Walsall, 1 mile(s). Tel: 33555 (0922)

WEST BROMWICH
Dartmouth Golf Club, Vale Street, West Bromwich, West Midlands. B71 4DW. Tel: 588 2131 (021)
Secretary: M Morton　　　　　　　Tel: 588 2131 (021)
Professional: C R Yates　　　　　Tel: 588 2131 (021)
Location: A4031, 1 mile from West Bromwich.

Cade's - Audi Golf Course Guide

Description: Meadowland, part undulating, part flat. Opening hole 617 yards.
9 holes, 6,060 yards, Par 71, S.S.S. 70, Course record 66.
Membership: 400
Visitors: Welcome. With members only at weekends. Some catering restrictions apply, please telephone in advance.
Green Fees: £16.50 per day.
Facilities: Lunch. Dinner. Bar Snacks. Full Catering. Changing Room. Golf Shop. Trolley Hire.
Class One Hotel: Moat House, West Bromwich, 1 mile(s). Tel: 553 6111 (021)
Class Two Hotel: Albion Hotel, West Bromwich, 3/4 mile(s). Tel: 500 5262 (021)

WEST BROMWICH
Sandwell Park Golf Club, Birmingham Road, West Bromwich, West Midlands. B71 4JJ. Tel: 553 0260 (021)
Secretary: J B Mawby   Tel: 553 4637 (021)
Professional: N Wylie   Tel: 553 4384 (021)
Location: On A41 close to junc 1 on M5.
Description: Old established parkland/heathland course.
18 holes, 6,121 yards, Par 71, S.S.S. 72, Course record 68.
Membership: 600
Visitors: Welcome. Handicap certificate required. Not weekends. No catering Mondays.
Green Fees: £30 per round weekday.
Facilities: Lunch. Dinner. Bar Snacks. Full Catering. Changing Room. Golf Shop. Club Hire. Trolley Hire.
Class One Hotel: Moat House, West Bromwich, 1 mile(s). Tel: 559 6111 (021)
Class Two Hotel: The Albion, West Bromwich, 1 1/2 mile(s). Tel: 5005262 (021)

WOLVERHAMPTON
Oxley Park Golf Club Ltd., Stafford Road, Bushbury, Wolverhampton, West Midlands. WV10 6DE. Tel: 20506 (0902)
Secretary: Mrs K Mann   Tel: 25892 (0902)
Professional: Mr L Burlison   Tel: 25445 (0902)
Location: 1 1/2 miles north of Wolverhampton on A449.
Description: Undulating parkland.
18 holes, 6,168 yards, Par 71, S.S.S. 70, Course record 64.
Membership: 620
Visitors: Welcome. Societies wednesdays, other times liaise with professional.
Green Fees: Weekdays £18 per round, £22 per day, £7 with member. Weekends £20 per round, £24 per day, £7 with member.
Facilities: Lunch. Dinner. Bar Snacks. Full Catering. Changing Room. Golf Shop. Trolley Hire.
Class One Hotel: The Goldthorn, Wolverhampton, 2 mile(s). Tel: 29216 (0902)

WOLVERHAMPTON
Patshull Park Hotel, Golf & Country Club, Pattingham, Near Wolverhampton, West Midlands. WV6 7HR. Tel: 700100 (0902)
Secretary: Mr Kimble   Tel: 700100 (0902)
Professional: Duncan J McDowall   Tel: 700342 (0902)
Location: 7 miles west of Wolverhampton.

Description: Nicely contoured parkland, lakeside with super trees.
18 holes, 6,400 yards, Par 72, S.S.S 71, Course record 61.
Membership: 500
Visitors: Welcome. Handicap certificate required. By prior arrangement.
Green Fees: Weekdays £22.50 per round, £37.50 for 36 holes. Weekends and Bank Holidays £27.50, £42.50 for 36 holes.
Facilities: Lunch. Dinner. Bar Snacks. Full Catering. Changing Room. Golf Shop. Club Hire. Driving Range. Trolley Hire. Buggy Hire.
Class One Hotel: Patshull Park Hotel, On Course, Tel: 700100 (0902)

WOLVERHAMPTON
Penn Golf Club Ltd., Penn Common, Penn, Wolverhampton, West Midlands. WV4 5JE. Tel: 341142 (0902)
Secretary: P W Thorrington   Tel: 256220 (0384)
Professional: A Briscas   Tel: 334072 (0902)
Location: Off A449, 3 miles south-west of Wolverhampton.
Description: Heathland.
18 holes, 6,465 yards, Par 70, S.S.S. 71, Course record 67.
Membership: 650
Visitors: Welcome. Handicap certificate required. Letter of Introduction required.
Green Fees: £20 per round, £25 per day.
Facilities: Lunch. Dinner. Bar Snacks. Full Catering. Changing Room. Golf Shop. Club Hire. Trolley Hire.
Class One Hotel: The Goldthorn, Wolverhampton, 2 mile(s). Tel: 29216 (0902)

WOLVERHAMPTON
Perton Park Golf Club, Wrottesley Park Road, Perton, Wolverhampton, West Midlands. WV6 7HL. Tel: 380103 (0902)
Secretary: E Greenway   Tel: 380073 (0902)
Location: Just off A454 Bridgnorth Road, or A41 Wolverhampton to Newport Road.
Description: Flat meadowland. New course opened July 1990.
18 holes, 7,007 yards, Par 73, S.S.S. 72.
Visitors: Welcome.
Green Fees: Weekdays £5, Saturdays £6, Sundays and Bank Holidays £7.
Facilities: Lunch. Dinner. Bar Snacks. Full Catering. Changing Room. Golf Shop. Club Hire. Driving Range. Trolley Hire. Buggy Hire.
Class One Hotel: Himley Country Club, Himley, 6 mile(s). Tel: 893755 (0902)

WOLVERHAMPTON
South Staffordshire Golf Club, Danescourt Road, Tettenhall, Wolverhampton, West Midlands. WV6 9BQ. Tel: 751065 (0902)
Secretary: R J Crofts   Tel: 751065 (0902)
Professional: J Rhodes   Tel: 754816 (0902)
Location: A41 north from Wolverhampton, 3 miles.
Description: Well established parkland course.
18 holes, 6,653 yards, Par 72, S.S.S. 72, Course record 67.

137

Membership: 500
Visitors: Welcome. Handicap certificate required. Not Tuesdays a.m. With member only at weekends before 11.30 a.m.
Green Fees: £25 per round or day.
Facilities: Lunch. Dinner. Bar Snacks. Full Catering. Changing Room. Golf Shop. Trolley Hire. Buggy Hire.
Class One Hotel: Mount, Tettenhall, 2 mile(s). Tel: 752055 (0902)
Class Two Hotel: Westwood, Wolverhampton, 1 mile(s). Tel: 753362 (0902)

WILTSHIRE

CORSHAM

Kingsdown Golf Club, Corsham, Wilts. SN14 9BS. Tel: 742530 (0225)
Secretary: S H Phipps   Tel: 742530 (0225)
Professional: Peter Evans   Tel: 742634 (0225)
Location: 5 miles east of Bath.
Description: Heathland with fringe of trees.
18 holes, 6,445 yards, Par 72, S.S.S. 71, Course record 66.
Membership: 630
Visitors: Welcome. Handicap certificate required. Not at weekends.
Green Fees: £22 per day.
Facilities: Lunch. Dinner. Bar Snacks. Full Catering. Changing Room. Golf Shop. Club Hire. Trolley Hire.
Class One Hotel: Leigh Park, Bradford-O-Avon, 5 mile(s). Tel: 4885 (02216)
Class Two Hotel: Widbrook Grange, Bradford-O-Avon, 5 mile(s). Tel: 4750 (02216)

DEVIZES

North Wilts Golf Club, Bishops Cannings, Devizes, Wilts. SN10 2LP. Tel: 860257 (0380)
Secretary: S A Musgrove   Tel: 860627 (0380)
Professional: G J Laing   Tel: 860330 (0380)
Location: 1 mile from A4 east of Calne, 5 miles from Devizes off A361.
Description: Downland with magnificent views.
18 holes, 6,451 yards, Par 72, S.S.S. 71, Course record 66.
Membership: 800
Visitors: Welcome.
Green Fees: Weekdays £18 per round, £25 per day. Weekends and Bank Holidays £30.
Facilities: Lunch. Dinner. Bar Snacks. Full Catering. Changing Room. Golf Shop. Club Hire. Trolley Hire.
Class One Hotel: Bear, Devizes, 5 mile(s). Tel: 727435 (0380)
Class Two Hotel: Landsdown Strand, Calne, 5 mile(s). Tel: 812488 (0249)

HIGHWORTH

Highworth Community Golf Centre, Swindon Road, Highworth, Wilts. SN6 7SJ. Tel: 766014 (0793)
Secretary: Tom Watt   Tel: 495761 (0793)
Professional: Kevin Pickett   Tel: 766014 (0793)
Description: Gently undulating parkland course. 9 hole golf course, with 9 hole pitch and putt.

9 holes, 3,120 yards, Par 35, S.S.S. 35, Course record 33.
Visitors: Welcome. Best to book in advance.
Green Fees: Weekdays £4.50, weekends £5.50.
Facilities: Changing Room. Golf Shop. Club Hire. Trolley Hire.
Class One Hotel: Crest, Swindon, 4 mile(s). Tel: 831333 (0793)
Class Two Hotel: Saracens Head, Highworth, 1 mile(s). Tel: 762064 (0793)

OGBOURNE ST.GEORGE

Swindon Golf Club, Ogbourne St George, Marlborough, Wilts. SN8 1TB. Tel: 84327 (0672)
Secretary: P V Dixon   Tel: 84327 (0672)
Professional: C Harraway   Tel: 84287 (0672)
Location: A345 between Swindon and Marlborough.
18 holes, 6,226 yards, Par 71, S.S.S. 70, Course record 66.
Membership: 800
Visitors: Welcome. Handicap certificate required. With member at weekends.
Green Fees: Weekdays £17 per round, £23 per day, with member £10, at weekends £15.
Facilities: Lunch. Dinner. Bar Snacks. Full Catering. Changing Room. Golf Shop. Club Hire. Trolley Hire.
Class One Hotel: Post House, Swindon, 6 mile(s). Tel: 524601 (0793)
Class Two Hotel: The Parklands, Ogbourne, 1/4 mile(s). Tel: 84555 (0672)

SALISBURY

Salisbury and South Wilts Golf Club, Netherhampton, Salisbury, Wilts. SP2 8PR. Tel: 742645 (0722)
Secretary: John Newcomb   Tel: 742645 (0722)
Professional: Gary Emerson   Tel: 742929 (0722)
Location: A3094 2 miles west of Salisbury.
Description: Undulating heathland.
18 holes, 6,528 yards, Par 71, S.S.S. 71, Course record 67.
Membership: 1000
Visitors: Welcome. Handicap certificate required. Advisable to telephone in advance.
Green Fees: Weekdays £23 per day, weekends and Bank Holidays £35 per day.
Facilities: Lunch. Dinner. Bar Snacks. Full Catering. Changing Room. Golf Shop. Club Hire. Trolley Hire.
Class One Hotel: White Hart, Salisbury, 2 1/2 mile(s). Tel: 327476 (0722)

SWINDON

Broome Manor Golf Complex, Pipers Way, Swindon, Wilts. SN3 1RG. Tel: 532403 (0793)
Secretary: Tom Watt   Tel: 495761 (0793)
Professional: Barry Sandry   Tel: 532403 (0793)
Description: Modern parkland design.
18 holes, 6,359 yards, Par 71, S.S.S. 70, Course record 66.
9 holes, 5,490 yards, Par 66, S.S.S. 67.
Visitors: Welcome. Best to book in advance.
Green Fees: 18 holes £7.60 weekdays, £9 weekends. 9 hole £4.50 weekdays, £5.50 weekends.
Facilities: Lunch. Dinner. Bar Snacks. Full Catering. Changing Room. Golf Shop. Club Hire. Driving Range. Trolley Hire.

Cade's - Audi Golf Course Guide

Class One Hotel: Goddard Arms, Swindon, 1 mile(s). Tel: 692313 (0793)
Class Two Hotel: Saracens Head, Highworth, 8 mile(s). Tel: 762064 (0793)

NORTH YORKSHIRE

EASINGWOLD
Easingwold Golf Club, Stillington Road, Easingwold, York, N Yorks. YO6 3ET. Tel: 21486 (0347)
Secretary: K C Hudson   Tel: 22474 (0347)
Professional: J Hughes   Tel: 21964 (0347)
Description: Flat parkland with many trees.
18 holes, 6,045 yards, Par 72, S.S.S. 70.
Membership: 600
Visitors: Welcome. Handicap certificate required.
Green Fees: Weekdays £20 per day, weekends and Bank Holidays £25 per day.
Facilities: Lunch. Dinner. Bar Snacks. Full Catering. Changing Room. Golf Shop. Trolley Hire.
Class One Hotel: The Garth, Easingwold, 2 mile(s). Tel: 22988 (0347)
Class Two Hotel: George, Easingwold, 1 1/2 mile(s). Tel: 21698 (0347)

FILEY
Filey Golf Course, The Clubhouse, West Avenue, Filey, N Yorks. YO11 3QH. Tel: 513116 (0723)
Secretary: T M Thompson   Tel: 513239 (0723)
Professional: D England   Tel: 513134 (0723)
Location: 1 mile south from centre of town.
Description: Links on cliff top.
Yellow 18 holes, 5,737 yards, Par 70, S.S.S. 67.
White 18 holes, 6,080 yards, Par 70, S.S.S. 69.
Membership: 950
Visitors: Welcome. Handicap certificate required. Not weekends, Bank Holidays or club competition days.
Green Fees: Weekdays £18, weekends £23.
Facilities: Lunch. Dinner. Bar Snacks. Full Catering. Changing Room. Golf Shop. Club Hire. Trolley Hire.
Class One Hotel: White Lodge, Filey, 1/2 mile(s). Tel: 514771 (0703)

HARROGATE
Crimple Valley Golf Club, Hookstone Wood Road, Harrogate, N Yorks. HG2 8PN. Tel: 883485 (0423)
Secretary: A M Grange   Tel: 883485 (0423)
Professional: R A Lumb   Tel: 883485 (0423)
Location: 1 mile south of town centre, turn off A61 at Appleyards Garage onto Hookstone Road, signposted to the right.
Description: Situated in Crimple Valley, gently sloping fairways in rural setting.
9 holes, 2,500 yards, Par , S.S.S. 33.
Visitors: Welcome. Some catering restrictions apply, please telephone in advance.
Green Fees: On application.
Facilities: Lunch. Golf Shop. Club Hire. Trolley Hire.

HARROGATE
Harrogate Golf Club, Forest Lane Head, Harrogate, N Yorks. HG2 7TF. Tel: 862999 (0423)
Secretary: J McDougall   Tel: 862999 (0423)
Professional: P Johnson   Tel: 862547 (0423)
Location: 2 miles form Harrogate on A59, Harrogate to Knaresborough Road.
Description: Undulating parkland.
18 holes, 6,241 yards, Par 69, S.S.S. 70.
Membership: 750
Visitors: Welcome. Handicap certificate required.
Green Fees: Weekdays £25 per round or day, weekends and Bank Holidays £35.
Facilities: Lunch. Dinner. Bar Snacks. Full Catering. Changing Room. Golf Shop. Club Hire. Trolley Hire.
Class One Hotel: Dower House, Knaresborough, 1 mile(s). Tel: 863302 (0423)

HARROGATE
Pannal Golf Club, Follifoot Road, Pannal, Harrogate, N Yorks. HG3 1ES. Tel: 871641 (0423)
Secretary: Mr T B Davey MBE   Tel: 872628 (0423)
Professional: Mr M Burgess   Tel: 872620 (0423)
Location: Off A61 Leeds to Harrogate Road, 3 miles south of Harrogate.
Description: Tree lined moorland/parkland. Championship course with wonderful panoramic views.
18 holes, 6,659 yards, Par 72, S.S.S. 72.
Membership: 780
Visitors: Welcome. Handicap certificate required. Tuesdays Ladies Day. Not before 9.30a.m. and not between 12p.m. and 1.30p.m. weekdays. Members and Guests have priority weekends.
Green Fees: Weekdays £28 per round, £35 per day. Weekends £35 per round.
Facilities: Lunch. Dinner. Bar Snacks. Full Catering. Changing Room. Golf Shop. Club Hire. Trolley Hire.
Class Two Hotel: Knox Mill House, Harrogate, 6 mile(s). Tel: 560650 (0423)

KNARESBOROUGH
Knaresborough Golf Club, Boroughbridge Road, Knaresborough, N Yorks. HG5 0QQ. Tel: 863219 (0423)
Secretary: Mr J I Barrow   Tel: 862690 (0423)
Professional: Mr K Johnstone   Tel: 864865 (0423)
Description: Undulating, open parkland, tree lined copses with hedges and small lakes.
18 holes, 6,232 yards, Par 70, S.S.S. 70, Course record 69.
Membership: 796
Visitors: Welcome. Weekdays not before 9.30a.m.. Not before 10a.m. and not between 12p.m. and 2p.m. weekends.
Green Fees: Weekdays £16 per round, £20 per day. Weekends £26 per round or day.
Facilities: Lunch. Dinner. Bar Snacks. Full Catering. Changing Room. Golf Shop. Trolley Hire.
Class One Hotel: The Dower House, Knaresborough, 2 1/2 mile(s). Tel: 863302 (0423)
Class Two Hotel: Toronto House, Knaresborough, 2 1/2 mile(s). Tel: 865919 (0423)

MALTON

Malton and Norton Golf Club, Welham Park, Malton, N Yorks. YO17 9QE. Tel: 692959 (0653)
Secretary: Mr W G Wade   Tel: 697912 (0653)
Professional: Mr S Robinson   Tel: 693882 (0653)
Location: Due south from Malton on Stamford Bridge.
Description: Open parkland, flat and undulating. Founded in 1910.
18 holes, 6,420 yards, Par 72, S.S.S. 71.
Membership: 750
Visitors: Welcome. Handicap certificate required. Letter of Introduction required.Thursdyas Ladies Day. Members always have priority.
Green Fees: Weekdays £18 per round or day. Weekends £23 per round or day.
Facilities: Lunch. Dinner. Bar Snacks. Full Catering. Changing Room. Golf Shop. Club Hire. Trolley Hire.
Class Two Hotel: The Mount, Malton, 1 mile(s). Tel: 692608 (0653)

RIPON

Masham Golf Club, Burnholme, Swinton Road, Masham, Ripon, N Yorks. HG4 4HT. Tel: 689379 (0765)
Secretary: Mrs M A Willis   Tel: 689491 (0765)
Professional: Miss J Furby   Tel: 689904 (0765)
Location: 1 mile south of Masham on Swinton Road.
Description: Tree lined parkland. The River Burn runs through the course. 9 holes played twice.
18 holes, 5,244 yards, Par 66, S.S.S. 66, Course record 69.
Membership: 310
Visitors: Welcome. With members only at weekends. Thursdays Ladies Day.
Green Fees: £15 per day.
Facilities: Lunch. Dinner. Bar Snacks. Full Catering. Changing Room.
Class One Hotel: Kings Head, Masham, 1 mile(s). Tel: 689295 (0765)

RIPON

Ripon City Golf Club, Palace Road, Ripon, N Yorks. HG4 3HH. Tel: 603640 (0765)
Secretary: J L Wright   Tel: 600070 (0765)
Professional: T Davis   Tel: 600411 (0765)
Location: 1 mile from town centre on Masham Road.
Description: Undulating parkland.
9 holes, 5,681 yards, Par 70, S.S.S. 68, Course record 64.
Membership: 550
Visitors: Welcome. Handicap certificate required. Starting sheets used weekends, check with professional 1 week before visiting.
Green Fees: Weekdays £12, weekends and Bank Holidays £20.
Facilities: Lunch. Dinner. Bar Snacks. Full Catering. Changing Room. Golf Shop. Trolley Hire.
Class One Hotel: Spa Hotel, Ripon, 1 1/2 mile(s). Tel: 602172 (0765)
Class Two Hotel: Fountains Guest House, Ripon, 1 mile(s). Tel: 600145 (0765)

SCARBOROUGH

Ganton Golf Club, Ganton, Scarborough, N Yorks. YO12 4PA. Tel: 70329 (0944)
Secretary: Mr R G Pryce   Tel: 70329 (0944)
Professional: Mr G Brown   Tel: 70260 (0944)
Location: 10 miles west of Scarborough on A64.
Description: Undulating heathland, links style, sand based. Championship course.
White 18 holes, 6,720 yards, Par 71, S.S.S. 71.
Yellow 18 holes, 6,455 yards, Par 73, S.S.S. 73.
Membership: 560
Visitors: Welcome. Handicap certificate required. Letter of Introduction required.With members only at weekends.
Green Fees: £35 per day.
Facilities: Lunch. Dinner. Bar Snacks. Full Catering. Changing Room. Golf Shop. Club Hire. Trolley Hire. Buggy Hire.
Class One Hotel: The Crescent, Scarborough, 1 Tel: 360929 (0723)

SCARBOROUGH

Scarborough North Cliff Golf Club, North Cliff Avenue, Scarborough, N Yorks.   YO12 6PP. Tel: 360786 (0723)
Secretary: J R Freeman   Tel: 360786 (0723)
Professional: S N Deller   Tel: 365920 (0723)
Location: 2 miles north of Scarborough on Coast Road.
Description: Parkland.
18 holes, 6,425 yards, Par 71, S.S.S. 71, Course record 66.
Membership: 860
Visitors: Welcome. Handicap certificate required. Not on competition days. Not Sundays before 10a.m..
Green Fees: Weekdays £20 per day, weekends and Bank Holidays £25 per day.
Facilities: Lunch. Dinner. Bar Snacks. Full Catering. Changing Room. Golf Shop. Trolley Hire.
Class One Hotel: Crescent, Scarborough, 2 mile(s). Tel: 360929 (0723)
Class Two Hotel: Overdale, Scarborough, 1/2 mile(s). Tel: 364865 (0723)

SCARBOROUGH

Scarborough South Cliff Golf Club Ltd, Deepdale Avenue, Scarborough, N Yorks.   YO11 2UE. Tel: 360522 (0723)
Secretary: Mr R Bramley   Tel: 374737 (0723)
Professional: Mr D Edwards   Tel: 365150 (0723)
Location: 1 mile south of Scarborough on Filey Road.
Description: Tree lined parkland with cliff top views.
18 holes, 6,085 yards, Par 70, S.S.S. 69, Course record 62.
Membership: 700
Visitors: Welcome. Handicap certificate required. Letter of Introduction required.Always contact Secretary in advance. Not before 9a.m. weekdays, 10a.m. Saturdays or 10.30a.m. Sundays.
Green Fees: Weekdays £19 per day, weekends £25 per day.
Facilities: Lunch. Dinner. Bar Snacks. Full Catering. Changing Room. Golf Shop. Club Hire. Trolley Hire.
Class Two Hotel: Southlands, Scarborough, 2 mile(s). Tel: 361461 (0723)

SELBY

Selby Golf Club, Mill Lane, Brayton Barff, Selby, N Yorks. YO8 9LD. Tel: 228622 (0757)
Secretary: B L C Moore Tel: 228622 (0757)
Professional: C A C Smith Tel: 228785 (0757)
Location: 3 miles south of Selby off A19 Selby to Doncaster Road.
Description: Inland links type course, very well draining.
18 holes, 6,246 yards, Par 70, Course record 65.
Membership: 740
Visitors: Welcome. Handicap certificate required. Not at weekends.
Green Fees: Weekdays £20 per round, £22 per day.
Facilities: Lunch. Dinner. Bar Snacks. Full Catering. Changing Room. Golf Shop. Club Hire. Trolley Hire. Buggy Hire.
Class One Hotel: Londesborough Arms, Selby, 3 mile(s). Tel: 707355 (0757)
Class Two Hotel: The Owl, Hambleton, 2 mile(s). Tel: 228374 (0757)

SETTLE

Settle Golf Club, Buck Haw Brow, Giggleswick, Settle, N Yorks. BD24 9EX. Tel: 823596 (0729)
Secretary: Mr R Bannler Tel: 823596 (0729)
Location: 1 mile north west of Settle on A65.
Description: Undulating moorland with scenic views of Giggleswick Scar.
9 holes, 4,489 yards, Par 64, S.S.S. 62, Course record 64.
Membership: 250
Visitors: Welcome. Some restrictions on Sunday during competitions. Wednesdays Ladies Day.
Green Fees: £7.50 per day.
Facilities: Changing Room.
Class One Hotel: Royal Oak, Settle, 1 mile(s). Tel: 822561 (0729)
Class Two Hotel: Liverpool House, Settle, 1 mile(s). Tel: 522247 (0729)

SKIPTON

Skipton Golf Club, North West By-Pass, Skipton, N Yorks. BD23 1LL. Tel: 793922 (0756)
Secretary: D Farnsworth Tel: 795657 (0756)
Location: On A65 2 miles north west of Skipton.
Description: Undulating with panoramic views. Water hazards from stream running through course.
18 holes, 6,010 yards, Par 70, S.S.S. 69, Course record 69.
Membership: 650
Visitors: Welcome. Restricted Thursdays and weekends. No catering Mondays.
Green Fees: On application.
Facilities: Lunch. Dinner. Bar Snacks. Full Catering. Changing Room. Golf Shop. Club Hire. Trolley Hire.
Class One Hotel: Randells, Skipton, 3 mile(s). Tel: 700100 (0756)
Class Two Hotel: The Devonshire Arms, Bolton Abbey, 5 mile(s). Tel: 710441 (0756)

YORK

Pike Hills Golf Club, Tadcaster Road, Askham Bryan, York, N Yorks. YO2 3UW. Tel: 706566 (0904)
Secretary: Mr G Rawlings Tel: 706566 (0904)
Professional: Mr I D Gradwell Tel: 708756 (0904)
Location: 3 miles west of York on A64 Leeds to Scarborough Road.
Description: Open parkland, flat and tree lined surrounding a nature reserve.
18 holes, 6,100 yards, Par 71, S.S.S. 69, Course record 69.
Membership: 600
Visitors: Welcome. Handicap certificate required. With members only at weekends. Tuesdays Ladies Day.
Green Fees: £18 per round or day.
Facilities: Lunch. Dinner. Bar Snacks. Full Catering. Changing Room. Golf Shop. Club Hire. Trolley Hire. Buggy Hire.
Class One Hotel: The Post House, York, 1 1/2 mile(s). Tel: 707921 (0904)

YORK

York Golf Club, Lordsmoor Lane, Strensall, York, N Yorks. YO3 5XF. Tel: 490304 (0904)
Secretary: F Appleyard Tel: 491840 (0904)
Professional: A B Mason Tel: 490304 (0904)
Description: Wooded heathland.
18 holes, 6,285 yards, S.S.S. 70, Course record 65.
Membership: 600
Visitors: Welcome. With members at weekends. Parties Mondays, Tuesdays p.m., Wednesdays, Thursdays and Sundays.
Green Fees: Weekdays £24, weekends £28.
Facilities: Lunch. Dinner. Bar Snacks. Full Catering. Changing Room. Golf Shop. Driving Range. Trolley Hire. Buggy Hire.

SOUTH YORKSHIRE

BARNSLEY

Silkstone Golf Club, Field Head, Silkstone, Barnsley, S Yorks. . Tel: 790328 (0226)
Secretary: Mr Depledge Tel: 287053 (0226)
Professional: Mr K Guy Tel: 790128 (0226)
Location: 3 miles north west of Barnsley centre on Manchester Road A628.
Description: Tree lined open parkland overlooking the moors of the Pennine Range.
18 holes, 6,200 yards, Par 70, S.S.S. 70, Course record 63.
Membership: 600
Visitors: Welcome. Handicap certificate required. With members only at weekends. Tuesdays Ladies Day.
Green Fees: £20 per day.
Facilities: Lunch. Dinner. Bar Snacks. Full Catering. Changing Room. Golf Shop. Trolley Hire.
Class One Hotel: The Ardsley Moat House, Ardsley, 3 mile(s). Tel: 289401 (0226)

DONCASTER

Austerfield Park Golf Club, Cross Lane, Austerfield, Doncaster, S Yorks. DN10 6RF. Tel: 710841 (0302)
Secretary: Alan Bradley Tel: 540928 (0709)
Professional: Chris Gray Tel: 710850 (0302)
Location: A614 Bawtry to Thorne Road, 2 miles from Bawtry on roundabout.

Description: Flat parkland.
18 holes, 6,457 yards, Par 73, S.S.S. 73, Course record 72.
Membership: 500
Visitors: Welcome. Weekends and competition days after 11a.m..
Green Fees: Weekdays £14, weekends £16.
Facilities: Lunch. Dinner. Bar Snacks. Full Catering. Changing Room. Golf Shop. Club Hire. Driving Range. Trolley Hire.
Class One Hotel: Crown, Bawtry, 2 mile(s). Tel: 710341 (0302)
Class Two Hotel: Three Counties, Bawtry, 2 mile(s). Tel: 711016 (0302)

DONCASTER
Crookhill Park Golf Course, Carr Lane, Conisborough, Doncaster, S Yorks. DN12 2AH. Tel: 862974 (0709)
Secretary: Mr M Belk   Tel: 862974 (0709)
Professional: Mr R Swaine   Tel: 862979 (0709)
Location: 4 miles north of Rotherham on the Rotherham to Doncaster Road.
Description: Undulating tree lined parkland with ditches and a large pond.
18 holes, 6,240 yards, Par 71, S.S.S. 68, Course record 66.
Membership: 450
Visitors: Welcome. Handicap certificate required. Letter of Introduction required.Bookings only in person one week in advance.
Green Fees: £7 per round.
Facilities: Lunch. Dinner. Bar Snacks. Full Catering. Changing Room. Golf Shop. Club Hire. Trolley Hire.
Class One Hotel: Earl of Strafford, Rotherham, 2 mile(s). Tel: 852737 (0709)

DONCASTER
Doncaster Town Moor Golf Club, Belle Vue Club, Belle Vue, Doncaster, S Yorks. DN4 5HT. Tel: 535286 (0302)
Secretary: Mr G Sampson   Tel: 538423 (0302)
Professional: Mr S Poole   Tel: 535286 (0302)
Location: 1 mile south of Doncaster on A638.
Description: Heathland/parkland situated in the middle of Doncaster racecourse. Played since 1895.
18 holes, 6,094 yards, Par 69, S.S.S. 69, Course record 65.
Membership: 553
Visitors: Welcome. Not on race days.
Green Fees: Weekdays £12 per round, £14 per day. Weekends £14 per round, £16 per day.
Facilities: Lunch. Dinner. Bar Snacks. Changing Room. Golf Shop. Club Hire. Trolley Hire.
Class One Hotel: Earl of Doncaster, Doncaster, 1/2 mile(s). Tel: 361371 (0302)
Class Two Hotel: The Park, Doncaster, 1/2 mile(s). Tel: 364008 (0302)

DONCASTER
Hickleton Golf Club, Hickleton, Near Doncaster, S Yorks. DN5 7BE. Tel: 892496 (0709)
Secretary: R Jowett   Tel: 896081 (0709)
Professional: Paul Shepherd   Tel: 895170 (0709)
Description: Undulating parkland.
Medal 18 holes, 6,403 yards, Par 71, S.S.S. 71, Course record 68.
Normal 18 holes, 6,231 yards, Par 71, S.S.S. 70.
Membership: 600
Visitors: Welcome.
Green Fees: Weekdays £17, weekends and Bank Holidays £25.
Facilities: Lunch. Dinner. Bar Snacks. Full Catering. Changing Room. Golf Shop. Caddies available.
Class One Hotel: The Moat House, Doncaster, 5 mile(s). Tel: 310331 (0302)

DONCASTER
Wheatley Golf Club, Armthorpe Road, Doncaster, S Yorks. . Tel: 831203 (0302)
Secretary: T A D Crumpton   Tel: 831203 (0302)
Professional: S Fox   Tel: 831655 (0302)
Location: 2 miles south east of Doncaster town centre.
Description: Parkland with tree lined fairways. Sandy sub-soil.
White 18 holes, 6,405 yards, Par 71, S.S.S. 71.
Yellow 18 holes, 6,220 yards, Par 71, S.S.S. 70.
Membership: 530
Visitors: Welcome. Handicap certificate required. Letter of Introduction required.No societies. Not Saturdays, Sundays or Bank Holidays.
Green Fees: Weekdays £17 per round, £21 per day. Weekends and Bank Holidays £21 per round, £25 per day.
Facilities: Lunch. Dinner. Bar Snacks. Full Catering. Changing Room. Golf Shop. Club Hire. Trolley Hire.

ROTHERHAM
Grange Park Golf Club, Upper Wortley Road, Rotherham, S Yorks. S61 2SJ. Tel: 558884 (0709)
Secretary: Mr R Charity   Tel: 583400 (0709)
Professional: Eric Clark   Tel: 559497 (0709)
Location: Tinsley junc off M1 (junc 34) take A6178 (Blackburn Road) onto Kimberworth Park Road and follow signs.
Description: Hilly parkland course. Municipal course with private club.
18 holes, 6,271 yards, Par 72, S.S.S. 71, Course record 69.
Membership: 300
Visitors: Welcome. No catering Mondays. Visiting parties must book in advance for catering. Closed some Sundays, always telephone in advance.
Green Fees: Weekdays £5.50 per round, weekends £6.50 per round.
Facilities: Lunch. Dinner. Bar Snacks. Full Catering. Changing Room. Golf Shop. Club Hire. Trolley Hire.

ROTHERHAM
Phoenix Golf Club, Pavilion Lane, Brinsworth, Rotherham, S Yorks. . Tel: 363864 (0709)
Secretary: J Burrows   Tel: 370759 (0709)
Professional: A Limb   Tel: 382624 (0709)
Location: M1 Tinsley roundabout Bawtry Road, 1 mile left hand side in Pavilion Lane.
Description: Parkland.
18 holes, 6,145 yards, Par 71, S.S.S. 69, Course record 66.
Visitors: Welcome. Handicap certificate required. After 10a.m. if not booked as a visiting party through the Secretary.

Green Fees: Weekdays £12, with member £6. Weekends £16, with member £8.
Facilities: Lunch. Dinner. Bar Snacks. Full Catering. Changing Room. Golf Shop. Club Hire. Driving Range. Trolley Hire.
Class One Hotel: Brecon, Rotherham, 1 1/2 mile(s). Tel: 828811 (0709)

ROTHERHAM

Rotherham Golf Club Ltd., Thrybergh Park, Thrybergh, Rotherham, S Yorks. S65 4NU. Tel: 850466 (0709)
Secretary: Mr F Green   Tel: 850812 (0709)
Professional: Mr S Thornhill   Tel: 850480 (0709)
Location: 3 1/2 miles east of Rotherham on A630 Rotherham to Doncaster Road.
Description: Open undulating tree lined parkland with ponds and ditches.
18 holes, 6,324 yards, Par 70, S.S.S. 70, Course record 66.
Membership: 450
Visitors: Welcome. Handicap certificate required. Wednesdays Ladies Day. Book with Professional for weekends.
Green Fees: Weekdays £22 per day, weekends £27 per round or day.
Facilities: Lunch. Dinner. Bar Snacks. Full Catering. Changing Room. Golf Shop. Club Hire. Trolley Hire. Buggy Hire.
Class One Hotel: The Beeches, Rotherham, 4 mile(s). Tel: 830630 (0709)
Class Two Hotel: The Regis, Rotherham, 3 mile(s). Tel: 376666 (0709)

ROTHERHAM

Sitwell Park Golf Club, Shrogswood Road, Rotherham, S Yorks. S60 4BY. Tel: 541096 (0709)
Secretary: G Simmonite   Tel: 541046 (0709)
Professional: N Taylor   Tel: 540961 (0709)
Location: M1 exit 33 A360, A361. M18 exit 1 A361.
Description: Undulating parkland.
18 holes, 6,203 yards, Par 71, S.S.S. 70, Course record 67.
Membership: 650
Visitors: Welcome. Not Saturdays. Sundays after 11.30a.m..
Green Fees: Weekdays £19 per round, weekends and Bank Holidays £22 per round, £26 per day.
Facilities: Lunch. Dinner. Bar Snacks. Full Catering. Changing Room. Golf Shop. Trolley Hire.
Class One Hotel: Consort, Thurcroft, 4 mile(s). Tel: 530022 (0709)
Class Two Hotel: Limes, Rotherham, 2 mile(s). Tel: 382446 (0709)

SHEFFIELD

Abbeydale Golf Club, Twentywell Lane, Sheffield, S Yorks. S17 4QA. Tel: 360763 (0742)
Secretary: Mrs K M Johnston   Tel: 360763 (0742)
Professional: N Perry   Tel: 365633 (0742)
Location: On A621 5 miles south of Sheffield.
Description: Parkland.
18 holes, 6,419 yards, Par 72, S.S.S. 71.
Membership: 700
Visitors: Welcome. Preferably by prior arrangement.
Green Fees: Weekdays £25, weekends £30.

Facilities: Lunch. Dinner. Bar Snacks. Full Catering. Changing Room. Golf Shop. Buggy Hire.
Class One Hotel: Sheffield Moat House, Sheffield, 2 mile(s). Tel: 375376 (0742)
Class Two Hotel: St Andrews Park, Sheffield, 4 mile(s). Tel: 500711 (0742)

SHEFFIELD

Beauchief Municipal Golf Club, Abbey Lane, Sheffield, S Yorks. S81 0DB. Tel: 367274 (0742)
Secretary: Mr J G Pearson   Tel: 306720 (0742)
Professional: Mr English   Tel: 620648 (0742)
Location: Between the Chesterfield Road and A621, 4 miles south of Sheffield.
Description: Open, hilly and tree lined parkland with a pond and some small streams. Views of the Peak District.
18 holes, 6,452 yards, Par 67, S.S.S. 66, Course record 65.
Membership: 450
Visitors: Welcome. Advisable to book 7 days in advance for weekends (in person only).
Green Fees: £6.95 per round.
Facilities: Lunch. Dinner. Bar Snacks. Full Catering. Changing Room. Golf Shop. Club Hire. Trolley Hire.
Class One Hotel: The Beauchief, Adjacent, Tel: 620500 (0742)

SHEFFIELD

Birley Wood Golf Course, Birley Lane, Sheffield, S Yorks. S12 3BP. Tel: 647262 (0742)
Secretary: Mr D Cronshaw   Tel: 471258 (0742)
Professional: Mr P Ball   Tel: 647262 (0742)
Location: 4 1/2 miles south east of Sheffield, just off the A616 towards Mosborough.
Description: Open plan golf course on undulating meadowland with varied features and good views.
18 holes, 5,483 yards, Par 68, S.S.S. 67, Course record 66.
Membership: 206
Visitors: Welcome. Must book in advance. Catering at Fairways Inn, next to course.
Green Fees: £6.95 per round.
Facilities: Lunch. Dinner. Bar Snacks. Full Catering. Changing Room. Club Hire. Trolley Hire.
Class One Hotel: Mosborough Hall, Sheffield, 1 1/2 mile(s). Tel: 484353 (0742)
Class Two Hotel: Critchleys Guest House, Sheffield, 3 mile(s). Tel: 364328 (0742)

SHEFFIELD

Dore and Totley Golf Club, The Clubhouse, Bradway Road, Sheffield, S Yorks. S17 4QR. Tel: 360492 (0742)
Secretary: Mrs Ward   Tel: 369872 (0742)
Professional: Mr Pearson   Tel: 366844 (0742)
Location: 6 miles south of Sheffield on A61.
Description: Flat parkland with many streams. Part of the course is surrounded by scenic Derbyshire countryside.
White 18 holes, 6,265 yards, Par 70, S.S.S. 70, Course record 67.
Yellow 18 holes, 6,042 yards, Par 70, S.S.S. 70.
Membership: 585
Visitors: Welcome. Handicap certificate required. Letter of Introduction required. Only by prior arrangement. With

members only at weekends. Wednesdays Ladies Day.
Green Fees: £20 per round.
Facilities: Lunch. Dinner. Bar Snacks. Full Catering. Changing Room. Golf Shop. Club Hire. Trolley Hire. Caddies available.
Class One Hotel: The Beauchief, Sheffield, 1 mile(s). Tel: 620500 (0742)

SHEFFIELD
Hallamshire Golf Club, Sandy Gate, Sheffield, S Yorks. S10 4LA. Tel: 302153 (0742)
Secretary: R Burns   Tel: 302153 (0742)
Professional: G Tickell   Tel: 305222 (0742)
Description: Moorland.
18 holes, 6,359 yards, S.S.S. 71, Course record 63.
Membership: 520
Visitors: Welcome. Handicap certificate required. No catering on Tuesdays. No visiting parties Wednesdays or weekends, only casuals.
Green Fees: Weekdays £27, weekends £32.
Facilities: Dinner. Bar Snacks. Full Catering. Changing Room. Golf Shop. Club Hire. Trolley Hire.
Class One Hotel: Forte Crest, Sheffield, 1 1/2 mile(s). Tel: 670067 (0742)

SHEFFIELD
Hillsborough Golf Club, Worral Road, Sheffield, S Yorks. S6 4BT. Tel: 343608 (0742)
Secretary: Mr G White   Tel: 349151 (0742)
Professional: Mr G Walker   Tel: 332666 (0742)
Location: 4 1/2 miles north of Sheffield on A61.
Description: Heathland. Local Championship course with scenic views of the reservoir.
18 holes, 6,204 yards, Par 70, S.S.S. 71, Course record 64.
Membership: 600
Visitors: Welcome. Handicap certificate required. Not before 9.30a.m. or between 12p.m. and 2p.m. every day. Tuesdays Ladies Day.
Green Fees: Weekdays £24 per round, weekends £35 per round.
Facilities: Lunch. Dinner. Bar Snacks. Full Catering. Changing Room. Golf Shop. Club Hire. Trolley Hire.
Class One Hotel: Middlewood Hall, Sheffield, 1 mile(s). Tel: 3919 (074286)

SHEFFIELD
Stocksbridge & District Golf Club, 30 Royd Lane, Deepcar, Sheffield, S Yorks. S30 5RZ. Tel: 882003 (0742)
Secretary: Stuart Lee   Tel: 882408 (0742)
Location: 11 miles from Sheffield on A616 Manchester Road.
Description: Moorland.
18 holes, 5,200 yards, Par 65, S.S.S. 65.
Membership: 300
Visitors: Welcome. No parties at weekends.
Green Fees: Weekdays £15, weekends £20.
Facilities: Lunch. Dinner. Bar Snacks. Changing Room.
Class One Hotel: Forte Crest, Sheffield, 11 mile(s). Tel: 670067 (0742)
Class Two Hotel: Rutland Hotel, Sheffield, 11 mile(s). Tel: 664411 (0742)

SHEFFIELD
Tankersley Park Golf Club, High Green, Sheffield, S Yorks. S30 4LG. Tel: 468247 (0742)
Secretary: P A Bagshaw   Tel: 468247 (0742)
Professional: I Kirk   Tel: 455583 (0742)
Location: M1 north to junc 35A, at island take A616 turn right into golf club. M1 south junc 36, at island take A61 SP Sheffield, take A616 club on
Description: Undulating parkland.
18 holes, 6,212 yards, Par 69, S.S.S. 70, Course record 64.
Membership: 700
Visitors: Welcome. Handicap certificate required. Weekdays without reservation but not before 3p.m. weekends. Society meeting by prior arrangement with the Secretary. No catering Mondays.
Green Fees: Weekdays £15.50 per round, weekends £20 per day.
Facilities: Lunch. Dinner. Bar Snacks. Full Catering. Changing Room. Golf Shop. Club Hire. Trolley Hire.
Class One Hotel: Staindrop Lodge, Chapeltown, 2 mile(s). Tel: 846727 (0742)
Class Two Hotel: Commercial, Chapeltown, 2 mile(s). Tel: 469066 (0742)

SHEFFIELD
Tinsley Park Golf Club (Municipal), High Hazels Park, Darnall, Sheffield, S Yorks. S9 4PE. Tel: 560237 (0742)
Secretary: C E Benson   Tel: 873110 (0742)
Professional: A P Highfield   Tel: 560237 (0742)
Description: Wooded undulating parkland course, easy walking.
18 holes, 6,064 yards, Par 71, S.S.S. 69.
Membership: 450
Visitors: Welcome.
Green Fees: £6.95 per round, reductions for OAP's and Juniors.
Facilities: Lunch. Dinner. Bar Snacks. Changing Room. Golf Shop. Club Hire. Trolley Hire.

SHEFFIELD
Wortley Golf Club, Hermit Hill Lane, Wortley, Sheffield, S Yorks. S30 4DF. Tel: 885294 (0742)
Secretary: J L Dalby   Tel: 885294 (0742)
Professional: J Tilson   Tel: 886490 (0742)
Location: Leave M1 at junc 35A or 36, course off A629 west of Wortley Village.
Description: Parkland.
18 holes, 5,983 yards, Par 69, S.S.S. 68.
Membership: 300
Visitors: Welcome. Handicap certificate required. Visiting parties Wednesdays and Fridays only by prior arrangement. Some catering restrictions apply, please telephone in advance.
Green Fees: Weekdays £19 per round or day, weekends and Bank Holidays £25.
Facilities: Lunch. Dinner. Bar Snacks. Changing Room. Golf Shop. Club Hire. Trolley Hire.

THORNE

Thorne Golf Club, Kirkton Lane, Thorne, Near Doncaster, S Yorks. DN8 5RJ. Tel: 812084 (0405)
Secretary: C Highfield   Tel: 815173 (0405)
Professional: E D Highfield   Tel: 812084 (0405)
Description: Parkland.
18 holes, 5,366 yards, Par 68, S.S.S. 66, Course record 65.
Membership: 300
Visitors: Welcome.
Green Fees: On application.
Facilities: Lunch. Dinner. Bar Snacks. Full Catering. Changing Room. Golf Shop. Club Hire. Trolley Hire.
Class Two Hotel: Belmont, Thorne, 1 mile(s). Tel: 812320 (0405)

WEST YORKSHIRE

BRADFORD

East Bierley Golf Club, South View Road, East Bierley, Bradford, W Yorks. BD4 6PP. Tel: 681023 (0274)
Secretary: M Welch   Tel: 683666 (0274)
Location: Off A650 Wakefield/Dewsbury/Bradford Road.
Description: Undulating moorland.
9 holes, 4,692 yards, Par 64, S.S.S. 63, Course record 61.
Membership: 300
Visitors: Welcome. Handicap certificate required. No Green Fees Sundays or Mondays after 3p.m..
Green Fees: £10.
Facilities: Lunch. Dinner. Bar Snacks. Full Catering. Changing Room.
Class One Hotel: Tong Village, Tong, 2 mile(s). Tel: 854646 (0532)
Class Two Hotel: Guide Post, Bradford, 2 mile(s). Tel: 607866 (0274)

BRADFORD

Headley Golf Club, Headley Lane, Thornton, Bradford, W Yorks. BD13 3LX. Tel: 833481 (0274)
Secretary: Mr J Clark   Tel: 832571 (0274)
Location: 4 miles west of Bradford off Thornton Road.
Description: Parkland/moorland with a stream.
9 holes, 4,914 yards, Par 64, S.S.S. 64, Course record 62.
Membership: 400
Visitors: Welcome. With members only at weekends. Ladies only Saturdays 12p.m. to 1.30p.m..
Green Fees: Weekdays £10 per round, £5 with a member. Weekends £7.
Facilities: Lunch. Dinner. Bar Snacks. Full Catering. Changing Room. Golf Shop.
Class One Hotel: Holdsworth House, Halifax, 3 mile(s). Tel: 240024 (0422)

BRADFORD

Northcliffe Golf Club, High Bank Lane, Shipley, Bradford, W Yorks. BD18 4LJ. Tel: 584085 (0274)
Secretary: R Anderson   Tel: 596731 (0274)

Professional: S Poot   Tel: 587193 (0274)
Location: 3 miles west of Bradford on A650 Bradford/Keighley Road.
Description: Undulating wooded parkland.
Yellow 18 holes, 5,839 yards, Par 71, S.S.S. 68.
White 18 holes, 6,104 yards, Par 71, S.S.S. 69, Course record 65.
Membership: 650
Visitors: Welcome. No catering Mondays, Clubhouse closed.
Green Fees: On application.
Facilities: Lunch. Dinner. Bar Snacks. Full Catering. Changing Room. Golf Shop. Club Hire. Trolley Hire.
Class One Hotel: Bankfield, Bingley, 1 1/2 mile(s). Tel: 567123 (0274)
Class Two Hotel: Park Drive, Heaton, 2 mile(s). Tel: 480194 (0274)

BRADFORD

West Bowling Golf Club, Newall Hall, Rooley Lane, Bradford, W Yorks. BD5 8LB. Tel: 724449 (0274)
Secretary: M E Lynn   Tel: 393207 (0274)
Professional: A P Swaine   Tel: 728036 (0274)
Location: Junc of M606 and Bradford ring road (east).
Description: Parkland.
18 holes, 5,657 yards, Par 69, S.S.S. 67.
Membership: 450
Visitors: Welcome. Handicap certificate required. Letter of Introduction required.Not Mondays or weekends. No catering on Mondays. Bar closed 2p.m. to 4p.m..
Green Fees: Weekdays £21, weekends £27.
Facilities: Lunch. Dinner. Bar Snacks. Full Catering. Changing Room. Golf Shop. Club Hire. Trolley Hire.
Class Two Hotel: Guide Post, Bradford, 1 mile(s). Tel: 607866 (0274)

BRADFORD

West Bradford Golf Club, Chellow Grange Road, Haworth Road, Bradford, W Yorks. BD9 6NP. Tel: 542767 (0274)
Secretary: D Ingham   Tel: 542767 (0274)
Professional: N Barber   Tel: 542102 (0274)
Description: Undulating.
18 holes, 5,788 yards, Par 69, S.S.S. 68, Course record 63.
Membership: 457
Visitors: Welcome.
Green Fees: Weekdays £14.50, weekends £20.50.
Facilities: Lunch. Dinner. Bar Snacks. Full Catering. Changing Room. Golf Shop. Trolley Hire.

ELLAND

Elland Golf Club, Hammerstone, Leach Lane, Elland, W Yorks. HX5 0TA. Tel: 372505 (0422)
Professional: M Allison   Tel: 374886 (0422)
Location: M62 junc 24 and follow signs for Blackley.
Description: Parkland.
9 holes, 5,630 yards, Par 66, S.S.S. 66, Course record 64.
Visitors: Welcome.
Green Fees: Weekdays £12, weekends £15.
Facilities: Lunch. Dinner. Bar Snacks. Full Catering. Changing Room. Golf Shop.

Cade's - Audi Golf Course Guide

HALIFAX

Halifax Golf Club, Union Lane, Ogden, Halifax, W Yorks. HX2 8XR. Tel: 244171 (0422)
Secretary: Mr J Clark Tel: 832571 (0274)
Professional: Mr S Foster Tel: 240047 (0422)
Location: 4 miles north of Halifax on the Halifax to Keighley Road.
Description: Undulating moorland with streams. Championship course with views over the Bronte Moors. A high course with the 12th hole 1,000 feet above sea level.
18 holes, 6,100 yards, Par 70, S.S.S. 70, Course record 64.
Membership: 700
Visitors: Welcome. Handicap certificate required. Only between 10a.m. and 11.30a.m. and 2p.m. to 3.30p.m. daily.
Green Fees: Weekdays £20 per day, £15 with a Handicap Certificate, £10 with a member. Weekends £30 per round or day, £25 with a Handicap Cert, £12 with a member.
Facilities: Lunch. Dinner. Bar Snacks. Full Catering. Changing Room. Golf Shop. Club Hire. Trolley Hire.
Class One Hotel: Holdsworth House, Halifax, 2 mile(s). Tel: 240024 (0422)
Class Two Hotel: Carlton House, Bradford, 2 mile(s). Tel: 833397 (0274)

HALIFAX

Lightcliffe Golf Club, Knowle Top Road, Lightcliffe, Halifax, W Yorks. HX3 8SW. Tel: 202459 (0422)
Secretary: T H Gooder Tel: 201051 (0422)
Professional: D W Lockett Tel: 202459 (0422)
Location: 3 miles from Halifax on Leeds Road A58.
Description: Meadowland.
9 holes, 5,467 yards, Par 68, S.S.S. 68, Course record 62.
Membership: 350
Visitors: Welcome. Handicap certificate required.
Green Fees: Weekdays £10, weekends and Bank Holidays £16.
Facilities: Lunch. Dinner. Bar Snacks. Full Catering. Changing Room. Golf Shop. Trolley Hire.
Class One Hotel: Forte Crest, Brighouse, 3 mile(s). Tel: 400400 (0484)
Class Two Hotel: Black Horse Inn, Brighouse, 3 1/2 mile(s). Tel: 713862 (0484)

HALIFAX

West End Golf Club (Halifax) Ltd., Paddock Lane, Highroad Well, Halifax, W Yorks. HX2 0NT. Tel: 353608 (0422)
Secretary: B R Thomas Tel: 341878 (0422)
Professional: D Rishworth Tel: 363293 (0422)
Location: West of Halifax town centre.
Description: Parkland.
18 holes, 6,003 yards, Par 68, S.S.S. 68, Course record 65.
Visitors: Welcome. Handicap certificate required. Not Saturdays.
Green Fees: Weekdays £15 per round, £18 per day. Weekends and Bank Holidays £18 per round, £23 per day.
Facilities: Lunch. Dinner. Bar Snacks. Full Catering. Changing Room. Golf Shop. Trolley Hire.
Class One Hotel: Imperial Crown, Halifax, 1 1/2 mile(s). Tel: 342342 (0422)

HEBDEN BRIDGE

Hebden Bridge Golf Club, Wadsworth, Hebden Bridge, W Yorks. HX7 8PH. Tel: 842896 (0422)
Secretary: R G Pogson Tel: 842896 (0422)
Location: 1 mile upwards from town centre past Birchcliffe Centre.
Description: Moorland with superb Pennine views.
9 holes, 5,202 yards, Par 68, S.S.S. 66, Course record 61.
Membership: 240
Visitors: Welcome. Not on major competition days (Summer Saturdays and Sundays).
Green Fees: Weekdays £7.50 per day, weekends £10 per day.
Facilities: Lunch. Dinner. Bar Snacks. Full Catering. Changing Room.
Class One Hotel: Carlton, Hebden Bridge, 1 1/2 mile(s). Tel: 844400 (0422)
Class Two Hotel: Hebden Lodge, Hebden Bridge, 1 1/2 mile(s). Tel: 845272 (0422)

HUDDERSFIELD

Crosland Heath Golf Club, Felk Stile Road, Crosland Hill, Huddersfield, W Yorks. HD4 7AF. Tel: 653216 (0484)
Secretary: Mr D Walker Tel: 653262 (0484)
Professional: Mr J Andrew Tel: 653877 (0484)
Location: 3 miles west of Huddersfield on A62.
Description: Flat tree lined moorland.
18 holes, 5,961 yards, Par 70, S.S.S. 70, Course record 63.
Membership: 350
Visitors: Welcome. Handicap certificate required. With members only on Saturdays. Prior arrangement required for Sunday. Wednesdays Ladies Day.
Green Fees: Weekdays £19.50 per round or day.
Facilities: Lunch. Dinner. Bar Snacks. Full Catering. Changing Room. Golf Shop. Club Hire. Trolley Hire.
Class One Hotel: The George, Huddersfield, 3 mile(s). Tel: 515444 (0484)

HUDDERSFIELD

Huddersfield Golf Club, Fixby Hall, Lightridge Road, Huddersfield, W Yorks. HD2 2EP. Tel: 420110 (0484)
Secretary: Miss D Rose Tel: 426203 (0484)
Professional: Mr P Carman Tel: 426463 (0484)
Location: 3 miles north of Huddersfield off M62.
Description: Tree lined, hilly heathland with scenic countryside views and extensively refurbished Georgian Manor House.
18 holes, 6,364 yards, Par 71, S.S.S. 71, Course record 67.
Membership: 750
Visitors: Welcome. Handicap certificate required. With members only at weekends. Tuesdays Ladies Day.
Green Fees: £25 per round, £35 per day.
Facilities: Lunch. Dinner. Bar Snacks. Full Catering. Changing Room. Golf Shop. Trolley Hire.
Class One Hotel: The Pennine Hilton, Huddersfield, 2 mile(s). Tel: 375431 (0422)
Class Two Hotel: The Ellasley Guest House, Huddersfield, 2 1/2 mile(s). Tel: 513171 (0484)

HUDDERSFIELD

Longley Park Golf Club, Maple Street, Aspley, Huddersfield, W Yorks. HD5 9AX. Tel: 426932 (0484)
Secretary: D Palliser Tel: 426932 (0484)
Professional: N Suckling Tel: 422304 (0484)
Description: Sheltered parkland near town centre.
9 holes, 5,324 yards, Par 66, S.S.S. 66, Course record 66.
Membership: 445
Visitors: Welcome. Handicap certificate required. Letter of Introduction required.Not Thursdays or weekends.
Green Fees: £11.50.
Facilities: Lunch. Dinner. Bar Snacks. Full Catering. Changing Room. Golf Shop. Trolley Hire.
Class One Hotel: Huddersfield Hotel, Huddersfield, 1/2 mile(s). Tel: 512111 (0484)

HUDDERSFIELD

Marsden Golf Course, Hemplow Mount Road, Marsden, Huddersfield, W Yorks. HD7 6NN. Tel: 844253 (0484)
Secretary: Mr Shaw Tel: 845869 (0484)
Location: 7 miles south west of Huddersfield on A62.
Description: Undulating moorland 1,000 feet above sea level. Scenic views of moorland reservoirs and valleys. 9 holes played off 18 tees.
9 holes, 5,700 yards, Par 68, S.S.S. 68, Course record 66.
Membership: 252
Visitors: Welcome. Handicap certificate required. With members only at weekends. Sundays Ladies Day.
Green Fees: £10 per day.
Facilities: Lunch. Dinner. Bar Snacks. Full Catering. Changing Room. Golf Shop.
Class One Hotel: The Hey Green, Marsden, 2 mile(s). Tel: 844235 (0484)

KEIGHLEY

Keighley Golf Club, Howden Park, Utley, Keighley, W Yorks. BD20 6DH. Tel: 603179 (0535)
Secretary: D F Coyle Tel: 604778 (0535)
Professional: S A Dixon Tel: 665370 (0535)
Description: Parkland.
18 holes, 6,149 yards, Par 69, S.S.S. 70, Course record 65.
Membership: 600
Visitors: Welcome. Handicap certificate required. Letter of Introduction required.Not weekends or Tuesdays. No catering or Bar Mondays.
Green Fees: £20 per round, £24 per day.
Facilities: Lunch. Dinner. Bar Snacks. Full Catering. Changing Room. Golf Shop. Club Hire. Trolley Hire.

KEIGHLEY

Riddlesden Golf Club, Howden Rough, Riddlesden, Keighley, W Yorks. BD20 5QN. Tel: 602148 (0535)
Secretary: Mrs K M Brooksbank Tel: 607646 (0535)
Location: A650 Keighley to Bradford Road.
Description: Moorland course with spectacular par 3's.
18 holes, 4,247 yards, Par 62, S.S.S. 61.
Membership: 300
Visitors: Welcome. Not between 10a.m. and 2p.m. Saturdays and only after 2p.m. Sundays.
Green Fees: Weekdays £8, weekends £12.
Facilities: Lunch. Dinner. Bar Snacks. Changing Room.

Class Two Hotel: Dalesgate, Keighley, 3 mile(s). Tel: 664930 (0535)

LEEDS

Alwoodley Golf Club, Wigton Lane, Leeds, W Yorks. LS17 8SA. Tel: 681680 (0532)
Location: North Leeds on A61 to Harrogate.
Description: Heathland.
18 holes, 6,686 yards, Par 72, S.S.S. 72, Course record 67.
Visitors: Welcome. Handicap certificate required. Letter of Introduction required.Not Tuesdays. Weekends only by arrangement.
Green Fees: Weekdays £35, weekends £45.
Facilities: Lunch. Dinner. Bar Snacks. Full Catering. Changing Room. Golf Shop. Club Hire. Trolley Hire.
Class One Hotel: Harewood Arms, Harewood, 2 mile(s). Tel: 886566 (0532)
Class Two Hotel: White Lodge, Leeds, 1/2 mile(s). Tel: 683361 (0532)

LEEDS

Garforth Golf Club, Long Lane, Garforth, Leeds, W Yorks. LS25 2DS. Tel: 860221 (0532)
Secretary: Mr F A Readman Tel: 863308 (0532)
Professional: Mr Findlater Tel: 862063 (0532)
Location: 5 miles east of Leeds on A63 or A64.
Description: Flat parkland with 2 brooks.
18 holes, 6,000 yards, Par 70, S.S.S. 70.
Membership: 500
Visitors: Welcome. Handicap certificate required. With members only at weekends.
Green Fees: £20 per round, £25 per day.
Facilities: Lunch. Dinner. Bar Snacks. Full Catering. Changing Room. Golf Shop. Club Hire. Trolley Hire.

LEEDS

Gotts Park Municipal Golf Course, Gotts House, Armley Ridge Road, Leeds, W Yorks. LS12 2QX. Tel: 638232 (0532)
Secretary: Mr M Gill Tel: 452069 (0532)
Professional: Mr J K Simpson Tel: 638232 (0532)
Location: 1 1/2 miles from city centre on the Bradford Road.
Description: Hilly parkland overlooking the Aire Valley.
18 holes, 4,960 yards, Par 65, S.S.S. 64, Course record 63.
Membership: 320
Visitors: Welcome. Book on the day, first come first serve.
Green Fees: Weekdays £5 per day, weekends £6.50 per day.
Facilities: Lunch. Bar Snacks. Changing Room. Golf Shop. Club Hire.
Class One Hotel: Holiday Inn, Leeds, 2 mile(s). Tel: 442200 (0532)

LEEDS

Horsforth Golf Club, Layton Road, Horsforth, Near Leeds, W Yorks. LS18 5EX. Tel: 581703 (0532)
Secretary: Mr C B Carrington Tel: 586819 (0532)
Professional: Mr L Turner Tel: 585200 (0532)
Location: From Leeds take A65 to Ilkley, 6 miles north west of Leeds.

Description: Tree lined rolling pasture. Challenging course but not too demanding.
18 holes, 6,243 yards, Par 71, S.S.S. 70, Course record 66.
Membership: 700
Visitors: Welcome. Handicap certificate required. Not at weekends or Bank Holidays. Tuesdays Ladies Day. Societies only at weekends.
Green Fees: Weekdays £20 per round, £22 per day. Groups at weekends £28.
Facilities: Lunch. Dinner. Bar Snacks. Full Catering. Changing Room. Golf Shop. Club Hire. Trolley Hire.
Class One Hotel: Chevin Lodge Country Park, Otley, 4 mile(s). Tel: 467818 (0943)

LEEDS

Howley Hall Golf Club, Scotchman Lane, Morley, Leeds, W Yorks. LS27 0NX. Tel: 472432 (0924)
Secretary: Mrs A Pepper   Tel: 478417 (0924)
Professional: Stephen Spinks   Tel: 473852 (0924)
Location: On B6123 turn onto A650 at the Halfway House Inn.
Description: Parkland.
18 holes, 6,443 yards, Par 71, S.S.S. 71, Course record 66.
Membership: 500
Visitors: Welcome. Handicap certificate required. With members only on Saturday.
Green Fees: Weekdays £18 per round, £22 per day. Weekends and Bank Holidays £25.
Facilities: Lunch. Dinner. Bar Snacks. Full Catering. Changing Room. Golf Shop. Club Hire. Buggy Hire.
Class One Hotel: Cedar Court, Wakefield, 5 mile(s). Tel: 276310 (0924)

LEEDS

Leeds Golf Club, Elmete Lane, Leeds, W Yorks. LS8 2LJ. Tel: 658775 (0532)
Secretary: G W Backhouse   Tel: 659203 (0532)
Professional: S Longster   Tel: 658786 (0532)
Location: 4 miles from city centre off A58 Leeds to Wetherby Road.
Description: Parkland.
18 holes, 6,097 yards, Par 69, S.S.S. 69, Course record 64.
Membership: 450
Visitors: Welcome. Handicap certificate required. With members only at weekends.
Green Fees: £19 per round, £25 per day.
Facilities: Lunch. Dinner. Bar Snacks. Full Catering. Changing Room. Golf Shop. Club Hire. Trolley Hire. Buggy Hire.

LEEDS

Moortown Golf Club Ltd., Harrogate Road, Alwoodley, Leeds, W Yorks. LS17 7DB. Tel: 681682 (0532)
Secretary: R H Brown   Tel: 686521 (0532)
Professional: B Hutchinson   Tel: 683636 (0532)
Location: 5 miles north of Leeds city centre on A61 Leeds to Harrogate Road.
Blue (Championship) 18 holes, 7,020 yards, Par 71, S.S.S. 74.
Yellow 18 holes, 6,515 yards, Par 71, S.S.S. 72.
Membership: 580
Visitors: Welcome. Handicap certificate required. By arrangement with the Secretary.
Green Fees: Weekdays £33 per round, £39 per day. Weekends and Bank Holidays £39 per round, £44 per day.
Facilities: Lunch. Dinner. Bar Snacks. Full Catering. Changing Room. Golf Shop. Trolley Hire.
Class One Hotel: Post House, Leeds, 6 mile(s). Tel: 842911 (0532)
Class Two Hotel: White Lodge, Leeds, 1/4 mile(s). Tel: 683561 (0532)

LEEDS

Roundhay Golf Club, Park Lane, Leeds, W Yorks. LS8 2EJ. Tel: 662695 (0532)
Secretary: R H McLauchlan   Tel: 492523 (0532)
Professional: J Pape   Tel: 661686 (0532)
Location: 4 1/2 miles north east of Leeds city centre, leave A58 at Oakwoods.
Description: Parkland.
9 holes, 5,322 yards, Par 70, S.S.S. 65, Course record 62.
Membership: 500
Visitors: Welcome. Tees must be booked at all times. Catering restriction - visitors must be introduced by a member.
Green Fees: Weekdays £5.80, weekends and Bank Holidays £6.15.
Facilities: Lunch. Dinner. Bar Snacks. Changing Room. Golf Shop. Club Hire. Trolley Hire.
Class One Hotel: Parcmont, Leeds, 1 1/2 mile(s). Tel: 655458 (0532)
Class Two Hotel: Clock, Leeds, 1 1/2 mile(s). Tel: 490304 (0532)

LEEDS

Sand Moor Golf Club, Alwoodley Lane, Leeds, W Yorks. LS17 7DJ. Tel: 681685 (0532)
Secretary: B F Precious   Tel: 685180 (0532)
Professional: J R Foss   Tel: 683925 (0532)
Description: Moorland overlooking picturesque Wharfedale.
18 holes, 6,429 yards, Par 71, S.S.S. 71, Course record 65.
Membership: 490
Visitors: Welcome. With members only at weekends. Ladies only Thursday mornings. Some catering restrictions apply, please telephone in advance.
Green Fees: £26 per round, £32 per day.
Facilities: Lunch. Dinner. Bar Snacks. Full Catering. Changing Room. Golf Shop. Club Hire. Trolley Hire.
Class One Hotel: Forte Crest, Bramhope, 5 mile(s). Tel: 842911 (0532)
Class Two Hotel: White Lodge, Alwoodley, 1 mile(s). Tel: 683561 (0532)

LEEDS

South Leeds Golf Club, Gypsy Lane, Leeds, W Yorks. LS11 5TU. Tel: 700479 (0532)
Secretary: Mr J McBride   Tel: 771676 (0532)
Professional: Mike Lewis   Tel: 702598 (0532)
Description: Parkland.
18 holes, 5,769 yards, Par 69, S.S.S. 68, Course record 65.
Membership: 443
Visitors: Welcome. Handicap certificate required. Not

weekends. No catering on Mondays.
Green Fees: Weekdays £17, weekends and Bank Holidays £25.
Facilities: Lunch. Dinner. Bar Snacks. Full Catering. Changing Room. Golf Shop. Trolley Hire.
Class One Hotel: Queen's, Leeds, 1 1/2 mile(s). Tel: 431323 (0532)
Class Two Hotel: Cross Keys, Morley, 2 mile(s). Tel: 380276 (0532)

MELTHAM
Meltham Golf Club, Thick Hollins Hall. Meltham, Huddersfield, W Yorks. HD7 3DQ. Tel: 850227 (0484)
Secretary: J Holdsworth   Tel: 850227 (0484)
Professional: P Davies   Tel: 851521 (0484)
Location: On B617 1/2 mile east of Meltham, 6 miles south west of Huddersfield.
Description: Gently sloping course in wooded valley.
18 holes, 6,202 yards, S.S.S. 70, Course record 62.
Membership: 480
Visitors: Welcome. Handicap certificate required. Not Saturdays.
Green Fees: Weekdays £18, weekends £22.
Facilities: Lunch. Dinner. Bar Snacks. Full Catering. Changing Room. Golf Shop. Trolley Hire.
Class One Hotel: Durker Roods, Meltham, 1 mile(s). Tel: 851413 (0484)
Class Two Hotel: Red Lion Inn, Holmfirth, 5 mile(s). Tel: 683449 (0484)

MIRFIELD
Dewsbury District Golf Club, The Pinnacle, Sands Lane, Mirfield, W Yorks. WF14 8HJ. Tel: 492399 (0924)
Secretary: D M Scott   Tel: 492399 (0924)
Professional: N P Hirst   Tel: 496030 (0924)
Location: Turn off A644 opposite Swan Inn, 2 miles west of Dewsbury.
Description: Undulating moorland/parkland with panoramic views over surrounding countryside.
18 holes, 6,256 yards, Par 71, S.S.S. 71, Course record 64.
Membership: 550
Visitors: Welcome. Handicap certificate required. With a member at weekends before 4.30p.m.. No catering or Bar on Mondays.
Green Fees: £18. Visiting party package (over 12 persons) £26 including coffee and biscuits.
Facilities: Lunch. Dinner. Bar Snacks. Full Catering. Changing Room. Golf Shop. Club Hire. Trolley Hire.
Class One Hotel: Forte Crest, Brighouse, 3 mile(s). Tel: 400400 (0484)
Class Two Hotel: The Woolpack, Dewsbury, 1 mile(s). Tel: 499999 (0924)

NORMANTON
Normanton Golf Club, Snydale Road, Normanton, W Yorks.
Secretary: Jack McElhinney   Tel: 702273 (0977)
Professional: Martin Evans   Tel: 220134 (0924)
Description: Flat with internal out of bounds for a true test of golfing skills. Also a large practice area.
Mens 9 holes, 5,288 yards, Par 66, S.S.S. 66.
Ladies 9 holes, 4,902 yards, Par 70, S.S.S. 69, Course record 67.
Membership: 300
Visitors: Welcome. Not Sundays. Visiting parties weekdays only.
Green Fees: Weekdays £8, £6 with a member. Saturdays and Bank Holidays £14, £12 with a member.
Facilities: Lunch. Dinner. Bar Snacks. Full Catering. Changing Room. Golf Shop.
Class Two Hotel: Black Swan, Normanton, 1/2 mile(s). Tel: 893294 (0924)

OTLEY
Otley Golf Club, West Busk Lane, Otley, W Yorks. l S21 3NG. Tel: 461015 (0943)
Secretary: A F Flowers   Tel: 465329 (0943)
Professional: S McNally   Tel: 463403 (0943)
Description: Attractive parkland course with expansive views over Wharfedale.
18 holes, 6,235 yards, Par 70, S.S.S. 70, Course record 66.
Membership: 650
Visitors: Welcome. Handicap certificate required. Not Tuesdays or Saturdays.
Green Fees: Weekdays £23, weekends £28.
Facilities: Lunch. Dinner. Bar Snacks. Full Catering. Changing Room. Golf Shop. Club Hire. Trolley Hire.
Class One Hotel: Chevin Lodge, Otley, 1/2 mile(s). Tel: 467818 (0943)
Class Two Hotel: Acacia House, Henston, 1/2 mile(s). Tel: 873688 (0943)

OUTLANE
Outlane Golf Club, Slack, Off Newhay Road, Outlane, Near Huddersfield, W Yorks. HD3 3YL. Tel: 374762 (0422)
Secretary: Mr G Boyle   Tel: 374762 (0422)
Professional: Mr D Chapman   Tel: 374762 (0422)
Location: A640 from Huddersfield through Outlane Village, entrance on the left just after the bus terminus.
Description: Semi-moorland course, enjoying panoramic views of the Pennines and West Yorkshire.
18 holes, 6,003 yards, Par 71, S.S.S. 69, Course record 67.
Membership: 500
Visitors: Welcome.
Green Fees: Weekdays £15, weekends and Bank Holidays £22. Reductions after 3p.m. on Sundays and playing with members.
Facilities: Lunch. Dinner. Bar Snacks. Full Catering. Changing Room. Golf Shop. Club Hire.
Class One Hotel: The Old Golf House, Outlane, 1/2 mile(s). Tel: 379311 (0422)
Class Two Hotel: Elm Crest Guest House, Edgerton, 1 1/2 mile(s). Tel: 530990 (0484)

PONTEFRACT
Pontefract and District Golf Club, Park Lane, Pontefract, W Yorks. WF8 4QS. Tel: 792241 (0977)
Secretary: W T Smith   Tel: 792115 (0977)
Professional: J Coleman   Tel: 706806 (0977)
Location: M62 exit 32, 1 mile from Pontefract on B6134.
Description: Parkland.
18 holes, 6,227 yards, Par 72, S.S.S. 70.

Membership: 750
Visitors: Welcome. Handicap certificate required. Letter of Introduction required.Not on Wednesdays, Saturdays or Sundays. No catering on Mondays.
Green Fees: Weekdays £22, weekends and Bank Holidays £27.
Facilities: Lunch. Dinner. Bar Snacks. Full Catering. Changing Room. Golf Shop. Trolley Hire.
Class Two Hotel: Parkside Inne, Pontefract, 1 mile(s). Tel: 709911 (0977)

PUDSEY

Woodhall Hills Golf Club Ltd., Woodhall Road, Calverley, Pudsey, W Yorks. LS28 5QY. Tel: 564771 (0532)
Secretary: Mr D Harkness   Tel: 554954 (0532)
Professional: Mr D Tear   Tel: 562857 (0532)
Location: 3 1/2 miles east of Bradford on A647 signposted Calverley.
Description: Undulating moorland.
18 holes, 6,102 yards, Par 71, S.S.S. 69, Course record 66.
Membership: 612
Visitors: Welcome. Not before 9.30a.m. weekdays or 10.30a.m. weekends. Tuesdays Ladies Day.
Green Fees: Weekdays £20.50 per round of day, weekends and Bank Holidays £25.50 per round or day.
Facilities: Lunch. Dinner. Bar Snacks. Full Catering. Changing Room. Golf Shop. Trolley Hire.
Class One Hotel: Tong Village Hotel, Tong, 5 mile(s). Tel: 854646 (0532)

RAWDON

Rawdon Golf and Lawn Tennis Club, Buckstone Drive, Rawdon, Leeds, W Yorks. LS19 6BD. Tel: 506040 (0532)
Secretary: Mr R Adams   Tel: 505017 (0532)
Professional: Mr S Wheldon   Tel: 873719 (0943)
Location: 6 miles north west of Leeds on A65 Leeds to Skipton Road.
Description: Open, undulating parkland.
9 holes, 5,982 yards, Par 72, S.S.S. 69, Course record 64.
Membership: 695
Visitors: Welcome. Handicap certificate required. With members only at weekends. Tuesdays Ladies Day.
Green Fees: £16 per day, £10 with a member.
Facilities: Lunch. Dinner. Bar Snacks. Full Catering. Changing Room. Golf Shop. Trolley Hire.

SCARCROFT

Scarcroft Golf Club, Syke Lane, Scarcroft, W Yorks. LS14 3BQ. Tel: 892263 (0532)
Secretary: Mr D Barwell   Tel: 892311 (0532)
Professional: Mr M Ross   Tel: 892780 (0532)
Location: 5 miles south west of Wetherby off A58.
Description: Undulating parkland with ditches. Views over the Yorkshire Moors.
18 holes, 6,426 yards, Par 71, S.S.S. 71, Course record 67.
Membership: 652
Visitors: Welcome. Handicap certificate required. Any day at the discretion of the club Secretary.
Green Fees: £25 per round, £30 per day.
Facilities: Lunch. Dinner. Bar Snacks. Full Catering. Changing Room. Golf Shop. Club Hire. Trolley Hire.

Class One Hotel: Harewood Arms, Harewood, 5 mile(s). Tel: 886566 (0532)

WAKEFIELD

City of Wakefield Golf Club, Lupset Park, Horbury Road, Wakefield, W Yorks. WF2 8QS. Tel: 374316 (0924)
Secretary: Mrs P Ambler   Tel: 367442 (0924)
Professional: Roger Holland   Tel: 360282 (0924)
Description: Undulating, partially wooded parkland.
18 holes, 6,299 yards, Par 72, S.S.S. 70, Course record 66.
Membership: 800
Visitors: Welcome. No catering on Thursdays.
Green Fees: Weekdays £6, weekends and Bank Holidays £8.
Facilities: Lunch. Dinner. Bar Snacks. Full Catering. Changing Room. Golf Shop. Club Hire. Trolley Hire.
Class One Hotel: Swallow Hotel, Wakefield, 3 mile(s). Tel: 372111 (0924)
Class Two Hotel: Parklands Hotel, Wakefield, 2 mile(s). Tel: 377407 (0924)

WAKEFIELD

Painthorpe House Golf & Country Club, Painthorpe Lane, Crigglestone, Wakefield, W Yorks. WF4 3HE. Tel: 255083 (0924)
Secretary: Mr H Kershaw   Tel: 274527 (0924)
Location: 3 miles west of Wakefield on the Huddersfield Road to Painthorpe.
Description: Meadowland course, undulating.
18 holes, 4,508 yards, Par 62, S.S.S. 62, Course record 64.
Membership: 200
Visitors: Welcome. Not on Saturdays. All day Sunday and Wednesday evenings competition days.
Green Fees: £3 per round, £5 per day.
Facilities: Lunch. Dinner. Bar Snacks. Full Catering. Changing Room. Caddies available.
Class One Hotel: Cedar Court, Wakefield, 1/2 mile(s). Tel: 276310 (0924)

WAKEFIELD

Wakefield Golf Club, Woodthorpe Lane, Sandal, Wakefield, W Yorks. WF2 6JH. Tel: 255104 (0924)
Secretary: D T Hall   Tel: 258778 (0924)
Professional: I M Right   Tel: 255308 (0924)
Description: Parkland.
18 holes, 6,611 yards, Par 72, S.S.S. 72, Course record 68.
Membership: 550
Visitors: Welcome. Handicap certificate required. Parties Mondays, Wednesdays, Thursdays and Fridays by arrangement. No catering on Mondays.
Green Fees: Weekdays £22 per round or day, weekends £25 per round or day.
Facilities: Lunch. Dinner. Bar Snacks. Full Catering. Changing Room. Golf Shop. Club Hire. Trolley Hire. Buggy Hire.
Class One Hotel: Cedar Court, Wakefield, 2 mile(s). Tel: 276310 (0924)
Class Two Hotel: Sandal Court, Wakefield, 1 mile(s). Tel: 258725 (0924)

WALES

CLWYD

DENBIGH
Bryn Morfydd Hotel Golf Club, Llanrhaeadr, Near Denbigh, Clwyd. LL16 4NP. Tel: 78280 (0745)
Secretary: C S Henderson   Tel: 78280 (0745)
Description: Mature parkland surrounding Country House Hotel. Spectacular views overlooking The Vale Of Clwyd.
Dukes 1992 9 holes, 5,144 yards, Par 70, S.S.S. 66.
Duchess 1982 9 holes, 1,190 yards, Par 27.
Membership: 200
Visitors: Welcome. Handicap certificate required.
Green Fees: Dukes £8 per 18 holes, Duchess £4 per 18 holes.
Facilities: Lunch. Dinner. Bar Snacks. Full Catering. Changing Room. Golf Shop. Club Hire. Trolley Hire.
Class Two Hotel: Bryn Morfydd Hotel, On course, Tel: 78280 (0745)

DENBIGH
Denbigh Golf Club, Henllan Road, Denbigh, Clwyd. LL16 5AA. Tel: 814159 (0745)
Secretary: G C Parry   Tel: 816669 (0745)
Professional: M D Jones   Tel: 814159 (0745)
Location: 1 mile outside town, on B5382.
Description: Undulating parkland.
18 holes, 5,580 yards, Par 68, S.S.S. 67, Course record 64.
Visitors: Welcome. Handicap certificate required.
Green Fees: On application.
Facilities: Lunch. Dinner. Bar Snacks. Full Catering. Changing Room. Golf Shop. Club Hire. Trolley Hire.
Class One Hotel: Oriel House, St Asaph, 3 mile(s). Tel: 582716 (0745)

FLINT
Flint Golf Club, Cornist Park, Flint, Clwyd. CH6 5HJ. Tel: 733461 (0352)
Secretary: Mr A Ryland   Tel: 733995 (0352)
Location: 1 mile south of Flint on A55.
Description: Undulating, wooded parkland with streams, 2 ponds and narrow fairways. 9 holes played off 18 tees.
9 holes, 5,819 yards, Par 69, S.S.S. 69, Course record 65.
Membership: 250
Visitors: Welcome. With members only at weekends. Wednesdays Ladies Day.
Green Fees: £10 per round.
Facilities: Lunch. Dinner. Bar Snacks. Full Catering. Changing Room.
Class One Hotel: Springfield, Pentre Halkyn, 1 1/2 mile(s). Tel: 780503 (0352)

HAWARDEN
Hawarden Golf Club, Groomsdale Lane, Hawarden, Deeside, Clwyd. CH5 3EH. Tel: 591447 (0244)
Secretary: T Hinks-Edwards   Tel: 531447 (0244)
Location: 10 miles west of Chester off A55.

Description: Undulating parkland.
9 holes, 5,630 yards, Par 68, S.S.S. 67, Course record 64.
Visitors: Welcome. Handicap certificate required. Letter of Introduction required. By appointment only.
Green Fees: £15.
Facilities: Lunch. Dinner. Bar Snacks. Full Catering. Changing Room. Golf Shop.
Class One Hotel: St David Park, Ewloe, 2 mile(s). Tel: 520800 (0244)

HOLYWELL
Holywell Golf Club, Brynford, Near Holywell, Clwyd. CH8 8LQ. Tel: 710040 (0352)
Secretary: E K Carney   Tel: 710040 (0352)
Professional: Martin Carty   Tel: 710040 (0352)
Description: Reasonably level on natural terrain, with bracken and gorse flanking the fairways.
18 holes, 6,005 yards, Par 70, S.S.S. 70, Course record 70.
Visitors: Welcome. Handicap certificate required. Parties by prior arrangement with the secretary. No visitors on competition days.
Green Fees: Weekdays £10, weekends and Bank Holidays £15.
Facilities: Lunch. Dinner. Bar Snacks. Full Catering. Changing Room. Golf Shop.
Class One Hotel: Stamford Gate Hotel, Holywell, 2 mile(s). Tel: 712942 (0352)
Class Two Hotel: Springfield, Halkyn, 2 mile(s). Tel: 780503 (0352)

LLANGOLLEN
Vale of Llangollen Golf Club Ltd., The Clubhouse, Llangollen, Clwyd.
Secretary: T F Ellis   Tel: 860040 (0978)
Professional: D I Vaughan   Tel: 860040 (0978)
Location: 1 1/4 miles east of LLangollen on A5.
18 holes, 6,661 yards, Par 72, S.S.S. 72.
Visitors: Welcome. Not on competition days. Telephone in advance.
Green Fees: Weekdays £18, weekends and Bank Holidays £23.
Facilities: Lunch. Dinner. Bar Snacks. Full Catering. Changing Room. Golf Shop. Club Hire. Trolley Hire. Buggy Hire.

MOLD
Mold Golf Club, Cilcain Road, Pantymwyn, Mold, Clwyd. CH7 5EH. Tel: 740318 (0352)
Secretary: Mr A Newall   Tel: 741513 (0352)
Professional: Mr M Carty   Tel: 740318 (0352)
Location: 3 miles north west of Mold on the Pantymwyn Road. Well signposted.
Description: Undulating, open parkland with magnificent views of the River Dee, Clwyd Mountain range and the Cheshire Plain.
18 holes, 5,521 yards, Par 67, S.S.S. 67, Course record 64.
Membership: 700
Visitors: Welcome. Weekends subject to availability.
Green Fees: Weekdays £15 per day, weekends and Bank Holidays £20 per day.
Facilities: Lunch. Dinner. Bar Snacks. Full Catering. Changing Room. Golf Shop. Club Hire. Trolley Hire.

Class One Hotel: Chequers, Northop, 3 mile(s). Tel: 816181 (0244)
Class Two Hotel: Brynawel Hotel, Mold, 3 mile(s). Tel: 758622 (0352)

MOLD

Padeswood and Buckley Golf Club, The Caia, Station Lane, Padeswood, Mold, Clwyd. CH7 4JD. Tel: 543636 (0244)
Secretary: Mr Peters	Tel: 550537 (0244)
Professional: Mr Ashton	Tel: 543636 (0244)
Location: 1 1/2 miles south of Buckley on A549.
Description: Open parkland with the River Alyn running through the course, many ditches, 60 bunkers and 3 lakes.
18 holes, 5,581 yards, Par 68, S.S.S. 66, Course record 66. Membership: 650
Visitors: Welcome. Letter of Introduction required. With members only at weekends.
Green Fees: £16.50 per round, £19 per day.
Facilities: Lunch. Dinner. Bar Snacks. Full Catering. Changing Room. Golf Shop. Club Hire. Trolley Hire.
Class One Hotel: St Davids Park Hotel, Ewloe, 3 mile(s). Tel: 520800 (0244)

MOLD

Old Padeswood Golf Club Ltd., Station Road, Padeswood, Mold, Clwyd. CH7 4JL. Tel: 547401 (0244)
Secretary: Mr B Hellen	Tel: 770506 (0352)
Professional: Mr T Davies	Tel: 547401 (0244)
Location: 3 miles south east of Mold on A5118 Chester to Mold Road.
Description: Gently undulating meadowland with 2 holes bordered by the River Alyn.
18 holes, 6,668 yards, Par 72, S.S.S. 72, Course record 66. Membership: 750
Visitors: Welcome. With members only at weekends.
Green Fees: Weekdays £12 per round, £20 per day. Weekends £20 per round.
Facilities: Lunch. Dinner. Bar Snacks. Full Catering. Changing Room. Golf Shop. Trolley Hire.

PRESTATYN

Prestatyn Golf Club, Marine Road East, Prestatyn, Clwyd. LL19 7HS. Tel: 854320 (0745)
Secretary: Roy Woodruff	Tel: 888353 (0745)
Professional: M Staton	Tel: 854320 (0745)
Location: A584 on approaching Prestatyn from Chester turn right at sign for Pontins Holiday Village and follow sign.
Description: Seaside links championship course.
18 holes, 6,792 yards, Par 72, S.S.S. 73, Course record 68. Membership: 650
Visitors: Welcome. Handicap certificate required. Not Tuesdays (Ladies day) or Saturdays, other weekdays and Sundays if Bona Fide member of a golf club. Society visits by arrangement.
Green Fees: Weekdays £16, weekends and Bank Holidays £20.
Facilities: Lunch. Dinner. Bar Snacks. Full Catering. Changing Room. Golf Shop. Club Hire. Trolley Hire.
Class One Hotel: Nant Hall, Prestatyn, 1/2 mile(s). Tel: 853901 (0745)

RHUDDLAN

Rhuddlan Golf Club, Meliden Road, Rhuddlan, Clwyd. LL18 6LB. Tel: 590217 (0745)
Secretary: Mr D Morris	Tel: 590217 (0745)
Professional: Mr Ian Worsley	Tel: 590898 (0745)
Location: 3 miles from St Asaph, A55, on roundabout top of Rhuddland High Street.
Description: Gently undulating parkland with fine views of Clwydian Hills, well bunkered with natural hazards.
White 18 holes, 6,487 yards, Par 71, S.S.S. 71, Course record 69.
Yellow 18 holes, 6,267 yards, Par 70, S.S.S. 70.
Visitors: Welcome. Handicap certificate required. Societies weekdays only. With members only on Sundays.
Green Fees: Weekdays £18 per day, weekends and Bank Holidays £25 per day.
Facilities: Lunch. Dinner. Bar Snacks. Full Catering. Changing Room. Golf Shop. Club Hire. Trolley Hire.
Class One Hotel: Talardy Park, St Asaph, 3 mile(s). Tel: 584957 (0745)
Class Two Hotel: Grange, Rhyl, 3 mile(s). Tel: 353174 (0745)

RHYL

Rhyl Golf Club, Coast Road, Rhyl, Clwyd. LL18 3RE. Tel: 353171 (0745)
Secretary: W Wilson	Tel: 353171 (0745)
Professional: M Carty
Description: Seaside links.
9 holes, 6,185 yards, Par 70, S.S.S. 69, Course record 65. Membership: 331
Visitors: Welcome. Handicap certificate required. Not Thursday afternoons or Saturday and Sunday competition days.
Green Fees: Weekdays £12, weekends and Bank Holidays £15.
Facilities: Lunch. Dinner. Bar Snacks. Full Catering. Changing Room. Golf Shop. Club Hire. Trolley Hire.
Class Two Hotel: Grange, Rhyl, 1 1/2 mile(s). Tel: 353174 (0745)

DYFED

AMMANFORD

Glynhir Golf Club, Glynhir Road, Llandybie, Ammanford, Dyfed. SA18 2NP. Tel: 850472 (0269)
Secretary: E P Rees	Tel: 851365 (0269)
Professional: Ian Roberts	Tel: 851010 (0269)
Location: 7 miles from the end of the M4, between Ammanford and Landybie on A483, turn right up Glynhir Road and proceed for about 2 miles.
Description: Undulating woodland/parkland course.
18 holes, 5,952 yards, Par 69, S.S.S. 69, Course record 66. Membership: 700
Visitors: Welcome. Handicap certificate required. Not Sundays. Societies by prior arrangement with the Secretary.
Green Fees: Summer weekdays £15, Saturdays and Bank Holidays £20.

Facilities: Lunch. Dinner. Bar Snacks. Full Catering. Changing Room. Golf Shop. Trolley Hire.
Class Two Hotel: The Mill At Glynhir, On course, Tel: 850672 (0269)

BORTH
Borth and Ynyslas Golf Club, Borth, Dyfed. SY24 5JS.
Tel: 871202 (0970)
Secretary: Ron Williams   Tel: 871325 (0970)
Professional: J G Lewis   Tel: 871557 (0970)
Description: Beautiful links course Oldest golf course in Wales. In the middle of Cardigan Bay. A very good test of golf.
18 holes, 6,110 yards, Par 70, S.S.S. 70, Course record 69.
Membership: 450
Visitors: Welcome. Handicap certificate required.
Green Fees: Weekdays £15, weekends, Bank Holidays and whole of August £20. 20% concession to visiting parties who book in advance.
Facilities: Lunch. Dinner. Bar Snacks. Full Catering. Changing Room. Golf Shop. Club Hire. Trolley Hire. Buggy Hire.
Class One Hotel: Cliff Haven, Borth, 1 mile(s). Tel: 871659 (0970)
Class Two Hotel: Railway, Borth, 3/4 mile(s). Tel: 871348 (0970)

CARMARTHEN
Carmarthen Golf Club, Blaenycoed Road, Carmarthen, Dyfed. SA33 6EH. Tel: 87214 (0267)
Secretary: Jonathan Coe   Tel: 87588 (0267)
Professional: Pat Gillis   Tel: 89493 (0267)
Location: 4 miles north-west of Carmarthen.
Description: Undulating parkland.
18 holes, 6,210 yards, Par 71, S.S.S. 71, Course record 68.
Membership: 700
Visitors: Welcome. Handicap certificate required. Tuesday is Ladies day.
Green Fees: On application.
Facilities: Lunch. Dinner. Bar Snacks. Full Catering. Changing Room. Golf Shop. Club Hire. Trolley Hire.
Class One Hotel: Royal Ivy Bush, Carmarthen, 5 mile(s). Tel: 235111 (0267)
Class Two Hotel: Falcon, Carmarthen, 4 mile(s). Tel: 234959 (0267)

HAVERFORDWEST
Haverfordwest Golf Club, Arnolds Down, Haverfordwest, Dyfed. SA61 2XQ. Tel: 763565 (0437)
Secretary: M A Harding   Tel: 764523 (0437)
Professional: A J Pile   Tel: 768409 (0437)
Location: Situated on main A40 trunk road, approx 1 mile east of town.
Description: Fairly flat parkland course with beautiful views over the Preseli Mountains.
18 holes, 6,005 yards, Par 70, S.S.S. 69, Course record 72.
Membership: 700
Visitors: Welcome. Handicap certificate required. Not after 4 p.m.. Full catering by arrangement.
Green Fees: Weekdays £14, weekends £20.
Facilities: Lunch. Dinner. Bar Snacks. Changing Room.

Golf Shop. Club Hire. Trolley Hire. Buggy Hire.
Class One Hotel: Hotel Mariners, Haverfordwest, 1 mile(s). Tel: 763353 (0437)
Class Two Hotel: Normandie, Haverfordwest, 1 mile(s). Tel: 762337 (0437)

LAMPETER
Cilgwyn Golf Club, Llangybi, Lampeter, Dyfed. SA48 8NN. Tel: 45286 (0570)
Secretary: Mr L B Evans   Tel: 422793 (0570)
Location: 4 1/2 miles south of Lampeter on A470.
Description: Open, undulating parkland with 3 lakes and a stream. Views of the Tregaron Hills.
9 holes, 5,327 yards, Par 68, S.S.S. 67, Course record 67.
Membership: 300
Visitors: Welcome. Advisable to book 10 days in advance for play at weekends. Wednesdays Ladies Day.
Green Fees: Weekdays £8 per day, weekends and Bank Holidays £10 per round.
Facilities: Bar Snacks. Full Catering. Changing Room. Golf Shop. Club Hire. Trolley Hire.
Class One Hotel: Black Lion Royal, Lampeter, 4 1/2 mile(s). Tel: 422172 (0570)

LLANELLI
Ashburnham Golf Club, Cliffe Terrace, Bury Port, Llanelli, Dyfed. SA16 0TH. Tel: 2269 (05546)
Secretary: D M Llewellyn   Tel: 2269 (05546)
Professional: R A Ryder   Tel: 3846 (05546)
Description: Championship links.
18 holes, 6,627 yards, Par 72, S.S.S. 72.
Membership: 800
Visitors: Welcome. Handicap certificate required. Not weekends.
Green Fees: £20 per round, £25 per day.
Facilities: Lunch. Dinner. Bar Snacks. Full Catering. Changing Room. Golf Shop. Trolley Hire.
Class Two Hotel: George Inn, Bury Port, 1 mile(s). Tel: 2211 (05546)

MILFORD HAVEN
Milford Haven Golf Club, Woodbine, Clay Lane, Milford Haven, Dyfed. . Tel: 692368 (0646)
Secretary: D G Britton   Tel: 697660 (0646)
Location: 1 mile west of town.
Description: Undulating parkland course, some fine waterside views.
18 holes, 6,030 yards, Par 71, S.S.S. 70, Course record 66.
Membership: 350
Visitors: Welcome. Check at weekends for start times. No catering Tuesdays.
Green Fees: Weekdays £12, weekends £15 (with members 50% discount at all times).
Facilities: Lunch. Dinner. Bar Snacks. Full Catering. Changing Room. Golf Shop. Club Hire. Trolley Hire.
Class One Hotel: Lord Nelson, Milford Haven, 2 mile(s). Tel: 695341 (0646)
Class Two Hotel: Sir Benfro Country Hotel, Milford Haven, 1 1/4 mile(s). Tel: 694242 (0646)

NEWPORT

Newport (Pembs) Golf Club, The Golf Club, Newport, Dyfed. SA42 0NR. Tel: 820244 (0239)
Secretary: Ron Dietrich   Tel: 820244 (0239)
Professional: Colin Parsons   Tel: 615359 (0239)
Location: 2 miles north of A487 Fishguard to Cardigan Road.
Description: Flat links course with superb scenery.
Gents 9 holes, 5,815 yards, Par 70, S.S.S. 68, Course record 68.
Ladies 9 holes, 4,938 yards, Par 72, S.S.S. 69, Course record 71.
Membership: 200
Visitors: Welcome.
Green Fees: £10 per day.
Facilities: Lunch. Dinner. Bar Snacks. Full Catering. Changing Room. Golf Shop. Club Hire. Trolley Hire.
Class One Hotel: Fishguard Bay Hotel, Fishguard, 8 mile(s). Tel: 873571 (0348)
Class Two Hotel: Golden Lion, Newport, 2 1/2 mile(s). Tel: 820321 (0239)

TENBY

Tenby Golf Club, The Burrows, Tenby, Dyfed. SA70 7NP. Tel: 2978 (0834)
Secretary: T R Arnold   Tel: 2978 (0834)
Professional: T Mountford   Tel: 4447 (0834)
Location: Between railway line and South Beach.
Description: Links.
Medal 18 holes, 6,232 yards, Par 69, S.S.S. 71.
Blue 18 holes, 5,634 yards, Par 69, S.S.S. 69.
Membership: 700
Visitors: Welcome. Handicap certificate required. Restricted during club competitions.
Green Fees: Weekdays £18, weekends and Bank Holidays £22.50.
Facilities: Lunch. Dinner. Bar Snacks. Full Catering. Changing Room. Golf Shop. Club Hire. Trolley Hire.
Class One Hotel: Kinloch Court, Tenby, 1/4 mile(s). Tel: 2777 (0834)
Class Two Hotel: Belgrave Hotel, Tenby, 1/4 mile(s). Tel: 2377 (0834)

MID GLAMORGAN

ABERDARE

Aberdare Golf Club, Abernant, Aberdare, Mid Glam. CF44 0RY. Tel: 871188 (0685)
Secretary: L Adler   Tel: 872797 (0685)
Professional: A Palmer   Tel: 878735 (0685)
Description: Mountain course with parkland features with view over Cynon Valley.
18 holes, 5,845 yards, Par 69, S.S.S. 69, Course record 63.
Membership: 550
Visitors: Welcome. Handicap certificate required. With members only on Saturdays. Sunday by arrangement with Secretary.
Green Fees: Weekdays £14, £8 with member. Weekends and Bank Holidays £18, £10 with member.
Facilities: Lunch. Dinner. Bar Snacks. Full Catering. Changing Room. Golf Shop. Trolley Hire.
Class One Hotel: Baverstock, Merthyr, 4 mile(s). Tel: 6221 (0685)
Class Two Hotel: Ty Andrew, Aberdare, 1 mile(s). Tel: 876603 (0685)

BARGOED

Bargoed Golf Club, Heolddu, Bargoed, Mid Glam. CF8 9GF. Tel: 830143 (0443)
Secretary: W Coleman   Tel: 822377 (0443)
Location: A469 Cardiff-Bargoed, 1/2 mile from Bargoed town centre.
Description: Mountain top course majority of which is on a level plain.
18 holes, 6,017 yards, Par 69, S.S.S. 69, Course record 65.
Membership: 479
Visitors: Welcome. Handicap certificate required. With members only at weekends.
Green Fees: £13, £8 with member.
Facilities: Lunch. Dinner. Bar Snacks. Full Catering. Changing Room.
Class One Hotel: Parc Hotel, Bargoed, 1/2 mile(s). Tel: 839828 (0443)

BRIDGEND

Southerndown Golf Club, Ewenny, Near Bridgend, Mid Glam. CF35 5BT. Tel: 880476 (0656)
Secretary: Mr K R Wilcox   Tel: 880476 (0656)
Professional: D McMonagle   Tel: 880326 (0656)
Location: Opposite Ogmore Castle ruins, 4 miles from Bridgend.
Description: Typical downland course with gorse, heather and firns. A championship course overlooking the Bristol Channel.
18 holes, 6,613 yards, Par 70, S.S.S. 73.
Membership: 700
Visitors: Welcome. Handicap certificate required. With members only on Sundays October to March.
Green Fees: Weekdays £24, weekends £30.
Facilities: Lunch. Dinner. Bar Snacks. Full Catering. Changing Room. Golf Shop. Trolley Hire.
Class One Hotel: The Heronston, Bridgend, 2 mile(s). Tel: 668811 (0656)
Class Two Hotel: Sea Lawn, Ogmore By Sea, 2 mile(s). Tel: 880311 (0656)

CAERPHILLY

Caerphilly Golf Club, Pencapel, Mountain Road, Caerphilly, Mid Glam. CF8 1HL. Tel: 863441 (0222)
Secretary: H M Matthews   Tel: 863441 (0222)
Location: 7 miles north of Cardiff on A469, 250 yards from rail and bus stations.
Description: Typical mountain course undulating 14 holes numbers 1, 3, 4 and 5 played twice.
18 holes, 6,028 yards, Par 73, S.S.S. 71, Course record 67.
Membership: 792
Visitors: Welcome. Handicap certificate required. Letter of Introduction required. No visitors at weekends or Bank Holidays unless playing with a member.
Green Fees: £16 per day, £10 with member.

Facilities: Lunch. Bar Snacks. Changing Room. Golf Shop.
Class One Hotel: Angel, Cardiff, 8 mile(s). Tel: 232633 (0222)

DOWLAIS
Morlais Castle Golf Club, Pant, Dowlais, Merthyr Tydfil, Mid Glam. CF48 2UY. Tel: 722822 (0685)
Secretary: J N Powell   Tel: 622822 (0685)
Location: Near Heads of Valley Road, Dowlais roundabout, follow direction signs for Brecon Mountian Railway.
Description: Very pleasant moorland course with outstanding views.
18 holes, 6,320 yards, Par 71, S.S.S. 71.
Membership: 450
Visitors: Welcome. Not Saturday afternoons and Sunday mornings. Society meetings contact Secretary. Some catering restrictions apply, please telephone in advance.
Green Fees: Weekdays £16 per day, weekends £20 per day.
Facilities: Lunch. Dinner. Bar Snacks. Changing Room.
Class Two Hotel: Tregenna Hotel, Merthyr Tydfil, 3 mile(s). Tel: 723627 (0685)

HENGOED
Bryn Meadows Golf & Country Club, The Bryn, Near Hengoed, Mid Glam. CF8 7SM. Tel: 225590 (0495)
Secretary: Mr B Mayo   Tel: 225590 (0495)
Professional: Mr Bruce Hunter   Tel: 221905 (0495)
Location: 1 mile south west of Blackwood on Ystrad Mynach Road.
Description: Undulating parkland with ditches surrounded by scenic views.
18 holes, 6,132 yards, Par 72, S.S.S. 69, Course record 69.
Membership: 450
Visitors: Welcome.
Green Fees: Weekdays £16 per day, weekends £20 per day.
Facilities: Lunch. Dinner. Bar Snacks. Full Catering. Changing Room. Golf Shop. Club Hire. Trolley Hire. Buggy Hire.
Class One Hotel: Bryn Meadows Country Club, On Course, Tel: 225590 (0495)

KENFIG
Pyle and Kenfig Golf Club, Waun-y-Mer, Kenfig, Mid Glam. CF33 4PU. Tel: 783093 (0656)
Secretary: R C.Thomas   Tel: 783093 (0656)
Professional: R Evans   Tel: 772446 (0656)
Location: 1 mile off junc 37 M4, 3 miles from Porthcawl.
Description: Seaside links.
18 holes, 6,650 yards, Par 71, S.S.S. 73, Course record 68.
Membership: 1100
Visitors: Welcome. Handicap certificate required. Letter of Introduction required.With members only at weekends.
Green Fees: £22 per round, £27 per day.
Facilities: Lunch. Dinner. Bar Snacks. Full Catering. Changing Room. Golf Shop. Trolley Hire.
Class One Hotel: Seabank, Porthcawl, 2 mile(s). Tel: 782261 (0656)
Class Two Hotel: Rose & Crown, Nottage, 1 mile(s). Tel: 784849 (0656)

LLANTRISANT
Llantrisant and Pontyclun Golf Club, Lanelay Road, Talbot Green, Llantrisant, Mid Glam. CF7 8HZ. Tel: 222148 (0443)
Secretary: Mr J Williams   Tel: 224601 (0443)
Professional: Mr N Watson   Tel: 228169 (0443)
Location: 8 miles west of Cardiff off M4 junc 34 to Llantrisant.
Description: 12 hole course with play from alternate tees. Undulating wooded parkland with beautiful scenery.
18 holes, 5,712 yards, Par 68, S.S.S. 68, Course record 65.
Membership: 600
Visitors: Welcome. Handicap certificate required. With members only at weekends.
Green Fees: £20 per day.
Facilities: Lunch. Bar Snacks. Full Catering. Changing Room. Golf Shop. Club Hire. Trolley Hire.
Class One Hotel: Miskin Manor, Miskin, 2 mile(s). Tel: 224204 (0443)

MAESTEG
Maesteg Golf Club, Mount Pleasant, Neath Road, Maesteg, Mid Glam. CF34 9PR. Tel: 732037 (0656)
Secretary: W H Hanford   Tel: 734106 (0656)
Professional: G Hughes   Tel: 735742 (0656)
Location: 1/2 mile out of Maesteg town centre on the Port Talbot Road (B4282).
Description: Reasonably flat hilltop course with scenic views of wooded hills and valleys down to Swansea Bay.
18 holes, 5,900 yards, Par 70, S.S.S. 69, Course record 69.
Membership: 700
Visitors: Welcome. Handicap certificate required. No societies at weekends and Bank Holiday weeks.
Green Fees: Weekdays £13.50, weekends £17.
Facilities: Lunch. Dinner. Bar Snacks. Full Catering. Changing Room. Golf Shop. Trolley Hire.
Class One Hotel: Court Coleman, Bridgend, 8 mile(s). Tel: 720212 (0656)
Class Two Hotel: Baglan Bay Hotel, Port Talbot, 8 mile(s). Tel: 813228 (0639)

MERTHYR TYDFIL
Merthyr Tydfil (Cilsanws) Golf Club, Cloth Hall Lane, Cefn Coed, Merthyr Tydfil, Mid Glam. CF48 2NU. Tel: 723308 (0685)
Secretary: Viv Price   Tel: 723308 (0685)
Location: 1/2 mile off A470 Merthyr to Bracon Road at Cefn Coed.
Description: Mountain top course in the Brecon Beacons National Park with panoramic views.
11 holes, 5,957 yards, Par 70, S.S.S. 69, Course record 66.
Membership: 180
Visitors: Welcome. Not Sunday afternoons.
Green Fees: Weekdays £10, weekends £12. Half fees with member.
Facilities: Dinner. Bar Snacks. Changing Room.
Class Two Hotel: Castle Hotel, Merthyr Tydfil, 2 mile(s). Tel: 722327 (0685)

MOUNTAIN ASH

Mountain Ash Golf Club, Cefn Pennar, Mountain Ash, Mid Glam. CF45 4DG. Tel: 472265 (0443)
Secretary: G Matthews　　　　　　Tel: 472265 (0443)
Professional: J Sim　　　　　　　Tel: 478770 (0443)
Description: Mountain course with panoramic views.
18 holes, 5,553 yards, Par 69, S.S.S. 68, Course record 65.
Membership: 500
Visitors: Welcome. Handicap certificate required. Letter of Introduction required. Weekends with members only.
Green Fees: £16.
Facilities: Lunch. Dinner. Bar Snacks. Full Catering. Changing Room. Golf Shop.
Class One Hotel: Baverstocks, Merthyr Tydfil, 6 mile(s). Tel: 6221 (0685)

PORTHCAWL

Royal Porthcawl Golf Club, Rest Bay, Porthcawl, Mid Glam. CF36 3UW. Tel: 782251 (0656)
Secretary: A Woolcott　　　　　　Tel: 782251 (0656)
Professional: Mr G Poor　　　　　Tel: 786984 (0656)
Location: 3 miles from M4 junc 37 follow signs for Porthcawl.
Description: Championship rated links.
18 holes, 6,691 yards, Par 72, S.S.S. 74, Course record 65.
Membership: 800
Visitors: Welcome. Handicap certificate required. With members only at weekends and Bank Holidays. Monday mornings Ladies only. Not Wednesdays between 12.30p.m. and 2.30p.m..
Green Fees: £30.
Facilities: Lunch. Dinner. Bar Snacks. Full Catering. Changing Room. Golf Shop. Club Hire. Trolley Hire.
Class One Hotel: Seabank, Porthcawl, 1 mile(s). Tel: 782261 (0656)
Class Two Hotel: Fairways, Porthcawl, 1 mile(s). Tel: 782085 (0656)

RHONDDA

Rhondda Golf Club, Golf House, Penrhys, Rhondda, Mid Glam. CF43 3PW. Tel: 441384 (0443)
Secretary: G Rees　　　　　　　Tel: 441384 (0443)
Professional: R Davies　　　　　Tel: 441385 (0443)
Description: Mountain course with fine views.
18 holes, 6,206 yards, Par 70, S.S.S. 70, Course record 67.
Membership: 700
Visitors: Welcome. Handicap certificate required. Weekends by prior arrangement.
Green Fees: Weekdays £15, with members £10. Weekends £20, with members £15.
Facilities: Lunch. Dinner. Bar Snacks. Full Catering. Changing Room. Golf Shop. Trolley Hire.

SOUTH GLAMORGAN

BARRY

Brynhill Golf Club, Port Road, Barry, S Glam. CF6 7PN. Tel: 720277 (0446)
Secretary: K Atkinson　　　　　Tel: 720277 (0446)
Professional: P Fountain　　　　Tel: 733660 (0446)
Location: Barry is approx 7 miles from M4 and 8 miles from Cardiff.
Description: Undulating meadowland course, some interesting par 3 and demanding par 4 and 5 holes.
18 holes, 6.077 yards, Par 71, S.S.S. 68.
Membership: 1000
Visitors: Welcome. Handicap certificate required.
Green Fees: £17 per day.
Facilities: Lunch. Dinner. Bar Snacks. Full Catering. Changing Room. Golf Shop. Club Hire. Trolley Hire.
Class One Hotel: Copthornes, Cardiff, 4 mile(s). Tel: 599100 (0222)
Class Two Hotel: Mountsorrel, Barry, 2 mile(s). Tel: 740069 (0446)

CARDIFF

Cardiff Golf Club, Cyncoed, Cardiff, S Glam. CF2 6SJ. Tel: 753067 (0222)
Secretary: Mr K Lloyd　　　　　Tel: 754772 (0222)
Professional: Mr T Hanson　　　Tel: 754772 (0222)
Location: 2 miles north east of Cardiff on the Cyncoed Road.
Description: Open parkland both flat and undulating with a stream running through the course.
18 holes, 6,013 yards, Par 70, S.S.S. 70, Course record 66.
Membership: 950
Visitors: Welcome. Handicap certificate required. With members only at weekends. Tuesdays Ladies Day.
Green Fees: £25 per round.
Facilities: Lunch. Dinner. Bar Snacks. Full Catering. Changing Room. Golf Shop. Trolley Hire.
Class One Hotel: Cardiff Moat House, Cardiff, 2 mile(s). Tel: 732520 (0222)
Class Two Hotel: Cedars, Cardiff, 1/2 mile(s). Tel: 764616 (0222)

CARDIFF

Llanishen Golf Club, Cwm, Lisvane, Cardiff, S Glam. CF4 5UD. Tel: 752205 (0222)
Secretary: Mr E Davies　　　　Tel: 755078 (0222)
Professional: Mr R A Jones　　 Tel: 755076 (0222)
Location: 5 miles north of Cardiff on Caerphilly Mountain.
Description: The oldest club in Cardiff. Spectacular views of the city and the Bristol Channel.
18 holes, 5,296 yards, Par 68, S.S.S. 66, Course record 64.
Membership: 900
Visitors: Welcome. Handicap certificate required. With members only at weekends. Wednesdays Ladies Day.
Green Fees: £20 per day.
Facilities: Lunch. Dinner. Bar Snacks. Full Catering. Changing Room. Golf Shop. Trolley Hire.
Class One Hotel: Phoenix, Cardiff, 1 mile(s). Tel: 764615 (0222)

CARDIFF

Wenvoe Castle Golf Club Ltd., Wenvoe, Cardiff, S Glam. CF5 6BE. Tel: 591094 (0222)
Secretary: Mr E J Dew　　　　Tel: 594371 (0222)
Professional: Mr Wyer　　　　 Tel: 593649 (0222)
Location: 2 miles west of Cardiff on A4050.

Description: Flat and undulating parkland.
18 holes, 6,422 yards, Par 72, S.S.S. 71, Course record 68.
Membership: 700
Visitors: Welcome. Handicap certificate required. Letter of Introduction required. With members only at weekends.
Green Fees: £20 per day.
Facilities: Lunch. Dinner. Bar Snacks. Full Catering. Changing Room. Golf Shop. Club Hire. Trolley Hire.

CARDIFF

Whitchurch (Cardiff) Golf Club, Pantmawr Road, Whitchurch, Cardiff, S Glam. CF4 6XD. Tel: 620125 (0222)
Secretary: Mr Bartlett   Tel: 620985 (0222)
Professional: Mr Clark   Tel: 614660 (0222)
Location: 4 miles north of Cardiff on A470 Merthyr Road.
Description: Championship course, tree lined undulating parkland.
18 holes, 6,319 yards, Par 71, S.S.S. 70, Course record 62.
Membership: 990
Visitors: Welcome. Handicap certificate required. Weekends subject to availability.
Green Fees: Weekdays £21 per day, weekends £26 per day.
Facilities: Lunch. Dinner. Bar Snacks. Full Catering. Changing Room. Golf Shop. Club Hire. Trolley Hire.
Class One Hotel: Masons Arms, Whitchurch, 1/2 mile(s). Tel: 692554 (0222)

PENARTH

Glamorganshire Golf Club, Lavernock Road, Penarth, S Glam. CF6 2UP. Tel: 707048 (0222)
Secretary: G C Crimp   Tel: 701185 (0222)
Professional: Mr A Kerr Smith   Tel: 707401 (0222)
Location: 1 mile west of Penarth on A4232 off M4 junc 33.
Description: Parkland with a stream. Spectacular views overlooking the Bristol Channel. Founded circa 1890.
18 holes, 6,150 yards, Par 70, S.S.S. 70, Course record 65.
Membership: 1020
Visitors: Welcome. Handicap certificate required. Weekends subject to availability.
Green Fees: Weekdays £22 per day, weekends and Bank Holidays £28 per day.
Facilities: Lunch. Dinner. Bar Snacks. Full Catering. Changing Room. Golf Shop. Club Hire. Driving Range. Trolley Hire.
Class One Hotel: Walton House Hotel, Penarth, 1/2 mile(s). Tel: 707782 (0222)
Class Two Hotel: The Glendale, Penarth, 1 mile(s). Tel: 709269 (0222)

WEST GLAMORGAN

GLYNNEATH

Glynneath Golf Club, Pennycraig, Pontneathvaughan, Near Glynneath, W Glam. SA11 5UG. Tel: 720452 (0639)
Secretary: R M Ellis   Tel: 720679 (0639)
Location: Turn off A465 trunk road to Glynneath, turn right at traffic lights onto B4242 for Portneathvaughan.
Description: Fairly flat, situated in Brecon National Park overlooking the vale of Neath. Attractive well kept course.

18 holes, 5,576 yards, Par 68, S.S.S. 67, Course record 66.
Membership: 560
Visitors: Welcome. Handicap certificate required. Every day. Societies Monday to Friday.
Green Fees: Weekdays £10 per day, weekends £16 per day.
Facilities: Bar Snacks. Changing Room. Golf Shop.

SWANSEA

Clyne Golf Club, 120 Owls Lodge Lane, Mayals, Swansea, W Glam. SA3 5DP. Tel: 401989 (0792)
Secretary: Brian R Player   Tel: 401989 (0792)
Professional: Mark Bevan   Tel: 402094 (0792)
Location:
Description: Moorland.
18 holes, 6,323 yards, Par 70, S.S.S. 71, Course record 64.
Membership: 950
Visitors: Welcome. Handicap certificate required.
Green Fees: Weekdays £18 per day, weekends £24 per day.
Facilities: Lunch. Dinner. Bar Snacks. Full Catering. Changing Room. Golf Shop. Trolley Hire.
Class One Hotel: Osborne, Mumbles, 3 mile(s). Tel: 366274 (0792)
Class Two Hotel: Parkway, Sketty, 4 mile(s). Tel: 201632 (0792)

SWANSEA

Langland Bay Golf Club, Langland Bay, Swansea, W Glam. SA3 4QR. Tel: 366023 (0792)
Secretary: Mr J Jenkins   Tel: 361721 (0792)
Professional: Mr T Lynch   Tel: 366186 (0792)
Location: 5 miles west of Swansea on the Mumbles Road.
Description: Undulating parkland with a lake and 80 bunkers. On the Gower coast, panoramic views of Ilfracombe, Swansea Bay and the Bristol Channel.
18 holes, 5,834 yards, Par 71, S.S.S. 69, Course record 62.
Membership: 700
Visitors: Welcome. Handicap certificate required. Not before 9.30a.m. and not between 1p.m. and 2p.m..
Green Fees: Weekdays £24 per day, weekends £26 per day.
Facilities: Lunch. Dinner. Bar Snacks. Full Catering. Changing Room. Golf Shop. Trolley Hire.
Class One Hotel: Langland Court, Langland Bay, 1/2 mile(s). Tel: 361545 (0792)

SWANSEA

Morriston Golf Club, 160 Class emont Road, Morriston, Swansea, W Glam. .
Secretary: W A Jefford   Tel: 796528 (0792)
Professional: Deryl Rees   Tel: 772335 (0792)
Description: Parkland.
18 holes, 5,581 yards, Par 68, S.S.S. 68, Course record 65.
Membership: 500
Visitors: Welcome. Handicap certificate required. Some catering restrictions apply.
Green Fees: Weekdays £18, with a member £12. Weekends and Bank Holidays £25, with a member £16.
Facilities: Lunch. Bar Snacks. Changing Room. Golf Shop. Club Hire. Trolley Hire.

Class One Hotel: Hilton, Swansea, 1 1/2 mile(s). Tel: 310330 (0792)
Class Two Hotel: Fforest Motel, Swansea, 1 1/2 mile(s). Tel: 588711 (0792)

SWANSEA

Palleg Golf Club, Lower Cwmtwrch, Swansea, W Glam. Tel: 842193 (0639)
Secretary: D W Moses   Tel: 862303 (0792)
Location: 15 miles from Swansea, 1 mile from A4067 Swansea to Brecon Road.
Description: Heathland course with panoramic views of the Black Mountains.
18 holes, 3,209 yards, Par 72.
Membership: 300
Visitors: Welcome. Not Saturdays in Summer, not Sunday mornings in Winter.
Green Fees: 18 holes weekdays £9, weekends and Bank Holidays £12.
Facilities: Bar Snacks. Changing Room.

SWANSEA

Pennard Golf Club, 2 Southgate Road, Southgate, Swansea, W Glam. SA3 2BT. Tel: 3131 (044128)
Secretary: J D Eccles   Tel: 3131 (044128)
Professional: M V Bennett   Tel: 3451 (044128)
Location: 8 miles south west of Swansea between A4067 and B4436.
Description: Cliff top links with undulating fairways. Magnificent views across the Bristol Channel.
18 holes, 6,289 yards, Par 71, S.S.S. 71, Course record 66.
Membership: 600
Visitors: Welcome. Handicap certificate required. No Societies weekends or Bank Holidays. Lunch and Dinner by prior arrangement only.
Green Fees: Weekdays £16, £12 with a member. Weekends and Bank Holidays £20, £15 with a member.
Facilities: Bar Snacks. Full Catering. Changing Room. Golf Shop. Club Hire. Trolley Hire.
Class One Hotel: Osborne, Langland, 5 mile(s). Tel: 366274 (0792)
Class Two Hotel: Winston Private Hotel, Bishopston, 2 mile(s). Tel: 2074 (044128)

GWENT

CHEPSTOW

St Pierre Hotel & Golf Club, St Pierre Park, Chepstow, Gwent. NP6 6YA. Tel: 625261 (0291)
Secretary: T Cleary   Tel: 625261 (0291)
Professional: R Doig   Tel: 625261 (0291)
Location: M4 junc 22, follow signs for Chepstow and take A48 Hotel on left hand side.
Description: Old course - 18th approach crosses 11 acre lake covering one of the finest parkland courses in the UK.
Old 18 holes, 6,748 yards, Par 71, S.S.S. 73, Course record 64.
Mathern 18 holes, 5,732 yards, Par 68, S.S.S. 68.
Membership: 850
Visitors: Welcome. Handicap certificate required.

Green Fees: Old course - £20 to £45. Mathern - £15 to £25.
Facilities: Lunch. Dinner. Bar Snacks. Full Catering. Changing Room. Golf Shop. Club Hire. Trolley Hire. Buggy Hire. Caddies available.
Class One Hotel: St Pierre, On Course, Tel: 625261 (0291)

CWMBRAN

Greenmeadow Golf Club, Treherbert Road, Croesygelliog, Cwmbran, Gwent. NP44 2BZ. Tel: 869321 (0633)
Professional: Mr C Coomes   Tel: 862626 (0633)
Location: 1 mile from Cwmbran centre.
Description: Undulating parkland with 5 ponds. 14 holes played off alternate tees.
18 holes, 5,597 yards, Par 68, S.S.S. 68, Course record 67.
Membership: 450
Visitors: Welcome. Handicap certificate required. Weekends subject to availability.
Green Fees: Weekdays £12 per day.
Facilities: Lunch. Dinner. Bar Snacks. Full Catering. Changing Room. Golf Shop. Trolley Hire. Buggy Hire.

LLANWERN

Llanwern Golf Club, Tennyson Avenue, Llanwern, Gwent. NP6 2DY. Tel: 412380 (0633)
Secretary: Mr D J Peak   Tel: 412029 (0633)
Professional: Mrs S Price   Tel: 413233 (0633)
Location: 4 miles east of Newport, 1 mile from M4 junc 24 in Llanwern Village.
Description: Parkland.
New 18 holes, 6,115 yards, Par 70, S.S.S. 69.
Old 9 holes, 5,237 yards, Par 67, S.S.S. 67.
Membership: 852
Visitors: Welcome. Handicap certificate required. Tuesdays Ladies Day. With members at weekends.
Green Fees: £20 per day.
Facilities: Lunch. Dinner. Bar Snacks. Full Catering. Changing Room. Golf Shop.
Class One Hotel: Stakis Country Court, Newport, 1 mile(s). Tel: 413733 (0633)

MONMOUTH

Monmouth Golf Course, Leasbrook Lane, Monmouth, Gwent. . Tel: 712212 (0600)
Secretary: P C Harris   Tel: 712941 (0600)
Description: Undulating parkland. 9 holes, changing to 18 late Summer 1992.
Mens 18 holes, 5,523 yards, Par 68, S.S.S. 66, Course record 65.
Ladies 18 holes, 4,874 yards, Par 70, S.S.S. 69, Course record 71.
Membership: 450
Visitors: Welcome. With members only at weekends.
Green Fees: Weekdays £10, weekends and Bank Holidays £15.
Facilities: Lunch. Bar Snacks. Full Catering. Changing Room. Golf Shop. Trolley Hire.
Class One Hotel: Pilgrim, Much Birch, 1 Tel: 540742 (0981)

MONMOUTH
The Rolls of Monmouth Golf Club, The Hendre, Monmouth, Gwent. NP5 4HG. Tel: 715353 (0600)
Secretary: Mr J D Ross   Tel: 715353 (0600)
Location: 4 miles west of Monmouth on B4233 Monmouth/Abergavenny Road.
Description: Outstanding wooded, hilly parkland course with lakes and streams, all contained within a private estate in a superb countryside setting.
18 holes, 6,723 yards, Par 72, S.S.S. 72, Course record 68.
Visitors: Welcome.
Green Fees: Weekdays £25 per day, weekends and Bank Holidays £30 per day.
Facilities: Lunch. Dinner. Bar Snacks. Full Catering. Changing Room. Golf Shop. Club Hire. Trolley Hire. Buggy Hire.
Class One Hotel: The King's Head, Monmouth, 4 mile(s). Tel: 712177 (0600)
Class Two Hotel: The Riverside, Monmouth, 4 mile(s). Tel: 715577 (0600)

NANTYGLO
West Monmouthshire Golf Club, Pond Road, Nantyglo, Gwent. NP3 6XF. Tel: 310233 (0495)
Secretary: Mr Allan Offers   Tel: 303663 (0495)
Location: 1 1/2 miles south of Brynmawr on A467.
Description: Mountain heathland course. Highest tee in Wales - 14th, 1,450 feet above sea level. Scenic views of Brecon Beacons.
18 holes, 6,550 yards, Par 71, S.S.S. 69, Course record 66.
Membership: 700
Visitors: Welcome. Handicap certificate required.
Green Fees: Weekdays £10 per day, Saturdays £12 per day, Sundays £17 per day.
Facilities: Lunch. Dinner. Bar Snacks. Full Catering. Changing Room. Golf Shop. Trolley Hire.
Class One Hotel: The Angel, Abergavenny, 7 mile(s). Tel: 7121 (0873)
Class Two Hotel: The Queen's, Blaina, 3 mile(s). Tel: 290491 (0495)

NEWPORT
Newport Golf Club, Great Oak, Rogerstone, Newport, Gwent. NP1 9FX. Tel: 892683 (0633)
Secretary: Mr A D Jones   Tel: 892643 (0633)
Professional: Mr R F Skuse   Tel: 893271 (0633)
Location: 4 miles west of Newport town centre on B4591 1 mile from M4 junc 27.
Description: Flat parkland with a pond, ditches and many bunkers. Championship course 1,200 feet above sea level.
White 18 holes, 6,431 yards, Par 72, S.S.S. 71, Course record 65.
Yellow 18 holes, 6,190 yards, Par 72, S.S.S. 69.
Membership: 780
Visitors: Welcome. Handicap certificate required. Letter of Introduction required. With members only at weekends. Tuesdays Ladies Day.
Green Fees: Weekdays £30 per day, weekends and Bank Holidays £40 per day.
Facilities: Lunch. Dinner. Bar Snacks. Full Catering. Changing Room. Golf Shop. Trolley Hire.
Class One Hotel: Newport Lodge, Newport, 1 1/2 mile(s). Tel: 821818 (0633)
Class Two Hotel: The Harris Hotel, Newport, 2 mile(s). Tel: 214247 (0633)

NEWPORT
Tredegar Park Golf Club Ltd., Bassaleg Road, Newport, Gwent. NP9 3PX. Tel: 895219 (0633)
Secretary: Mr Howell   Tel: 894433 (0633)
Professional: Mr Morgan   Tel: 894517 (0633)
Location: 2 miles north west of Newport off M4 junc 28.
Description: Flat parkland with many bunkers. A fast stream and River Ebbw run through the course.
18 holes, 6,095 yards, Par 71, S.S.S. 70.
Membership: 800
Visitors: Welcome. Handicap certificate required. Subject to availability.
Green Fees: Weekdays £22 per day, weekends £27.50 per day.
Facilities: Lunch. Dinner. Bar Snacks. Full Catering. Changing Room. Golf Shop. Club Hire. Trolley Hire.

RHYMNEY
Tredegar and Rhymney Golf Club, Cwmtysswg, Rhymney, Gwent. NP2 3BQ. Tel: 840743 (0685)
Secretary: Viv Davies   Tel: 6096 (049525)
Location: Junc of A4048 and A465 Heads of the Valley Road.
Description: Mountain course with lovely views of the Rhymney Valley.
9 holes, 5,564 yards, Par 68, S.S.S. 68, Course record 67.
Membership: 200
Visitors: Welcome. Handicap certificate required.
Green Fees: Weekdays £10, weekends and Bank Holidays £12.50.
Facilities: Bar Snacks. Changing Room.
Class One Hotel: Castle, Merthyr Tydfil, 1 Tel: 722327 (0685)

GWYNEDD

ABERDOVEY
Aberdovey Golf Club, Aberdovey, Gwynedd. LL35 0RT. Tel: 767493 (0654)
Secretary: John Griffiths   Tel: 767493 (0654)
Professional: John Davies   Tel: 767602 (0654)
Location: On A493 west end of Aberdovey adjacent to the railway station.
Description: Championship links.
18 holes, 6,445 yards, Par 71, S.S.S. 71, Course record 67.
Membership: 800
Visitors: Welcome. Handicap certificate required. Reserved for members 8a.m. to 9.30a.m. and 12.30p.m. to 2.30p.m. daily and for Ladies Wednesdays a.m..
Green Fees: Weekdays from £14 per round, weekends £30 per day.
Facilities: Lunch. Dinner. Bar Snacks. Full Catering. Changing Room. Golf Shop. Trolley Hire. Buggy Hire. Caddies available.
Class One Hotel: Trefeddian, Aberdovey, 1/4 mile(s). Tel: 767213 (0654)

ABERSOCH

Abersoch Golf Club, Golf Road, Abersoch, Gwynedd. LL53 7EY. Tel: 812622 (0758)
Secretary: B Guest   Tel: 812622 (0758)
Location: In Village turn left to Beach.
Description: Partly parkland, mostly links along shoreside.
18 holes, 5,819 yards, Par 69, S.S.S. 68.
Membership: 632
Visitors: Welcome. Handicap certificate required. Must book in advance.
Green Fees: £15 any day.
Facilities: Lunch. Dinner. Bar Snacks. Full Catering. Changing Room. Golf Shop. Trolley Hire.

AMLWCH

Bull Bay Golf Club, Bull Bay, Amlwch, Anglesey, Gwynedd. LL68 9RY. Tel: 830213 (0407)
Secretary: Rennie Tickle   Tel: 830960 (0407)
Professional: Neil Dunroe   Tel: 831188 (0407)
Location: On A5025 1 mile outside Amlwch.
Description: Seaside links.
18 holes, 6,132 yards, Par 70, S.S.S. 70, Course record 66.
Membership: 800
Visitors: Welcome. Handicap certificate required. Limited numbers at weekends.
Green Fees: £15 per day, £20 Fridays and weekends.
Facilities: Lunch. Dinner. Bar Snacks. Full Catering. Changing Room. Golf Shop. Club Hire. Trolley Hire.
Class One Hotel: Trecastell, Bull Bay, 1/4 mile(s). Tel: 830651 (0407)
Class Two Hotel: Bull Bay Hotel, Bull Bay, 1 mile(s). Tel: 830223 (0407)

BALA

Bala (Penlan) Golf Club, Penlan, Bala, Gwynedd. LL23 7SR. Tel: 520359 (0678)
Secretary: Martin Wright   Tel: 520057 (0678)
Location: Turn right just outside Bala on main Dolgellau Road and follow signs to course, approx 1/2 mile south west of Bala.
Description: Upland course with views of Bala Lake and surrounding countryside.
10 holes, 4,970 yards, Par 66, S.S.S. 64, Course record 66.
Membership: 200
Visitors: Welcome. Some restrictions at weekends, advisable to telephone in advance. Catering by arrangement for groups only.
Green Fees: £10.
Facilities: Changing Room. Golf Shop. Club Hire.
Class One Hotel: White Lion Royal Hotel, Bala, 1 mile(s). Tel: 520314 (0678)

BEAUMARIS

Baron Hill Golf Club, Beaumaris, Anglesey, Gwynedd. Tel: 810231 (0248)
Secretary: A Pleming   Tel: 714646 (0248)
Location: Turn left on approach to Beaumaris from Menai Bridge on A545.
Description: Situated above Beaumaris, a testing 9 hole course with a fair sprinkling of gorse and heather.
9 holes, 5,519 yards, Par 68, S.S.S. 67, Course record 63.
Membership: 420
Visitors: Welcome. Handicap certificate required. Competitions most Sundays. Tee reserved for Ladies Tuesdays 10.30a.m. to 12.30p.m.. Clubhouse closed due to fire, please telephone for fa
Green Fees: £10, £5 with a member.
Class One Hotel: Bulkeley, Beaumaris, 1 mile(s). Tel: 810415 (0248)
Class Two Hotel: The Bishop's Gate, Beaumaris, 1 mile(s). Tel: 810302 (0248)

BETWS-Y-COED

Betws-Y-Coed Golf Club, Betws-Y-Coed, Gwynedd. LL24 0AL. Tel: 710556 (0690)
Secretary: G B Archer   Tel: 202 (06903)
Location: Turn north off A5 for 1/4 mile in Village centre.
Description: Flat parkland in picturesque setting between Afon Llugwy and Afon Conwy.
9 holes, 4,996 yards, Par 64, S.S.S. 64, Course record 63.
Membership: 350
Visitors: Welcome. Handicap certificate required. Advisable to check availability at weekends.
Green Fees: Weekdays £12.50, weekends £17.50.
Facilities: Lunch. Dinner. Bar Snacks. Full Catering. Changing Room. Trolley Hire.
Class One Hotel: Royal Oak, Betws-Y-Coed, 1/2 mile(s). Tel: 710219 (0690)
Class Two Hotel: Fairy Glen, Betws-Y-Coed, 1 1/2 mile(s). Tel: 710269 (0690)

CONWY

Conwy (Caernarvonshire) Golf Club, Morfa, Conwy, Gwynedd. LL32 8ER. Tel: 593400 (0492)
Secretary: E C Roberts   Tel: 592423 (0492)
Professional: P Lees   Tel: 593225 (0492)
Location: 1/2 mile west of Conwy off A55.
Description: Typical seaside course lying between Conwy Mountain and the sea. Founded in 1890, one of the oldest courses in Wales.
White 18 holes, 6,901 yards, Par 72, S.S.S. 73, Course record 69.
Yellow 18 holes, 6,458 yards, Par 72, S.S.S. 71.
Visitors: Welcome. Handicap certificate required. Restricted at weekends and competition days. Some catering restrictions apply, please telephone in advance.
Green Fees: Weekdays £18 per day, weekends and Bank Holidays £23 per day.
Facilities: Lunch. Dinner. Bar Snacks. Full Catering. Changing Room. Golf Shop. Club Hire. Trolley Hire.
Class One Hotel: Royal, Llandudno, 4 mile(s). Tel: 876084 (0492)
Class Two Hotel: Castle Bank, Conwy, 1 mile(s). Tel: 593888 (0492)

HARLECH
Royal St Davids Golf Club, Harlech, Gwynedd. LL46 2UB. Tel: 780203 (0766)
Secretary: R I Jones　　　　　　Tel: 780361 (0766)
Professional: John Barnett　　　Tel: 780857 (0766)
Location: A496 Lower Harlech to Barmouth Road.
Description: Seaside championship links course.
18 holes, 6,427 yards, Par 69, S.S.S. 71.
Visitors: Welcome. Handicap certificate required. Letter of Introduction required.
Green Fees: Weekdays £20 per day, weekends and Bank Holidays £25 per day.
Facilities: Lunch. Dinner. Bar Snacks. Full Catering. Changing Room. Golf Shop. Trolley Hire. Buggy Hire.
Class One Hotel: St David's, Harlech, 1/2 mile(s). Tel: 780366 (0766)
Class Two Hotel: Castle Cottage, Harlech, 1 mile(s). Tel: 780479 (0766)

LLANDUDNO
Rhos-on-Sea Golf Club, Penrhyn Bay, Llandudno, Gwynedd. LL30 3PU. Tel: 549100 (0492)
Secretary: Mr Graham J Robinson　　Tel: 544551 (0492)
Professional: Mr Mike Greenough　　Tel: 548115 (0492)
Location: A55 to Colwyn Bay. Follow signs to Rhos-on-Sea, 1 mile past on Coast Road in Penrhyn Bay.
Description: Flat seaside parkland course.
18 holes, 6,064 yards, S.S.S. 69.
Membership: 600
Visitors: Welcome.
Green Fees: Weekdays £15, weekends £20.
Facilities: Lunch. Dinner. Bar Snacks. Full Catering. Changing Room. Golf Shop. Club Hire.
Class Two Hotel: Dormy House, On Course, 0 mile(s). Tel: 549100 (0492)

LLANGEFNI
Llangefni Golf Course, Llangefni, Isle of Anglesey, Gwynedd. . Tel: 722193 (0248)
Professional: Mr P Lovell　　　　Tel: 722193 (0248)
Location: 500 yards from centre of Llangefni on B5111.
Description: Short parkland course with 11 bunkers, good for beginners and offering a test to the established golfer.
9 holes, 1,300 yards, Par 28.
Visitors: Welcome.
Green Fees: Weekdays £2 per round, weekends £3 per round.
Facilities: Changing Room. Golf Shop. Club Hire. Trolley Hire.
Class One Hotel: Plas Eithin Hotel, Menai Bridge, 5 mile(s). Tel: 713451 (0248)

NEFYN
Nefyn and District Golf Club, Morfa Nefyn, Pwllheli, Gwynedd. LL53 6DA. Tel: 720966 (0758)
Secretary: Lt Col R Parry　　　　Tel: 720966 (0758)
Professional: John Pilkington　　Tel: 720218 (0758)
Location: Lleyn Peninsula, 20 miles west of Caernarfon.
Description: 18 hole seaside course, with further 9 hole course under construction.
18 holes, 6,301 yards, Par 72, S.S.S. 71, Course record 67.

Membership: 800
Visitors: Welcome. Handicap certificate required. Advisable to check with Secretary or Professional.
Green Fees: Weekdays £16 per round, £20 per day. Weekends and Bank Holidays £22.50 per day.
Facilities: Lunch. Dinner. Bar Snacks. Full Catering. Changing Room. Golf Shop. Club Hire. Trolley Hire. Buggy Hire.

PENMAENMAWR
Penmaenmawr Golf Club, Conwy Old Road, Penmaenmawr, Gwynedd. LL34 6RD. Tel: 623330 (0492)
Secretary: Mrs J Dryhurst-Jones　　Tel: 623330 (0492)
Location: A55 express way to first Penmaenmawr turn-off, then second left, first right and first left.
Description: Parkland in a small valley with magnificent views of sea and mountains. 9 holes played off 18 tees.
9 holes, 5,306 yards, Par 67, S.S.S. 66, Course record 66.
Membership: 520
Visitors: Welcome. Not Saturdays or Bank Holidays.
Green Fees: Weekdays £12, Sundays £16.
Facilities: Bar Snacks. Changing Room.
Class One Hotel: Caerlyr Hall, Penmaenmawr, 1/8 mile(s). Tel: 623518 (0492)
Class Two Hotel: Split Willow, Llanfair Fechan, 4 mile(s). Tel: 680647 (0248)

PWLLHELI
Pwllheli Golf Club, Golf Road, Pwllheli, Gwynedd. LL53 5PS. Tel: 612520 (0758)
Secretary: Mr R E Williams　　　　Tel: 612520 (0758)
Professional: G D Verity　　　　　Tel: 612520 (0758)
Location: 20 miles south of Caernarfon on A499.
Description: Parkland and links, 2 lakes and streams, many bunkers. Panoramic views of Mountains and the sea.
18 holes, 6,091 yards, Par 69, S.S.S. 69, Course record 66.
Membership: 820
Visitors: Welcome. Subject to availability. Tuesdays Ladies Day.
Green Fees: Weekdays £18 per day, weekends £22 per day.
Facilities: Lunch. Dinner. Bar Snacks. Full Catering. Changing Room. Golf Shop. Trolley Hire.
Class One Hotel: Bron Eifion Country House, Criccieth, 6 mile(s). Tel: 522385 (0766)
Class Two Hotel: Bryn Eisteddford Hotel, Clynnog, 10 mile(s). Tel: 86421 (0286)

RHOSNEIGR
Anglesey Golf Club, Station Road, Rhosneigr, Anglesey, Gwynedd. LL64 5QX. Tel: 810219 (0407)
Secretary: Arfon Jones　　　　　Tel: 811202 (0407)
Professional: Paul Lovell　　　　Tel: 811202 (0407)
Location: Turn south off A5 between Gwalchmai and Bryngwran onto A4080. In about 3 miles turn right at Llanfaelog Church, about 1 mile from course.
Description: Low lying links course on common land stabilised dunes.
18 holes, 5,713 yards, Par 68, S.S.S. 68.
Visitors: Welcome. Not between 8a.m. and 9.30a.m. and 11.30a.m. to 1.30p.m. Saturdays and Sundays, or 11.30a.m.

to 1.30p.m. Tuesdays or 4p.m. to 6p.m. Wednesdays.
Green Fees: Weekdays £10.50, weekends £12.50.
Facilities: Lunch. Dinner. Bar Snacks. Full Catering. Changing Room. Golf Shop. Club Hire. Trolley Hire.
Class One Hotel: Beach Hotel, Trearddur Bay, 6 mile(s). Tel: 860332 (0407)
Class Two Hotel: Maelog Lake Hotel, Rhosneigr, 1 mile(s). Tel: 810204 (0407)

TREARDDUR BAY
Holyhead Golf Club, Trearddur Bay, Anglesey, Gwynedd. LL65 2YG. Tel: 762119 (0407)
Secretary: David Entwhistle   Tel: 763279 (0407)
Professional: Paul Capper   Tel: 762022 (0407)
Description: Designed by James Braid, a tough test of golf with gorse, heather and narrow fairways.
18 holes, 6,058 yards, Par 70, S.S.S. 70, Course record 64.
Visitors: Welcome. Handicap certificate required.
Green Fees: Weekdays £17, weekends £20.
Facilities: Lunch. Dinner. Bar Snacks. Full Catering. Changing Room. Golf Shop. Trolley Hire.
Class One Hotel: Trearddur Bay Hotel, Trearddur Bay, 1 1/2 mile(s). Tel: 860301 (0407)
Class Two Hotel: Dormy House, On Course, 0 mile(s). Tel: 763279 (0407)

POWYS

BUILTH WELLS
Builth Wells Golf Club, Golf Club Road, Builth Wells, Powys. LD2 3NF. Tel: 553296 (0982)
Secretary: R A Jones   Tel: 553296 (0982)
Professional: Bill Evans   Tel: 553293 (0982)
Location: On A483 west of Builth, close to the town.
Description: Undulating parkland.
18 holes, 5,386 yards, Par 66, S.S.S. 67, Course record 66.
Membership: 400
Visitors: Welcome. Handicap certificate required. Restricted on competition days.
Green Fees: £14 to £18.
Facilities: Lunch. Dinner. Bar Snacks. Full Catering. Changing Room. Golf Shop. Club Hire. Trolley Hire.

BUILTH WELLS
Rhosgoch Golf Club, Rhosgoch, Builth Wells, Powys. Tel: 851251 (0497)
Secretary: Mr Dance   Tel: 22286 (0544)
Location: 4 miles north of Hay-on-Wye on B4594.
Description: Hilly parkland with 3 large ponds. Extensive views of Black Mountains and Brecon Beacons.
9 holes, 4,842 yards, Par 68, S.S.S. 64, Course record 72.
Membership: 190
Visitors: Welcome.
Green Fees: Weekdays £7 per day, weekends £10 per day.
Facilities: Lunch. Dinner. Bar Snacks. Full Catering. Changing Room. Club Hire. Trolley Hire.
Class Two Hotel: Rosgoch Golf Club, On Course, Tel: 851251 (0497)

CRADOC
Cradoc Golf Club, Penoyre Park, Cradoc, Brecon, Powys. Tel: 623658 (0874)
Secretary: G S W Davies   Tel: 623658 (0874)
Professional: D Beattie   Tel: 625524 (0874)
Location: 2 miles north of Brecon. B4520 Upper Chapel Road.
Description: Parkland in Brecon Beacons National Park.
18 holes, 6,301 yards, Par 71, S.S.S. 71, Course record 65.
Membership: 730
Visitors: Welcome. Handicap certificate required. With members only on Sundays.
Green Fees: Weekdays £15, weekends and Bank Holidays £18.
Facilities: Lunch. Dinner. Bar Snacks. Full Catering. Changing Room. Golf Shop. Trolley Hire.
Class One Hotel: Lake Hotel, Llangammarch, 2 Tel: 202 (05912)
Class Two Hotel: Lansdown, Brecon, 2 mile(s). Tel: 623321 (0874)

KNIGHTON
Knighton Golf Club, Ffryd, Knighton, Powys. . Tel: 528646 (0547)
Secretary: E Bright   Tel: 528684 (0547)
Description: Hilly course.
9 holes, 2,660 yards, Par 34, S.S.S. 33, Course record 32.
Membership: 150
Visitors: Welcome. Handicap certificate required. Not Saturdays p.m. and not Sundays.
Green Fees: Weekdays £8, weekends £10.
Facilities: Bar Snacks. Changing Room.
Class One Hotel: Knighton Hotel, Knighton, 1 mile(s). Tel: 520530 (0547)
Class Two Hotel: Red Lion, Knighton, 1 mile(s). Tel: 528231 (0547)

MACHYNLLETH
Machynlleth Golf Club, Ffordd-Y-Drenewydd, Machynlleth, Powys. SY20 8UH. Tel: 702000 (0654)
Secretary: Gary Holdsworth   Tel: 703264 (0654)
Description: Undulating 9 hole meadowland course.
9 holes, 5,726 yards, Par 68, S.S.S. 67, Course record 66.
Membership: 250
Visitors: Welcome. Handicap certificate required. Not between 1p.m. and 3p.m. Thursdays and not between 8a.m. and 11.30a.m. Sundays.
Green Fees: £10 per day, £35 per week. Juniors half price with a member.
Facilities: Lunch. Dinner. Bar Snacks. Changing Room. Driving Range. Trolley Hire.
Class Two Hotel: Wynnstay, Machynlleth, 1 mile(s). Tel: 702941 (0654)

NEWTOWN
St Giles Golf Club, Pool Road, Newtown, Powys. SY16 3AJ. Tel: 625844 (0686)
Secretary: Mr T Hall   Tel: 625091 (0686)

Cade's - Audi Golf Course Guide

Professional: Mr P Owen Tel: 625844 (0686)
Location: At side of A458 from Welshpool.
Description: Parkland.
9 holes, 5,936 yards, Par 70, S.S.S. 68, Course record 63.
Membership: 450
Visitors: Welcome. Handicap certificate required. Ladies Day Thursday. Restricted on Saturdays during competitions. No catering on Mondays.
Green Fees: Weekdays £10 per day, weekends £12.50. Reduction of £2.50 if playing with a member.
Facilities: Lunch. Dinner. Bar Snacks. Full Catering. Changing Room. Golf Shop. Club Hire. Trolley Hire.
Class One Hotel: Elephant and Castle, Newtown, 1 mile(s). Tel: 626271 (0686)
Class Two Hotel: The Bell, Newtown, 1 mile(s). Tel: 625540 (0686)

WELSHPOOL

Welshpool Golf Club, Y Golfa, Welshpool, Powys. . Tel: 83249 (0938)
Secretary: D B Pritchard Tel: 552215 (0938)
Description: Rather hilly with very beautiful scenery.
18 holes, 5,708 yards, Par 70, S.S.S. 69, Course record 68.
Visitors: Welcome. Handicap certificate required. Some restrictions at weekends, advisable to telephone for confirmation.
Green Fees: Weekdays £10, weekends £15.
Facilities: Lunch. Dinner. Bar Snacks. Full Catering. Changing Room. Golf Shop.
Class One Hotel: Golfa Hall, Welshpool, 2 mile(s). Tel: 553399 (0938)
Class Two Hotel: Kaye, Welshpool, 3 mile(s). Tel: 552693 (0938)

Cade's - Audi Golf Course Guide

Audi Coupe 2.8E quattro

Cade's - Audi Golf Course Guide

SCOTLAND

BORDERS

DUNS
Duns Golf Club, Hardens Road, Duns, Borders.
Secretary: A Campbell Tel: 82717 (0361)
Location: 1 mile west of Duns, off A6105 signposted to Longformacus.
Description: Upland.
9 holes, 5,826 yards, Par 68, S.S.S. 68, Course record 66.
Membership: 300
Visitors: Welcome. Not Tuesdays after 3p.m., also restrictions on club competition days. Bar Snacks at weekends only.
Green Fees: Weekdays £8, weekends £10. Juniors £1.50 per day.
Facilities: Changing Room. Trolley Hire.

INNERLEITHEN
Innerleithen Golf Club, Leithen Water, Leithen Road, Innerleithen, Borders. EH44 6NL. Tel: 830951 (0896)
Secretary: S Wyse Tel: 830071 (0896)
Location: On A72 6 mles from Peebles.
Description: Situated in a valley, challenging course but easy walking.
9 holes, 5,910 yards, Par 68, S.S.S. 68, Course record 67.
Membership: 200
Visitors: Welcome. Catering by arrangement.
Green Fees: Weekdays £7, weekends £9.
Facilities: Lunch. Dinner. Bar Snacks. Changing Room.
Class One Hotel: Peebles Hydro, Peebles, 5 mile(s). Tel: 20602 (0721)
Class Two Hotel: Tweed Valley, Walkerburn, 3 mile(s). Tel: 636 (089687)

JEDBURGH
Jedburgh Golf Club, Dunion Road, Jedburgh, Borders. TD8 6LA. Tel: 63587 (0835)
Secretary: R Strachan Tel: 64175 (0835)
Professional: S Farquharson Tel: 63338 (0835)
Location: 3/4 mile out of town on the Hawick Road B3658.
Description: Undulating, many new trees, small tricky greens.
9 holes, 5,555 yards, Par 68, S.S.S. 67, Course record 62.
Membership: 225
Visitors: Welcome. Weekends restricted by competitions. Catering at weekends only.
Green Fees: £10 per day.
Facilities: Lunch. Dinner. Bar Snacks. Full Catering. Changing Room. Golf Shop.
Class One Hotel: Jedforest, Jedburgh, 4 mile(s). Tel: 274 (08354)
Class Two Hotel: Glenbank, Jedburgh, 1 mile(s). Tel: 62258 (0835)

KELSO
Kelso Golf Club, Borrymoss Road, Kelso, Borders. . Tel: 223009 (0573)
Secretary: John Payne Tel: 223009 (0573)
Location: Within Kelso Racecourse.
Description: Flat parkland.
18 holes, 6,066 yards, Par 70, S.S.S. 69.
Membership: 450
Visitors: Welcome. Closed on race days. Some catering restrictions apply, please telephone in advance. Caddies by prior arrangement.
Green Fees: Weekdays £10 per round, £12 per day. Weekends £12 per round, £18 per day. Weekly ticket £40.
Facilities: Lunch. Dinner. Bar Snacks. Full Catering. Changing Room.
Class One Hotel: Cross Keys, Kelso, 1 1/2 mile(s). Tel: 23303 (0573)
Class Two Hotel: Queen's Head, Kelso, 1 1/2 mile(s). Tel: 24636 (0573)

LAUDER
Lauder Golf Club, Galashiels Road, Lauder, Borders. TD26 6QD.
Secretary: D Dickson Tel: 526 (05782)
Location: On A68 25 miles south of Edinburgh.
Description: 9 hole course designed by Mr W Park Jnr. of Musselburgh on a gently sloping hill.
9 holes, 6,002 yards, Par 72, S.S.S. 70, Course record 70.
Membership: 180
Visitors: Welcome. Restrictions on Wednesday evenings and Sunday mornings.
Green Fees: Weekdays - Adults £5, Juniors £2. Weekends - Adults £6, Juniors £3.
Facilities: Changing Room.
Class One Hotel: Lauderdale, Lauder, 1 mile(s). Tel: 231 (05782)
Class Two Hotel: The Black Bull, Lauder, 1/2 mile(s). Tel: 208 (05782)

NEWCASTLETON
Newcastleton Golf Club, Holm Hill, Newcastleton, Borders.
Secretary: F J Ewart Tel: 75257 (03873)
Location: 2 minutes from Newcastleton Main Street.
Description: Hilly with splendid views of Newcastleton and Liddesdale Valley.
9 holes, 5,748 yards, Par 70, S.S.S. 68, Course record 64.
Visitors: Welcome. Catering provided in local Hotel.
Green Fees: £5 per round or day, £20 per week.
Facilities: Changing Room.

PEEBLES
Peebles Golf Club, Kirkland Street, Peebles, Borders. EH45 8EU. Tel: 20197 (0721)
Secretary: R Reeves Tel: 20197 (0721)
Description: Open with some treed areas.
18 holes, 6,137 yards, Par 70, S.S.S. 69.

Membership: 633
Visitors: Welcome.
Green Fees: Weekdays £10 per round, £15 per day. Weekends £16 per round, £22 per day.
Facilities: Lunch. Bar Snacks. Full Catering. Changing Room. Golf Shop. Club Hire. Trolley Hire. Buggy Hire.
Class One Hotel: Peebles Hydro, Peebles, 2 mile(s). Tel: 20602 (0721)
Class Two Hotel: Kingsmuir, Peebles, 1 1/2 mile(s). Tel: 20151 (0721)

ST BOSWELLS

St Boswells Golf Club, Ashleabank, St Boswells, Borders. TD6 0AT. Tel: 22359 (0835)
Secretary: G B Ovens   Tel: 22359 (0835)
Location: 1/4 mile off A68 trunk road at St Boswells Green.
Description: Flat with attractive scenery alongside River Tweed.
9 holes, 2,625 yards, Par 66, S.S.S. 65, Course record 61.
Membership: 310
Visitors: Welcome. Not after 4p.m. weekdays or on competition days.
Green Fees: Weekdays £8 per round or day, weekends £10 per round or day.
Facilities: Changing Room. Club Hire.
Class One Hotel: Dryburgh Abbey, St Boswells, 2 mile(s). Tel: 22261 (0835)
Class Two Hotel: Buccleuch Arms, St Boswells, 1/2 mile(s). Tel: 22243 (0835)

WEST LINTON

West Linton Golf Club, West Linton, Borders. EH46 7HN. Tel: 60463 (0968)
Secretary: G Scott   Tel: 60970 (0968)
Professional: R Tickle   Tel: 60256 (0968)
Location: Off A702 approx 17 miles south west of Edinburgh.
Description: Scenic moorland course in peaceful countryside with uninterrupted views of Pentland Hills and Moorfoot Hills. Fairly flat but a good test of golf.
18 holes, 6,132 yards, Par 69, S.S.S. 69, Course record 67.
Membership: 600
Visitors: Welcome. Not before 1p.m. weekends. No catering on Tuesdays.
Green Fees: Weekdays £13 per round, £18 per day. Weekends £20 per round.
Facilities: Lunch. Dinner. Bar Snacks. Full Catering. Changing Room. Golf Shop. Trolley Hire.
Class One Hotel: Dolphinton House, Dolphinton, 3 mile(s). Tel: 82286 (0968)
Class Two Hotel: Medwin House, West Linton, 1/4 mile(s). Tel: 60542 (0968)

CENTRAL

ABERFOYLE

Aberfoyle Golf Club, Braeval, Aberfoyle, Central. FK8 3UY. Tel: 493 (08772)
Secretary: R Steele   Tel: 638 (08772)
Description: Hilly and scenic.

18 holes, 5,205 yards, S.S.S. 68.
Membership: 600
Visitors: Welcome. Not before 10.30a.m. Saturdays or Sundays.
Green Fees: Weekdays £12 per round, £15 per day. Weekends £15 per round, £20 per day.
Facilities: Lunch. Full Catering. Changing Room. Golf Shop. Driving Range.
Class One Hotel: Inverard, Aberfoyle, 1 mile(s). Tel: 229 (08772)

ALLOA

Alloa Golf Club, Schawpark, Sauchie, Alloa, Central. FK10 3AX. Tel: 722745 (0259)
Secretary: A M Frame   Tel: 50100 (0259)
Professional: Bill Bennett   Tel: 724476 (0259)
Location: 5 miles from Kincardine Bridge, 9 miles from Stirling.
Description: Undulating parkland.
18 holes, 6,240 yards, Par 70, S.S.S. 70, Course record 63.
Membership: 820
Visitors: Welcome. Must be members of a recognised club. Wednesdays Ladies Day. Not before 11.30a.m. weekends.
Green Fees: Weekdays £12 per round, £20 per day. Weekends £24 per day or £15 after 2p.m..
Facilities: Lunch. Dinner. Bar Snacks. Full Catering. Changing Room. Golf Shop. Club Hire. Trolley Hire.
Class Two Hotel: Royal Oak, Alloa, 1 mile(s). Tel: 722423 (0259)

ALLOA

Braehead Golf Club, Cambus, By Alloa, Central. FK10 2NT. Tel: 722078 (0259)
Secretary: Paul MacMichael   Tel: 722078 (0259)
Professional: Paul Brookes   Tel: 722078 (0259)
Location: 1 mile west of Alloa on the A907.
Description: Parkland course with a fine variety of interesting and challenging holes. Outstanding views to Ochil Hills and Forth Valley.
18 holes, 6,041 yards, Par 70, S.S.S. 69, Course record 64.
Membership: 800
Visitors: Welcome. Advisable to telephone in advance. Some catering restrictions apply, please telephone in advance.
Green Fees: Weekdays £12 per round, £17 per day. Weekends £17 per round, £22 per day.
Facilities: Lunch. Dinner. Bar Snacks. Full Catering. Changing Room. Golf Shop. Club Hire. Trolley Hire.
Class One Hotel: Royal, Bridge of Allan, 5 mile(s). Tel: 832284 (0786)
Class Two Hotel: Dunmar, Alloa, 0 mile(s). Tel: 214339 (0259)

ALVA

Alva Golf Club, Beauclerc, Alva, Central. Tel: 760431 (0259)
Location: On A91 Stirling to St Andrews Road.
Description: Hilly.
9 holes, 4,574 yards, S.S.S. 64.
Membership: 280

Cade's - Audi Golf Course Guide

Visitors: Welcome. Restrictions on competition days. Thursday evenings Ladies only.
Green Fees: On application.
Facilities: Bar Snacks. Changing Room.
Class One Hotel: Johnstone Arms, Alva, 1/2 mile(s). Tel: 62884 (0259)
Class Two Hotel: Alva Glen Hotel, Alva, 1/2 mile(s). Tel: 60223 (0259)

DOLLAR
Dollar Golf Club, Brewlands House, Dollar, Central. FK14 7EA. Tel: 42400 (0259)
Secretary: M B Shea   Tel: 42400 (0259)
Description: Short hillside course with panoramic views of the Devon Valley.
18 holes, 5,144 yards, Par 68, S.S.S. 66, Course record 63.
Membership: 400
Visitors: Welcome.
Green Fees: Weekdays £6 per round, £10 per day. Weekends £13 per day.
Facilities: Lunch. Dinner. Bar Snacks. Full Catering. Changing Room. Club Hire.
Class Two Hotel: Castle Campbell, Dollar, 1/2 mile(s). Tel: 42519 (0259)

DRYMEN
Strathendrick Golf Club, Glasgow Road, Drymen, Central.
Secretary: T F Turner   Tel: 60860 (0360)
Description: Hilly parkland.
9 holes, 4,962 yards, Par 66, S.S.S. 65, Course record 62.
Membership: 460
Visitors: Welcome. With members only. Restrictions on competition days.
Green Fees: On application.
Facilities: Changing Room.
Class One Hotel: Buchanan Highland, Drymen, 1/2 mile(s). Tel: 60588 (0360)

DUNBLANE
Dunblane New Golf Club, Perth Road, Dunblane, Central. FK15 0LJ. Tel: 823711 (0786)
Secretary: R S MacCrae   Tel: 823711 (0786)
Professional: R M Jamieson   Tel: 823711 (0786)
Location: At Fourways roundabout, Dunblane centre.
Description: Undulating parkland.
18 holes, 5,939 yards, Par 69, S.S.S. 68, Course record 63.
Membership: 700
Visitors: Welcome. Not Saturdays.
Green Fees: £15 per round, £23 per day.
Facilities: Lunch. Dinner. Bar Snacks. Full Catering. Changing Room. Golf Shop. Club Hire. Trolley Hire.
Class One Hotel: Dunblane Hydro, Dunblane, 1/4 mile(s). Tel: 822551 (0786)
Class Two Hotel: Stirling Arms, Dunblane, 1/2 mile(s). Tel: 822156 (0786)

KILLIN
Killin Golf Club, Killin, Central.   FK21 8TX. Tel: 312 (05672)
Secretary: S Chisholm   Tel: 235 (08383)

Description: Very scenic parkland course some hilly holes.
9 holes, 2,500 yards, Par 66, S.S.S. 65, Course record 61.
Visitors: Welcome. Juniors must be accompanied by an adult.
Green Fees: From £7.50 per round.
Facilities: Lunch. Dinner. Bar Snacks. Full Catering. Changing Room. Club Hire. Trolley Hire.

LARBERT
Falkirk Tryst Golf Club, 86 Burnhead Road, Larbert, Central. FK5 4BD. Tel: 562415 (0324)
Secretary: R D Wallace   Tel: 562054 (0324)
Location: Situated in Larbert, approx 3 miles north of Falkirk, mid-way between Edinburgh and Glasgow.
Description: Flat, sandy soil, links type course with trees, gorse and bushes.
18 holes, 6,053 yards, Par 70, S.S.S. 69, Course record 64.
Membership: 650
Visitors: Welcome. With members only at weekends.
Green Fees: £10 per round, £15 per day.
Facilities: Lunch. Dinner. Bar Snacks. Full Catering. Changing Room. Golf Shop. Trolley Hire. Buggy Hire.
Class One Hotel: Park, Falkirk, 3 mile(s). Tel: 28331 (0324)
Class Two Hotel: Commercial, Larbert, 1 1/2 mile(s). Tel: 562398 (0324)

LARBERT
Glenbervie Golf Club Ltd., Stirling Road, Larbert, Central. FK5 4SJ. Tel: 562605 (0324)
Secretary: Mrs Mary Purves   Tel: 562605 (0324)
Professional: John Chillas   Tel: 562725 (0324)
Location: Half way between Falkirk and Stirling on the Stirling Road.
Description: Flat parkland.
18 holes, 6,469 yards, Par 71, S.S.S. 71.
Membership: 600
Visitors: Welcome. Not at weekends. Societies Tuesdays and Thursdays only by prior arrangement.
Green Fees: £20 per round, £28 per day.
Facilities: Lunch. Dinner. Bar Snacks. Full Catering. Changing Room. Golf Shop. Trolley Hire.

STIRLING
Stirling Golf Club, Queen's Road, Stirling, Central. FK8 2AA. Tel: 64098 (0786)
Secretary: W C McArthur   Tel: 64098 (0786)
Professional: I Collins   Tel: 71490 (0786)
Location: Within 1 mile of Stirling town centre, close to M9 motorway.
Description: Parkland course with superb panoramic views of Stirling Castle and the Grampian Mountains.
Kings Park 18 holes, 6,438 yards, Par 72, S.S.S. 71, Course record 65.
Membership: 1000
Visitors: Welcome. Handicap certificate required. Letter of Introduction required. Weekends on application.
Green Fees: £15.50 per round, £21.50 per day.
Facilities: Lunch. Dinner. Bar Snacks. Full Catering. Changing Room. Golf Shop. Trolley Hire. Buggy Hire. Caddies

available.
Class One Hotel: Golden Lion, Stirling, 1/2 mile(s). Tel: 75351 (0786)
Class Two Hotel: Garfield, Stirling, 1/8 mile(s). Tel: 73730 (0786)

DUMFRIES & GALLOWAY

ANNAN

Powfoot Golf Club, Cummertrees, Annan, Dumfries & Galloway. DG12 5QE. Tel: 227 (04617)
Secretary: Mr R Anderson Tel: 202866 (0461)
Professional: Gareth Dick Tel: 327 (04617)
Location: On A74 from Eaglesfield turn off to Annan, turn right out of Annan, take first left at top of hill on Low Road to Dumfries. Follow River Solway.
Description: Links and parkland. Championship course. 18 holes, 6,200 yards, Par 71, S.S.S. 70, Course record 63.
Membership: 750
Visitors: Welcome. Must book in advance for 3 or more players. Not on Saturdays. Not before 2.45p.m. Sundays.
Green Fees: Weekdays £14 per round, £23 per day. Sundays £15.
Facilities: Lunch. Dinner. Bar Snacks. Full Catering. Changing Room. Golf Shop. Club Hire. Trolley Hire. Caddies available.
Class One Hotel: Powfoot Golf Hotel, On Course, Tel: 254 (04617)
Class Two Hotel: Northfield House, Annan, 4 mile(s). Tel: 2851 (046120)

DALBEATTIE

Colvend Golf Club, Sandyhills, Colvend, Dalbeattie, Dumfries & Galloway. DG5 4PY. Tel: 398 (055663)
Secretary: Mr J B Henderson Tel: 610878 (0556)
Location: 6 miles from Dalbeattie on the A710 Solway Coast Road.
Description: 9 challenging holes over a picturesque course. Superb views over the Galloway Hills and the Solway Firth. 18 holes, 4,480 yards, Par 66, S.S.S. 63, Course record 63.
Visitors: Welcome. Members competitions Apr-Sept at 2p.m. Tuesdays and 5.30p.m. Thursdays, also some Sundays.
Green Fees: Adults - £10 per day. Juniors - £5 per day. Juniors pay full fee at weekends.
Facilities: Lunch. Dinner. Bar Snacks. Full Catering. Changing Room. Club Hire. Trolley Hire.
Class One Hotel: Clonyard, Dalbeattie, 2 1/2 mile(s). Tel: 372 (055663)
Class Two Hotel: Maxwell Arms, Dalbeattie, 6 mile(s). Tel: 610431 (0556)

DUMFRIES

Dumfries and County Golf Club, Nunfield, Edinburgh Road, Dumfries & Galloway. DG1 1JX. Tel: 53585 (0387)
Secretary: E C Pringle Tel: 53585 (0387)
Professional: Gordon Gray Tel: 68918 (0387)
Location: 1 mile from Dumfries on the Edinburgh Road.
Description: Undulating parkland.
18 holes, 5,928 yards, Par 69, S.S.S. 68.
Membership: 600
Visitors: Welcome. Handicap certificate required. Not at weekends and Bank Holidays. Tuesdays Ladies Day.
Green Fees: £18 per day.
Facilities: Lunch. Dinner. Bar Snacks. Full Catering. Changing Room. Golf Shop. Club Hire. Trolley Hire.
Class One Hotel: Cairndale Hotel, Dumfries, 1 mile(s). Tel: 54111 (0387)
Class Two Hotel: Station Hotel, Dumfries, 1 mile(s). Tel: 54316 (0387)

DUMFRIES

Dumfries & Galloway Golf Club, 2 Laurieston Avenue, Dumfries, Dumfries & Galloway. DG2 7NY. Tel: 53582 (0387)
Secretary: Jack Donnachie Tel: 63848 (0387)
Professional: Joe Fergusson Tel: 56902 (0387)
Location: On outskirts of Dumfries towards Castle Douglas.
Description: Undulating parkland with beautiful scenic views.
18 holes, 5,813 yards, Par 68, S.S.S. 68, Course record 62.
Membership: 800
Visitors: Welcome. Always by prior arrangement. Tuesdays Ladies day. No parties at weekends. No catering Mondays.
Green Fees: Weekdays £16, weekends £20.
Facilities: Lunch. Dinner. Bar Snacks. Full Catering. Changing Room. Golf Shop. Club Hire. Trolley Hire.
Class One Hotel: Cairndale, Dumfries, 1 mile(s). Tel: 54111 (0387)
Class Two Hotel: Dalston, Dumfries, 1/4 mile(s). Tel: 54422 (0387)

DUMFRIES

Southerness Golf Club, Southerness, Dumfries & Galloway. DG2 8AZ. Tel: 677 (038788)
Location: Near Dumfries on Solway coast road towards Southerness.
Description: Links.
18 holes, 6,554 yards, Par 69, S.S.S. 72, Course record 65.
Membership: 600
Visitors: Welcome. Handicap certificate required. Always book in advance.
Green Fees: Weekdays £20, weekends and Bank Holidays £26.
Facilities: Lunch. Dinner. Bar Snacks. Full Catering. Changing Room. Trolley Hire.
Class One Hotel: Cavens House, Kirkbean, 2 mile(s). Tel: 234 (038782)

GATEHOUSE OF FLEET

Gatehouse of Fleet Golf Club, Laurieston Road, Gatehouse of Fleet, Castle Douglas, Dumfries & Galloway. DG7 2HS.

Secretary: A McCreath Tel: 814281 (0557)
Location: 1/4 mile from Gatehouse.
Description: Sloping and wooded.
9 holes, 2,400 yards, Par 66, S.S.S. 63, Course record 60.
Membership: 294
Visitors: Welcome. Not Sunday mornings.
Green Fees: £8, Juniors £4.
Facilities: Changing Room.
Class One Hotel: Murray Arms, Gatehouse, 1/4 mile(s). Tel: 814207 (0557).

GLENLUCE

Wigtownshire Golf Club, Mains of Park, Glenluce, Dumfries and Galloway. DG8 0NN. Tel: 420 (05813).
Secretary: Robin McCubbin Tel: 589 (05813)
Location: On A75 8 mile east from Stranraer.
Description: Natural links course, quite well bunkered, greens second to none.
18 holes, 5,715 yards, Par 70, S.S.S. 68, Course record 66.
Membership: 350
Visitors: Welcome. Members have priority times each day, please telephone in advance for booking.
Green Fees: Weekdays £11 per round, £14 per day. Weekends £13 per round, £16 per day.
Facilities: Lunch. Dinner. Bar Snacks. Full Catering. Changing Room. Trolley Hire.
Class One Hotel: North West Castle, Stranraer, 8 mile(s). Tel: 4413 (0776)
Class Two Hotel: Glenbay, Glenluce, 2 mile(s). Tel: 581 (05813)

LANGHOLM

Langholm Golf Club, Whitaside, Langholm, Dumfries & Galloway. DG13 0JS.
Secretary: Mr Alan Edgar Tel: 80878 (03873)
Description: Hillside.
9 holes, 5,744 yards, Par 70, S.S.S. 68, Course record 66.
Visitors: Welcome. Restrictions weekends during competitions.
Green Fees: £8 per round or day, £4 with a member.
Facilities: Lunch. Bar Snacks. Changing Room.
Class Two Hotel: Eskdale, Langholm, 1/2 mile(s). Tel: 81178 (03873)

LOCKERBIE

Lockerbie Golf Club, Corrie Road, Lockerbie, Dumfries & Galloway. DG11 2ND. Tel: 3363 (05762)
Secretary: J Thomson Tel: 2462 (05762)
Location: Corrie Road, 1/4 mile from Lockerbie.
Description: 18 hole parkland featuring the only pond in Dumfries & Galloway which comes into play on 3 holes.
Gents 18 holes, 5,327 yards, Par 67, S.S.S. 66, Course record 64.
Ladies 18 holes, 5,279 yards, Par 71, S.S.S. 71, Course record 69.
Membership: 600
Visitors: Welcome. Handicap certificate required. Letter of Introduction required.No 36 hole bookings on Sundays.
Green Fees: Weekdays £12, weekends £15.
Facilities: Lunch. Dinner. Bar Snacks. Full Catering. Changing Room. Trolley Hire.

Class One Hotel: Queen's, Lockerbie, 1 1/2 mile(s). Tel: 3005 (05762)
Class Two Hotel: Kings Arms, Lockerbie, 1 mile(s). Tel: 2410 (05762)

MOFFAT

Moffat Golf Club, Coatshill, Moffat, Dumfries & Galloway. DG10 9SB. Tel: 20020 (0683)
Secretary: T A Rankin Tel: 20020 (0683)
Description: Hilly moorland.
18 holes, 5,000 yards, Par 67, S.S.S. 64, Course record 60.
Membership: 400
Visitors: Welcome. Only by prior arrangement.
Green Fees: Weekdays £12 per day, weekends £22 per day.
Facilities: Lunch. Dinner. Bar Snacks. Full Catering. Changing Room. Golf Shop. Club Hire. Trolley Hire.
Class One Hotel: Auchen, Beattock, 1 1/2 mile(s). Tel: 407 (06833)
Class Two Hotel: Annandale Arms, Moffat, 3/4 mile(s). Tel: 20013 (0683)

NEW GALLOWAY

New Galloway Golf Club, New Galloway, Castle Douglas, Dumfries & Galloway. DG7 3RN. Tel: 737 (06442)
Secretary: A R Brown Tel: 455 (06443)
Location: 1 mile from A713 Castle Douglas to Ayr Road.
Description: Superb 9 hole course with excellent tees and greens, the views over Loch Ken and indeed in every direction are spectacular. Founded in 1902. Mixed woodland and moorland.
9 holes, 2,529 yards, S.S.S. 65, Course record 65.
Membership: 235
Visitors: Welcome. Must give way to competitors on club competition days (normally Sundays).
Green Fees: £8 per day or round, £10 per day or round on Sundays.
Facilities: Changing Room.
Class One Hotel: Leamington, New Galloway, 1/4 mile(s). Tel: 327 (06442)
Class Two Hotel: Cairn Edward, New Galloway, 1 mile(s). Tel: 244 (06442)

NEWTON STEWART

Newton Stewart Golf Club, Kirroughtree Avenue, Minnigaff, Newton Stewart, Dumfries & Galloway. DG8 6PL. Tel: 2172 (0671)
Secretary: D Matthewson Tel: 3236 (0671)
Description: Scenic parkland.
9 holes, 5,402 yards, Par 68, S.S.S. 67, Course record 64.
Membership: 240
Visitors: Welcome. Handicap certificate required. Tuesdays p.m. reserved for Ladies. No visitors during open competitions.
Green Fees: Weekdays £8 per day, weekends and Bank Holidays £12 per day.
Facilities: Lunch. Bar Snacks. Changing Room.
Class One Hotel: Cally Palace, Gatehouse, 12 mile(s). Tel: 814341 (0557)
Class Two Hotel: Bruce, Newton Stewart, 2 mile(s). Tel: 2294 (0671)

PORTPATRICK

Portpatrick (Dunskey) Golf Club, Golf Course Road, Portpatrick, Dumfries & Galloway. DG9 8SU. Tel: 273 (077681)
Secretary: J A Horberry   Tel: 273 (077681)
Location: A77 and A75 follow signs to Portpatrick, fork right at War Memorial, then signposted on left.
Description: Links type, set on cliffs overlooking Irish Sea. Voted No.1 holiday course by Golf World magazine.
18 holes, 5,732 yards, Par 70, S.S.S. 68, Course record 65.
9 holes, 1,442 yards, Par 27, S.S.S. 27, Course record 23.
Visitors: Welcome. Handicap certificate required. Reserved for members - Weekdays, 9.30-10.00 a.m. and 1.00-2.00 p.m.. Weekends, 9.00-10.30 a.m. and 12.30-2.00 p.m..
Green Fees: Weekdays 18 holes £12 per round, £18 per day, weekends £15 per round, £22 per day. 9 holes £4 per round, £8 per day. Juniors half price.
Facilities: Lunch. Dinner. Bar Snacks. Full Catering. Changing Room. Golf Shop. Club Hire. Trolley Hire. Buggy Hire. Caddies available.
Class One Hotel: Fernhill Golf, Portpatrick, 1/4 mile. Tel: 81220 (0776)
Class Two Hotel: Inglenook Guest House, Portpatrick, 1/4 mile. Tel: 81231 (0776)

STRANRAER

Stranraer Golf Club, Leswalt, Stranraer, Dumfries & Galloway. . Tel: 87245 (0776)
Secretary: W I Wilson CA   Tel: 3539 (0776)
Location: 3 miles from Stranraer on A718.
Description: Undulating parkland.
18 holes, 6,358 yards, Par 70, S.S.S. 71.
Membership: 500
Visitors: Welcome. Always book in advance.
Green Fees: Weekdays £15 per round, £20 per day. Weekends £20 per round, £25 per day.
Facilities: Lunch. Dinner. Bar Snacks. Full Catering. Changing Room. Golf Shop. Trolley Hire.
Class One Hotel: Northwest Castle, Stranraer, 3 mile(s). Tel: 4413 (0776)
Class Two Hotel: Fernhill, Port Patrick, 5 mile(s). Tel: 220 (077681)

THORNHILL

Thornhill Golf Club, Blacknest, Thornhill, Dumfries & Galloway. DG3 5DW. Tel: 30546 (0848)
Secretary: Stuart Moscrop   Tel: 30151 (0848)
Location: 15 miles north of Dumfries on A76 Glasgow to Kilmarnock Road.
Description: Fairly level parkland, easy walking.
18 holes, 6,011 yards, Par 71, S.S.S. 69, Course record 65.
Membership: 630
Visitors: Welcome. Handicap certificate required. Always book in advance. Weekend parties restricted to 18 to 20 persons must tee off between 9.30a.m. and 2p.m.. Tuesdays Ladies Day.
Green Fees: Weekdays £12 per day, weekends £18 per day.
Facilities: Lunch. Bar Snacks. Changing Room. Trolley Hire.

Class One Hotel: Cairndale, Dumfries, 15 mile(s). Tel: 54111 (0387)
Class Two Hotel: Gillbank Guest House, Thornhill, 1 mile(s). Tel: 30597 (0848)

WIGTOWN

Wigtown and Bladnoch Golf Club, Lightlands Terrace, Wigtown, Dumfries and Galloway. . Tel: 3354 (09884)
Secretary: J Bateman   Tel: 650 (098884)
Location: 1/4 mile from Wigtown Centre on Bladnoch Road.
Description: Scenic part hilly parkland.
9 holes, 2,731 yards, Par 68, S.S.S. 67, Course record 61.
Membership: 130
Visitors: Welcome.
Green Fees: Weekdays £7 per day, weekends £10 per round.
Facilities: Lunch. Bar Snacks. Changing Room.

FIFE

ABERDOUR

Aberdour Golf Club, Seaside Place, Aberdour, Fife. KY3 0TX. Tel: 860256 (0383)
Secretary: Mr J J Train   Tel: 860080 (0383)
Professional: Gordon McCallum   Tel: 860256 (0383)
Location: In centre of Aberdour signposted on Shore Road.
Description: Parkland.
18 holes, 5,469 yards, Par 67, S.S.S. 67.
Membership: 580
Visitors: Welcome. Not on Saturdays. Advance booking for parties.
Green Fees: Weekdays £13 per round, £18 per day. Sundays £14 per round, £18 per day.
Facilities: Lunch. Dinner. Bar Snacks. Full Catering. Changing Room. Golf Shop. Trolley Hire.
Class Two Hotel: Woodside, Aberdour, Tel: 860328 (0383)

ANSTRUTHER

Anstruther Golf Club, Marsfield, Shore Road, Anstruther, Fife. KY10 3DZ. Tel: 310956 (0333)
Secretary: A B Cleary   Tel: 310956 (0333)
Location:
Description: 9 hole seaside links.
9 holes, 2,259 yards, Par 62, S.S.S. 63, Course record 61.
Membership: 600
Visitors: Welcome. Handicap certificate required. Not during competition days. Many facilities exist only during summer months, please telephone in advance.

Green Fees: Weekdays £10 per 18 holes, weekends £14 per 18 holes.
Facilities: Lunch. Dinner. Bar Snacks. Changing Room. Trolley Hire.
Class One Hotel: The Craws Nest, Anstruther, 1/4 mile(s). Tel: 310691 (0333)
Class Two Hotel: Spindrift, Anstruther, 1/4 mile(s). Tel: 310573 (0333)

BURNTISLAND

Burntisland Golf House Club, Dodhead, Burntisland, Fife. KY3 9EY. Tel: 874093 (0592)
Secretary: Ian McClean   Tel: 874093 (0592)
Professional: Jacky Montgomery   Tel: 873247 (0592)
Description: Parkland.
18 holes, 5,497 yards, Par 69, S.S.S. 69, Course record 65.
Membership: 780
Visitors: Welcome. Prior booking required.
Green Fees: Weekdays £12.50 per round, £18 per day. Weekends £18 per round, £28 per day.
Facilities: Lunch. Dinner. Bar Snacks. Full Catering. Changing Room. Golf Shop. Trolley Hire.
Class One Hotel: Inchview, Burntisland, 1 mile(s). Tel: 872239 (0592)
Class Two Hotel: Kingswood, Burntisland, 1 1/2 mile(s). Tel: 872329 (0592)

CRAIL

Crail Golfing Society (Balcomie Links), Balcomie Clubhouse, Crail, Fife. KY10 3XN. Tel: 50278 (0333)
Secretary: Mrs C W Penhale   Tel: 50686 (0333)
Professional: Graeme Lennie   Tel: 50960 (0333)
Location: A917, 10 miles south-east of St Andrews.
Description: Parkland/links, every hole within sight of the sea.
18 holes, 5,720 yards, Par 69, S.S.S. 68, Course record 64.
Membership: 1100
Visitors: Welcome. Restrictions on certain competition days. Caddies by arrangement.
Green Fees: Weekdays £16 per round, £24 per day. Weekends £20 per round, £30 per day.
Facilities: Lunch. Dinner. Bar Snacks. Full Catering. Changing Room. Golf Shop. Club Hire. Trolley Hire.
Class One Hotel: The Craws Nest, Anstruther, 7 mile(s). Tel: 310691 (0333)
Class Two Hotel: Balcomie Links Hotel, Crail, 2 mile(s). Tel: 50237 (0333)

CUPAR

Cupar Golf Club, Hilltarvit, Cupar, Fife.   . Tel: 53549 (0334)
Secretary: J P McAndrew   Tel: 54312 (0334)
Description: 9 hole hillside parkland, possibly the oldest 9 hole club in the World, founded in 1855.
9 holes, 4,500 yards, Par 68, S.S.S. 65, Course record 61.
Membership: 400
Visitors: Welcome. Handicap certificate required.
Green Fees: Weekdays £10, Sundays £12.
Facilities: Lunch. Bar Snacks. Changing Room.
Class One Hotel: Fernie Castle, Lethan, 3 mile(s). Tel: 381 (030781)

Cade's - Audi Golf Course Guide

DUNFERMLINE

Dunfermline Golf Club, Pitfirrane, Crossford, Dunfermline, Fife. KY12 8QV. Tel: 723534 (0383)
Secretary: H Mathston   Tel: 723534 (0383)
Professional: S Craig   Tel: 723534 (0383)
Location: 2 miles west of Dunfermline at Crossford on A994.
Description: Undulating parkland.
18 holes, 5,813 yards, Par 75, S.S.S. 72, Course record 64.
Membership: 520
Visitors: Welcome. Handicap certificate required. Weekdays only. Not between 10.00 a.m. and noon, or between 2.00-4.00 p.m.. Some catering restrictions apply, please telephone in advance.
Green Fees: £15 per round, £25 per day.
Facilities: Lunch. Dinner. Bar Snacks. Full Catering. Changing Room. Golf Shop. Trolley Hire.
Class One Hotel: Keavil House, Croossford, 1/2 mile(s). Tel: 736258 (0383)

DUNFERMLINE

Pitreavie (Dunfermline) Golf Club, Queensferry Road, Dunfermline, Fife. KY11 5PR. Tel: 722591 (0383)
Secretary: Mr D Carter   Tel: 722591 (0383)
Professional: Jim Forrester   Tel: 723151 (0383)
Location: Exit junc 2 M90, golf lies on dual carriageway between Rosyth and Dunfermline.
Description: Parkland with views overlooking Firth of Forth.
18 holes, 6,086 yards, Par 70, S.S.S. 69, Course record 65.
Membership: 700
Visitors: Welcome. No Ladies prior to 1.00 p.m. weekends or between 4.00-6.00 p.m. weekdays.
Green Fees: Weekdays £12 per round, £17 per day. Weekends £22 per day.
Facilities: Lunch. Dinner. Bar Snacks. Full Catering. Changing Room. Golf Shop. Club Hire. Trolley Hire.
Class One Hotel: King Malcolm, Dunfermline, 1/4 mile(s). Tel: 722611 (0383)
Class Two Hotel: Hillview House, Dunfermline, 1/2 mile(s). Tel: 726278 (0383)

ELIE

Golf House Club, Elie, Fife. KY9 1AS. Tel: 330301 (0333)
Secretary: A Sneddon   Tel: 330301 (0333)
Professional: R Wilson   Tel: 330955 (0333)
Location: A915 10 miles east of Leven, 13 miles south of St Andrews.
Description: Links.
18 holes, 6,241 yards, Par 70, S.S.S. 70, Course record 63.
Membership: 600
Visitors: Welcome. Handicap certificate required. No visiting parties at weekends or during the months of June, July and August.
Green Fees: Weekdays £20 per round, £27.50 per day. Weekends £30 per round, £37.50 per day.
Facilities: Lunch. Dinner. Bar Snacks. Full Catering. Changing Room. Golf Shop. Club Hire. Driving Range Trolley Hire.
Class One Hotel: The Golf Hotel, Adjacent, 0 mile(s). Tel: 330209 (0333)

171

KINCARDINE
Tulliallan Golf Club, Alloa Road, Kincardine, Fife. FK10 4BB. Tel: 30396 (0259)
Secretary: J S McDowall Tel: 485420 (0324)
Professional: S Kelly Tel: 30798 (0259)
Location: On A977 from Kincardine Bridge to Kinross.
Description: Parkland.
18 holes, 5,965 yards, Par 69, S.S.S. 69, Course record 63.
Membership: 525
Visitors: Welcome. Always book with Professional in advance.
Green Fees: Weekdays £13 per round, £17 per day. Weekends £17 per round, £21 per day.
Facilities: Lunch. Bar Snacks. Changing Room. Golf Shop. Trolley Hire.

KINGHORN
Kinghorn Golf Club, MacDuff Crescent, Kinghorn, Fife. KY3 9RE. Tel: 890345 (0592)
Secretary: J P Robertson Tel: 890345 (0592)
Location: A92, 3 miles west of Kirkcaldy.
Description: Links.
18 holes, 5,217 yards, Par 65, S.S.S. 67.
Membership: 150
Visitors: Welcome. Parties 12 to 35 in writing to secretary. Some catering restrictions apply, please telephone in advance.
Green Fees: Weekdays £7 per round, £9.40 per day. Weekends £10 per round, £12 per day.
Facilities: Lunch. Dinner. Bar Snacks. Full Catering. Changing Room.
Class One Hotel: Inchview, Burntisland, 2 mile(s). Tel: 872239 (0592)
Class Two Hotel: Longboat, Kinghorn, 1 mile(s). Tel: 890625 (0592)

KIRKCALDY
Dunnikier Park Golf Club, Dunnikier Way, Kirkcaldy, Fife. KY1 3LP. Tel: 261599 (0592)
Secretary: Robert Waddell Tel: 200627 (0592)
Professional: Jacky Montgomery Tel: 205916 (0592)
Location: A92, 2 miles north of Kirkcaldy town centre.
Description: Wooded parkland.
18 holes, 6,601 yards, Par 72, S.S.S. 72, Course record 65.
Membership: 600
Visitors: Welcome.
Green Fees: Weekdays £10, £13 per day. Weekends £15 per day.
Facilities: Lunch. Dinner. Bar Snacks. Full Catering. Changing Room. Golf Shop. Trolley Hire.
Class One Hotel: Dean Park, Kirkcaldy, 1 1/2 mile(s). Tel: 261635 (0592)
Class Two Hotel: Ollerton, Kirkcaldy, 2 mile(s). Tel: 264086 (0592)

KIRKCALDY
Kirkcaldy Golf Club, Balwearie, Kirkcaldy, Fife. KY2 5LT. Tel: 260370 (0592)

Secretary: J I Brodley Tel: 205240 (0592)
Professional: P Hodgson Tel: 203258 (0592)
Location: South-west end of town adjacent to Beveridge Park.
18 holes, 6,004 yards, Par 71, S.S.S. 70, Course record 67.
Membership: 700
Visitors: Welcome. Handicap certificate required. Not Saturdays.
Green Fees: Weekdays £12 per round, £18 per day. Weekends £15 per round, £21 per day.
Facilities: Lunch. Dinner. Bar Snacks. Full Catering. Changing Room. Golf Shop. Trolley Hire.
Class One Hotel: Dean park, Kirkcaldy, 2 mile(s). Tel: 261635 (0592)
Class Two Hotel: Strathearn, Kirkcaldy, 1 1/2 mile(s). Tel: 52210 (0592)

LADYBANK
Ladybank Golf Club, Annsmuir, Ladybank, Fife. KY7 7RA. Tel: 30814 (0337)
Secretary: A M Dick Tel: 30814 (0337)
Professional: M J Gray Tel: 30725 (0337)
Location: On B9129, off A91 west from St Andrews and Cupar.
Description: Wooded heathland. Ladybank is used regularly as a qualifying course when the British Open is held at St Andrews.
18 holes, 6,641 yards, Par 71, S.S.S. 72.
Membership: 800
Visitors: Welcome. No booked parties at weekends. Caddies available during school holidays.
Green Fees: £23 per round, £31 per day.
Facilities: Lunch. Dinner. Bar Snacks. Full Catering. Changing Room. Golf Shop. Club Hire. Trolley Hire. Buggy Hire.
Class One Hotel: Fernie Castle, Lethan, 4 mile(s). Tel: 381 (033781)
Class Two Hotel: Lomond Hills, Freuchie, 3 mile(s). Tel: 57329 (0337)

LEVEN
Leven Links, The Promenade, Leven, Fife. KY8 4HS. Tel: 428859 (0333)
Secretary: B Jackson Tel: 428859 (0333)
Professional: G Finlayson Tel: 426881 (0333)
Location: A915 Kirkcaldy to Leven, at roundabout on promenade continue straight on for 1/4 mile, Leven Links on left hand side of road.
Description: Played by 2 clubs, Leven golfing society and Leven Thistle Golf Club.
18 holes, 6,435 yards, Par 71, S.S.S. 71, Course record 64.
Membership: 1200
Visitors: Welcome. Not Sats. Suns after 10.30 a.m., weekdays after 9.30 a.m. Max players in one party Suns 2, weekdays 45. Booking via Starter Tel: 21390 (0333).
Green Fees: Weekdays £16 per round, £22.50 per day. Weekends £20 per round, £30 per day.
Facilities: Lunch. Dinner. Bar Snacks. Full Catering. Changing Room. Golf Shop. Club Hire. Trolley Hire. Caddies available.
Class One Hotel: New Caledonian, Leven, 1/2 mile(s). Tel: 424101 (0333)

Cade's - Audi Golf Course Guide

Class Two Hotel: Mount Stuart Guest House, Elie, 6 mile(s). Tel: 330653 (0333)

LEVEN
Lundin Golf Club, Lundin Links, Leven, Fife. KY8 6BA. Tel: 320202 (0333)
Secretary: Mr McBride   Tel: 320202 (0333)
Professional: David K Webster   Tel: 320051 (0333)
Location: 10 miles from St Andrews on coast road.
Description: Seaside links.
18 holes, 6,377 yards, Par 71, Course record 65.
Membership: 800
Visitors: Welcome. Handicap certificate required. Not on Sundays. Some restrictions on Saturdays. Always telephone in advance.
Green Fees: Weekdays £18 per round, £27 per day. Saturdays £25 per round. Weekly ticket £80.
Facilities: Lunch. Dinner. Bar Snacks. Full Catering. Changing Room. Golf Shop. Club Hire. Trolley Hire. Caddies available.
Class One Hotel: The Old Manor, Lundin Links, 1/4 mile(s). Tel: 320368 (0333)

ST ANDREWS
St Andrews Eden Course, Links Management Committee of St Andrews Fife. KY16 9JA. Tel: 74296 (0334)
Secretary: Mr A Beveridge   Tel: 75757 (0334)
Location: Outskirts of St Andrews on Dundee road, 10 miles south of Dundee.
Description: Undulating links course, established since 1914.
18 holes, 6,315 yards, Par 70, S.S.S. 70.
Visitors: Welcome.
Green Fees: £12 per round. Reservation fee £5.
Facilities: Changing Room. Golf Shop. Club Hire. Trolley Hire. Caddies available.

ST ANDREWS
St Andrews Jubilee Course, Links Management Committee of St Andrews Fife. KY16 9JA. Tel: 73938 (0334)
Secretary: Mr A Beveridge   Tel: 73938 (0334)
Location: West Sands of St Andrews, 10 miles south of Dundee.
Description: Undulating links. Major amateur championship course.
18 holes, 6,805 yards, Par 72, S.S.S. 73.
Visitors: Welcome.
Green Fees: £14 per round. Reservation fee £5.
Facilities: Golf Shop. Club Hire. Trolley Hire. Caddies available.

ST ANDREWS
St Andrews New Course, Links Management Committee of St Andrews, Fife. KY16 9JA. Tel: 73938 (0334)
Secretary: Mr A Beveridge   Tel: 75757 (0334)
Location: Adjacent to Old Course, 10 miles south of Dundee.

Description: Undulating links. Major amateur championship course dating back to 1896.
18 holes, 6,604 yards, Par 71, S.S.S. 72.
Visitors: Welcome. Advisable to contact starter for tee availability. Reservations in writing three months in advance.
Green Fees: £14 per round. Reservation fee £5.
Facilities: Golf Shop. Club Hire. Trolley Hire. Caddies available.

ST ANDREWS
St Andrews Old Course, Links Management Committee of St Andrews, Fife. KY16 9JA. Tel: 73393 (0334)
Secretary: Mr A Beveridge   Tel: 75757 (0334)
Location: 10 miles south of Dundee.
Description: Links.
18 holes, 6,566 yards, Par 72, S.S.S. 72, Course record 62.
Visitors: Welcome. Handicap certificate required. Letter of Introduction required. Closed Sundays.
Green Fees: £34. Reservation fee £20.
Facilities: Golf Shop. Club Hire. Trolley Hire. Caddies available.

ST ANDREWS
St Andrews Links, Links Management Committee of St Andrews, Fife. KY16 9JA. Tel: 75757 (0334)
Location: Situated on the east coast alongside St Andrews, 50 miles north of Edinburgh Airport.
Description: Undulating links. Championship course - 1990 British Open held here. Course dates back to 1400.
18 holes, 6,566 yards, Par 72, S.S.S. 72.
Visitors: Welcome. Handicap certificate required. Letter of Introduction required. Must book in writing 8 - 10 months in advance. A £20 reservation fee is required of which £10 is refundable.
Green Fees: £34 per round.
Facilities: Lunch. Dinner. Bar Snacks. Full Catering. Changing Room. Golf Shop. Club Hire. Trolley Hire. Caddies available.
Class One Hotel: St Andrews Old Course Hotel, St Andrews, 1/2 mile(s). Tel: 74371 (0334)

THORNTON
Thornton Golf Club, Thornton, Fife. KY1 4DW. Tel: 771111 (0592)
Secretary: N Robertson   Tel: 771111 (0592)
Location: Thornton lies midway between Kirkcaldy and Glenrothes. Access to club via Station Road in Thornton.
Description: Undulating parkland.
18 holes, 5,589 yards, Par 70, S.S.S. 69, Course record 65.
Membership: 630
Visitors: Welcome.
Green Fees: On application.
Facilities: Lunch. Dinner. Bar Snacks. Full Catering. Changing Room. Trolley Hire.
Class One Hotel: Balbirnie House, Glenrothes, 5 mile(s). Tel: 610066 (0592)
Class Two Hotel: Crown, Thornton, 2 mile(s). Tel: 774416 (0592)

GRAMPIAN

ABERDEEN
Deeside Golf Club, Golf Road, Bieldside, Aberdeen, Grampian. Tel: 867697 (0224)
Secretary: Dr. N M Scott   Tel: 869457 (0224)
Professional: Mr F Coutts   Tel: 861041 (0224)
Location: On Braemar Road in the village of Bieldside.
Description: Parkland with panoramic views of the River Dee which also runs through the course.
18 holes, 5,972 yards, Par 72, S.S.S. 69, Course record 64.
Membership: 500
Visitors: Welcome. Handicap certificate required. Tuesdays and Fridays Ladies Day. Not before 4p.m. weekends.
Green Fees: Weekdays £17 per day, weekends £19 per day.
Facilities: Lunch. Dinner. Bar Snacks. Full Catering. Changing Room. Golf Shop. Club Hire. Trolley Hire.

ABERDEEN
Links Golf Course, Golf Road, Aberdeen, Grampian. .
Tel: 633464 (0224)
Secretary: G S Hunter   Tel: 633464 (0224)
Description: Links.
18 holes, 6,433 yards, Par 72, S.S.S. 71, Course record 64.
Membership: 600
Visitors: Welcome.
Green Fees: On application.
Facilities: Lunch. Bar Snacks. Full Catering. Changing Room. Golf Shop. Driving Range. Trolley Hire.

ABERDEEN
Murcar Golf Club, Murcar, Bridge of Don, Aberdeen, Grampian. AB23 8BD. Tel: 704345 (0224)
Secretary: R Matthews   Tel: 704354 (0224)
Professional: A White   Tel: 704370 (0224)
Location: On A92 approx 6 miles from Aberdeen.
Description: Typical links.
18 holes, 6,241 yards, Par 71, S.S.S. 70, Course record 65.
Visitors: Welcome. Handicap certificate required. Not saturdays. Not before 10.00 a.m. Sundays, Wednesdays not before 12p.m.. Snacks only on Tuesdays.
Green Fees: Weekdays before 11.30 a.m. £12.50, after 11.30 a.m. £20 per round or day. Sundays £22.50.
Facilities: Lunch. Dinner. Bar Snacks. Full Catering. Changing Room. Golf Shop. Trolley Hire.

ABERDEEN
Royal Aberdeen Golf Club, Links road, Bridge of Don, Aberdeen, Grampian. AB23 8AT. Tel: 702571 (0224)
Secretary: Mr Webster   Tel: 702571 (0224)
Professional: Mr Macaskill   Tel: 702221 (0224)
Location: 4 miles north-east of Aberdeen centre on the Fraserburgh road.
Description: Traditional undulating Scottish links championship course. The sixth oldest course in the world established in 1780.
Balgownie Links 18 holes, 6,407 yards, Par 70, S.S.S. 71, Course record 63
Silver Burn 18 holes, 4,066 yards, Par 64, S.S.S. 60.
Membership: 500
Visitors: Welcome. Letter of Introduction required. Always by arrangement with professional. Not Sats before 3.30p.m..
Green Fees: Balgownie Links: £25 per round, £30 per day. Silver Burn: £12.50 per round, £15 per day.
Facilities: Lunch. Dinner. Bar Snacks. Full Catering. Changing Room. Golf Shop. Club Hire. Trolley Hire.
Class One Hotel: Udny Arms, Newburgh, 1 Tel: 89444 (03586)
Class Two Hotel: Brentwood Villa, Aberdeen, 1 1/2 mile(s). Tel: 480633 (0224)

ABOYNE
Aboyne Golf Club, Formaston Park, Aboyne, Grampian. AB34 5HP. Tel: 86328 (03398)
Secretary: Mrs MacLean   Tel: 87078 (03398)
Professional: Mr I Wright   Tel: 86328 (03398)
Location: 12 miles west of Banchory on A93.
Description: Parkland both flat and undulating. Panoramic views of the Grampian Hills and Aboyne Loch.
18 holes, 5,910 yards, Par 68, S.S.S. 69, Course record 69.
Membership: 900
Visitors: Welcome. Subject to availability.
Green Fees: Weekdays £13 per round, £17 per day. Weekends £20 per day.
Facilities: Lunch. Dinner. Bar Snacks. Full Catering. Changing Room. Golf Shop. Club Hire. Trolley Hire.
Class One Hotel: Balnacoil Hotel, Aboyne, 1 1/2 mile(s). Tel: 86806 (03398)

ABOYNE
Tarland Golf Club, Aberdeen Road, Tarland, Aboyne, Grampian. . Tel: 81413 (03398)
Secretary: Jim Honeyman   Tel: 81413 (03398)
Location: 30 miles west of Aberdeen on A974, 6 miles north of Aboyne on B9094.
Description: Easy walking, difficult upland course.
9 holes, 5,888 yards, Par 67, S.S.S. 68, Course record 69.
Membership: 240
Visitors: Welcome. No reservations at weekends. Advise telephone call before travelling.
Green Fees: Weekdays £8, weekends £10 (under review).
Facilities: Bar Snacks. Full Catering. Changing Room. Trolley Hire.

ALFORD
Alford Golf Club, Montgarrie Road, Alford, Grampian. AB33 8AE. Tel: 62178 (09755)
Secretary: Mrs M J Ball   Tel: 62843 (09755)
Location: A944, 26 miles west of Aberdeen.
Description: Flat parkland. 9 hole course extending to 18 holes in August 1992.
9 holes, 5,964 yards, Par 70, S.S.S. 68, Course record 68.
Membership: 400
Visitors: Welcome. Thursday 5.00-7.30 p.m. Ladies competitions. Telephone for availability at weekends. Some catering restrictions apply, please telephone in advance.
Green Fees: Weekdays £6 per round, £8 per day. Weekends £9.50 per round, £12.50 per day.
Facilities: Lunch. Dinner. Bar Snacks. Changing Room.

BANCHORY
Banchory Golf Club, Kinneskie Road, Banchory, Grampian. AB31 3TA. Tel: 2365 (03302)
Professional: D W Smart   Tel: 2447 (03302)
Location: 18 miles west of Aberdeen on Deeside.
Description: Parkland.
18 holes, 5,245 yards, Par 67, S.S.S. 66, Course record 60.
Membership: 950
Visitors: Welcome. No societies catered for at weekends.
Green Fees: Weekdays £16.50, weekends £18.50.
Facilities: Lunch. Dinner. Bar Snacks. Full Catering. Changing Room. Golf Shop. Club Hire. Trolley Hire. Buggy Hire. Caddies available.
Class One Hotel: Invery House, Banchory, 2 mile(s). Tel: 4782 (03302)
Class Two Hotel: Burnett Arms, Banchory, 1/2 mile(s). Tel: 4944 (03302)

BANFF
Duff House Royal Golf Club, The Barnyards, Banff, Grampian. AB45 3SX. Tel: 812062 (0261)
Secretary: Mr K T Morrison   Tel: 812062 (0261)
Professional: Mr R S Strachan   Tel: 812075 (0261)
Location: Adjacent to A98 in the town of Banff.
Description: Flat parkland course, well bunkered with large two-tier greens designed by Dr McKenzie.
18 holes, 6,161 yards, Par 68, S.S.S. 69, Course record 63.
Membership: 700
Visitors: Welcome. Handicap certificate required. Some restricted times at weekends and evenings in July and August.
Green Fees: Weekdays £9 per round, £14 per day. Weekends £15 per round, £20 per day.
Facilities: Lunch. Dinner. Bar Snacks. Full Catering. Changing Room. Golf Shop. Trolley Hire.
Class One Hotel: Banff Springs, Banff, 1/2 mile(s). Tel: 812881 (0261)
Class Two Hotel: Carmelite House, Banff, 1/4 mile(s). Tel: 812152 (0261)

BRAEMAR
Braemar Golf Club, Cluniebank Road, Braemar, Grampian. AB35 5XX. Tel: 41618 (03397)
Secretary: John Pennet   Tel: 704471 (0224)
Location: 1 mile from village centre opposite Fife Arms Hotel.
Description: Reasonably flat parkland with a river running through.
18 holes, 4,916 yards, Par 65, S.S.S. 64, Course record 61.
Membership: 400
Visitors: Welcome. Book 24 hours in advance for weekends play.
Green Fees: Weekdays £9 per round, £12 per day. Weekends £15 per round, £18 per day.
Facilities: Lunch. Dinner. Bar Snacks. Full Catering. Changing Room. Golf Shop. Club Hire. Trolley Hire.
Class One Hotel: Fife Arms, Braemar, 1 mile(s). Tel: 41644 (03397)
Class Two Hotel: Moorfield, Braemar, 1 mile(s). Tel: 41244 (03397)

Cade's - Audi Golf Course Guide

CULLEN
Cullen Golf Club, The Links, Cullen, Buckie, Grampian. AB56 2SM. Tel: 40685 (0542)
Secretary: Ian Findlay   Tel: 40174 (0542)
Location: Off A98, midway between Aberdeen and Inverness on Moray Firth coast, on west side of town.
Description: Seaside natural links course with elevated section, natural rock landscaping and sandy beach coming in to play at several holes. Interesting hidden holes. Superlative views of Moray Firth.
18 holes, 4,610 yards, Par 63, S.S.S. 62, Course record 58.
Membership: 550
Visitors: Welcome. Society meetings catered for. Possible restrictions on club competition days (Wcds and Sats). Member of Moray D.Council Rover Golf Ticket Scheme.
Green Fees: Weekdays £7 per day, weekends £10 per day also weekly and fortnightly tickets available.
Facilities: Lunch. Dinner. Bar Snacks. Full Catering. Changing Room.
Class One Hotel: Cullen Bay Hotel, Cullen, 1/2 mile(s). Tel: 40432 (0542)
Class Two Hotel: Royal Oak, Cullen, 1/4 mile(s). Tel: 40252 (0542)

DUFFTOWN
Dufftown Golf Club, Mether Cluny, Dufftown, Grampian. Tel: 20325 (0340)
Secretary: A Stuart   Tel: 20165 (0340)
Location: 1 mile from centre of Dufftown on Tomintoul Road B9009.
Description: Hilly course with superb views, includes some challenging holes.
18 holes, 5,300 yards, Par 67, S.S.S. 67, Course record 68.
Membership: 233
Visitors: Welcome. Some restrictions competition days (Wednesday evenings and Sundays). Some catering restrctions apply, please telephone in advance.
Green Fees: Weekdays £7, weekends £8, all week £25. Juniors half price.
Facilities: Lunch. Dinner. Bar Snacks. Changing Room. Club Hire. Trolley Hire.
Class One Hotel: Craigellachie Hotel, Craigellachie, 5 mile(s). Tel: 881204 (0840)

ELGIN
Elgin Golf Club, Hardhillock, Birnie Road, Elgin, Grampian. IV30 3SX. Tel: 542338 (0343)
Secretary: Mr D J Chambers   Tel: 542338 (0343)
Professional: Mr I P Rodger   Tel: 542884 (0343)
Location: 1/2 mile south of Elgin on Rothers-on-Spey Road.
Description: Undulating parkland. Inland course with prevailing westerly winds. Many bunkers and panoramic views of Speyside Hills.
18 holes, 6,401 yards, Par 69, S.S.S. 71, Course record 64.
Membership: 980
Visitors: Welcome. Handicap certificate required. Subject to availability. Caddies available subject to 7 days notice.
Green Fees: Weekdays £13 per round, £19 per day. Weekends £18.50 per round, £26.50 per day.
Facilities: Lunch. Dinner. Bar Snacks. Full Catering. Chang-

175

ing Room. Golf Shop. Trolley Hire.
Class One Hotel: The Mansion House, Elgin, 1 mile(s). Tel: 548811 (0343)
Class Two Hotel: Braelossie, Elgin, 1 mile(s). Tel: 547181 (0343)

ELLON
Newburgh-on-Ythan Golf Club, C/O 51 Mavis Bank, Newburgh, Ellon, Grampian. AB41 0FB. Tel: 89438 (03586)
Secretary: Andrew C Stevenson   Tel: 89438 (03586)
Location: 12 miles north of Aberdeen on the A975 Cruden Bay Road.
Description: Links.
9 holes, 6,300 yards, Par 72, S.S.S. 70, Course record 69.
Membership: 350
Visitors: Welcome. Course closed Tuesdays from 4.30p.m..
Green Fees: Weekdays £10, weekends £12.
Class One Hotel: Udny Arms, Newburgh, Tel: 89444 (03586)
Class Two Hotel: Ythan Hotel, Newburgh, Tel: 89272 (03586)

FOCHABERS
Garmouth and Kingston Golf Club, Garmouth, Fochabers, Grampian. IV32 7NJ. Tel: 388 (034387)
Secretary: A Robertson   Tel: 231 (034387)
Description: Parkland, part links suitable for elderly or disabled.
18 holes, 5,656 yards, Par 67, S.S.S. 67, Course record 64.
Membership: 350
Visitors: Welcome. Restricted during club competitions. Tuesdays tee reserved for Ladies from 5p.m. to 7p.m..
Green Fees: Weekdays £10 per round, £12 per day. Weekends £14 per round, £18 per day.
Facilities: Lunch. Dinner. Bar Snacks. Full Catering. Changing Room.
Class One Hotel: Garmouth Hotel, Garmouth, 1/4 mile(s). Tel: 226 (034387)

FOCHABERS
Spey Bay Golf Club, Spey Bay, By Fochabers, Grampian. IV32 7PN. Tel: 820424 (0343)
Location: Turn off A96 at Fochabers to Spey Bay, 3 miles.
Description: Gently undulating links course.
18 holes, 6,059 yards, Par 71, S.S.S. 69.
Visitors: Welcome. Not between 8.30 - 9.30a.m. and 12.15 - 2.15p.m..
Green Fees: Monday to Saturday £7. Sundays £8.50. Free to hotel residents.
Facilities: Lunch. Dinner. Bar Snacks. Full Catering. Changing Room. Club Hire. Driving Range. Trolley Hire.
Class One Hotel: Spey Bay Hotel, On Course, Tel: 820424 (0343)
Class Two Hotel: Cluny, Buckie, 7 mile(s). Tel: 32922 (0542)

FORRES
Forres Golf Club, Muiryshade, Forres, Grampian. IV36 0RD. Tel: 672949 (0309)
Secretary: David F Black   Tel: 672949 (0309)

Professional: Sandy Aird   Tel: 672250 (0309)
Location: 1 mile south of town centre.
Description: Wooded parkland with some hilly parts.
18 holes, 6,203 yards, Par 70, S.S.S. 69, Course record 63.
Membership: 950
Visitors: Welcome. Restricted weekends due to members competitions, contact Secretary in advance.
Green Fees: W/days £11 per day, w/ends £16.50 per day.
Facilities: Lunch. Dinner. Bar Snacks. Full Catering. Changing Room. Golf Shop. Club Hire. Trolley Hire.
Class One Hotel: The Ramnee Hotel, Forres, 1 mile(s). Tel: 672410 (0309)
Class Two Hotel: Park, Forres, 1 mile(s). Tel: 675328 (0309)

HOPEMAN
Hopeman Golf Club, Hopeman, By Elgin, Grampian. IV30 1PP. Tel: 830578 (0343)
Secretary: W H Dunbar   Tel: 830687 (0343)
Location: 6 miles north of Elgin on the Hopeman B9012.
Description: A links style course, parkland, ditches, 45 bunkers, spectaclar views of the Moray Firth.
18 holes, 6,125 yards, Par 66, S.S.S. 67, Course record 65.
Membership: 530
Visitors: Welcome. Tuesdays Ladies Day. Members and guests have priority at weekends. Caddies available with 7 days notice.
Green Fees: Weekdays £10 per round or day, weekends £15 per round.
Facilities: Lunch. Dinner. Bar Snacks. Full Catering. Changing Room. Golf Shop. Club Hire. Trolley Hire.
Class One Hotel: Station Hotel, Hopeman, 1/2 mile(s). Tel: 830258 (0343)

INVERALLOCHY
Inverallochy Golf Club, Inverallochy, Near Fraserburgh, Grampian. Tel: 2324 (03465)
Location: 5 miles from Fraserburgh.
Description: Links.
18 holes, 5,137 yards, Par 64, S.S.S. 65, Course record 60.
Visitors: Welcome.
Green Fees: Weekdays £5, weekends £7.
Class One Hotel: Station, Fraserburgh, 5 mile(s). Tel: 23343 (0346)

INVERURIE
Inverurie Golf Club, Blackhall Road, Inverurie, Grampian. AB51 9JH. Tel: 24080 (0467)
Secretary: John Ramage   Tel: 21291 (0467)
Location: Off A96 at Inverurie.
Description: Parkland with some wooded areas.
18 holes, 5,096 yards, Par 66, S.S.S. 65, Course record 63.
Membership: 700
Visitors: Welcome. Handicap certificate required. Not Saturday mornings.
Green Fees: Weekdays £8 per day, weekends £12 per day.
Facilities: Lunch. Dinner. Bar Snacks. Full Catering. Changing Room. Golf Shop. Trolley Hire.
Class One Hotel: Strathburn, Inverurie, 1/2 mile(s). Tel: 24422 (0467)

Class Two Hotel: Kintorr Arms, Inverurie, 1 mile(s) Tel: 21367 (0467)

KEITH

Keith Golf Club, Fife Park, Keith, Grampian. . Tel: 2469 (05422)
Secretary: Graeme Morrison   Tel: 2696 (05422)
Location: On A96 within the town.
Description: Undulating parkland with scenic views of surrounding countryside.
18 holes, 5,797 yards, Par 69, S.S.S. 68.
Visitors: Welcome.
Green Fees: Weekdays £8, weekends £10.
Facilities: Lunch. Dinner. Bar Snacks. Full Catering. Changing Room.

KEMNAY

Kemnay Golf Club, Monymusk Road, Kemnay, Grampian. AB51 9NB. Tel: 42225 (0467)
Secretary: Mr D Imrie   Tel: 43047 (0467)
Location: Situated on the western boundary of Kemnay Village.
Description: Undulating parkland with a stream flowing through the course surrounded by mature pine, beech and sycamore trees. Views of the Bennachie Hills.
9 holes, 5,502 yards, Par 68, S.S.S. 67, Course record 64.
Membership: 420
Visitors: Welcome. With members only on Sunday mornings and Monday, Tuesday and Thursday evenings.
Green Fees: Weekdays £8 per round or day, weekends £10 per round or day.
Facilities: Lunch. Bar Snacks. Full Catering. Changing Room.
Class One Hotel: Pittodrie House, Pitcaple, 6 mile(s). Tel: 444 (04676)

LAURENCEKIRK

Auchenblae Golf Course, Auchenblae, Laurencekirk, Grampian. AB30 1BU. Tel: 8869 (05617)
Secretary: Alistair Robertson   Tel: 8869 (05617)
Location: 5 miles north of Laurencekirk on A94, 2 miles west of Fordoun.
Description: Parkland. Easy to play with some difficult holes.
9 holes, 2,174 yards, Par 32, S.S.S. 30.
Membership: 80
Visitors: Welcome. Not on Wednesday or Friday evenings after 5.30p.m..
Green Fees: Weekdays £5, Saturdays £6, Sundays £6.50.
Class One Hotel: Drumtolhty Hotel, Auchenblae, 1 mile(s). Tel: 407 (05612)

LOSSIEMOUTH

Moray Golf Club, Stotfield Road, Lossiemouth, Grampian. IV31 6QS. Tel: 812018 (0343)
Secretary: Mr J Hamilton   Tel: 812018 (0343)
Professional: Mr A Thomson   Tel: 813330 (0343)
Location: 1 mile north of Lossiemouth centre on the Elgin Road.
Description: Links type seaside course flat but surrounded by sand dunes.
New 18 holes, 6,005 yards, Par 69, S.S.S. 69, Course record 67.
Old 18 holes, 6,643 yards, Par 71, S.S.S. 72, Course record 67.
Membership: 1200
Visitors: Welcome. Handicap certificate required. Members and guests have priority at weekends.
Green Fees: New - Weekdays £12 per day, weekends £18 per day. Old - Weekdays £18 per day, weekends £25 per day.
Facilities: Lunch. Dinner. Bar Snacks. Full Catering. Changing Room. Golf Shop. Trolley Hire.
Class One Hotel: The Stotfield, Adjacent, Tel: 812011 (0343)

OLDMELDRUM

Oldmeldrum Golf Club, Kirkbrae, Oldmeldrum, Grampian. AB51 0DJ. Tel: 2648 (06512)
Secretary: D Petrie   Tel: 2383 (06512)
Location: 17 miles from Aberdeen on A947 towards Banff.
Description: Undulating parkland with tree lined fairways and water features.
18 holes, 5,988 yards, Par 70, S.S.S. 69, Course record 71.
Membership: 600
Visitors: Welcome. Restrictions during club competitions, please telephone in advance. Catering by arrangement.
Green Fees: W/days £10 per day, w/ends £15 per day.
Facilities: Lunch. Dinner. Bar Snacks. Full Catering. Changing Room.
Class One Hotel: Meldrum House, Oldmeldrum, 1 mile(s). Tel: 2294 (06512)
Class Two Hotel: Meldrum Arms, Oldmeldrum, 1/2 mile(s). Tel: 2238 (06512)

PETERHEAD

Cruden Bay Golf Club, Cruden Bay, Peterhead, Grampian. AB42 7NN. Tel: 812285 (0779)
Secretary: Ian A D McPherson   Tel: 812285 (0779)
Professional: Robbie Stewart   Tel: 812414 (0779)
Description: Traditional seaside links ranked in the top 50 in Britain.
Cruden Bay 18 holes, 6,370 yards, Par 70, S.S.S. 71, Course record 63.
St Olaf 9 holes, 4,710 yards, Par 64, S.S.S. 62.
Membership: 1000
Visitors: Welcome. Handicap certificate required. Not before 3.30p.m. on weekend competition days. Set times on non competition days, please telephone in advance.
Green Fees: Weekdays £18.50, weekends £25.50.
Facilities: Lunch. Dinner. Bar Snacks. Full Catering. Changing Room. Golf Shop. Club Hire. Trolley Hire. Caddies available.
Class One Hotel: Waterside Inn, Peterhead, 1 Tel: 71121 (0779)
Class Two Hotel: Red House, Cruden Bay, 8 mile(s). Tel: 812215 (0779)

PETERHEAD

Peterhead Golf Club, Craigewan Links, Peterhead, Grampian. AB42 6LT. Tel: 72149 (0779)
Secretary: Mr A Brandie   Tel: 73350 (0779)

Location: North end of town, at mouth of River Ugie.
Description: Natural seaside links.
Old Course 18 holes, 6,185 yards, Par 70, S.S.S. 70, Course record 64.
New Course 9 holes, 2,750 yards, Par 60, S.S.S. 60.
Membership: 525
Visitors: Welcome. Handicap certificate required. No Societies etc. on Saturdays.
Green Fees: Weekdays £10 per day, weekends £14 per day.
Facilities: Lunch. Dinner. Bar Snacks. Full Catering. Changing Room.
Class One Hotel: Waterside Inn, Peterhead, 2 mile(s). Tel: 71121 (0779)
Class Two Hotel: Caledonian, Peterhead, 1 mile(s). Tel: 73277 (0779)

STONEHAVEN
Stonehaven Golf Club, Cowie, Stonehaven, Grampian. AB3 2RH. Tel: 62124 (0569)
Secretary: R O Blair   Tel: 62124 (0569)
Location:
Description: Inland type course with exceptional sea views.
18 holes, 5,128 yards, Par 66, S.S.S. 65, Course record 61.
Membership: 830
Visitors: Welcome. Not Saturdays.
Green Fees: Weekdays £13, weekends £18.
Facilities: Lunch. Dinner. Bar Snacks. Full Catering. Changing Room. Golf Shop.
Class One Hotel: Commodore, Stonehaven, 1/2 mile(s). Tel: 62930 (0569)
Class Two Hotel: County, Stonehaven, 1 mile(s). Tel: 64386 (0569)

TURRIFF
Turriff Golf Club, Rosehall, Turriff, Grampian. AB53 7BB. Tel: 62982 (0888)
Secretary: J D Stott   Tel: 62982 (0888)
Professional: R Smith   Tel: 63025 (0888)
Location: Signposted from A947 at south side of Turriff.
Description: Parkland course alongside River Deveron.
18 holes, 6,145 yards, Par 69, S.S.S. 69, Course record 64.
Visitors: Welcome. Handicap certificate required.
Green Fees: Weekdays £9 per round, £13 per day. Weekends £13 per round, £16 per day.
Facilities: Lunch. Dinner. Bar Snacks. Full Catering. Changing Room. Golf Shop. Club Hire. Trolley Hire.
Class One Hotel: Banff Springs, Banff, 12 mile(s). Tel: 812881 (0261)
Class Two Hotel: Union, Turriff, 1 mile(s). Tel: 63704 (0888)

WESTHILL
Westhill Golf Club, Westhill Heights, Westhill, Skene, Grampian. AB32 6UZ. Tel: 743361 (0224)
Secretary: John L Webster   Tel: 740957 (0224)
Professional: Ronnie McDonald Tel: 740159 (0224)
Description: Undulating parkland, hilly in places.
18 holes, 5,921 yards, Par 69, S.S.S. 69, Course record 66.
Membership: 625

Visitors: Welcome. Not Saturdays. Not weekdays between 4p.m. and 7p.m.. Catering by arrangement with club Steward.
Green Fees: Weekdays £8 per round, £11 per day. Sundays and Bank Holidays £10 per round, £13 per day.
Facilities: Lunch. Dinner. Bar Snacks. Full Catering. Changing Room. Golf Shop. Trolley Hire.
Class One Hotel: Westhill Hotel, Westhill, 1 mile(s). Tel: 740388 (0224)

HIGHLAND

BONAR BRIDGE
Bonar Bridge-Ardgay Golf Club, Market Stance, Migdale Road, Bonar Bridge, Highland. .
Secretary: Mr A Turner   Tel: 248 (054982)
Location: 40 miles north of Inverness on A9.
Description: 9 hole heathland course in magnificent setting with loch and mountain views.
18 holes, 4,626 yards, Par 66, S.S.S. 63.
Membership: 300
Visitors: Welcome. May be closed for major competitions at weekends, please telephone in advance.
Green Fees: £6 per day.
Facilities: Changing Room.
Class Two Hotel: Kincardine House, Ardgay, 2 mile(s). Tel: 471 (08632)

DORNOCH
Royal Dornoch Golf Club, The Clubhouse, Golf Road, Dornoch, Highland. IV25 3LW. Tel: 810219 (0862)
Secretary: Mr Walker   Tel: 810219 (0862)
Professional: Mr Skinner   Tel: 810902 (0862)
Location: Signposted in Dornoch.
Description: Links type championship course, undulating with many bunkers. Rated 11th best course in the world by Golf World Magazine in 1992.
18 holes, 6,112 yards, Par 70, S.S.S. 72, Course record 67.
Membership: 900
Visitors: Welcome. Handicap certificate required. Letter of Introduction required. Members and guest have priority. Subject to availability, please telphone in advance.
Green Fees: Weekdays £25 per round, £45 per day. Weekends £30 per round, £55 per day.
Facilities: Lunch. Dinner. Bar Snacks. Full Catering. Changing Room. Golf Shop. Club Hire. Trolley Hire. Caddies available.
Class One Hotel: Royal Golf Hotel, Adjacent, Tel: 810283 (0862)

DURNESS
Durness Golf Course, Balnakiel, Durness, Highland. IV27 4PQ.
Secretary: Lucy MacKay   Tel: 364 (097181)
Location: 57 miles north west of Lairg on A838.
Description: Links course with final hole played over deep intimidating gulley. 9 greens played off 18 tees.
9 holes, 5,545 yards, Par 70, S.S.S. 68, Course record 72.
Membership: 100
Visitors: Welcome. Restrictions some Sunday mornings

during competitions. Course closed during Lambing season (approx Mid-April to Mid-May).
Green Fees: £6 per day, £24 per week.
Facilities: Changing Room. Club Hire. Trolley Hire.
Class Two Hotel: Parkhill, Durness, 1 mile(s). Tel: 209 (097181)

FORT AUGUSTUS
Fort Augustus Golf Club, Fort Augustus, Highland. PH32 4DT. Tel: 6460 (0320)
Secretary: Mr Aitchison　　　　　　Tel: 6460 (0320)
Location: 3/4 mile west of Fort Augustus on A84 Inverness/Fort William Road.
Description: 9 holes played off 18 tees. Undulating moorland, a tight course bordered by the Caledonian Canal, pine trees and heather.
9 holes, 5,454 yards, Par 67, S.S.S. 68, Course record 69.
Membership: 150
Visitors: Welcome. Not Saturday afternoons or Tuesday and Wednesday evenings. Caddies available with 2 days notice.
Green Fees: £5 per round.
Facilities: Bar Snacks. Full Catering. Changing Room. Club Hire. Trolley Hire.
Class Two Hotel: Lovat Arms, Fort Augustus, 3/4 mile(s). Tel: 6206 (0320)

GAIRLOCH
Gairloch Golf Club, Gairloch, Highland.　. Tel: 2407 (0445)
Secretary: Mr J Dingwall　　　　　Tel: 2315 (0445)
Location: In the central parish of Gairloch on the Ullapool to Inverness Road.
Description: 9 holes played twice. Undulating parkland/links.
9 holes, 5,700 yards, Par 64.
Membership: 250
Visitors: Welcome. No non-golfers.
Green Fees: £10 per day.
Facilities: Changing Room. Golf Shop. Club Hire. Trolley Hire.
Class One Hotel: Gairloch Hotel, Gairloch, 1/2 mile(s). Tel: 2001 (0445)

GOLSPIE
Golspie Golf Course, Ferry Road, Golspie, Highland. KW10 6ST. Tel: 633266 (0408)
Secretary: Mrs Marie MacLeod　　　Tel: 633266 (0408)
Location: Off A9, 1/2 mile from Golspie.
Description: Fairly flat seaside links, wooded with heather and the Lochy pond providing the hazards.
18 holes, 5,836 yards, Par 68, S.S.S. 68, Course record 64.
Membership: 420
Visitors: Welcome. Parties must book in advance. Caddies by prior arrangement.
Green Fees: £14 per day.
Facilities: Lunch. Bar Snacks. Full Catering. Changing Room. Golf Shop. Trolley Hire.
Class One Hotel: Royal Dornoch Hotel, Dornoch, 12 mile(s). Tel: 810283 (0862)
Class Two Hotel: Stags Head, Golspie, 3/4 mile(s). Tel: 633245 (0408)

GRANTOWN-ON-SPEY
Grantown-on-Spey Golf Club, The Clubhouse, Golf Course Road, Grantown-on-Spey, Highland. PH26 3HY. Tel: 2079 (0479)
Secretary: D W Elms　　　　　　Tel: 2715 (0479)
Professional: W Mitchell　　　　　Tel: 2398 (0479)
Description: Open parkland with wooded central section.
18 holes, 5,745 yards, Par 70, S.S.S. 67, Course record 60.
Membership: 500
Visitors: Welcome. Weekdays not between 5.30p.m. and 6.30p.m.. Weekends not before 10a.m., not between 1p.m. and 2p.m. or 5p.m. and 6p.m..
Green Fees: Weekdays £13 per day, weekends £16 per day.
Facilities: Lunch. Dinner. Bar Snacks. Full Catering. Changing Room. Golf Shop. Club Hire. Trolley Hire.
Class One Hotel: Ben Mhor, Grantown, 1/2 mile(s). Tel: 2056 (0479)
Class Two Hotel: Tyree House, Grantown, 1/2 mile(s). Tel: 2615 (0479)

HELMSDALE
Helmsdale Golf Club, Golf Road, Helmsdale, Highland. KW8 6JA. Tel: 240 (04312)
Secretary: Mr J MacKay　　　　　Tel: 240 (04312)
Location: 80 miles north of Inverness on the A9 to John O'Groats.
Description: 9 holes played twice. Flat meadowland with gorse and heather. Challenging course with the River Helmsdale running along side.
9 holes, 3,650 yards, Par 62, S.S.S. 62, Course record 60.
Membership: 80
Visitors: Welcome.
Green Fees: £3 per day, £10 per week, £15 per fortnight.
Facilities: Bar Snacks. Full Catering. Changing Room. Caddies available.
Class One Hotel: Bridge, Helmsdale, 1/8 mile(s). Tel: 219 (04312)

INVERNESS
Inverness Golf Club, Culcaboch Road, Inverness, Highland. IV2 3XQ. Tel: 233422 (0463)
Secretary: Mr J Fraser　　　　　Tel: 239882 (0463)
Professional: Mr A P Thomson　　Tel: 231989 (0463)
Location: 1 mile south of Inverness town centre on old A9.
Description: Open parkland with a stream running through the course, scenic views. Golf club dates back to 1883.
18 holes, 6,226 yards, Par 69, S.S.S. 70, Course record 64.
Membership: 1052
Visitors: Welcome. Handicap certificate required. Thursdays Ladies Day. Not Saturdays (competition day).
Green Fees: Weekdays £14 per round, £18 per day. Weekends £17 per round, £20 per day.
Facilities: Lunch. Dinner. Bar Snacks. Full Catering. Changing Room. Golf Shop. Club Hire. Trolley Hire. Caddies available.
Class One Hotel: Kings Mill, Inverness, 1 mile(s). Tel: 239882 (0463)

KINGUSSIE

Kingussie Golf Club, Gynack Road, Kingussie, Highland. PH21 1LR. Tel: 661600 (0540)
Secretary: W M Cook   Tel: 661600 (0540)
Location: 1/2 mile from town centre, turn at Duke of Gordon Hotel.
Description: Upland course with spectacular scenery.
18 holes, 5,555 yards, Par 66, S.S.S. 67, Course record 64.
Membership: 660
Visitors: Welcome. Members only 8.30a.m. to 9.30a.m., 12.30p.m. to 1.30p.m. and 5.30p.m. to 6.30p.m. at weekends. No Four-balls at weekends.
Green Fees: Weekdays £10 per round, £13 per day. Weekends £12 per round, £16 per day.
Facilities: Lunch. Bar Snacks. Full Catering. Changing Room. Golf Shop. Club Hire. Trolley Hire.
Class One Hotel: Duke of Gordon, Kingussie, 1/2 mile(s). Tel: 661302 (0540)
Class Two Hotel: Columba House, Kingussie, 3/4 mile(s). Tel: 661402 (0540)

MUIR OF ORD

Muir of Ord Golf Club, Great North Road, Muir of Ord, Highland. IV6 7SX. Tel: 870825 (0463)
Secretary: Mr G Reid   Tel: 870859 (0463)
Professional: Mr A Thompson   Tel: 870825 (0463)
Location: 12 miles north of Inverness on A862.
Description: Heathland/moorland. Established in 1875. Situated in the foothills of Ben Wyvis.
18 holes, 5,202 yards, Par 67, S.S.S. 65, Course record 61.
Membership: 750
Visitors: Welcome. Handicap certificate required. Subject to availability of tees. Caddies available with 2 days notice.
Green Fees: Weekdays £10 per day, weekends £12 per day.
Facilities: Lunch. Bar Snacks. Full Catering. Changing Room. Golf Shop. Club Hire. Trolley Hire.
Class One Hotel: Ord Arms, Miur Of Ord, 1 mile(s). Tel: 870286 (0463)
Class Two Hotel: Tarradale, Muir Of Ord, 1 mile(s). Tel: 870226 (0463)

NAIRN

Nairn Dunbar Golf Club, Lochloy Road, Nairn, Highland. IV12 5AE. Tel: 52741 (0667)
Secretary: Mrs MacLennan   Tel: 52741 (0667)
Professional: Mr B Mason   Tel: 53964 (0667)
Description: Links championship course, established in 1899. Attractive and challenging.
18 holes, 6,431 yards, Par 71, S.S.S. 71, Course record 68.
Membership: 700
Visitors: Welcome. Subject to availability of tees.
Green Fees: Weekdays £15 per day, weekends £20 per day.
Facilities: Lunch. Dinner. Bar Snacks. Full Catering. Changing Room. Golf Shop. Club Hire. Trolley Hire.
Class One Hotel: Golf View, Nairn, 1 mile(s). Tel: 52301 (0667)
Class Two Hotel: Links, Nairn, 1/2 mile(s). Tel: 52231 (0667)

NAIRN

Nairn Golf Club, Seabank Road, Nairn, Highland. IV12 4HB. Tel: 53208 (0667)
Secretary: Jim Somerville   Tel: 53208 (0667)
Professional: Robin Fyfe   Tel: 52787 (0667)
Description: Traditional links championship course with gorse and abundant heather.
Nairn 18 holes, 6,722 yards, Par 72, S.S.S. 72, Course record 65.
Newton 9 holes, 1,918 yards, Par 30.
Membership: 1040
Visitors: Welcome. Handicap certificate required.
Green Fees: Weekdays £23 per round, £33 per day. Weekends £28 per round, £38 per day.
Facilities: Lunch. Dinner. Bar Snacks. Full Catering. Changing Room. Golf Shop. Club Hire. Trolley Hire.
Class One Hotel: Golf View, Nairn, 1/4 mile(s). Tel: 52301 (0667)
Class Two Hotel: Altonburn, Nairn, 1/2 mile(s). Tel: 52051 (0667)

NETHYBRIDGE

Abernethy Golf Club, Nethybridge, Highland. PH25 3EB. Tel: 305 (047982)
Secretary: Bill Templeton   Tel: 214 (047982)
Location: On B970 1/2 mile from village on road to Grantown-on-Spey.
Description: 9 hole course. Pine woods and scenic views of River Spey and Valley.
9 holes, 4,986 yards, Par 66, S.S.S. 66, Course record 61.
Membership: 260
Visitors: Welcome. Some restrictions at weekends.
Green Fees: Weekdays £8, weekends £12, £50 per week.
Facilities: Lunch. Bar Snacks. Changing Room. Club Hire. Trolley Hire.
Class One Hotel: Nethy Bridge Hotel, Nethy Bridge, 1/4 mile(s). Tel: 203 (047982)
Class Two Hotel: Heatherbrae, Nethy Bridge, 1 1/4 mile(s). Tel: 345 (047982)

PORTMAHOMACK

Tarbat Golf Club, Portmahomack, Highland. IV20 1YB. Tel: 236 (086287)
Secretary: D C Wilson   Tel: 236 (086287)
Location: 10 miles east of Tain on A9.
Description: Seaside links.
9 holes, 5,654 yards, Par 63, S.S.S. 65.
Membership: 140
Visitors: Welcome. Handicap certificate required. Restrictions on Saturdays.
Green Fees: Weekdays £5 per day, weekends £6 per day. £20 per week.
Facilities: Changing Room.
Class One Hotel: Caledonian, Portmahomack, 1/2 mile(s). Tel: 345 (086287)
Class Two Hotel: Castle, Portmahomack, 1/2 mile(s). Tel: 263 (086287)

Cade's - Audi Golf Course Guide

REAY
Reay Golf Club, Clubhouse, Reay, Highland. KW14 /RE. Tel: 244 (084781)
Description: Scotland's most northerly links course.
18 holes, 6,250 yards, Par 69, S.S.S. 68, Course record 65.
Membership: 300
Visitors: Welcome. Lunch during Summer only.
Green Fees: £8 per day.
Facilities: Lunch. Bar Snacks. Changing Room.
Class One Hotel: Pentland, Thurso, 10 mile(s). Tel: 63102 (0847)
Class Two Hotel: Mrs Riley, Reay, Tel: 394 (084781)

SCONSER
Isle of Skye Golf Club, Sconser, Isle of Skye, Highland. . Tel: 2000 (0478)
Secretary: I Stephen Tel: 2000 (0478)
Location: 20 miles from Ferry on road to Portree.
Description: Seaside course situated at foot of Cuillin Hills with spectacular views of Raasay and North Skye.
9 holes, 4,500 yards, Par 66, S.S.S. 63, Course record 59.
Membership: 150
Visitors: Welcome. Members only competitions 10a.m. to 2p.m. Saturdays.
Green Fees: £7 per day, £12 per two days, £20 per three days.
Facilities: Changing Room. Club Hire.
Class One Hotel: Cuillin Hills Hotel, Portree, 14 mile(s). Tel: 2003 (0478)
Class Two Hotel: Sconser Lodge, Sconser, Tel: 300 (047852)

THURSO
Thurso Golf Club, Newlands of Geise, By Thurso, Highland. KW14 7XF. Tel: 63807 (0847)
Secretary: J R Owens Tel: 64030 (0847)
Location: 2 miles west of Thurso.
Description: Parkland with commanding views of Pentland Firth.
18 holes, 5,818 yards, Par 69, S.S.S. 69, Course record 63.
Membership: 400
Visitors: Welcome. Not Thursday evenings or Saturday mornings.
Green Fees: £10.
Facilities: Lunch. Dinner. Bar Snacks. Full Catering. Changing Room. Golf Shop. Club Hire. Trolley Hire. Caddies available.
Class One Hotel: Pentland, Thurso, 2 mile(s). Tel: 63102 (0847)
Class Two Hotel: St Clair Hotel, Thurso, 2 mile(s). Tel: 66481 (0847)

WICK
Wick Golf Club, Reiss, By Wick, Highland. KW1 4RW. Tel: 2726 (0955)
Secretary: Mrs M Abernethy Tel: 2702 (0955)
Location: Off A9, 3 1/2 miles north of Wick.
Description: Typical links in attractive situation with panoramic view of Sinclair Bay. Established in 1870, one of the top links courses in the north.
18 holes, 5,976 yards, Par 69, S.S.S. 69, Course record 63.

Membership: 350
Visitors: Welcome. Restrictions during club competitions (Wednesday and Thursday evenings).
Green Fees: £10 per day.
Facilities: Bar Snacks. Changing Room.
Class One Hotel: Mackays, Wick, 4 mile(s). Tel: 2323 (0955)

LOTHIAN

ABERLADY
Kilspindie Golf Club, Aberlady, Lothian. EH32 0QP. Tel: 216 (08757)
Secretary: Mr H F Brown Tel: 358 (08757)
Professional: Mr G Sked Tel: 695 (08752)
Location: Off A198 Edinburgh to North Berwick road, 17 miles south-east of Edinburgh.
Description: Flat links course alongside River Forth.
18 holes, 5,410 yards, Par 70, S.S.S. 66, Course record 61.
Membership: 700
Visitors: Welcome. Handicap certificate required. Subject of availability of tees. Caddies available, one days notice required.
Green Fees: Weekdays £16 per round, £22 per day. Weekends £20 per round, £26 per day.
Facilities: Lunch. Dinner. Bar Snacks. Full Catering. Changing Room. Golf Shop. Club Hire. Trolley Hire.
Class One Hotel: Kilspindie House, Aberlady, 1 mile(s). Tel: 682 (08757)

ABERLADY
Luffness New Golf Club, Aberlady, Lothian. EH32 0QA. Tel: 843114 (0620)
Secretary: Lt Col J G Tedford Tel: 843336 (0620)
Location: 25 miles south of Edinburgh on A198, 1 mile outside Aberlady on Gullane Road.
Description: Links. Royal and ancient selected championship course.
18 holes, 6,122 yards, Par 69, S.S.S. 69, Course record 63.
Membership: 710
Visitors: Welcome. Handicap certificate required. Letter of Introduction required. Not at weekends, Bank Holidays and Edinburgh Holidays. No LGU tees. Some catering restrictions apply, please telephone in advance.
Green Fees: On application.
Facilities: Lunch. Dinner. Full Catering. Changing Room. Caddies available.
Class One Hotel: Marine Hotel, North Berwick, 5 mile(s). Tel: 2406 (0620)
Class Two Hotel: Mallard, Gullane, 1 mile(s). Tel: 842288 (0620)

BATHGATE
Bathgate Golf Club, Edinburgh Road, Bathgate, Lothian. EH48 1BA. Tel: 52232 (0506)
Secretary: Mr W Gray Tel: 630505 (0506)
Professional: Mr S Strachan Tel: 630553 (0506)
Location: 1/2 mile east of centre of Bathgate.
Description: Flat parkland with a stream. Home course of

181

Eric Brown and Bernard Gallagher. Established in 1892. 18 holes, 6,328 yards, Par 71, S.S.S. 70, Course record 64.
Membership: 850
Visitors: Welcome. Subject to availability of tees.
Green Fees: Weekdays £11 per round, £14 per day. Weekends £22 per day.
Facilities: Lunch. Dinner. Bar Snacks. Full Catering. Changing Room. Golf Shop. Club Hire. Trolley Hire.
Class One Hotel: Golden Circle, Bathgate, 1 mile(s). Tel: 53771 (0506)
Class Two Hotel: Fairweigh Inn, Bathgate, 1/4 mile(s). Tel: 52835 (0506)

DALKEITH

Broomieknowe Golf Club, 36 Golf Course Road, Bonnyrigg, Dalkeith, Lothian. EH19 2HZ. Tel: 663 9317 (031)
Secretary: Mr I Nimmo   Tel: 663 9317 (031)
Professional: Mr M Patchett   Tel: 660 2035 (031)
Location: 2 miles west of Dalkeith on A6094.
Description: Flat parkland course. Established in 1906. Designed by James Braid.
18 holes, 5,754 yards, Par 68, S.S.S. 68, Course record 64.
Membership: 500
Visitors: Welcome. Not before 10a.m. weekends.
Green Fees: Weekdays £14 per round, £20 per day. Weekends £20 per round.
Facilities: Lunch. Dinner. Bar Snacks. Full Catering. Changing Room. Golf Shop. Club Hire. Trolley Hire.
Class One Hotel: Dalhousie Castle, Bonnyrigg, 1 mile(s). Tel: 20153 (0875)

DALKEITH

Newbattle Golf Club, Abbey Road, Dalkeith, Mid Lothian. Tel: 663 2123 (031)
Secretary: Mr H G Stanners   Tel: 663 2123 (031)
Professional: Mr D Torrence   Tel: 660 1631 (031)
Location: On the edge of Dalkeith 1/2 mile from the town centre.
Description: Woodland course.
18 holes, 6,012 yards, Par 69, S.S.S. 69, Course record 63.
Membership: 700
Visitors: Welcome. Handicap certificate required. With members only at weekends.
Green Fees: Weekdays £12 per round, £20 per day.
Facilities: Lunch. Dinner. Bar Snacks. Full Catering. Changing Room. Golf Shop. Trolley Hire.

DUNBAR

Dunbar Golf Club, East Links, Dunbar, Lothian. EH42 1LP. Tel: 62317 (0368).
Secretary: Don Thompson   Tel: 62317 (0368)
Professional: Derek Small   Tel: 62086 (0368)
Location: A1 Berwick to Edinburgh, turn off for Dunbar, 1/2 mile east of town centre.
Description: Links championship course, used for final qualifier of 1992 open.
18 holes, 6,426 yards, Par 71, S.S.S. 71.
Membership: 800
Visitors: Welcome. Not Thursdays. Weekdays not before 9.30a.m. and not between 12.30p.m. and 2p.m.. Weekends not before 10a.m. and not between 12p.m. and 2p.m..
Green Fees: Weekdays £20 per day, weekends £35 per day.
Facilities: Lunch. Dinner. Bar Snacks. Full Catering. Changing Room. Golf Shop. Club Hire. Trolley Hire. Caddies available.
Class Two Hotel: Hillside, Dunbar, 1/2 mile(s). Tel: 62071 (0368)

DUNBAR

Winterfield Golf Club, North Road, Dunbar, East Lothian. EH42 1AU. Tel: 62280 (0368)
Secretary: Mr O'Donnell   Tel: 62280 (0368)
Professional: Mr K Phillips   Tel: 63562 (0368)
Location: 1 mile north of Dunbar on the North Road.
Description: Undulating links type course overlooking the East Lothian coast line. 8 par 3's. A demanding course.
18 holes, 5,141 yards, Par 65, S.S.S. 65, Course record 61.
Membership: 250
Visitors: Welcome. Not before 10a.m. or between 12p.m. and 2p.m. or after 6p.m. Saturdays.
Green Fees: Weekdays £8.15 per round, £10.50 per day. Weekends £10 per round, £15.60 per day.
Facilities: Lunch. Dinner. Bar Snacks. Full Catering. Changing Room. Golf Shop. Club Hire. Trolley Hire. Caddies available.
Class One Hotel: The Hillside, Dunbar, 1 mile(s). Tel: 62071 (0368)

EDINBURGH

Baberton Golf Club, Baberton Aveune, Juniper Green, Edinburgh, Lothian. EH14 9DU. Tel: 453 3361 (031)
Secretary: Mr Horberry   Tel: 453 4911 (031)
Professional: Mr K Kelly   Tel: 453 3555 (031)
Location: 5 miles west of Edinburgh on A70.
Description: Undulating parkland. Established in 1893.
18 holes, 6,098 yards, Par 69, S.S.S. 69, Course record 64.
Membership: 950
Visitors: Welcome. Not after 4p.m.. With members only at weekends.
Green Fees: £17 per round, £25 per day.
Facilities: Lunch. Dinner. Bar Snacks. Full Catering. Changing Room. Golf Shop. Trolley Hire.
Class One Hotel: Braid Hills, Edinburgh, 4 mile(s). Tel: 447 8888 (031)

EDINBURGH

Bruntsfield Links Golfing Society, 32 Barnton Avenue, Davidsons Mains, Edinburgh, Lothian. EH4 6JH.
Secretary: Lt Col M B Hext   Tel: 336 1479 (031)
Professional: Mr B MacKenzie   Tel: 336 2050 (031)
Description: Flat parkland. The 4th Oldest club in the world which dates back to 1761. Men only.
18 holes, 6,407 yards, Par 71, S.S.S. 71, Course record 65.
Visitors: Welcome. Handicap certificate required. Letter of Introduction required. Must apply in writing.
Green Fees: On application.
Facilities: Lunch. Dinner. Full Catering. Changing Room. Golf Shop. Club Hire.

EDINBURGH
Craigmillar Park Golf Club, 1 Observatory Road, Edinburgh, Lothian. EH9 3HG. Tel: 667 0047 (031)
Secretary: Mrs J H Smith　　　　　Tel: 667 0047 (031)
Professional: B J McGhee　　　　Tel: 667 0047 (031)
Location: A702 from city centre on Mayfield Road, turn right at Kings buildings.
Description: Parkland.
18 holes, 5,859 yards, Par 70, S.S.S. 68, Course record 64.
Membership: 700
Visitors: Welcome. Handicap certificate required. Letter of Introduction required. Weekdays only, must clear first tee before 3.30p.m..
Green Fees: £12 per round, £18 per day.
Facilities: Lunch. Dinner. Bar Snacks. Full Catering. Changing Room. Golf Shop. Club Hire. Driving Range. Trolley Hire.

EDINBURGH
Duddingston Golf Club Ltd., Duddingston Road West, Edinburgh, Lothian. EH15 3QD. Tel: 661 1005 (031)
Secretary: Mr J C Small　　　　　Tel: 661 7688 (031)
Professional: Mr A MacLean　　　Tel: 661 4301 (031)
Location: 2 miles east of Edinburgh city centre off A1.
Description: Undulating parkland. Established in 1895.
18 holes, 6,647 yards, Par 72, S.S.S. 72, Course record 64.
Membership: 600
Visitors: Welcome. All male club. No Ladies changing rooms. With members only at weekends.
Green Fees: £18 per round, £24 per day.
Facilities: Lunch. Dinner. Bar Snacks. Full Catering. Changing Room. Golf Shop. Club Hire. Trolley Hire.
Class One Hotel: King's Manor, Edinburgh, 1 mile(s). Tel: 669 0444 (031)

EDINBURGH
Kingsknowe Golf Club, 326 Lanark Road, Edinburgh, Lothian. EH14 2JD. Tel: 441 1144 (031)
Location: On Lanark Rd in western suburbs of Edinburgh.
Description: Well kept parkland course.
18 holes, 5,979 yards, Par 69, S.S.S. 69, Course record 64.
Membership: 774
Visitors: Welcome. No catering on Tuesdays.
Green Fees: Weekdays £14 per round, £18 per day. Weekends £20 per round.
Facilities: Lunch. Dinner. Bar Snacks. Full Catering. Changing Room. Golf Shop. Club Hire. Trolley Hire.
Class One Hotel: Post House, Edinburgh, 3 mile(s). Tel: 334 0390 (031)
Class Two Hotel: Orwell Lodge, Edinburgh, 1 1/2 mile(s). Tel: 229 1044 (031)

EDINBURGH
Liberton Golf Club, Kingston Grange, 297 Gilmerton Road, Edinburgh, Lothian. EH16 5UJ. Tel: 664 3009 (031)
Secretary: Mr Poole　　　　　　　Tel: 664 3009 (031)
Professional: Mr Seath　　　　　 Tel: 664 1056 (031)
Location: 2 miles south of city on the Gilmerton Road.
Description: Undulating parkland with a stream and many bunkers. A tight course.
18 holes, 5,299 yards, Par 66, S.S.S. 66, Course record 61.

Visitors: Welcome. With members only at weekends.
Green Fees: Weekdays £12.50 per round, £18 per day.
Facilities: Lunch. Dinner. Bar Snacks. Full Catering. Changing Room. Golf Shop. Club Hire. Trolley Hire.

EDINBURGH
Lothianburn Golf Club, 106A Biggar Road, Edinburgh, Lothian. EH10 2DU. Tel: 445 2206 (031)
Secretary: W F A Jardine　　　　　Tel: 445 5067 (031)
Professional: Paul Morton　　　　Tel: 445 2288 (031)
Location: 400 yards south of Edinburgh City By-Pass at Lothianburn junc.
Description: Hilly course with magnificent views over surrounding area.
18 holes, 5,750 yards, Par 71, S.S.S. 69, Course record 63.
Membership: 700
Visitors: Welcome. Handicap certificate required. Some restrictions in force at weekends. Societies welcome. No hot meals on Wednesdays.
Green Fees: Weekdays £8 per round, £12 per day. Weekends £11 per round, £15 per day.
Facilities: Lunch. Dinner. Bar Snacks. Full Catering. Changing Room. Golf Shop.
Class One Hotel: Braid Hills, Edinburgh, 2 1/2 mile(s). Tel: 447 8888 (031)

EDINBURGH
Merchants of Edinburgh Golf Club, 10 Craighill Gardens, Edinburgh, Lothian. EH10 5PY. Tel: 447 1219 (031)
Secretary: A M Montgomery　　　Tel: 447 1219 (031)
Professional: C A Imlah　　　　　Tel: 447 8709 (031)
Description: Short hilly course.
18 holes, 4,889 yards, Par 64, S.S.S. 64, Course record 61.
Visitors: Welcome. Not after 4p.m. weekdays unless with a member. Some catering restrictions apply, please telephone in advance.
Green Fees: On application.
Facilities: Lunch. Dinner. Bar Snacks. Changing Room. Golf Shop.

EDINBURGH
Mortonhall Golf Club, Braid Road, Edinburgh, Lothian. EH10 6PB. Tel: 447 2411 (031).
Secretary: Mr P T Ricketts　　　　Tel: 447 6974 (031)
Professional: Mr D Horn　　　　　Tel: 447 5185 (031)
Location: 2 miles south of Edinburgh centre.
Description: Championship course, Scottish amateur strokeplay championship held here. Undulating parkland well bunkered with a pond and views of the Firth of Forth.
18 holes, 6,597 yards, Par 72, S.S.S. 71, Course record 66.
Membership: 500
Visitors: Welcome. Handicap certificate required. Letter of Introduction required.
Green Fees: Weekdays £20 per round, £25 per day. Weekends £30 per round, £35 per day.
Facilities: Lunch. Dinner. Bar Snacks. Full Catering. Changing Room. Golf Shop. Club Hire. Trolley Hire. Buggy Hire.
Class One Hotel: Braid Hills, Edinburgh, 1/2 mile(s). Tel: 447 8888 (031)
Class Two Hotel: Rowand Guest House, Morningside, 1 mile(s). Tel: 447 4089 (031)

EDINBURGH
Murrayfield Golf Club, 43 Murrayfield Road, Edinburgh, Lothian. EH12 6EU. Tel: 337 3478 (031)
Secretary: Mr J P Bullen Tel: 337 3478 (031)
Professional: Mr J Fisher Tel: 337 3479 (031)
Location: 2 1/2 miles west of Edinburgh centre on A8 Glasgow Road.
Description: Undulating parkland with views of the River Forth and Pentland Hills.
18 holes, 5,725 yards, Par 70, S.S.S. 68, Course record 64.
Membership: 1020
Visitors: Welcome. Handicap certificate required. Letter of Introduction required. With members only at weekends. Always by prior arrangement with the Secretary.
Green Fees: £18 per round, £24 per day.
Facilities: Lunch. Dinner. Bar Snacks. Full Catering. Changing Room. Golf Shop. Club Hire. Trolley Hire.
Class One Hotel: Ellersly Hotel, Edinburgh, 1/4 mile(s). Tel: 337 6888 (031)

EDINBURGH
Portobello Golf Club, Stanley Street, Portobello, Edinburgh, Lothian. EH15 1JJ. Tel: 669 4361 (031)
Secretary: Alastair Cook Tel: 669 5271 (031)
Location: On A1 at Milton Road East.
Description: Parkland.
9 holes, 2,400 yards, Par 32, S.S.S. 32.
Membership: 76
Visitors: Welcome.
Green Fees: £3.
Facilities: Club Hire.
Class One Hotel: Carlton Highland, Edinburgh, 3 1/2 mile(s). Tel: 556 7277 (031)
Class Two Hotel: King's Manor, Edinburgh, 1/2 mile(s). Tel: 669 0444 (031)

EDINBURGH
Ravelston Golf Club, 24 Ravelston Dykes Road, Edinburgh, Lothian. EH4 5NZ. Tel: 315 2486 (031)
Secretary: Mr F Phillips Tel: 315 2486 (031)
Location: 4 miles west of Edinburgh centre towards Queensferry.
Description: Undulating parkland with bunkers. Designed by James Braid.
9 holes, 5,200 yards, Par 66, S.S.S. 66, Course record 66.
Membership: 610
Visitors: Welcome. Letter of Introduction required. With members only at weekends.
Green Fees: Weekdays £12.50 per round (18 holes).
Facilities: Bar Snacks. Changing Room.

EDINBURGH
Silverknowes Golf Club, Silverknowes, Parkway, Edinburgh, Lothian. EH4 5AT. Tel: 336 3843 (031)
Secretary: Mr D W Scobie Tel: 336 5359 (031)
Location: 5 miles north of Edinburgh on the Queensferry Road.
Description: Flat parkland course. Established in 1957. Last hole is 601 yards long. Views across the Firth of Forth.
18 holes, 6,216 yards, Par 71, S.S.S. 70.
Membership: 464

Visitors: Welcome. Not on competition days (usually weekends).
Green Fees: £6 per round, £12 per day.
Facilities: Lunch. Bar Snacks. Full Catering.
Class One Hotel: Commodore, Adjacent, 0 mile(s). Tel: 336 1700 (031)

EDINBURGH
Swanston Golf Course, 111 Swanston Road, Edinburgh, Lothian. EH10 7DS. Tel: 445 2239 (031)
Secretary: John Allan Tel: 445 2239 (031)
Description: Hilly parkland on lower slopes of the Pentland Hills.
18 holes, 5,024 yards, Par 66, S.S.S. 66, Course record 63.
Visitors: Welcome. Not weekends or competition days.
Green Fees: Weekdays £8 per round, £12 per day. Weekends £10 per round, £15 per day.
Facilities: Lunch. Dinner. Bar Snacks. Full Catering. Changing Room. Golf Shop.
Class One Hotel: Braid Hills, Edinburgh, 1 1/4 mile(s). Tel: 447 8888 (031)
Class Two Hotel: Orwell Lodge, Edinburgh, 2 mile(s). Tel: 229 1044 (031)

EDINBURGH
Torphin Hill Golf Club, Torphin Road, Edinburgh, Lothian. EH13 0PG. Tel: 441 1100 (031)
Secretary: E H Marchant Tel: 441 4061 (031)
18 holes, 5,012 yards, Par 67, S.S.S. 66, Course record 65.
Membership: 500
Visitors: Welcome.
Green Fees: Weekdays £10 per day, w/ends £16 per day.
Facilities: Lunch. Dinner. Bar Snacks. Full Catering. Changing Room. Club Hire. Driving Range.
Class One Hotel: Braid Hills, Edinburgh, 2 mile(s). Tel: 447 8888 (031)
Class Two Hotel: Orwell Lodge, Edinburgh, 1 1/2 mile(s). Tel: 229 1044 (031)

FAULDHOUSE
Greenburn Golf Club, 6 Greenburn Road, Fauldhouse, Lothian. EH47 9AY. Tel: 70292 (0501)
Secretary: Mr Derek Watson Tel: 71154 (0501)
Professional: Mr Howard Ferguson Tel: 71187 (0501)
Location: 4 miles south from junc 4 (eastbound) and 5 (westbound) M8, Harthill and Whitburn turn offs.
Description: Moorland.
18 holes, 6,210 yards, Par 71, S.S.S. 70, Course record 65.
Membership: 600
Visitors: Welcome. No parties on Saturdays except on non-competition days, check with Secretary.
Green Fees: Weekdays £11 per round, £16.50 per day. Weekends £13 per round, £19.50 per day.
Facilities: Lunch. Dinner. Bar Snacks. Full Catering. Changing Room. Golf Shop. Trolley Hire.
Class One Hotel: Hillcroft, Whitburn, 4 mile(s). Tel: 4018 (0501)

GULLANE
Gullane Golf Club, Gullane, Lothian. EH31 2BB. Tel: 842255 (0620)

Secretary: A J B Taylor Tel: 842255 (0620)
Professional: Mr J M Hume Tel: 843111 (0620)
Location: 18 miles east of Edinburgh on A198 Edinburgh to North Berwick Road.
One 18 holes, 6,466 yards, Par 71, S.S.S. 71.
Two 18 holes, 6,244 yards, Par 70, S.S.S. 70.
Visitors: Welcome. No catering Mondays. Catering by arrangement with Club Master.
Green Fees: On application.

GULLANE

The Honorable Company of Edinburgh Golfers, Muirfield, Gullane, Lothian. EH31 2EG. Tel: 842123 (0620)
Secretary: Gp Cpt Prideaux Tel: 842123 (0620)
Location: East side of Gullane, 5 miles west of North Berwick.
Description: Championship links course, hosts of the Open in 1992 for the 14th time. Established in 1891.
18 holes, 6,970 yards, Par 71, S.S.S. 71, Course record 71.
Membership: 550
Visitors: Welcome. Handicap certificate required. Letter of Introduction required. Tuesday, Thursday and Friday mornings only. Not during July and August. Maximum handicaps - Ladies 24, Gents 18.
Green Fees: £45 per round, £60 per day.
Facilities: Lunch. Full Catering. Changing Room. Club Hire. Trolley Hire. Buggy Hire. Caddies available.

HADDINGTON

Haddington Golf Club, Amisfield Park, Haddington, Lothian. Tel: 3627 (062082)
Secretary: T Shaw Tel: 3627 (062082)
Professional: J Sandilands Tel: 2727 (062082)
Location: 1/4 mile from Haddington off A1.
Description: Tree lined inland course.
18 holes, 6,280 yards, Par 71, S.S.S. 70, Course record 65.
Membership: 600
Visitors: Welcome. Restrictions apply, please telephone Secretary in advance.
Green Fees: £12 - £16.
Facilities: Lunch. Dinner. Bar Snacks. Full Catering. Changing Room. Golf Shop. Club Hire. Trolley Hire.
Class One Hotel: Maitlandfield, Haddington, 1/4 mile(s). Tel: 229 1467 (031)
Class Two Hotel: Mrs Richards, Haddington, 1/4 mile(s). Tel: 5663 (062082)

KIRKNEWTON

Dalmahoy Hotel Golf & Country Club, Kirknewton, Lothian. EH27 8EB. Tel: 333 4105 (031)
Secretary: Miss J Wilson Tel: 333 4105 (031)
Professional: Mr S Maxwell Tel: 333 4105 (031)
Location: 7 miles west of Edinburgh.
Description: Undulating parkland with a lake and bunkers. Championship course.
18 holes, 6,664 yards, Par 72, S.S.S. 72, Course record 68
Membership: 700
Visitors: Welcome. Handicap certificate required. Members with guests and residents only at weekends. Caddies available with 7 days notice.
Green Fees: £30 per round.

Facilities: Lunch. Dinner. Bar Snacks. Full Catering. Changing Room. Golf Shop. Club Hire. Trolley Hire. Buggy Hire.
Class One Hotel: Dalmahoy Hotel, On Course, Tel: 333 1845 (031)

LINLITHGOW

Linlithgow Golf Club, Braehead, Linlithgow, Lothian. EH49 6QF. Tel: 842585 (0506)
Secretary: Mrs A Bird Tel: 842585 (0506)
Professional: Derek Smith Tel: 844356 (0506)
Location: Off M9 about 20 miles west of Edinburgh.
Description: Parkland with panoramic views.
18 holes, 5,729 yards, Par 70, S.S.S. 68.
Membership: 430
Visitors: Welcome. Not Saturdays. Maximum 24 visitors on Sundays.
Green Fees: Weekdays £10 per round, £14 per day. Sundays £14 per round, £17 per day.
Facilities: Lunch. Dinner. Bar Snacks. Full Catering. Changing Room. Golf Shop. Trolley Hire.
Class One Hotel: Star & Garter, Linlithgow, 1 1/2 mile(s). Tel: 845485 (0506)

LIVINGSTON

Deer Park Golf and Country Club, Golf Course Road, Livingston, Lothian. EH54 8PG. Tel: 31037 (0506)
Secretary: Mr Clark Tel: 31037 (0506)
Professional: Mr Yule Tel: 38843 (0506)
Location: 2 miles north of Livingston off M8.
Description: Undulating parkland. Championship course. Hosts of the Scottish Championship 1990.
18 holes, 6,775 yards, Par 72, S.S.S. 72, Course record 66.
Membership: 500
Visitors: Welcome.
Green Fees: Weekdays £14 per round, £19 per day. Weekends £22 per round, £31 per day.
Facilities: Lunch. Dinner. Bar Snacks. Full Catering. Changing Room. Golf Shop. Club Hire. Trolley Hire. Buggy Hire.
Class One Hotel: The Hilton, Livingston, 2 mile(s). Tel: 31222 (0506)
Class Two Hotel: White Croft Guest House, East Culver, 3 mile(s). Tel: 881810 (0506)

LONGNIDDRY

Longniddry Golf Club, Links Road, Longniddry, Lothian. EH32 0NL. Tel: 52141 (0875)
Secretary: Mr G C Dempster CA Tel: 52141 (0875)
Professional: Mr J Gray Tel: 52228 (0875)
Location: 13 miles east of Edinburgh on A1.
Description: Undulating, part links, part parkland. A number of difficult Par 4's. Coastal position which overlooks the Firth of Forth.
18 holes, 6,219 yards, Par 68, S.S.S. 70, Course record 63.
Membership: 900
Visitors: Welcome. Handicap certificate required. With members only at weekends.
Green Fees: Weekdays £20 per round, £30 per day.
Facilities: Lunch. Dinner. Bar Snacks. Full Catering. Changing Room. Golf Shop. Club Hire. Driving Range. Trolley Hire.

Class One Hotel: Marine, North Berwick, 12 mile(s). Tel: 2406 (0620)
Class Two Hotel: Kilspindie House, Aberlady, 4 mile(s). Tel: 682 (08757)

MUSSELBURGH

Musselburgh Golf Club, Monktonhall, Musselburgh, Lothian. EH21 6SA. Tel: 665 2005 (031).
Secretary: Mr G McGill   Tel: 665 2005 (031)
Professional: Mr T Stangoe   Tel: 665 7055 (031)
Location: 1/2 mile west of Musselburgh centre on A1 from Edinburgh.
Description: Flat wooded parkland designed by James Braid in 1937. A championship course.
18 holes, 6,614 yards, Par 71, S.S.S. 72, Course record 66.
Membership: 800
Visitors: Welcome. Handicap certificate required. Not before 9.30a.m.. Caddies available with 24 hours notice.
Green Fees: £13 per round, £20 per day.
Facilities: Lunch. Dinner. Bar Snacks. Full Catering. Changing Room. Golf Shop. Club Hire. Trolley Hire. Buggy Hire.

NEWBRIDGE

Ratho Park Golf Club, Ratho, Newbridge, Lothian. EH28 8NX. Tel: 333 1252 (031)
Secretary: J C McLafferty   Tel: 333 1752 (031)
Professional: Alan Pate   Tel: 333 1406 (031)
Location: 8 miles west of Edinburgh on the Glasgow road A8, adjacent to Edinburgh Airport.
Description: Undulating parkland course designed by James Braid in 1928, overlooking the Pentland Hills.
18 holes, 5060 yards, Par 70, S.S.S. 69, Course record 61.
Membership: 850
Visitors: Welcome. Handicap certificate required. Subject to availability. Parties of 8 or more, only from Monday to Thursday.
Green Fees: Weekdays £16.50 per round, £25 per day. Weekends £30 per day.
Facilities: Lunch. Dinner. Bar Snacks. Full Catering. Changing Room. Golf Shop. Trolley Hire.
Class One Hotel: Norton House Hotel, Edinburgh, 2 mile(s). Tel: 333 1275 (031)

NORTH BERWICK

Glen Golf Club, Tantallon Terrace, North Berwick, Lothian. EH39 4LE. Tel: 2221 (0620)
Secretary: D R Montgomery   Tel: 2221 (0620)
Location: 1 miles east of A198.
Description: Seaside links with magnificent panoramic views.
East Links 18 holes, 6,094 yards, Par 69, S.S.S. 69, Course record 64.
Membership: 600
Visitors: Welcome.
Green Fees: Weekdays 310.50 per round, £14.50 per day. Weekends £13.50 per round, £18.50 per day.
Facilities: Lunch. Bar Snacks. Full Catering. Changing Room. Golf Shop. Club Hire. Trolley Hire. Caddies available.

Class One Hotel: Nether Abbey, North Berwick, 1 1/2 mile(s). Tel: 2802 (0620)
Class Two Hotel: Fairways, North Berwick, 1 mile(s). Tel: 2241 (0620)

NORTH BERWICK

North Berwick Golf Club, New Clubhouse, Beach Road, North Berwick, Lothian. EH39 4BB. Tel: 5040 (0620)
Secretary: William Gray   Tel: 5040 (0620)
Professional: David Huish   Tel: 3233 (0620)
Location: A1 from Edinburgh to Meadowmill roundabout then take the A198 to North Berwick.
Description: Links course stretching along the shores of the Firth of Forth.
18 holes, 6,315 yards, Par 71, S.S.S. 70.
Membership: 377
Visitors: Welcome. Handicap certificate required. No party bookings on Saturdays. Dinner by arrangement.
Green Fees: Weekdays £20 per round, £30 per day. Weekends and Public Holidays £30 per round, £40 per day.
Facilities: Lunch. Bar Snacks. Full Catering. Changing Room. Golf Shop. Club Hire. Trolley Hire. Caddies available.
Class One Hotel: Marine Hotel, North Berwick, 1/2 mile(s). Tel: 2406 (0620)
Class Two Hotel: Point Garry, North Berwick, 1/8 mile(s). Tel: 2380 (0620)

PENICUIK

Glencorse Golf Club, Milton Bridge, Penicuik, Lothian. EH26 0RD. Tel: 77189 (0968)
Secretary: D A McNiven   Tel: 77189 (0968)
Professional: C Jones   Tel: 76481 (0968)
Location: On A701 9 miles south of Edinburgh.
Description: Parkland with burn effecting 10 holes.
18 holes, 5,205 yards, Par 64, S.S.S. 66, Course record 61.
Membership: 660
Visitors: Welcome. Handicap certificate required. Not during club competitions (most weekends).
Green Fees: Weekdays £15 per round, £20 per day. Weekends and Bank Holidays £20 per round.
Facilities: Lunch. Dinner. Bar Snacks. Full Catering. Changing Room. Golf Shop. Club Hire. Trolley Hire.
Class One Hotel: Braid Hills, Edinburgh, 6 mile(s). Tel: 447 8888 (031)
Class Two Hotel: Original, Roslin, 2 mile(s). Tel: 440 2514 (031)

SOUTH QUEENSFERRY

Dundas Parks Golf Club, Dundas Estate, South Queensferry, Lothian.
Secretary: Keith D Love   Tel: 331 1416 (031)
Description: Gently undulating parkland course with delightful views and excellent fairways.
9 holes, 6,024 yards, Par 70, S.S.S. 69, Course record 66.
Membership: 600
Visitors: Welcome. Letter of Introduction required. Not at weekends. Always by prior arrangement with the Secretary.

Cade's - Audi Golf Course Guide

Green Fees: £8 per day.
Facilities: Changing Room.
Class One Hotel: Forth Bridges Moat House, Sth Queensferry, 1 1/2 mile(s). Tel: 331 1199 (031)
Class Two Hotel: Hawes Inn, Sth Queensferry, 2 mile(s). Tel: 331 1100 (031)

WEST CALDER

Harburn Golf Club, Harburn, West Calder, Lothian. EH55 8RS. Tel: 871256 (0506)
Secretary: Mr Vinter   Tel: 871131 (0506)
Professional: Mr S Crookston Tel: 871582 (0506)
Location: On A71 from Edinburgh towards Kilmarnock.
Description: Well bunkered, undulating moorland course, 700 to 800 feet above sea level, in secluded peaceful setting.
18 holes, 5,800 yards, Par 69, S.S.S. 68, Course record 64.
Membership: 600
Visitors: Welcome. Subject to availability.
Green Fees: Weekdays £11 per round, £16 per day. Weekends £16 per round, £22 per day.
Facilities: Lunch. Dinner. Bar Snacks. Full Catering. Changing Room. Golf Shop. Trolley Hire.
Class One Hotel: Hilton National, Livingston, 4 mile(s). Tel: 31222 (0506)

WHITBURN

Polkemmet Golf Course, Polkemmet Country Park, Whitburn, Lothian. EH47 0AD. Tel: 43905 (0501)
Location: On north side of B7066 half way between Whitburn and Harthill.
Description: Inland course set within old former private estate. Tree lined with seasonal displays of rhododendrons. Course operated by Local Authority.
9 holes, 3,237 yards, Par 37.
Visitors: Welcome.
Green Fees: Summer - Monday to Saturday £2.10, Sunday £2.70. Winter - £1.65 any day.
Facilities: Lunch. Dinner. Bar Snacks. Club Hire. Driving Range. Trolley Hire.
Class One Hotel: Golden Circle, Bathgate, 5 mile(s). Tel: 53771 (0506)
Class Two Hotel: Hilcroft, Whitburn, 1 1/2 mile(s). Tel: 40818 (0501)

WINCHBURGH

Niddry Castle Golf Club, Castle Road, Winchburgh, Lothian. EH52 6RQ. Tel: 891097 (0506)
Secretary: A Brockbank   Tel: 891134 (0506)
Location: Off A803 on Kirkliston to Linlithgow Road.
Description: Undulating parkland.
9 holes, 5,450 yards, Par 70, S.S.S. 67.
Membership: 360
Visitors: Welcome. Not before 2 p.m. on competition days (i.e. most Saturdays and some Sundays).
Green Fees: Weekdays £6 per round, weekends £8.50 per round.
Facilities: Changing Room.
Class One Hotel: Houstoun, Uphall, 4 mile(s). Tel: 853831 (0506)

ORKNEYS

KIRKWALL

Orkney Golf Club, Grain Bank, Kirkwall, Orkney.
Tel: 872457 (0856)
Secretary: L Howard   Tel: 874165 (0856)
Location: Western boundary of Kirkwall.
Description: Parkland.
18 holes, 5,406 yards, Par 70, S.S.S. 68, Course record 65.
Membership: 330
Visitors: Welcome.
Green Fees: £8 per day, £30 per week, £40 per fortnight. (Juniors £2-£5-£10).
Facilities: Bar Snacks. Club Hire. Trolley Hire.
Class One Hotel: Ayre, Kirkwall, 1/4 mile(s). Tel: 873001 (0856)
Class Two Hotel: J Thornton, Kirkwall, 1/4 mile(s). Tel: 874761 (0856)

STRATHCLYDE

ALEXANDRIA

Vale of Leven Golf Club, Northfield Road, Bonhill, Alexandria, Strathclyde. G83 9ET. Tel: 52351 (0389)
Secretary: W McKinlay   Tel: 52508 (0389)
Location: Off A82 at Bonhill, follow signs to Clubhouse, approx 1 mile.
Description: Moorland overlooking Loch Lomond with splendid views.
Northfield 18 holes, 5,165 yards, Par 67, S.S.S. 66, Course record 61.
Membership: 690
Visitors: Welcome. Handicap certificate required. Not Saturdays between April 1st and September 30th.
Green Fees: Weekdays £8.50 per round, £12 per day. Weekends £11 per round, £16 per day.
Facilities: Lunch. Dinner. Bar Snacks. Full Catering. Changing Room. Golf Shop.
Class One Hotel: Cameron House, Alexandria, 2 mile(s). Tel: 55565 (0389)
Class Two Hotel: Tullichewan, Balloch, 1 1/2 mile(s). Tel: 52052 (0389)

AYR

Belleisle Golf Course, Doonfoot Road, Ayr, Strathclyde. KA7 4DU. Tel: 41258 (0292)
Secretary: Mrs Fraser Wilson Tel: 42136 (0292)
Professional: Mr D Gemmall   Tel: 41314 (0292)
Location: 1 1/2 miles south west of Ayr on A77.
Description: Flat parkland course with a stream, many bunkers. Championship course designed by James Braid. Open in 1927.
Belleisle 18 holes, 6,552 yards, Par 70, S.S.S. 71, Course record 63.
Seafield 18 holes, 5,369 yards, Par 66, S.S.S. 65, Course record 63.
Membership: 350

Visitors: Welcome. Handicap certificate required. All players must be over 17. Saturdays 7.30a.m. to 9.30a.m. and 12.30p.m. to 2.30p.m. Season Ticket holders only.
Green Fees: Belleisle £12 per round, £18 per day. Seafield £9 per round, £14 per day.
Facilities: Lunch. Dinner. Bar Snacks. Full Catering. Changing Room. Golf Shop. Club Hire. Trolley Hire. Caddies available.
Class One Hotel: Belleisle Hotel, Adjacent, Tel: 42331 (0292)
Class Two Hotel: The Dunn Thing, Ayr, 1 1/2 mile(s). Tel: 284531 (0292)

AYR

Dalmilling Golf Club, Westwood Avenue, Ayr, Strathclyde. KA8 0QY. Tel: 263893 (0292)
Professional: Philip Cheyney   Tel: 263893 (0292)
Location: On A77 north east boundary, 1 mile from town centre.
Description: Gently undulating meadowland.
18 holes, 5,752 yards, Par 69, S.S.S. 68.
Visitors: Welcome. Not before 9.30a.m. weekends. Please telephone in advance.
Green Fees: £9 per round, £16 per day.
Facilities: Lunch. Bar Snacks. Full Catering. Changing Room. Golf Shop. Club Hire. Trolley Hire.
Class Two Hotel: Abbotsford, Ayr, 4 mile(s). Tel: 261506 (0292)

BLACKWATERFOOT

Shiskine Golf and Tennis Club, Blackwaterfoot, Isle of Arran, Strathclyde. KA27 8EP. Tel: 86226 (0770)
Secretary: Mrs Crawford   Tel: 86293 (0770)
Location: 10 miles from Brodrick in an easterley direction, signposted Shiskine.
Description: 12 holes played off alternate tees. A links type natural course with views of the Kilbrannan Sound.
12 holes, 2,990 yards, Par 42, S.S.S. 41, Course record 40.
Membership: 200
Visitors: Welcome. Handicap certificate required. Advisable to book 1 or 2 days in advance.
Green Fees: £8 per round.
Facilities: Lunch. Dinner. Bar Snacks. Full Catering. Changing Room. Golf Shop. Club Hire. Trolley Hire.
Class One Hotel: The Kinloch, Blackwaterfoot, 1 mile(s). Tel: 86444 (0770)
Class Two Hotel: Blackwaterfoot Hotel, Blackwaterfoot, 1/2 mile(s). Tel: 86202 (0770)

BRIDGE OF WEIR

Ranfurly Castle Golf Club Ltd., Golf Road, Bridge of Weir, Strathclyde. PA11 3HN. Tel: 612609 (0505)
Secretary: Mr J Walker   Tel: 612609 (0505)
Professional: Alastair Forrow   Tel: 614795 (0505)
Location: 7 miles west of Paisley.
Description: Moorland.
18 holes, 6,284 yards, Par 70, S.S.S. 70, Course record 65.
Membership: 360
Visitors: Welcome. Handicap certificate required. With members only at weekends and Glasgow Public Holidays.

Visiting parties on Tuesdays only.
Green Fees: £20 per round, £25 per day.
Facilities: Lunch. Dinner. Bar Snacks. Full Catering. Changing Room. Golf Shop. Club Hire. Trolley Hire.
Class One Hotel: Gryffe Arms, Bridge of Weir, 1 mile(s). Tel: 613360 (0505)

CAMPBELTOWN

Machrihanish Golf Club, Machrihanish, By Campbeltown, Strathclyde. PA28 6PG. Tel: 81213 (0586)
Secretary: Mrs A Anderson   Tel: 81213 (0586)
Professional: Mr K Campbell   Tel: 81277 (0586)
Location: 6 miles west of Campbeltown on A83.
Description: Undulating links style championship course.
18 holes, 6,228 yards, Par 70, S.S.S. 70, Course record 66.
9 holes, 2,000 yards, Par 32.
Membership: 600
Visitors: Welcome. Not between 12p.m & 1.45p.m weekdays. Only between 9.30a.m. & 11a.m., and 2.40p.m. & 4p.m. at weekends. Caddies available with 2 days notice.
Green Fees: Weekdays £13.50 per round, weekends £18 per day.
Facilities: Lunch. Dinner. Bar Snacks. Full Catering. Changing Room. Golf Shop. Club Hire. Trolley Hire.
Class Two Hotel: Seafield Hotel, Campbeltown, 6 mile(s). Tel: 54385 (0586)

CARDROSS

Cardross Golf Club, Main Road, Cardross, Dumbarton, Strathclyde. G82 5LB. Tel: 841213 (0389)
Secretary: Mr R Evans CA   Tel: 841754 (0389)
Professional: Mr R Craig   Tel: 841350 (0389)
Location: 6 miles west of Dumbarton on the Helensburgh road.
Description: Undulating parkland with views overlooking the Firth of Clyde.
18 holes, 6,469 yards, Par 71, S.S.S. 71, Course record 63.
Membership: 850
Visitors: Welcome. With members only at weekends.
Green Fees: £15 per round, £25 per day.
Facilities: Lunch. Dinner. Bar Snacks. Full Catering. Changing Room. Golf Shop. Trolley Hire.
Class One Hotel: Commodore Toby, Helensburgh, 3 mile(s). Tel: 76924 (0436)
Class Two Hotel: Kirkton House, Cardross, 2 mile(s). Tel: 841951 (0389)

CARRADALE

Carradale Golf Club, Woodbine Cottage, Torrisdale, Carradale, Strathclyde. PA28 6QT. Tel: 387 (05833)
Secretary: Dr J A Duncan   Tel: 387 (05833)
Location: 15 miles north of Campeltown on the B842.
Description: A short but very demanding 9 holes, built on the east side of the Kintyre Peninsula, marvellous views of the Isle of Arran and Ailsa Craig.
9 holes, 2,387 yards, Par 66, S.S.S. 63, Course record 62.
Membership: 310
Visitors: Welcome. Catering in the Carradale Hotel adjacent to the first tee.
Green Fees: £5 per day, £25 per week, £35 per fortnight.
Facilities: Club Hire. Trolley Hire.

Class Two Hotel: Carradale Hotel, Adjacent, Tel: 223 (05833)

CLYDEBANK

Clydebank and District Golf Club, Glasgow Road, Hardgate, Clydebank, Strathclyde. G81 5XR. Tel: 73289 (0389)
Secretary: Mr W Manson	Tel: 72832 (0389)
Location: 3 miles north of Clydebank on A7 to Balloch.
Description: Undulating parkland.
18 holes, 5,896 yards, Par 68, S.S.S. 68, Course record 64.
Membership: 856
Visitors: Welcome. Handicap certificate required. Letter of Introduction required.Not after 4p.m. With members only at weekends.
Green Fees: £12 per round.
Facilities: Lunch. Dinner. Bar Snacks. Full Catering. Changing Room. Golf Shop. Club Hire. Trolley Hire.
Class Two Hotel: Cameron, Hardgate, 1/2 mile(s). Tel: 73535 (0389)

COATBRIDGE

Drumpellier Golf Club Ltd., Drumpellier Avenue, Coatbridge, Strathclyde. ML5 1RX. Tel: 428723 (0236)
Secretary: W Brownlie	Tel: 424625 (0236)
Professional: K Hutton	Tel: 432971 (0236)
Description: Parkland.
18 holes, 5,930 yards, Par 71, S.S.S. 70, Course record 63.
Membership: 740
Visitors: Welcome. Handicap certificate required. Letter of Introduction required.With members only on Thursdays and at weekends.
Green Fees: On application.
Facilities: Lunch. Dinner. Bar Snacks. Full Catering. Changing Room. Golf Shop. Club Hire. Trolley Hire.
Class One Hotel: Coatbridge Hotel, Coatbridge, 1 mile(s). Tel: 424392 (0236)
Class Two Hotel: Georgian, Coatbridge, 2 mile(s). Tel: 422621 (0236)

COLONSAY

Colonsay Golf Club, Isle of Colonsay, Strathclyde. PA61 7YP. Tel: 316 (09512)
Secretary: K Byrne	Tel: 316 (09512)
Location: On the west coast of the Island.
Description: 19th Century traditional course on natural machair, a magnificent Hebridean setting.
18 holes, 4,775 yards, Par .
Membership: 120
Visitors: Welcome. Everyone invited to become full members at £5 per family per year, nothing else to pay.
Green Fees: None. (See visitors).
Class One Hotel: The Hotel, I O Colonsay, 2 mile(s). Tel: 316 (09512)
Class Two Hotel: Sea View, I O Colonsay, 1 mile(s). Tel: 315 (09512)

CRAIGNURE

Craignure Golf Club, Scallastle, Craignure, Strathclyde. Tel: 370 (06802)
Secretary: Sheila Campbell	Tel: 370 (06802)
Location: 1 mile north of the ferry terminal at Craignure on the Isle of Mull
Description: A holiday links course with views of Ben Nevis.
9 holes, 2,454 yards, Par 66, S.S.S. 64.
Membership: 75
Visitors: Welcome. Some restrictions Sunday afternoons during competitions.
Green Fees: £6 per day.
Facilities: Changing Room. Club Hire.
Class One Hotel: Isle of Mull Hotel, Craignure, 1/2 mile(s). Tel: 351 (06802)
Class Two Hotel: Ardnadrochat, Loch Don, 4 mile(s). Tel: 370 (06802)

DOUGLAS WATER

Douglas Water Golf Club, Ayr Road, Rigside, Douglas Water, Strathclyde. ML11 9LY. Tel: 361 (055588)
Secretary: Mr R McMillan	Tel: 2295 (0555)
Location: 5 miles south of Lanark towards Ayr.
Description: Hilly and undulating.
18 holes, 2,894 yards, Par , S.S.S. 69, Course record 63.
Membership: 150
Visitors: Welcome. Restricted Saturdays during competitions.
Green Fees: Weekdays £5 per round, £7 per day. Weekends £7 per day.
Facilities: Bar Snacks. Changing Room.

DUNOON

Cowal Golf Club, Ardenslate Road, Kirn, Dunoon, Strathclyde. PA23 7SR. Tel: 5673 (0369)
Secretary: Brian Chatham	Tel: 5673 (0369)
Professional: Russell Weir	Tel: 2395 (0369)
Description: Beautiful moorland course with superb views over the Firth of Clyde.
18 holes, 6,251 yards, Par 70, S.S.S. 70, Course record 63.
Membership: 600
Visitors: Welcome. Handicap certificate required.
Green Fees: Weekdays £12, weekends £15 per round.
Facilities: Lunch. Dinner. Bar Snacks. Full Catering. Changing Room. Golf Shop. Club Hire. Trolley Hire.

GLASGOW

Alexandra Golf Club, Sannox Gardens, Glasgow, Strathclyde. G31 3SE. Tel: 554 1204 (041)
Secretary: G McArthur	Tel: 554 1204 (041)
Professional: S Wilson	Tel: 554 1204 (041)
Location: M8 off slip road to Alexandra Parade.
Description: Wooded parkland, hilly with hidden hazards.
9 holes, 2,281 yards, Par 39, Course record 35.
Membership: 50
Visitors: Welcome. Handicap certificate required. Letter of Introduction required.
Green Fees: Adults - £1.55. Juniors - 80p. OAP's - 50p.
Facilities: Lunch. Dinner. Bar Snacks. Changing Room. Driving Range.
Class One Hotel: Copthorne, Glasgow, 1 mile(s). Tel: 332 6711 (041)
Class Two Hotel: Buchanan, Glasgow, 1 mile(s). Tel: 332 7284 (041)

GLASGOW
Bearsden Golf Club, Thorn Road, Bearsden, Glasgow, Strathclyde. G61 4BP. Tel: 942 2351 (041)
Secretary: Mr W S Chalmers Tel: 942 4480 (041)
Location: 5 miles north west of Glasgow on Drymen Road.
Description: 9 hole course played twice on alternate greens and tees.
9 holes, 6,014 yards, Par 68, S.S.S. 69, Course record 66.
Membership: 420
Visitors: With members only.
Green Fees: £20 per round.
Facilities: Lunch. Bar Snacks. Full Catering. Changing Room.

GLASGOW
Bishopbriggs Golf Club, Brackenbrae Road, Bishopbriggs, Glasgow, Strathclyde. G64 2DX. Tel: 772 4510 (041)
Secretary: John Magin Tel: 772 8938 (041)
Location: 1/4 mile from Bishopbriggs Cross, A803 5 miles north of Glasgow city centre.
Description: Fairly flat parkland.
18 holes, 6,041 yards, Par 69, S.S.S. 69, Course record 63.
Membership: 650
Visitors: Welcome. Handicap certificate required. Letter of Introduction required. With members only at weekends. Always book in advance.
Green Fees: £18 per day.
Facilities: Lunch. Dinner. Bar Snacks. Full Catering. Changing Room.
Class One Hotel: Garfield House, Stepps, 4 mile(s). Tel: 779 2111 (041)
Class Two Hotel: Lion, Bishopbriggs, 1 mile(s). Tel: 772 2108 (041)

GLASGOW
Bothwell Castle Golf Club, Blantyre Road, Bothwell, Glasgow, Strathclyde. . Tel: 853177 (0698)
Secretary: Mr Watson Tel: 852395 (0698)
Professional: Mr W Walker Tel: 852052 (0698)
Location: 1 1/2 miles north of Hamilton on M74.
Description: Flat parkland in the Bothwell Castle estate, with ditches and streams. A trying course, well bunkered.
18 holes, 6,243 yards, Par 71, S.S.S. 70, Course record 64.
Membership: 1100
Visitors: Welcome. Handicap certificate required. Letter of Introduction required. Weekdays only between 9a.m. and 3p.m.. With members only at weekends.
Green Fees: £14 per round, £21 per day.
Facilities: Lunch. Dinner. Bar Snacks. Full Catering. Changing Room. Golf Shop. Club Hire. Trolley Hire.
Class One Hotel: Silvertrees, Bothwell, 1/4 mile(s). Tel: 852311 (0698)

GLASGOW
Cathkin Braes Golf Club, Rutherglen, Glasgow, Strathclyde. G73 4SE. Tel: 634 4007 (041)
Secretary: Mr G L Stevenson Tel: 634 6605 (041)
Professional: Mr S Bree Tel: 634 0650 (041)
Location: 3 miles south of Glasgow centre on the East Kilbride road.

Description: Heathland with many trees and water hazards. Club established in 1888.
18 holes, 6,208 yards, Par 71, S.S.S. 71, Course record 67.
Membership: 800
Visitors: Welcome. With members only at weekends.
Green Fees: £16 per round, £25 per day.
Facilities: Lunch. Dinner. Bar Snacks. Full Catering. Changing Room. Golf Shop. Club Hire. Trolley Hire.
Class One Hotel: Mc Donald, Newton Mearns, 3 mile(s). Tel: 638 2225 (041)
Class Two Hotel: Stuart, East Kilbride, 2 mile(s). Tel: 21161 (03552)

GLASGOW
Cawder Golf Club, Cadder Road, Bishopbriggs, Glasgow, Strathclyde. G64 3QD. Tel: 772 7101 (041)
Secretary: Mr G T Stoddart Tel: 772 5167 (041)
Professional: Mr K Stevely Tel: 772 7102 (041)
Location: 1 1/4 miles west of Bishopbriggs on the Glasgow road.
Description: Undulating parkland. Championship standard with water hazards.
Cawder 18 holes, 6,295 yards, Par 70, S.S.S. 71, Course record 68.
Keir 18 holes, 5,877 yards, Par 68, S.S.S. 68, Course record 63.
Membership: 1250
Visitors: Welcome. Handicap certificate required. Letter of Introduction required. With members only at weekends.
Green Fees: £21 per day.
Facilities: Lunch. Dinner. Bar Snacks. Full Catering. Changing Room. Golf Shop. Club Hire. Trolley Hire.
Class One Hotel: Holiday Inn, Glasgow, 6 mile(s). Tel: 226 5577 (041)
Class Two Hotel: Glazert Bank, Lennoxtown, 6 mile(s). Tel: 310790 (0360)

GLASGOW
Clober Golf Club, Craigton Road, Milngavie, Glasgow, Strathclyde. . Tel: 956 1685 (041)
Secretary: Mr John Anderson Tel: 956 1685 (041)
Location: 8 miles from Glasgow.
Description: Parkland.
18 holes, 4,763 yards, Par 65, S.S.S. 65.
Membership: 650
Visitors: Welcome. Not at weekends. Monday to Thursday before 4.30p.m., Friday before 4p.m., last Tuesday of the month March to September before 4p.m..
Green Fees: £8 per round.
Facilities: Lunch. Dinner. Bar Snacks. Full Catering. Changing Room. Golf Shop. Trolley Hire. Buggy Hire.
Class One Hotel: Black Bull Thistle, Milngavie, 1 mile(s). Tel: 956 2291 (041)

GLASGOW
Cowglen Golf Club, 301 Barrhead Road, Glasgow, Strathclyde. G43 1AA. Tel: 632 0556 (041)
Secretary: R J G Jamieson Tel: 266600 (0292)
Professional: J McTear Tel: 649 9401 (041)
Location: South west of Glasgow follow signs for Borrell Collection.

Cade's - Audi Golf Course Guide

Description: Undulating parkland.
18 holes, 6,016 yards, Par 69, S.S.S. 69, Course record 65.
Membership: 770
Visitors: Welcome. Handicap certificate required. Letter of Introduction required. With members only at weekends.
Green Fees: £14 per round, £21 per day.
Facilities: Lunch. Dinner. Bar Snacks. Full Catering. Changing Room. Golf Shop. Driving Range. Caddies available.
Class One Hotel: Tinto Firs Thistle, Glasgow, 1 mile(s). Tel: 637 2353 (041)

GLASGOW

Crow Wood Golf Club, Garnkirk House, Cumbernauld Road, Muirhead, Glasgow, Strathclyde. G69 9JF. Tel: 779 2011 (041)
Secretary: I McInnes   Tel: 779 4954 (041)
Professional: S Forbes   Tel: 779 1943 (041)
Location: North east of Glasgow off the A80 to Stirling, 10 miles from the centre of Glasgow.
Description: Wooded parkland.
18 holes, 6,249 yards, Par 71, S.S.S. 70, Course record 62.
Membership: 700
Visitors: Welcome. Weekdays only with at least 24 hours notice to Secretary.
Green Fees: £14 per round, £21 per day.
Facilities: Lunch. Dinner. Bar Snacks. Full Catering. Changing Room. Golf Shop. Trolley Hire.
Class One Hotel: Crow Wood House, Adjacent, Tel: 779 3861 (041)
Class Two Hotel: Moodiesburn House, Moodiesburn, 1 mile(s). Tel: 873172 (0236)

GLASGOW

Dougalston Golf Course, Strathblane Road, Milngavie, Glasgow, Strathclyde. G62 8HJ. Tel: 956 5750 (041)
Secretary: W McInnes   Tel: 956 5750 (041)
Location: A81 1/2 mile north of Milngavie, 5 miles north of Glasgow.
Description: Tree lined, 5 greens with adjacent ponds.
18 holes, 6,483 yards, Par 72, S.S.S. 71, Course record 71.
Visitors: Welcome.
Green Fees: Weekdays £9 per round, £12 per day. Weekends and Bank Holidays £10 per round, £14 per day.
Facilities: Lunch. Dinner. Bar Snacks. Full Catering. Changing Room. Club Hire. Trolley Hire.
Class One Hotel: Black Bull, Milngavie, 2 mile(s). Tel: 956 2291 (041)
Class Two Hotel: Bamkell Farm, Milngavie, 1/4 mile(s). Tel: 956 1733 (041)

GLASGOW

Eastwood Golf Club, Loganswell, Newton Mearns, Glasgow, Strathclyde. G77 6RX. Tel: 261 (03555)
Secretary: C B Scouler   Tel: 280 (03555)
Professional: K McWade   Tel: 285 (03555)
Location: 4 miles south of Newton Mearns, on road to Kilmarnock.
Description: Moorland.
18 holes, 5,864 yards, Par 68, S.S.S. 68.
Membership: 900
Visitors: Welcome. Handicap certificate required. Letter of Introduction required. Parties only by arrangement.
Green Fees: £16 per round, £24 per day.
Facilities: Lunch. Dinner. Bar Snacks. Full Catering. Changing Room. Golf Shop. Trolley Hire.
Class One Hotel: McDonald Thistle, Whitecraigs, 6 mile(s). Tel: 638 2225 (041)

GLASGOW

Haggs Castle Golf Club, 70 Dumbreck Road, Glasgow, Strathclyde. G41 4SN. Tel: 427 0480 (041)
Secretary: Mr I Harvey   Tel: 427 1157 (041)
Professional: Mr J McAlister   Tel: 427 3355 (041)
Location: 4 miles south of Glasgow centre on M8 and M77.
Description: Flat parkland championship course with ditches, well bunkered.
18 holes, 6,464 yards, Par 72, S.S.S. 65, Course record 65.
Membership: 960
Visitors: Welcome. Handicap certificate required. With members only at weekends. Caddies available with 7 days notice.
Green Fees: £24 per round, £36 per day.
Facilities: Lunch. Dinner. Bar Snacks. Full Catering. Changing Room. Golf Shop. Club Hire. Trolley Hire. Buggy Hire.
Class One Hotel: Sherbrook Castle, Glasgow, 1 mile(s). Tel: 427 4227 (041)

GLASGOW

Hayston Golf Club, Campsie Road, Kirkintilloch, Glasgow, Strathclyde. G66 1RN. Tel: 776 1244 (041)
Secretary: Mr J Carmichael   Tel: 775 0723 (041)
Professional: Mr S Barnett   Tel: 775 0882 (041)
Location: 8 miles north of Glasgow on A803.
Description: Undulating moorland and parkland.
18 holes, 6,042 yards, Par 70, S.S.S. 69.
Membership: 800
Visitors: Welcome. Handicap certificate required. Letter of Introduction required. With members only at weekends. Caddies available with 3 or 4 days notice.
Green Fees: £20 per day, £12 per round.
Facilities: Lunch. Dinner. Bar Snacks. Full Catering. Changing Room. Golf Shop. Club Hire. Trolley Hire.
Class One Hotel: Broadcroft, Kirkintilloch, 1 mile(s). Tel: 775 0398 (041)

GLASGOW

Hilton Park Golf Club, Stockiemuir Road, Milngavie, Glasgow, Strathclyde. G62 7HB. Tel: 956 4657 (041)
Secretary: Mrs J A Dawson   Tel: 956 4657 (041)
Professional: W McCondichie   Tel: 956 5125 (041)
Location: A809, approx 5 miles north west of Glasgow.
Description: Moorland.
Hilton 18 holes, 6,007 yards, Par 70, S.S.S. 70.
Allander 18 holes, 5,374 yards, Par 69, S.S.S. 67.
Visitors: Welcome. Handicap certificate required. By prior arrangement only. No weekends, Fridays, Bank Holidays or 2nd and 4th Tuesdays of the month.
Green Fees: £18 per round, £24 per two rounds.
Facilities: Lunch. Dinner. Bar Snacks. Full Catering. Changing Room. Golf Shop. Club Hire. Trolley Hire.

GLASGOW

Knightswood Golf Club, Lincoln Avenue, Glasgow, Strathclyde. G13 8QD. Tel: 959 1129 (041)
Secretary: Mr N McCraig   Tel: 950 1235 (041)
Location: 5 miles west of Glasgow on Great Western Road.
Description: 9 hole course played twice from alternate tees. Undulating parkland. Established in 1920. Municipal course.
9 holes, 5,240 yards, Par 33, S.S.S. 66, Course record 29.
Membership: 82
Visitors: Welcome.
Green Fees: £3.40 per round for 18 holes, £1.70 per round 'or 9 holes.
Facilities: Bar Snacks. Changing Room.

GLASGOW

The Whitecraigs Golf Club, 72 Ayr Road, Giffnock, Glasgow, Strathclyde. G46 6SW. Tel: 639 1681 (041)
Secretary: Mr R Miller   Tel: 639 4530 (041)
Professional: Mr W Watson   Tel: 639 2140 (041)
Location: 10 miles south of Glasgow on A77 Ayr Road.
Description: Hilly parkland with 2 small streams. Established in 1905.
18 holes, 6,280 yards, Par 70, S.S.S. 70, Course record 65.
Membership: 1050
Visitors: Welcome. Letter of Introduction required. With members only at weekends.
Green Fees: £23 per round, £29 per day.
Facilities: Lunch. Dinner. Bar Snacks. Full Catering. Changing Room. Golf Shop. Club Hire. Trolley Hire.
Class One Hotel: MacDonald Thistle, Giffnock, 1 1/2 mile(s). Tel: 628 2225 (041)

GLASGOW

Williamwood Golf Club, Clarkston Road, Glasgow, Strathclyde. G44 3YR. Tel: 637 1783 (041)
Secretary: R G Cuthbert   Tel: 226 4311 (041)
Professional: J Gardner   Tel: 637 2715 (041)
18 holes, 5,878 yards, S.S.S. 68, Course record 61.
Visitors: Welcome. Only if introduced by and playing with a member.
Green Fees: On application.
Facilities: Lunch. Dinner. Bar Snacks. Full Catering. Changing Room. Golf Shop. Trolley Hire.

GLASGOW

Windyhill Golf Club, Baljaffray Road, Bearsden, Glasgow, Strathclyde. G61 4QQ. Tel: 942 2349 (041)
Secretary: A J Miller   Tel: 942 2349 (041)
Professional: R Collinson   Tel: 942 7157 (041)
Location: 8 miles from Glasgow city centre, north west of Bearsden.
Description: Undulating parkland/moorland course with unrivalled views of the Glasgow area.
18 holes, 6,254 yards, Par 71, S.S.S. 70, Course record 66.
Membership: 700
Visitors: Welcome. Handicap certificate required. With a member only at weekends. No catering Tuesdays.
Green Fees: £15 per day.
Facilities: Lunch. Dinner. Bar Snacks. Full Catering. Changing Room. Golf Shop. Trolley Hire.
Class One Hotel: Black Bull, Milngavie, 2 mile(s). Tel: 956 2291 (041)
Class Two Hotel: Kirkhouse Inn, Strathblane, 6 mile(s). Tel: 70621 (0360)

GOTT BAY

Vaul Golf Club, Scarinish, Isle of Tiree, Strathclyde. PA77 6XH.
Secretary: N J MacArthur   Tel: 339 (08792)
Location: 4 hour ferry journey from Oban, or 45 minute flight from Glasgow Airport.
Description: Links.
9 holes, 2,911 yards, Par 36, S.S.S. 35.
Membership: 100
Visitors: Welcome. Handicap certificate required. No Sunday Golf. Catering facilities exist at Hotel.
Green Fees: Islanders £40 per annum, Mainland members £30 per annum, Juniors £5 per annum.
Facilities: Lunch. Dinner. Bar Snacks. Club Hire.
Class Two Hotel: Lodge, Kirkapol, 1/2 mile(s). Tel: 368 (08792)

GREENOCK

Greenock Golf Club, Forsyth Street, Greenock, Strathclyde. PA16 8RE. Tel: 20793 (0475)
Secretary: Mr E Black   Tel: 20793 (0475)
Professional: Mr G Ross   Tel: 87236 (0475)
Location: 23 miles west of Glasgow on M8.
Description: The 18 hole course, designed by James Braid, comprises of hilly moorland and dates back to 1890. Superb views overlooking the River Clyde.
18 holes, 5,888 yards, Par 68, S.S.S. 68, Course record 64.
9 holes, 2,149 yards, Par 32, S.S.S. 32, Course record 29.
Membership: 740
Visitors: Welcome. Handicap certificate required. Letter of Introduction required. With members only on Saturdays.
Green Fees: Weekdays £11 for 18 holes, Sundays £18 per day.
Facilities: Lunch. Dinner. Bar Snacks. Full Catering. Changing Room. Golf Shop. Club Hire. Trolley Hire.
Class One Hotel: The Stakis Gantock, Gourock, 7 mile(s). Tel: 34671 (0475)

HAMILTON

Hamilton Golf Club, Riccarton, Ferniegair, Hamilton, Strathclyde. . Tel: 282872 (0698)
Secretary: Mr P E Soutter   Tel: 286131 (0698)
Professional: Mr Moir   Tel: 282324 (0698)
Location: 1 1/2 miles south of Hamilton on A74.
Description: Flat parkland course designed by James Braid.
18 holes, 6,243 yards, Par 70, S.S.S. 70, Course record 63.
Membership: 900
Visitors: Welcome. Letter of Introduction required. With members only at weekends.
Green Fees: £15 per round, £25 per day.
Facilities: Lunch. Dinner. Bar Snacks. Full Catering. Changing Room. Golf Shop. Trolley Hire.
Class One Hotel: Avonbridge Hotel, Hamilton, 2 mile(s). Tel: 285001 (0698)

HAMILTON

Strathclyde Park Golf Club, Mote Hill, Hamilton, Strathclyde. Tel: 66155 (0698)
Secretary: Kevin Will					Tel: 825363 (0698)
Professional: Ken Davidson			Tel: 283994 (0698)
Location: M74 north, Hamilton/Motherwell exit, 2nd exit at roundabout, turn right at next roundabout into Golf Course.
Description: Wooded parkland.
9 holes, 3,147 yards, Par 72, S.S.S. 70, Course record 67.
Visitors: Welcome. A booking system operates, telephone to book time on day of play, lines open from 8.45a.m. until course is fully booked.
Green Fees: £1.80.
Facilities: Lunch. Dinner. Bar Snacks. Full Catering. Changing Room. Golf Shop. Driving Range.

HELENSBURGH

Helensburgh Golf Club, 25 East Abercromby Street, Helensburgh, Strathclyde. G84 9JD. Tel: 74173 (0436)
Secretary: Mrs A McEwan			Tel: 74173 (0436)
Professional: Mr R Farrell			Tel: 75505 (0436)
Location: 17 miles west of Glasgow on the Loch Lomond road.
Description: Undulating moorland course with views of Loch Lomond and River Clyde.
Middle 18 holes, 6,058 yards, Par 69, S.S.S. 64, Course record 64.
Box 18 holes, 5,715 yards, Par 69, S.S.S. 64.
Membership: 450
Visitors: Welcome. With members only at weekends.
Green Fees: £15 per round, £23 per day.
Facilities: Lunch. Dinner. Bar Snacks. Full Catering. Changing Room. Golf Shop. Club Hire. Trolley Hire.
Class One Hotel: Commodore Toby, Helensburgh, 1 1/2 mile(s). Tel: 76924 (0436)

IRVINE

Glasgow Gailes Golf Club, Gailes, Irvine, Strathclyde. KA11 5AE. Tel: 311347 (0294)
Secretary: D W Deas				Tel: 942 2011 (041)
Professional: J Steven				Tel: 942 8507 (041)
Location: 1 mile south of Irvine off Troon Road.
Description: Championship links course.
18 holes, 6,493 yards, Par 71, S.S.S. 71, Course record 62.
Membership: 1200
Visitors: Welcome. Handicap certificate required. Letter of Introduction required. Not Saturdays or Sundays before 2.30p.m.. Please telephone Secretary for reservation.
Green Fees: Weekdays £27 per round, £30 per day. Weekends £33 per round.
Facilities: Lunch. Dinner. Bar Snacks. Full Catering. Changing Room. Trolley Hire. Caddies available.

IRVINE

Irvine Golf Club, Bogside, Irvine, Strathclyde. KA12 8SN. Tel: 75979 (0294)
Secretary: Andrew Morton			Tel: 75979 (0294)
Professional: Keith Erskine			Tel: 75626 (0294)
Location: Off Kilwinning Road in Irvine.
Description: Links.
18 holes, 6,480 yards, Par 71, S.S.S. 71, Course record 65.

Membership: 590
Visitors: Welcome. Not before 3p.m. weekends.
Green Fees: Weekdays £23 per round, £28 per day. Weekends £28.
Facilities: Lunch. Dinner. Bar Snacks. Full Catering. Changing Room. Golf Shop. Driving Range. Trolley Hire. Caddies available.
Class One Hotel: Hospitality Inn, Irvine, 2 mile(s). Tel: 74272 (0294)
Class Two Hotel: Redburn, Irvine, 2 mile(s). Tel: 76792 (0294)

IRVINE

Irvine Ravenspark Golf Club, 13 Kidsneuk Lane, Irvine, Strathclyde. KA12 8SR. Tel: 71293 (0294)
Secretary: Mr G Robertson			Tel: 54617 (0294)
Professional: Mr P Bond			Tel: 76467 (0294)
Location: 1/2 mile west of town centre on A77.
Description: Flat parkland. Club established in 1907.
18 holes, 6,720 yards, Par 71, S.S.S. 65, Course record 65.
Membership: 550
Visitors: Welcome. Handicap certificate required. Not before 3p.m. Saturdays. Caddies available with 24 hours notice.
Green Fees: W/days £9 per day, w/ends £16 per day.
Facilities: Lunch. Dinner. Bar Snacks. Full Catering. Golf Shop. Trolley Hire.
Class One Hotel: Hospitality Inn, Irvine, 1 mile(s). Tel: 74272 (0294)
Class Two Hotel: Golf Hotel, Irvine, 1/3 mile(s). Tel: 78633 (0294)

JOHNSTONE

Cochrane Castle Golf Club, Craigston, Johnstone, Strathclyde. PA5 0HF. Tel: 22010 (0505)
Secretary: Mr Cowan				Tel: 20146 (0505)
Professional: Stuart Campbell		Tel: 28465 (0505)
Location: 15 miles west of Glasgow on A737.
Description: Undulating parkland with streams. The foothills of Gleniffer Braes forms part of the course.
18 holes, 6,226 yards, Par 70, S.S.S. 70, Course record 66.
Membership: 600
Visitors: Welcome. With members only at weekends.
Green Fees: £14 per round, £18 per day.
Facilities: Lunch. Dinner. Bar Snacks. Full Catering. Changing Room. Golf Shop. Trolley Hire.
Class One Hotel: Lynnhurst, Johnstone, 1 mile(s). Tel: 24331 (0505)
Class Two Hotel: Ashburn Guest House, Milliken Park, 1 mile(s). Tel: 5447 (05057)

KILMARNOCK

Caprington Golf Club, Ayr Road, Kilmarnock, Strathclyde. KA1 4UW. Tel: 23702 (0563)
Secretary: Mr McCulloch			Tel: 23702 (0563)
Location: 2 miles south of town on the Ayr road A76.
Description: Undulating wooded parkland.
18 holes, 5,700 yards, Par 69, S.S.S. 68, Course record 64.
Membership: 400
Visitors: Welcome. With members only on Saturdays.

Green Fees: Weekdays £6 per round, £10 per day. Sundays £15 per day.
Facilities: Lunch. Dinner. Bar Snacks. Full Catering. Changing Room. Golf Shop. Trolley Hire.
Class One Hotel: Foxbar Hotel, Kilmarnock, 2 mile(s). Tel: 25701 (0563)

KILSYTH

Kilsyth Lennox Golf Club, Tak-Ma-Doon Road, Kilsyth, Strathclyde. . Tel: 822910 (0236)
Secretary: Alan Stevenson   Tel: 823213 (0236)
Location: 1 mile from town on the Tak-Ma-Doon Road.
Description: Hillside course, at present 9 holes extending to 18 during 1992.
9 holes, 5,944 yards, Par 70, S.S.S. 69, Course record 65.
Membership: 400
Visitors: Welcome. Not Saturdays.
Green Fees: £10 for 18 holes.
Facilities: Lunch. Bar Snacks. Golf Shop.
Class One Hotel: Coachman, Kilsyth, 1 mile(s). Tel: 821649 (0236)

KINGARTH

Bute Golf Club, Kingarth, Isle of Bute, Strathclyde. .
Secretary: Mr J M Burnside   Tel: 648 (070083)
Location: 8 miles south of Rothsay on A845.
Description: Links course with magnificent scenery.
9 holes, 2,497 yards, Par 68, S.S.S. 64, Course record 65.
Membership: 220
Visitors: Welcome. Not before 12.30p.m. on Saturdays.
Green Fees: £3 per day.
Class Two Hotel: Kingarth Hotel, Kingarth, 1/4 mile(s). Tel: 662 (070083)

LAMLASH

Lamlash Golf Club, Lamlash, Isle of Arran, Strathclyde. KA27 8JU. Tel: 600296 (0770)
Secretary: J Henderson   Tel: 600272 (0770)
Location: 3 miles south of Ferry Terminal.
Description: Undulating heathland.
18 holes, 4,611 yards, Par 64, S.S.S. 63, Course record 62.
Membership: 390
Visitors: Welcome.
Green Fees: Weekdays £18 per day, weekends £9 per day.
Facilities: Lunch. Dinner. Bar Snacks. Full Catering. Changing Room. Golf Shop.
Class One Hotel: Glenisle, Lamlash, 3/4 mile(s). Tel: 559 (07706)
Class Two Hotel: Marine House, Lamlash, 1/4 mile(s). Tel: 298 (07706)

LANARK

Carnwath Golf Club, 1 Main Street, Carnwath, Lanark, Strathclyde. . Tel: 840251 (0555)
Secretary: Mr D Craig   Tel: 840251 (0555)
Location: 6 miles east of Lanark.
Description: Hilly parkland with ditches and a stream, overlooking mills, moorland and pine forests.
18 holes, 5,953 yards, Par 70, S.S.S. 69, Course record 64.
Membership: 400

Visitors: Welcome. Handicap certificate required. Subject to availability. Saturdays competition day.
Green Fees: Weekdays £15 per day, weekends £18 per day.
Facilities: Lunch. Dinner. Bar Snacks. Full Catering. Changing Room. Golf Shop. Trolley Hire.
Class Two Hotel: Old Bush, Adjacent, 0 mile(s). Tel: 840238 (0555)

LANARK

Lanark Golf Club, The Moor, Whitelees Road, Lanark, Strathclyde. ML11 7RX. Tel: 3219 (0555)
Secretary: George H Cuthill   Tel: 3219 (0555)
Professional: Ron Wallace   Tel: 61456 (0555)
Description: Tough moorland course, used regularly for the British Open Regional Qualifier.
Old Course 18 holes, 6,423 yards, Par 70, S.S.S. 71, Course record 64.
Membership: 850
Visitors: Welcome. Parties Mondays to Wednesdays, up to 14 on Thursdays and Fridays. No visitors after 4p.m. weekdays or at all weekends without a member.
Green Fees: £16 per round, £25 per day.
Facilities: Lunch. Dinner. Bar Snacks. Full Catering. Changing Room. Golf Shop. Club Hire. Trolley Hire. Buggy Hire.
Class One Hotel: Popinjay, Crossford, 7 mile(s). Tel: 441 (055586)
Class Two Hotel: Clydesdale, Biggar, 1 mile(s). Tel: 20015 (0899)

LARGS

Largs Golf Club, Irvine Road, Largs, Strathclyde. KA30 8EU. Tel: 673594 (0475)
Secretary: F Gilmour   Tel: 672497 (0475)
Professional: R Collinson   Tel: 686192 (0475)
Description: Parkland with scenic views of Cumbria and the Isle of Arran.
18 holes, 6,270 yards, Par 70, S.S.S. 70.
Membership: 900
Visitors: Welcome. Society days Tuesdays and Thursdays.
Green Fees: £24 per day, £18 per round.
Facilities: Lunch. Dinner. Bar Snacks. Full Catering. Changing Room. Golf Shop. Club Hire. Trolley Hire.
Class One Hotel: Brisbane, Largs, 1 mile(s). Tel: 687200 (0475)
Class Two Hotel: Haylie Hotel, Largs, 1/2 mile(s). Tel: 673207 (0475)

LARGS

Routenburn Golf Club, Routenburn Road, Largs, Strathclyde. K30 8SQ. Tel: 673230 (0475)
Secretary: Mr E Smeaton   Tel: 673230 (0475)
Professional: Mr McQueen   Tel: 687240 (0475)
Location: 25 miles west of Glasgow on M8 to Greenock.
Description: Undulating parkland with magnificent views.
18 holes, 5,604 yards, Par 68, S.S.S. 67, Course record 63.
Membership: 450
Visitors: Welcome. Not between 7.30a.m. and 2.30p.m. Saturdays (members only).
Green Fees: Weekdays £4.60 per round, weekends £8.20

per round.
Facilities: Lunch. Dinner. Bar Snacks. Full Catering. Changing Room. Golf Shop. Club Hire. Trolley Hire.
Class One Hotel: Brisbane, Largs, 1/2 mile(s). Tel: 687200 (0475)
Class Two Hotel: Willowbank, Largs, 1/4 mile(s). Tel: 672311 (0475)

LENZIE
Lenzie Golf Club, 19 Crosshill Road, Lenzie, Strathclyde. G66 5DA. Tel: 776 1535 (041)
Secretary: John A Chisholm   Tel: 776 6020 (041)
Professional: Jim McCallum   Tel: 777 7748 (041)
Location: 7 miles north east of Glasgow, 2 miles from main Glasgow to Perth Road.
Description: Parkland/moorland.
18 holes, 5,984 yards, Par 69, S.S.S. 69, Course record 64.
Membership: 830
Visitors: Welcome. Letter of Introduction required. With members only at weekends.
Green Fees: £12.50 per round, £20 per day.
Facilities: Lunch. Dinner. Bar Snacks. Full Catering. Changing Room. Golf Shop. Trolley Hire.
Class One Hotel: Holiday Inn, Glasgow, 7 mile(s). Tel: 226 5577 (041)
Class Two Hotel: Crow Wood House, Muirhead, 2 mile(s). Tel: 779 3861 (041)

LESMAHAGOW
Hollandbush Golf Club, Acretop Head, Lesmahagow, Strathclyde. . Tel: 893484 (0555)
Secretary: J Hamilton   Tel: 82222 (0555)
Professional: I Rae   Tel: 893646 (0555)
Description: Parkland/moorland.
18 holes, 6,110 yards, Par 71, S.S.S. 70, Course record 63.
Membership: 600
Visitors: Welcome.
Green Fees: Weekdays £5 per round, £7 per day. Weekends £9 per day.
Facilities: Lunch. Dinner. Bar Snacks. Full Catering. Changing Room. Golf Shop. Club Hire. Trolley Hire.
Class Two Hotel: Craignethan, Lesmahagow, 2 mile(s). Tel: 892333 (0555)

LOCHWINNOCH
Lochwinnoch Golf Club, Burnfoot Road, Lochwinnoch, Strathclyde. PA12 4AN. Tel: 842153 (0505)
Secretary: Mrs E McBride   Tel: 842153 (0505)
Professional: Mr G Reilly   Tel: 843029 (0505)
Location: 3 miles north of Johnstone on the Howwood Road.
Description: Undulating parkland.
18 holes, 6,202 yards, Par 70, S.S.S. 70, Course record 67.
Membership: 500
Visitors: Welcome. Handicap certificate required. With members only at weekends and Bank Holidays.
Green Fees: Weekdays £13 per day.
Facilities: Lunch. Dinner. Bar Snacks. Full Catering. Changing Room. Golf Shop. Club Hire. Trolley Hire.
Class One Hotel: Lynnhurst, Johnstone, 3 mile(s). Tel: 24331 (0505)

OBAN
Glencruitten Golf Club, Glencruitten Road, Oban, Strathclyde. PA34 4PU. Tel: 62868 (0631)
Secretary: Mr C M Jarvie   Tel: 62308 (0631)
Location: 1 mile south of Oban off the Loch Gilphead Road.
Description: Hilly parkland with streams on every hole.
18 holes, 4,452 yards, Par 61, S.S.S. 63, Course record 55.
Membership: 550
Visitors: Welcome. Thursdays Ladies Day. Mens competitions on Saturdays.
Green Fees: Weekdays £9 per round, weekends £10.50 per round.
Facilities: Lunch. Dinner. Bar Snacks. Full Catering. Changing Room. Golf Shop. Club Hire.
Class One Hotel: Argyll Hotel, Oban, 1 mile(s). Tel: 62353 (0631)

PAISLEY
Barshaw Golf Club, Barshaw Park, Glasgow Road, Paisley, Strathclyde. . Tel: 889 2908 (041)
Secretary: W Collins   Tel: 884 2533 (041)
Location: 1 mile from Paisley Cross towards Glasgow.
Description: Level and sloping parkland.
18 holes, 5,703 yards, Par 68, S.S.S. 67, Course record 64.
Membership: 80
Visitors: Welcome. No par 5's on the card.
Green Fees: Adults - £4.50, Juniors - £2.25.
Facilities: Changing Room.
Class One Hotel: Brabloch, Paisley, 3/4 mile(s). Tel: 889 5577 (041)

PAISLEY
Elderslie Golf Club, 63 Main Road, Elderslie, Paisley, Strathclyde. PA5 9AZ. Tel: 22835 (0505)
Secretary: Mr W Muirhead   Tel: 23956 (0505)
Professional: Mr A Armstrong   Tel: 20032 (0505)
Location: On A737 2 miles west of Paisley, close to Glasgow Airport.
Description: An undulating woodland course, a good test of golf. Established in 1909.
18 holes, 6,037 yards, Par 70, S.S.S. 69, Course record 61.
Membership: 809
Visitors: Welcome. Letter of Introduction required. With members only at weekends.
Green Fees: £15.50 per round, £21 per day.
Facilities: Lunch. Dinner. Bar Snacks. Full Catering. Changing Room. Golf Shop. Club Hire. Trolley Hire.
Class One Hotel: Excelsior, Glasgow, 6 mile(s). Tel: 887 1212 (041)
Class Two Hotel: Lynhurst, Johnstone, 2 mile(s). Tel: 24331 (0505)

PRESTWICK
Prestwick Golf Club, 2 Links Road, Prestwick, Strathclyde. KA9 1QG. Tel: 77404 (0292)
Secretary: Mr Donaldson   Tel: 77404 (0292)
Professional: Mr F C Rennie   Tel: 79483 (0292)
Location: Adjacent to railway station in Prestwick, 1 mile south of Airport.
Description: Typical links course, home of British Open.

Established in 1851.
18 holes, 6,544 yards, Par 71, S.S.S. 71, Course record 68.
Membership: 580
Visitors: Welcome. Handicap certificate required. Letter of Introduction required. With members only at weekends. Only by prior arrangement.
Green Fees: £45 per round.
Facilities: Lunch. Dinner. Bar Snacks. Full Catering. Changing Room. Golf Shop. Club Hire. Trolley Hire. Caddies available.

ROTHESAY
Rothesay Golf Club, Canada Hill, Rothesay, Isle of Bute, Strathclyde. PA20 9HN.
Secretary: J Barker   Tel: 503744 (0700)
Professional: J Dougal   Tel: 503554 (0700)
Description: Scenic hillside course overlooking bays and sea lochs. One of Scotland's most scenic island courses, designed by James Braid and Ben Sayers.
18 holes, 5,370 yards, Par 69, S.S.S. 67.
Membership: 300
Visitors: Welcome. Essential to book with Professional weekends April to September.
Green Fees: Weekdays £10, weekends £15.
Facilities: Lunch. Dinner. Bar Snacks. Full Catering. Changing Room. Golf Shop. Club Hire. Trolley Hire.

SHOTTS
Shotts Golf Club, Blairhead, Benhar Road, Shotts, Strathclyde. ML7 5BJ. Tel: 20431 (0501)
Secretary: Jack McDermott   Tel: 20431 (0501)
Location: Off M8 at junc B7057. Travel 1 mile on Benar road.
Description: Wooded moorland.
18 holes, 6,125 yards, Par 70, S.S.S. 70, Course record 64.
Membership: 950
Visitors: Welcome. Some restrictions apply at weekends, advisable to telephone in advance.
Green Fees: Weekdays £14 per day, weekends £16 per day.
Facilities: Lunch. Dinner. Bar Snacks. Full Catering. Changing Room. Golf Shop. Club Hire.

SOUTHEND
Dunaverty Golf Club, Southend, By Campbeltown, Strathclyde. PA28 6RG. Tel: 677 (058683)
Secretary: John Galbraith   Tel: 698 (058683)
Location: 10 miles south of Campbeltown.
Description: Undulating links.
18 holes, 4,799 yards, Par 66, S.S.S. 64, Course record 59.
Membership: 350
Visitors: Welcome.
Green Fees: £7 per round.
Facilities: Lunch. Full Catering. Changing Room. Golf Shop.
Class One Hotel: White Hart, Campbeltown, 1 Tel: 552440 (0586).
Class Two Hotel: Argyll Arms, Southend, 1 mile(s). Tel: 622 (058683)

STEVENSTON
Ardeer Golf Club, Greenhead, Stevenston, Strathclyde. KA20 4JX. Tel: 64542 (0294)
Secretary: Mr W F Hand   Tel: 63538 (0294)
Professional: Bob Rogers   Tel: 601327 (0294)
Location: Off main Greenock Road between Glasgow and Ayr heading west.
Description: Undulating parkland with beautiful scenery.
18 holes, 6,630 yards, Par 72, S.S.S. 72, Course record 64.
Membership: 600
Visitors: Welcome. Handicap certificate required. Not Wednesdays or Saturdays. Restrictions some Sundays.
Green Fees: Weekdays £12 per round, £18 per day. Weekends and Bank Holidays £14 per round, £24 per day.
Facilities: Lunch. Dinner. Bar Snacks. Full Catering. Changing Room. Golf Shop. Trolley Hire.
Class One Hotel: Hospitality Inn, Irvine, 3 mile(s). Tel: 74272 (0294)
Class Two Hotel: Ellwood Guest House, Ardrossan, 3 mile(s). Tel: 61130 (0294)

STRATHAVEN
Strathaven Golf Club, Glasgow Road, Strathaven, Strathclyde. ML10 6NL. Tel: 20539 (0357)
Secretary: Mr Wallace   Tel: 20421 (0357)
Professional: Mr McCrorie   Tel: 21812 (0357)
Location: 7 miles west of Hamilton, follow signs to Strathaven.
Description: Undulating parkland. Established in 1908.
18 holes, 6,226 yards, Par 71, S.S.S. 70, Course record 66.
Membership: 1000
Visitors: Welcome. Handicap certificate required. Not at weekends. Monday to Friday only before 4p.m..
Green Fees: £17 per round, £24 per day.
Facilities: Lunch. Dinner. Bar Snacks. Full Catering. Changing Room. Golf Shop. Trolley Hire.
Class One Hotel: Strathaven Hotel, Strathaven, 1 mile(s). Tel: 21778 (0357)
Class Two Hotel: Springvale, Strathaven, 1/2 mile(s). Tel: 21131 (0357)

TARBERT
Tarbert Golf Club, Kilberry Road, Tarbert, Strathclyde. PA29 6TT. Tel: 820565 (0880)
Secretary: John Reid   Tel: 820565 (0880)
Location: 1 mile south of Tarbert on A83, turn right onto B8042.
Description: Hilly woodland with spectacular views.
9 holes, 2,240 yards, Par 66, S.S.S. 64, Course record 61.
Membership: 120
Visitors: Welcome. Tees reserved most Saturdays.
Green Fees: 9 holes £4, 18 holes £6, Day £8.
Class One Hotel: Tarbert Hotel, Tarbert, 1 mile(s). Tel: 820264 (0880)
Class Two Hotel: West Loch, Tarbert, 1/2 mile(s). Tel: 820283 (0880)

TOBERMORY
Tobermory Golf Club, Tobermory, Isle of Mull, Strathclyde. PA75 6PE.
Secretary: Dr W H Clegg   Tel: 2013 (0688)

Description: Testing, very hilly with panoramic views. Unsuitable for trolleys.
9 holes, 2,233 yards, Par 64, S.S.S. 64.
Membership: 110
Visitors: Welcome. Some restrictions on competition days.
Green Fees: £7.50 per day, £25 per week, £40 per fortnight.
Facilities: Changing Room. Club Hire.
Class One Hotel: Western Isles, Tobermory, 1/2 mile(s). Tel: 2091 (0688)

TROON
Kilmarnock (Barassie) Golf Club, 29 Hillhouse Road, Barassie, Troon, Strathclyde. KA10 6SY. Tel: 313920 (0292)
Secretary: R L Bryce   Tel: 313920 (0292)
Professional: W R Lockie   Tel: 311322 (0292)
Location: 2 miles from Troon opposite Barassie Railway Station.
Description: Links.
Long 18 holes, 6,473 yards, Par 71, S.S.S. 71, Course record 63.
Short 18 holes, 6,177 yards, Par 69, S.S.S. 69.
Membership: 650
Visitors: Welcome. Not Wednesdays, Fridays, Saturdays or Sundays a.m..
Green Fees: £35 per day.
Facilities: Lunch. Dinner. Bar Snacks. Full Catering. Changing Room. Golf Shop. Club Hire. Trolley Hire.
Class One Hotel: Piersland House, Troon, 2 1/2 mile(s). Tel: 314747 (0292)
Class Two Hotel: Tower Hotel, Troon, 1/2 mile(s). Tel: 311142 (0292)

TROON
Royal Troon Golf Club, Craigend Road, Troon, Strathclyde. KA10 6EP. Tel: 311555 (0292)
Secretary: Mr J D Montgomerie   Tel: 311555 (0292)
Professional: Mr R B Anderson   Tel: 313281 (0292)
Location: 3 miles off A74 Prestwick Road south of Prestwick Airport.
Description: Flat, exposed links championship course. Founded in 1878.
18 holes, 7,097 yards, Par 72, S.S.S. 74, Course record 70.
Membership: 800
Visitors: Welcome. Handicap certificate required. Letter of Introduction required. By prior application and only on Mondays, Tuesdays and Thursdays between 9a.m. and 11a.m..
Green Fees: £65 per day.
Facilities: Lunch. Dinner. Bar Snacks. Full Catering. Changing Room. Golf Shop. Club Hire. Trolley Hire. Caddies available.
Class One Hotel: The Marine Highland, Troon, Tel: 314444 (0292)

TROON
Troon Municipal, Harling Drive, Troon, Strathclyde. KA10 7NF. Tel: 312464 (0292)
Description: Links with some trees.

Lochgreen 18 holes, 6,785 yards, Par 73, S.S.S. 73, Course record 65.
Darley 18 holes, 6,501 yards, Par 71, S.S.S. 71, Course record 64.
Membership: 200
Visitors: Welcome. Handicap certificate required.
Green Fees: Lochgreen and Darley - £12 per round, £18 per day. Fullerton - £8 per round, £14 per day.
Facilities: Lunch. Dinner. Bar Snacks. Full Catering. Changing Room. Golf Shop. Club Hire. Trolley Hire.
Class One Hotel: South Beach, Troon, 1/2 mile(s). Tel: 312033 (0292)
Class Two Hotel: Ardneil, Troon, 1 mile(s). Tel: 311611 (0292)

TURNBERRY
Turnberry Hotel, Golf Courses & Spa, Turnberry, Strathclyde. KA26 9LT. Tel: 31000 (0655)
Secretary: R L Hamblett   Tel: 31000 (0655)
Professional: R S Jamieson   Tel: 31000 (0655)
Description: 2 championship 18 hole links courses, primarily for use of Hotel guests.
Ailsa 18 holes, 6,950 yards, Par 70, S.S.S. 72.
Arran 18 holes, 6,249 yards, Par 69, S.S.S. 70.
Visitors: Welcome.
Green Fees: On application.
Facilities: Lunch. Dinner. Bar Snacks. Full Catering. Changing Room. Golf Shop. Club Hire. Trolley Hire. Caddies available.
Class One Hotel: Turnberry Hotel, On Course, Tel: 31000 (0655)

WEST KILBRIDE
West Kilbride Golf Club, 33-35 Fullerton Drive, Seamill, West Kilbride, Strathclyde. KA23 9HT. Tel: 823128 (0294)
Secretary: Mr E D Jefferies   Tel: 823911 (0294)
Professional: Mr G Howie   Tel: 823042 (0294)
Location: On A78 Greenock to Ayr coast road at Seamill.
Description: Flat links course with beautiful views across Isle of Arran.
18 holes, 6,452 yards, Par 71, S.S.S. 71, Course record 67.
Membership: 900
Visitors: Welcome. Handicap certificate required. With members only at weekends.
Green Fees: £25 per round or day, £16 between 1.30p.m. and 5p.m..
Facilities: Lunch. Dinner. Bar Snacks. Full Catering. Changing Room. Golf Shop. Trolley Hire.
Class One Hotel: Hospitality Inn, Irvine, 8 mile(s). Tel: 74272 (0294)
Class Two Hotel: Femill Hydro, Seamill, 1/4 mile(s). Tel: 822217 (0294)

WHITING BAY
Whiting Bay Golf Club, Golf Course Road, Whiting Bay, Brodick, Strathclyde. FA27 8QR. Tel: 487 (07707)
Secretary. Irene L'Anson   Tel: 487 (07707)
Description: Hilly parkland course, no bunkers or water hazards. Views of the Clyde coast line. Established in 1895.
18 holes, 4,405 yards, Par 64, S.S.S. 63, Course record 58.
Membership: 300

Visitors: Welcome. Letter of Introduction required.
Green Fees: £5.54 per round, £6.50 per day.
Facilities: Lunch. Bar Snacks. Full Catering. Changing Room. Golf Shop. Club Hire.
Class One Hotel: Grange House, Whiting Bay, 1/2 mile(s). Tel: 263 (07707)
Class Two Hotel: Viewbank, Whiting Bay, 1/2 mile(s). Tel: 326 (07707)

WISHAW
Wishaw Golf Club, 55 Cleland Road, Wishaw, Strathclyde. ML2 7PH. Tel: 372869 (0698)
Secretary: D D Gallacher   Tel: 372869 (0698)
Professional: J Campbell   Tel: 358247 (0698)
Location: 1 minute from town centre.
Description: Parkland.
18 holes, 6,051 yards, Par 69, S.S.S. 69, Course record 63.
Membership: 953
Visitors: Welcome. Not Saturdays. After 10.30a.m. Sundays and before 4p.m. weekdays.
Green Fees: £10 per round, £15 per day. Sunday £20 per day.
Facilities: Lunch. Dinner. Bar Snacks. Full Catering. Changing Room. Golf Shop. Trolley Hire.
Class One Hotel: The Moorings, Motherwell, 4 mile(s). Tel: 58131 (0698)
Class Two Hotel: The Bentley, Motherwell, 4 mile(s). Tel: 65588 (0698)

TAYSIDE

ABERFELDY
Aberfeldy Golf Club, Taybridge Drive, Aberfeldy, Tayside. PH15 2BP. Tel: 820535 (0887)
Secretary: Angus M Stewart   Tel: 820117 (0887)
Location: 1/2 mile north west of Aberfeldy centre on A827.
Description: 9 holes played of alternate tees. Flat parkland adjacent to River Tay. Beautiful scenery. Established in 1895.
9 holes, 5,466 yards, Par 67, S.S.S. 67, Course record 65.
Membership: 300
Visitors: Welcome. Subject to availability. Restrictions on competition days.
Green Fees: £10 per round, £14 per day.
Facilities: Lunch. Dinner. Bar Snacks. Full Catering. Changing Room. Golf Shop. Trolley Hire.

ABERFELDY
Taymouth Castle Golf Course, By Aberfeldy, Tayside. PH15 2NT. Tel: 228 (08873)
Professional: Mr Marshall   Tel: 20910 (0887)
Location: 6 miles west of Aberfeldy on Aberfeldy to Killin Road.
Description: Flat parkland with 2 streams and a lake. The River Tay runs along side.
18 holes, 6,044 yards, Par 69, S.S.S. 69, Course record 63.
Membership: 200
Visitors: Welcome. Booking required by Societies for weekend play.

Green Fees: £13 per round.
Facilities: Lunch. Dinner. Bar Snacks. Full Catering. Changing Room. Golf Shop. Club Hire. Trolley Hire. Buggy Hire.
Class One Hotel: Kenmore Hotel, Adjacent. Tel: 205 (08873)
Class Two Hotel: Weem, Aberfeldy, 6 mile(s). Tel: 20381 (0887)

ARBROATH
Arbroath Golf Course, Elliot, By Arbroath, Tayside. . Tel: 75837 (0241)
Secretary: Tom Pullar   Tel: 75837 (0241)
Professional: Lindsay Ewart   Tel: 75837 (0241)
Location: On A92 Dundee to Arbroath Road, 1 mile west of Arbroath.
Description: Seaside links.
18 holes, 6,098 yards, Par 70, S.S.S. 69, Course record 66.
Membership: 650
Visitors: Welcome. Not before 10a.m. weekends. Clubhouse closed Thursday until 7.30p.m..
Green Fees: On application.
Facilities: Lunch. Dinner. Bar Snacks. Full Catering. Changing Room. Golf Shop. Club Hire. Trolley Hire. Caddies available.
Class One Hotel: Hotel Seaforth, Arbroath, 2 mile(s). Tel: 72232 (0241)
Class Two Hotel: Inverpark, Arbroath, 2 mile(s). Tel: 73378 (0241)

ARBROATH
Letham Grange Golf Club, Colliston, By Arbroath, Tayside. DD11 4RL. Tel: 373 (024189)
Secretary: Mrs H MacDougall   Tel: 373 (024189)
Professional: David F G Scott   Tel: 373 (024189)
Old 18 holes, 6,954 yards, Par 73, S.S.S. 73.
New 18 holes, 5,528 yards, Par 68, S.S.S. 68.
Membership: 850
Visitors: Welcome. Not before 10.30a.m. weekends or between 12.30p.m. and 2p.m., not before 10a.m. Tuesdays.
Green Fees: On application.
Facilities: Lunch. Dinner. Bar Snacks. Full Catering. Changing Room. Golf Shop. Club Hire. Trolley Hire. Buggy Hire.
Class One Hotel: Letham Grange, On Course. Tel: 373 (024189)
Class Two Hotel: Colliston Inn, Colliston, 2 mile(s). Tel: 232 (024189)

AUCHTERARDER
Auchterarder Golf Club, Orchil Road, Auchterarder, Tayside. PH3 1LS. Tel: 62804 (0764)
Secretary: W M Campbell   Tel: 62804 (0764)
Professional: K Salmoni   Tel: 63711 (0764)
Location: Off A9 Auchterarder By-Pass.
Description: Parkland.
18 holes, 5,778 yards, Par 69, S.S.S. 68, Course record 65.
Membership: 650
Visitors: Welcome. Restrictions only on major competition days.
Green Fees: Weekdays £12 per round, £17 per day. Weekends £18 per round, £25 per day.

AUCHTERARDER

Gleneagles Hotel Golf Courses, Auchterarder, Tayside. PH3 1NF. Tel: 62231 (0764)
Professional: Ian Marchbank　　　Tel: 62231 (0764)
Location: 50 miles north west of Edinburgh on M90 to Perth and 50 miles north west of Glasgow on M8.
Description: Undulating heathland championship course, home of the Bell Scottish Open every year. Opened in 1919.
Kings White 18 holes, 6,471 yards, Par 70, S.S.S. 71, Course record 65.
Kings Yellow 18 holes, 6,125 yards, Par 68, S.S.S. 69.
Visitors: Welcome. All players must be either members or residents at the Hotel.
Green Fees: £35 per round.
Facilities: Lunch. Dinner. Bar Snacks. Full Catering. Changing Room. Golf Shop. Club Hire. Driving Range. Trolley Hire. Caddies available.
Class One Hotel: Gleneagles, On Course. Tel: 62231 (0764)

BARRY

Panmure Golf Club, Barry, Near Carnoustie, Tayside. DD7 7RT. Tel: 53120 (0241)
Professional: Mr T Shiel　　　Tel: 53120 (0241)
Location: 10 miles east of Dundee, follow signs for Carnoustie.
Description: Rolling links course with narrow fairways and small greens.
18 holes, 6,317 yards, Par 70, S.S.S. 70, Course record 66.
Membership: 500
Visitors: Welcome. With members only on Saturdays. Caddies available with 3 days notice.
Green Fees: £20 per round, £30 per 2 rounds.
Facilities: Lunch. Dinner. Bar Snacks. Full Catering. Changing Room. Golf Shop. Trolley Hire.
Class One Hotel: The Glencoe, Carnoustie, 2 mile(s). Tel: 53273 (0241)
Class Two Hotel: The Carlogie, Carnoustie, 4 mile(s). Tel: 53185 (0241)

BLAIR ATHOLL

Blair Atholl Golf Club, Blair Atholl, Tayside. PH18 5TG. Tel: 407 (079681)
Secretary: Mr J A McGregor　　　Tel: 274 (079681)
Location: 7 miles north of Pitlochry, just off A9.
Description: Flat parkland.
9 holes, 5,710 yards, Par 70, S.S.S. 69, Course record 65.
Membership: 300
Visitors: Welcome.
Green Fees: Weekdays £7 per round, weekends £8 per round.
Facilities: Lunch. Bar Snacks. Changing Room. Club Hire. Trolley Hire. Buggy Hire.
Class One Hotel: Tilt, Blair Atholl, 1/4 mile(s). Tel: 333 (079681)
Class Two Hotel: Atholl Arms, Blair Atholl, 1/2 mile(s). Tel: 250 (079681)

BLAIRGOWRIE

Alythe Golf Club, Alythe, Blairgowrie, Tayside. PH11 8JJ.
Secretary: Mr Sullivan　　　Tel: 2268 (08283)
Professional: Mr T Melville　　　Tel: 2411 (08283)
Location: 17 miles east of Perth off Aberdeen Road to Meigle.
Description: Undulating heathland with ditches and streams. Well bunkered.
18 holes, 6,226 yards, Par 70, S.S.S. 70, Course record 67.
Membership: 900
Visitors: Welcome. Handicap certificate required. Not before 10a.m. weekends.
Green Fees: Weekdays £15 per round, £20 per day. Weekends £20 per round, £25 per day.
Facilities: Lunch. Dinner. Bar Snacks. Full Catering. Changing Room. Golf Shop. Club Hire. Trolley Hire.
Class One Hotel: The Land of Loyle, Alythe, 1 1/2 mile(s). Tel: 3151 (08283)
Class Two Hotel: Alythe Hotel, Alythe, 1 1/2 mile(s). Tel: 2447 (08283)

BLAIRGOWRIE

Dalmunzie Golf Course, Spittal O'Glenshee, Blairgowrie, Tayside. PH10 7QG. Tel: 885224 (0250)
Description: Highest course in the Country, spectacular mountain scenery.
9 holes, 2,035 yards, Par 30, S.S.S. 30.
Membership: 50
Visitors: Welcome. Tees reserved Sundays between 10.30 a.m. and 12 noon. Dinner only if booked.
Green Fees: £7 per day.
Facilities: Lunch. Dinner. Club Hire.
Class One Hotel: Dalmunzie House, On course. Tel: 885224 (0250)

BRECHIN

Brechin Golf and Squash Club, Trinity, By Brechin, Tayside. DD9 7PD. Tel: 2383 (03562)
Secretary: Mr A B May　　　Tel: 2326 (03562)
Professional: Mr B Young　　　Tel: 5270 (03562)
Location: 1 mile north east of Brechin on Aberdeen Road A94.
Description: Undulating parkland with scenic views of Grampian Hills. Short hole course. Established in 1893.
18 holes, 5,200 yards, Par 65, S.S.S. 66, Course record 64.
Membership: 680
Visitors: Welcome. Not between 12.30p.m. and 1.45p.m.. With members only at weekends. Wednesdays Ladies Day.
Green Fees: Weekdays £11 per round, £16 per day. Weekends £14 per round, £22 per day.
Facilities: Lunch. Dinner. Bar Snacks. Full Catering. Changing Room. Golf Shop. Club Hire. Trolley Hire.
Class Two Hotel: The Northern, Brechin, 1 mile(s). Tel: 2156 (03562)

CARNOUSTIE

Carnoustie Golf Links, Links Parade, Carnoustie, Tayside. DD7 7JE. Tel: 53249 (0241)
Secretary: Earle J C Smith   Tel: 53789 (0241)
Location: 12 miles east of Dundee by A92 on A930.
Description: Flat, championship, links course played since 1560. Testing finish because of the Barry Burn (stream). Reputed to be the most difficult finish in golf.
Championship 18 holes, 6,936 yards, Par 72, S.S.S. 74, Course record 65.
Burnside 18 holes, 6,020 yards, Par 68, S.S.S. 69.
Visitors: Welcome. Handicap certificate required. With members only before 1.30p.m. Saturdays or before 11a.m. Sundays. Caddies available with a days notice.
Green Fees: Championship - £31 per round, £54 per day. Burnside - £12 per round, £20 per day. Buddon Links - £7 per round, £10 per day.
Facilities: Lunch. Dinner. Bar Snacks. Full Catering. Changing Room. Golf Shop. Club Hire. Trolley Hire.
Class One Hotel: Glencoe Hotel, Carnoustie, 1/8 mile(s). Tel: 53273 (0241)

CRIEFF

Comrie Golf Club, Comrie, Crieff, Tayside. PH6 2HJ. Tel: 70544 (0764)
Secretary: D G McGlashan   Tel: 70544 (0764)
Location: 6 miles from Crieff on Crieff-Locharnhead road at east side of village.
9 holes, 5,966 yards, Par 70, S.S.S. 69, Course record 64.
Membership: 320
Visitors: Welcome. Tee reserved for members Monday and Tuesday evenings.
Green Fees: Weekdays £18, weekends £12 per day.
Facilities: Lunch. Bar Snacks. Changing Room. Club Hire. Trolley Hire.
Class One Hotel: Comrie Hotel, Comrie, 1/2 mile(s). Tel: 70239 (0764)
Class Two Hotel: Royal, Comrie, 1/2 mile(s). Tel: 70200 (0764)

CRIEFF

Crieff Golf Club Ltd., Perth Road, Crieff, Tayside. PH7 3LR. Tel: 2909 (0764)
Secretary: Mr L J Rundle   Tel: 2397 (0764)
Professional: Mr J M Stark   Tel: 2909 (0764)
Description: Founded in 1891. Open all year round.
Ferntower 18 holes, 6,402 yards, Par 71, S.S.S. 71, Course record 67.
Dornock 9 holes, 2,386 yards, Par 64, S.S.S. 63.
Visitors: Welcome. Handicap certificate required. Some restrictions, advisable to telephone in advance for reservation. Trollies and Buggies banned from 1st November to 31st March.
Green Fees: Weekdays £14 per round, £23 per day. Weekends £16 per round. (To be confirmed). Weekly and fortnightly tickets available.
Facilities: Lunch. Dinner. Bar Snacks. Changing Room. Golf Shop. Club Hire. Trolley Hire. Buggy Hire.
Class Two Hotel: Murray Park, Crieff, 1 mile(s). Tel: 3731 (0764)

CRIEFF

Muthill Golf Club, Peat Road, Muthill, Crieff, Tayside. PH5 2AD. Tel: 523 (076481)
Secretary: W H Gordon   Tel: 3319 (0764)
Location: 3 miles from Crieff off A822, 1/4 mile off main road, signposted at north end of village.
Description: Parkland.
9 holes, 4,700 yards, Par 66, S.S.S. 63, Course record 61.
Membership: 400
Visitors: Welcome. Restricted during competitions and matches (mostly evenings).
Green Fees: Weekdays £7 per day, weekends £10 per day.
Facilities: Changing Room.
Class One Hotel: Drummond Arms, Muthill, 1/2 mile(s). Tel: 451 (076481)
Class Two Hotel: Commercial, Muthill, 1/2 mile(s). Tel: 263 (076481)

CRIEFF

St Fillans Golf Club, South Loch Earn Road, St Fillans, Crieff, Tayside. PH6 2NG. Tel: 83312 (0764)
Secretary: A J N Abercrombie   Tel: 3643 (0764)
Professional: J Stark   Tel: 83312 (0764)
Location: On A85 from Crieff to Crianlarich, 13 miles west of Crieff.
Description: Parkland with one small hill, magnificent scenery.
9 holes, 5,862 yards, Par 68, S.S.S. 67, Course record 66.
Membership: 400
Visitors: Welcome. No visiting parties at weekends during July and August.
Green Fees: Weekdays £8 per round, £10 per day. Weekends £12 per round, £14 per day.
Facilities: Lunch. Bar Snacks. Full Catering. Changing Room. Golf Shop. Club Hire. Trolley Hire.
Class One Hotel: Comrie Hotel, Comrie, 6 mile(s). Tel: 70239 (0764)
Class Two Hotel: The Clachan Cottage, Lochearnhead, 6 mile(s). Tel: 247 (05673)

DUNDEE

Camperdown Golf Club, Camperdown House, Camperdown Park, Dundee, Tayside. DD2 4TF. Tel: 623398 (0382)
Secretary: Mr K McCreery   Tel: 642925 (0382)
Professional: Mr R Brown   Tel: 623398 (0382)
Location: 2 miles north west of Dundee city centre on Coupar to Angus Road.
Description: Undulating, wooded parkland course. A championship course, hosting the qualifying round of the Scottish Amateur Championship.
18 holes, 6,900 yards, Par 70, S.S.S. 71, Course record 64.
Membership: 370
Visitors: Welcome. Caddies available with 3 days notice.
Green Fees: £9.50 per day.
Facilities: Lunch. Dinner. Bar Snacks. Full Catering. Changing Room. Golf Shop.
Class Two Hotel: The Shaftesbury, Dundee, 2 mile(s). Tel: 69216 (0382)

DUNDEE

Downfield Golf Club, Turnberry Aveune, Dundee, Tayside. DD2 3QP. Tel: 825595 (0382)
Secretary: B F Mole   Tel: 825595 (0382)
Professional: C Waddell   Tel: 89246 (0382)
Location: North west of city on A923.
Description: Undulating wooded heathland course. Venue for Scottish Amateur Championship in 1991.
18 holes, 6,804 yards, Par 73, S.S.S. 73.
Membership: 550
Visitors: Welcome. Not weekends. Always book in advance.
Green Fees: £22 per round, £33 per day.
Facilities: Full Catering. Changing Room. Golf Shop. Club Hire. Driving Range. Trolley Hire. Caddies available.
Class One Hotel: Swallow, Dundee, 2 mile(s). Tel: 641122 (0382)
Class Two Hotel: Barton House, Dundee, 2 mile(s). Tel: 23521 (0382)

DUNKELD

Dunkeld and Birnam Golf Club, Fungarth, Dunkeld, Tayside. PH8 0HU. Tel: 524 (03502)
Secretary: Mrs W A Sinclair   Tel: 564 (03502)
Location: 1 mile north of Dunkeld on the A923.
Description: Undulating heathland with scenic views of the surrounding hills and lochs.
9 holes, 5,240 yards, Par 68, S.S.S. 66, Course record 64.
Membership: 300
Visitors: Welcome.
Green Fees: Weekdays £8 per round, £10 per day. Weekends £14 per day.
Facilities: Lunch. Dinner. Bar Snacks. Full Catering. Changing Room. Club Hire. Trolley Hire.

DUNNING

Dunning Golf Club, Rollo Park, Dunning, Tayside, PH2 0QX.
Secretary: Miss C Westwood   Tel: 312 (076484)
Location: 10 miles west of Perth.
Description: Parkland.
9 holes, 4,836 yards, Par 66, S.S.S. 64.
Membership: 555
Visitors: Welcome. Not after 5p.m. weekdays unless accompanied by a member. Not before 4p.m. Saturday. Not before 1p.m. Sunday.
Green Fees: £7 per round/day. £4 junior.
Facilities: Changing Room. Trolley Hire.
Class One Hotel: Gleneagles, Auchterarder, 7 mile(s). Tel: 62231 (0764)
Class Two Hotel: Dunning Hotel, Dunning, 1/4 mile(s). Tel: 242 (076484)

KINROSS

Green Hotel Golf Course, The Muirs, Kinross, Tayside. KY13 7AS. Tel: 63467 (0577)
Secretary: Mrs S M Stewart   Tel: 63467 (0577)
Professional: Mr S Geraghty   Tel: 63467 (0577)
Description: Wooded parkland.
Red 18 holes, 6,257 yards, Par 72, S.S.S. 70.
Blue 18 holes, 6,456 yards, Par 71, S.S.S. 71.

_____Cade's - Audi Golf Course Guide

Visitors: Welcome.
Green Fees: Weekdays £12 per round, £18 per day. Weekends £18 per round, £25 per day.
Facilities: Lunch. Dinner. Bar Snacks. Full Catering. Changing Room. Golf Shop. Club Hire. Trolley Hire.
Class One Hotel: Green Hotel, Kinross, 1/4 mile(s). Tel: 63467 (0577)
Class Two Hotel: Kirklands, Kinross, 1/3 mile(s). Tel: 63313 (0577)

MILNATHORT

Milnthort Golf Club, South Street, Milnthort, Tayside. KY13 7XX. Tel: 64069 (0577)
Secretary: Mrs E Sunners   Tel: 62328 (0577)
Location: 1/2 mile from M90 south, 1 1/2 miles from M90 north.
Description: Parkland.
9 holes, 5,969 yards, Par 71, S.S.S. 69.
Membership: 500
Visitors: Welcome. Some catering restrictions apply, please telephone in advance.
Green Fees: Weekdays £10 per day, weekends £15 per day.
Facilities: Bar Snacks. Full Catering. Changing Room.
Class One Hotel: Windlestrae, Kinross, 1 mile(s). Tel: 63217 (0577)

MONIFIETH

Broughty Golf Club, Princes Street, Monifieth, Tayside. DD5 4AW. Tel: 532147 (0382)
Secretary: S J Gailey   Tel: 730014 (0382)
Professional: Ian McLeod   Tel: 532945 (0382)
Location: A930 from Dundee (5 miles) to Monifieth. Turn right in town centre down to links (sign).
Description: Seaside links courses, fairly flat with som tree lined fairways, lots of bunkers. Two 18 hole courses shared by 4 clubs.
Medal 18 holes, 6,657 yards, Par 71, S.S.S. 72.
Ashludie 18 holes, 5,123 yards, Par 68, S.S.S. 66.
Membership: 1500
Visitors: Welcome. Handicap certificate required. Not before 2p.m. Saturdays. No parties on Saturdays. Not before 10a.m. on Sundays. Limited parties on Sundays. No catering Tuesdays or Thursdays.
Green Fees: Medal; £16 per round, £24 per day. Sundays £18 per round, £27.60 per day. Ashludie; £10 per round, £15 per day. Sundays £11 per round, £16.50 per day.
Facilities: Lunch. Dinner. Bar Snacks. Full Catering. Changing Room. Golf Shop. Club Hire. Trolley Hire.
Class One Hotel: Angus Thistle, Dundee, 5 mile(s). Tel: 26874 (0382)
Class Two Hotel: Panmure, Monifieth. Tel: 532911 (0382)

MONTROSE

Montrose Links Trust, Traill Drive, Montrose, Tayside. DD10 8SW. Tel: 72932 (0674)
Secretary: Mrs M Stewart   Tel: 72932 (0674)
Professional: K Stables   Tel: 72634 (0674)
Location: Halfway between Dundee and Aberdeen on A92.

201

Description: Links.
Medal 18 holes, 6,443 yards, Par 71, S.S.S. 71, Course record 64.
Broomfield 18 holes, 4,815 yards, Par 66, S.S.S. 63.
Membership: 1100
Visitors: Welcome. Handicap certificate required. Medal Course: No parties on Saturdays or before 10a.m. on Sundays. Broomfield Course: No restrictions.
Green Fees: Medal: W/days £11 round, £18 day. W/ends £16 round, £25 day. Broomfield: Weekdays £6.50 round, £10 day. Weekends £10 round, £15 day.
Facilities: Lunch. Dinner. Bar Snacks. Full Catering. Changing Room. Golf Shop. Club Hire. Trolley Hire.
Class One Hotel: Park, Montrose, 1/2 mile(s). Tel: 73415 (0674)
Class Two Hotel: Limes, Montrose, 1/2 mile(s). Tel: 77236 (0674)

PERTH
Craigie Hill Golf Club (1982) Ltd., Cherrybank, Perth, Tayside. PH2 0NE. Tel: 24377 (0738)
Secretary: W A Miller   Tel: 20829 (0738)
Professional: F Smith   Tel: 22644 (0738)
Location: West of town, access from M90 and the A9.
Description: Hilly course with interesting and challenging holes and spectacular views.
18 holes, 5,379 yards, Par 66, S.S.S. 66, Course record 60.
Membership: 670
Visitors: Welcome. By arrangement only. Not saturdays.
Green Fees: Weekdays £9 per round, £14 per day. Sunday £18 per day only. Visitor with member £4 per round.
Facilities: Lunch. Dinner. Bar Snacks. Changing Room. Golf Shop. Trolley Hire.

PERTH
King James VI Golf Club, Moncrieffe Island, Perth, Tayside. PH2 8NR. Tel: 25170 (0738)
Secretary: Mrs D Barraclough   Tel: 32460 (0738)
Professional: Tony Coles   Tel: 32460 (0738)
Location: Island in River Tay in the centre of Perth.
Description: Parkland.
18 holes, 5,661 yards, Par 68, S.S.S. 68, Course record 63.
Membership: 675
Visitors: Welcome. Not Saturdays.
Green Fees: Weekdays £11.50 per round, £17.50 per day. Sundays £23 per day.
Facilities: Lunch. Dinner. Bar Snacks. Full Catering. Changing Room. Golf Shop. Trolley Hire. Buggy Hire.
Class One Hotel: Salutation, Perth, 1 mile(s). Tel: 30066 (0738)
Class Two Hotel: Sunbank House, Perth 1, 1 mile(s). Tel: 24882 (0738)

PITLOCHRY
Pitlochry Golf Course, Pitlochry, Tayside. PH16 5QY. Tel: 2942 (0796)
Secretary: Mr I McDougall   Tel: 2863 (0796)
Professional: Mr G Hampton   Tel: 2792 (0796)
Location: 24 miles north of Perth on A9 to Inverness.
Description: Hilly parkland course with spectacular views of the Tay Valley.

18 holes, 5,811 yards, Par 69, S.S.S. 68.
Membership: 500
Visitors: Welcome. Handicap certificate required. Subject to availability.
Green Fees: Weekdays £13, weekends £16.
Facilities: Lunch. Dinner. Bar Snacks. Full Catering. Changing Room. Golf Shop. Club Hire. Trolley Hire.
Class One Hotel: Pitlochry Hydro, Pitlochry, 1/2 mile(s). Tel: 2666 (0796)
Class Two Hotel: Atholl Palace, Pitlochry, 1/2 mile(s). Tel: 2400 (0796)

SCONE
Murrayshall Golf Course, Murrayshall, Scone, By Perth, Tayside. PH2 7PH. Tel: 52784 (0738)
Professional: Neil MacKintosh   Tel: 52784 (0738)
Description: Undulating tree lined parkland.
18 holes, 6,446 yards, Par 72, S.S.S. 71, Course record 68.
Membership: 300
Visitors: Welcome.
Green Fees: Weekdays £20 per round, £30 per day. Weekendfs £25 per round, £40 per day.
Facilities: Lunch. Dinner. Bar Snacks. Full Catering. Changing Room. Golf Shop. Club Hire. Driving Range. Trolley Hire. Buggy Hire. Caddies available.
Class One Hotel: Murrayshall County House, Scone. Tel: 51171 (0738)
Class Two Hotel: The Wheel Inn, Scone, 1 mile(s). Tel: 51518 (0738)

STRATHTAY
Strathtay Golf Club, Strathtay, Tayside.   . Tel: 367 (08874)
Secretary: Mr J B Armstrong Payne   Tel: 367 (08874)
Location: 4 miles west of A9 towards Aberfeldy on A827.
Description: Hilly parkland with scenic views over the River Tay.
9 holes, 6,700 yards, Par 63, S.S.S. 63, Course record 59.
Membership: 220
Visitors: Welcome. Letter of Introduction required. Competitions on Sunday afternoons.
Green Fees: Weekdays £6 per day, weekends £8 per day.
Facilities: Bar Snacks. Changing Room.
Class One Hotel: Grandtully Hotel, Grandtully, 1/4 mile(s). Tel: 207 (08874)

NORTHERN IRELAND

Please note:

The information provided in this section has been supplied by by the Northern Ireland Tourist Board and therefore varies in presentation slightly from the information in previous sections.

There is only accommodation listed where a club has provided the relevant information. Course descriptions are not as full. You are especially advised to verify any facility that you particularly require directly with the course secretary. Green fees should also be confirmed as these may not be current.

COUNTY ANTRIM

ANTRIM
Massereene Golf Club, 51 Lough Road, Antrim, Co. Antrim, Northern Ireland. BT41 4DQ. Tel: 28096 (08494)
Secretary: Marie Agnew   Tel: 28096 (08494)
Professional: Jim Smyth   Tel: 28096 (08494)
Location: 1 1/2 miles south of Antrim town centre.
Description: Parkland.
18 holes, 6,614 yards, S.S.S. 72.
Visitors: Welcome. Not Wednesdays, Fridays or Saturdays. Snooker.
Green Fees: Weekdays £15, weekends £18.
Facilities: Lunch. Dinner. Bar Snacks. Full Catering. Changing Room. Golf Shop. Club Hire. Trolley Hire.
Class One Hotel: Dunadry Inn, Antrim, 4 mile(s). Tel: 32474 (08494)

BALLYCASTLE
Ballycastle Golf Club, Cushendall Road, Ballycastle, Co. Antrim, Northern Ireland. BT54 6QP. Tel: 62536 (02657)
Secretary: T J Sheehan   Tel: 62536 (02657)
Professional: T N Stewart   Tel: 62536 (02657)
Location: 1/2 mile south east of town centre.
Description: Seaside course.
18 holes, 5,692 yards, S.S.S. 68.
Visitors: Welcome. Bar. Some catering restrictions apply, please telephone in advance.
Green Fees: Weekdays £11, weekends and Bank Holidays £16.
Facilities: Changing Room. Golf Shop. Trolley Hire.

Class One Hotel: Marine, Ballycastle, 1/8 mile(s). Tel: 62222 (02657)
Class Two Hotel: Hillsea, Ballycastle, 1/4 mile(s). Tel: 62385 (02657)

BALLYCLARE
Ballyclare Golf Club, 25 Springvale Road, Ballyclare, Co. Antrim, Northern Ireland. BT39 9JW. Tel: 22696 (09603)
Secretary: H McConnell   Tel: 23465 (09603)
Location: 2 miles north of town centre.
Description: Parkland.
18 holes, 5,699 yards, S.S.S. 71.
Membership: 440
Visitors: Welcome. Not Thursdays or Saturdays. Best Days - Mondays, Tuesdays and Wednesdays. Societies welcome.
Green Fees: Weekdays £12, with a member £5. Weekends £18, with a member £8. Special rates for Societies.
Facilities: Lunch. Dinner. Bar Snacks. Full Catering. Changing Room. Trolley Hire. Buggy Hire.
Class One Hotel: Country House, Kells, 5 mile(s). Tel: 891663 (0266)
Class Two Hotel: N Berry, Adjacent, 0 mile(s). Tel: 42419 (09603)

BALLYMENA
Ballymena Golf Club, 128 Raceview Road, Ballymena, Co. Antrim, Northern Ireland. BT42 4HY. Tel: 861487 (0266)

Secretary: Michael J MacCrory Tel: 861487 (0266)
Professional: James Gallagher Tel: 861487 (0266)
Location: 2 miles east of town centre on A42.
Description: Parkland.
18 holes, 5,654 yards, S.S.S. 67.
Membership: 500
Visitors: Welcome. Not Tuesdays or Saturdays. Societies welcome. Snooker. Bowls.
Green Fees: Weekdays £11, with a member £7. Sundays and Bank Holidays £13.50, with a member £8.50.
Facilities: Lunch. Dinner. Bar Snacks. Full Catering. Changing Room. Golf Shop. Club Hire. Trolley Hire.
Class One Hotel: Adair Arms, Ballymena, 3 mile(s). Tel: 653674 (0266)
Class Two Hotel: Tullymore, Broughshane, 1 mile(s). Tel: 861233 (0266)

BALLYMENA

Cushendall Golf Club, Shore Road, Cushendall, Ballymena, Co. Antrim, Northern Ireland. BT44 0NG. Tel: 71318 (02667)
Secretary: Shaun McLaughlin Tel: 73366 (0266)
Location: 25 north of Larne on A2.
Description: Seaside course.
9 holes, 4,706 yards, S.S.S. 63.
Visitors: Welcome. Best Days - Mondays, Thursdays and Fridays. Bar. Catering by arrangement.
Green Fees: Weekdays £8, weekends and Bank Holidays £10.

CARRICKFERGUS

Carrickfergus Golf Club, 35 North Road, Carrickfergus, Co. Antrim, Northern Ireland. BT38 8LP. Tel: 63713 (09603)
Secretary: I D Jardine Tel: 62203 (09603)
Professional: Raymond Stevenson Tel: 51803 (09603)
Location: 9 miles north east of Belfast on A2.
Description: Parkland.
18 holes, 5,759 yards, S.S.S. 68.
Membership: 812
Visitors: Welcome. Not at weekends. Societies welcome. Snooker.
Green Fees: Weekdays £12, with a member £7. Sundays £17, with a member £10.
Facilities: Lunch. Dinner. Bar Snacks. Full Catering. Changing Room. Golf Shop. Club Hire. Trolley Hire.
Class One Hotel: Coast Road Hotel, Carrickfergus, 1 mile(s). Tel: 51021 (09603)
Class Two Hotel: Dobbins Inn, Carrickfergus, 1 mile(s). Tel: 51905 (09603)

CARRICKFERGUS

Greenisland Golf Club, 156 Upper Road, Greenisland, Carrickfergus, Co. Antrim, Northern Ireland. BT38 8RW. Tel: 862236 (0232)
Secretary: James Wyness Tel: 862236 (0232)
Location: 8 miles north east of Belfast.
Description: Meadowland.
9 holes, 5,918 yards, S.S.S. 68.
Visitors: Welcome. Not on Saturdays. Snooker and pool.

Lunch and dinner by arrangement.
Green Fees: Weekdays £8, weekends £12.
Facilities: Bar Snacks.

LARNE

Cairndhu Golf Club, 192 Coast Road, Ballygally, Larne, Co. Antrim, Northern Ireland. BT40 2QG. Tel: 83324 (0574)
Secretary: Josephine Robinson Tel: 83324 (0574)
Professional: R Walker Tel: 83324 (0574)
Location: 4 miles north of Larne on A2.
Description: Undulating parkland.
18 holes, 6,112 yards, S.S.S. 69.
Visitors: Welcome. Best Days - Weekdays. Societies welcome. Snooker.
Green Fees: Weekdays £10, Sundays £15.
Facilities: Bar Snacks. Club Hire.

LARNE

Larne Golf Club, 54 Ferris Bay Road, Islandmagee, Larne, Co. Antrim, Northern Ireland. BT40 3RT. Tel: 82228 (09603)
Secretary: J B Stewart Tel: 72043 (09603)
Location: 6 miles north of Whitehead on Peninsula.
Description: Seaside course.
9 holes, 6,066 yards, S.S.S. 69.
Membership: 430
Visitors: Welcome. Handicap certificate required. Best Days - Mondays to Thursdays. Societies welcome Monday to Thursday and Sundays by arrangement. Snooker.
Green Fees: Weekdays £8, weekends £12. With a member 50% discount.
Facilities: Lunch. Dinner. Bar Snacks. Full Catering. Changing Room.

LISBURN

Aberdelghy Golf Course, Bells Lane, Lambeg, Lisburn, Co. Antrim, Northern Ireland. BT27 4QH. Tel: 662738 (0846)
Secretary: Ian Murdoch Tel: 662738 (0846)
Location: 1 1/4 miles north of Lisburn on A1.
Description: Parkland.
9 holes, 4,832 yards, S.S.S. 65.
Visitors: Welcome. Societies welcome.
Green Fees: Weekdays £2.50 for 9 holes, £4.50 for 18 holes. Weekends and Bank Holidays £3 for 9 holes, £5 for 18 holes.
Facilities: Club Hire.

LISBURN

Lisburn Golf Club, 68 Eglantine Road, Lisburn, Co. Antrim, Northern Ireland. BT27 5RQ. Tel: 677216 (0846)
Secretary: T C McCullough Tel: 677216 (0846)
Professional: B R Campbell Tel: 677217 (0846)
Location: 2 miles south of town centre.
Description: Meadowland.
18 holes, 6,572 yards, S.S.S. 72.
Visitors: Welcome. With members only at weekends. Societies welcome Mondays and Thursdays.
Green Fees: Weekdays £15, weekends £8 with a member.
Facilities: Lunch. Dinner. Club Hire.

Cade's - Audi Golf Course Guide

NEWTOWNABBEY
Ballyearl Golf and Leisure Centre, 585 Doagh Road, Newtownabbey, Co. Antrim, Northern Ireland. BT36 8RZ. Tel: 848287 (0232)
Secretary: Tom Armstrong   Tel: 848287 (0232)
Professional: Jim Robinson   Tel: 848287 (0232)
Location: 6 miles north of Belfast on A5 at Mossley turn off.
Description: Parkland.
9 holes, 1,269 yards, Par 27 .
Visitors: Welcome. Squash courts. Sun beds. Hi-tech fitness suite.
Green Fees: Weekdays £2.50, weekends and Bank Holidays £3.
Facilities: Club Hire. Driving Range.

NEWTOWNABBEY
Belfast Parks Golf Course, 614 Antrim Road, Newtownabbey, Co. Antrim, Northern Ireland. BT36 8RS. Tel: 43799 (02313)
Secretary: David Fitzgerald   Tel: 43799 (02313)
Location: 6 miles north west of Belfast on A6.
Description: Meadowland.
9 holes, 1,760 yards, Par 30.
Visitors: Welcome. Societies welcome. Putting green.
Green Fees: Weekdays £3.30 for 18 holes, weekends and Bank Holidays £4.40 for 18 holes. Putting Green - Adults 55p, Children 35p.

PORTBALLINTRAE
Bushfoot Golf Club, 50 Bushfoot Road, Portballintrae, Co. Antrim, Northern Ireland. BT57 8RR. Tel: 31317 (02657)
Secretary: Dr P Ritchie   Tel: 31317 (02657)
Location: 1 mile north of Bushmills.
Description: Seaside course.
9 holes, 5,572 yards, S.S.S. 67.
Visitors: Welcome. Best Days - Weekdays. Societies welcome weekdays only by prior arrangement. Snooker. Pitch and Putt.
Green Fees: Weekdays £9, weekends and Bank Holidays £12.
Facilities: Bar Snacks.

PORTRUSH
Ballyreagh Golf Course, Glen Road, Off Ballyreagh Road, Portrush, Co. Antrim, Northern Ireland. BT56 8LX. Tel: 822028 (0265)
Professional: Bob Cockroft   Tel: 823812 (0265)
Location: 1 1/2 miles east of Portstewart on A2.
Description: Seaside course.
9 holes, 1,323 yards, Par 27.
Visitors: Welcome. Societies welcome. Pitch and Putt. Snacks.
Green Fees: Weekdays £2.50, July, August, weekends and Bank Holidays £3.30.
Facilities: Club Hire.

PORTRUSH
Royal Portrush Golf Club, Dunluce Road, Portrush, Co. Antrim, Northern Ireland. BT56 8JQ. Tel: 823314 (0265)
Secretary: Miss W Erskine   Tel: 822311 (0265)
Professional: Mr D Stevenson   Tel: 823335 (0265)
Location: 1/2 mile from Portrush on coast road.
Description: 3 links courses.
Dunluce 18 holes, 6,680 yards, S.S.S. 72.
Valley 18 holes, 6,278 yards, S.S.S. 70.
Membership: 1400
Visitors: Welcome. Handicap certificate required. Not between 12.30p.m. and 2p.m. weekdays. Not before 10a.m. Sundays. Saturday is competition day.
Green Fees: Weekdays - Dunluce £25, Valley £12, Skerries £1. Weekends and Bank Holidays - Dunluce £30, Valley £16, Skerries £1.
Facilities: Lunch. Dinner. Bar Snacks. Full Catering. Changing Room. Golf Shop. Club Hire. Trolley Hire. Caddies available.
Class One Hotel: Magherabouy Hotel, Portrush, 1 mile(s). Tel: 823507 (0265)
Class Two Hotel: Vally Magarry Guest House, Portrush, 1 mile(s). Tel: 823535 (0265)

WHITEHEAD
Bentra Golf Club, Slaughterford Road, Whitehead, Co. Antrim, Northern Ireland. BT38 9TG. Tel: 78996 (09603)
Secretary: A Phair   Tel: 51604 (09603)
Location: 7 miles north east of Carrickfergus.
Description: Parkland.
9 holes, 6,310 yards, S.S.S. 70.
Visitors: Welcome. Best Days - Summer weekdays, any day in winter.
Green Fees: Weekdays £4.25, weekends and Bank Holidays £5.75.
Facilities: Lunch. Dinner. Club Hire. Driving Range.

WHITEHEAD
Whitehead Golf Club, McCreas Brae, Whitehead, Co. Antrim, Northern Ireland. BT38 9NZ. Tel: 53631 (09603)
Secretary: J M Niblock   Tel: 53792 (09603)
Location: 1/2 mile north of Whitehead.
Description: Undulating parkland.
18 holes, 6,426 yards, S.S.S. 71.
Visitors: Welcome. Not Saturdays. With members only on Sundays. Societies welcome Monday to Friday and Sundays, advance booking required. Snooker.
Green Fees: Weekdays £10, Sundays and Bank Holidays £15, with a member £6.
Facilities: Bar Snacks.

COUNTY ARMAGH

ARMAGH
County Armagh Golf Club, 4 Newry Road, Armagh, Co. Armagh, Northern Ireland. BT60 1EN. Tel: 525861 (0861)
Secretary: P Reid   Tel: 525425 (0861)
Professional: Alan Rankin   Tel: 525864 (0861)
Location: In Palace Demesne.
Description: Parkland.
18 holes, 6,120 yards, S.S.S. 69.
Visitors: Welcome. Best Days - Weekdays. Societies welcome, telephone B Hughes 525861 (0861). Practice

205

fairway. Snooker.
Green Fees: Weekdays £9, weekends £12.
Facilities: Lunch. Dinner. Bar Snacks.

CRAIGAVON

Tandragee Golf Club, Markethill Road, Tandragee, Craigavon, Co. Armagh, Northern Ireland. BT62 2ER. Tel: 841272 (0762)
Secretary: Austin Best   Tel: 840274 (0762)
Professional: John Black   Tel: 840727 (0762)
Location: In the town.
Description: Parkland.
18 holes, 6,084 yards, S.S.S. 69.
Visitors: Welcome. Not on Saturdays. Ladies only Thursday afternoons. Societies welcome. No catering Mondays. Practice fairway. Pool Table.
Green Fees: Weekdays £8, Sundays £11.
Facilities: Bar Snacks.

CULLYHANNA

Ashfield Golf Club, Freeduff, Cullyhanna, Co. Armagh, Northern Ireland. BT35 0NA. Tel: 861315 (0693)
Secretary: Elizabeth Quinn   Tel: 868180 (0693)
Professional: Erill Maney   Tel: 861315 (0693)
Location: 4 miles north of Crossmaglen off B30.
Description: Parkland.
18 holes, 5,645 yards, Par 68.
Visitors: Welcome. Best Days - Weekdays. Societies welcome. Lunch and dinner by arrangement.
Green Fees: Weekdays £5, weekends £7.
Facilities: Bar Snacks. Club Hire. Driving Range.

LURGAN

Craigavon Golf and Ski Centre, Turmoyra Lane, Lurgan, Co. Armagh, Northern Ireland. BT66 6NG. Tel: 326606 (0762)
Secretary: V P McCorry   Tel: 326606 (0762)
Professional: Des Paul   Tel: 326606 (0762)
Location: 2 miles north of Lurgan.
Description: Parkland.
18 holes, 6,496 yards, S.S.S. 72.
9 holes, yards, Par 27.
Visitors: Welcome. Societies welcome. 12 hole Pitch and Putt. Putting green.
Green Fees: Weekdays £6, weekends £8.
Facilities: Lunch. Dinner. Club Hire. Driving Range.

LURGAN

Lurgan Golf Club, The Demesne, Lurgan, Co. Armagh, Northern Ireland. BT67 9BN. Tel: 322087 (0762)
Secretary: Gail Turkington   Tel: 322087 (0762)
Professional: D Paul   Tel: 322087 (0762)
Location: In the town.
Description: Parkland.
18 holes, 6,385 yards, S.S.S. 70.
Visitors: Welcome. Best Days - Mondays, Thursdays and Fridays. Societies welcome.
Green Fees: Weekdays £11, weekends £13.50.
Facilities: Lunch. Dinner. Bar Snacks.

PORTADOWN

Portadown Golf Club, 192 Gilford Road, Portadown, Co. Armagh, Northern Ireland. BT63 5LF. Tel: 355356 (0762)
Secretary: Lily Holloway   Tel: 355356 (0762)
Professional: Paul Stevenson   Tel: 355356 (0762)
Location: 3 miles south east of town centre.
Description: Parkland.
18 holes, 6,147 yards, S.S.S. 70.
Visitors: Welcome. Not Tuesdays or Saturdays. Squash, Snooker, Pool, Indoor Bowls. Practice fairway. Putting green. Societies welcome by advance booking.
Green Fees: Weekdays £8, Sundays and Bank Holidays £12.
Facilities: Lunch. Dinner. Bar Snacks. Club Hire.

BELFAST

BELFAST

Balmoral Golf Club, 518 Lisburn Road, Belfast, Northern Ireland. BT9 6GX. Tel: 381514 (0232)
Secretary: M P Fitzmaurice   Tel: 381514 (0232)
Professional: Geoff Bleakley   Tel: 381514 (0232)
Location: 3 miles south west of city centre.
Description: Parkland.
18 holes, 6,238 yards, S.S.S. 70.
Visitors: Welcome. Not Saturdays. Best days Mondays and Thursdays.
Green Fees: Weekdays £12, Wednesdays £14.50, weekends £18.
Facilities: Lunch. Dinner. Bar Snacks. Full Catering. Changing Room. Golf Shop. Club Hire. Trolley Hire.
Class One Hotel: Europa, Belfast, 2 mile(s). Tel: 327000 (0232)
Class Two Hotel: Beech Lawns, Dunmurry, 2 mile(s). Tel: 612974 (0232)

BELFAST

Belvoir Golf Club, 73 Church Road, Newtownbreda, Belfast, Northen Ireland. BT8 4AN. Tel: 491693 (0232)
Secretary: W I Davidson   Tel: 646113 (0232)
Professional: Maurice Kelly   Tel: 646714 (0232)
Location: 3 miles south of city centre.
Description: Parkland.
18 holes, 6,276 yards, S.S.S. 70.
Membership: 1100
Visitors: Welcome. Best Days Monday, Tuesday and Thursday. Visiting Societies by arrangement. Restrictions on Saturdays during competitions. Fridays Ladies Day.
Green Fees: Mondays, Tuesdays, Thursdays or Fridays £25. Wednesdays, Sundays and Bank Holidays £30.
Facilities: Lunch. Dinner. Bar Snacks. Full Catering. Changing Room. Golf Shop. Club Hire. Trolley Hire.
Class One Hotel: Drumkeen, Belfast, 1/2 mile(s). Tel: 491321 (0232)
Class Two Hotel: Parador, Belfast, 1 mile(s). Tel: 491883 (0232)

Cade's - Audi Golf Course Guide

BELFAST
Cliftonville Golf Club, 44 Westland Road, Belfast, Northern Ireland. BT14 6NH. Tel: 744158 (0232)
Secretary: J M Henderson   Tel: 744158 (0232)
Location: 2 1/2 miles north west of city centre.
Description: Parkland.
9 holes, 6,205 yards, S.S.S. 70.
Visitors: Welcome. Not Saturdays. With members only Sunday mornings. Societies welcome. Practice fairway. Snooker.
Green Fees: Weekdays £9, Sundays £11.
Facilities: Bar Snacks.

BELFAST
Dunmurry Golf Club, 91 Dunmurry Lane, Dunmurry, Belfast, Northern Ireland. BT17 9JS. Tel: 610834 (0232)
Secretary: Cyril Mackerell   Tel: 610834 (0232)
Professional: Paul Leonard   Tel: 621314 (0232)
Location: 4 miles south west of city centre.
Description: Parkland.
18 holes, 5,832 yards, S.S.S. 68.
Membership: 840
Visitors: Welcome. Handicap certificate required. Best Days - Tuesdays and Thursdays. Societies welcome but not Fridays and Saturdays. Saturdays after 5p.m.. No Catering Mondays.
Green Fees: Weekdays £13, Sunday £17.
Facilities: Lunch. Dinner. Bar Snacks. Full Catering. Changing Room. Golf Shop. Club Hire. Trolley Hire.

BELFAST
Fortwilliam Golf Club, Downview Avenue, Belfast, Northern Ireland. BT15 4EZ. Tel: 370770 (0232)
Secretary: R J Campbell   Tel: 370770 (0232)
Professional: Peter Hanna   Tel: 370770 (0232)
Location: 3 miles north of city centre.
Description: Parkland.
18 holes, 5,771 yards, S.S.S. 68.
Visitors: Welcome. Best Times - Weekday mornings. Societies welcome preferably Thursdays. Practice fairway. Snooker.
Green Fees: Weekdays £12, weekends and Bank Holidays £17.
Facilities: Bar Snacks.

BELFAST
Gilnahirk Golf Club, Manns Corner, Upper Braniel Road, Gilnahirk, Belfast, Northern Ireland. BT5 7EX. Tel: 448477 (0232)
Secretary: H Moore   Tel: 448477 (0232)
Professional: Ken Gray   Tel: 448477 (0232)
Location: 4 1/2 miles south east of city centre.
Description: Parkland.
9 holes, 5,904 yards, S.S.S. 68.
Visitors: Welcome. Putting green. Practice nets.
Green Fees: Weekdays £2.60 for 9 holes, £4.50 for 18 holes. Weekends £3.40 for 9 holes, £5.50 for 18 holes.
Facilities: Club Hire.

BELFAST
Knock Golf Club, Summerfield, Dundonald, Belfast, Northern Ireland. BT16 0QX. Tel: 483251 (0232)
Secretary: S G Managh   Tel: 483251 (0232)
Professional: Gordon Fairweather   Tel: 483825 (0232)
Location: 4 miles east of city centre.
Description: Parkland.
18 holes, 6,392 yards, S.S.S. 71.
Membership: 880
Visitors: Welcome. Best Times - Monday, Wednesday and Thursday mornings. Tuesday and Friday afternoons. With members only on Saturdays. Societies by arrangement.
Green Fees: Weekdays £17, with a member £8 Weekends and Bank Holidays £22, with a member £11.
Facilities: Lunch. Dinner. Bar Snacks. Full Catering. Changing Room. Golf Shop. Club Hire. Trolley Hire.
Class One Hotel: Stormont, Belfast, 1 mile(s). Tel: 658621 (0232)

BELFAST
Knockbracken Golf and Country Club, 24 Ballymaconaghy Road, Belfast, Northern Ireland. BT8 4SB. Tel: 792108 (0232)
Secretary: Malcolm Grose   Tel: 792108 (0232)
Location: 4 1/2 miles south south east of city centre.
Description: Undulating parkland.
18 holes, 5,312 yards, S.S.S. 68.
Visitors: Welcome. Not before 1.30p.m. Saturdays. Societies welcome. Don Patterson Golf School. Putting. Bowling Alleys. Snooker. Ski-ing.
Green Fees: Weekdays £8, with a member £6. Weekends and Bank Holidays £10, with a member £8.
Facilities: Bar Snacks. Club Hire. Driving Range.

BELFAST
Malone Golf Club, 240 Upper Malone Road, Dunmurry, Belfast, Northern Ireland. BT17 9LB. Tel: 612758 (0232)
Secretary: T Aitken   Tel: 612758 (0232)
Professional: P M O'Hagan   Tel: 612758 (0232)
Location: 4 1/2 miles south of city centre.
Description: Parkland courses.
18 holes, 6,433 yards, S.S.S. 71.
9 holes, 5,784 yards, S.S.S. 68.
Visitors: Welcome. Not Tuesdays, Wednesdays or Saturdays on 18 hole course.
Green Fees: Weekdays £8 for 9 holes, £19 for 18 holes. Weekends and Bank Holidays £9 for 9 holes, £22 for 18 holes.
Facilities: Lunch. Dinner. Bar Snacks.

BELFAST
Ormeau Golf Club, 149 Ravenhill Road, Belfast, Northern Ireland. BT6 0BN. Tel: 641069 (0232)
Secretary: Robert Burnett   Tel: 641069 (0232)
Location: 2 miles south east of city centre.
Description: Parkland.
9 holes, 5,306 yards, S.S.S. 66.
Visitors: Welcome. Not Tuesdays or Saturdays. Bar.
Green Fees: Weekdays £5, weekends and Bank Holidays £7.50.

207

BELFAST

Shandon Park Golf Club, 73 Shandon Park, Belfast, Northern Ireland. BT5 6NY. Tel: 401856 (0232)
Secretary: H Wallace　　　　　　Tel: 401856 (0232)
Professional: B C Wilson　　　　Tel: 797859 (0232)
Location: 4 miles east of city centre.
Description: Parkland.
18 holes, 6,249 yards, S.S.S. 70.
Visitors: Welcome. Not Saturdays. Societies welcome Mondays and Fridays.
Green Fees: Weekdays £14, weekends £18.
Facilities: Bar Snacks. Club Hire.

COUNTY DOWN

ARDGLASS

Ardglass Golf Club, Castle Place, Ardglass, Co. Down, Northern Ireland. BT30 7TP. Tel: 841219 (0396)
Secretary: Alan Cannon　　　　Tel: 841219 (0396)
Professional: Kevin Dorrian　　Tel: 841319 (0396)
Location: In the town.
Description: Seaside course.
18 holes, 5,974 yards, S.S.S. 69.
Visitors: Welcome. Best Days - Weekdays. Societies welcome by arrangement.
Green Fees: Weekdays £10, with a member £6. Weekends £15, with a member £7.50.
Facilities: Lunch. Dinner. Bar Snacks.

BALLYNAHINCH

Spa Golf Club, 20 Grove Road, Ballynahinch, Co. Down, Northern Ireland. BT24 8PN. Tel: 562365 (0238)
Secretary: J Glass　　　　　　Tel: 812340 (0232)
Location: 1 mile south of town centre.
Description: Parkland.
18 holes, 6,494 yards, S.S.S. 72.
Visitors: Welcome. Best Days - Monday to Thursday. Societies welcome Mondays, Tuesdays and Thursdays and a.m. Sundays. Full catering by arrangement.
Green Fees: Weekdays £11, weekends and Bank Holidays £14.
Facilities: Lunch. Bar Snacks. Full Catering. Changing Room.
Class One Hotel: Mill Brook, Ballynahinch, 1 mile(s). Tel: 562828 (0238)
Class Two Hotel: White Horse, Ballynahinch, 1/2 mile(s). Tel: 562225 (0238)

BANBRIDGE

Banbridge Golf Club, 116 Huntly Road, Banbridge, Co. Down, Northern Ireland. BT32 3UR. Tel: 62342 (08206)
Secretary: Thomas Fee　　　　Tel: 23831 (08206)
Location: 1 1/2 miles north west of Banbridge town centre.
Description: Parkland.
12 holes, 5,879 yards, S.S.S. 68.
Visitors: Welcome. Shortly extending to 18 holes. Not Saturdays. Best Days - Wednesdays and Fridays. Lunch and dinner by arrangement.

Green Fees: Weekdays £7, Sundays £12 .
Facilities: Bar Snacks. Changing Room. Driving Range. Trolley Hire. Buggy Hire. Caddies available.
Class One Hotel: Belmont, Banbridge, 2 mile(s). Tel: 62517 (08206)
Class Two Hotel: Downshire Arms, Banbridge, 1 1/2 mile(s). Tel: 22638 (08206)

BANGOR

Bangor Golf Club, Broadway, Bangor, Co. Down, Northern Ireland. BT20 4RH. Tel: 270922 (0247)
Secretary: David Wilson　　　　Tel: 270922 (0247)
Professional: N V Drew　　　　Tel: 462164 (0247)
Location: In the town.
Description: Undulating parkland.
18 holes, 6,490 yards, S.S.S. 71.
Membership: 1030
Visitors: Welcome. Best Days - Mondays, Wednesdays and Fridays. Societies welcome Mondays and Wednesdays, please book in advance.
Green Fees: Weekdays £15, with a member £7.50. Weekends £21, with a member £9.50.
Facilities: Lunch. Dinner. Bar Snacks. Full Catering. Changing Room. Golf Shop. Trolley Hire.
Class One Hotel: Culloden, Holywood, 8 mile(s). Tel: 5223 (02317)
Class Two Hotel: Royal, Bangor, 1 mile(s). Tel: 271866 (0247)

BANGOR

Carnalea Golf Club, Station Road, Bangor, Co. Down, Northern Ireland. BT19 1EZ. Tel: 270368 (0247)
Secretary: Joseph Crozier　　　Tel: 270368 (0247)
Professional: M McGee　　　　Tel: 270368 (0247)
Location: 1 1/2 miles west of Bangor.
Description: Seaside meadowland.
18 holes, 5,548 yards, S.S.S. 67.
Membership: 1100
Visitors: Welcome. Every day.
Green Fees: Weekdays £9, weekends and Bank Holidays £12.
Facilities: Lunch. Dinner. Bar Snacks. Full Catering. Changing Room. Golf Shop. Club Hire. Trolley Hire.
Class One Hotel: Crawfordsburn Inn, Crawfordsburn, 1/2 mile(s). Tel: 853255 (0247)
Class Two Hotel: Abbeyview Heights, Bangor, 3/4 mile(s). Tel: 472119 (0247)

BANGOR

Helen's Bay Golf Club, Golf Road, Helen's Bay, Bangor, Co. Down, Northern Ireland. BT19 1TL. Tel: 852815 (0247)
Secretary: John H Ward　　　　Tel: 852601 (0247)
Professional: Thomas Loughran　Tel: 853313 (0247)
Location: 12 miles east of Belfast.
Description: Seaside course.
9 holes, 5,638 yards, S.S.S. 67.
Visitors: Welcome. Not Mondays. With members only on Saturdays.
Green Fees: Weekdays £10, Sundays and Bank Holidays £15.
Facilities: Lunch. Dinner. Bar Snacks.

DONAGHADEE

Donaghadee Golf Club, Warren Road, Donaghadee, Co. Down, Northern Ireland. BT21 0PQ. Tel: 883624 (0247).
Secretary: C D McCutcheon   Tel: 883624 (0247)
Professional: Gordon Drew   Tel: 883624 (0247)
Location: 6 miles east of Bangor on A2.
Description: Undulating seaside course.
18 holes, 6,098 yards, S.S.S. 69.
Visitors: Welcome. Best Days - Mondays and Wednesdays.
Green Fees: Weekdays £10, weekends £12.
Facilities: Bar Snacks. Club Hire.

DOWNPATRICK

Bright Castle Golf Club, 14 Coniamstown Road, Bright, Downpatrick, Co. Down, Northern Ireland. BT30 8LU. Tel: 841319 (0396)
Secretary: Raymond Reid   Tel: 841319 (0396)
Location: 5 miles south east of Downpatrick.
Description: Parkland.
18 holes, 7,300 yards, S.S.S. 74.
Visitors: Welcome. Societies welcome. Snacks.
Green Fees: Weekdays £6, weekends £7.

DOWNPATRICK

Downpatrick Golf Club, 43 Saul Road, Downpatrick, Co. Down, Northern Ireland. BT30 6PA. Tel: 615947 (0396)
Secretary: Danny McGreevy   Tel: 612152 (0396)
Location: 1 mile north east of town centre.
Description: Undulating.
18 holes, 5,834 yards, S.S.S. 68.
Membership: 830
Visitors: Welcome. Thursdays Ladies Day. Weekends not before 3p.m..
Green Fees: Weekdays £13, with a member £9. Weekends £16, with a member £11.
Facilities: Lunch. Dinner. Full Catering. Changing Room. Golf Shop. Club Hire. Trolley Hire. Caddies available.
Class One Hotel: Abbey Lodge, Downpatrick, 2 mile(s). Tel: 614511 (0396)
Class Two Hotel: Denvirs, Downpatrick, 1 mile(s). Tel: 612012 (0396)

HOLYWOOD

Holywood Golf Club, Nun's Walk, Demesne Road, Holywood, Co. Down, Northern Ireland. BT18 9DX. Tel: 3135 (02317)
Secretary: Gerald Magennis   Tel: 3135 (02317)
Professional: Michael Bannon   Tel: 3135 (02317)
Location: 1 mile south of town centre.
Description: Undulating parkland.
18 holes, 5,885 yards, S.S.S. 68.
Visitors: Welcome. Not Thursdays or Saturdays. Societies welcome Monday, Tuesdays, Wednesdays, Fridays and Sundays. Practice fairway.
Green Fees: Weekdays £12, Sundays £17.
Facilities: Lunch. Dinner. Bar Snacks.

HOLYWOOD

Royal Belfast Golf Club, Station Road, Craigavad, Holywood, Co. Down, Northern Ireland. B I 18 0BT. Tel: 428165 (0232)
Secretary: Ian Piggot   Tel: 428165 (0232)
Professional: D Carson   Tel: 428165 (0232)
Location: 8 miles north east of Belfast on A2.
Description: Parkland.
18 holes, 5,963 yards, S.S.S. 69.
Visitors: Welcome. Letter of Introduction required. Not before 4.30p.m. Saturdays. Snooker. Squash. Practice fairway.
Green Fees: Weekdays £20, weekends £25.
Facilities: Lunch. Dinner. Bar Snacks.

MAZE

Down Royal Park Golf Club, Dunygarton Road, Maze, Co. Down, Northern Ireland. BT27 5RT. Tel: 621339 (0846)
Secretary: Nigel F Ewing   Tel: 621176 (0846)
Location: Within Down Royal Racecourse.
Description: Parkland.
18 holes, 6,824 yards, Par 72.
Visitors: Welcome. Societies welcome.
Green Fees: Weekdays £8.50, Saturdays £9.50 and Sundays £11.50.
Facilities: Lunch. Dinner. Bar Snacks.

NEWCASTLE

Royal County Down Golf Club, Newcastle, Co. Down, Northern Ireland. BT33 0AN. Tel: 23314 (03967)
Secretary: Peter E Rolph   Tel: 23314 (03967)
Professional: Ernie Jones   Tel: 23314 (03967)
Location: 30 miles south of Belfast on A2.
Description: Links courses.
18 holes, 6,968 yards, S.S.S. 73.
18 holes, 4,087 yards, S.S.S. 60.
Visitors: Welcome. Handicap certificate required. Best Days - Mondays, Tuesdays, Thursdays and Fridays.
Green Fees: One - Weekdays, Winter £25, Summer £35, weekends and Bank Holidays, Winter £30, Summer £40. Two - Weekdays £7, weekends and Bank Holiday
Facilities: Lunch. Dinner. Bar Snacks. Full Catering. Changing Room. Golf Shop. Club Hire. Trolley Hire. Caddies available.
Class One Hotel: Slieve Donard, Newcastle, 1/8 mile(s). Tel: 23681 (03967)
Class Two Hotel: Brook Cottage, Newcastle, 1 mile(s). Tel: 22204 (03967)

NEWRY

Kilkeel Golf Club, Mourne Park, Ballyardle, Newry, Co. Down, Northern Ireland. BT34 4LB. Tel: 62296 (06937)
Secretary: S W Rutherford   Tel: 73660 (06937)
Location: 3 miles west of town on A2.
Description: Undulating parkland.
9 holes, 6,151 yards, S.S.S. 69.
Membership: 450
Visitors: Welcome. Not Tuesdays or Saturdays. Societies welcome. Snooker and pool. Practice fairway.
Green Fees: Weekdays £12, weekends and Bank Holi-

days £15.
Facilities: Lunch. Dinner. Bar Snacks. Full Catering. Changing Room.
Class One Hotel: Slieve Donand, Newcastle, 16 mile(s). Tel: 23681 (03967)
Class Two Hotel: Cranfield House, Kilkeel, 3 mile(s). Tel: 62327 (06937)

NEWRY
Newry Golf Club, 11 Forkhill Road, Newry, Co. Down, Northern Ireland. BT35 8LZ. Tel: 63871 (0693)
Secretary: Michael Heaney   Tel: 62120 (0693)
Location: 1 1/2 miles south of town centre.
Description: Parkland.
9 holes, 2,014 yards, Par 27.
Visitors: Welcome. Societies welcome. Snooker and pool. Practice fairway. Pitch and Putt.
Green Fees: Weekdays £3, weekends £4.
Facilities: Lunch. Dinner. Bar Snacks.

NEWTOWNARDS
Clandeboye Golf Club, Tower Road, Conlig, Newtownards, Co. Down, Northern Ireland. BT23 3PN. Tel: 271767 (0247)
Secretary: Ian Marks   Tel: 271767 (0247)
Professional: Peter Gragory   Tel: 271750 (0247)
Location: 2 miles south of Bangor on A21.
Description: Parkland/heathland courses.
Dufferin 18 holes, 6,469 yards, S.S.S. 72.
Ava 18 holes, 5,656 yards, S.S.S. 67.
Visitors: Welcome. With members only at weekends. Societies welcome April - September Mondays, Tuesdays, Wednesdays and Fridays. October - March Mondays and Wednesdays.
Green Fees: Dufferin - Weekdays £13, weekends £18. Ava - Weekdays £11, weekends £14.
Facilities: Lunch. Dinner. Bar Snacks. Club Hire. Driving Range.

NEWTOWNARDS
Kirkistown Castle Golf Club, 142 Main Road, Cloughey, Newtownards, Co. Down, Northern Ireland. BT22 1JA. Tel: 71233 (02477)
Professional: J Peden   Tel: 71233 (02477)
Location: Take A20 south from Newtownards, then B173 south from Kircubbin.
Description: Links.
18 holes, 6,157 yards, S.S.S. 70.
Membership: 840
Visitors: Welcome. Best Days - Weekdays. Restrictions at weekends during competitions.
Green Fees: On application.
Facilities: Lunch. Dinner. Bar Snacks. Full Catering. Changing Room. Golf Shop. Trolley Hire. Buggy Hire.
Class One Hotel: Portaferry Hotel, Portaferry, 5 mile(s). Tel: 28131 (02477)

NEWTOWNARDS
Mahee Island Golf Club, Mahee Island, Comber, Newtownards, Co. Down, Northern Ireland. BT23 6EP. Tel: 541234 (0238)

Secretary: Thomas Reid   Tel: 541234 (0238)
Location: 14 miles south east of Belfast on A22, 1/4 mile south of Comber turn left, 6 miles to Island.
Description: Undulating meadowland.
9 holes, 5,570 yards, S.S.S. 67.
Visitors: Welcome. Best Days - Tuesdays and Fridays. Societies welcome, please telephone in advance. Catering by arrangement. Practice net. Pitch and Putt.
Green Fees: Weekdays £8, weekends and Bank Holidays £12.
Facilities: Club Hire.

NEWTOWNARDS
Scrabo Golf Club, 233 Scrabo Road, Newtownards, Co. Down, Northern Ireland. BT23 4SL. Tel: 812355 (0247)
Secretary: George Graham   Tel: 812355 (0247)
Professional: Billy Todd   Tel: 812355 (0247)
Location: 2 1/2 miles south west of Newtownards, take road to Scrabo Monument.
Description: Undulating.
18 holes, 6,233 yards, S.S.S. 71.
Visitors: Welcome. Best Days - Mondays, Tuesdays and Thursdays, Sundays after 5p.m.. Societies welcome.
Green Fees: On application.
Facilities: Lunch. Dinner. Bar Snacks. Full Catering. Changing Room. Golf Shop. Trolley Hire. Buggy Hire. Caddies available.
Class One Hotel: Strangford Arms, Newtownards, 2 mile(s). Tel: 814141 (0247)

WARRENPOINT
Warrenpoint Golf Club, Lower Dromore Road, Warrenpoint, Co. Down, Northern Ireland. BT34 3LN. Tel: 53695 (06937)
Secretary: John Mahon   Tel: 53695 (06937)
Professional: Nigel Shaw   Tel: 52371 (06937)
Location: 1 mile west of town centre.
Description: Parkland.
18 holes, 6,288 yards, S.S.S. 70.
Membership: 1100
Visitors: Welcome. Handicap certificate required. Best Days - Mondays, Thursdays and Fridays. Not on Saturdays. Snooker. Squash. Practice area.
Green Fees: Weekdays £12, weekends £18.
Facilities: Lunch. Dinner. Bar Snacks. Full Catering. Changing Room. Golf Shop. Club Hire. Trolley Hire.
Class One Hotel: Carlingford Bay, Warrenpoint, 1 mile(s). Tel: 53521 (06937)
Class Two Hotel: Diplomat, Warrenpoint, 1 mile(s). Tel: 53629 (06937)

COUNTY FERMANAGH

ENNISKILLEN
Ashwoods Golf Centre, Ashwoods, Enniskillen, Co. Fermanagh, Northern Ireland. BT74. Tel: 325321 (0365)
Secretary: Peggy McManus   Tel: 322908 (0365)
Professional: Thomas Loughran   Tel: 325321 (0365)
Location: 1 1/2 miles south west of Enniskillen on A4.

Description: Meadowland.
9 holes, 1,150 yards, Par 27.
Visitors: Welcome. Societies welcome. Practice fairway. Pitch and Putt.
Green Fees: £3.
Facilities: Club Hire. Driving Range.

ENNISKILLEN

Castle Hume Golf Course, Castle Hume, Enniskillen, Co. Fermanagh, Northern Ireland. BT74. Tel: 89205 (0365)
Secretary: Alan Cathcart   Tel: 89205 (0365)
Location: 2 1/2 miles north of Enniskillen on A46.
Description: Parkland.
9 holes, 3,450 yards, Par 36.
Visitors: Welcome. Every day.
Green Fees: On application.
Facilities: Club Hire.

ENNISKILLEN

Enniskillen Golf Club, Castle Coole, Enniskillen, Co. Fermanagh, Northern Ireland. BT74 6HZ. Tel: 325250 (0365)
Secretary: Brendan O'Neil   Tel: 325250 (0365)
Location: In Castle Coole estate.
Description: Meadowland.
18 holes, 5,476 yards, S.S.S. 69.
Membership: 500
Visitors: Welcome. Tuesdays Ladies Day. Saturday is competition day, visitors must give way. Societies welcome. Lunch and dinner by arrangement.
Green Fees: £8.50 per day.
Facilities: Bar Snacks. Changing Room. Club Hire. Trolley Hire.
Class One Hotel: Killyhevlin Hotel, Enniskillen, 1 mile(s). Tel: 323481 (0365)
Class Two Hotel: Belmore Court Motel, Enniskillen, 1/2 mile(s). Tel: 326633 (0365)

COUNTY LONDONDERRY

AGHADOWEY

Brown Trout Golf and Country Inn, 209 Agivey Road, Aghadowey, Co. Londonderry, Northern Ireland. BT51 4AD. Tel: 868209 (0265)
Secretary: Gerry McIlwaine   Tel: 868209 (0265)
Professional: Ken Revie   Tel: 868209 (0265)
Location: 6 miles north of Kilrea.
Description: Meadowland.
9 holes, 5,400 yards. S.S.S. 68.
Visitors: Welcome. Societies welcome.
Green Fees: Weekdays £5, weekends £7.
Facilities: Lunch. Dinner. Bar Snacks.

CASTLEROCK

Castlerock Golf Club, 65 Circular Road, Castlerock, Co. Londonderry, Northern Ireland. BT51 4TJ. Tel: 848314 (0265)
Secretary: Geoffrey McBride   Tel: 848314 (0265)

Professional: Bobby Kelly   Tel: 848314 (0265)
Location: 6 miles west of Coleraine on A2.
Description: Links courses.
18 holes, 6,694 yards, S.S.S. 72.
9 holes, 2,706 yards, Par 35.
Visitors: Welcome. Best Days - 18 hole weekdays, 9 hole any day. Societies welcome Monday to Friday.
Green Fees: 18 holes - Weekdays £11, after 4p.m. £6. Weekends and Bank Holidays £22, after 4p.m. £10. 9 holes - Weekdays £4 per day, weekends £7 per day
Facilities: Lunch. Dinner. Bar Snacks. Club Hire.

COLERAINE

Kilrea Golf Club, 38 Drumagarner Road, Kilrea, Coleraine, Co. Londonderry, Northern Ireland. BT51 5TB.
Secretary: W McIlmoyle   Tel: 71397 (02665)
Location: 1/2 mile south west of village.
Description: Undulating inland course.
9 holes, 4,326 yards, S.S.S. 62.
Visitors: Welcome. Best Days - Weekdays except Tuesday and Wednesday afternoons. Closed Sundays.
Green Fees: £5.

KILREA

Manor Golf and Fishing Club, 69 Bridge Street, Kilrea, Co. Londonderry, Northern Ireland. BT51 5RR. Tel: 40205 (02665)
Secretary: Philip McIntyre   Tel: 40205 (02665)
Location: 1/2 mile south east of village on A54.
Description: Parkland.
9 holes, 3,686 yards, S.S.S. 60.
Visitors: Welcome. Every day.
Green Fees: On application.

LIMAVADY

Benone Golf Course, 53 Benone Avenue, Limavady, Co. Londonderry, Northern Ireland. BT49 0LQ. Tel: 50555 (05047)
Secretary: Colin Smith   Tel: 50555 (05047)
Location: 2 1/2 miles west of Downhill on A2.
Description: Seaside course.
9 holes, 1,427 yards, Par 27.
Visitors: Welcome. Snacks. Practice range. Tennis. Caravan Park. Children's activity park, with heated splash pool.
Green Fees: Weekdays £1.80 per day, weekends and Bank Holidays £2.30 per day.
Facilities: Club Hire.

LONDONDERRY

City of Derry Golf Club, 49 Victoria Road, Londonderry, Co. Londonderry, Northern Ireland. BT47 2PU. Tel: 46369 (0504)
Secretary: Patrick J Doherty   Tel: 41493 (0504)
Professional: Michael Doherty   Tel: 311496 (0504)
Location: 2 miles south of city centre.
Description: Parkland courses.
Prehen 18 holes, 6,406 yards, S.S.S. 71.
Dunhugh 9 holes, 4,708 yards, S.S.S. 63.
Visitors: Welcome. Weekdays before 4.30p.m., weekends always telephone in advance. Dunhugh - No restric-

tions. Societies welcome by arrangement. Practice area.
Green Fees: Prehen - Weekdays £11, weekends and Bank Holidays £13. Dunhugh - £5. Juniors £3.
Facilities: Lunch. Dinner. Bar Snacks.

MAGHERAFELT

Moyola Park Golf Club, Shanemullagh, Castledawson, Magherafelt, Co. Londonderry, Northern Ireland. BT45 8DG. Tel: 68468 (0648)
Secretary: Lawrence Hastings   Tel: 68468 (0648)
Professional: Vivian Teague   Tel: 68830 (0648)
Location: 3 miles north east of Magherafelt.
Description: Parkland.
18 holes, 6,517 yards, S.S.S. 71.
Visitors: Welcome. Societies welcome.
Green Fees: Weekdays £11, weekends and Bank Holidays £14.
Facilities: Lunch. Dinner. Bar Snacks. Club Hire.

PORTSTEWART

Portstewart Golf Club, 117 Strand Road, Portstewart, Co. Londonderry, Northern Ireland. BT55 7PG. Tel: 2015 (026583)
Secretary: Michael Moss   Tel: 2015 (026583)
Professional: Alan Hunter   Tel: 2015 (026583)
Location: 1 mile west of town centre.
Description: Links courses.
18 holes, 6,784 yards, S.S.S. 72.
18 holes, 4,733 yards, S.S.S. 62.
Visitors: Welcome. Best Days - Weekdays. Societies welcome by arrangement. Indoor bowling. Snooker. Practice fairway.
Green Fees: One - Weekdays £15, weekends £20. Two - Weekdays £6, weekends £8. Three - Weekdays £9, weekends £12.
Facilities: Lunch. Dinner. Bar Snacks. Club Hire.

COUNTY TYRONE

COOKSTOWN

Killymoon Golf Club, 200 Killymoon Road, Cookstown, Co. Tyrone, Northern Ireland. BT80 8TW. Tel: 63762 (06487)
Secretary: Les Hodgett   Tel: 62254 (06487)
Professional: Barry Hamill   Tel: 63460 (06487)
Location: Southern outskirts of the town.
Description: Parkland.
18 holes, 6,015 yards, S.S.S. 69.
Visitors: Welcome. Best Days - Mondays, Tuesdays, Wednesdays and Fridays. Thursdays Ladies Day. Societies welcome. Practice fairway.
Green Fees: Weekdays £10, Sundays and Bank Holidays £14.
Facilities: Lunch. Dinner. Bar Snacks.

DUNGANNON

Dungannon Golf Club, 34 Springfield Lane, Dungannon, Co. Tyrone, Northern Ireland. BT70 1QX. Tel: 22098 (08687)
Secretary: L R P Agnew   Tel: 27338 (08687)

Location: 1 mile west of town centre.
Description: Undulating parkland.
18 holes, 5,904 yards, S.S.S. 68.
Membership: 834
Visitors: Welcome. Not Saturdays (competition days). Societies welcome.
Green Fees: Weekdays £7, weekends and Bank Holidays £10.
Facilities: Lunch. Dinner. Bar Snacks. Full Catering. Changing Room. Golf Shop.
Class One Hotel: Inn on the Park, Dungannon, 1 mile(s). Tel: 25151 (08687)

FINTONA

Fintona Golf Club, Ecclesville Demesne, Fintona, Co. Tyrone, Northern Ireland. BT78 2AF. Tel: 841480 (0662)
Secretary: Gerry McNulty   Tel: 841514 (0662)
Location: In the village.
Description: Parkland.
9 holes, 6,250 yards, S.S.S. 70.
Membership: 320
Visitors: Welcome. Best Days - Midweek. Societies welcome. Lunch and dinner by arrangement. Snooker. Putting green.
Green Fees: £10 per day, £5 with a member.
Facilities: Bar Snacks.
Class One Hotel: Royal Arms, Omagh, 9 mile(s). Tel: 242119 (0662)
Class Two Hotel: Valley, Fivemiletown, 10 mile(s). Tel: 21505 (03655)

NEWTOWNSTEWART

Newtownstewart Golf Club, 38 Golf Course Road, Newtownstewart, Co. Tyrone, Northern Ireland. BT78 4HU. Tel: 61466 (06626)
Secretary: Daphne Magee   Tel: 61829 (06626)
Location: 2 miles south west of town centre on B84.
Description: Undulating parkland.
18 holes, 5,980 yards, S.S.S. 69.
Visitors: Welcome. Best Days - Mondays, Tuesdays and Fridays. Lunch and dinner by arrangement.
Green Fees: Weekdays £6, weekends £8.
Facilities: Bar Snacks. Club Hire. Trolley Hire.

OMAGH

Omagh Golf Club, 83a Dublin Road, Omagh, Co. Tyrone, Northern Ireland. BT78 1HQ. Tel: 243160 (0662)
Secretary: Joseph A McElholm   Tel: 241442 (0662)
Location: Southern outskirts of the town.
Description: Undulating parkland.
18 holes, 5,774 yards, S.S.S. 68.
Membership: 600
Visitors: Welcome. Not Saturdays in Summer (competition days). Societies welcome.
Green Fees: Weekdays £10, Sundays and Bank Holidays £12.
Facilities: Bar Snacks. Changing Room.
Class One Hotel: Royal Arms, Omagh, 3/4 mile(s). Tel: 243262 (0662)
Class Two Hotel: Silver Birch, Omagh, 1 1/2 mile(s). Tel: 242520 (0662)

STRABANE
Strabane Golf Club, 33 Ballycolman Road, Strabane, Co. Tyrone, Northern Ireland. BT82 9PH. Tel: 382271 (0504)
Secretary: Jim Harron　　　　Tel: 382271 (0504)
Location: 1 mile south of town centre.
Description: Parkland.
18 holes, 5,969 yards, Par , S.S.S. 69.
Visitors: Welcome. Best Days - Weekdays (Mondays and Wednesdays mornings only). Societies welcome by prior arrangement. Catering by arrangement. Practice area. Bar.
Green Fees: Weekdays £6, weekends £10, with a member £6.

Cade's - Audi Golf Course Guide

Audi 80 TDI

REPUBLIC OF IRELAND

Please note:

The information provided in this section has been supplied by by the Irish Tourist Board and therefore varies in presentation slightly from the information in previous sections.

There is no accommodation listed, course descriptions are not as full and all prices are shown in Irish Pounds. You are especially advised to verify any facility that you particularly require directly with the course secretary. Green fees should also be confirmed as these may not be current.

COUNTY CARLOW

CARLOW
Carlow Golf Club, Deerpark, Carlow, Co. Carlow, Eire. .Tel: 31695 (0503)
Secretary: Margaret Meaney   Tel: 31695 (0503)
Professional: Andrew Gilbert   Tel: 41745 (0503)
Location: On the Dublin Road 2 miles north of Carlow town.
Description: Inland.
18 holes, yards, Par 70.
Visitors: Welcome. Best Days - Weekdays.
Green Fees: Weekdays IR£13, weekends and Bank Holidays IR£17.
Facilities: Lunch. Dinner. Bar Snacks. Club Hire. Trolley Hire.

COUNTY CAVAN

DRUMELLIS
County Cavan Golf Club, Arnmore House, Drumellis, Co. Cavan, Eire. . Tel: 31283 (049)
Secretary: T O'Reilly   Tel: 31283 (049)
Location: 1 mile from Cavan town.
Description: Inland.
18 holes, yards, Par 70.
Visitors: Welcome. Best Days - Mondays, Tuesdays and Thursdays.
Green Fees: Weekdays IR£6, weekends IR£8.
Facilities: Lunch. Dinner. Bar Snacks. Club Hire. Trolley Hire.

COUNTY CLARE

ENNIS
Ennis Golf Club, Drumbiggle, Ennis, Co. Clare, Eire. . Tel: 24074 (065)
Secretary: James Cooney   Tel: 29637 (065)
Professional: Martin Ward   Tel: 20690 (065)
Location: 15 miles from Shannon Airport, 3/4 mile from Ennis.
Description: Inland.
18 holes, yards, Par 69.
Visitors: Welcome. Not Tuesdays or Sundays.
Green Fees: IR£14.
Facilities: Lunch. Dinner. Bar Snacks. Club Hire. Trolley Hire.

LAHINCH
Lahinch Golf Club, Lahinch, Co. Clare, Eire. . Tel: 81003 (065)
Secretary: Alan H Reardon   Tel: 81003 (065)
Professional: R McCavery   Tel: 81003 (065)
Location: 35 miles from Shannon Airport.
Description: Seaside championship course.
Old 18 holes, 6,675 yards, Par 72, S.S.S. 73.
Castle 18 holes, 5,218 yards, S.S.S. 67.
Visitors: Welcome. Every day.
Green Fees: Old - IR£25. Castle - IR£15.
Facilities: Lunch. Dinner. Bar Snacks. Club Hire. Trolley Hire.

NEWMARKET ON FERGUS
Dromoland Golf Club, Newmarket on Fergus, Ennis, Co. Clare, Eire. . Tel: 71144 (061)
Secretary: James Healy   Tel: 71144 (061)
Location: 10 miles from Shannon Airport, in grounds of

Dromoland Castle Hotel.
Description: Inland.
18 holes, 6,098 yards, Par 71.
Visitors: Welcome. Every day. Catering facilities exist in Dromoland Castle Hotel.
Green Fees: IR£15 per day.
Facilities: Club Hire. Trolley Hire.

SHANNON
Shannon Golf Club, Shannon Airport, Co. Clare, Eire. .Tel: 61020 (061)
Secretary: John Quigley   Tel: 61849 (061)
Professional: Artie Pyke   Tel: 61551 (061)
Location: 1/2 mile from Shannon Airport Terminal building, 14 miles from Limerick and Ennis.
Description: Inland.
18 holes, yards, Par 72.
Visitors: Welcome. Best Days - Weekdays.
Green Fees: Weekdays IR£18, weekends IR£20.
Facilities: Lunch. Dinner. Bar Snacks. Club Hire. Trolley Hire.

COUNTY CORK

BANDON
Bandon Golf Club, Castlebernard, Bandon, Co. Cork, Eire. . Tel: 41111 (023)
Secretary: B O'Neill   Tel: 41111 (023)
Professional: P O'Boyle   Tel: 42224 (023)
Location: 1 mile from Bandon, 20 miles from Cork.
Description: Inland.
18 holes, 5,496 yards, Par 70, S.S.S. 69.
Visitors: Welcome. Best Days - Weekdays.
Green Fees: Weekdays IR£12, weekends IR£15.
Facilities: Lunch. Dinner. Bar Snacks. Club Hire. Trolley Hire.

CHARLEVILLE
Charleville Golf Club, Ardmore, Charleville, Co. Cork, Eire. . Tel: 81257 (063)
Secretary: Tony Murphy   Tel: 81257 (063)
Location: 1/2 mile from Charleville, 35 miles from Cork.
Description: Inland.
18 holes, 6,430 yards, Par 71, S.S.S. 70.
Visitors: Welcome. Best Days - Mondays, Wednesdays and Fridays.
Green Fees: IR£10.
Facilities: Lunch. Bar Snacks. Trolley Hire.

CORK
Cork Golf Club, Little Island, Co. Cork, Eire. . Tel: 353451 (021)
Secretary: Matt Sands   Tel: 353451 (021)
Professional: David Higgins   Tel: 353451 (021)
Location: 5 miles east of Cork city, 1/2 mile off main Cork to Youghal Road.
Description: Inland.
18 holes, 6,612 yards, Par 72, S.S.S. 72.
Visitors: Welcome. Best Days - Mondays, Tuesdays, Wednesdays and Fridays.
Green Fees: Weekdays IR£20, weekends and Bank Holidays IR£22.
Facilities: Lunch. Dinner. Bar Snacks. Club Hire. Trolley Hire.

CORK
Douglas Golf Club, Douglas, Co. Cork, Eire. Tel: 891086 (021)
Secretary: Brian Barrett   Tel: 895297 (021)
Professional: G Nicholson   Tel: 362055 (021)
Location: 3 miles from Cork city centre.
Description: Inland.
18 holes, 5,772 yards, Par 70, S.S.S. 68.
Visitors: Welcome. Best Days - Mondays, Thursdays and Fridays.
Green Fees: Weekdays IR£14, weekends IR£15.
Facilities: Lunch. Dinner. Bar Snacks. Club Hire. Trolley Hire.

CORK
Harbour Point Golf Club, Little Island, Co. Cork, Eire. . Tel: 353094 (021)
Secretary: Sean K Power   Tel: 353094 (021)
Location: 4 miles east of Cork city centre.
Description: Inland.
18 holes, yards, Par 72.
Visitors: Welcome. Every day.
Green Fees: Weekdays IR£20, weekends IR£22.
Facilities: Lunch. Dinner. Bar Snacks. Club Hire. Trolley Hire.

CORK
Mahon Municipal Golf Club, Blackrock, Co. Cork, Eire. . Tel: 362480 (021)
Secretary: Tim O'Connor   Tel: 362480 (021)
Location: On Douglas Road, 2 miles from Cork city centre.
Description: Inland.
18 holes, yards, Par 67.
Visitors: Welcome. Not Saturdays or Sunday mornings.
Green Fees: Weekdays IR£6.50, weekends IR£7.50.
Facilities: Lunch. Dinner. Bar Snacks. Club Hire. Trolley Hire.

CORK
Muskerry Golf Club, Carrigrohane, Co. Cork, Eire. . Tel: 385297 (021)
Secretary: J J Moynihan   Tel: 385297 (021)
Professional: Martin Lehane   Tel: 385104 (021)
Location: 7 miles north west of Cork.
Description: Inland.
18 holes, 6,308 yards, Par 71, S.S.S. 70.
Visitors: Welcome. Not Wednesday afternoons or Thursday mornings. With members only at weekends. Lunch and dinner by arrangement.
Green Fees: Weekdays IR£16.
Facilities: Bar Snacks. Club Hire.

FERMOY
Fermoy Golf Club, Fermoy, Co. Cork, Eire. . Tel: 31472 (025)
Secretary: Patrick McCarthy   Tel: 31472 (025)
Location: At Corrin Cross 3 miles from Fermoy.
Description: Inland.
18 holes, 5,550 yards, Par 70, S.S.S. 70.
Visitors: Welcome. Best days - Weekdays.
Green Fees: Weekdays IR£10, weekends IR£20.
Facilities: Lunch. Dinner. Bar Snacks. Club Hire. Trolley Hire.

MALLOW
Mallow Golf Club, Ballellis, Mallow, Co. Cork, Eire. . Tel: 21145 (022)
Secretary: Brian Wall   Tel: 21972 (022)
Professional: Sean Conway   Tel: 21145 (022)
Location: 21 miles north of Cork city centre.
Description: Inland.
18 holes, 6,404 yards, Par 72, S.S.S. 71.
Visitors: Welcome. Best Days - Mondays, Wednesdays, Thursdays and Fridays.
Green Fees: Weekdays IR£10, weekends IR£12.
Facilities: Lunch. Dinner. Bar Snacks. Club Hire. Trolley Hire.

MIDLETON
East Cork Golf Club, Midleton, Co. Cork, Eire. . Tel: 631687 (021)
Secretary: Maurice Moloney   Tel: 631687 (021)
Location: 1 mile from Midleton on Fermoy Road.
Description: Inland.
18 holes, 4,874 yards, Par 69, S.S.S. 65.
Visitors: Welcome. Best Days - Weekdays.
Green Fees: IR£10.
Facilities: Lunch. Bar Snacks. Club Hire. Trolley Hire.

MONKSTOWN
Monkstown Golf Club, Monkstown, Co. Cork, Eire. . Tel: 841225 (021)
Secretary: Joe Curtin   Tel: 841376 (021)
Professional: Batt Murphy   Tel: 841686 (021)
Location: 8 miles from Cork city centre.
Description: Inland.
18 holes, 6,181 yards, Par 70, S.S.S. 69.
Visitors: Welcome. Best Days - Mondays, Wednesday afternoons, Thursdays and Fridays.
Green Fees: Weekdays IR£15, weekends IR£16.
Facilities: Lunch. Dinner. Bar Snacks. Club Hire. Trolley Hire.

YOUGHAL
Youghal Golf Club, Knockavery, Youghal, Co. Cork, Eire. Tel: 92787 (024)
Secretary: Margaret O'Sullivan   Tel: 92787 (024)
Location: 1/2 mile from Youghal.
Description: Inland.
18 holes, 6,206 yards, Par 70, S.S.S. 69.
Visitors: Welcome. Best Days - Weekdays, not Wednesdays. Dinner by arrangement.
Green Fees: IR£12.
Facilities: Trolley Hire.

COUNTY DONEGAL

ARDARA
Narin and Portnoo Golf Club, Narin-Portnoo, Co. Donegal, Eire. . Tel: 45107 (075)
Secretary: D T McBride   Tel: 45107 (075)
Location: 8 miles from Glenties, 6 miles from Ardara.
Description: Seaside.
18 holes, 5,700 yards, Par 69, S.S.S. 68.
Visitors: Welcome. Best Days - Weekdays.
Green Fees: Weekdays IR£8, weekends IR£10.
Facilities: Bar Snacks.

BALLINTRA
Donegal Town Golf Club, Murvagh, Ballintra, Co. Donegal, Eire. . Tel: 34054 (073)
Secretary: Jim Nixon   Tel: 22166 (073)
Location: 7 miles from Donegal town centre on Ballyshannon to Donegal Town Road.
Description: Seaside.
18 holes, 7,271 yards, Par 73, S.S.S. 73.
Visitors: Welcome. Every Day.
Green Fees: Weekdays IR£12, weekends IR£15.
Facilities: Dinner. Bar Snacks.

BALLYBOFEY
Ballybofey and Stranorlar Golf Club, Ballybofey, Co. Donegal, Eire. . Tel: 31093 (074)
Secretary: P Carr   Tel: 31104 (074)
Location: 1/4 mile from Stranorlar.
Description: Inland.
18 holes, 5,922 yards, Par 68, S.S.S. 69.
Visitors: Welcome. Best Days - Weekdays.
Green Fees: IR£8.
Facilities: Bar Snacks.

BALLYLIFFEN
Ballyliffen Golf Club, Ballyliffen, Co. Donegal, Eire. . Tel: 76119 (077)
Secretary: Karl J O'Doherty   Tel: 74417 (077)
Location: 1 mile from Ballyliffen, 4 miles from Carndonagh.
Description: Inland.
18 holes, 6,611 yards, Par 71, S.S.S. 71.
Visitors: Welcome. Best Days - Weekdays.
Green Fees: Weekdays IR£7, weekends IR£10.
Facilities: Bar Snacks. Trolley Hire.

BUNCRANA
North West Golf Club, Fahan, Lifford, Co. Donegal, Eire. Tel: 61027 (077)
Secretary: Dudley Coyle   Tel: 61027 (077)
Professional: Seamus McBriarty   Tel: 61027 (077)
Location: 2 miles south of Buncrana and 12 miles from Derry.
Description: Seaside.

18 holes, 6,203 yards, Par 69, S.S.S. 69.
Visitors: Welcome. Best Days - Weekdays.
Green Fees: Weekdays IR£5, weekends IR£10.
Facilities: Lunch. Dinner. Bar Snacks.

BUNDORAN
Bundoran Golf Club, Bundoran, Co. Donegal, Eire. . Tel: 41302 (072)
Secretary: L McDivitt   Tel: 41302 (072)
Professional: David Robinson   Tel: 41302 (072)
Location: 24 miles north of Sligo town centre, 32 miles from Enniskillen.
Description: Seaside.
18 holes, yards, Par 70.
Visitors: Welcome. Best Days - Weekdays. All catering facilities provided in the Great Northern Hotel.
Green Fees: Weekdays IR£10, weekends IR£12. Special reductions for groups. Free for residents of Great Northern Hotel.
Facilities: Club Hire. Trolley Hire.

DOWNINGS
Rosapenna Golf Club, Downings, Co. Donegal, Eire. . Tel: 55301 (074)
Secretary: Frank T Casey   Tel: 55301 (074)
Professional: Simon Byrne   Tel: 55301 (074)
Location: 1 mile from Downings.
Description: Seaside.
18 holes, 6,254 yards, Par 70, S.S.S. 71.
Visitors: Welcome. Every Day. Dinner in Hotel.
Green Fees: Weekdays IR£10, weekends and Bank Holidays IR£12.
Facilities: Bar Snacks. Club Hire. Trolley Hire. Buggy Hire.

DUNFANAGHY
Dunfanaghy Golf Club, Dunfanaghy, Co. Donegal, Eire. Tel: 36335 (074)
Secretary: Michael Murray   Tel: 35243 (074)
Location: On main road 1/2 mile from Dunfanaghy.
Description: Seaside.
18 holes, 5,523 yards, Par 68, S.S.S. 66.
Visitors: Welcome. Not on Sundays.
Green Fees: Weekdays IR£7, Saturdays IR£8. Reductions for groups by arrangement.
Facilities: Bar Snacks.

LETTERKENNY
Letterkenny Golf Club, Barnhill, Letterkenny, Co. Donegal, Eire. . Tel: 21150 (074)
Secretary: Hugh O'Kane   Tel: 21144 (074)
Location: 2 miles from Letterkenny on Ramelton Road.
Description: Inland.
18 holes, 6,299 yards, Par 70, S.S.S. 69.
Visitors: Welcome. Best Days - Weekdays.
Green Fees: IR£8.
Facilities: Bar Snacks.

PORTSALON
Portsalon Golf Club, Portsalon, Co. Donegal, Eire. Tel: 59102 (074)

Secretary: Michael Kerr   Tel: 59102 (074)
Location: 20 miles from Letterkenny.
Description: Seaside.
18 holes, 5,522 yards, Par 69, S.S.S. 67.
Visitors: Welcome. Best Days - Weekdays.
Green Fees: IR£6.
Facilities: Lunch. Bar Snacks.

COUNTY DUBLIN

BALBRIGGAN
Balbriggan Golf Club, Balbriggan, Co. Dublin, Eire. . Tel: 412173 (01)
Secretary: Leslie Cashell   Tel: 412229 (01)
Location: 1/2 mile south of Balbriggan off Dublin Road.
Description: Inland.
18 holes, 6,233 yards, Par 71, S.S.S. 70.
Visitors: Welcome. Best Days - Weekdays, not on Tuesdays. Lunch and dinner by arrangement.
Green Fees: Weekdays IR£12, weekends IR£15.
Facilities: Bar Snacks. Trolley Hire.

BALLYBOUGHAL
Hollywood Golf Club, Hollywood, Ballyboughal, Co. Dublin, Eire. . Tel: 433406 (01)
Secretary: Kathleen Kelly   Tel: 433406 (01)
Professional: Mel Flanagan   Tel: 438332 (01)
Location: 12 miles north of Dublin city centre off the Dublin to Belfast Road.
Description: Inland.
18 holes, yards, Par 72.
Visitors: Welcome. Every Day.
Green Fees: Weekdays IR£5.
Facilities: Lunch. Dinner. Bar Snacks. Trolley Hire.

BRITTAS
Slade Valley Golf Club, Lynch Park, Brittas, Co. Dublin, Eire. . Tel: 582183 (01)
Secretary: Patrick Maguire   Tel: 582207 (01)
Professional: Gerry Egan   Tel: 582207 (01)
Location: 9 miles west of Dublin city centre.
Description: Inland.
18 holes, 5,955 yards, Par 69, S.S.S. 69.
Visitors: Welcome. Best Days - Mondays, Thursdays and Fridays.
Green Fees: Weekdays IR£12.
Facilities: Lunch. Dinner. Bar Snacks. Club Hire. Trolley Hire.

CLOGHRAN
Forrest Little Golf Club, Cloghran, Co. Dublin, Eire. . Tel: 401183 (01)
Secretary: Anthony Greany   Tel: 401763 (01)
Professional: Tony Judd   Tel: 407670 (01)
Location: 6 miles from city centre.
Description: Inland.
18 holes, 6,394 yards, Par 70, S.S.S. 70.
Visitors: Welcome. Best Days - Weekdays, preferably mornings.

Green Fees: Weekdays IR£16.
Facilities: Bar Snacks. Club Hire. Trolley Hire.

CLONDALKIN
Newlands Golf Club, Clondalkin, Co. Dublin, Eire. . Tel: 593157 (01)
Secretary: Tony O'Neill　　　　Tel: 593157 (01)
Professional: Paul Heeney　　　Tel: 593538 (01)
Location: 6 miles from Dublin city, at Newlands Cross on Naas Road.
Description: Inland.
18 holes, 6,210 yards, Par 71, S.S.S. 70.
Visitors: Welcome. Best days - Mondays, Thursdays and Fridays.
Green Fees: IR£20.
Facilities: Lunch. Dinner. Bar Snacks. Club Hire. Trolley Hire.

DONABATE
Beaverstown Golf Club, Beaverstown, Donabate, Co. Dublin, Eire. . Tel: 436439 (01)
Secretary: Eddie Smyth　　　　Tel: 436439 (01)
Location: 15 miles north of Dublin.
Description: Inland.
18 holes, yards, Par 71.
Visitors: Welcome. Best Days - Mondays, Thursdays and Fridays.
Green Fees: Weekdays IR£12, weekends IR£15.
Facilities: Lunch. Dinner. Bar Snacks. Trolley Hire.

DONABATE
Corballis Public Golf Course, Corballis, Donabate, Co. Dublin, Eire. Tel: 436583 (01)
Secretary: Paddy Boylan　　　　Tel: 436583 (01)
Location: 12 miles north of Dublin, 4 miles from Swords.
Description: Seaside.
18 holes, 4,953 yards, Par 65, S.S.S. 64.
Visitors: Welcome. Every day.
Green Fees: Weekdays IR£6, weekends IR£7.
Facilities: Trolley Hire.

DONABATE
Donabate Golf Club, Donabate, Co. Dublin, Eire. Tel: 436346 (01)
Secretary: Nancy Campion　　　Tel: 436346 (01)
Professional: Hugh Jackson　　Tel: 436346 (01)
Location: 16 miles from Dublin, 5 miles north of Dublin Airport.
Description: Inland.
18 holes, 6,191 yards, Par 70, S.S.S. 69.
Visitors: Welcome. Best Days - Weekdays, not Wednesdays.
Green Fees: IR£15.
Facilities: Lunch. Dinner. Bar Snacks. Club Hire. Trolley Hire.

DONABATE
Island Golf Club, Corballis, Donabate, Co. Dublin, Eire. . Tel: 436104 (01)
Secretary: Liam O'Connor　　　Tel: 436462 (01)
Location: 15 miles north of Dublin near Donabate.

Description: Seaside.
18 holes, 6,599 yards, Par 71, S.S.S. 72.
Visitors: Welcome. Best Days - Mondays, Tuesdays and Fridays.
Green Fees: IR£21.
Facilities: Lunch. Dinner. Bar Snacks.

DUBLIN
Clontarf Golf Club, Donnycarney House, Malahide, Dublin 3, Co. Dublin, Eire. Tel: 331892 (01)
Secretary: M G O'Brien　　　　Tel: 331892 (01)
Professional: Joe Craddock　　Tel: 331877 (01)
Location: 2 1/2 miles from city centre.
Description: Inland.
18 holes, 5,938 yards, Par 69, S.S.S. 68.
Visitors: Welcome. Best Days - Tuesday to Friday. Not at weekends.
Green Fees: Weekdays IR£15.
Facilities: Lunch. Dinner. Bar Snacks. Trolley Hire.

DUBLIN
Elm Park Golf and Sports Club, Nutley House, Dublin 4, Co. Dublin, Eire. Tel: 269 3438 (01)
Secretary: H Montag　　　　　Tel: 269 3438 (01)
Professional: Seamus Green　　Tel: 269 2650 (01)
Location: 3 1/2 miles from city centre.
Description: Inland.
18 holes, 5,911 yards, Par 69, S.S.S. 68.
Visitors: Welcome. Always telephone Professional for availability.
Green Fees: Weekdays IR£22, weekends IR£25.
Facilities: Lunch. Dinner. Bar Snacks. Golf Shop. Club Hire. Trolley Hire.

DUBLIN
Milltown Golf Club, Lower Churchtown Road, Dublin 14, Co. Dublin, Eire. Tel: 976090 (01)
Secretary: B Cassidy　　　　　Tel: 976090 (01)
Professional: Christy Greene　Tel: 977072 (01)
Location: 4 miles south of city centre.
Description: Inland.
18 holes, 6,217 yards, Par 71, S.S.S. 69.
Visitors: Welcome. Best days - Mondays and Thursdays.
Green Fees: IR£25.
Facilities: Lunch. Dinner. Bar Snacks. Golf Shop. Trolley Hire.

DUBLIN
Royal Dublin Golf Club, Bull Island, Dollymount, Dublin 3, Co. Dublin, Eire. Tel: 336346 (01)
Secretary: John A Lambe　　　Tel: 336346 (01)
Professional: Leonard Owens　Tel: 336477 (01)
Location: 3 1/2 miles north of Dublin city centre.
Description: Seaside.
18 holes, 6,858 yards, Par 73, S.S.S. 73.
Visitors: Welcome. Best Days - Weekdays, but not on Wednesdays.
Green Fees: Weekdays IR£30, weekends IR£40.
Facilities: Lunch. Dinner. Bar Snacks. Golf Shop. Club Hire. Trolley Hire.

DUBLIN

St Annes Golf Club, North Bull Island, Dollymount, Dublin 3, Co. Dublin, Eire. Tel: 336471 (01)
Secretary: Joe Carberry　　　　　　Tel: 336471 (01)
Professional: Paddy Skerritt　　　　Tel: 314138 (01)
Location: 4 1/2 miles north east of Dublin city centre.
Description: Seaside.
18 holes, 5,940 yards, Par 71, S.S.S. 68.
Visitors: Welcome. Best Days - Monday and Wednesday mornings, Thursdays and Fridays. Lunch and dinner by arrangement.
Green Fees: Weekdays IR£15, weekends IR£20.
Facilities: Bar Snacks.

DUN LAOGHAIRE

Dun Laoghaire Golf Club, Eglinton Park, Tivoli Road, Dun Laoghaire, Co. Dublin, Eire. Tel: 280 3916 (01)
Secretary: T Stewart　　　　　　Tel: 280 3916 (01)
Professional: O Mulhall　　　　　Tel: 280 1694 (01)
Location: 7 miles from Dublin city centre, 1/2 mile from Dun Laoghaire.
Description: Inland.
18 holes, 6,059 yards, Par 70, S.S.S. 69.
Visitors: Welcome. Best Days - Weekdays, not Thursdays.
Green Fees: IR£21.
Facilities: Dinner. Bar Snacks. Golf Shop. Club Hire. Trolley Hire.

HOWTH

Deerpark Hotel Golf Courses, Howth, Co. Dublin, Eire. . Tel: 322624 (01)
Secretary: David Tighe　　　　　　Tel: 322624 (01)
Location: 8 miles north of Dublin.
Description: Inland.
18 holes, yards, Par 70.
9 holes, yards, Par 35.
Visitors: Welcome. Every Day.
Green Fees: Weekdays IR£5.70, weekends IR£7.25.
Facilities: Lunch. Dinner. Bar Snacks. Club Hire. Trolley Hire.

HOWTH

Howth Golf Club, Carrickbrack Road, Sutton, Dublin 13, Co. Dublin, Eire. Tel: 323055 (01)
Secretary: Ann MacNeice　　　　　Tel: 323055 (01)
Professional: John McGuirk　　　　Tel: 393895 (01)
Location: Sutton side of the Hill of Howth. 1 1/2 miles from Sutton.
Description: Inland.
18 holes, 6,168 yards, Par 71, S.S.S. 69.
Visitors: Welcome. Best Days - Mondays, Tuesdays and Fridays.
Green Fees: Weekdays IR£15.
Facilities: Bar Snacks. Golf Shop.

KILTERNAN

Kilternan Golf Club, Kilternan Hotel, Enniskerry Road, Kilternan, Co. Dublin, Eire. Tel: 955542 (01)
Secretary: Terry Bradley　　　　　Tel: 955542 (01)
Professional: Bryan Malone　　　　Tel: 955542 (01)

Description: Inland.
18 holes, yards, Par 68.
Visitors: Welcome. Weekdays and Saturday and Sunday afternoons.
Green Fees: Weekdays IR£9, weekends IR£11.
Facilities: Lunch. Dinner. Bar Snacks. Golf Shop. Club Hire. Trolley Hire.

LUCAN

Hermitage Golf Club, Lucan, Co. Dublin, Eire. Tel: 626 8491 (01)
Secretary: Denis Kane　　　　　　Tel: 626 8491 (01)
Professional: David Daly　　　　　Tel: 626 8491 (01)
Location: 2 miles from Lucan.
Description: Inland.
18 holes, 6,578 yards, Par 71, S.S.S. 71.
18 holes, 6,179 yards, S.S.S. 70.
Visitors: Welcome. Best Days - Weekdays.
Green Fees: Weekdays IR£20, weekends IR£30.
Facilities: Lunch. Dinner. Bar Snacks. Golf Shop. Club Hire. Trolley Hire.

LUCAN

Lucan Golf Club, Celbridge Road, Lucan, Co. Dublin, Eire. Tel: 628 2106 (01)
Secretary: Gordon Long　　　　　Tel: 628 2106 (01)
Location: 8 miles west of Dublin on Celbridge Road.
Description: Inland.
18 holes, 6,300 yards, Par 71, S.S.S. 70.
Visitors: Welcome. Best Days - Mondays, Tuesdays and Fridays. Dinner by arrangement.
Green Fees: Weekdays IR£15.
Facilities: Lunch. Bar Snacks.

MALAHIDE

Malahide Golf Club, Beechwood, The Grange, Malahide, Co. Dublin, Eire. Tel: 461611 (01)
Secretary: John O'Donovan　　　　Tel: 461611 (01)
Professional: David Barton　　　　Tel: 461611 (01)
Location: 9 miles north east of Dublin city centre.
Description: Seaside courses.
18 holes, 5,568 yards, Par 71, S.S.S. 67.
9 holes, yards, Par 35.
Visitors: Welcome. Every day except Sundays (time sheet in operation).
Green Fees: Weekdays IR£21, weekends and Bank Holidays IR£31.
Facilities: Lunch. Dinner. Bar Snacks. Golf Shop. Club Hire. Trolley Hire.

PORTMARNOCK

Portmarnock Golf Club, Portmarnock, Co. Dublin, Eire. . Tel: 323082 (01)
Secretary: Walter Bornemann　　　Tel: 323082 (01)
Professional: Joey Purcell　　　　Tel: 325157 (01)
Location: 10 miles north of city centre.
Description: Seaside courses.
Old 18 holes, 6,064 yards, Par 72, S.S.S. 73.
New 9 holes, yards, Par 36.
Visitors: Welcome. Best Days - Moondays, Tuesdays and Fridays.

Green Fees: Weekdays IR£35, weekends IR£45. Ladies (weekdays only) IR£15.
Facilities: Lunch. Dinner. Bar Snacks. Golf Shop. Club Hire. Trolley Hire.

RATHCOOLE
Beech Park Golf Club, Johnstown, Rathcoole, Co. Dublin, Eire. Tel: 580522 (01)
Secretary: M O'Halloran   Tel: 580522 (01)
Location: 2 miles from Rathcool on Kilteel Road.
Description: Inland.
18 holes, yards, Par 72.
Visitors: Welcome. Best Days - Mondays, Thursdays and Fridays.
Green Fees: Weekdays IR£12.
Facilities: Lunch. Dinner. Bar Snacks. Trolley Hire.

RATHFARNHAM
Castle Golf Club, Woodside Drive, Rathfarnham, Dublin 14, Co. Dublin, Eire. Tel: 904207 (01)
Secretary: Leslie Blackburne   Tel: 905835 (01)
Professional: David Kinsella   Tel: 933444 (01)
Location: In Rathfarnham, 5 miles from Dublin city centre.
Description: Inland.
18 holes, 6,240 yards, Par 70, S.S.S. 69.
Visitors: Welcome. Best Days - Mondays, Wednesday mornings, Thursdays and Fridays.
Green Fees: IR£22.
Facilities: Lunch. Dinner. Bar Snacks. Golf Shop. Trolley Hire.

RATHFARNHAM
Edmondstown Golf Club, Rathfarnham, Dublin 16, Co. Dublin, Eire. Tel: 932461 (01)
Secretary: Selwyn S Davies   Tel: 931082 (01)
Professional: A Crofton   Tel: 941049 (01)
Location: 7 miles from city centre.
Description: Inland.
18 holes, 6,159 yards, Par 70, S.S.S. 69.
Visitors: Welcome. Best days - Weekdays.
Green Fees: Weekdays IR£16, weekends IR£20.
Facilities: Lunch. Dinner. Bar Snacks. Golf Shop. Club Hire. Trolley Hire.

RATHFARNHAM
Grange Golf Club, Rathfarnham, Dublin 16, Co. Dublin, Eire. Tel: 932889 (01)
Secretary: James A O'Donoghue   Tel: 932889 (01)
Professional: W Sullivan   Tel: 932299 (01)
Location: 6 miles from city centre.
Description: Inland.
18 holes, 5,517 yards, Par 68, S.S.S. 69.
Visitors: Welcome. Best Days - Weekdays.
Green Fees: Weekdays IR£22, weekends IR£25.
Facilities: Lunch. Dinner. Bar Snacks. Golf Shop. Trolley Hire.

RATHFARNHAM
Stackstown Golf Club, Rathfarnham, Dublin 16, Co. Dublin, Eire. Tel: 942338 (01)
Secretary: Kieran Lawlor   Tel: 941993 (01)

Location: 9 miles south of Dublin city on Kellystown Road in Rathfarnham.
Description: Inland.
18 holes, yards, Par 72.
Visitors: Welcome. Best Days - Weekdays.
Green Fees: Weekdays IR£12, weekends IR£15.
Facilities: Lunch. Dinner. Bar Snacks.

SKERRIES
Skerries Golf Club, Skerries, Co. Dublin, Eire. Tel: 491567 (01)
Secretary: John Harte   Tel: 491567 (01)
Professional: Jimmy Kinsella   Tel: 490925 (01)
Location: 18 miles north of Dublin.
Description: Inland.
18 holes, 5,852 yards, Par 71, S.S.S. 70.
Visitors: Welcome. Best Days - Mondays, Thursdays and Fridays.
Green Fees: Weekdays IR£15, weekends IR£18.
Facilities: Lunch. Dinner. Bar Snacks. Golf Shop. Club Hire. Trolley Hire.

TALLAGHT
Ballyinascorney Golf Club, Bohernabreena, Tallaght, Dublin 24, Co. Dublin, Eire. Tel: 512516 (01)
Secretary: G Murphy   Tel: 512516 (01)
Location: 10 miles south west of Dublin.
Description: Inland.
18 holes, yards, Par 68.
Visitors: Welcome. Best Days - Weekdays. Bar.
Green Fees: IR£10.

COUNTY GALWAY

ATHENRY
Athenry Golf Club, Palmerstown, Oranmore, Co Galway, Eire. Tel: 94466 (091)
Secretary: Pat Burkitt   Tel: 94681 (091)
Location: 5 miles from Athenry on the Oranmore road and 19 miles from Galway.
Description: Inland.
18 holes, 5,448 yards, Par 68, S.S.S. 67.
Visitors: Welcome. Not Sundays.
Green Fees: Weekdays IR£10.
Facilities: Bar Snacks. Club Hire.

BALLINASLOE
Ballinasloe Golf Club, Rossgloss, Ballinasloe, Co Galway, Eire. Tel: 42126 (0905)
Secretary: W O'Rourke   Tel: 42435 (0905)
Location: 2 miles from Ballinasloe on Portumna road.
Description: Inland.
18 holes, 5,622 yards, Par 68, S.S.S. 67.
Visitors: Welcome. Best days - Weekdays. Dinner by arrangement.
Green Fees: IR£10.
Facilities: Lunch. Bar Snacks. Trolley Hire.

BALLYCONNEELY

Connemara Golf Club, Ballyconeely, Clifden, Co Galway, Eire. Tel: 23502 (095)
Secretary: Matt Killilea   Tel: 23502 (095)
Location: 8 miles from Clifton.
Description: Seaside.
18 holes, 6,620 yards, Par 72, S.S.S. 75.
Visitors: Welcome. Not Sundays.
Green Fees: IR£16.
Facilities: Lunch. Dinner. Bar Snacks. Club Hire. Trolley Hire.

GALWAY

Galway Golf Club, Blackrock, Co Galway, Eire.   Tel: 22169 (091)
Secretary: William C Caulfield   Tel: 22169 (091)
Professional: Don Wallace   Tel: 23038 (091)
Location: 2 miles from City Centre.
Description: Seaside.
18 holes, 6,354 yards, Par 69, S.S.S. 70.
Visitors: Welcome. Best days - Weekdays except Tuesdays.
Green Fees: IR£20.
Facilities: Lunch. Dinner. Bar Snacks. Golf Shop. Club Hire. Trolley Hire.

OUGHTERARD

Oughterard Golf Club, Oughterard, Co Galway, Eire. Tel: 82131 (091)
Secretary: John Walters   Tel: 82381 (091)
Professional: Michael Ryan   Tel: 82626 (091)
Location: 1 mile from Oughterard on Galway road, 15 miles from Galway.
Description: Inland.
18 holes, yards, Par 72.
Visitors: Welcome. Best days - Weekdays.
Green Fees: Weekdays IR£12, weekends IR£15.
Facilities: Lunch. Dinner. Bar Snacks. Golf Shop. Club Hire. Trolley Hire.

TUAM

Tuam Golf Club, Barnacurragh, Tuam, Co Galway, Eire. Tel: 24354 (093)
Secretary: Padraig King   Tel: 28364 (093)
Location: 1/2 mile from Tuam on Athenry road.
Description: Inland.
18 holes, 6,321 yards, Par 73, S.S.S. 70.
Visitors: Welcome. Best days - Weekdays.
Green Fees: IR£10.
Facilities: Bar Snacks. Golf Shop. Club Hire. Trolley Hire.

COUNTY KERRY

ARDFERT

Tralee Golf Club, West Barrow, Ardfert, Tralee, Co Kerry, Eire. Tel: 36379 (066)
Secretary: Peter Colleran   Tel: 36379 (066)
Location: 8 miles from Tralee on Fenit to Churchill road.
Description: Seaside.
18 holes, 6,499 yards, Par 71, S.S.S. 71.
Visitors: Welcome. Best days - Weekdays.
Green Fees: Weekdays IR£22, weekends IR£30.
Facilities: Lunch. Dinner. Bar Snacks. Club Hire. Trolley Hire.

BALLYBUNION

Ballybunion Golf Club, Ballybunion, Co Kerry, Eire. Tel: 27146 (068)
Secretary: Sean Welsh   Tel: 27611 (068)
Professional: Ted Higgins   Tel: 27209 (068)
Location: 1 mile from Ballybunion.
Description: Seaside.
Old 18 holes, 6,542 yards, Par 71, S.S.S. 72.
New 18 holes, 6,477 yards, Par 71, S.S.S. 72.
Visitors: Welcome. Best days - Weekdays. One course open each Sunday.
Green Fees: Old Course IR£30, New Course IR£20. Both courses IR£40.
Facilities: Lunch. Dinner. Bar Snacks. Golf Shop. Club Hire. Trolley Hire.

BALLYFERRITER

Ballyferriter Golf Club, Ballyferriter, Co Kerry, Eire. . Tel: 56255 (066)
Secretary: G Partington   Tel: 56255 (066)
Professional: Dermot O'Connor   Tel: 56255 (066)
Location: Western end of Dingle Peninsula, 10 miles from Dingle.
Description: Inland.
18 holes, yards, Par 72.
Visitors: Welcome. Everyday. Catering facilites in Hotel.
Green Fees: IR£14.
Facilities: Golf Shop. Club Hire. Trolley Hire.

GLENBEIGH

Dooks Golf Club, Dooks, Glenbeigh, Co Kerry, Eire . Tel: 68205 (066)
Secretary: Michael Shanahan   Tel: 67370 (066)
Location: 4 miles from Killorglin on Ring of Kerry road.
Description: Seaside.
18 holes, 6,021 yards, Par 70, S.S.S. 68.
Visitors: Welcome. Best days - Weekdays.
Green Fees: IR£14.
Facilities: Lunch. Dinner. Bar Snacks. Club Hire. Trolley Hire.

KILLARNEY

Killarney Golf and Fishing Club, Killarney, Co Kerry, Eire. Tel: 31034 (064)
Secretary: Tom Prendergast   Tel: 31034 (064)
Professional: Tony Coveney   Tel: 31615 (064)
Location: 3 miles west of Killarney Town.
Description: Inland.
Killeen 18 holes, 6,909 yards, Par 72, S.S.S. 73.
Mahonys Point 18 holes, 6,734 yards, Par 72, S.S.S. 71.
Visitors: Welcome. Best days - Mondays to Saturdays.
Green Fees: 18 holes IR£20. Weekdays both courses IR£32, weekends IR£40.
Facilities: Lunch. Dinner. Bar Snacks. Golf Shop. Club Hire. Trolley Hire.

WATERVILLE

Waterville Golf Club, Waterville, Co Kerry Eire. Tel: 4102 (0667)
Secretary: Noel Cronin　　　　　Tel: 4102 (0667)
Professional: Liam Higgins　　　Tel: 4102 (0667)
Location: On shore of Ballinskelligs Bay, 1 mile from Waterville.
Description: Seaside.
18 holes, 7,184 yards, Par 74, S.S.S. 74.
Visitors: Welcome. Best days - Weekdays.
Green Fees: Monday to Thursday IR£25, Fridays and weekends IR£30.
Facilities: Lunch. Dinner. Bar Snacks. Golf Shop. Club Hire. Trolley Hire. Buggy Hire.

COUNTY KILDARE

DONADEA

Knockanally Golf Club, Donadea, Co Kildare, Eire. Tel: 69322 (045)
Secretary: Noel A Lyons　　　　Tel: 69322 (045)
Professional: Peter Hickey　　　Tel: 69322 (045)
Location: 4 miles from Prosperous, 23 miles from Dublin.
Description: Inland.
18 holes, yards, Par 72.
Visitors: Welcome. Everyday.
Green Fees: Weekdays IR£10, weekends IR£15.
Facilities: Bar Snacks. Golf Shop. Club Hire. Trolley Hire.

KILDARE

Curragh Golf Club, Curragh, Co Kildare, Eire. Tel: 41238 (045)
Secretary: Ann Cullerton　　　　Tel: 41714 (045)
Professional: Phil Lawlor　　　　Tel: 41896 (045)
Location: 2 miles from Newbridge, 3 miles from Kildare.
Description: Inland.
18 holes, 6,565 yards, Par 72, S.S.S. 71.
Visitors: Welcome. Best days - Mondays, Thursdays and Fridays.
Green Fees: Weekdays IR£12, weekends and Bank Holidays IR£15.
Facilities: Lunch. Dinner. Bar Snacks. Golf Shop. Club Hire. Trolley Hire.

KILL

Four Lakes Golf Club, Kill, Co Kildare, Eire. Tel: 66003 (045)
Secretary: Peter Carey　　　　　Tel: 66003 (045)
Location: 1 mile from Kill, 17 miles from Dublin.
Description: Inland.
18 holes, yards, Par 69
Visitors: Welcome. Best days - Weekdays. Dinner by arrangement.
Green Fees: Weekdays IR£6, weekends IR£8
Facilities: Lunch. Bar Snacks. Club Hire. Trolley Hire.

NAAS

Castlewarden Golf and Country Club, Castlewarden, Kill, Co Kildare, Eire. Tel: 589254 (01)
Secretary: Brian Tighe　　　　　Tel: 624 2175 (01)
Professional: Tommy Halpin　　Tel: 588219 (01)
Location: Off Naas dual carriageway, between Newlands Cross and Naas.
Description: Inland.
18 holes, yards, Par 73.
Visitors: Welcome. Best days - Weekdays.
Green Fees: Weekdays IR£10.
Facilities: Lunch. Dinner. Bar Snacks. Golf Shop. Club Hire.

SALLINS

Bodenstown Golf Club, Bodenstown, Sallins, Co Kildare, Eire. Tel: 97096 (045)
Secretary: Bernadette Mather　Tel: 97096 (045)
Location: 5 miles from Naas.
Description: Inland.
18 holes, yards, Par 72.
Visitors: Welcome. Best days - Weekdays.
Green Fees: IR£8.
Facilities: Bar Snacks. Trolley Hire.

STRAFFAN

Kildare Country Club, Straffan, Co Kildare, Eire. Tel: 627 3111 (01)
Secretary: Eddie Fallon　　　　Tel: 627 3111 (01)
Professional: Ernie Jones　　　Tel: 627 3111 (01)
Location: 23 miles west of Dublin, off Naas dual carriageway.
Description: Inland.
18 holes, yards, Par 72.
Visitors: Welcome. Everyday.
Green Fees: Residents IR£55 per day, non-residents IR£110 including full day use at the club.
Facilities: Lunch. Dinner. Bar Snacks. Golf Shop. Club Hire. Trolley Hire. Caddies available.

COUNTY KILKENNY

KILKENNY

Kilkenny Golf Club, Glendine, Co Kilkenny, Eire. Tel: 22125 (056)
Secretary: Sean O'Neill　　　　Tel: 22125 (056)
Professional: Michael Kavanagh　Tel: 61730 (056)
Location: 1 mile from city centre.
Description: Inland.
18 holes, 6,400 yards, Par 71, S.S.S. 70.
Visitors: Welcome. Best days - Weekdays except Tuesdays.
Green Fees: Weekdays IR£12, weekends and Bank Holidays IR£15.
Facilities: Lunch. Dinner. Bar Snacks. Golf Shop. Club Hire. Trolley Hire.

THOMASTOWN

Mount Juliet Golf and Country Club, Thomastown, Co Kilkenny, Eire. Tel: 24725 (056)
Secretary: Katherine MacCann　Tel: 24725 (056)
Professional: Keith Mongan　　Tel: 24725 (056)

Location: 10 miles south of Kilkenny.
Description: Parkland.
18 holes, yards, Par 72.
Visitors: Welcome. Everyday.
Green Fees: Residents IR£35, non-residents IR£55.
Facilities: Lunch. Dinner. Bar Snacks. Golf Shop. Club Hire. Trolley Hire.

COUNTY LAOIS

PORTLAOISE
Heath Golf Club, Portlaoise, Co Laois, Eire. Tel: 46533 (0502)
Secretary: Fran Conway   Tel: 46533 (0502)
Professional: Eddie Doyle   Tel: 46622 (0502)
Location: 5 miles north-east of Portlaoise.
Description: Inland.
18 holes, 6,286 yards, Par 71, S.S.S. 70.
Visitors: Welcome. Best days - Weekdays. Dinner by arrangement.
Green Fees: Weekdays IR£8, weekends IR£12.
Facilities: Lunch. Bar Snacks. Golf Shop. Club Hire. Trolley Hire.

COUNTY LIMERICK

LIMERICK
Castleroy Golf Club, Castleroy, Co Limerick, Eire. Tel: 335753 (061)
Secretary: Laurence Hayes   Tel: 335753 (061)
Professional: Noel Cassidy   Tel: 338283 (061)
Location: 3 miles from Limerick City on Dublin road.
Description: Inland.
18 holes, 6,340 yards, Par 69, S.S.S. 71.
Visitors: Welcome. Best days - Mondays, Wedsnesdays and Fridays.
Green Fees: Weekdays IR£20.
Facilities: Lunch. Dinner. Bar Snacks. Golf Shop. Club Hire. Trolley Hire.

LIMERICK
Limerick Golf Club, Ballyclough, Co Limerick, Eire . Tel: 44083 (061)
Secretary: Declan McDonagh   Tel: 45146 (061)
Professional: John Cassidy   Tel: 42492 (061)
Location: 3 miles south of Limerick City in Ballyclough.
Description: Inland.
18 holes, 6,551 yards, Par 71, S.S.S. 71.
Visitors: Welcome. Best days - Mondays, Wednesdays and Fridays.
Green Fees: Weekdays IR£20.
Facilities: Lunch. Dinner. Bar Snacks. Golf Shop. Trolley Hire.

COUNTY LONGFORD

LONGFORD
County Longford Golf Club, Dublin Road, Longford, Co Longford, Eire. Tel: 46310 (043)
Secretary: Alan Mitchell   Tel: 46310 (043)
Location: On Dublin road, 1 mile from Longford town centre.
Description: Inland.
18 holes, 6,028 yards, Par 70, S.S.S. 68.
Visitors: Welcome. Everyday.
Green Fees: Weekdays IR£8, weekends IR£10. Group rates negotiable. Lunch and Dinner by arrangement.
Facilities: Bar Snacks.

COUNTY LOUTH

ARDEE
Ardee Golf Club, Townparks, Ardee, Co Louth, Eire. Tel: 53227 (041)
Secretary: Seamus Kelly   Tel: 53227 (041)
Location:
Description: Inland.
18 holes, 6,100 yards, Par 69, S.S.S. 69.
Visitors: Welcome. Best days - except Wednesdays.
Green Fees: IR£12.
Facilities: Dinner. Bar Snacks. Golf Shop. Trolley Hire.

DROGHEDA
County Louth Golf Club, Baltray, Drogheda, Co Louth, Eire. Tel: 22329 (041)
Secretary: Michael Delany   Tel: 22329 (041)
Professional: P McGuirk   Tel: 22444 (041)
Location: 3 1/2 miles from Drogheda.
Description: Seaside.
18 holes, 6,728 yards, Par 74, S.S.S. 72.
Visitors: Welcome. Best days - Weekdays except Tuesdays.
Green Fees: Weekdays IR£20, weekends IR£25.
Facilities: Lunch. Dinner. Bar Snacks. Golf Shop. Trolley Hire.

DUNDALK
Dundalk Golf Club, Dundalk, Co Louth, Eire. Tel: 21731 (042)
Secretary: Joe Carroll   Tel: 21731 (042)
Professional: Jimmy Cassidy   Tel: 22102 (042)
Location: 2 miles south of Dundalk near the Village of Blackrock.
Description: Inland.
18 holes, 6,740 yards, Par 72, S.S.S. 72.
Visitors: Welcome. Best days - Weekdays except Tuesdays.
Green Fees: Weekdays IR£15, weekends IR£18.
Facilities: Lunch. Dinner. Bar Snacks. Golf Shop. Trolley Hire.

GREENORE

Greenore Golf Club, Dundalk, Co Louth, Eire. Tel: 73212 (042)
Secretary: Peter Savage   Tel: 73212 (042)
Location: 16 miles from Dundalk.
Description: Seaside.
18 holes, 6,140 yards, Par 71, S.S.S. 71.
Visitors: Welcome. Best days - Weekdays.
Green Fees: Weekdays IR£8, weekends and Bank Holidays IR£14.
Facilities: Lunch. Dinner. Bar Snacks.

COUNTY MAYO

CASTLEBAR

Castlebar Golf Club, Rocklands, Castlebar, Co Mayo, Eire. Tel: 21649 (094)
Secretary: Brian MacDonald   Tel: 22430 (094)
Location: 1 mile from Castlebar on Belcarra road.
Description: Inland.
18 holes, 6,109 yards, Par 71, S.S.S. 69.
Visitors: Welcome. Best days - Weekdays.
Green Fees: IR£10.
Facilities: Lunch. Bar Snacks. Club Hire. Trolley Hire.

WESTPORT

Westport Golf Club, Westport, Co Mayo, Eire. Tel: 25113 (098)
Secretary: Paschal Quinn   Tel: 25113 (098)
Professional: Alex Melia   Tel: 25113 (098)
Location: 2 miles from Westport.
Description: Inland.
18 holes, 6,706 yards, Par 73, S.S.S. 71.
Visitors: Welcome. Best days - Weekdays.
Green Fees: Weekdays IR£12, weekends IR£15.
Facilities: Lunch. Dinner. Bar Snacks. Golf Shop. Club Hire. Trolley Hire.

COUNTY MEATH

DUNSHAUGHLIN

Blackbush Golf Club, Thomastown, Dunshaughlin, Co Meath, Eire. Tel: 250021 (01)
Secretary: Michael Cummins   Tel: 250021 (01)
Location: 1/2 mile from Dunshaughlin Village on main Dublin to Navan road.
Description: Inland.
18 holes, yards, Par 72.
Visitors: Welcome. Best days - Weekdays. Not Tuesdays p.m., Wednesdays or Thursdays.
Green Fees: Weekdays IR£10, weekends IR£12.
Facilities: Lunch. Dinner. Bar Snacks.

KELLS

Headfort Golf Club, Kells, Co Meath, Eire.   Tel: 40146 (046)
Secretary: P Curran   Tel: 40857 (046)
Professional: Brendan McGovern   Tel: 40639 (046)
Location: 1/4 mile from Kells, 40 miles from Dublin.
Description: Inland.
18 holes, 6,393 yards, Par 72, S.S.S. 70.
Visitors: Welcome. Best days - Weekdays except Tuesdays. Lunch and Dinner by prior arrangement.
Green Fees: Weekdays IR£10, weekends and Bank Holidays IR£15.
Facilities: Bar Snacks. Golf Shop. Trolley Hire.

LAYTOWN

Laytown and Bettystown Golf Club, Laytown, Co Meath, Eire. Tel: 27170 (041)
Secretary: Stella Garvey   Tel: 27170 (041)
Professional: Bobby Brown   Tel: 27563 (041)
Location: 1 3/4 miles from Laytown.
Description: Seaside.
18 holes, 6,200 yards, Par 70, S.S.S. 69.
Visitors: Welcome. Best days - Tuesdays, Wednesdays and Thursdays.
Green Fees: Weekdays IR£13, weekends and Bank Holidays IR£18.
Facilities: Lunch. Dinner. Bar Snacks. Golf Shop. Club Hire. Trolley Hire.

NAVAN

Royal Tara Golf Club, Bellinter, Navan, Co Meath, Eire. Tel: 25244 (046)
Secretary: Des Foley   Tel: 25244 (046)
Professional: Adam Whiston   Tel: 25244 (046)
Location: 6 miles from Navan.
Description: Inland.
18 holes, yards, Par 71, S.S.S. 70.
Visitors: Welcome. Best days - Mondays, Thursdays and Fridays.
Green Fees: Weekdays IR£10, weekends and Bank Holidays IR£12.
Facilities: Lunch. Dinner. Bar Snacks. Golf Shop. Club Hire. Trolley Hire.

TRIM

Trim Golf Club, Newtownmoynagh, Trim, Co Meath, Eire. Tel: 31463 (046)
Secretary: Peter J Darby   Tel: 31438 (046)
Location: 3 miles from Trim on Longford road.
Description: Inland.
18 holes, yards, Par 71.
Visitors: Welcome. Best days - Weekdays except Thursdays.
Green Fees: Weekdays IR£8, weekends IR£12.
Facilities: Lunch. Dinner. Bar Snacks. Trolley Hire.

COUNTY MONAGHAN

CARRICKMACROSS

Nuremore Golf Club, Carrickmacross, Co Monaghan, Eire. Tel: 62125 (042)
Secretary: Sean Egan   Tel: 62125 (042)
Location: 1 mile south of Carrickmacross on main Dublin road.

Description: Parkland.
18 holes, 5959 yards, Par 73, S.S.S. 69.
Visitors: Welcome. Best days - Weekdays. Catering provided at nearby Hotel.
Green Fees: Weekdays IR£5, weekends IR£6.

COUNTY OFFALY

BIRR

Birr Golf Club, Birr, Co Offaly, Eire. Tel: 20082 (0509)
Secretary: P R O'Gorman   Tel: 20082 (0509)
Location: 2 miles from Birr town.
Description: Inland.
18 holes, 6,262 yards, Par 70, S.S.S. 70.
Visitors: Welcome. Best days - Weekdays. Dinner by arrangement.
Green Fees: IR£10.
Facilities: Lunch. Bar Snacks.

TULLAMORE

Tullamore Golf Club, Tullamore, Co Offaly, Eire.
Tel:21439 (0506)
Secretary: W M Rossiter   Tel: 21310 (0506)
Professional: John Kelly   Tel: 21439 (0506)
Location: 2 miles from Tullamore town.
Description: Inland.
18 holes, 6,414 yards, Par 72, S.S.S. 71.
Visitors: Welcome. Best days - Weekdays except Tuesdays.
Green Fees: Weekdays IR£10, weekends IR£12.
Facilities: Lunch. Dinner. Bar Snacks. Golf Shop. Club Hire. Trolley Hire.

COUNTY SLIGO

ENNISCRONE

Enniscrone Golf Club, Enniscrone, Co Sligo, Eire. Tel: 36297 (096)
Secretary: John M Fleming   Tel: 36243 (096)
Location: 1/2 mile from Enniscrone on Ballina road.
Description: Seaside.
18 holes, 6,487 yards, Par 72, S.S.S. 72.
Visitors: Welcome. Best days - Weekdays. Weekends by arrangement.
Green Fees: IR£15. Ladies IR£10.
Facilities: Bar Snacks. Club Hire. Trolley Hire.

ROSSES POINT

County Sligo Golf CLub, Rosses Point, Co Sligo, Eire.
.Tel: 331892 (01)
Secretary: M G O'Brien   Tel: 331892 (01)
Professional: Joe Craddock   Tel: 331877 (01)
Location: 2 1/2 miles from city centre.
Description: Inland.
18 holes, 6,544 yards, Par 69, S.S.S. 72.

Visitors: Welcome. Best days - Tuesdays to Fridays. Not weekends.
Green Fees: IR£15.
Facilities: Lunch. Dinner. Bar Snacks. Golf Shop. Trolley Hire.

STRANDHILL

Strandhill Golf Club, Strandhill, Co Sligo, Eire : Tel: 68188 (071)
Secretary: Tony McConnell   Tel: 43221 (071)
Location: 5 miles from Sligo, 1/4 mile from Strandhill.
Description: Seaside.
18 holes, 5,950 yards, Par 69, S.S.S. 69.
Visitors: Welcome. Everyday. Dinner by arrangement.
Green Fees: Weekdays IR£10, weekends IR£12.
Facilities: Lunch. Bar Snacks.

COUNTY TIPPERARY

CLONMEL

Clonmel Golf Club, Lyreanearla, Mountain Road, Clonmel, Co Tipperary, Eire. Tel: 21138 (052)
Secretary: William O'Sullivan   Tel: 24050 (052)
Professional: Robert Hayes   Tel: 24050 (052)
Location: 3 miles south-east of Clonmel.
Description: Inland.
18 holes, 6,330 yards, Par 71.
Visitors: Welcome. Best days - Weekdays.
Green Fees: Weekdays IR£10, weekends IR£12.
Facilities: Lunch. Dinner. Bar Snacks. Golf Shop. Club Hire. Trolley Hire.

NENAGH

Nenagh Golf Club, Graigue, Nenagh, Co Tipperary, Eire.
Tel: 31476 (067)
Secretary: Paddy Heffernan   Tel: 31771 (067)
Professional: John Coyle   Tel: 33242 (067)
Location: Beechwood, 5 miles from Nenagh.
Description: Inland.
18 holes, 5,648 yards, Par 69, S.S.S. 67.
Visitors: Welcome. Best days - Weekdays.
Green Fees: Weekdays IR£12 (except Wednesdays), Saturdays and Wednesdays IR£10, Sundays and Bank Holidays IR£15.
Facilities: Bar Snacks. Golf Shop. Club Hire. Trolley Hire.

THURLES

Thurles Golf Club, Thurles, Co Tipperary, Eire. Tel: 21983 (0504)
Secretary: Tom Ryan   Tel: 23787 (0504)
Professional: Sean Hunt   Tel: 21983 (0504)
Location: On Thurles to Cork road, 1 mile from Thurles.
Description: Inland.
18 holes, 6,300 yards, Par 71, S.S.S. 70.
Visitors: Welcome. Best days - Mondays, Wednesdays, Thursdays and Fridays.
Green Fees: Weekdays IR£10, weekends IR£13.
Facilities: Lunch. Bar Snacks. Golf Shop. Club Hire. Trolley Hire.

Cade's - Audi Golf Course Guide

COUNTY WATERFORD

TRAMORE
Tramore Golf Club, Newtown Hill, Tramore, Co Waterford, Eire. Tel: 86170 (051)
Secretary: James Cox   Tel: 86170 (051)
Professional: Paul McDaid   Tel: 81706 (051)
Location: 1 mile from Tramore, 8 miles from Waterford.
Description: Inland.
18 holes, 6,660 yards, Par 72, S.S.S. 71.
Visitors: Welcome. Best days - Weekdays.
Green Fees: Weekdays IR£16, weekends IR£20.
Facilities: Lunch. Dinner. Bar Snacks. Golf Shop. Club Hire. Trolley Hire.

WATERFORD
Waterford Golf Club, Newrath, Co Waterford, Eire. Tel: 76748 (051)
Secretary: Joe Condon   Tel: 76748 (051)
Professional: E Condon   Tel: 78489 (051)
Location: 1 mile north of Waterford City.
Description: Inland.
18 holes, 6,237 yards, Par 71, S.S.S. 69.
Visitors: Welcome. Best days - Weekdays.
Green Fees: Weekdays IR£12, weekends and Bank Holidays IR£15.
Facilities: Lunch. Dinner. Bar Snacks. Golf Shop. Club Hire. Trolley Hire.

COUNTY WESTMEATH

ATHLONE
Athlone Golf Club, Hodson Bay, Athlone, Co Westmeath, Eire. Tel: 92073 (0902)
Secretary: Daniel Clarke   Tel: 75366 (0902)
Professional: Martin Quinn   Tel: 92073 (0902)
Location: 3 miles from Athlone town, off Roscommon road.
Description: Inland.
18 holes, 6,450 yards, Par 70, S.S.S. 70.
Visitors: Welcome. Best days - Mondays, Wednesdays, Thursdays and Fridays.
Green Fees: IR£10.
Facilities: Lunch. Dinner. Bar Snacks. Golf Shop. Club Hire.

MULLINGAR
Mullingar Golf Club, Mullingar, Co Westmeath, Eire. Tel: 48366 (044)
Secretary: Anne Scully   Tel: 48366 (044)
Professional: John Burns   Tel: 48366 (044)
Location: 3 miles from Mullingar.
Description: Inland.
18 holes, 6450 yards, Par 72, S.S.S. 71.
Visitors: Welcome. Best days - Weekdays except Wednesdays.
Green Fees: Weekdays IR£12, weekends IR£18.
Facilities: Lunch. Dinner. Bar Snacks. Golf Shop. Club Hire. Trolley Hire.

COUNTY WEXFORD

ENNISCORTHY
Enniscorthy Golf Club, Knockmarshall, Enniscorthy, Co Wexford, Eire. Tel: 33191 (054)
Secretary: Anne Byrne   Tel: 35257 (054)
Location: 1 1/2 miles from Enniscorthy, of Enniscorthy to New Ross road.
Description: Inland.
18 holes, 6,220 yards, Par 70, S.S.S. 70.
Visitors: Welcome. Best days - Weekdays.
Green Fees: Weekdays IR£8, weekends IR£10.
Facilities: Lunch. Dinner Bar Snacks. Trolley Hire.

GOREY
Courtown Golf Club, Kiltennel, Gorey, Co Wexford, Eire. Tel: 25166 (055)
Secretary: J Sheehan   Tel: 25166 (055)
Professional: John Cooke   Tel: 25166 (055)
Location: 4 miles from Gorey, 1 mile from Courtown.
Description: Inland.
18 holes, 6,398 yards, Par 71, S.S.S. 70.
Visitors: Welcome. Best days - Weekdays except Tuesdays.
Green Fees: Weekdays IR£11, weekends IR£15.
Facilities: Lunch. Dinner. Bar Snacks. Golf Shop. Club Hire. Trolley Hire.

ROSSLARE
Rosslare Golf Club, Rosslare, Co Wexford, Eire.   Tel: 32113 (053)
Secretary: J F Hall   Tel: 32370 (053)
Professional: Austin Skerritt   Tel: 32238 (053)
Location: 10 miles south of Wexford town.
Description: Seaside.
18 holes, 6,502 yards, Par 74, S.S.S. 71.
Visitors: Welcome. Best days - Weekdays except Tuesdays.
Green Fees: Weekdays IR£15, weekends and Bank Holidays IR£20.
Facilities: Lunch. Dinner. Bar Snacks. Golf Shop. Club Hire. Trolley Hire.

WEXFORD
Wexford Golf Club, Mulgannon, Co Wexford, Eire. Tel: 42238 (053)
Secretary: M O'Keeffe   Tel: 41967 (053)
Professional: Noel Leahy   Tel: 45723 (053)
Location: 1/4 mile from Wexford on Mulgannon road.
Description: Inland.
18 holes, 6,038 yards, Par 70, S.S.S. 69.
Visitors: Welcome. Best days - Weekdays except Thursdays. Full catering by prior arrangement.
Green Fees: Weekdays IR£12, weekends and bank Holidays IR£14.
Facilities: Bar Snacks. Golf Shop. Trolley Hire.

COUNTY WICKLOW

ARKLOW
Arklow Golf Club, Abbeylands, Arklow, Co Wicklow, Eire. Tel: 32492 (0402)
Secretary: Brendan Timmons   Tel: 32971 (0402)
Location: 1/2 mile from Arklow town centre.
Description: Seaside.
18 holes, 5,963 yards, Par 68, S.S.S. 68.
Visitors: Welcome. Best days - Weekdays.
Green Fees: Weekdays IR£10, weekends and Bank Holidays IR£12.
Facilities: Lunch. Dinner. Bar Snacks.

BRAY
Old Connor Golf Club, Ferndale Road, Bray, Co Wicklow, Eire. Tel: 2826055 (01)
Secretary: Kevin O'Byrne   Tel: 2826055 (01)
Professional: Niall Murray   Tel: 2820822 (01)
Location: 12 miles from Dublin.
Description: Inland.
18 holes, yards, Par 72.
Visitors: Welcome. Best days - Mondays, Thursdays and Fridays.
Green Fees: IR£15.
Facilities: Lunch. Dinner. Bar Snacks. Golf Shop. Club Hire. Trolley Hire.

BRAY
Woodbrook Golf Club, Bray, Co Wicklow, Eire. Tel: 2824799 (01)
Secretary: Derek Smyth   Tel: 2824799 (01)
Professional: W Kinsella   Tel: 2824799 (01)
Location: 3 miles from Bray, 12 miles from Dublin.
Description: Inland.
18 holes, 6,541 yards, Par 72, S.S.S. 71.
Visitors: Welcome. Best days - Weekdays except Tuesdays and Wednesdays (by prior arrangement only).
Green Fees: Weekdays IR£22, weekends IR£30.
Facilities: Lunch. Dinner. Bar Snacks. Golf Shop. Club Hire. Trolley Hire.

DELGANY
Delgany Golf Club, Delgany, Greystones, Co Wicklow, Eire. Tel: 2874536 (01)
Secretary: Joseph Deally   Tel: 2874536 (01)
Professional: E Darcy   Tel: 2874697 (01)
Location: 3/4 mile from Delgany village.
Description: Inland.
18 holes, 5,946 yards, Par 69, S.S.S. 69.
Visitors: Welcome. Best days - Mondays, Thursdays and Fridays.
Green Fees: Weekdays IR£15, weekends and Bank Holidays IR£20.
Facilities: Lunch. Dinner. Bar Snacks. Golf Shop. Club Hire. Trolley Hire.

GREYSTONES
Greystones Golf Club, Greystones, Co Wicklow, Eire. Tel: 2874136 (01)
Secretary: Oliver Walsh   Tel: 2874136 (01)
Professional: Kevin Daly   Tel: 2875308 (01)
Location: 20 miles from Dublin.
Description: Inland.
18 holes, 5,227 yards, Par 69, S.S.S. 67.
Visitors: Welcome. Best days - Mondays, Tuesdays and Friday mornings. Dinner for group bookings only.
Green Fees: Weekdays IR£16, weekends IR£20.
Facilities: Bar Snacks. Golf Shop. Club Hire. Trolley Hire.

WICKLOW
Blainroe Golf Club, Blainroe, Co Wicklow, Eire. Tel: 68168 (0404)
Secretary: William O'Sullivan   Tel: 68168 (0404)
Professional: John McDonald   Tel: 68168 (0404)
Location: 3 miles south of Wicklow town on Arklow coast road.
Description: Inland.
18 holes, 6,681 yards, Par 72, S.S.S. 72.
Visitors: Welcome. Best days - Weekdays except Mondays.
Green Fees: Weekdays IR£14, weekends IR£19.
Facilities: Bar Snacks. Golf Shop. Club Hire. Trolley Hire.

A Complete Directory of AUDI Dealerships Throughout Britain and Ireland

ENGLAND

AVON
Motor Services (Bath) Limited, Locksbrook Road, Bath, Avon, BA1 3EU. Tel:(0225) 428000.
White Tree Garage, 156 Cheltenham Road, Redland, Bristol, Avon, BS6 5RL. Tel:(0272) 248051.
Anthony Ince (Weston) Limited, Winterstoke Road, Weston-Super-Mare, Avon, BS24 9AA. Tel:(0934) 632541.

BEDFORDSHIRE
F Vindis & Sons, 332 Ampthill Road, Bedford, Beds, MK42 9RU. Tel:(0234) 327932.

BERKSHIRE
Normans of Maidenhead, Maidenhead Bridge, Bath Road, Maidenhead, Berks, SL6 0AH. Tel:(0628) 72323.
Ridgeway Garages (Newbury) Limited, St John's Garage, 22 Newtown Road, Berks, RG14 7BL. Tel:(0635) 41911.
Marshall's Garage (Reading) Limited, Oxford Road, Tilehurst, Reading, Berks, RG3 6TQ. Tel:(0734) 418181.
The Royal Berks Motor Co., Erleigh Road, Reading, Berks, RG1 5NJ. Tel:(0734) 666111.
Windrush Garage Limited, 57 Farnham Road, Slough, Berks, SL1 3TN. Tel:(0753) 533914.

BUCKINGHAMSHIRE
Keith Garages Limited, Bicester Road, Aylesbury, Bucks, HP19 3AL. Tel:(0296) 28001.
Rye Mill Garage Limited, 70/76 London Road, High Wycombe, Bucks, HP11 1DD. Tel:(0494) 450611.
Munn & Chapman Limited, Chalfont Station Garage, Little Chalfont, Bucks, HP7 9PN. Tel:(0494) 763456.
Wayside Garages Limited, 3 Denbigh Road, Bletchley, Milton Keynes, Bucks, MK1 1DE. Tel:(0908) 641535.

CAMBRIDGESHIRE
Birch's Garage Limited, 383 Milton Road, Cambridge, Cambs, CB4 1SR. Tel:(0223) 424472.
F Vindis & Sons, 25/27 High Street, Sawston, Cambridge, Cambs, CB2 4BG. Tel:(0223) 833110.
F Vindis & Sons, Low Road, St Ives, Huntingdon, Cambs, PE17 4EL. Tel:(0480) 61019.
Cooks, Storeys Bar Road, Peterborough, Cambs, PE1 5YS. Tel:(0733) 312213.

CHANNEL ISLANDS
St Martins Garage, Grande Rue, St Martins, Guernsey, Channel Isles, CI1. Tel:(0481) 35533.
Five Oaks Garage Limited, Five Oaks, St Saviour, Jersey, Channel Isles. Tel:(0534) 69911.

CHESHIRE
Dane Motor Company (Chester) Limited, Sealand Road, Chester, Cheshire, CH1 4LD. Tel:(0244) 390033.
L C Charles Limited, Oak Street, Crewe, Cheshire, CW2 7BZ. Tel:(0270) 213241.
Smith Knight Fay, Stockport Road, Gee Cross, Hyde, Cheshire, SK14 5ET. Tel:(061) 368 0413.
Charles Barber & Sons Limited, Station Road, Northwich, Cheshire, CW9 5LR. Tel:(0606) 46061.
Smith Knight Fay, Green Lane, Stockport, Cheshire, SK4 2JN. Tel:(061) 480 6695.
Hartwell Warrington, Milner Street, Warrington, Cheshire, WA5 1AD. Tel:(0925) 55300.

CLEVELAND
Lookers, Ormesby Road, Park End, Middlesbrough, Cleveland, TS3 0DZ. Tel:(0642) 317971.

CORNWALL
Helston Garages Limited, Meneage Street, Helston, Cornwall, TR13 8RD. Tel:(0326) 573415.

CUMBRIA
Harper & Hebson Limited, Viaduct Estate, Carlisle, Cumbria, CA2 5BH. Tel:(0228) 511317.
Hadwins (Lindale) Limited, Lindale, Grange over Sands, Cumbria, LA11 6LP. Tel:(05395) 34242.

DERBYSHIRE
International Cars of Alfreton, Hall Street, Alfreton, Derbys, DE5 7BU. Tel:(0773) 832176/7.
Links Garage, 3 The Front, Fairfield, Buxton, Derbys, SK17 7EQ. Tel:(0298) 70431/3.
Merlin (Chatsworth) Limited, Broombank Road, Sheepbridge, Chesterfield, Derbys, S41 9BJ. Tel:(0246) 260060.
Arlington of Derby, Sir Frank Whittle Road, Derby, Derbys, DE2 4AW. Tel:(0332) 290022.

DEVON
Mann Egerton, Trusham Road, Marsh Barton, Exeter, Devon, EX2 8QQ. Tel:(0392) 215151.
North Devon Motorhaven, Two Rivers Industrial Estate, Braunton Road, Barnstaple, Devon, EX31 1JY. Tel: (0271) 79711
Renwicks Garages, The Avenue, Newton Abbot, Devon, TQ12 2DE. Tel:(0626) 52641.
Renwicks Garages, Durnford Street, Stonehouse, Plymouth, Devon, PL1 3QF. Tel:(0752) 668351.

DORSET

Mann Egerton (Christchurch) Limited, Somerford Road, Christchurch, Dorset, BH23 3QE. Tel:(0202) 476871.
Loders Garage (Dorchester) Limited, The Grove, Dorchester, Dorset, DT1 1XU. Tel:(0305) 267881.
Diamond, Cabot Lane, Creekmoor Industrial Estate, Poole, Dorset, BH17 7DE. Tel:(0202) 603883.

COUNTY DURHAM

Mill Garages Faverdale, West Auckland Road, Faverdale, Darlington, Co. Durham, DL3 0UX. Tel:(0325) 353737.
Minories Garages Limited, 20 Alma Place, Gilesgate Moor, Durham, Co. Durham, DH1 2HN. Tel:(091) 386 7215.

ESSEX

Abridge Dealer Group, Market Place, Abridge, Essex, RM4 1UA. Tel:(037881) 2722/4.
Grange Motors (Brentwood) Limited, 2 Brook Street, Brentwood, Essex, CM14 5LU. Tel:(0277) 216161.
Nigel Grogan Limited, 112 Parkway, Chelmsford, Essex, CM2 7PW. Tel:(0245) 268826.
Maryan & Brading, Comet Way, Southend on Sea, Essex, SS2 6XR. Tel:(0702) 421142.

GLOUCESTERSHIRE

Skipper of Cheltenham Limited, Tewkesbury Road, Cheltenham, Gloucs, GL51 9AH. Tel:(0242) 222233.
Northfield Garage (Cirencester), Kingsmeadow, Cricklade Road, Cirencester, Gloucs, GL7 1NP. Tel:(0285) 650222.
Northfield Garage (Tetbury) Limited, London Road, Tetbury, Gloucs, GL8 8HN. Tel:(0666) 502473.

GREATER MANCHESTER

Ian Skelly (Manchester) Limited, Great Ancoates Street, Manchester, Greater Manchester, M4 7DF. Tel:(061) 274 3636.
Gilbert Lawton Limited, Cross Street, Washway Road, Sale, Greater Manchester, M33 1BU. Tel:(061) 973 3399.

HAMPSHIRE

Martins of Basingstoke, The Hatch, London Road, Basingstoke, Hants, RG24 0AD. Tel:(0256) 24444.
Peter Cooper (Southampton) Limited, Botley Road, Hedge End, Southampton, Hants, SO3 2FN. Tel:(0489) 783434.
Testwood Motors Limited, 331 Salisbury Road, Totton, Southampton, Hants, SO4 3ZU. Tel:(0703) 663333.
Winchester Motor Co. Limited, 43 Saint Cross Road, Winchester, Hants, SO23 9PU. Tel:(0962) 66331/4.

HEREFORD AND WORCESTERSHIRE

Black & White Garages, Harvington, Evesham, Here/Worcs, WR11 5LX. Tel:(0386) 870612.
South Hereford Garages Limited, Centurion Way, Roman Road, Hereford, Here/Worcs, HR1 1LQ. Tel:(0432) 352424.
Jaffar Motors (International) Limited, Evesham Road, Crabbs Cross, Redditch, Here/Worcs, B97 5JW. Tel:(0527) 544554.
Listers of Worcester, Hallow Road, Hallow, Worcester, Here/Worcs, WR2 4LB. Tel:(0905) 640512.

HERTFORDSHIRE

L J Sheppard Limited, Dane Street, Bishop's Stortford, Herts, CM23 3BX. Tel:(0279) 757700.
Executive Motors (St Albans) Limited, Executive House, 229/233 Hatfield Road, St Albans, Herts, AL1 4TB. Tel:(0727) 836366.
Harper Euro Cars (Stevenage) Limited, Lytton Way, Stevenage, Herts, SG1 3LN. Tel:(0438) 746400.
Douglas Stewart Limited, Britannia Road, Waltham Cross, Herts, EN8 7NZ. Tel:(0992) 712323.
Vernons of Watford, 68 Chalk Hill, Watford, Herts, WD1 4BY. Tel:(0923) 55055.

HUMBERSIDE

Triangle Motor Company Limited, 170 Anlaby Road, Hull, North Humberside, HU3 2JN. Tel:(0482) 23631.
F Cross & Sons Limited, Brigg Road, Scunthorpe, South Humberside, DN15 6TZ. Tel:(0724) 842011.

ISLE OF MAN

Corkills Garage, 1 Main Road, Onchan, Isle of Man. Tel:(0624) 676809.

ISLE OF WIGHT

Esplanade Newport, Medina Avenue, Newport, Isle of Wight, PO30 1HG. Tel:(0983) 523232.

KENT

EuroCharing, School Road, Charing, Ashford, Kent, TN27 0JN. Tel:(023) 371 2141.
Autobahn Beckenham Limited, 1 Wickham Road, Beckenham, Kent, BR3 2JS. Tel:(081) 650 7276.
Euro Canterbury, Westminster Road, Vauxhall Road Estate, Canterbury, Kent, CT1 1HF. Tel:(0227) 763200.
Whitehouse Bexley, Westmount Garage, 138 Blendon Road, Bexley, Kent, DA5 1BZ. Tel:(081) 301 3050.
Whitehouse Dartford, 555-571 Princes Road, Dartford, Kent, DA1 1YT. Tel:(0322) 77231.
Hollis Motors, 1 Crabble Hill, Buckland, Dover, Kent, CT17 0RS. Tel:(0304) 206710.
MCS Medway Limited, Bailey Drive, Gillingham Business Park, Gillingham, Kent, ME8 0PZ. Tel:(0634) 378988.
MCS Maidstone Limited, George Street & Upper Stone Street, Maidstone, Kent, ME15 6NY. Tel:(0622) 750821.
Wolfe Garage Otford, Sevenoaks Road, Otford, Kent, TN14 5PA. Tel:(09592) 5222.
Rawsons Euro Cars Limited, 302 Vale Road, Tonbridge, Kent, TN9 1SZ. Tel:(0732) 355822.

LANCASHIRE

Coulthurst & Grimshaw Limited, 759/854 Whalley New Road, Blackburn, Lancs, BB1 9BD. Tel:(0254) 240621.

Cade's - Audi Golf Course Guide

McMillans of Bolton Limited, Morris Street, Mill Street Industrial Estate, off Bury New Road, Bolton, Lancs, BL2 2BL. Tel:(0204) 31464.
Lookers Burnley, Accrington Road, Burnley, Lancs, BB11 4AS. Tel:(0282) 53731.
John Wallwork, Bell Lane, Bury, Lancs, BL9 6DL. Tel:(061) 797 9121.
Cumberland View Garage Limited, Mellishaw Lane, Morecambe, Lancs, LA3 3EN. Tel:(0524) 415833.
Lookers, 390 Manchester Road, Hollingwood, Oldham, Lancs, OL9 7PQ. Tel:(061) 652 7131.
Fairways (A.G.) Limited, Blackpool Road, Ribbleton, Preston, Lancs, PR2 6BX. Tel:(0772) 702288.
Fairways of St Annes Limited, Heeley Road, St Annes, Lancs, FY8 2LS. Tel:(0253) 726714.
Rigby Turner Limited, Station Road, Haydock, St Helens, Lancs, WA11 0JN. Tel:(0744) 26126.

LEICESTERSHIRE
Ashby & Mann Limited, 94/106 Upper Bond Street, Hinckley, Leics, LE10 1RL. Tel:(0455) 637934.
Castles Dover Street Limited, Dover Street, Leicester, Leics, LE1 6PT. Tel:(0533) 556262.
Arthur Prince Limited, Belton Road, Loughborough, Leics, LE11 1JB. Tel:(0509) 217080.
Victor Wood of Melton Limited, Leicester Road, Melton Mowbray, Leics, LE13 0DA. Tel:(0664) 60251.

LINCOLNSHIRE
Stanwell Boston Limited, 45 Main Ridge East, Boston, Lincs, PE21 6ST. Tel:(0205) 363867.
D C Cook (Lincoln) Limited, Newark Road, Lincoln, Lincs, LN5 8NU. Tel:(0522) 531881.
Loveday & Bennett Limited, Fairfield Industrial Estate, Tattershall Way, Louth, Lincs, LN11 0YA. Tel:(0507) 600929.

LONDON
Lonsdale Garages Limited, 42/46 Lonsdale Road, Barnes, London, SW13 9JS. Tel:(081) 748 1366.
Dovercourt Battersea, 100 York Road, Battersea, London, SW11 3RT. Tel:(071) 228 6444.
Scotts of Sloane Square, 214/224 Pavilion Road, Sloane Square, Chelsea, London, SW1X 0AN. Tel:(071) 730 2131.
The Colindale Centre, 155/159 Edgware Road, Colindale, London, NW9 6NL. Tel:(081) 205 0131.
Alan Day (Finchley) Limited, 252/256 Regents Park Road, Finchley, London, N3 3HN. Tel:(081) 349 0022.
Normand (Continental), 405 King Street, Hammersmith, London, W6 9NQ. Tel:(081) 741 0161.
Contim Heathrow Limited, 554 London Road, Ashford, Middlesex, TW15 3AE. Tel:(0784) 250051.
Contim Harrow Limited, Shaftesbury Avenue, Harrow, Middlesex, HA2 0AT. Tel:(081) 864 0838.
Contim Hayes Limited, 505/509 Uxbridge Road, Hayes, Middlesex, UB4 8HH. Tel:(081) 848 0202/5.
Northway Garage, Wembley Park Works, North End Road, Wembley Park, Middlesex, HA9 0AD. Tel:(081) 900 1622.

Dovercourt Plaistow, 259 Plaistow Road, Plaistow, London, E15 3EU. Tel:(081) 534 7661.
F C Purser Limited, 434/452 Old Kent Road, Southwark, London, SE1 5AG. Tel:(071) 231 0031.
Dovercourt St John's Wood, 30/34 St John's Wood Road, St John's Wood, London, NW8 7HE. Tel:(071) 286 8000.
Scotts of Stockwell, 187-191 Clapham Road, Stockwell, London, SW9 0QE. Tel:(071) 737 7133.
Whites Wimbledon, S Wimbledon Service Station, 194 Merton Road, Wimbledon, London, SW19 1EQ. Tel:(081) 543 5244/7.

MERSEYSIDE
Cheshire Brothers Limited, 129 Mount Road, Bebington, Merseyside, L63 8PU. Tel:(051) 608 6466.
Ian Skelly (Liverpool) Limited, 66/72 Mill Lane, Liverpool, Merseyside, L13 4DS. Tel:(051) 228 0919.
Tom England & Sons Limited, Moor Lane, Thornton, Liverpool, Merseyside, L23 4ON. Tel:(051) 931 2861.

NORFOLK
Cookes of Fakenham Limited, Norwich Road, Fakenham, Norfolk, NR21 8SL. Tel:(0328) 864951.
Poplar Garage, Norfolk Street, Kings Lynn, Norfolk, PE30 1AE. Tel:(0553) 760911.
Robinsons Autoservices Limited, Heigham Causeway, Heigham Street, Norwich, Norfolk, NR2 4LX. Tel:(0603) 612111.

NORTHAMPTONSHIRE
W Grose Eurocar, Scirocco Close, Boughton Green Road, Northampton, Northants, NN3 1AP. Tel:(0604) 494121.
Autohaus Limited, The Embankment, Wellingborough, Northants, NN8 1LD. Tel:(0933) 443030.

NORTHUMBERLAND
A Carr & Son (Hexham) Limited, Station Garage, Hexham, Northumberland, NE46 1EZ. Tel:(0434) 606781.

NOTTINGHAMSHIRE
John Fox Limited, Vernon Road, Basford, Notts, NG6 0AA. Tel:(0602) 789291.
Newbolds Garage (Mansfield) Limited, 206 Chesterfield Road North, Mansfield, Notts, NG19 7JF. Tel:(0623) 26272.
Heron Newark Limited, Northern Road, Newark, Notts, NG24 2ET. Tel:(0636) 704484.
Bristol Street Motors (Nottingham) Limited, 180 Loughborough Road, West Bridgford, Nottingham, Notts, NG2 7JB. Tel:(0602) 813813.

OXFORDSHIRE
Clover Leaf Cars (Henley) Limited, Newtown Road, Henley on Thames, Oxon, RG9 1HG Tel:(0491) 573555.
Spirit Motor Company, 9/16 Southam Road, Banbury, Oxon, OX16 7EE. Tel:(0295) 250141.
Motorworld, 2 Oxford Road, Kidlington, Oxon, OX5 1AA. Tel:(0867) 53732.

SHROPSHIRE
Enterprise, Hollybush Road, Bridgnorth, Salop, WV16 4AZ. Tel:(0746) 764343.
Shrewsbury Motors, Featherbed Lane, Shrewsbury, Salop, SY1 4NQ. Tel:(0743) 52471.
Hardy's of Telford, Trench Road, Trench, Telford, Salop, TF2 8AA. Tel:(0952) 608066.

SOMERSET
Silver Street Motors LImited, Silver Street, Taunton, Somerset, TA1 3DL. Tel:(0823) 288371.
Loders Garage, Houndstone Business Park, Yeovil, Somerset, BA22 8RT. Tel:(0935) 20881.

STAFFORDSHIRE
Brincars Limited, Delta Way, Watling Street, Cannock, Staffs, WS11 3BE. Tel:(0543) 506216.
Premier Garage, Broad Street, Leek, Staffs, ST13 5NS. Tel:(0538) 399499.
Autobon Limited, Brunswick Street, Newcastle-under-Lyme, Staffs, ST5 1HQ. Tel:(0782) 617321.
Brown & Frewer Limited, Friars Terrace, Stafford, Staffs, ST17 4AU. Tel:(0785) 223232.
Pinkstone of Stoke, Victoria Road, Fenton, Stoke-on-Trent, Staffs, ST4 2LS. Tel:(0782) 416666.

SUFFOLK
Northgate Motors Limited, Northern Way, Bury St Edmunds, Suffolk, IP32 6NL. Tel:(0284) 763441.
Mann Egerton, 88 Princes Street, Ipswich, Suffolk, IP1 1RX. Tel:(0473) 214231.
Simpsons Garage (Lowestoft) Limited, Cooke Road, South Lowestoft Industrial Estate, Lowestoft, Suffolk, NR33 7NA. Tel:(0502) 516831.

SURREY
Whites Camberley, Whites Corner, 177 London Road, Camberley, Surrey, GU15 3LG. Tel:(0276) 691200.
Bell & Colvill (Caterham) Limited, 119/123 Croydon Road, Caterham, Surrey, CR3 6PE. Tel:(0883) 348013.
Thomson & Taylor (Brooklands) Limited, 42 Portsmouth Road, Cobham, Surrey, KT11 1JB. Tel:(0932) 864493.
Lockyear Motors Limited, Ewhurst, Cranleigh, Surrey, GU6 7QY. Tel:(0483) 277696.
Leathwoods Limited, 203 St James Road, Croydon, Surrey, CR0 2BZ. tel:(081) 684 8222/4.
Deepdene Dorking, 285/293 High Street, Dorking, Surrey, RH4 1RN. Tel:(0306) 885588.
Drift Bridge Garage Limited, Reigate Road, Epsom, Surrey, KT17 3LA. Tel:(0737) 360111.
Whites Haslemere, Hindhead Road, Haslemere, Surrey, GU27 1LE. Tel:(0428) 53811.
Colborne Garages Limited, Portsmouth Road, Ripley, Surrey, GU23 6HP. Tel:(0483) 224361.
John Ashley Motors Limited, 78 Portsmouth Road, Surbiton, Surrey, KT6 5PT. Tel:(081) 390 3441.

EAST SUSSEX
Wadham Kenning, 154 Old Shoreham Road, Hove, Brighton, E Sussex, BN3 7BR. Tel:(0273) 26264.
Skinners (Eastbourne) Limited, Hammonds Drive, Lottbridge Drove, Eastbourne, E Sussex, BN23 6PW. Tel:(0323) 647141.

WEST SUSSEX
Whyke Motors Limited, 51/54 Bognor Road, Chichester, W Sussex, PO19 2NG. Tel:(0243) 787684.
MCS Crawley Limited, Overdene Drive, Ifield, Crawley, W Sussex, RH11 8DU. Tel:(0293) 515551.
Sidlow Garages, London Road, East Grinstead, W Sussex, RH19 1QH. Tel:(0342) 315722.
Caffyns plc, 341 Goring Road, Goring-by-Sea, W Sussex, BN12 4NX. Tel:(0903) 504440.
Caffyns plc, Station Garage, Market Place, Haywards Heath, W Sussex, RH16 1DB. Tel:(0444) 451511.

TYNE & WEAR
Reg Vardy plc, Hepburn Gardens, Felling, Newcastle-upon-Tyne, Tyne & Wear, NE10 0AD. Tel:(091) 495 0088.
Benfield Motors, The Fossway, Byker, Newcastle-upon-Tyne, Tyne & Wear, NE6 2XG. Tel:(091) 265 7121.
Mill Garages Northeast, Newcastle Road, Sunderland, Tyne & Wear, SR5 1QE. Tel:(091) 548 0235.
Colebrook & Burgess Limited, The Silverlink, Silverlink Business Park, Wallsend, Tyne & Wear, NE28 9ND. Tel:(091) 295 0555.

WARWICKSHIRE
Listers of Stratford-on-Avon, Western Road, Stratford-on-Avon, Warwicks, CV37 0AH. Tel:(0789) 294477.
Tollbar Warwick, 1 Coventry Road, St Johns, Warwick, Warwicks, CV34 4LJ. Tel:(0926) 400999.

WEST MIDLANDS
Hartwell Smithfield, Digbeth, Birmingham, West Midlands, B5 5DX. Tel:(021) 643 7341.
Stonehouse Motors Limited, Barnes Hill, California, Birmingham, West Midlands, B29 5UP. Tel:(021) 427 6201.
Listers of Coventry (Motors) Limited, Swanswell Garage, Spon End, Coventry, West Midlands, CV1 3HF. Tel:(0203) 525555.
Quicks of Oldbury, Oldbury Ringway, Oldbury, West Midlands, B69 2AR. Tel:(021) 511 1122.
Philip Mist (Automobiles) Limited, Kings Garage, 45-51 Kings Road, Sutton Coldfield, West Midlands, B73 5AB. Tel:(021) 355 1261/5.
Willenhall Coachcraft, 348 Wolverhampton Road West, Willenhall, West Midlands, WV13 2RN. Tel:(0902) 608773.
Wolverhampton Motor Services, Raby Street, Wolverhampton, West Midlands, WV2 1BL. Tel:(0902) 54602.

WILTSHIRE
Anthony Ince Limited, 16 Lower Road, Churchfields, Salisbury, Wilts, SP2 7QE. Tel:(0722) 327162.

Mann Egerton, Eldene Drive, Swindon, Wilts, SN3 3TW. Tel:(0793) 531333/6.

NORTH YORKSHIRE
Massingberd (Harrogate) Limited, Ripon Road, Harrogate, N Yorks, HG1 2BX. Tel:(0423) 505141.
Massingberd (Northallerton) Limited, Darlington Road, Northallerton, N Yorks, DL6 2PN. Tel:(0609) 771011.
Layerthorpe Limited, 100 Layerthorpe, York, N Yorks, YO3 7XY. Tel:(0904) 646651.

SOUTH YORKSHIRE
T Hayselden (Barnsley) Limited, Wilthorpe Road, Barnsley, S Yorks, S75 1JA. Tel:(0226) 299494.
T Hayselden (Doncaster), York Road Roundabout, Doncaster, S Yorks, DN5 8AN. Tel:(0302) 364141.
Gilders Listerdale, Bawtry Road, Wickersley, Rotherham, S Yorks, S66 0JL. Tel:(0709) 543462.
J Gilder & Co. Limited, 1 Ecclesall Road South, Banner Cross, Sheffield, S Yorks, S11 9PA. Tel:(0742) 670670.

WEST YORKSHIRE
Trust Motors, Ingleby Road, Bradford, W Yorks, BD8 9AP. Tel:(0274) 494100.
Lightcliffe Motors Limited, Denholme Gate Road, Hipperholme, Halifax, W Yorks, HX3 8HX. Tel:(0422) 205611.
Carnell Huddersfield, Bradford Road, Huddersfield, W Yorks, HD1 6DY. Tel:(0484) 542001.
Trust Motors, Gelderd Road, Leeds, W Yorks, LS12 6BJ. Tel:(0532) 633431.
Massingberd (Otley) Limited, Leeds Road, Otley, W Yorks, LS21 3BG. Tel:(0943) 463361.
J.C.T. 600 (Wakefield) Limited, Waldorf Way, Denby Dale Road, Wakefield, W Yorks, WF2 8DH. Tel:(0924) 291129.

WALES

CLWYD
Dane Motor Company (Wrexham) Limited, Rhosrobin, Wrexham, Clwyd, LL11 4YL. Tel:(0978) 291177.

DYFED
Forge Garage, Perrots Garage, Perrots Road, Haverfordwest, Dyfed, SA61 2HD. Tel:(0437) 760500.

MID GLAMORGAN
Sinclair Garages (Bridgend) Limited, Tremains Road, Bridgend, Mid Glam, CF31 1TZ. Tel:(0656) 664241.

SOUTH GLAMORGAN
Hartwell, 13-15 Hadfield Road, Cardiff, S Glam, CF1 8XG. Tel:(0222) 224848.

WEST GLAMORGAN
Sinclair Garages (Port Talbot) Limited, Dan-y-Bryn Road, Port Talbot, W Glam, SA13 1AL. Tel:(0639) 887948.

Sinclair Garages Limited, Gorseinon Road, Penllegaer, Gorseinon, Swansea, W Glam, SA4 1GW. Tel:(0792) 894951.

GWENT
Hartwell, Seven Stiles Avenue, Newport Retail Park, Newport, Gwent, NP9 0QQ. Tel:(0633) 270727.

GWYNEDD
Pentraeth Limited, Henfford Garage, Menai Bridge, Anglesey, Gwynedd, LL59 5RW. Tel:(0248) 712002.

SCOTLAND

BORDERS
Thornwood Motors (Hawick) Limited, 4-8 Commercial Road, Hawick, Borders, TD9 7BD. Tel:(0450) 73211.

CENTRAL
Carron Motors, 84 Grahams Road, Falkirk, Central, FK2 7DL. Tel:(0324) 611622.
Abercromby, Kerse Road, Stirling, Central, FK7 7RT. Tel:(0786) 72222.

FIFE
Barnetts of Kirkcaldy, Mitchelston Industrial Estate, Kirkcaldy, Fife, KY1 3NF. Tel:(0592) 55100.

GRAMPIAN
Specialist Cars (Aberdeen) Limited, 116 Stanley Street, Aberdeen, Grampian, AB1 6UQ. Tel:(0224) 592255.
Hawco & Sons Limited, 41/43 Blackfriars Road, Elgin, Grampian, IV30 1TY. Tel:(0343) 544977/9.

HIGHLAND
Hawco & Sons Limited, Harbour Road, Inverness, Highland, IV1 1UF. Tel:(0463) 236111.

LOTHIAN
Inch Engineering (Bathgate) Limited, Blackburn Road, Bathgate, Lothian, EH48 2EQ. Tel:(0506) 54090.
Abercromby, Seafield Road East, Edinburgh, Lothian, EH15 1EN. Tel:(031) 657 1234
Sloan of Edinburgh, 454 Gorgie Road, Edinburgh, Lothian, EH11 2RN. Tel:(031) 346 1661.

STRATHCLYDE
Ingram Motoring Centre (Ayr), 24 Dalblair Road, Ayr, Strath, KA7 1UN. Tel:(0292) 269522/3.
Ian Skelly (Glasgow) Limited, 29 Dalmarnock Road, Rutherglen, Glasgow, Strath, G73 1AE. Tel:(041) 647 0511.
Lex, 512 Kilmarnock Road, Glasgow, Strath, G43 2BP. Tel:(041) 637 2241.

Lex, 459 Crow Road, Glasgow, Strath, G11 7DQ. Tel:(041) 954 1577.
Arnold Clark Automobiles Limited, 60/64 East Hamilton Street, Greenock, Strath, PA15 2UA. Tel:(0475) 83535.
Ingram Motoring Centre (Paisley), 15 Rowan Street, Paisley, Strath, PA2 6RS. Tel:(041) 8899 4551.
Ian Skelly (Wishaw) Limited, Bogside, Newmains, Wishaw, Strath, ML2 9PW. Tel:(0698) 358221.

TAYSIDE
Lex, Douglas Street, Dundee, Tayside, DD1 5AN. Tel:(0382) 200222.
Cameron Motors (Perth) Limited, 166 Dunkeld Road, Perth, Tayside, PH1 5AS. Tel:(0738) 36036.

NORTHERN IRELAND

COUNTY ANTRIM
Isaac Agnew Limited, 1 Boucher Road, Belfast, Co. Antrim, BT12 6HR. Tel:(0232) 234477.
David Prentice Limited, 225 Hillsborough Road, Sprucefield, Lisburn, Co. Antrim, BT27 5RJ. Tel:(0846) 665252.
Isaac Agnew (Mallusk) Limited, 45 Mallusk Road, Newtownabbey, Co. Antrim, BT36 8PS. Tel:(0232) 342111.

COUNTY DOWN
P & R Motor Sales, 6/7 Merchant's Quay, Newry, Co. Down, BT35 6AL. Tel:(0693) 67722.

COUNTY FERMANAGH
Modern Motors, 74 Forthill Street, Enniskillen, Co. Fermanagh, BT74 6AW. Tel:(0365) 322974.

COUNTY DERRY (LONDONDERRY)
The Brook Garage (Coleraine) Limited, 113 Ballycastle Road, Coleraine, Co. Londonderry, BT52 2DY. Tel:(0265) 44837.

COUNTY TYRONE
T J Hamilton & Co., 50 Union Street, Cookstown, Co. Tyrone, BT60 8NN. Tel:(06487) 62488.

INDEX

Abbey Hill Golf Club	32	Atherstone Golf Club	132
Abbey Park Golf and Country Club	79	Athlone Golf Club	227
Abbeydale Golf Club	143	Auchenblae Golf Course	177
Abbotsley Golf Club	34	Auchterarder Golf Club	198
Aberdare Golf Club	154	Austerfield Park Golf Club	141
Aberdelghy Golf Course	204	Axe Cliff Golf Club	45
Aberdour Golf Club	170	Aycliffe Golf Course & Driving Range	53
Aberdovey Golf Club	159	Baberton Golf Club	182
Aberfeldy Golf Club	198	Backworth Golf Club	131
Aberfoyle Golf Club	166	Badgemore Park Golf Club	109
Abernethy Golf Club	180	Bala (Penlan) Golf Club	160
Abersoch Golf Club	160	Balbriggan Golf Club	218
Aboyne Golf Club	174	Ballards Gore Golf Club	57
Accrington Golf Club	92	Ballinasloe Golf Club	221
Airlinks Golf Club	62	Ballybofey and Stranorlar Golf Club	217
Aldenham Golf Club	83	Ballybunion Golf Club	222
Alderney Golf Club	35	Ballycastle Golf Club	203
Alexandra Golf Club	189	Ballyclare Golf Club	203
Alford Golf Club	174	Ballyearl Golf and Leisure Centre	205
Allendale Golf Club	105	Ballyferriter Golf Club	222
Alloa Golf Club	166	Ballyinascorney Golf Club	221
Alnesbourne Priory Golf Club	117	Ballyliffen Golf Club	217
Alnwick Golf Club	104	Ballymena Golf Club	203
Alsager Golf and Country Club	115	Ballyreagh Golf Course	205
Alston Moor Golf Club	41	Balmoral Golf Club	206
Alton Golf Club	72	Bamburgh Castle Golf Club	104
Alva Golf Club	166	Banbridge Golf Club	208
Alwoodley Golf Club	147	Banchory Golf Club	175
Alythe Golf Club	199	Bandon Golf Club	216
Ampfield Par Three Golf Club	72	Bangor Golf Club	208
Andover Golf Club	72	Banstead Downs Golf Club	123
Anglesey Golf Club	161	Bargoed Golf Club	154
Anstruther Golf Club	170	Barlaston Golf Club	113
Arbroath Golf Course	198	Barnard Castle Golf Club	51
Ardee Golf Club	224	Barnham Broom Hotel, Golf & C. Club	102
Ardeer Golf Club	196	Baron Hill Golf Club	160
Ardglass Golf Club	208	Barshaw Golf Club	195
Arkley Golf Club	80	Basildon Golf Club	54
Arklow Golf Club	228	Batchwood Golf Club	83
Ashburnham Golf Club	153	Bathgate Golf Club	181
Ashfield Golf Club	206	Bawburgh Golf Club	101
Ashford (Kent) Golf Club	88	Beacon Park Golf Club	96
Ashley Wood Golf Club	49	Beaconsfield Golf Club Ltd.	31
Ashridge Golf Club	80	Beamish Park Golf Club	53
Ashton and Lea Golf Club	95	Bearsden Golf Club	190
Ashton on Mersey Golf Club	70	Bearsted Golf Club	90
Ashton-in-Makerfield Golf Club	66	Beau Desert Golf Club Ltd.	114
Ashton-under-Lyne Golf Club	66	Beauchief Municipal Golf Club	143
Ashwoods Golf Centre	210	Beauport Park Golf Club	126
Aspley Guise & Woburn Sands Golf Club	28	Beaverstown Golf Club	219
Athenry Golf Club	221	Bedlingtonshire Golf Club	105
		Beech Park Golf Club	221
		Beeston Fields Golf Club	107
		Belfast Parks Golf Course	205

Belfry (The)	136	Bridlington Golf Club	84
Belhus Park Golf Club	56	Bridport and West Dorset Golf Club	49
Belleisle Golf Course	187	Bright Castle Golf Club	209
Bellingham Golf Club	105	Brighton and Hove Golf Club	125
Belmont House Golf Club	78	Bristol and Clifton Golf Club	27
Belton Park Golf Club	97	Broadstone (Dorset) Golf Club	49
Belvoir Golf Club	206	Brockenhurst Manor Golf Club	73
Benone Golf Course	211	Bromley Golf Club	59
Bentley Golf Club	54	Brookmans Park Golf Club	81
Bentra Golf Club	205	Broome Manor Golf Complex	138
Berkhamsted Golf Club	80	Broomieknowe Golf Club	182
Berkshire Golf Club	29	Brough Golf Club	85
Berwick-upon-Tweed (Goswick) G. C.	105	Broughty Golf Club	201
Betws-Y-Coed Golf Club	160	Brown Trout Golf and Country Inn	211
Bexley Heath Golf Club	59	Bruntsfield Links Golfing Society	182
Birch Grove Golf Club	55	Bryn Meadows Golf & Country Club	155
Birchwood Golf Club	38	Bryn Morfydd Hotel Golf Club	151
Birley Wood Golf Course	143	Brynhill Golf Club	156
Birr Golf Club	226	Builth Wells Golf Club	162
Bishop Auckland Golf Club	51	Bull Bay Golf Club	160
Bishopbriggs Golf Club	190	Bulwell Forest Golf Club	106
Bishopswood Golf Club	72	Bundoran Golf Club	218
Blackburn Golf Club	92	Bungay and Waveney Valley Golf Club	116
Blackbush Golf Club	225	Burford Golf Club	109
Blackley Golf Club	69	Burghill Valley Golf Club	78
Blackpool North Shore Golf Club	92	Burley Golf Club	75
Blackpool Park Golf Club	93	Burnham and Berrow Golf Club	112
Blackwell Grange Golf Club	52	Burnham-on-Crouch Golf Club Ltd.	54
Blainroe Golf Club	228	Burnley Golf Club	93
Blair Atholl Golf Club	199	Burntisland Golf House Club	171
Blankney Golf Club	97	Burton-on-Trent Golf Club	114
Blyth Golf Club	105	Bury Golf Club	67
Bodenstown Golf Club	223	Bush Hill Park Golf Club	65
Boldon Golf Club Ltd.	130	Bushey Hall Golf Club	81
Bonar Bridge-Ardgay Golf Club	178	Bushfoot Golf Club	205
Borth and Ynyslas Golf Club	153	Bute Golf Club	194
Boston Golf Club	97	Caerphilly Golf Club	154
Bothwell Castle Golf Club	190	Cairndhu Golf Club	204
Bournemouth & Meyrick Park Golf Club	49	Calderfield Golf Club Ltd.	136
Brackenwood Golf Club	99	Camberley Heath Golf Club	120
Braehead Golf Club	166	Cambridge Moat House Hotel Golf Club	33
Braemar Golf Club	175	Came Down Golf Club	50
Braeside Golf Club	58	Camperdown Golf Club	200
Braintree Golf Club	54	Cannock Park Golf Club	114
Bramhall Golf Club Ltd.	67	Canons Brook Golf Club	56
Bramley Golf Club	122	Canwick Park Golf Club	97
Bramshaw Golf Club	74	Cape Cornwall Golf and Country Club	40
Brancepeth Castle Golf Club	52	Caprington Golf Club	193
Brandhall Golf Club	135	Cardiff Golf Club	156
Branston Golf Club	114	Cardross Golf Club	188
Breadsall Priory Hotel Golf & C. Club	44	Carlow Golf Club	215
Brean Golf Club	112	Carmarthen Golf Club	153
Brechin Golf and Squash Club	199	Carnalea Golf Club	208
Brickendon Grange Golf & Country Club	82	Carnoustie Golf Links	200

Cade's - Audi Golf Course Guide

Carnwath Golf Club	194	Colchester Golf Club	55
Carradale Golf Club	188	Cold Ashby Golf Club	103
Carrickfergus Golf Club	204	Collingtree Park Golf Club	104
Castle Eden and Peterlee Golf Club	38	Colne Golf Club	93
Castle Golf Club	221	Colonsay Golf Club	189
Castle Hume Golf Course	211	Colvend Golf Club	168
Castle Point Golf Club	54	Comrie Golf Club	200
Castlebar Golf Club	225	Connemara Golf Club	222
Castlerock Golf Club	211	Consett and District Golf Club	52
Castleroy Golf Club	224	Conwy (Caernarvonshire) Golf Club	160
Castlewarden Golf and Country Club	223	Cooden Beach Golf Club	124
Cathkin Braes Golf Club	190	Copthorne Golf Course	128
Cavendish Golf Club Ltd.	44	Corballis Public Golf Course	219
Cawder Golf Club	190	Corhampton Golf Club	75
Chadwell Springs Golf Club	83	Corinthian Golf Club	90
Channels Golf Club	55	Cork Golf Club	216
Chapel-En-Le-Frith Golf Club	44	Cosby Golf Club	96
Charleville Golf Club	216	Costessey Park Golf Club	102
Cheadle Golf Club	68	Cotswold Edge Golf Club	58
Cherry Lodge Golf Club	88	Coulsdon Court	59
Cherwell Edge Course	109	County Armagh Golf Club	205
Chesfield Downs Family Golf Centre	81	County Cavan Golf Club	215
Cheshunt Golf Club	81	County Longford Golf Club	224
Chessington Golf Club	59	County Louth Golf Club	224
Chester-le-Street Golf Club	52	County Sligo Golf CLub	226
Chigwell Golf Club	55	Courtown Golf Club	227
Childwall Golf Club Ltd. (The)	100	Coventry Hearsall Golf Club	133
Chiltern Forest Golf Club	31	Cowal Golf Club	189
Chipping Norton Golf Club	109	Cowdray Park Golf Club	129
Chipping Sodbury Golf Club	28	Cowes Golf Club	87
Chislehurst Golf Club	59	Cowglen Golf Club	190
Chorley Golf Club	93	Cradoc Golf Club	162
Chorlton-cum-Hardy Golf Club	68	Craigavon Golf and Ski Centre	206
Christchurch Golf Club	50	Craigie Hill Golf Club (1982) Ltd.	202
Chulmleigh Golf Course	46	Craigmillar Park Golf Club	183
Church Stretton Golf Club	110	Craignure Golf Club	189
Churston Golf Club	46	Crail Golfing Soc. (Balcomie Links)	171
Cilgwyn Golf Club	153	Cranbrook Golf Club	89
City of Derry Golf Club	211	Cray Valley Golf Club	63
City of Newcastle Golf Club	130	Craythorne Golf Centre	114
City of Wakefield Golf Club	150	Crewe Golf Club	36
Clandeboye Golf Club	210	Crieff Golf Club Ltd.	200
Cleethorpes Golf Club	85	Crimple Valley Golf Club	139
Clevedon Golf Club	28	Croham Hurst Golf Club	60
Cleveland Golf Club	39	Crook Golf Club	52
Cliftonville Golf Club	207	Crookhill Park Golf Course	142
Clober Golf Club	190	Crosland Heath Golf Club	146
Clonmel Golf Club	226	Crow Wood Golf Club	191
Clontarf Golf Club	219	Crowborough Beacon Golf Club	125
Close House Golf Club	130	Cruden Bay Golf Club	177
Clydebank and District Golf Club	189	Cullen Golf Club	175
Clyne Golf Club	157	Cupar Golf Club	171
Cochrane Castle Golf Club	193	Curragh Golf Club	223
Cockermouth Golf Club	41	Cushendall Golf Club	204

Dale Hill Golf Club	127	Dundalk Golf Club	224
Dalmahoy Hotel Golf & Country Club	185	Dundas Parks Golf Club	186
Dalmilling Golf Club	188	Dunfanaghy Golf Club	218
Dalmunzie Golf Course	199	Dunfermline Golf Club	171
Dalston Hall Golf Club	41	Dungannon Golf Club	212
Darenth Valley Golf Club Ltd.	91	Dunham Forest Golf and Country Club	66
Darlington Golf Club	52	Dunkeld and Birnam Golf Club	201
Dartford Golf Club Ltd.	89	Dunmurry Golf Club	207
Dartmouth Golf Club	136	Dunnikier Park Golf Club	172
Darwen Golf Club	93	Dunning Golf Club	201
Davenport Golf Club	37	Duns Golf Club	165
Davyhulme Park Golf Club	71	Dunscar Golf Club	67
Deane Golf Club	66	Dunstable Downs Golf Club	28
Deer Park Golf and Country Club	185	Dunstanburgh Castle Golf Club	104
Deerpark Hotel Golf Courses	220	Dunwood Manor Golf Club	75
Deeside Golf Club	174	Durness Golf Course	178
Delgany Golf Club	228	Dyke Golf Club	125
Denbigh Golf Club	151	Ealing Golf Club	61
Dereham Golf Club	102	Easingwold Golf Club	139
Dewsbury District Golf Club	149	East Berkshire Golf Club	30
Dinsdale Spa Golf Club	52	East Bierley Golf Club	145
Dollar Golf Club	167	East Brighton Golf Club	125
Donabate Golf Club	219	East Cork Golf Club	217
Donaghadee Golf Club	209	East Dorset Golf Club	51
Doncaster Town Moor Golf Club	142	Eastbourne Downs Golf Club	126
Donegal Town Golf Club	217	Eastwood Golf Club	191
Dooks Golf Club	222	Eaton Golf Club	102
Dore and Totley Golf Club	143	Edmondstown Golf Club	221
Dorking Golf Club	121	Edwalton Municipal Golf & Social Club	108
Dougalston Golf Course	191	Effingham Golf Club	121
Douglas Golf Club	216	Elderslie Golf Club	195
Douglas Water Golf Club	189	Elgin Golf Club	175
Down Royal Park Golf Club	209	Elland Golf Club	145
Downes Crediton Golf Club	46	Ellesmere Golf Club	72
Downfield Golf Club	201	Elm Park Golf and Sports Club	219
Downpatrick Golf Club	209	Elsham Golf Club	85
Downshire Golf Course	31	Eltham Warren Golf Club	60
Drayton Park Golf Club	116	Ely City Golf Course	34
Droitwich Golf and Country Club	77	Enfield Golf Club	60
Dromoland Golf Club	215	Enmore Park Golf Club	112
Druids Heath Golf Club Ltd.	136	Ennis Golf Club	215
Drumpellier Golf Club Ltd.	189	Enniscorthy Golf Club	227
Duddingston Golf Club Ltd.	183	Enniscrone Golf Club	226
Dudley Golf Club	100	Enniskillen Golf Club	211
Duff House Royal Golf Club	175	Enville Golf Club	135
Dufftown Golf Club	175	Epsom Golf Club	121
Dukinfield Golf Club	68	Erewash Valley Golf Club	44
Dulwich and Sydenham Golf Club	60	Exeter Golf and Country Club	46
Dumfries and County Golf Club	168	Fairfield Golf and Sailing Club	66
Dumfries & Galloway Golf Club	168	Fairlop Waters Golf Club	58
Dun Laoghaire Golf Club	220	Fakenham Golf Club	102
Dunaverty Golf Club	196	Falkirk Tryst Golf Club	167
Dunbar Golf Club	182	Falmouth Golf Club	39
Dunblane New Golf Club	167	Farnham Golf Club Ltd.	121

Cade's - Audi Golf Course Guide

Faversham Golf Club Ltd.	89	Gog Magog Golf Club	34
Felixstowe Ferry Golf Club	117	Golf House Club	171
Fermoy Golf Club	217	Golspie Golf Course	179
Ferndown Golf Club	50	Goodwood Golf Club	128
Fernfell Golf and Country Club	121	Goring and Streatley Golf Club	31
Filey Golf Course	139	Gorleston Golf Club	102
Filton Golf Club	27	Gosforth Golf Club	130
Finchley Golf Club	61	Gosport and Stokes Bay Golf Club	73
Fintona Golf Club	212	Gotts Park Municipal Golf Course	147
Fishwick Hall Golf Club	95	Grange Golf Club (*Coventry - W/Mids*)	133
Flackwell Heath Golf Club Ltd.	32	Grange Golf Club (*Rathfarnham - Eire*)	221
Flamborough Head Golf Club	84	Grange Park Golf Club	
Fleetland Golf Club	73	(*Scunthorpe - Humberside*)	86
Fleetwood Golf Club	93	Grange Park Golf Club	
Flint Golf Club	151	(*Rotherham - South Yorks*)	142
Forest of Arden Hotel, Golf & C. Club	134	Grange Park Golf Club (*St Helens - Mersey*)	101
Formby Golf Club	99	Grange-Over-Sands Golf Club	42
Formby Ladies' Golf Club	99	Grantown-on-Spey Golf Club	179
Fornham Park Golf and Country Club	116	Great Salterns Municipal Golf Course	75
Forres Golf Club	176	Great Yarmouth and Caister Golf Club	101
Forrest Little Golf Club	218	Green Hotel Golf Course	201
Forrester Park Golf Club	56	Greenburn Golf Club	184
Fort Augustus Golf Club	179	Greenisland Golf Club	204
Fortwilliam Golf Club	207	Greenmeadow Golf Club	158
Fosseway Golf Club	27	Greenmount Golf Club	67
Four Lakes Golf Club	223	Greenock Golf Club	192
Freshwater Bay Golf Club	88	Greenore Golf Club	225
Frilford Heath Golf Club	108	Greystones Golf Club	228
Fulwell Golf Club	61	Grims Dyke Golf Club	63
Fynn Valley Golf Club	117	Grimsby Golf Club	85
Gairloch Golf Club	179	Gullane Golf Club	184
Galway Golf Club	222	Habberley Golf Club	78
Ganstead Park Golf Club	85	Haddington Golf Club	185
Ganton Golf Club	140	Hadley Wood Golf Club	80
Garesfield Golf Club	129	Haggs Castle Golf Club	191
Garforth Golf Club	147	Hagley Country Club Golf Club	78
Garmouth and Kingston Golf Club	176	Haigh Hall Golf Club	71
Gatehouse of Fleet Golf Club	168	Hainault Forest Golf Club	55
Gathurst Golf Club	71	Halesowen Golf Club	133
Gay Hill Golf Club	78	Halifax Golf Club	146
Gerrards Cross Golf Club	32	Hallamshire Golf Club	144
Ghyll Golf Club	92	Haltwhistle Golf Course	105
Gilnahirk Golf Club	207	Hamilton Golf Club	192
Girton Golf Club	33	Hampstead Golf Club	61
Glamorganshire Golf Club	157	Handsworth Golf Club	134
Glasgow Gailes Golf Club	193	Harborne Golf Club	134
Glen Golf Club	186	Harbour Point Golf Club	216
Glenbervie Golf Club Ltd.	167	Harburn Golf Club	187
Glencorse Golf Club	186	Harewood Downs Golf Club	32
Glencruitten Golf Club	195	Harrogate Golf Club	139
Gleneagles Hotel Golf Courses	199	Hartley Wintney Golf Club	73
Glynhir Golf Club	152	Hartsbourne Golf and Country Club	81
Glynneath Golf Club	157	Haverfordwest Golf Club	153
Goal Farm Golf Club	123	Haverhill Golf Club	117

239

Club	Page	Club	Page
Hawarden Golf Club	151	Honiton Golf Club	47
Hawkhurst Golf Club	89	Honorable Company Of Edinburgh Golfers	185
Hawkstone Park Leisure Ltd.	111	Hopeman Golf Club	176
Haydock Park Golf Club	100	Hornsea Golf Club	85
Hayling Golf Club	74	Horsenden Hill Golf Club	61
Hayston Golf Club	191	Horsforth Golf Club	147
Haywards Heath Golf Club	128	Houghton-le-Spring Golf Club	130
Hazel Grove Golf Club	70	Houldsworth Golf Club	68
Hazlemere Golf and Country Club Ltd.	32	Howley Hall Golf Club	148
Headfort Golf Club	225	Howth Golf Club	220
Headley Golf Club	145	Huddersfield Golf Club	146
Heath Golf Club	224	Hull Golf Club	86
Heaton Moor Golf Club	70	Hunstanton Golf Club	102
Hebden Bridge Golf Club	146	Huyton and Prescot Golf Club	99
Helensburgh Golf Club	193	Ifield Golf and Country Club	128
Helen's Bay Golf Club	208	Ilford Golf Club	62
Helmsdale Golf Club	179	Ilfracombe Golf Club	47
Helsby Golf Club	36	Ilkeston Borough Golf Club	45
Henbury Golf Club	27	Immingham Golf Club	86
Hendon Golf Club	62	Ingestre Park Golf Club	115
Henley Golf Club	109	Innerleithen Golf Club	165
Herefordshire Golf Club	78	Inverallochy Golf Club	176
Hermitage Golf Club	220	Inverness Golf Club	179
Hessle Golf Club	85	Inverurie Golf Club	176
Heswall Golf Club	99	Ipswich Golf Club	117
Heworth Golf Club	130	Irvine Golf Club	193
Hexham Golf Club	105	Irvine Ravenspark Golf Club	193
Heysham Golf Club	94	Island Golf Club	219
Hickleton Golf Club	142	Isle of Purbeck Golf Club	50
Highcliffe Castle Golf Club	50	Isle of Skye Golf Club	181
Highgate Golf Club	62	Ivinghoe Golf Club	29
Highwoods Golf Club	124	Jedburgh Golf Club	165
Highworth Community Golf Centre	138	John O'Gaunt Golf Club	29
Hill Barn Golf Course	129	Kedleston Park Golf Club	45
Hill Valley Golf and Country Club	112	Keighley Golf Club	147
Hillingdon Golf Club	62	Keith Golf Club	177
Hillsborough Golf Club	144	Kelso Golf Club	165
Hillside Golf Club	100	Kemnay Golf Club	177
Hilton Park Golf Club	191	Kendal Golf Club	42
Hinckley Golf Club	96	Keswick Golf Club Ltd.	42
Hindhead Golf Club	122	Kettering Golf Club	103
Hindley Hall Golf Club	71	Kidderminster Golf Club	78
Hobson Municipal Golf Club	130	Kildare Country Club	223
Holiday Inn Golf Club	65	Kilkeel Golf Club	209
Hollandbush Golf Club	195	Kllkenny Golf Club	223
Hollingbury Park Golf Club	125	Killarney Golf and Fishing Club	222
Hollywood Golf Club	218	Killin Golf Club	167
Holme Hall Golf Club	86	Killiow Park Golf Club	41
Holsworthy Golf Club	47	Killymoon Golf Club	212
Holtye Golf Club	128	Kilmarnock (Barassie) Golf Club	197
Holyhead Golf Club	162	Kilrea Golf Club	211
Holywell Golf Club	151	Kilspindie Golf Club	181
Holywood Golf Club	209	Kilsyth Lennox Golf Club	194
Home Park Golf Club	61	Kilternan Golf Club	220

Cade's - Audi Golf Course Guide

Kilton Forest Golf Club	108	Letterkenny Golf Club	218
King Edward Bay Golf Club	87	Leven Links	172
King James VI Golf Club	202	Lewes Golf Club	127
Kinghorn Golf Club	172	Liberton Golf Club	183
Kings Norton Golf Club Ltd.	77	Lightcliffe Golf Club	146
Kingsdown Golf Club	138	Limerick Golf Club	224
Kingsknowe Golf Club	183	Limpsfield Chart Golf	123
Kington Golf Club	79	Lindrick Golf Club	108
Kingussie Golf Club	180	Lingdale Golf Club	97
Kirby Muxloe Golf Club	96	Lingfield Park Golf Club	122
Kirkby Lonsdale Golf Club	42	Links Country Park Hotel & Golf Club	101
Kirkcaldy Golf Club	172	Links Golf Club	118
Kirkistown Castle Golf Club	210	Links Golf Course	174
Knaresborough Golf Club	139	Linlithgow Golf Club	185
Knebworth Golf Club	82	Liphook Golf Club	74
Knighton Golf Club	162	Lisburn Golf Club	204
Knighton Heath Golf Club	49	Little Aston Golf Club	135
Knights Grange Sports Complex	38	Little Chalfont Golf Club	32
Knightswood Golf Club	192	Little Hay Golf Complex	82
Knock Golf Club	207	Little Lakes Golf Club	77
Knockanally Golf Club	223	Llangefni Golf Course	161
Knockbracken Golf and Country Club	207	Llanishen Golf Club	156
Knole Park Golf Club	91	Llantrisant and Pontyclun Golf Club	155
Knowle Golf Club	27	Llanwern Golf Club	158
La Moye Golf Club	35	Llanymynech Golf Club	110
Ladbrook Park Golf Club Ltd.	135	Lobden Golf Club	69
Ladybank Golf Club	172	Lochwinnoch Golf Club	195
Lahinch Golf Club	215	Lockerbie Golf Club	169
Lakeside Golf Club	115	London Scottish Golf Club	65
Laleham Golf Course	120	Longcliffe Golf Club	96
Lamlash Golf Club	194	Longley Park Golf Club	147
Lanark Golf Club	194	Longniddry Golf Club	185
Lancaster Golf and Country Club	94	Longridge Golf Club	95
Langholm Golf Club	169	Lothianburn Golf Club	183
Langland Bay Golf Club	157	Loughton Golf Club	56
Langley Park Golf Club	58	Lowes Park Golf Club Ltd.	67
Lansdown Golf Club	27	Lucan Golf Club	220
Lansil Golf Club	94	Ludlow Golf Club	110
Largs Golf Club	194	Luffenham Heath Golf Club	98
Larne Golf Club	204	Luffness New Golf Club	181
Lauder Golf Club	165	Lullingstone Park Golf Club	63
Lavender Park	29	Lundin Golf Club	173
Laytown and Bettystown Golf Club	225	Lurgan Golf Club	206
Leatherhead Golf Club	122	Lyme Regis Golf Club	50
Leeds Castle Golf Course	90	Macclesfield Golf Club	37
Leeds Golf Club	148	Machrihanish Golf Club	188
Leek Golf Club	114	Machynlleth Golf Club	162
Lee-on-the-Solent Golf Club	74	Maesteg Golf Club	155
Leigh Golf Club	38	Mahee Island Golf Club	210
Leighton Buzzard Golf Club	29	Mahon Municipal Golf Club	216
Lenzie Golf Club	195	Maidenhead Golf Club	30
Leominster Golf Club	79	Malahide Golf Club	220
Letchworth Golf Club	82	Maldon Golf Club	56
Letham Grange Golf Club	198	Malkins Bank Golf Club	38

Mallow Golf Club	217	Moyola Park Golf Club	212
Malone Golf Club	207	Muir of Ord Golf Club	180
Malton and Norton Golf Club	140	Mullingar Golf Club	227
Manchester Golf Club	69	Murcar Golf Club	174
Mangotsfield Golf Club	28	Murrayfield Golf Club	184
Mannings Heath Golf Club	128	Murrayshall Golf Course	202
Manor Golf and Fishing Club	211	Muskerry Golf Club	216
Mansfield Woodhouse Golf Club	107	Musselburgh Golf Club	186
Mapperley Golf Club	107	Muswell Hill Golf Club	66
March Golf Club	34	Muthill Golf Club	200
Market Drayton Golf Club	110	Nairn Dunbar Golf Club	180
Market Rasen and District Golf Club	97	Nairn Golf Club	180
Marsden Golf Course	147	Narin and Portnoo Golf Club	217
Maryport Golf Club	42	Nefyn and District Golf Club	161
Masham Golf Club	140	Nelson Golf Club	95
Massereene Golf Club	203	Nenagh Golf Club	226
Maxstoke Park Golf Club	133	New Forest Golf Club	75
Maylands Golf Club	63	New Galloway Golf Club	169
Mellor and Townscliffe Golf Club	70	Newark Golf Club	107
Meltham Golf Club	149	Newbattle Golf Club	182
Mendip Golf Club Ltd.	113	Newbold Comyn Golf Club	132
Meon Valley Golf and Country Club	76	Newburgh-on-Ythan Golf Club	176
Merchants of Edinburgh Golf Club	183	Newbury and Crookham Golf Club	30
Mere Golf and Country Club	37	Newcastleton Golf Club	165
Merthyr Tydfil (Cilsanws) Golf Club	155	Newlands Golf Club	219
Mickleover Golf Club	45	Newport Golf Club	159
Mid-Herts Golf Club	84	Newport (Pembs) Golf Club	154
Milford Haven Golf Club	153	Newquay Golf Club	39
Mill Hill Golf Club	62	Newry Golf Club	210
Mill Ride Golf Club	30	Newton Abbot (Stover) Golf Club	47
Millbrook Golf Course	28	Newton Green Golf Club	120
Milltown Golf Club	219	Newton Stewart Golf Club	169
Milnthort Golf Club	201	Newtownstewart Golf Club	212
Minchinhampton Golf Club	57	Niddry Castle Golf Club	187
Minehead and West Somerset Golf Club	113	Normanby Golf Club	86
Mitcham Golf Club	62	Normanton Golf Club	149
Moffat Golf Club	169	North Berwick Golf Club	186
Mold Golf Club	151	North Foreland Golf Club	88
Monkstown Golf Club	217	North Hants Golf Club	73
Monmouth Golf Course	158	North Middlesex Golf Club	65
Montrose Links Trust	201	North Oxford Golf Club	110
Moor Hall Golf Club	136	North Shore Hotel and Golf Club	98
Moor Park Golf Club	82	North Warwickshire Golf Club Ltd.	134
Moortown Golf Club Ltd.	148	North West Golf Club	217
Morecambe Golf Club	94	North Wilts Golf Club	138
Morlais Castle Golf Club	155	North Worcestershire Golf Club	134
Morray Golf Club	177	Northampton Golf Club	103
Morriston Golf Club	157	Northamptonshire County Golf Club	103
Mortonhall Golf Club	183	Northcliffe Golf Club	145
Moseley Golf Club	134	Northenden Golf Club	69
Mount Juliet Golf and Country Club	223	Nottingham City Golf Club	106
Mount Oswald Golf Club	53	Notts. (Hollinwell) Golf Club Ltd.	107
Mountain Ash Golf Club	156	Nuneaton Golf Club	132
Mowsbury Golf Club	28	Nuremore Golf Club	225

Oak Park Golf Complex	73	Porters Park Golf Club	82
Okehampton Golf Club	47	Portmarnock Golf Club	220
Old Connor Golf Club	228	Portobello Golf Club	184
Old Fold Manor Golf Club	80	Portpatrick (Dunskey) Golf Club	170
Old Padeswood Golf Club Ltd.	152	Portsalon Golf Club	218
Old Thorns Golf Course & Hotel	74	Portsmouth Golf Club	76
Oldmeldrum Golf Club	177	Portstewart Golf Club	212
Omagh Golf Club	212	Potters Bar Golf Club	82
Ombersley Golf Club	77	Poulton Park Golf Club	38
Onneley Golf Club	36	Powfoot Golf Club	168
Orkney Golf Club	187	Prenton Golf Club	99
Ormeau Golf Club	207	Prestatyn Golf Club	152
Ormonde Fields Golf Club	44	Prestbury Golf Club	37
Orsett Golf Club	57	Preston Golf Club	95
Orton Meadows Golf Course	34	Prestwick Golf Club	195
Osborne Golf Club	87	Prince's Golf Club	90
Oswestry Golf Club	111	Purley Chase Golf and Country Club	132
Otley Golf Club	149	Pwllheli Golf Club	161
Oughterard Golf Club	222	Pyecombe Golf Club	125
Outlane Golf Club	149	Pyle and Kenfig Golf Club	155
Oxley Park Golf Club Ltd.	137	Pype Hayes Golf Club	136
Padeswood and Buckley Golf Club	152	Queens Park Golf Course	36
Painswick Golf Club	58	Quiet Waters Golf and Country Club	56
Painthorpe House Golf & Country Club	150	Radcliffe-on-Trent Golf Club	108
Palleg Golf Club	158	Ramsey Golf Course	87
Panmure Golf Club	199	Ranfurly Castle Golf Club Ltd.	188
Pannal Golf Club	139	Ratho Park Golf Club	186
Panshanger Municipal Golf Club	84	Ravelston Golf Club	184
Parkstone Golf Club	50	Rawdon Golf and Lawn Tennis Club	150
Pastures Golf Club	45	Reading Golf Club	30
Patshull Park Hotel, Golf & C. Club	137	Reay Golf Club	181
Peacehaven Golf Club	127	Redbourn Golf Club	83
Peebles Golf Club	165	Redditch Golf Club	79
Peel Golf Club	87	Redhill and Reigate Golf Club	123
Penmaenmawr Golf Club	161	Reigate Heath Golf Club	123
Penn Golf Club Ltd.	137	Renishaw Park Golf Club	45
Pennard Golf Club	158	Retford Golf Club Ltd.	108
Pennington Golf Club	68	Rhondda Golf Club	156
Penrith Golf Club	42	Rhosgoch Golf Club	162
Penwortham Golf Club Ltd.	95	Rhos-on-Sea Golf Club	161
Perranporth Golf Club	40	Rhuddlan Golf Club	152
Perton Park Golf Club	137	Rhyl Golf Club	152
Peterhead Golf Club	177	Rickmansworth Public Golf Course	83
Petersfield Golf Club	75	Riddlesden Golf Club	147
Phoenix Golf Club	142	Ringway Golf Club (The)	66
Pike Hills Golf Club	141	Ripon City Golf Club	140
Piltdown Golf Club	127	Robin Hood Golf Club	135
Pinner Hill Golf Club	63	Rochdale Golf Club	69
Pitlochry Golf Course	202	Rochester and Cobham Park Golf Club	90
Pitreavie (Dunfermline) Golf Club	171	Rolls Of Monmouth Golf Club (The)	159
Polkemmet Golf Course	187	Romiley Golf Club	70
Pontefract and District Golf Club	149	Rookery Park Golf Club	118
Ponteland Golf Club	106	Rosapenna Golf Club	218
Portadown Golf Club	206	Rossendale Golf Club	94

Rosslare Golf Club	227	Scunthorpe Golf Club	87
Ross-on-Wye Golf Club	79	Seacroft Golf Club	98
Rothbury Golf Club	106	Seaford Golf Club	127
Rotherham Golf Club Ltd.	143	Seahouses Golf Club	106
Rothesay Golf Club	196	Seascale Golf Club	43
Roundhay Golf Club	148	Seaton Carew Golf Club	38
Routenburn Golf Club	194	Sedbergh Golf Club	43
Rowlands Castle Golf Club	74	Selby Golf Club	141
Royal Aberdeen Golf Club	174	Selsdon Park Hotel Golf Course	60
Royal Ashdown Forest New Course	126	Selsey Golf Club	129
Royal Belfast Golf Club	209	Settle Golf Club	141
Royal Cinque Ports Golf Club	89	Shandon Park Golf Club	208
Royal County Down Golf Club	209	Shanklin and Sandown Golf Club	88
Royal Cromer Golf Club	101	Shannon Golf Club	216
Royal Dornoch Golf Club	178	Shaw Hill Hotel Golf & Country Club	93
Royal Dublin Golf Club	219	Sheerness Golf Club	91
Royal Eastbourne Golf Club	126	Sherwood Forest Golf Club	107
Royal Forest of Dean Golf Club	57	Shifnal Golf Club	111
Royal Guernsey Golf Club	35	Shillinglee Park Golf Club	122
Royal Jersey Golf Club	35	Shirland Golf Club	45
Royal Liverpool Golf Club	99	Shirley Golf Club	135
Royal Lytham and St Annes Golf Club	94	Shirley Park Golf Club	60
Royal North Devon Golf Club	48	Shiskine Golf and Tennis Club	188
Royal Porthcawl Golf Club	156	Shooters Hill Golf Club	64
Royal Portrush Golf Club	205	Shotts Golf Club	196
Royal St Davids Golf Club	161	Shrewsbury Golf Club	111
Royal St Georges Golf Club	91	Sickleholme Golf Club	44
Royal Tara Golf Club	225	Sidmouth Golf Club	48
Royal Troon Golf Club	197	Silecroft Golf Club	42
Royal Winchester Golf Club	76	Silkstone Golf Club	141
Royal Worlington & Newmarket G C	117	Silloth on Solway Golf Club	43
Rugby Golf Club	132	Silverdale Golf Club	95
Ruislip Golf Club	64	Silverknowes Golf Club	184
Runcorn Golf Club	37	Sittingbourne & Milton Regis G C	91
Rushcliffe Golf Club	106	Sitwell Park Golf Club	143
Rushden Golf Club	104	Skerries Golf Club	221
Rushmere Golf Club	118	Skipton Golf Club	141
Ruxley Park Golf Centre Ltd.	63	Slade Valley Golf Club	218
Ryde Golf Club	88	Sleaford Golf Club	98
Rye Golf Course	127	South Leeds Golf Club	148
Saddleworth Golf Club	69	South Moor Golf Club	53
Sale Golf Club	70	South Shields Golf Club	131
Salisbury and South Wilts Golf Club	138	South Staffordshire Golf Club	137
Sand Moor Golf Club	148	Southampton Golf Club	76
Sandilands Golf Club	98	Southerndown Golf Club	154
Sandown Golf Centre	121	Southerness Golf Club	168
Sandwell Park Golf Club	137	Southfield Golf Club	110
Sandy Lodge Golf Club	63	Southport Municipal Golf Club	100
Sapey Golf Club	77	Southport Old Links Golf Club	101
Saunton Golf Club	46	Southwold Golf Club	118
Scarborough North Cliff Golf Club	140	Spa Golf Club	208
Scarborough South Cliff Golf Club Ltd	140	Spey Bay Golf Club	176
Scarcroft Golf Club	150	St Andrews Eden Course	173
Scrabo Golf Club	210	St Andrews Jubilee Course	173

St Andrews Links Course	173	Tarbat Golf Club	180
St Andrews New Course	173	Tarbert Golf Club	196
St Andrews Old Course	173	Tarland Golf Club	174
St Annes Golf Club	220	Tavistock Golf Club	48
St Augustines Golf Club	90	Taymouth Castle Golf Course	198
St Austell Golf Club	40	Tehidy Park Golf Club	39
St Boswells Golf Club	166	Telford Hotel, Golf and Country Club	111
St Enodoc Golf Club	41	Tenby Golf Club	154
St Fillans Golf Club	200	Tenterden Golf Club	92
St George's Hill Golf Club	124	Thetford Golf Club	103
St Giles Golf Club	162	Theydon Bois Golf Club	56
St Mellion Golf and Country Club	40	Thorne Golf Club	145
St Pierre Hotel & Golf Club	158	Thornhill Golf Club	170
Stackstown Golf Club	221	Thornton Golf Club	173
Staddon Heights Golf Club	47	Thorpe Hall Golf Club	57
Stafford Castle Golf Club	115	Thorpe Wood Golf Course	34
Stand Golf Club	71	Three Locks Golf Club	33
Stanedge Golf Club	44	Thurles Golf Club	226
Stanmore Golf Club	64	Thurlestone Golf Club	48
Stapleford Abbotts Golf Club	57	Thurso Golf Club	181
Stirling Golf Club	167	Tidworth Garrison Golf Club	76
Stockport Golf Club	71	Tinsley Park Golf Club (Municipal)	144
Stocksbridge & District Golf Club	144	Tiverton Golf Club	48
Stocksfield Golf Club	106	Tobermory Golf Club	196
Stoke by Nayland Golf Club	55	Tolladine Golf Club	80
Stoke Rochford Golf Club	97	Torphin Hill Golf Club	184
Stone Golf Club	116	Torquay Golf Club	48
Stoneham Golf Club	76	Towerlands Gold Club	54
Stonehaven Golf Club	178	Tralee Golf Club	222
Stourbridge Golf Club	135	Tramore Golf Club	227
Stowmarket Golf Club	118	Tredegar and Rhymney Golf Club	159
Strabane Golf Club	213	Tredegar Park Golf Club Ltd.	159
Strandhill Golf Club	226	Treloy Golf Club	40
Stranraer Golf Club	170	Trent Park Golf Club	64
Strathaven Golf Club	196	Trentham Golf Club	115
Strathclyde Park Golf Club	193	Trentham Park Golf Club	116
Strathendrick Golf Club	167	Trevose Golf and Country Club	40
Strathtay Golf Club	202	Trim Golf Club	225
Strawberry Hill Golf Club	64	Troon Municipal	197
Stressholme Golf Club	53	Truro Golf Club	41
Sudbury Golf Club	65	Tuam Golf Club	222
Sunningdale Golf Club	31	Tullamore Golf Club	226
Surbiton Golf Club	59	Tulliallan Golf Club	172
Sutton Park Municipal Golf Club	86	Tunbridge Wells Golf Club	92
Swaffham Golf Club	103	Turnberry Hotel, Golf Courses & Spa	197
Swanston Golf Course	184	Turriff Golf Club	178
Swindon Golf Club *(Dudley - West Mids)*	133	Tyrrells Wood Golf Club	122
Swindon Golf Club *(Ogbourne St G. - Wilts)*	138	Tytherington Club (The)	37
Swinley Forest Golf Club	30	Ulverston Golf Club Ltd.	43
Swinton Park Golf Club	71	Upton-By-Chester Golf Club	35
Tadmarton Heath Golf Club	109	Uttoxeter Golf Club	116
Tandragee Golf Club	206	Vale of Leven Golf Club	187
Tandridge Golf Club	123	Vale of Llangollen Golf Club Ltd.	151
Tankersley Park Golf Club	144	Vaul Golf Club	192

Cade's - Audi Golf Course Guide

Ventnor Golf Club	88	Whalley Golf Club	92
Verulam Golf Club	83	Wheatley Golf Club	142
Vivary Park Golf Course	113	Whickham Golf Club Ltd.	131
Wakefield Golf Club	150	Whipsnade Golf Club	81
Waldringfield Heath Golf Club	120	Whitburn Golf Club	131
Wallsend Golf Club	131	Whitchurch (Cardiff) Golf Club	157
Walmer and Kingsdown Golf Club	89	Whitecraigs Golf Club (The)	192
Walmersley Golf Club	67	Whitefield Golf Club	71
Walsall Golf Club	136	Whitehead Golf Club	205
Walton Hall Municipal Golf Club	36	Whiteleaf Golf Club Ltd.	33
Walton Heath Golf Club	123	Whitewebbs Golf Club	61
Wanstead Golf Club	64	Whiting Bay Golf Club	197
Wareham Golf Club	51	Whitley Bay Golf Club	132
Warley Park Golf Club	54	Whittaker Golf Club	69
Warren Golf Club	46	Whittington Barracks Golf Club	115
Warrenpoint Golf Club	210	Wick Golf Club	181
Warwick Golf Club	133	Wigan Golf Club	72
Waterford Golf Club	227	Wigtown and Bladnoch Golf Club	170
Waterlooville Golf Club	75	Wigtownshire Golf Club	169
Waterville Golf Club	223	Willesley Park Golf Club Ltd.	96
Wavendon Golf Centre	33	Williamwood Golf Club	192
Welcombe Hotel and Golf Course	132	Willingdon Golf Club	126
Wellingborough Golf Club	104	Wimbledon Common Golf Club	65
Wells (Somerset) Golf Club	113	Wimbledon Park Golf Club	65
Welshpool Golf Club	163	Windermere Golf Club	43
Welwyn Garden City Golf Club	84	Windlemere Golf Club	124
Wentworth Club Ltd.	124	Windwhistle Golf, Squash & C Club Ltd	112
Wenvoe Castle Golf Club Ltd.	156	Windyhill Golf Club	192
Werneth Low Golf Club	68	Winterfield Golf Club	182
Wessex Golf Centre	51	Wishaw Golf Club	198
West Berkshire Golf Club	30	Woburn Golf and Country Club	33
West Bowling Golf Club	145	Wood Valley Golf Club	116
West Bradford Golf Club	145	Woodbridge Golf Club	120
West Byfleet Golf Club	124	Woodbrook Golf Club	228
West Cornwall Golf Club	40	Woodcote Park Golf Club	60
West Derby Golf Club	100	Woodhall Hills Golf Club	150
West End Golf Club (Halifax) Ltd.	146	Woodhall Spa Golf Club	98
West Essex Golf Club	59	Woodham Golf and Country Club	53
West Herts Golf Club Ltd.	84	Woolton Golf Club	100
West Hill Golf Club	120	Worcestershire Golf Club Ltd. (The)	79
West Hove Golf Course	126	Worfield Golf Club	112
West Kilbride Golf Club	197	Workington Golf Club	43
West Linton Golf Club	166	Worksop Golf Club	108
West Malling Golf Club	90	Worsley Golf Club	68
West Monmouthshire Golf Club	159	Worthing Golf Club	129
West Sussex Golf Club	129	Wortley Golf Club	144
Westerhope Golf Club	131	Wrangaton (South Devon) Golf Club	48
Westhill Golf Club	178	Wrekin Golf Club	111
Weston Turville Golf and Squash Club	31	Wrotham Heath Golf Club	91
Westonbirt Golf Course	58	Wyboston Lakes Golf Club	29
Westport Golf Club	225	Yelverton Golf Club	49
Westwood Golf Club	114	Yeovil Golf Club	113
Wexford Golf Club	227	York Golf Club	141
Weymouth Golf Club	51	Youghal Golf Club	217

ATTENTION AUDI OWNERS!

The Audi Quattro Cup

An Annual Golf Tournament
Exclusive to Audi Owners.

Anybody wishing to take part should contact:

Mike Brosnan at the Tournament Office
on 071 - 537 - 2051

Vorsprung durch technik

MAP SECTION

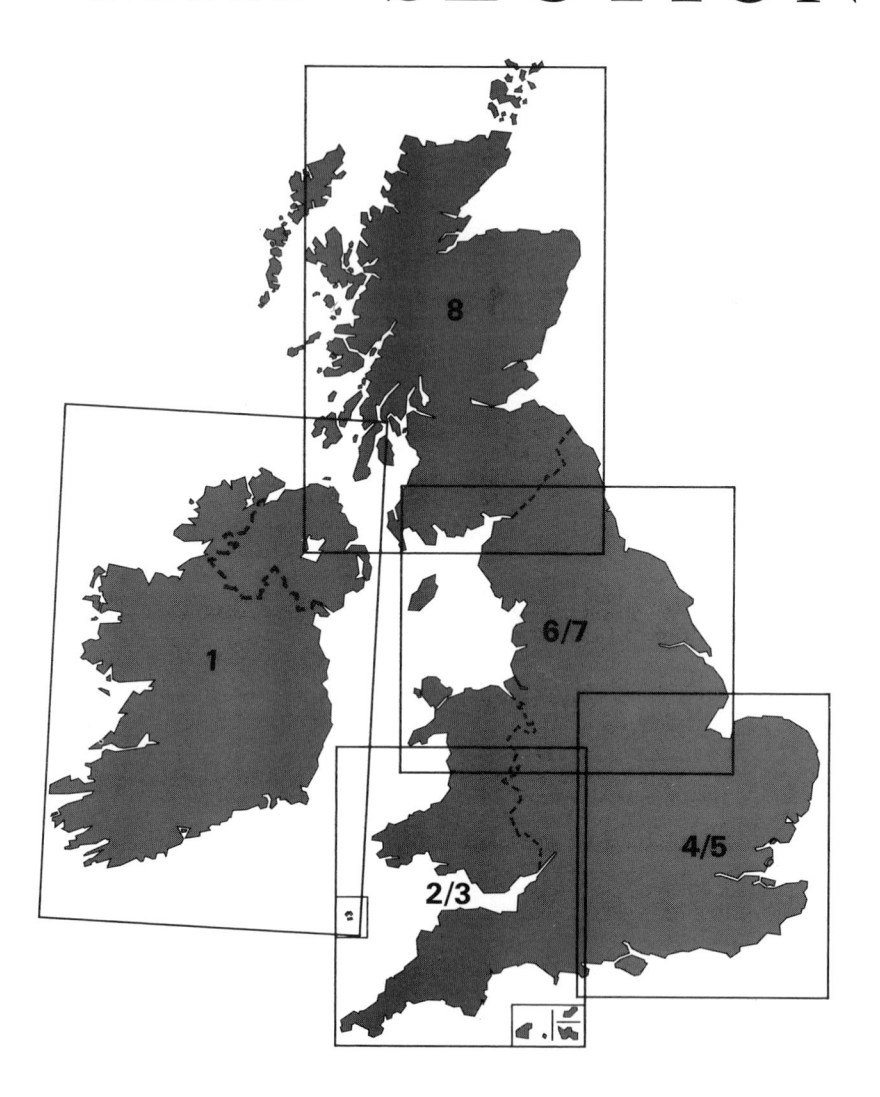

RELUM

Maps designed and produced by GEOprojects (UK) Ltd., Reading, Berkshire. RG1 4QS. © GEOprojects (UK) Ltd.

RELUM

Coleraine
Limavady
Ballymoney
Londonderry
LONDONDERRY
ANTRIM
Letterkenny
Ballymena
Larne
DONEGAL
Maghera
Strabane
Carrickfergus
Antrim
Donegal
TYRONE
Bangor
Cookstown
Omagh
BELFAST
Ballyshannon
Dungannon
Lurgan
Portadown
DOWN
Enniskillen
Armagh
Sligo
FERMANAGH
ARMAGH
Downpatrick
Monaghan
Newcastle
Newry
Ballina
SLIGO
Clones
Warrenpoint
MONAGHAN
Castleblayney
MAYO
Boyle
LEITRIM
Cavan
Dundalk
Newport
Swinford
Carrick-on-Shannon
CAVAN
Castlebar
LOUTH
Westport
ROSCOMMON
LONGFORD
Claremorris
Castlerea
Longford
Ceanannas Mor
Navan
Drogheda
Roscommon
MEATH
Letterfrack
Mullingar
Clifden
Tuam
Swords
WESTMEATH
Oughterard
Athlone
Moate
GALWAY
DUBLIN
Ballinasloe
Galway
Salthill
Tullamore
KILDARE
DUBLIN
Naas
Bray
Loughrea
OFFALY
Kildare
Birr
Port Laoise
Lisdoonvarna
Mountrath
Wicklow
Ennistymon
Roscrea
Athy
LAOIS
WICKLOW
Ennis
CLARE
Nenagh
Carlow
Arklow
Tullow
CARLOW
Kilkee
Thurles
Kilrush
Limerick
Kilkenny
TIPPERARY
Adare
KILKENNY
LIMERICK
Cashel
Enniscorthy
Listowel
Newcastle West
Tipperary
WEXFORD
Cahir
Clonmel
New Ross
Abbeyfeale
Wexford
Rosslare
Tralee
Castleisland
Mitchelstown
Waterford
KERRY
Mallow
Fermoy
WATERFORD
Glenbeigh
Killarney
Dungarvan
CORK
Cahirciveen
Kenmare
Macroom
Cork
Youghal
Waterville
Parknasilla
Inishannon
Bantry
Clonakilty
Skibereen
0 10 20 30 40 50 Kilometres
0 10 20 30 Miles

1

2

0 10 20 30 40 50 Kilometres
0 10 20 30 Miles
RELUM
6
4
SHROPSHIRE
POWYS
HEREFORD AND WORCESTER
GLOUCESTERSHIRE
DYFED
GWENT
WEST GLAMORGAN
MID GLAMORGAN
SOUTH GLAMORGAN
AVON
Dolgellau
Barmouth
Tywyn
Aberdovey
Machynlleth
Welshpool
Montgomery
Newtown
Llanidloes
Aberystwyth
Aberaeron
New Quay
Tregaron
Lampeter
Cardigan
Newcastle Emlyn
Llandyssul
Fishguard
St David's
Haverfordwest
Broad Haven
Narberth
Milford Haven
Pembroke
Saundersfoot
Tenby
Manorbier
St Clears
Carmarthen
Llandeilo
Llandovery
Llanelli
Swansea
Neath
Port Talbot
Porthcawl
Bridgend
Llantwit Major
Barry
Penarth
Cardiff
Caerphilly
Pontypridd
Rhondda
Merthyr Tydfil
Pontypool
Newport
Chepstow
Clevedon
Bristol
Tormarton
Chippenham
Malmesbury
Wotton-under-Edge
Stroud
Lydney
Cinderford
Coleford
Symonds Yat
Monmouth
Abergavenny
Crickhowell
Brecon
Sennybridge
Llanwrtyd Wells
Builth Wells
Painscastle
Hay-on-Wye
Llandrindod Wells
Rhayader
Presteigne
Knighton
Kington
Craven Arms
Ludlow
Church Stretton
Bridgnorth
Shrewsbury
Wellington
Telford
Wolverhampton
Stafford
Stourbridge
Kidderminster
Stourport-on-Severn
Droitwich
Leominster
Worcester
Malvern
Hereford
Ledbury
Ross-on-Wye
Tewkesbury
Cheltenham
Gloucester
M4
M5
M50
M54
M6
A40
A44
A48
A49
A470
A483
A487

ISLES OF SCILLY
TRESCO
ST MARTIN'S
Hugh Town
ST MARY'S
ST AGNES
0 5 10 15 Kilometres
0 5 10 Miles
CHANNEL ISLANDS
0 5 10 15 Kilometres
0 5 10 Miles
ALDERNEY
St Anne
GUERNSEY
St Peter Port
SARK
JERSEY
St Aubin
St Helier
A1
5
CORNWALL
DEVON
SOMERSET
DORSET
Weston-super-Mare
Bath
Melksham
Trowbridge
Warminster
Axbridge
Cheddar
Wedmore
Radstock
Frome
Wells
Shepton Mallet
Burnham-on-Sea
Highbridge
Glastonbury
Street
Bruton
Minehead
Watchet
Williton
Bridgwater
Wincanton
Mere
Somerton
Langport
Taunton
Ilchester
Shaftesbury
Wellington
Bampton
Ilminster
Yeovil
Sherborne
Sturminster Newton
Chard
Crewkerne
Blandford Forum
Honiton
Axminster
Charmouth
Bridport
Lyme Regis
Bere Regis
Dorchester
Wareham
Weymouth
Burton Bradstock
Ottery St Mary
Sidmouth
Seaton
Budleigh Salterton
Exmouth
Dawlish
Teignmouth
Newton Abbot
Torquay
Paignton
Brixham
Dartmouth
Torcross
Kingsbridge
Salcombe
Hope Cove
Bigbury
Modbury
Totnes
South Brent
Ivybridge
Plymouth
Buckfastleigh
Ashburton
Bovey Tracey
Chudleigh
Widecombe
Moretonhampstead
Chagford
Exeter
Crediton
Cullompton
Tiverton
Okehampton
Winkleigh
Eggesford
Chulmleigh
South Molton
Dulverton
Exford
Simonsbath
Dunster
Porlock
Lynmouth
Lynton
Woody Bay
Combe Martin
Ilfracombe
Woolacombe
Croyde
Barnstaple
Westward Ho!
Bideford
Torrington
Clovelly
Holsworthy
Bude
Crackington Haven
Boscastle
Tintagel
Launceston
Port Isaac
Camelford
Polzeath
Padstow
Wadebridge
Bodmin
Gunnislake
Callington
Tavistock
Calstock
Mawgan Porth
St Columb Major
Newquay
Liskeard
Saltash
Lostwithiel
Looe
Portwrinkle
Cawsand
Fowey
Polperro
Perranporth
St Austell
Mitchell
St Agnes
Mevagissey
Portreath
Redruth
Truro
St Ives
Hayle
Camborne
St Mawes
St Just
Marazion
Penzance
Whitsand Bay
Land's End
Helston
Falmouth
Praa Sands
Helford
Mullion
Coverack
Lizard
M5
A30
A38
A39
A361
A377
A396
A3072
A386
A390
A385
A380
A35
A354
A37
A303
A350
A36
A368
A394
A31
A3

4

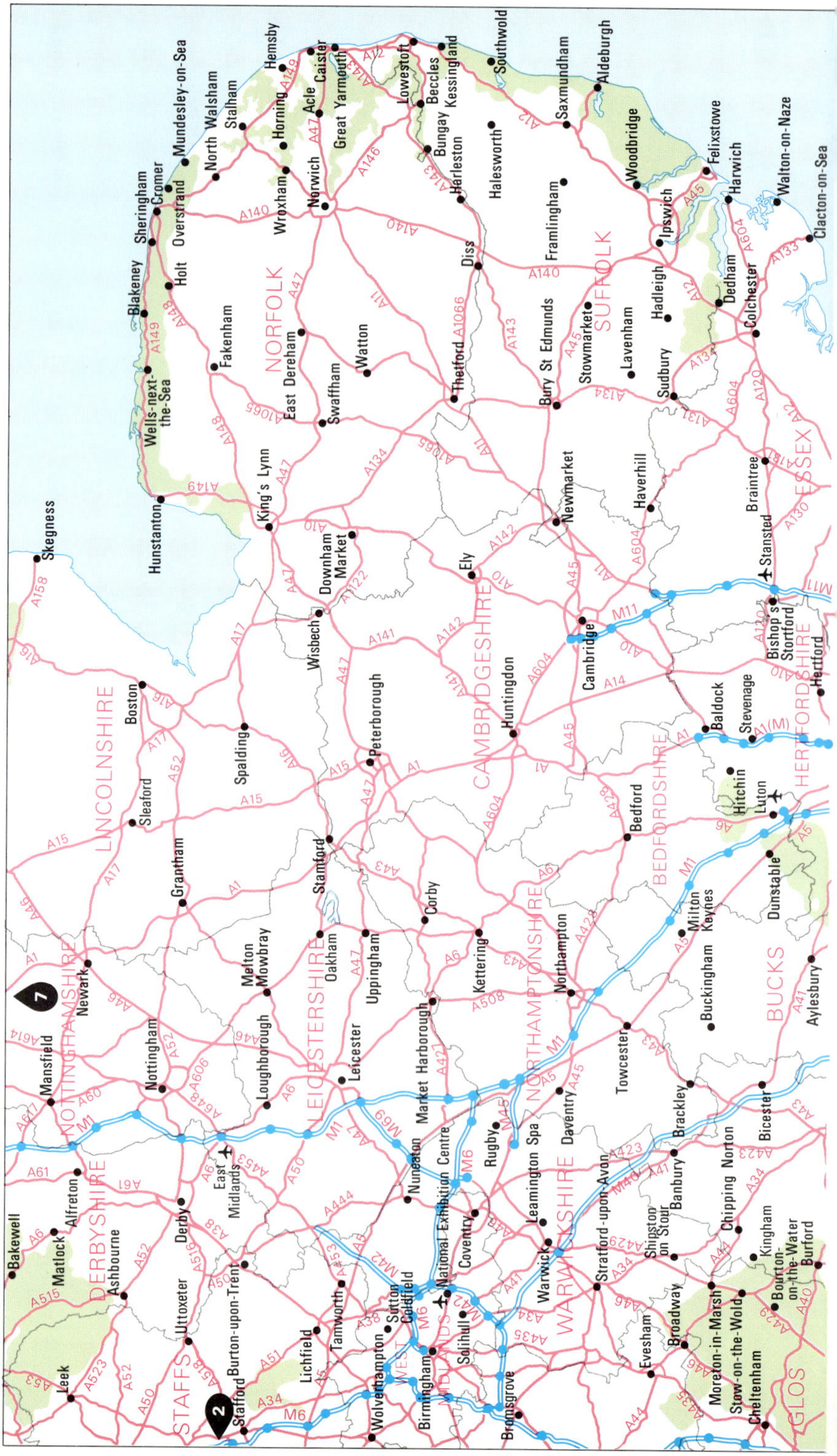

NORFOLK
SUFFOLK
ESSEX
CAMBRIDGESHIRE
LINCOLNSHIRE
NOTTINGHAMSHIRE
DERBYSHIRE
LEICESTERSHIRE
NORTHAMPTONSHIRE
BEDFORDSHIRE
HERTFORDSHIRE
BUCKS
WARWICKSHIRE
WEST MIDLANDS
STAFFS
GLOS
Hemsby
Mundesley-on-Sea
North Walsham
Stalham
Horning
Acle
Caister
Great Yarmouth
Lowestoft
Beccles
Kessingland
Southwold
Bungay
Harleston
Halesworth
Saxmundham
Aldeburgh
Woodbridge
Felixstowe
Harwich
Walton-on-Naze
Clacton-on-Sea
Sheringham
Cromer
Overstrand
Wroxham
Norwich
Framlingham
Ipswich
Blakeney
Holt
Diss
Hadleigh
Dedham
Colchester
Fakenham
East Dereham
Watton
Thetford
Bury St Edmunds
Stowmarket
Lavenham
Sudbury
Wells-next-the-Sea
Swaffham
Haverhill
Braintree
Newmarket
King's Lynn
Hunstanton
Skegness
Downham Market
Ely
Stansted
Bishop's Stortford
Wisbech
Cambridge
Hertford
Boston
Peterborough
Huntingdon
Baldock
Stevenage
Spalding
Hitchin
Luton
Sleaford
Bedford
Stamford
Dunstable
Grantham
Corby
Milton Keynes
Oakham
Uppingham
Kettering
Northampton
Melton Mowbray
Buckingham
Aylesbury
Newark
Mansfield
Nottingham
Loughborough
Leicester
Market Harborough
Towcester
Daventry
Brackley
Bicester
Rugby
Leamington Spa
Banbury
Alfreton
East Midlands
Nuneaton
National Exhibition Centre
Coventry
Stratford-upon-Avon
Chipping Norton
Shipston on Stour
Kingham
Bakewell
Matlock
Ashbourne
Derby
Burton-upon-Trent
Uttoxeter
Tamworth
Sutton Coldfield
Warwick
Bourton-on-the-Water
Burford
Leek
Lichfield
Solihull
Broadway
Moreton-in-Marsh
Stow-on-the-Wold
Stafford
Wolverhampton
Birmingham
Bromsgrove
Evesham
Cheltenham
M1
M6
M11
M42
M45
M40
M69
M5
A1(M)
2
7

OXFORDSHIRE
BERKSHIRE
WILTSHIRE
HAMPSHIRE
SURREY
GREATER LONDON
KENT
WEST SUSSEX
EAST SUSSEX
ISLE OF WIGHT
LONDON
Witney
Oxford
Cirencester
Abingdon
Wantage
Wallingford
Malmesbury
Swindon
Chippenham
Hungerford
Marlborough
Melksham
Devizes
Newbury
Henley-on-Thames
High Wycombe
Reading
Maidenhead
Slough
Windsor
Bracknell
Heathrow
Beaconsfield
Rickmansworth
Watford
Hemel Hempstead
St Albans
Hatfield
Epping
Chelmsford
Maldon
Burnham-on-Crouch
Brentwood
Basildon
Romford
Southend-on-Sea
Brentford
Richmond
Kingston Upon Thames
Bromley
Croydon
Weybridge
Epsom
Woking
Dartford
Gravesend
Rochester
Gillingham
Chatham
Sheerness
Whitstable
Herne Bay
Margate
Broadstairs
Ramsgate
Faversham
Canterbury
Sandwich
Deal
Dover
Folkestone
Hythe
Dymchurch
New Romney
Ashford
Tenterden
Maidstone
Sevenoaks
Tonbridge
Tunbridge Wells
Hawkhurst
Crowborough
Heathfield
Battle
Rye
Winchelsea
Hastings
Bexhill-on-Sea
Hailsham
Eastbourne
Lewes
Newhaven
Seaford
Brighton
Hove
Shoreham-by-Sea
Worthing
Steyning
Uckfield
East Grinstead
Haywards Heath
Crawley
Gatwick
Reigate
Dorking
Horsham
Guildford
Aldershot
Farnham
Basingstoke
Andover
Amesbury
Salisbury
Winchester
Alton
Hindhead
Haslemere
Petersfield
Midhurst
Petworth
Pulborough
Arundel
Chichester
Littlehampton
Bognor Regis
Selsey
Hayling Island
Havant
Southsea
Portsmouth
Gosport
Fareham
Southampton
Eastleigh
Romsey
Fordingbridge
Lyndhurst
Brockenhurst
Ringwood
Wimborne
Christchurch
Lymington
New Milton
Bournemouth
Poole
Wareham
Studland
Swanage
Cowes
Ryde
Yarmouth
Totland Bay
Freshwater
Newport
Sandown
Shanklin
Ventnor
Chale
St Lawrence
3
RELUM
0 10 20 30 40 50 Kilometres
0 10 20 30 Miles

6

DUMFRIES AND GALLOWAY

Girvan, New Galloway, Newton Stewart, Wigtown, Port William, Castle Douglas, Gatehouse of Fleet, Kirkcudbright, Dalbeattie, Dumfries, Annan, Gretna, Langholm, Lockerbie, Longtown, Brampton, Carlisle, Silloth

CUMBRIA

Wigton, Maryport, Cockermouth, Bassenthwaite, Workington, Thornthwaite, Keswick, Penrith, Whitehaven, Ennerdale Bridge, Ullswater, Brampton, Appleby, Shap, Kirkby Stephen, Gosforth, Little Langdale, Ambleside, Troutbeck, Seascale, Hawkshead, Windermere, Ravenglass, Coniston, Kendal, Broughton-in-Furness, Newby Bridge, Sedbergh, Millom, Ulverston, Kirkby Lonsdale, Barrow-in-Furness, Grange-over-Sands, Ingleton, Carnforth, Morecambe, Settle, Lancaster

Greenhead, Alston

ISLE OF MAN

Ramsey, Peel, Douglas, Port Erin, Castletown, Port St Mary

LANCASHIRE

Fleetwood, Clitheroe, Blackpool, Lytham St Annes, Preston, Blackburn, Southport, Chorley, Ormskirk, Bolton, Formby, Wigan

GREATER MANCHESTER

Manchester, Warrington, Knutsford

MERSEYSIDE

Hoylake, Liverpool, Birkenhead, Widnes

ANGLESEY

Amlwch, Holyhead, Llanerchymedd, Llandudno, Colwyn Bay, Prestatyn, Menai Bridge, Beaumaris, Conwy, Rhyl, Abergele, Llangefni, Bangor, Ellesmere Port, Northwich

CHESHIRE

Chester, Crewe, Nantwich, Newcastle-under-Lyme

GWYNEDD

Caernarvon, Llanrwst, Llanberis, Betws-y-Coed, Denbigh, Mold, Ruthin

CLWYD

Corwen, Wrexham, Ellesmere, Whitchurch, Wem, Market Drayton

Nefyn, Portmadoc, Criccieth, Ffestiniog, Penrhyndeudraeth, Bala, Llangollen, Pwllheli, Llanbedrog, Harlech, Oswestry, Abersoch, Aberdaron, Dolgellau, Barmouth, Wellington, Telford

SHROPSHIRE

Welshpool, Shrewsbury

POWYS

Tywyn, Machynlleth

© GEOprojects (U.K.) Ltd
Crown Copyright Reserved

0 10 20 30 40 50 Kilometres
0 10 20 30 Miles
RELUM
UMBERLAND
TYNE AND WEAR
DURHAM
CLEVELAND
NORTH YORKSHIRE
HUMBERSIDE
WEST YORKSHIRE
SOUTH YORKSHIRE
DERBYSHIRE
NOTTINGHAMSHIRE
LINCOLNSHIRE
STAFFORDSHIRE
LEICESTERSHIRE
Morpeth
Ashington
Whitley Bay
Tynemouth
South Shields
Corbridge
Hexham
Newcastle-upon-Tyne
Sunderland
Washington
Consett
Durham
Peterlee
Hartlepool
Bishop Auckland
Redcar
Saltburn-by-the-Sea
Middleton-in-Teesdale
Middlesbrough
Stockton-on-Tees
Barnard Castle
Darlington
Guisborough
Whitby
Stokesley
Richmond
Hawes
Leyburn
Northallerton
Middleham
Scarborough
Cayton Bay
Thirsk
Helmsley
Pickering
Filey
Ripon
Castle Howard
Malton
Flamborough
Sledmere
Bridlington
Grassington
Huby
Driffield
Knaresborough
Stamford Bridge
Skipton
Harrogate
Wetherby
York
Hornsea
Keighley
Ilkley
Beverley
Bingley
Bradford
Leeds
Selby
Heptonstall
Hull
Withernsea
Halifax
Goole
Wakefield
Huddersfield
Scunthorpe
Grimsby
Cleethorpes
Holmfirth
Barnsley
Oldham
Doncaster
Glossop
Rotherham
Stockport
Gainsborough
Market Rasen
Louth
Sheffield
Mablethorpe
Whaley Bridge
Castleton
Worksop
Buxton
Alford
Macclesfield
Chesterfield
Lincoln
Bakewell
Horncastle
Mansfield
Woodhall Spa
Skegness
Congleton
Matlock
Leek
Alfreton
Newark
Ashbourne
Sleaford
Stoke-on-Trent
Boston
Nottingham
Uttoxeter
Derby
Grantham
East Midlands
Stafford
Burton-upon-Trent
Spalding
Loughborough
Melton Mowbray
Lichfield
Wisbech
Stamford
Oakham
Tamworth
Leicester
Uppingham
Peterborough
4

7

8